386™ DX MICROPROCESSOR PROGRAMMER'S REFERENCE MANUAL

1990

Intel Corporation makes no warranty for the use of its products and assumes no responsibility for any errors which may appear in this document nor does it make a commitment to update the information contained herein.

Intel retains the right to make changes to these specifications at any time, without notice.

Contact your local sales office to obtain the latest specifications before placing your order.

The following are trademarks of Intel Corporation and may only be used to identify Intel products:

376, 386, 387, 486, 4-SITE, Above, ACE51, ACE96, ACE186, ACE196, ACE960, BITBUS, COMMputer, CREDIT, Data Pipeline, DVI, ETOX, FaxBACK, Genius, i, i, i486, i750, i860, ICE, iCEL, ICEVIEW, iCS, iDBP, iDIS, I²ICE, iLBX, iMDDX, iMMX, Inboard, Insite, Intel, intel, Intel386, intelBOS, Intel Certified, Intelevision, inteligent Identifier, inteligent Programming, Intellec, Intellink, iOSP, iPAT, iPDS, iPSC, iRMK, iRMX, iSBC, iSBX, iSDM, iSXM, Library Manager, MAPNET, MCS, Megachassis, MICROMAINFRAME, MULTIBUS, MULTICHANNEL, MULTIMODULE, MultiSERVER, ONCE, OpenNET, OTP, PRO750, PROMPT, Promware, QUEST, QueX, Quick-Erase, Quick-Pulse Programming, Ripplemode, RMX/80, RUPI, Seamless, SLD, SugarCube, ToolTALK, UPI, Visual Edge, VLSiCEL, and ZapCode, and the combination of ICE, iCS, iRMX, iSBC, iSBX, iSXM, MCS, or UPI and a numerical suffix.

MDS is an ordering code only and is not used as a product name or trademark. MDS® is a registered trademark of Mohawk Data Sciences Corporation.

MULTIBUS is a patented Intel bus.

CHMOS and HMOS are patented processes of Intel Corp.

Intel Corporation and Intel's FASTPATH are not affiliated with Kinetics, a division of Excelan, Inc. or its FASTPATH trademark or products.

Additional copies of this manual or other Intel literature may be obtained from:

Intel Corporation
Literature Sales
P.O. Box 7641
Mt. Prospect, IL 60056-7641

©INTEL CORPORATION 1989

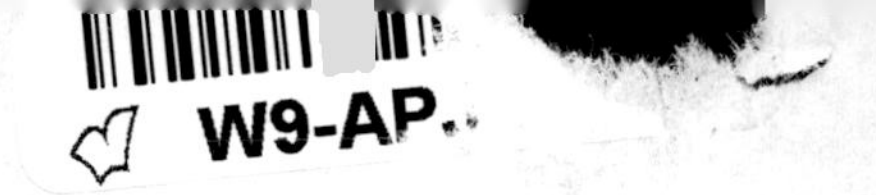

U.S. and CANADA LITERATURE ORDER FORM

NAME: ______________________________

COMPANY: ______________________________

ADDRESS: ______________________________

CITY: ____________ STATE: ________ ZIP: ________

COUNTRY: ______________________________

PHONE NO.: ( ) ______________________________

ORDER NO.	TITLE	QTY.		PRICE		TOTAL
			×		=	
			×		=	
			×		=	
			×		=	
			×		=	
			×		=	
			×		=	
			×		=	
			×		=	
			×		=	

Subtotal ________

Must Add Your Local Sales Tax ________

Postage: add 10% of subtotal → Postage ________

Total ________

Pay by check, money order, or include company purchase order with this form ($100 minimum).We also accept VISA, MasterCard or American Express. Make payment to Intel Literature Sales. Allow 2-4 weeks for delivery.

☐ VISA ☐ MasterCard ☐ American Express Expiration Date ________

Account No. ______________________________

Signature ______________________________

Mail To: Intel Literature Sales
P.O. Box 7641
Mt. Prospect, Il 60056-7641

International Customers outside the U.S. and Canada should use the International order form or contact their local Sales Office or Distributor.

For phone orders in the U.S. and Canada
Call Toll Free: (800) 548-4725

Prices good until 12/31/90.

Source HB

INTERNATIONAL LITERATURE ORDER FORM

NAME: ____________________

COMPANY: ____________________

ADDRESS: ____________________

CITY: ____________________ STATE: __________ ZIP: __________

COUNTRY: ____________________

PHONE NO.: (   ) ____________________

ORDER NO.	TITLE	QTY.		PRICE		TOTAL
			×		=	
			×		=	
			×		=	
			×		=	
			×		=	
			×		=	
			×		=	
			×		=	
			×		=	
			×		=	

Subtotal __________

Must Add Your Local Sales Tax __________

Total __________

PAYMENT

Cheques should be made payable to your local Intel Sales Office

Other forms of payment may be available in your country. Please contact the Literature Coordinator at your local Intel Sales Office for details.

The completed form should be marked to the attention of the LITERATURE COORDINATOR and returned to your local Intel Sales Office.

CUSTOMER SUPPORT

INTEL'S COMPLETE SUPPORT SOLUTION WORLDWIDE

Customer Support is Intel's complete support service that provides Intel customers with hardware support, software support, customer training, consulting services and network management services. For detailed information contact your local sales offices.

After a customer purchases any system hardware or software product, service and support become major factors in determining whether that product will continue to meet a customer's expectations. Such support requires an international support organization and a breadth of programs to meet a variety of customer needs. As you might expect, Intel's customer support is quite extensive. It can start with assistance during your development effort to network management. 100 Intel sales and service offices are located worldwide — in the U.S., Canada, Europe and the Far East. So wherever you're using Intel technology, our professional staff is within close reach.

HARDWARE SUPPORT SERVICES

Intel's hardware maintenance service, starting with complete on-site installation will boost your productivity from the start and keep you running at maximum efficiency. Support for system or board level products can be tailored to match your needs, from complete on-site repair and maintenance support economical carry-in or mail-in factory service.

Intel can provide support service for not only Intel systems and emulators, but also support for equipment in your development lab or provide service on your product to your end-user/customer.

SOFTWARE SUPPORT SERVICES

Software products are supported by our Technical Information Phone Service (TIPS) that has a special toll free number to provide you with direct, ready information on known, documented problems and deficiencies, as well as work-arounds, patches and other solutions.

Intel's software support consists of two levels of contracts. Standard support includes TIPS (Technical Information Phone Service), updates and subscription service (product-specific troubleshooting guides and; *COMMENTS Magazine*). Basic support consists of updates and the subscription service. Contracts are sold in environments which represent product groupings (e.g., iRMX® environment).

CONSULTING SERVICES

Intel provides field system engineering consulting services for any phase of your development or application effort. You can use our system engineers in a variety of ways ranging from assistance in using a new product, developing an application, personalizing training and customizing an Intel product to providing technical and management consulting. Systems Engineers are well versed in technical areas such as microcommunications, real-time applications, embedded microcontrollers, and network services. You know your application needs; we know our products. Working together we can help you get a successful product to market in the least possible time.

CUSTOMER TRAINING

Intel offers a wide range of instructional programs covering various aspects of system design and implementation. In just three to ten days a limited number of individuals learn more in a single workshop than in weeks of self-study. For optimum convenience, workshops are scheduled regularly at Training Centers worldwide or we can take our workshops to you for on-site instruction. Covering a wide variety of topics, Intel's major course categories include: architecture and assembly language, programming and operating systems, BITBUS™ and LAN applications.

NETWORK MANAGEMENT SERVICES

Today's networking products are powerful and extremely flexible. The return they can provide on your investment via increased productivity and reduced costs can be very substantial.

Intel offers complete network support, from definition of your network's physical and functional design, to implementation, installation and maintenance. Whether installing your first network or adding to an existing one, Intel's Networking Specialists can optimize network performance for you.

TABLE OF CONTENTS

PART II—SYSTEMS PROGRAMMING

CHAPTER 4
SYSTEM ARCHITECTURE

CHAPTER 15
VIRTUAL-8086 MODE

CHAPTER 16
MIXING 16-BIT AND 32-BIT CODE

PART IV—INSTRUCTION SET

CHAPTER 17
386™ DX MICROPROCESSOR INSTRUCTION SET

Figures

Figures

Tables

Introduction to the 386™ DX Microprocessor 1

CHAPTER 1
INTRODUCTION TO THE 386™ DX MICROPROCESSOR

The 386™ DX microprocessor is an advanced 32-bit processor optimized for multitasking operating systems and other computation-intensive applications. The 32-bit registers and buses support 32-bit addresses and data. The processor can address up to 4 gigabytes of physical memory and 64 terabytes of virtual memory.

The 386 DX microprocessor includes:

- 32-bit integer processor for performing arithmetic and logical operations
- interface to the 387™ numerics coprocessor, an external floating-point arithmetic unit for supporting the 32-, 64-, and 80-bit formats specified in IEEE standard 754
- segmentation, a form of memory management for creating independent, protected address spaces
- paging, a form of memory management which provides access to data structures larger than the available memory space by keeping them partly in memory and partly on disk
- instruction backup for allowing a program to be restarted following an exception (necessary for supporting demand-paged virtual memory)
- pipelined instruction execution for allowing the interpretation of different instructions to be overlapped
- debugging registers for hardware support of instruction and data breakpoints

The Intel386™ architecture is an extension of Intel's 16-bit architecture to 32 bits. The native mode of execution is a powerful 32-bit instruction set which takes full advantage of a completely 32-bit architecture. Object-code compatibility with the 8086 and 80286 processors are provided through different modes of execution. Programs running in the compatibility mode for the 8086 processor can run with 32-bit programs when multitasking is used. In addition to the 386 DX microprocessor, which has a 32-bit data bus, the Intel386 architecture is available in two implementations with a 16-bit external data bus:

- 386 DX Microprocessor – The complete architecture of the 386 DX microprocessor adapted for midrange personal computers, which are sensitive to the higher system cost of a 32-bit bus.
- 376™ Embedded Processor – A reduced form of the 386 DX microprocessor optimized for embedded applications, such as process controllers. The 376 processor lacks the paging and 8086-compatibility features provided in the 386 DX microprocessor. The 376 processor is available in a surface-mount plastic package, which provides the lowest cost and smallest form factor for any implementation of the Intel386 architecture.

Both processors can run programs written for the 386 DX microprocessor, but with some reduction in performance due to the narrower bus. Both processors can use the 387™ SX numerics coprocessor, which is an implementation of the 387 coprocessor with a 16-bit interface.

1.1 ORGANIZATION OF THIS MANUAL

This book presents the Intel386 architecture in four parts:

Part I – Application Programming
Part II – System Programming
Part III – Compatibility
Part IV – Instruction Set
Appendices

These divisions are determined by the architecture and by the ways programmers use this book. The first three parts are explanatory, showing the purpose of architectural features, developing terminology and concepts, and describing instructions as they relate to specific purposes or to specific architectural features. The remaining parts are reference material for programmers developing software for the 386 DX microprocessor.

The first three parts cover the operating modes and protection mechanism of the 386 DX microprocessor. The distinction between application programming and system programming is related to the protection mechanism of the 386 DX microprocessor. One purpose of protection is to prevent applications from interfering with the operating system. For this reason, certain registers and instructions are inaccessible to application programs. The features discussed in Part I are those which are accessible to applications; the features in Part II are available only to programs running with special privileges, or programs running on systems where the protection mechanism is not used.

The mode of the 386 DX microprocessor affects which instructions and architectural features are accessible. The 386 DX microprocessor has three modes for running programs:

Protected mode uses the native 32-bit instruction set of the processor. In this mode all instructions and architectural features are available.

Real-address mode (also called "real mode") emulates the programming environment of the 8086 processor, with a few extensions (such as the ability to break out of this mode). Reset initialization places the processor into real mode.

Virtual-8086 mode (also called "V86 mode") is another form of 8086 emulation mode. Unlike real-address mode, virtual-8086 mode is compatible with protection and memory management. The processor can enter virtual-8086 mode from protected mode to run a program written for the 8086 processor, then leave virtual-8086 mode and re-enter protected mode to continue a program which uses the 32-bit instruction set.

The features available to application programs in protected mode and to all programs in virtual-8086 mode are the same. These features are described in Part I of this book. The additional features available to system programs in protected mode are described in Part II. Part III describes real-address mode and virtual-8086 mode, as well as how to run a mix of 16-bit and 32-bit programs.

1.1.1 Part I—Application Programming

This part presents the architecture used by application programmers.

Chapter 2—Basic Programming Model: Introduces the models of memory organization. Defines the data types. Presents the register set used by applications. Introduces the stack. Explains string operations. Defines the parts of an instruction. Explains address calculations. Introduces interrupts and exceptions as they apply to application programming.

Chapter 3—Application Instruction Set: Surveys the instructions commonly used for application programming. Considers instructions in functionally related groups; forexample, string instructions are considered in one section, while control-transfer instructions are considered in another. Explains the concepts behind the instructions. Details of individual instructions are deferred until Part IV, the instruction-set reference.

1.1.2 Part II—System Programming

This part presents the Intel386 architectural features used by operating systems, device drivers, debuggers, and other software which support application programs.

Chapter 4—System Architecture: Describes the features of the 386 DX microprocessor used by system programmers. Introduces the remaining registers and data structures of the 386 DX microprocessor which were not discussed in Part I. Introduces the system-oriented instructions in the context of the registers and data structures they support. References the chapters in which each register, data structure, and instruction is discussed in more detail.

Chapter 5—Memory Management: Presents details of the data structures, registers, and instructions which support segmentation. Explains how system designers can choose between an unsegmented ("flat") model of memory organization and a model with segmentation.

Chapter 6—Protection: Discusses protection as it applies to segments. Explains the implementation of privilege rules, stack switching, pointer validation, user and supervisor modes. Protection aspects of multitasking are deferred until the following chapter.

Chapter 7—Multitasking: Explains how the hardware of the 386 DX microprocessor supports multitasking with context-switching operations and intertask protection.

Chapter 8—Input/Output: Describes the I/O features of the 386 DX microprocessor, including I/O instructions, protection as it relates to I/O, and the I/O permission bit map.

Chapter 9—Exceptions and Interrupts: Explains the basic interrupt mechanisms of the 386 DX microprocessor. Shows how interrupts and exceptions relate to protection. Discusses all possible exceptions, listing causes and including information needed to handle and recover from each exception.

Chapter 10 – Initialization: Defines the condition of the processor after reset initialization. Explains how to set up registers, flags, and data structures. Contains an example of an initialization program.

Chapter 11 – Coprocessing and Multiprocessing: Explains the instructions and flags which support multiple processors with shared memory and floating-point arithmetic coprocessors.

Chapter 12 – Debugging: Tells how to use the debugging registers of the 386 DX microprocessor.

1.1.3 Part III – Compatibility

This part explains the features of the architecture which support 16-bit programming. All three execution modes have support for 16-bit programming: 16-bit operations can be performed in protected mode using the operand size prefix, programs written for the 8086 processor or the real mode of the 80286 processor can run in real mode on the 386 DX microprocessor, and a virtual machine monitor can be used to emulate real mode using virtual-8086 mode, even while multitasking with 32-bit programs.

Chapter 13 – Executing 80286 Programs: Because the 386 DX microprocessor supports a superset of the programming environment of the 80286 processor, an application can be ported to the 386 DX microprocessor along with its operating system. It is also possible to port only the application, for use with a 32-bit operating system.

Chapter 14 – Real-Address Mode: Explains the real mode of the 386 DX microprocessor. In this mode, the 386 DX microprocessor appears as a fast real-mode 80286 processor or a fast 8086 processor enhanced with additional instructions.

Chapter 15 – Virtual-8086 Mode: The 386 DX microprocessor can switch rapidly between protected mode and virtual-8086 mode, which allows multitasking among programs running in different modes.

Chapter 16 – Mixing 16-Bit and 32-Bit Code: Even within a program or task, the 386 DX microprocessor can mix 16-bit and 32-bit modules. Any particular module can use both 16-bit and 32-bit operands and addresses.

1.1.4 Part IV – Instruction Set

Parts I and II present the instruction set as it relates to specific aspects of the architecture. Part III discusses compatibility with programs written for Intel 16-bit processors. Part IV presents the instructions in alphabetical order, with the detail needed by assembly-language programmers and programmers of debuggers, compilers, operating systems, etc. Instruction descriptions include an algorithmic description of operations, effect of flag settings, effect on flag settings, effect of operand and address-size attributes, and exceptions which may be generated.

1.1.5 Appendices

The appendices present tables of encodings and other details in a format designed for quick reference by programmers.

1.2 RELATED LITERATURE

The following books contain additional material related to the Intel386 family:

Introduction to the 80386, Order Number 231252
386™ DX Microprocessor Hardware Reference Manual, Order Number 231732
80386 Processor System Software Writer's Guide, Order Number 231499
386™ DX Microprocessor High-Performance 32-Bit CHMOS Microprocessor with Integrated Memory Management, Order Number 231630
376™ Embedded Processor Programmer's Reference Manual, Order Number 240314
80387 Programmer's Reference Manual, Order Number 231917
376™ High-Performance 32-Bit Embedded Processor, Order Number 240182
386™ SX Microprocessor, Order Number 240187
Microprocessor and Peripheral Handbook (vol. 1), Order Number 230843

The *386™ DX Microprocessor Hardware Reference Manual* is the companion of this book for use by hardware designers. It contains information which may be useful to programmers, especially system programmers. For example, software may be affected by these features of the hardware design:

- Asserting (or not asserting) the READY# input in response to bus cycles to unimplemented addresses.
- Asserting (or not asserting) the READY# input in response to write cycles to ROM.
- Assignment of the memory space to different bus sizes (16 or 32 bits).
- Assignment of the memory space to different forms of memory, such as EPROM, dynamic RAM, and fast static RAM.
- Assignment of user-defined interrupt vectors.
- Placement of I/O ports in the physical memory space, or in a separate I/O address space.
- Response of hardware to receiving a halt indication from the processor.
- Response of hardware to receiving a shutdown indication from the processor.
- Running the built-in self-test (BIST). This test can be invoked only from hardware, and the result of the test can be read only by software.

The data sheet contains the latest information regarding device parameters (voltage levels, bus cycle timing, priority of simultaneous exceptions and interrupts, etc.). The data sheet is found in the *Microprocessor and Peripheral Handbook (vol. 1)*.

1.3 NOTATIONAL CONVENTIONS

This manual uses special notation for data-structure formats, for symbolic representation of instructions, and for hexadecimal numbers. A review of this notation makes the manual easier to read.

1.3.1 Bit and Byte Order

In illustrations of data structures in memory, smaller addresses appear toward the bottom of the figure; addresses increase toward the top. Bit positions are numbered from right to left. The numerical value of a set bit is equal to two raised to the power of the bit position. The 386 DX microprocessor is a "little endian" machine; this means the bytes of a word are numbered starting from the least significant byte. Figure 1-1 illustrates these conventions.

Numbers are usually expressed in decimal notation (base 10). When hexadecimal (base 16) numbers are used, they are indicated by an 'H' suffix.

1.3.2 Undefined Bits and Software Compatibility

In many register and memory layout descriptions, certain bits are marked as *reserved*. When bits are marked as undefined or reserved, it is essential for compatibility with future processors that software treat these bits as having a future, though unknown, effect. Software should follow these guidelines in dealing with reserved bits:

- Do not depend on the states of any reserved bits when testing the values of registers which contain such bits. Mask out the reserved bits before testing.
- Do not depend on the states of any reserved bits when storing to memory or to a register.

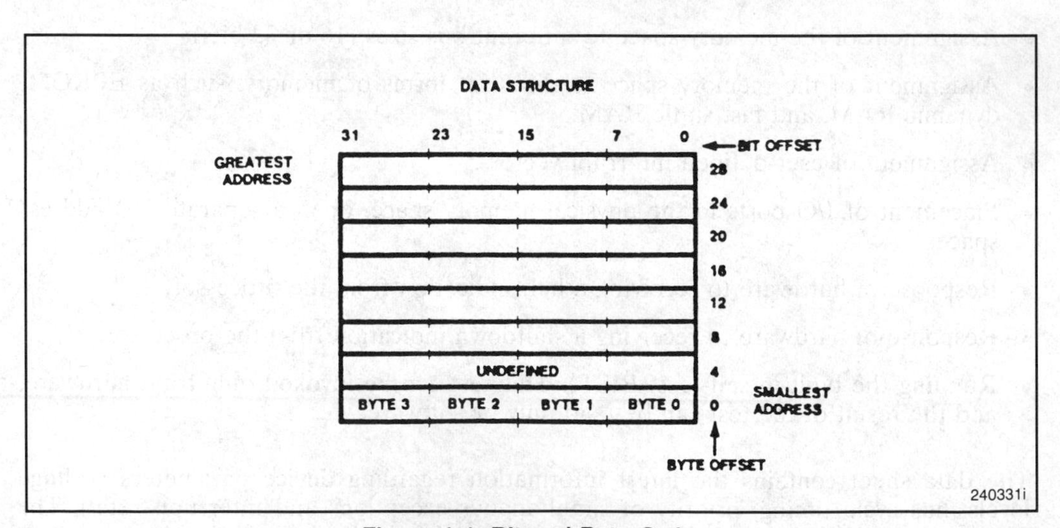

Figure 1-1. Bit and Byte Order

- Do not depend on the ability to retain information written into any reserved bits.
- When loading a register, always load the reserved or undefined bits with the values indicated in the documentation, if any, or reload them with values previously stored from the same register. (This means to store the register contents, modify only the necessary bits, and then load the new value into the register.)

NOTE

Depending upon the values of reserved register bits will make software dependent upon the unspecified manner in which the 386 DX microprocessor handles these bits. Depending upon reserved values risks incompatibility with future processors. ***AVOID ANY SOFTWARE DEPENDENCE UPON THE STATE OF RESERVED 386 DX MICROPROCESSOR REGISTER BITS.***

1.3.3 Instruction Operands

When instructions are represented symbolically, a subset of the assembly language for the 386 DX microprocessor is used. In this subset, an instruction has the following format:

label: mnemonic argument1, argument2, argument3

where:

- A *label* is an identifier which is followed by a colon.
- A *mnemonic* is a reserved name for a class of instruction opcodes which have the same function.
- The operands *argument1*, *argument2*, and *argument3* are optional. There may be from zero to three operands, depending on the opcode. When present, they take the form of either literals or identifiers for data items. Operand identifiers are either reserved names of registers or are assumed to be assigned to data items declared in another part of the program (which may not be shown in the example).

When two operands are present in an arithmetic or logical instruction, the right operand is the source and the left operand is the destination. Some assembly languages put the source and destination in reverse order.

For example:

```
LOADREG: MOV EAX, SUBTOTAL
```

In this example LOADREG is a label, MOV is the mnemonic identifier of an opcode, EAX is the destination operand, and SUBTOTAL is the source operand.

1.3.4 Hexadecimal Numbers

Base 16 numbers are represented by a string of hexadecimal digits followed by the character H. A hexadecimal digit is a character from the set (0, 1, 2, 3, 4, 5, 6, 7, 8, 9, A, B, C, D, E, F). A leading zero is added if the number would otherwise begin with one of the digits **A-F**. For example, 0FH is equivalent to the decimal number 15.

1.3.5 Segmented Addressing

Intel processors use byte addressing. This means memory is organized and accessed as a sequence of bytes. Whether one or more bytes are being accessed, a byte number is used to address memory. The memory which can be addressed with this number is called an *address space*.

Intel processors also support segmented addressing. This is a form of addressing where a program may have many independent address spaces, called *segments*. For example, a program can keep its code (instructions) and stack in separate segments. Code addresses would always refer to the code space, and stack addresses would always refer to the stack space. An example of the notation used to show segmented addresses is shown below.

CS:EIP

This example refers to a byte within the code segment. The byte number is held in the EIP register.

1.3.6 Exceptions

An exception is an event which occurs when an instruction causes an error. For example, an attempt to divide by zero generates an exception. There are several different types of exceptions, and some of these types may provide error codes. An error code reports additional information about the error. Error codes are produced only for some exceptions. An example of the notation used to show an exception and error code is shown below.

#PF(fault code)

This example refers to a page-fault exception under conditions where an error code naming a type of fault is reported. Under some conditions, exceptions which produce error codes may not be able to report an accurate code. In this case, the error code is zero, as shown below.

#PF(0)

Part I
Applications Programming

Basic Programming Model 2

CHAPTER 2
BASIC PROGRAMMING MODEL

This chapter describes the application programming environment of the 386™ DX microprocessor as seen by assembly language programmers. The chapter introduces programmers to those features of the Intel386™ architecture which directly affect the design and implementation of application programs.

The basic programming model consists of these parts:

- Memory organization
- Data types
- Registers
- Instruction format
- Operand selection
- Interrupts and exceptions

Note that input/output is not included as part of the basic programming model. System designers may choose to make I/O instructions available to applications or may choose to reserve these functions for the operating system. For this reason, the I/O features of the 386 DX microprocessor are discussed in Part II.

This chapter contains a section for each feature of the architecture normally visible to applications.

2.1 MEMORY ORGANIZATION

The memory on the bus of a 386 DX microprocessor is called *physical memory*. It is organized as a sequence of 8-bit bytes. Each byte is assigned a unique address, called a *physical address*, which ranges from zero to a maximum of $2^{32} - 1$ (4 gigabytes). Memory management is a hardware mechanism for making reliable and efficient use of memory. When memory management is used, programs do not directly address physical memory. Programs address a memory model, called *virtual memory*.

Memory management consists of segmentation and paging. Segmentation is a mechanism for providing multiple, independent address spaces. Paging is a mechanism to support a model of a large address space in RAM using a small amount of RAM and some disk storage. Either or both of these mechanisms may be used. An address issued by a program is a *logical address*. Segmentation hardware translates a logical address into an address for a continuous, unsegmented address space, called a *linear address*. Paging hardware translates a linear address into a physical address.

Memory may appear as a single, addressable space like physical memory. Or, it may appear as one or more independent memory spaces, called *segments*. Segments can be assigned specifically for holding a program's code (instructions), data, or stack. In fact, a single program may have up to 16,383 segments of different sizes and kinds. Segments can be used to increase the reliability of programs and systems. For example, a program's stack can be put into a different segment than its code to prevent the stack from growing into the code space and overwriting instructions with data.

Whether or not multiple segments are used, logical addresses are translated into linear addresses by treating the address as an offset into a segment. Each segment has a *segment descriptor*, which holds its base address and size limit. If the offset does not exceed the limit, and no other condition exists which would prevent reading the segment, the offset and base address are added together to form the linear address.

The linear address produced by segmentation is used directly as the physical address if bit 31 of the CR0 register is clear (the CR0 register is discussed in Chapter 4). This register bit controls whether paging is used or not used. If the bit is set, the paging hardware is used to translate the linear address into the physical address.

The paging hardware gives another level of organization to memory. It breaks the linear address space into fixed blocks of 4K bytes, called *pages*. The logical address space is mapped into the linear address space, which is mapped into some number of pages. A page may be in memory or on disk. When a logical address is issued, it is translated into an address for a page in memory, or an exception is issued. An exception gives the operating system a chance to read the page from disk and update the page mapping. The program which generated the exception then can be restarted without generating an exception.

If multiple segments are used, they are part of the programming environment seen by application programmers. If paging is used, it is normally invisible to the application programmer. It only becomes visible when there is an interaction between the application program and the paging algorithm used by the operating system. When all of the pages in memory are used, the operating system uses its paging algorithm to decide which memory pages should be sent to disk. All paging algorithms (except random algorithms) have some kind of worst-case behavior which may be exercised by some kinds of application programs.

The architecture of the 386 DX microprocessor gives designers the freedom to choose a different memory model for each program, even when more than one program is running at the same time. The model of memory organization can range between the following extremes:

- A "flat" address space where the code, stack, and data spaces are mapped to the same linear addresses. To the greatest extent possible, this eliminates segmentation by allowing any type of memory reference to access any type of data.
- A segmented address space with separate segments for the code, data, and stack spaces. As many as 16,383 linear address spaces of up to 4 gigabytes each can be used.

Both models can provide memory protection. Models intermediate between these extremes also can be chosen. The reasons for choosing a particular memory model and the manner in which system programmers implement a model are discussed in Part II—System Programming.

2.1.1 Unsegmented or "Flat" Model

The simplest memory model is the flat model. Although there isn't a mode bit or control register which turns off the segmentation mechanism, the same effect can be achieved by mapping all segments to the same linear addresses. This will cause all memory operations to refer to the same memory space.

In a flat model, segments may cover the entire 4 gigabyte range of physical addresses, or they may cover only those addresses which are mapped to physical memory. The advantage of the smaller address space is it provides a minimum level of hardware protection against software bugs; an exception will occur if any logical address refers to an address for which no memory exists.

2.1.2 Segmented Model

In a segmented model of memory organization, the logical address space consists of as many as 16,383 segments of up to 4 gigabytes each, or a total as large as 2^{46} bytes (64 terabytes). The processor maps this 64 terabyte logical address space onto the physical address space (up to 4 gigabytes) by the address translation mechanism described in Chapter 5. Application programmers may ignore the details of this mapping. The advantage of the segmented model is that offsets within each address space are separately checked and access to each segment can be individually controlled.

A pointer into a segmented address space consists of two parts (see Figure 2-1).

1. A *segment selector*, which is a 16-bit field which identifies a segment.
2. An *offset*, which is a 32-bit byte address within a segment.

The processor uses the segment selector to find the linear address of the beginning of the segment, called the *base address*. Programs access memory using fixed offsets from this base address, so an object-code module may be loaded into memory and run without changing the addresses it uses (dynamic linking). The size of a segment is defined by the programmer, so a segment can be exactly the size of the module it contains.

2.2 DATA TYPES

Bytes, words, and doublewords are the principal data types (see Figure 2-2). A byte is eight bits. The bits are numbered 0 through 7, bit 0 being the least significant bit (LSB).

A word is two bytes occupying any two consecutive addresses. A word contains 16 bits. The bits of a word are numbered from 0 through 15, bit 0 again being the least significant bit. The byte containing bit 0 of the word is called the *low byte*; the byte containing bit 15 is called the *high byte*. On the 386 DX microprocessor, the low byte is stored in the byte with the lower address. The address of the low byte also is the address of the word. The address of the high byte is used only when the upper half of the word is being accessed separately from the lower half.

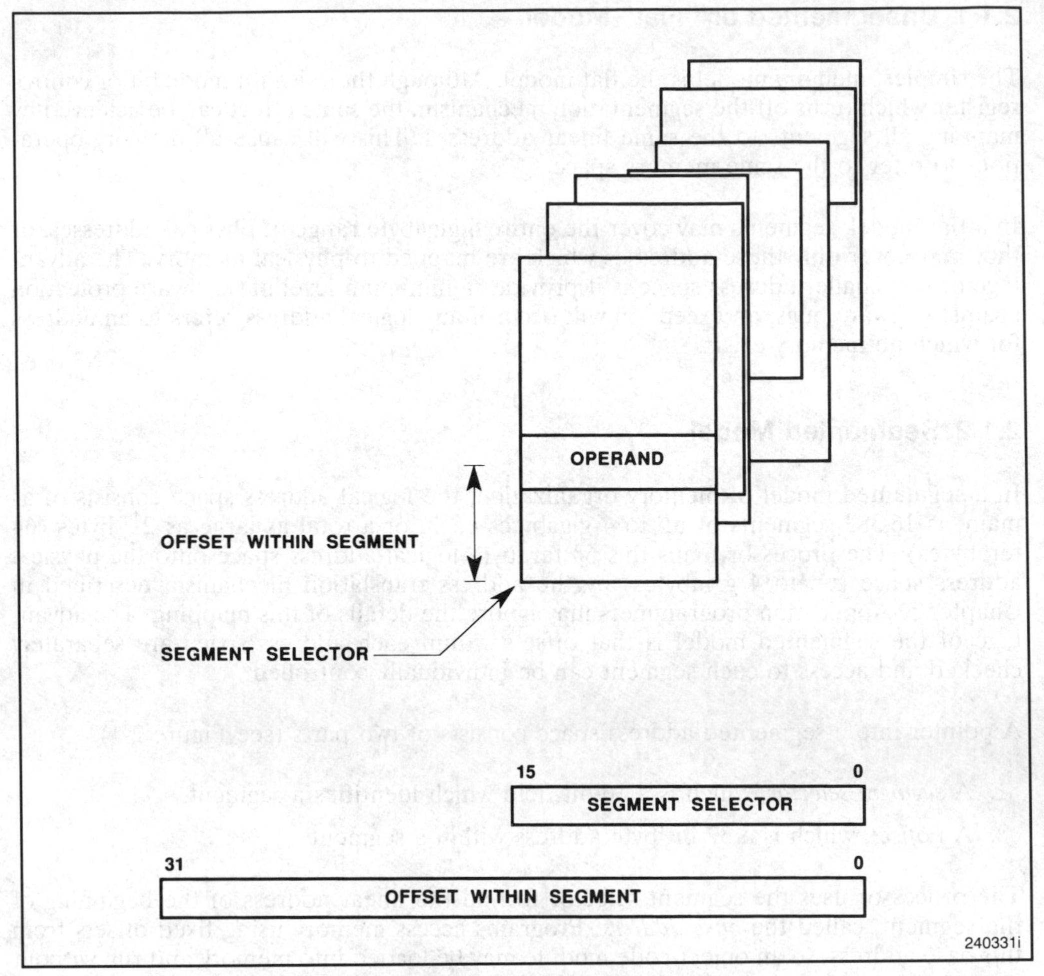

Figure 2-1. Segmented Addressing

A doubleword is four bytes occupying any four consecutive addresses. A doubleword contains 32 bits. The bits of a doubleword are numbered from 0 through 31, bit 0 again being the least significant bit. The word containing bit 0 of the doubleword is called the *low word*; the word containing bit 31 is called the *high word*. The low word is stored in the two bytes with the lower addresses. The address of the lowest byte is the address of the doubleword. The higher addresses are used only when the upper word is being accessed separately from the lower word, or when individual bytes are being accessed. Figure 2-3 illustrates the arrangement of bytes within words and doublewords.

Note that words do not need to be aligned at even-numbered addresses and doublewords do not need to be aligned at addresses evenly divisible by four. This allows maximum flexibility in data structures (e.g., records containing mixed byte, word, and doubleword items) and efficiency in memory utilization. Because the 386 DX microprocessor has a 32-bit data bus, communication between processor and memory takes place

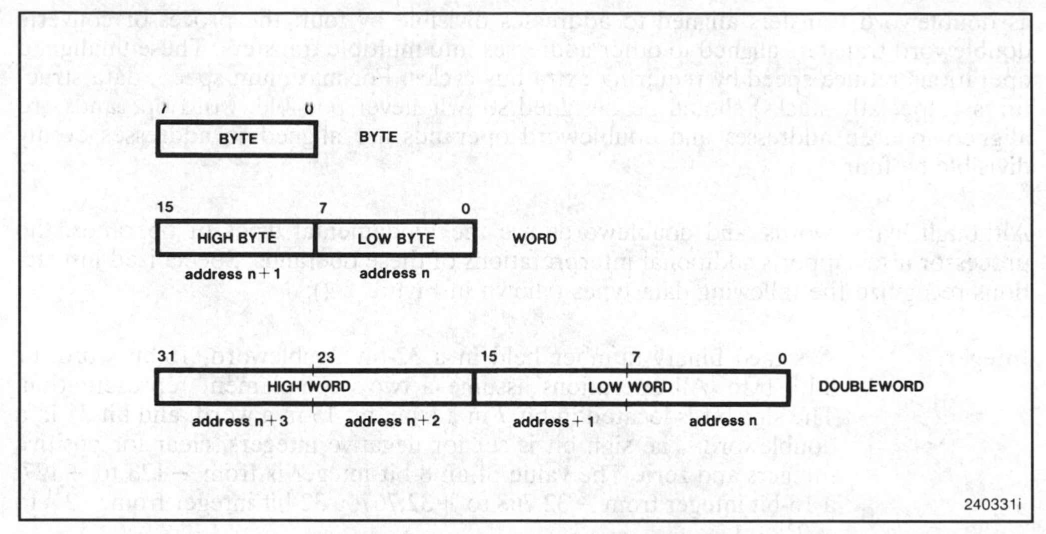

Figure 2-2. Fundamental Data Types

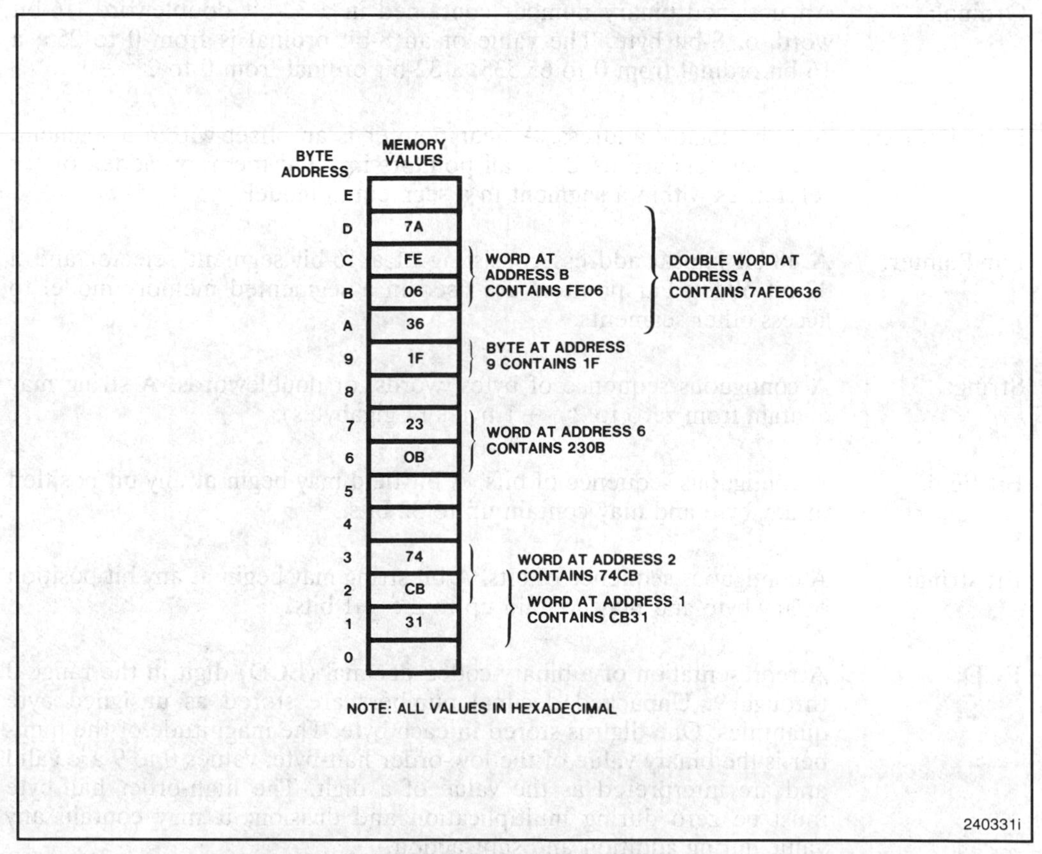

Figure 2-3. Bytes, Words, and Doublewords in Memory

as doubleword transfers aligned to addresses divisible by four; the processor converts doubleword transfers aligned to other addresses into multiple transfers. These unaligned operations reduce speed by requiring extra bus cycles. For maximum speed, data structures (especially stacks) should be designed so, whenever possible, word operands are aligned to even addresses and doubleword operands are aligned to addresses evenly divisible by four.

Although bytes, words, and doublewords are the fundamental types of operands, the processor also supports additional interpretations of these operands. Specialized instructions recognize the following data types (shown in Figure 2-4):

Integer: A signed binary number held in a 32-bit doubleword, 16-bit word, or 8-bit byte. All operations assume a two's complement representation. The sign bit is located in bit 7 in a byte, bit 15 in a word, and bit 31 in a doubleword. The sign bit is set for negative integers, clear for positive integers and zero. The value of an 8-bit integer is from −128 to +127; a 16-bit integer from −32,768 to +32,767; a 32-bit integer from -2^{31} to $+2^{31}-1$.

Ordinal: An unsigned binary number contained in a 32-bit doubleword, 16-bit word, or 8-bit byte. The value of an 8-bit ordinal is from 0 to 255; a 16-bit ordinal from 0 to 65,535; a 32-bit ordinal from 0 to $2^{32}-1$.

Near Pointer: A 32-bit logical address. A near pointer is an offset within a segment. Near pointers are used for all pointers in a flat memory model, or for references within a segment in a segmented model.

Far Pointer: A 48-bit logical address consisting of a 16-bit segment selector and a 32-bit offset. Far pointers are used in a segmented memory model to access other segments.

String: A contiguous sequence of bytes, words, or doublewords. A string may contain from zero to $2^{32}-1$ bytes (4 gigabytes).

Bit field: A contiguous sequence of bits. A bit field may begin at any bit position of any byte and may contain up to 32 bits.

Bit string: A contiguous sequence of bits. A bit string may begin at any bit position of any byte and may contain up to $2^{32}-1$ bits.

BCD: A representation of a binary-coded decimal (BCD) digit in the range 0 through 9. Unpacked decimal numbers are stored as unsigned byte quantities. One digit is stored in each byte. The magnitude of the number is the binary value of the low-order half-byte; values 0 to 9 are valid and are interpreted as the value of a digit. The high-order half-byte must be zero during multiplication and division; it may contain any value during addition and subtraction.

Packed BCD: A representation of binary-coded decimal digits, each in the range 0 to 9. One digit is stored in each half-byte, two digits in each byte. The digit in bits 4 to 7 is more significant than the digit in bits 0 to 3. Values 0 to 9 are valid for a digit.

2.3 REGISTERS

The 386 DX microprocessor contains sixteen registers which may be used by an application programmer. As Figure 2-5 shows, these registers may be grouped as:

1. General Registers. These eight 32-bit registers are free for use by the programmer.
2. Segment registers. These registers hold segment selectors associated with different forms of memory access. For example, there are separate segment registers for access to code and stack space. These six registers determine, at any given time, which segments of memory are currently available.
3. Status and control registers. These registers report and allow modification of the state of the 386 DX microprocessor.

2.3.1 General Registers

The general registers; are the 32-bit registers EAX, EBX, ECX, EDX, EBP, ESP, ESI, and EDI. These registers are used to hold operands for logical and arithmetic operations. They also may be used to hold operands for address calculations (except the ESP register cannot be used as an index operand). The names of these registers are derived from the names of the general registers on the 8086 processor, the AX, BX, CX, DX, BP, SP, SI, and DI registers. As Figure 2-5 shows, the low 16 bits of the general registers can be referenced using these names.

Operations which specify a general register as a destination can change part or all of the register. If a destination register has more bytes than the operand, the upper part of the register is left unchanged. Instructions which use a 16-bit general register require the 16-bit operand size prefix. The prefix is a byte with the value 67H placed before the rest of the instruction. Instruction opcodes use a single bit to select either 8- or 32-bit operands. Selection of 16-bit operands is infrequent enough that an instruction prefix is a more efficient instruction encoding than one in which an additional bit in the opcode is used. This, together with byte alignment of instructions, provides greater code density than with word-aligned instruction sets. The 386 DX microprocessor has many one-, two-, and three-byte instructions which would be two- and four-byte instructions in a word-aligned instruction set.

Each byte of the 16-bit registers AX, BX, CX, and DX also have other names. The byte registers are named AH, BH, CH, and DH (high bytes) and AL, BL, CL, and DL (low bytes).

All of the general-purpose registers are available for address calculations and for the results of most arithmetic and logical operations; however, a few instructions assign specific registers to hold operands. For example, string instructions use the contents of

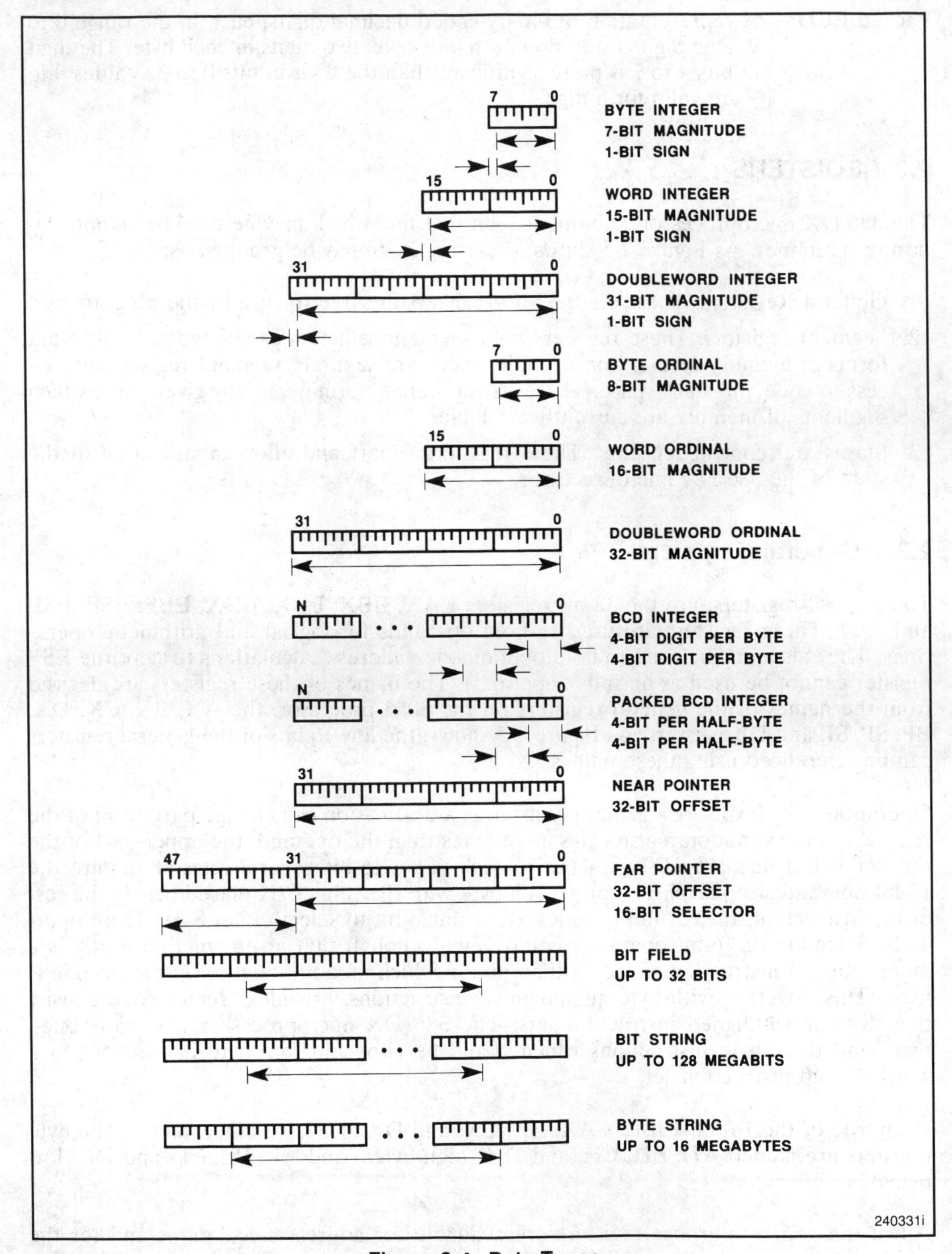

Figure 2-4. Data Types

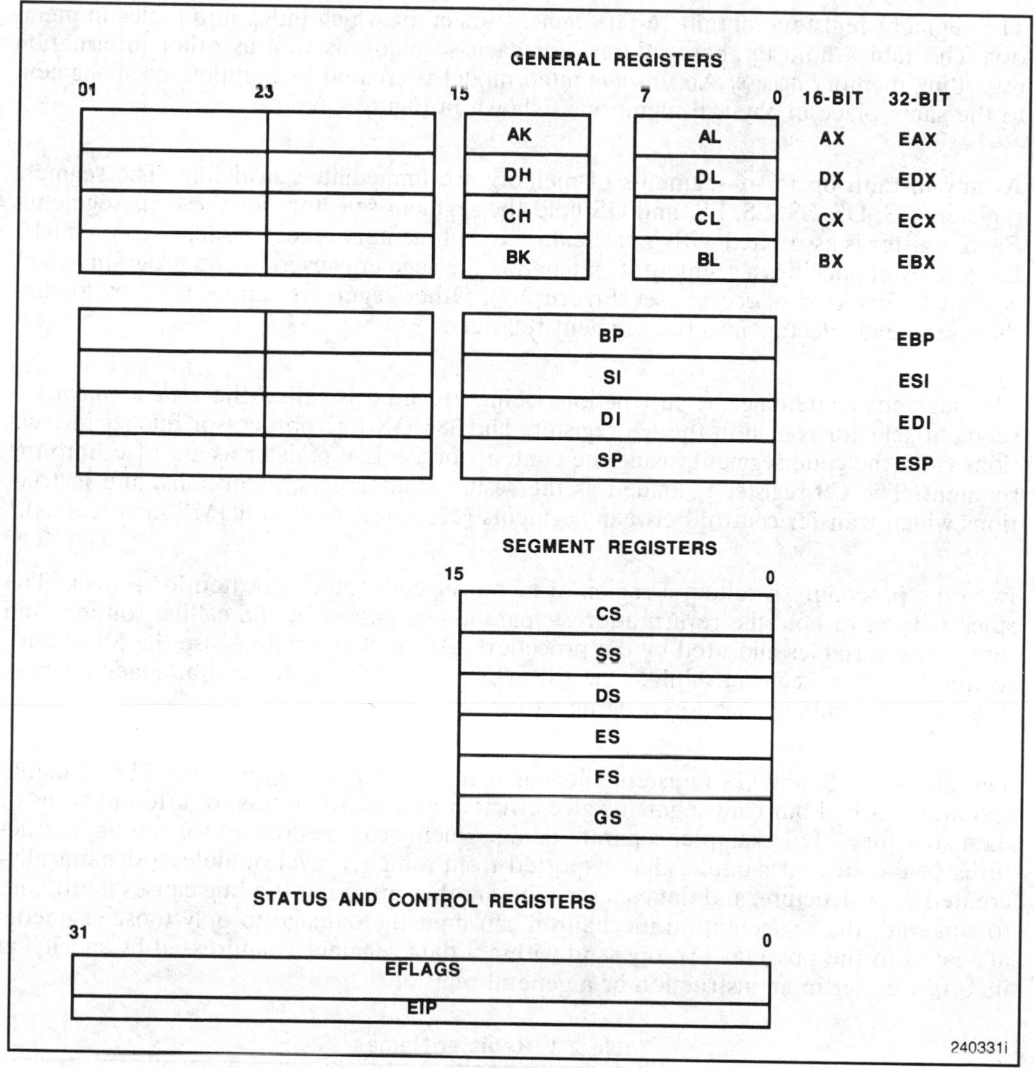

Figure 2-5. Application Register Set

the ECX, ESI, and EDI registers as operands. By assigning specific registers for these functions, the instruction set can be encoded more compactly. The instructions using specific registers include: double-precision multiply and divide, I/O, strings, translate, loop, variable shift and rotate, and stack operations.

2.3.2 Segment Registers

Segmentation gives system designers the flexibility to choose among various models of memory organization. Implementation of memory models is the subject of Part II— System Programming.

The segment registers contain 16-bit segment selectors, which index into tables in memory. The tables hold the base address for each segment, as well as other information regarding memory access. An unsegmented model is created by mapping each segment to the same place in physical memory, as shown in Figure 2-6.

At any instant, up to six segments of memory are immediately available. The segment registers CS, DS, SS, ES, FS, and GS hold the segment selectors for these six segments. Each register is associated with a particular kind of memory access (code, data, or stack). Each register specifies a segment, from among the segments used by the program, which is used for its kind of access (see Figure 2-7). Other segments can be used by loading their segment selectors into the segment registers.

The segment containing the instructions being executed is called the *code segment*. Its segment selector is held in the CS register. The 386 DX microprocessor fetches instructions from the code segment, using the contents of the EIP register as an offset into the segment. The CS register is loaded as the result of interrupts, exceptions, and instructions which transfer control between segments (e.g., the CALL and JMP instructions).

Before a procedure is called, a region of memory needs to be allocated for a stack. The stack is used to hold the return address, parameters passed by the calling routine, and temporary variables allocated by the procedure. All stack operations use the SS register to find the stack segment. Unlike the CS register, the SS register can be loaded explicitly, which permits application programs to set up stacks.

The DS, ES, FS, and GS registers allow as many as four data segments to be available simultaneously. Four data segments give efficient and secure access to different types of data structures. For example, separate data segments can be created for the data structures of the current module, data exported from a higher-level module, a dynamically-created data structure, and data shared with another program. If a bug causes a program to run wild, the segmentation mechanism can limit the damage to only those segments allocated to the program. An operand within a data segment is addressed by specifying its offset either in an instruction or a general register.

Table 2-1. Register Names

8-Bit	16-Bit	32-Bit
AL	AX	EAX
AH		
BL	BX	EBX
BH		
CL	CX	ECX
CH		
DL	DX	EDX
DH		
	SI	ESI
	DI	EDI
	BP	EBP
	SP	ESP

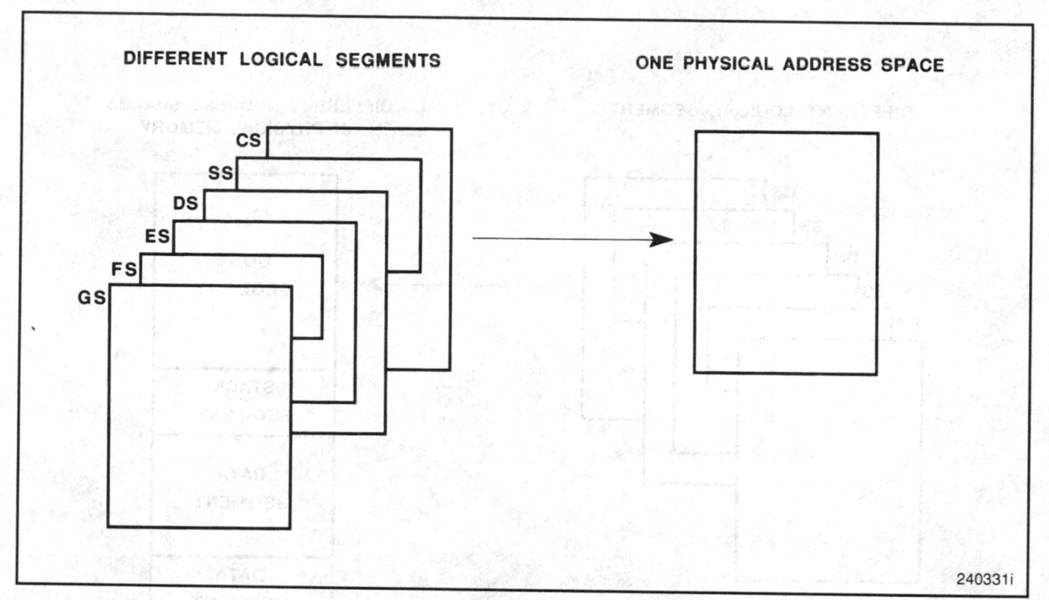

Figure 2-6. An Unsegmented Memory

Depending on the structure of data (i.e., the way data is partitioned into segments), a program may require access to more than four data segments. To access additional segments, the DS, ES, FS, and GS registers can be loaded by an application program during execution. The only requirement is to load the appropriate segment register before accessing data in its segment.

A base address is kept for each segment. To address data within a segment, a 32-bit offset is added to the segment's base address. Once a segment is selected (by loading the segment selector into a segment register), an instruction only needs to specify the offset. Simple rules define which segment register is used to form an address when only an offset is specified.

2.3.3 Stack Implementation

Stack operations are supported by three registers:

1. **Stack Segment (SS) Register:** Stacks reside in memory. The number of stacks in a system is limited only by the maximum number of segments. A stack may be up to 4 gigabytes long, the maximum size of a segment on the 386 DX microprocessor. One stack is available at a time—the stack whose segment selector is held in the SS register. This is the current stack, often referred to simply as "the" stack. The SS register is used automatically by the processor for all stack operations.
2. **Stack Pointer (ESP) Register:** The ESP register holds an offset to the top-of-stack (TOS) in the current stack segment. It is used by PUSH and POP operations, subroutine calls and returns, exceptions, and interrupts. When an item is pushed onto

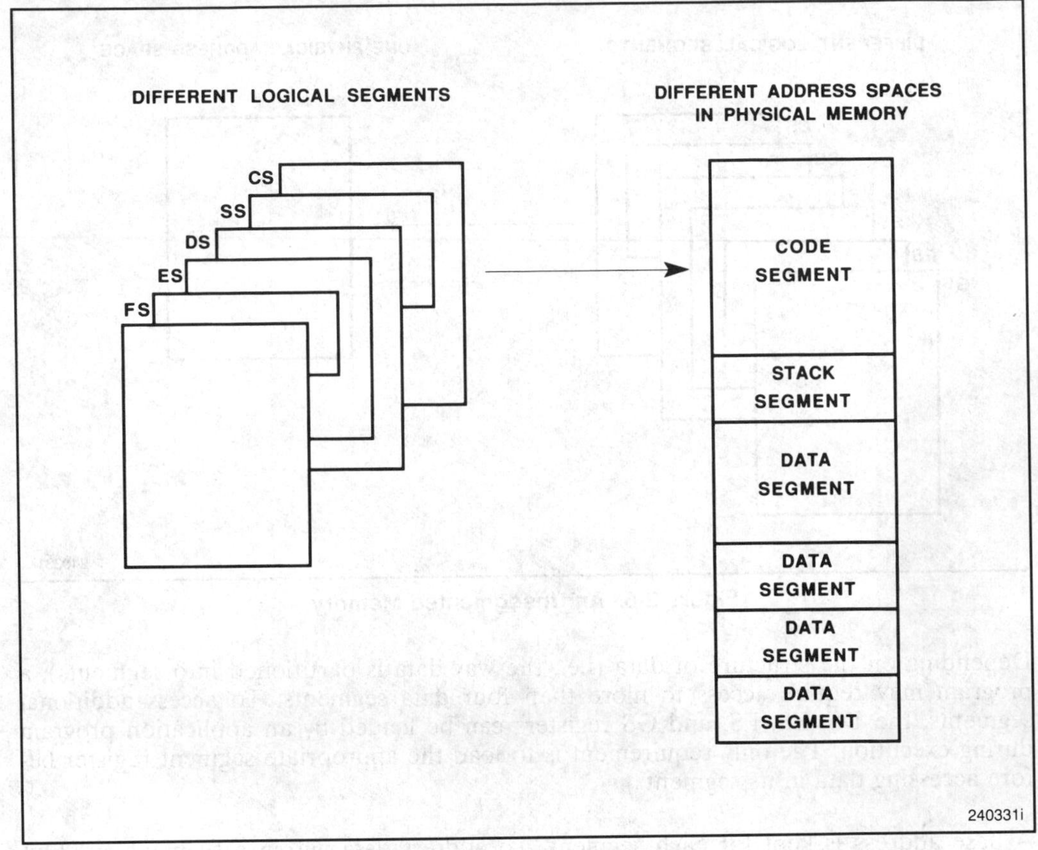

Figure 2-7. A Segmented Memory

the stack (see Figure 2-8), the processor decrements the ESP register, then writes the item at the new TOS. When an item is popped off the stack, the processor copies it from the TOS, then increments the ESP register. In other words, the stack grows *down* in memory toward lesser addresses.

3. **Stack-Frame Base Pointer (EBP) Register:** The EBP register typically is used to access data structures passed on the stack. For example, on entering a subroutine the stack contains the return address and some number of data structures passed to the subroutine. The subroutine adds to the stack whenever it needs to create space for temporary local variables. As a result, the stack pointer moves around as temporary variables are pushed and popped. If the stack pointer is copied into the base pointer before anything is pushed on the stack, the base pointer can be used to reference data structures with fixed offsets. If this is not done, the offset to access a particular data structure would change whenever a temporary variable is allocated or de-allocated.

   When the EBP register is used to address memory, the current stack segment is selected (i.e., the SS segment). Because the stack segment does not have to be

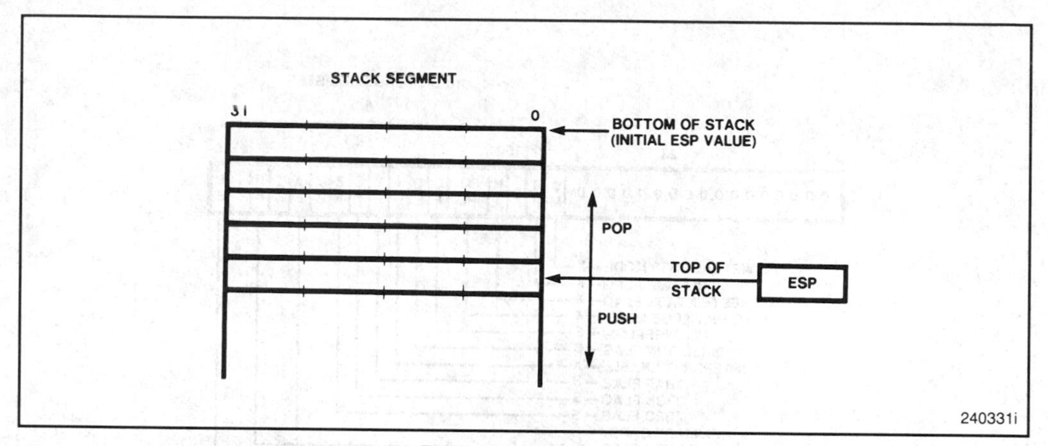

Figure 2-8. Stacks

specified, instruction encoding is more compact. The EBP register also can be used to address other segments.

Instructions, such as the ENTER and LEAVE instructions, are provided which automatically set up the EBP register for convenient access to variables.

2.3.4 Flags Register

Condition codes (e.g., carry, sign, overflow) and mode bits are kept in a 32-bit register named EFLAGS. Figure 2-9 defines the bits within this register. The flags control certain operations and indicate the status of the 386 DX microprocessor.

The flags may be considered in three groups: status flags, control flags, and system flags. Discussion of the system flags occurs in Part II.

2.3.4.1 STATUS FLAGS

The status flags of the EFLAGS register report the kind of result produced from the execution of arithmetic instructions. The MOV instruction does not affect these flags. Conditional jumps and subroutine calls allow a program to sense the state of the status flags and respond to them. For example, when the counter controlling a loop is decremented to zero, the state of the ZF flag changes, and this change can be used to suppress the conditional jump to the start of the loop.

The status flags are shown in Table 2-2.

2.3.4.2 CONTROL FLAG

The control flag DF of the EFLAGS register controls string instructions.

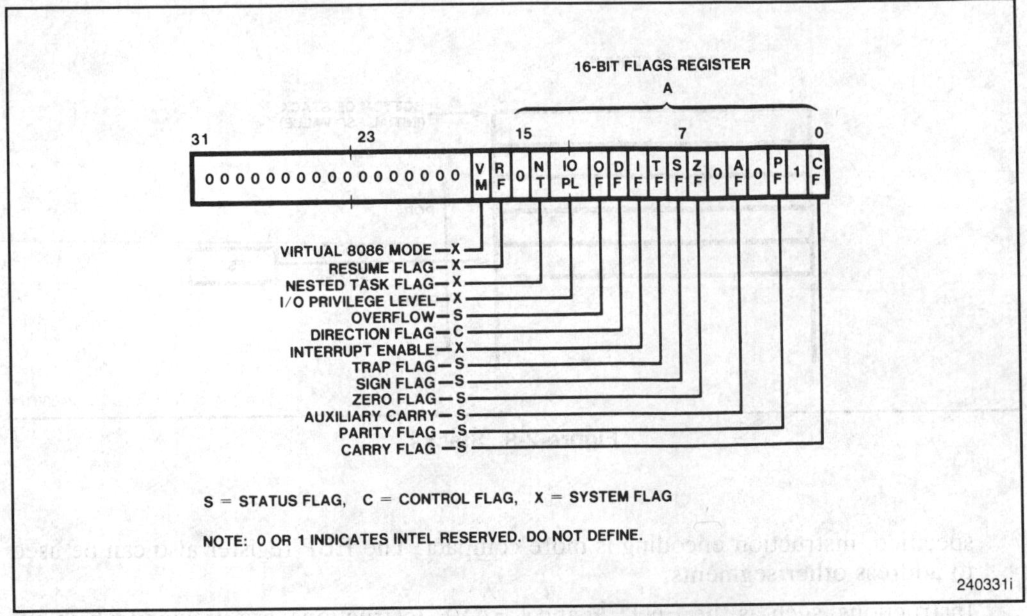

Figure 2-9. EFLAGS Register

Table 2-2. Status Flags

Name	Purpose	Condition Reported
OF	overflow	Result exceeds positive or negative limit of number range
SF	sign	Result is negative (less than zero)
ZF	zero	Result is zero
AF	auxiliary carry	Carry out of bit position 3 (used for BCD)
PF	parity	Low byte of result has even parity (even number of set bits)
CF	carry flag	Carry out of most significant bit of result

DF (Direction Flag, bit 10)

Setting the DF flag causes string instructions to auto-decrement, that is, to process strings from high addresses to low addresses. Clearing the DF flag causes string instructions to auto-increment, or to process strings from low addresses to high addresses.

2.3.4.3 INSTRUCTION POINTER

The instruction pointer (EIP) register contains the offset into the current code segment for the next instruction to execute. The instruction pointer is not directly available to the programmer; it is controlled implicitly by control-transfer instructions (jumps, returns, etc.), interrupts, and exceptions.

2.4 INSTRUCTION FORMAT

The information encoded in an instruction includes a specification of the operation to be performed, the type of the operands to be manipulated, and the location of these operands. If an operand is located in memory, the instruction also must select, explicitly or implicitly, the segment which contains the operand.

An instruction may have various parts and formats. The exact format of instructions is shown in Appendix B; the parts of an instruction are described below. Of these parts, only the opcode is always present. The other parts may or may not be present, depending on the operation involved and the location and type of the operands. The parts of an instruction, in order of occurrence, are listed below:

- **Prefixes:** one or more bytes preceding an instruction which modify the operation of the instruction. The following prefixes can be used by application programs:
  1. Segment override – explicitly specifies which segment register an instruction should use, instead of the default segment register.
  2. Address size – switches between 16- and 32-bit addressing. Either size can be the default; this prefix selects the non-default size.
  3. Operand size – switches between 16- and 32-bit data size. Either size can be the default; this prefix selects the non-default size.
  4. Repeat – used with a string instruction to cause the instruction to be repeated for each element of the string.

- **Opcode:** specifies the operation performed by the instruction. Some operations have several different opcodes, each specifying a different form of the operation.

- **Register specifier:** an instruction may specify one or two register operands. Register specifiers occur either in the same byte as the opcode or in the same byte as the addressing-mode specifier.

- **Addressing-mode specifier:** when present, specifies whether an operand is a register or memory location; if in memory, specifies whether a displacement, a base register, an index register, and scaling are to be used.

- **SIB (scale, index, base) byte:** when the addressing-mode specifier indicates an index register will be used to calculate the address of an operand, a SIB byte is included in the instruction to encode the base register, the index register, and a scaling factor.

- **Displacement:** when the addressing-mode specifier indicates a displacement will be used to compute the address of an operand, the displacement is encoded in the instruction. A displacement is a signed integer of 32, 16, or 8 bits. The 8-bit form is used in the common case when the displacement is sufficiently small. The processor extends an 8-bit displacement to 16 or 32 bits, taking into account the sign.

- **Immediate operand:** when present, directly provides the value of an operand. Immediate operands may be bytes, words, or doublewords. In cases where an 8-bit immediate operand is used with a 16- or 32-bit operand, the processor extends the eight-bit operand to an integer of the same sign and magnitude in the larger size. In the same way, a 16-bit operand is extended to 32-bits.

2.5 OPERAND SELECTION

An instruction acts on zero or more operands. An example of a zero-operand instruction is the NOP instruction (no operation). An operand can be held in any of these places:

- In the instruction itself (an immediate operand).
- In a register (in the case of 32-bit operands, EAX, EBX, ECX, EDX, ESI, EDI, ESP, or EBP; in the case of 16-bit operands AX, BX, CX, DX, SI, DI, SP, or BP; in the case of 8-bit operands AH, AL, BH, BL, CH, CL, DH, or DL; the segment registers; or the EFLAGS register for flag operations). Use of 16-bit register operands requires use of the 16-bit operand size prefix (a byte with the value 67H preceding the instruction).
- In memory.
- At an I/O port.

Immediate operands and operands in registers can be accessed more rapidly than operands in memory because memory operands require extra bus cycles. Register and immediate operands are available on-chip, the latter because they are prefetched as part of interpreting the instruction.

Of the instructions which have operands, some specify operands implicitly; others specify operands explicitly; still others use a combination of both. For example:

Implicit operand: `AAM`

By definition, AAM (ASCII adjust for multiplication) operates on the contents of the AX register.

Explicit operand: `XCHG EAX, EBX`

The operands to be exchanged are encoded in the instruction with the opcode.

Implicit and explicit operands: `PUSH COUNTER`

The memory variable COUNTER (the explicit operand) is copied to the top of the stack (the implicit operand).

Note that most instructions have implicit operands. All arithmetic instructions, for example, update the EFLAGS register.

An instruction can *explicitly* reference one or two operands. Two-operand instructions, such as MOV, ADD, and XOR, generally overwrite one of the two participating operands with the result. This is the difference between the *source operand* (the one unaffected by the operation) and the *destination operand* (the one overwritten by the result).

For most instructions, one of the two explicitly specified operands—either the source or the destination—can be either in a register or in memory. The other operand must be in a register or it must be an immediate source operand. This puts the explicit two-operand instructions into the following groups:

- Register to register
- Register to memory
- Memory to register
- Immediate to register
- Immediate to memory

Certain string instructions and stack manipulation instructions, however, transfer data from memory to memory. Both operands of some string instructions are in memory and are specified implicitly. Push and pop stack operations allow transfer between memory operands and the memory-based stack.

Several three-operand instructions are provided, such as the IMUL, SHRD, and SHLD instructions. Two of the three operands are specified explicitly, as for the two-operand instructions, while a third is taken from the ECX register or supplied as an immediate. Other three-operand instructions, such as the string instructions when used with a repeat prefix, take all their operands from registers.

2.5.1 Immediate Operands

Certain instructions use data from the instruction itself as one (and sometimes two) of the operands. Such an operand is called an *immediate* operand. It may be a byte, word, or doubleword. For example:

```
SHR PATTERN, 2
```

One byte of the instruction holds the value 2, the number of bits by which to shift the variable PATTERN.

```
TEST PATTERN, 0FFFF00FFH
```

A doubleword of the instruction holds the mask which is used to test the variable PATTERN.

```
IMUL CX, MEMWORD, 3
```

A word in memory is multiplied by an immediate 3 and stored into the CX register.

All arithmetic instructions (except divide) allow the source operand to be an immediate value. When the destination is the EAX or AL register, the instruction encoding is one byte shorter than with the other general registers.

2.5.2 Register Operands

Operands may be located in one of the 32-bit general registers (EAX, EBX, ECX, EDX, ESI, EDI, ESP, or EBP), in one of the 16-bit general registers (AX, BX, CX, DX, SI, DI, SP, or BP), or in one of the 8-bit general registers (AH, BH, CH, DH, AL, BL, CL, or DL). An instruction which uses 16-bit register operands must use the 16-bit operand size prefix (a byte with the value 67H before the remainder of the instruction).

The 386 DX microprocessor has instructions for referencing the segment registers (CS, DS, ES, SS, FS, and GS). These instructions are used by application programs only if segmentation is being used.

The 386 DX microprocessor also has instructions for changing the state of individual flags in the EFLAGS register. Instructions have been provided for setting and clearing flags which often need to be accessed. The other flags, which are not accessed so often, can be changed by pushing the contents of the EFLAGS register on the stack, making changes to it while it's on the stack, and popping it back into the register.

2.5.3 Memory Operands

Instructions with explicit operands in memory must reference the segment containing the operand and the offset from the beginning of the segment to the operand. Segments are specified using a segment-override prefix, which is a byte placed at the beginning of an instruction. If no segment is specified, simple rules assign the segment by default. The offset is specified in one of the following ways:

1. Most instructions which access memory contain a byte for specifying the addressing method of the operand. The byte, called the *modR/M byte*, comes after the opcode and specifies whether the operand is in a register or in memory. If the operand is in memory, the address is calculated from a segment register and any of the following values: a base register, an index register, a scaling factor, and a displacement. When an index register is used, the modR/M byte also is followed by another byte to specify the index register and scaling factor. This form of addressing is the most flexible.

2. A few instructions select segments by default:

   A MOV instruction with the AL or EAX register as either source or destination can address memory with a doubleword encoded in the instruction. This special form of the MOV instruction allows no base register, index register, or scaling factor to be used. This form is one byte shorter than the general-purpose form.

   String operations address memory in the DS segment using the ESI register, (the MOVS, CMPS, OUTS, LODS, and SCAS instructions) or using the ES segment and EDI register (the MOVS, CMPS, INS, and STOS instructions).

   Stack operations address memory in the SS segment using the ESP register (the PUSH, POP, PUSHA, PUSHAD, POPA, POPAD, PUSHF, PUSHFD, POPF, POPFD, CALL, RET, IRET, and IRETD instructions, exceptions, and interrupts).

2.5.3.1 SEGMENT SELECTION

Explicit specification of a segment is optional. If a segment is not specified using a segment-override prefix, the processor automatically chooses a segment according to the rules of Table 2-3. (If a flat model of memory organization is used, the rules for selecting segments are not apparent to application programs.)

Table 2-3. Default Segment Selection Rules

Type of Reference	Segment Used Register Used	Default Selection Rule
Instructions	Code Segment CS register	Automatic with instruction fetch.
Stack	Stack Segment LSS register	All stack pushes and pops. Any memory reference which uses ESP or EBP as a base register.
Local Data	Data Segment DS register	All data references except when relative to stack or string destination.
Destination Strings	E-Space Segment ES register	Destination of string instructions.

Different kinds of memory access have different default segments. Data operands usually use the main data segment (the DS segment). However, the ESP and EBP registers are used for addressing the stack, so when either register is used, the stack segment (the SS segment) is selected.

Segment-override prefixes are used to override the default segment selection. Segment-override prefixes are provided for each of the segment registers. Only the following special cases have a default segment selection which is not affected by a segment-override prefix:

- Destination strings in string instructions use the ES segment
- Stack operands use the SS segment
- Instruction fetches use the CS segment

2.5.3.2 EFFECTIVE-ADDRESS COMPUTATION

The modR/M byte provides the most flexible form of addressing. Instructions which have a modR/M byte after the opcode are the most common in the instruction set. For memory operands specified by a modR/M byte, the offset within the selected segment is the sum of three components:

- A displacement
- A base register
- An index register (the index register may be multiplied by a factor of 2, 4, or 8)

The offset which results from adding these components is called an *effective address*. Each of these components may have either a positive or negative value. Figure 2-10 illustrates the full set of possibilities for modR/M addressing.

The displacement component, because it is encoded in the instruction, is useful for relative addressing by fixed amounts, such as:

- Location of simple scalar operands.
- Beginning of a statically allocated array.
- Offset to a field within a record.

The base and index components have similar functions. Both use the same set of general registers. Both can be used for addressing which changes during program execution, such as:

- Location of procedure parameters and local variables on the stack.
- The beginning of one record among several occurrences of the same record type or in an array of records.
- The beginning of one dimension of multiple dimension array.
- The beginning of a dynamically allocated array.

The uses of general registers as base or index components differ in the following respects:

- The ESP register cannot be used as an index register.
- When the ESP or EBP register is used as the base, the SS segment is the default selection. In all other cases, the DS segment is the default selection.

The scaling factor permits efficient indexing into an array when the array elements are 2, 4, or 8 bytes. The scaling of the index register is done in hardware at the time the address is evaluated. This eliminates an extra shift or multiply instruction.

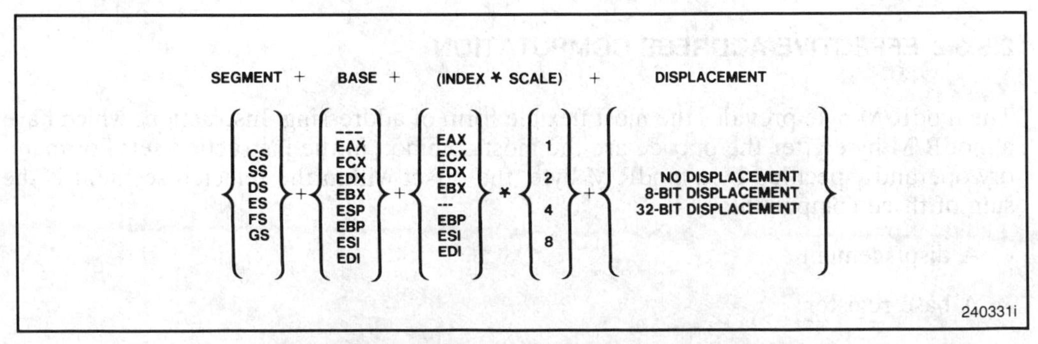

Figure 2-10. Effective Address Computation

The base, index, and displacement components may be used in any combination; any of these components may be null. A scale factor can be used only when an index also is used. Each possible combination is useful for data structures commonly used by programmers in high level languages and assembly language. Suggested uses for some combinations of address components are described below.

DISPLACEMENT

The displacement alone indicates the offset of the operand. This form of addressing is used to access a statically allocated scalar operand. A byte, word, or doubleword displacement can be used.

BASE

The offset to the operand is specified indirectly in one of the general registers, as for "based" variables.

BASE + DISPLACEMENT

A register and a displacement can be used together for two distinct purposes:

1. Index into static array when the element size is not 2, 4, or 8 bytes. The displacement component encodes the offset of the beginning of the array. The register holds the results of a calculation to determine the offset to a specific element within the array.
2. Access a field of a record. The base register holds the address of the beginning of the record, while the displacement is an offset to the field.

An important special case of this combination is access to parameters in a procedure activation record. A procedure activation record is the stack frame created when a subroutine is entered. In this case, the EBP register is the best choice for the base register, because it automatically selects the stack segment. This is a compact encoding for this common function.

(INDEX * SCALE) + DISPLACEMENT

This combination is an efficient way to index into a static array when the element size is 2, 4, or 8 bytes. The displacement addresses the beginning of the array, the index register holds the subscript of the desired array element, and the processor automatically converts the subscript into an index by applying the scaling factor.

BASE + INDEX + DISPLACEMENT

Two registers used together support either a two-dimensional array (the displacement holds the address of the beginning of the array) or one of several instances of an array of records (the displacement is an offset to a field within the record).

BASE + (INDEX * SCALE) + DISPLACEMENT

This combination provides efficient indexing of a two-dimensional array when the elements of the array are 2, 4, or 8 bytes in size.

2.6 INTERRUPTS AND EXCEPTIONS

The 386 DX microprocessor has two mechanisms for interrupting program execution:

1. *Exceptions* are synchronous events which are responses of the processor to certain conditions detected during the execution of an instruction.
2. *Interrupts* are asynchronous events typically triggered by external devices needing attention.

Interrupts and exceptions are alike in that both cause the processor to temporarily suspend the program being run in order to run a program of higher priority. The major distinction between these two kinds of interrupts is their origin. An exception is always reproducible by re-executing the program which caused the exception, while an interrupt can have a complex, timing-dependent relationship with programs.

Application programmers normally are not concerned with handling exceptions or interrupts. The operating system, monitor, or device driver handles them. More information on interrupts for system programmers may be found in Chapter 9. Certain kinds of exceptions, however, are relevant to application programming, and many operating systems give application programs the opportunity to service these exceptions. However, the operating system defines the interface between the application program and the exception mechanism of the 386 DX microprocessor. Table 2-4 lists the interrupts and exceptions.

- A divide-error exception; results when the DIV or IDIV instruction is executed with a zero denominator or when the quotient is too large for the destination operand. (See Chapter 3 for more information on the DIV and IDIV instructions.)
- A debug exception may be sent back to an application program if it results from the TF (trap) flag.
- A breakpoint exception results when an INT3 instruction is executed. This instruction is used by some debuggers to stop program execution at specific points.
- An overflow exception results when the INTO instruction is executed and the OF (overflow) flag is set. See Chapter 3 for a discussion of the INTO instruction.
- A bounds-check exception results when the BOUND instruction is executed with an array index which falls outside the bounds of the array. See Chapter 3 for a discussion of the BOUND instruction.
- The coprocessor-not-available exception occurs if the program contains instructions for a coprocessor, but no coprocessor is present in the system.
- A coprocessor-error exception is generated when a coprocessor detects an illegal operation.

Table 2-4. Exceptions and Interrupts

Vector Number	Description
0	Divide Error
1	Debugger Call
2	NMI Interrupt
3	Breakpoint
4	INTO-detected Overflow
5	BOUND Range Exceeded
6	Invalid Opcode
7	Coprocessor Not Available
8	Double Fault
9	Coprocessor Segment Overrun
10	Invalid Task State Segment
11	Segment Not Present
12	Stack Exception
13	General Protection
15	(Intel® reserved. Do not use.)
16	Coprocessor Error
17-31	(Intel reserved. Do not use.)
32-255	Maskable Interrupts

The INT instruction generates an interrupt whenever it is executed; the processor treats this interrupt as an exception. Its effects (and the effects of all other exceptions) are determined by exception handler routines in the application program or the operating system. The INT instruction itself is discussed in Chapter 3. See Chapter 9 for a more complete description of exceptions.

Exceptions caused by segmentation and paging are handled differently than interrupts. Normally, the contents of the program counter (EIP register) are saved on the stack when an exception or interrupt is generated. But exceptions resulting from segmentation and paging restore the contents of some processor registers to their state *before* interpretation of the instruction began. The saved contents of the program counter address the instruction which caused the exception, rather than the instruction after it. This lets the operating system fix the exception-generating condition and restart the program which generated the exception. This mechanism is completely transparent to the program.

Application Programming 3

CHAPTER 3
APPLICATION PROGRAMMING

This chapter is an overview of the instructions which programmers can use to write application software for the 386™ DX microprocessor. The instructions are grouped by categories of related functions.

The instructions not discussed in this chapter normally are used only by operating-system programmers. Part II describes these instructions.

These instruction descriptions are for the 386 DX microprocessor in protected mode. The instruction set in this mode is a 32-bit superset of the instruction set used in Intel 16-bit processors. In real-address mode or virtual-86 mode, the 386 DX microprocessor appears to have the architecture of a fast, enhanced 16-bit processor with instruction set extensions. See Chapters 13, 14, 15, and 16 for more information about running the 16-bit instruction set. All of the instructions described in this chapter are available in all modes.

The instruction set description in Chapter 17 contains more detailed information on all instructions, including encoding, operation, timing, effect on flags, and exceptions which may be generated.

3.1 DATA MOVEMENT INSTRUCTIONS

These instructions provide convenient methods for moving bytes, words, or doublewords between memory and the processor registers. They come in three types:

1. General-purpose data movement instructions.
2. Stack manipulation instructions.
3. Type-conversion instructions.

3.1.1 General-Purpose Data Movement Instructions

MOV (Move) transfers a byte, word, or doubleword from the source operand to the destination operand. The MOV instruction is useful for transferring data along any of these paths:

- To a register from memory
- To memory from a register
- Between general registers
- Immediate data to a register
- Immediate data to memory

The MOV instruction cannot move from memory to memory or from a segment register to a segment register. Memory-to-memory moves can be performed, however, by the string move instruction MOVS. A special form of the MOV instruction is provided for transferring data between the AL or EAX registers and a location in memory specified by a 32-bit offset encoded in the instruction. This form of the instruction does not allow a segment override, index register, or scaling factor to be used. The encoding of this form is one byte shorter than the encoding of the general-purpose MOV instruction. A similar encoding is provided for moving an 8-, 16-, or 32-bit immediate into any of the general registers.

XCHG (Exchange) swaps the contents of two operands. This instruction takes the place of three MOV instructions. It does not require a temporary location to save the contents of one operand while the other is being loaded. The XCHG instruction is especially useful for implementing semaphores or similar data structures for process synchronization.

The XCHG instruction can swap two byte operands, two word operands, or two doubleword operands. The operands for the XCHG instruction may be two register operands, or a register operand and a memory operand. When used with a memory operand, XCHG automatically activates the LOCK signal. (See Chapter 11 for more information on bus locking.)

3.1.2 Stack Manipulation Instructions

PUSH (Push) decrements the stack pointer (ESP register), then copies the source operand to the top of stack (see Figure 3-1). The PUSH instruction often is used to place parameters on the stack before calling a procedure. Inside a procedure, it can be used to reserve space on the stack for temporary variables. The PUSH instruction operates on memory operands, immediate operands, and register operands (including segment registers). A special form of the PUSH instruction is available for pushing a 32-bit general register on the stack. This form has an encoding which is one byte shorter than the general-purpose form.

PUSHA (Push All Registers) saves the contents of the eight general registers on the stack (see Figure 3-2). This instruction simplifies procedure calls by reducing the number of instructions required to save the contents of the general registers. The processor pushes the general registers on the stack in the following order: EAX, ECX, EDX, EBX, the initial value of ESP before EAX was pushed, EBP, ESI, and EDI. The effect of the PUSHA instruction; is reversed using the POPA instruction.

POP (Pop) transfers the word or doubleword at the current top of stack (indicated by the ESP register) to the destination operand, and then increments the ESP register to point to the new top of stack. See Figure 3-3. POP moves information from the stack to a general register, segment register, or to memory. A special form of the POP instruction is available for popping a doubleword from the stack to a general register. This form has an encoding which is one byte shorter than the general-purpose form.

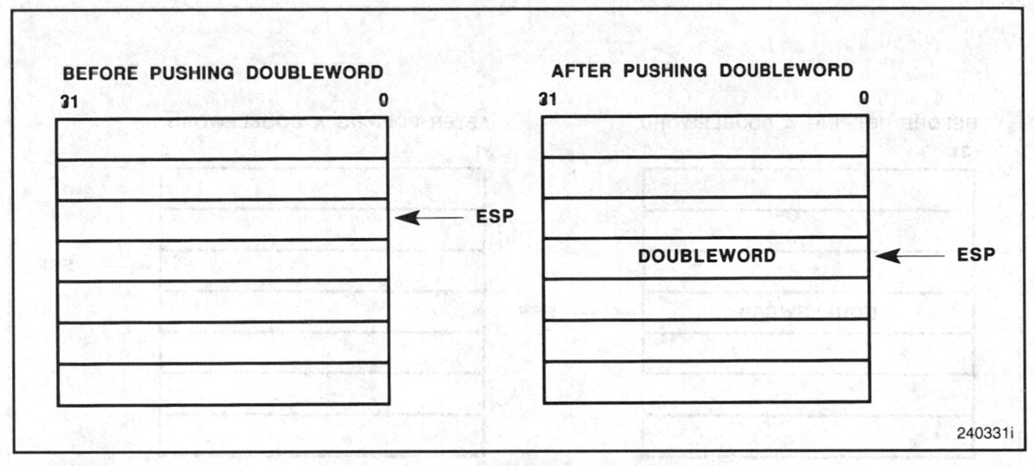

Figure 3-1. PUSH Instruction

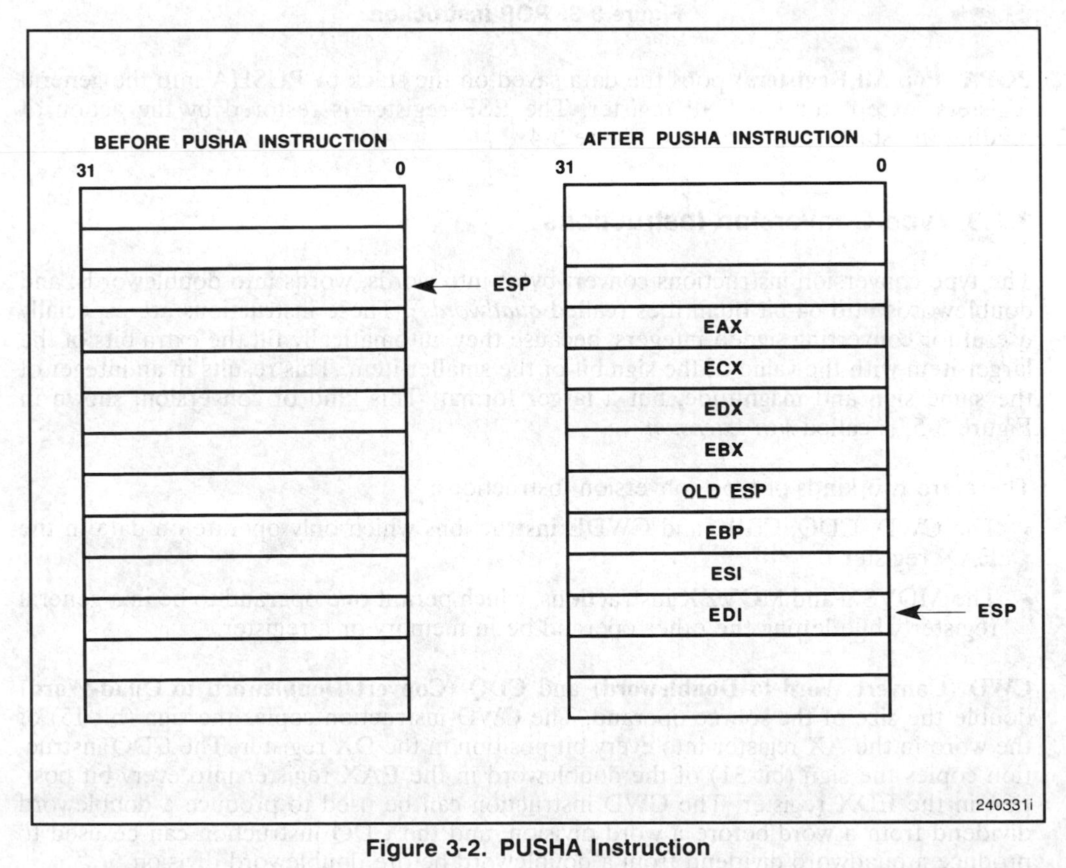

Figure 3-2. PUSHA Instruction

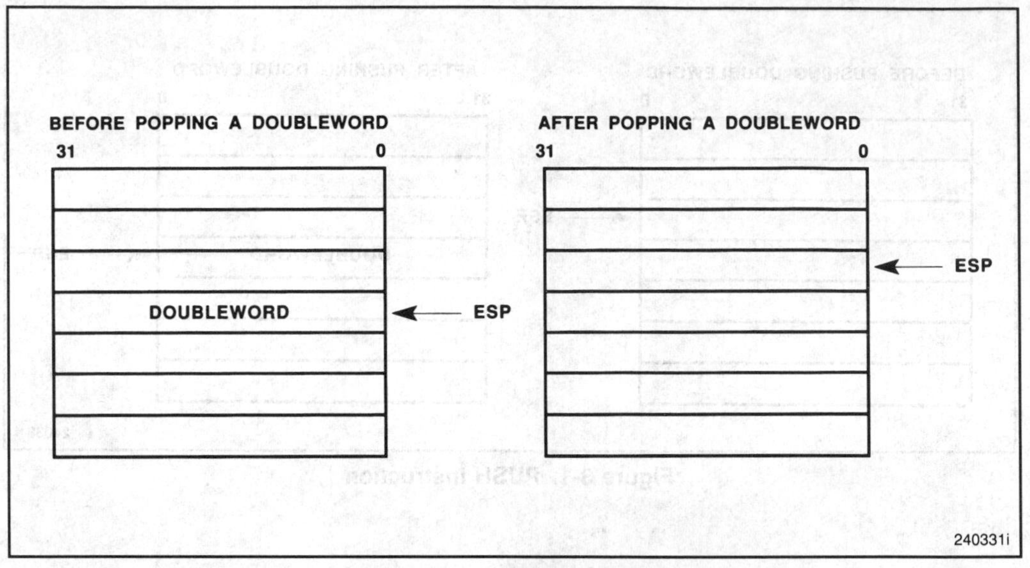

Figure 3-3. POP Instruction

POPA (Pop All Registers) pops the data saved on the stack by PUSHA into the general registers, except for the ESP register. The ESP register is restored by the action of reading the stack (popping). See Figure 3-4.

3.1.3 Type Conversion Instructions

The type conversion instructions convert bytes into words, words into doublewords, and doublewords into 64-bit quantities (called *quadwords*). These instructions are especially useful for converting signed integers, because they automatically fill the extra bits of the larger item with the value of the sign bit of the smaller item. This results in an integer of the same sign and magnitude, but a larger format. This kind of conversion, shown in Figure 3-5, is called *sign extension*.

There are two kinds of type conversion instructions:

- The CWD, CDQ, CBW, and CWDE instructions which only operate on data in the EAX register.
- The MOVSX and MOVZX instructions, which permit one operand to be in a general register while letting the other operand be in memory or a register.

CWD (Convert Word to Doubleword) and **CDQ (Convert Doubleword to Quad-Word)** double the size of the source operand. The CWD instruction copies the sign (bit 15) of the word in the AX register into every bit position in the DX register. The CDQ instruction copies the sign (bit 31) of the doubleword in the EAX register into every bit position in the EDX register. The CWD instruction can be used to produce a doubleword dividend from a word before a word division, and the CDQ instruction can be used to produce a quadword dividend from a doubleword before doubleword division.

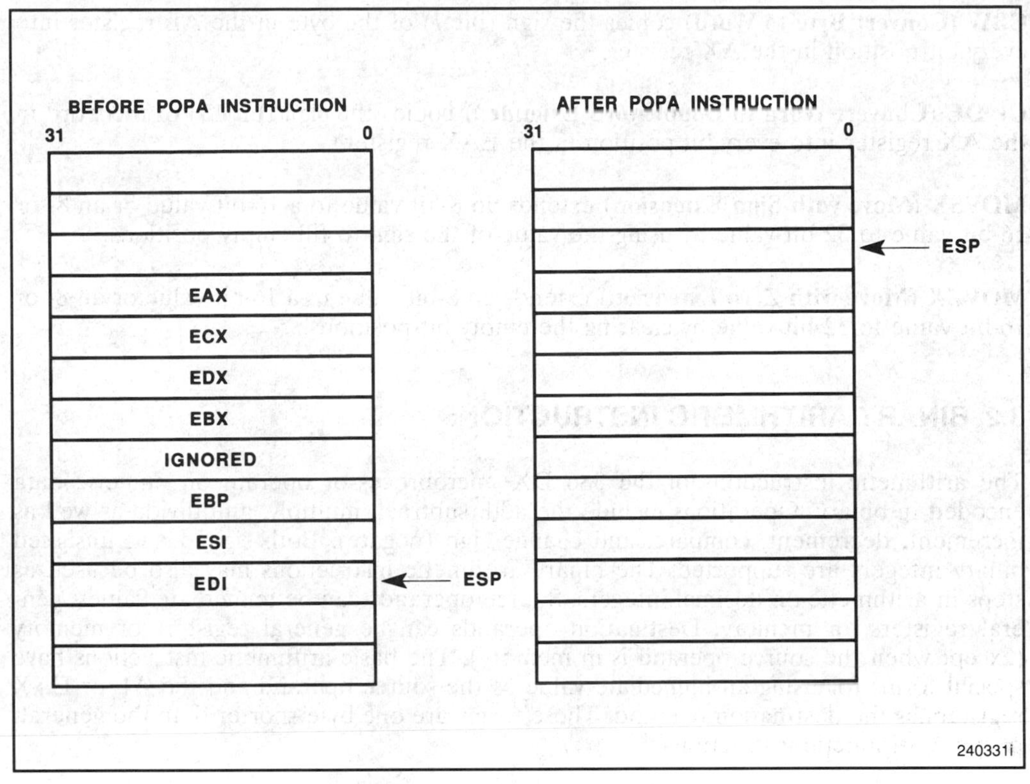

Figure 3-4. POPA Instruction

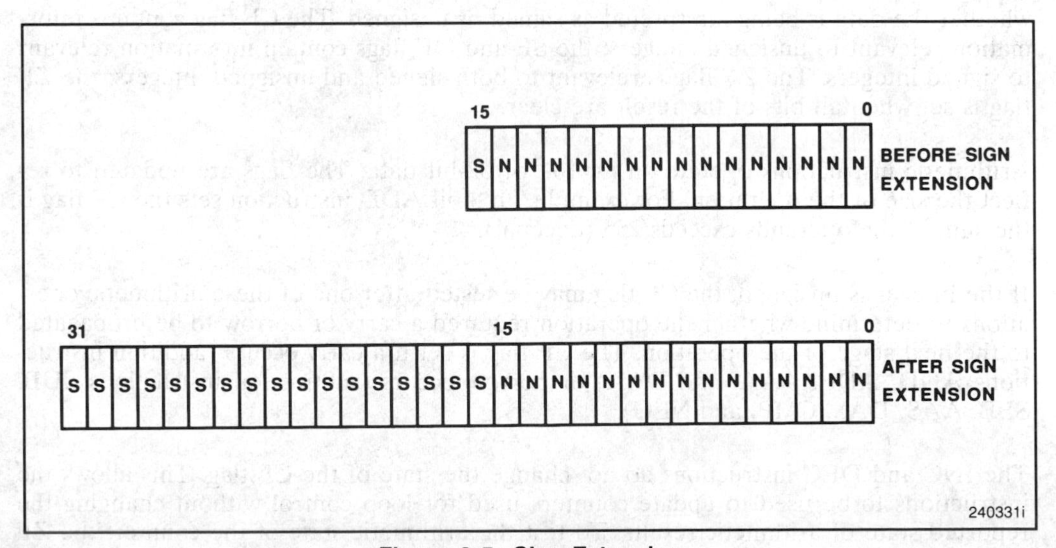

Figure 3-5. Sign Extension

CBW (Convert Byte to Word) copies the sign (bit 7) of the byte in the AL register into every bit position in the AX register.

CWDE (Convert Word to Doubleword Extended) copies the sign (bit 15) of the word in the AX register into every bit position in the EAX register.

MOVSX (Move with Sign Extension) extends an 8-bit value to a 16-bit value or an 8- or 16-bit value to 32-bit value by using the value of the sign to fill empty positions.

MOVZX (Move with Zero Extension) extends an 8-bit value to a 16-bit value or an 8- or 16-bit value to 32-bit value by clearing the empty bit positions.

3.2 BINARY ARITHMETIC INSTRUCTIONS

The arithmetic instructions of the 386 DX microprocessor operate on numeric data encoded in binary. Operations include the add, subtract, multiply, and divide as well as increment, decrement, compare, and change sign (negate). Both signed and unsigned binary integers are supported. The binary arithmetic instructions may also be used as steps in arithmetic on decimal integers. Source operands can be immediate values, general registers, or memory. Destination operands can be general registers or memory (except when the source operand is in memory). The basic arithmetic instructions have special forms for using an immediate value as the source operand and the AL or EAX registers as the destination operand. These forms are one byte shorter than the general-purpose arithmetic instructions.

The arithmetic instructions update the ZF, CF, SF, and OF flags to report the kind of result which was produced. The kind of instruction used to test the flags depends on whether the data is being interpreted as signed or unsigned. The CF flag contains information relevant to unsigned integers; the SF and OF flags contain information relevant to signed integers. The ZF flag is relevant to both signed and unsigned integers; the ZF flag is set when all bits of the result are clear.

Arithmetic instructions operate on 8-, 16-, or 32-bit data. The flags are updated to reflect the size of the operation. For example, an 8-bit ADD instruction sets the CF flag if the sum of the operands exceeds 255 (decimal).

If the integer is unsigned, the CF flag may be tested after one of these arithmetic operations to determine whether the operation required a carry or borrow to be propagated to the next stage of the operation. The CF flag is set if a carry occurs (addition instructions ADD, ADC, AAA, and DAA) or borrow occurs (subtraction instructions SUB, SBB, AAS, DAS, CMP, and NEG).

The INC and DEC instructions do not change the state of the CF flag. This allows the instructions to be used to update counters used for loop control without changing the reported state of arithmetic results. To test the arithmetic state of the counter, the ZF flag can be tested to detect loop termination, or the ADD and SUB instructions can be used to update the value held by the counter.

The SF and OF flags support signed integer arithmetic. The SF flag has the value of the sign bit of the result. The most significant bit (MSB) of the magnitude of a signed integer is the bit next to the sign—bit 6 of a byte, bit 14 of a word, or bit 30 of a doubleword. The OF flag is set in either of these cases:

- A carry was generated from the MSB into the sign bit but no carry was generated out of the sign bit (addition instructions ADD, ADC, INC, AAA, and DAA). In other words, the result was greater than the greatest positive number which could be represented in two's complement form.
- A carry was generated from the sign bit into the MSB but no carry was generated into the sign bit (subtraction instructions SUB, SBB, DEC, AAS, DAS, CMP, and NEG). In other words, the result was smaller than the smallest negative number which could be represented in two's complement form.

These status flags are tested by either kind of conditional instruction: J*cc* (jump on condition *cc*) or SET*cc* (byte set on condition).

3.2.1 Addition and Subtraction Instructions

ADD (Add Integers) replaces the destination operand with the sum of the source and destination operands. The OF, SF, ZF, AF, PF, and CF flags are affected.

ADC (Add Integers with Carry) replaces the destination operand with the sum of the source and destination operands, plus 1 if the CF flag is set. If the CF flag is clear, the ADC instruction performs the same operation as the ADD instruction. An ADC instruction is used to propagate carry when adding numbers in stages, for example when using 32-bit ADD instructions to sum quadword operands. The OF, SF, ZF, AF, PF, and CF flags are affected.

INC (Increment) adds 1 to the destination operand. The INC instruction preserves the state of the CF flag. This allows the use of INC instructions to update counters in loops without disturbing the status flags resulting from an arithmetic operation used for loop control. The ZF flag can be used to detect when carry would have occurred. Use an ADD instruction with an immediate value of 1 to perform an increment which updates the CF flag. A one-byte form of this instruction is available when the operand is a general register. The OF, SF, ZF, AF, and PF flags are affected.

SUB (Subtract Integers) subtracts the source operand from the destination operand and replaces the destination operand with the result. If a borrow is required, the CF flag is set. The operands may be signed or unsigned bytes, words, or doublewords. The OF, SF, ZF, AF, PF, and CF flags are affected.

SBB (Subtract Integers with Borrow) subtracts the source operand from the destination operand and replaces the destination operand with the result, minus 1 if the CF flag is set. If the CF flag is clear, the SBB instruction performs the same operation as the SUB instruction. An SBB instruction is used to propagate borrow when subtracting numbers in stages, for example when using 32-bit SUB instructions to subtract one quadword operand from another. The OF, SF, ZF, AF, PF, and CF flags are affected.

DEC (Decrement) subtracts 1 from the destination operand. The DEC instruction preserves the state of the CF flag. This allows the use of the DEC instruction to update counters in loops without disturbing the status flags resulting from an arithmetic operation used for loop control. Use a SUB instruction with an immediate value of 1 to perform a decrement which updates the CF flag. A one-byte form of this instruction is available when the operand is a general register. The OF, SF, ZF, AF, and PF flags are affected.

3.2.2 Comparison and Sign Change Instruction

CMP (Compare) subtracts the source operand from the destination operand. It updates the OF, SF, ZF, AF, PF, and CF flags, but does not modify the source or destination operands. A subsequent J*cc* or SET*cc* instruction can test the flags.

NEG (Negate) subtracts a signed integer operand from zero. The effect of the NEG instruction is to change the sign of a two's complement operand while keeping its magnitude. The OF, SF, ZF, AF, PF, and CF flags are affected.

3.2.3 Multiplication Instructions

The 386 DX microprocessor has separate multiply instructions for unsigned and signed operands. The MUL instruction operates on unsigned integers, while the IMUL instruction operates on signed integers as well as unsigned.

MUL (Unsigned Integer Multiply) performs an unsigned multiplication of the source operand and the AL, AX, or EAX register. If the source is a byte, the processor multiplies it by the value held in the AL register and returns the double-length result in the AH and AL registers. If the source operand is a word, the processor multiplies it by the value held in the AX register and returns the double-length result in the DX and AX registers. If the source operand is a doubleword, the processor multiplies it by the value held in the EAX register and returns the quadword result in the EDX and EAX registers. The MUL instruction sets the CF and OF flags when the upper half of the result is non-zero; otherwise, the flags are cleared. The state of the SF, ZF, AF, and PF flags is undefined.

IMUL (Signed Integer Multiply) performs a signed multiplication operation. The IMUL instruction has three forms:

1. A one-operand form. The operand may be a byte, word, or doubleword located in memory or in a general register. This instruction uses the EAX and EDX registers as implicit operands in the same way as the MUL instruction.
2. A two-operand form. One of the source operands is in a general register while the other may be in a general register or memory. The result replaces the general-register operand.
3. A three-operand form; two are source operands and one is the destination. One of the source operands is an immediate value supplied by the instruction; the second may be in memory or in a general register. The result is stored in a general register.

The immediate operand is a two's complement signed integer. If the immediate operand is a byte, the processor automatically sign-extends it to the size of the second operand before performing the multiplication.

The three forms are similar in most respects:

- The length of the product is calculated to twice the length of the operands.
- The CF and OF flags are set when significant bits are carried into the upper half of the result. The CF and OF flags are cleared when the upper half of the result is the sign-extension of the lower half. The state of the SF, ZF, AF, and PF flags is undefined.

However, forms 2 and 3 differ because the product is truncated to the length of the operands before it is stored in the destination register. Because of this truncation, the OF flag should be tested to ensure that no significant bits are lost. (For ways to test the OF flag, see the JO, INTO, and PUSHF instructions.)

Forms 2 and 3 of IMUL also may be used with unsigned operands because, whether the operands are signed or unsigned, the lower half of the product is the same. The CF and OF flags, however, cannot be used to determine if the upper half of the result is non-zero.

3.2.4 Division Instructions

The 386 DX microprocessor has separate division instructions for unsigned and signed operands. The DIV instruction operates on unsigned integers, while the IDIV instruction operates on both signed and unsigned integers. In either case, a divide-error exception is generated if the divisor is zero or if the quotient is too large for the AL, AX, or EAX register.

DIV (Unsigned Integer Divide) performs an unsigned division of the AL, AX, or EAX register by the source operand. The dividend (the accumulator) is twice the size of the divisor (the source operand); the quotient and remainder have the same size as the divisor, as shown in Table 3-1.

Non-integral results are truncated toward 0. The remainder is always smaller than the divisor. For unsigned byte division, the largest quotient is 255. For unsigned word division, the largest quotient is 65,535. For unsigned doubleword division the largest quotient is $2^{32}-1$. The state of the OF, SF, ZF, AF, PF, and CF flags is undefined.

Table 3-1. Operands for Division

Operand Size (Divisor)	Dividend	Quotient	Remainder
Byte	AX register	AL register	AH register
Word	DX and AX	AX register	DX register
Doubleword	EDX and EAX	EAX register	EDX register

IDIV (Signed Integer Divide) performs a signed division of the accumulator by the source operand. The IDIV instruction uses the same registers as the DIV instruction.

For signed byte division, the maximum positive quotient is +127, and the minimum negative quotient is −128. For signed word division, the maximum positive quotient is +32,767, and the minimum negative quotient is −32,768. For signed doubleword division the maximum positive quotient is $2^{32}-1$, the minimum negative quotient is -2^{31}. Nonintegral results are truncated towards 0. The remainder always has the same sign as the dividend and is less than the divisor in magnitude. The state of the OF, SF, ZF, AF, PF, and CF flags is undefined.

3.3 DECIMAL ARITHMETIC INSTRUCTIONS

Decimal arithmetic is performed by combining the binary arithmetic instructions (already discussed in the prior section) with the decimal arithmetic instructions. The decimal arithmetic instructions are used in one of the following ways:

- To adjust the results of a previous binary arithmetic operation to produce a valid packed or unpacked decimal result.
- To adjust the inputs to a subsequent binary arithmetic operation so that the operation will produce a valid packed or unpacked decimal result. These instructions operate only on the AL or AH registers. Most use the AF flag.

3.3.1 Packed BCD Adjustment Instructions

DAA (Decimal Adjust after Addition) adjusts the result of adding two valid packed decimal operands in the AL register. A DAA instruction must follow the addition of two pairs of packed decimal numbers (one digit in each half-byte) to obtain a pair of valid packed decimal digits as results. The CF flag is set if a carry occurs. The SF, ZF, AF, PF, and CF flags are affected. The state of the OF flag is undefined.

DAS (Decimal Adjust after Subtraction) adjusts the result of subtracting two valid packed decimal operands in the AL register. A DAS instruction must always follow the subtraction of one pair of packed decimal numbers (one digit in each half-byte) from another to obtain a pair of valid packed decimal digits as results. The CF flag is set if a borrow is needed. The SF, ZF, AF, PF, and CF flags are affected. The state of the OF flag is undefined.

3.3.2 Unpacked BCD Adjustment Instructions

AAA (ASCII Adjust after Addition) changes the contents of the AL register to a valid unpacked decimal number, and clears the upper 4 bits. An AAA instruction must follow the addition of two unpacked decimal operands in the AL register. The CF flag is set and the contents of the AH register are incremented if a carry occurs. The AF and CF flags are affected. The state of the OF, SF, ZF, and PF flags is undefined.

AAS (ASCII Adjust after Subtraction) changes the contents of the AL register to a valid unpacked decimal number, and clears the upper 4 bits. An AAS instruction must follow the subtraction of one unpacked decimal operand from another in the AL register. The CF flag is set and the contents of the AH register are decremented if a borrow is needed. The AF and CF flags are affected. The state of the OF, SF, ZF, and PF flags is undefined.

AAM (ASCII Adjust after Multiplication) corrects the result of a multiplication of two valid unpacked decimal numbers. An AAM instruction must follow the multiplication of two decimal numbers to produce a valid decimal result. The upper digit is left in the AH register, the lower digit in the AL register. The SF, ZF, and PF flags are affected. The state of the AF, OF, and CF flags is undefined.

AAD (ASCII Adjust before Division) modifies the numerator in the AH and AL registers to prepare for the division of two valid unpacked decimal operands, so that the quotient produced by the division will be a valid unpacked decimal number. The AH register should contain the upper digit and the AL register should contain the lower digit. This instruction adjusts the value and places the result in the AL register. The AH register will be clear. The SF, ZF, and PF flags are affected. The state of the AF, OF, and CF flags is undefined.

3.4 LOGICAL INSTRUCTIONS

The logical instructions have two operands. Source operands can be immediate values, general registers, or memory. Destination operands can be general registers or memory (except when the source operand is in memory). The logical instructions modify the state of the flags. Short forms of the instructions are available when the an immediate source operand is applied to a destination operand in the AL or EAX registers. The group of logical instructions includes:

- Boolean operation instructions
- Bit test and modify instructions
- Bit scan instructions
- Rotate and shift instructions
- Byte set on condition

3.4.1 Boolean Operation Instructions

The logical operations are performed by the AND, OR, XOR, and NOT instructions.

NOT (Not) inverts the bits in the specified operand to form a one's complement of the operand. The NOT instruction is a unary operation which uses a single operand in a register or memory. NOT has no effect on the flags.

The AND, OR, and XOR instructions perform the standard logical operations "and," "or," and "exclusive or." These instructions can use the following combinations of operands:

- Two register operands
- A general register operand with a memory operand
- An immediate operand with either a general register operand or a memory operand

The AND, OR, and XOR instructions clear the OF and CF flags, leave the AF flag undefined, and update the SF, ZF, and PF flags.

3.4.2 Bit Test and Modify Instructions

This group of instructions operates on a single bit which can be in memory or in a general register. The location of the bit is specified as an offset from the low end of the operand. The value of the offset either may be given by an immediate byte in the instruction or may be contained in a general register.

These instructions first assign the value of the selected bit to the CF flag. Then a new value is assigned to the selected bit, as determined by the operation. The state of the OF, SF, ZF, AF, and PF flags is undefined. Table 3-2 defines these instructions.

3.4.3 Bit Scan Instructions

These instructions scan a word or doubleword for a set bit and store the bit index (an integer representing the bit position) of the first set bit into a register. The bit string being scanned may be in a register or in memory. The ZF flag is set if the entire word is clear, otherwise the ZF flag is cleared. In the former case, the value of the destination register is left undefined. The state of the OF, SF, AF, PF, and CF flags is undefined.

BSF (Bit Scan Forward) scans low-to-high (from bit 0 toward the upper bit positions).

BSR (Bit Scan Reverse) scans high-to-low (from the uppermost bit toward bit 0).

3.4.4 Shift and Rotate Instructions

The shift and rotate instructions rearrange the bits within an operand.

Table 3-2. Bit Test and Modify Instructions

Instruction	Effect on CF Flag	Effect on Selected Bit
BT (Bit Test)	CF flag ← Selected Bit	no effect
BTS (Bit Test and Set)	CF flag ← Selected Bit	Selected Bit ← 1
BTR (Bit Test and Reset)	CF flag ← Selected Bit	Selected Bit ← 0
BTC (Bit Test and Complement)	CF flag ← Selected Bit	Selected Bit ← - (Selected Bit)

These instructions fall into the following classes:

- Shift instructions
- Double shift instructions
- Rotate instructions

3.4.4.1 SHIFT INSTRUCTIONS

Shift instructions apply an arithmetic or logical shift to bytes, words, and doublewords. An arithmetic shift right copies the sign bit into empty bit positions on the upper end of the operand, while a logical shift right fills clears the empty bit positions. An arithmetic shift is a fast way to perform a simple calculation. For example, an arithmetic shift right by one bit position divides an integer by two. A logical shift right divides an unsigned integer or a positive integer, but a signed negative integer loses its sign bit.

The arithmetic and logical shift right instructions, SAR and SHR, differ only in their treatment of the bit positions emptied by shifting the contents of the operand. Note that there is no difference between an arithmetic shift left and a logical shift left. Two names, SAL and SHL, are supported for this instruction in the assembler.

A count specifies the number of bit positions to shift an operand. Bits can be shifted up to 31 places. A shift instruction can give the count in any of three ways. One form of shift instruction always shifts by one bit position. The second form gives the count as an immediate operand. The third form gives the count as the value contained in the CL register. This last form allows the count to be a result from a calculation. Only the low five bits of the CL register are used.

When the number of bit positions to shift is zero, no flags are affected. Otherwise, the CF flag is left with the value of the last bit shifted out of the operand. In a single-bit shift, the OF flag is set if the value of the uppermost bit (sign bit) was changed by the operation. Otherwise, the OF flag is cleared. After a shift of more than one bit position, the state of the OF flag is undefined. On a shift of one or more bit positions, the SF, ZF, PF, and CF flags are affected, and the state of the AF flag is undefined.

SAL (Shift Arithmetic Left) shifts the destination byte, word, or doubleword operand left by one bit position or by the number of bits specified in the count operand (an immediate value or a value contained in the CL register). Empty bit positions are cleared. See Figure 3-6.

SHL (Shift Logical Left) is another name for the SAL instruction. It is supported in the assembler.

SHR (Shift Logical Right) shifts the destination byte, word, or doubleword operand right by one bit position or by the number of bits specified in the count operand (an immediate value or a value contained in the CL register). Empty bit positions are cleared. See Figure 3-7.

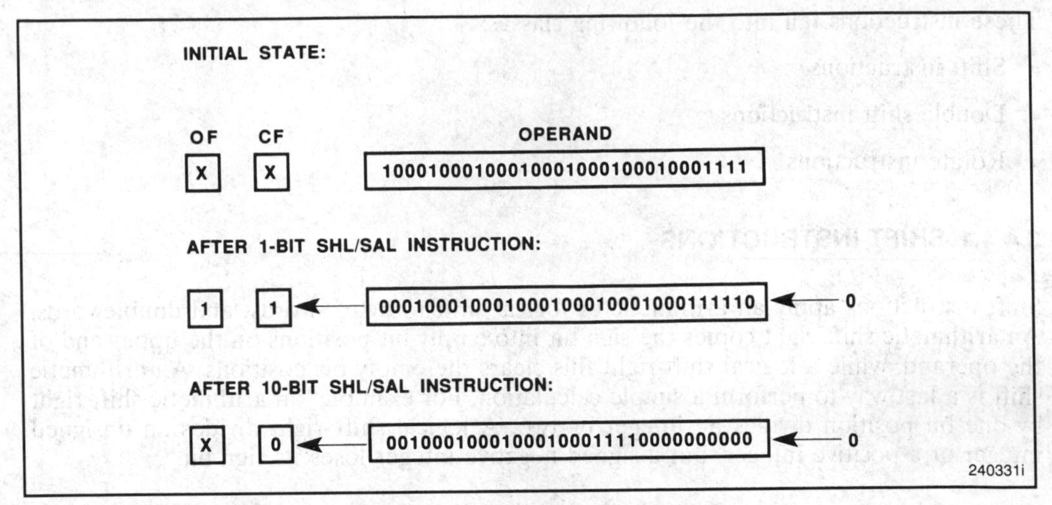

Figure 3-6. SHL/SAL Instruction

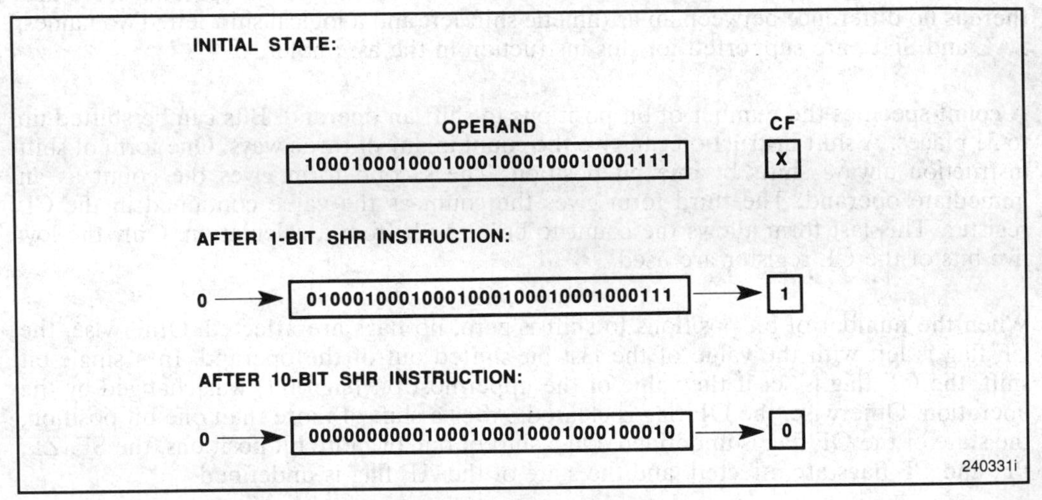

Figure 3-7. SHR Instruction

SAR (Shift Arithmetic Right) shifts the destination byte, word, or doubleword operand to the right by one bit position or by the number of bits specified in the count operand (an immediate value or a value contained in the CL register). The sign of the operand is preserved by clearing empty bit positions if the operand is positive, or setting the empty bits if the operand is negative. See Figure 3-8.

Even though this instruction can be used to divide integers by an integer power of two, **the type of division is not the same as that produced by the IDIV instruction**. The quotient from the IDIV instruction is rounded toward zero, whereas the "quotient" of the SAR instruction is rounded toward negative infinity. This difference is apparent only for negative numbers. For example, when the IDIV instruction is used to divide -9 by 4,

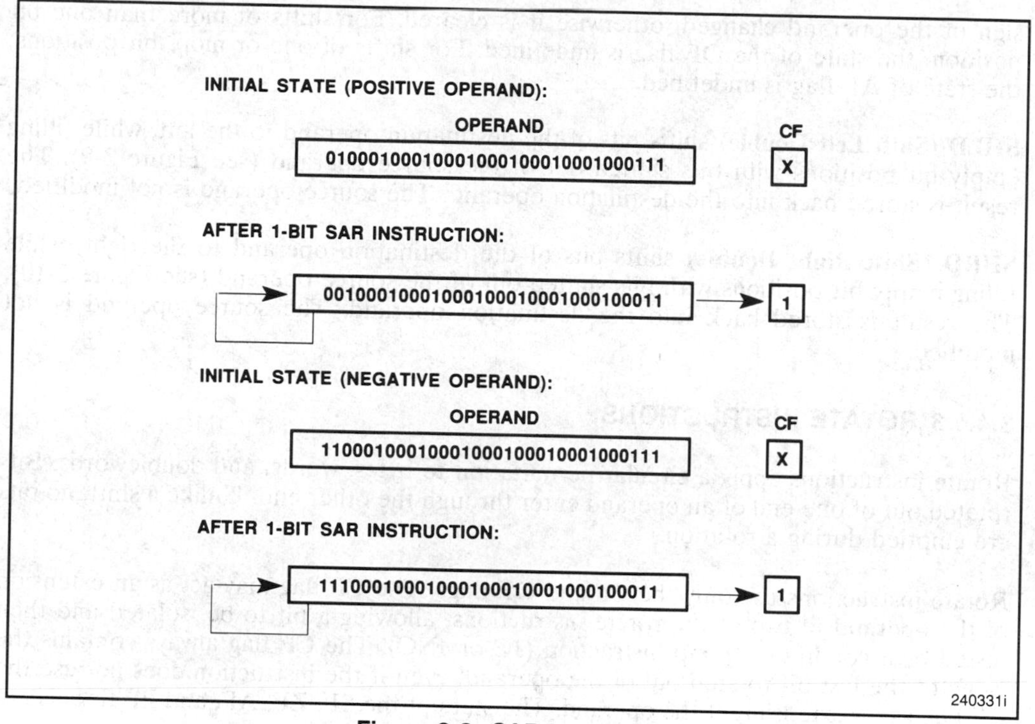

Figure 3-8. SAR Instruction

the result is −2 with a remainder of −1. If the SAR instruction is used to shift −9 right by two bits, the result is −3. The "remainder" of this kind of division is +13; however, the SAR instruction stores only the high-order bit of the remainder (in the CF flag).

3.4.4.2 DOUBLE-SHIFT INSTRUCTIONS

These instructions provide the basic operations needed to implement operations on long unaligned bit strings. The double shifts operate either on word or doubleword operands, as follows:

- Take two word operands and produce a one-word result (32-bit shift).
- Take two doubleword operands and produce a doubleword result (64-bit shift).

Of the two operands, the source operand must be in a register while the destination operand may be in a register or in memory. The number of bits to be shifted is specified either in the CL register or in an immediate byte in the instruction. Bits shifted out of the source operand fill empty bit positions in the destination operand, which also is shifted. Only the destination operand is stored.

When the number of bit positions to shift is zero, no flags are affected. Otherwise, the CF flag is set to the value of the last bit shifted out of the destination operand, and the SF, ZF, and PF flags are affected. On a shift of one bit position, the OF flag is set if the sign of the operand changed, otherwise it is cleared. For shifts of more than one bit position, the state of the OF flag is undefined. For shifts of one or more bit positions, the state of AF flag is undefined.

SHLD (Shift Left Double) shifts bits of the destination operand to the left, while filling empty bit positions with bits shifted out of the source operand (see Figure 3-9). The result is stored back into the destination operand. The source operand is not modified.

SHRD (Shift Right Double) shifts bits of the destination operand to the right, while filling empty bit positions with bits shifted out of the source operand (see Figure 3-10). The result is stored back into the destination operand. The source operand is not modified.

3.4.4.3 ROTATE INSTRUCTIONS

Rotate instructions apply a circular permutation to bytes, words, and doublewords. Bits rotated out of one end of an operand enter through the other end. Unlike a shift, no bits are emptied during a rotation.

Rotate instructions use only the CF and OF flags. The CF flag may act as an extension of the operand in two of the rotate instructions, allowing a bit to be isolated and then tested by a conditional jump instruction (JC or JNC). The CF flag always contains the value of the last bit rotated out of the operand, even if the instruction does not use the CF flag as an extension of the operand. The state of the SF, ZF, AF, and PF flags is not affected.

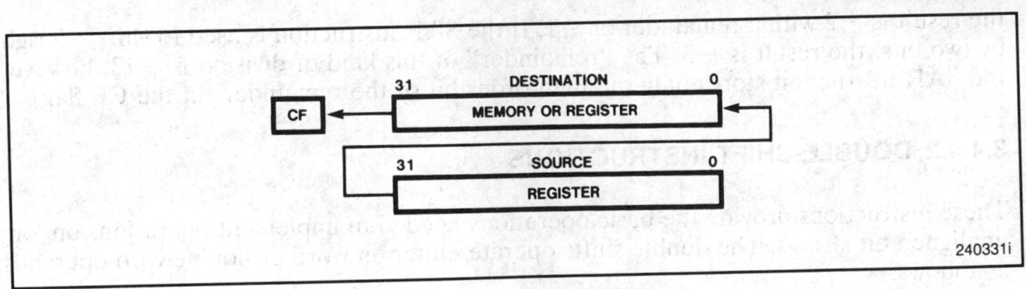

Figure 3-9. SHLD Instruction

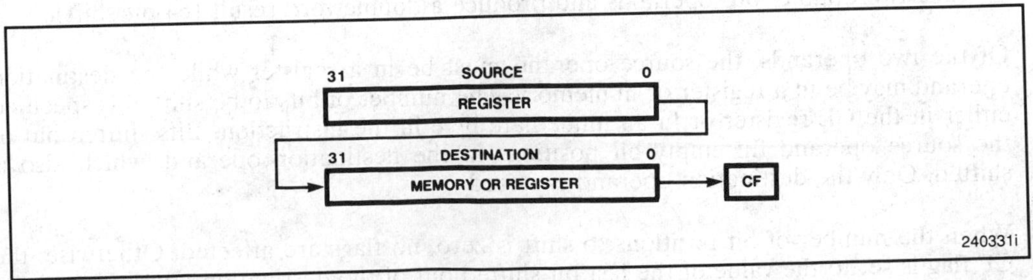

Figure 3-10. SHRD Instruction

In a single-bit rotation, the OF flag is set if the operation changes the uppermost bit (sign bit) of the destination operand. If the sign bit retains its original value, the OF flag is cleared. After a rotate of more than one bit position, the value of the OF flag is undefined.

ROL (Rotate Left) rotates the byte, word, or doubleword destination operand left by one bit position or by the number of bits specified in the count operand (an immediate value or a value contained in the CL register). For each bit position of the rotation, the bit which exits from the left of the operand returns at the right. See Figure 3-11.

ROR (Rotate Right) rotates the byte, word, or doubleword destination operand right by one bit position or by the number of bits specified in the count operand (an immediate value or a value contained in the CL register). For each bit position of the rotation, the bit which exits from the right of the operand returns at the left. See Figure 3-12.

RCL (Rotate Through Carry Left) rotates bits in the byte, word, or doubleword destination operand left by one bit position or by the number of bits specified in the count operand (an immediate value or a value contained in the CL register).

This instruction differs from ROL in that it treats the CF flag as a one-bit extension on the upper end of the destination operand. Each bit which exits from the left side of the operand moves into the CF flag. At the same time, the bit in the CF flag enters the right side. See Figure 3-13.

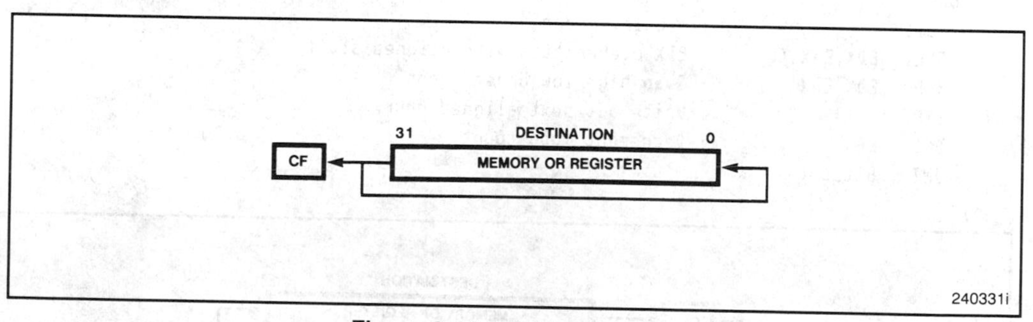

Figure 3-11. ROL Instruction

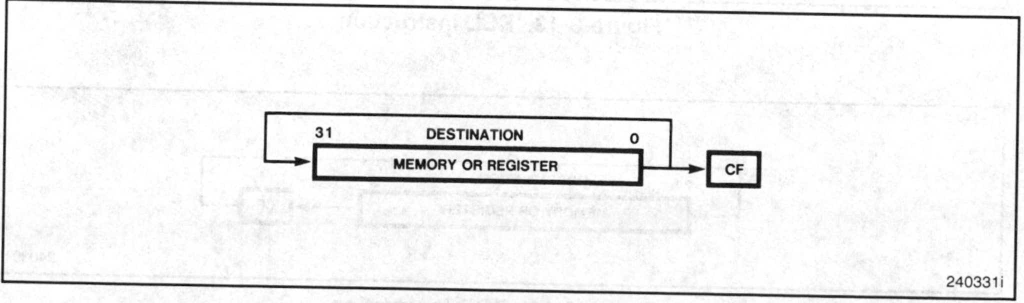

Figure 3-12. ROR Instruction

RCR (Rotate Through Carry Right) rotates bits in the byte, word, or doubleword destination operand right by one bit position or by the number of bits specified in the count operand (an immediate value or a value contained in the CL register).

This instruction differs from ROR in that it treats CF as a one-bit extension on the lower end of the destination operand. Each bit which exits from the right side of the operand moves into the CF flag. At the same time, the bit in the CF flag enters the left side. See Figure 3-14.

3.4.4.4 FAST "BIT BLT" USING DOUBLE-SHIFT INSTRUCTIONS

One purpose of the double shift instructions is to implement a bit string move, with arbitrary misalignment of the bit strings. This is called a "bit blt" (BIT BLock Transfer). A simple example is to move a bit string from an arbitrary offset into a doubleword-aligned byte string. A left-to-right string is moved 32 bits at a time if a double shift is used inside the move loop.

```
        MOV   ESI,ScrAddr
        MOV   EDI,DestAddr
        MOV   EBX,WordCnt
        MOV   CL,RelOffset       ; relative offset Dest-Src
        MOV   EDX, [ESI]         ; load first word of source
        ADD   ESI,4              ; bump source address
BltLoop:
        LODS                     ; new low order part
        SHLD  EDX,EAX,CL         ; EDX overwritten with aligned stuff
        XCHG  EDX,EAX            ; Swap high/low order words
        STOS                     ; Write out next aligned chunk
        DEC   EBX                ; Decrement loop count
        JNZ   BltLoop
```

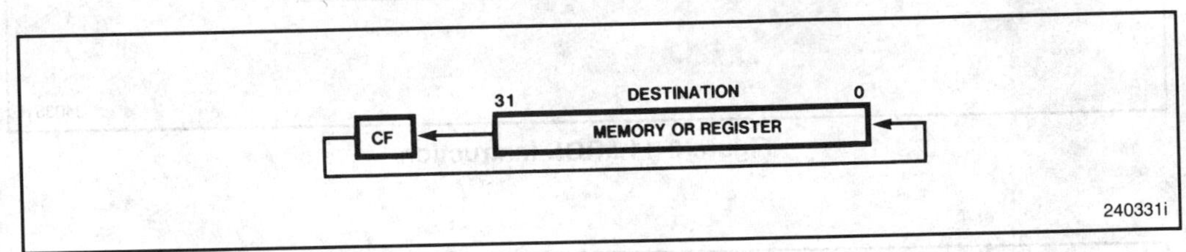

Figure 3-13. RCL Instruction

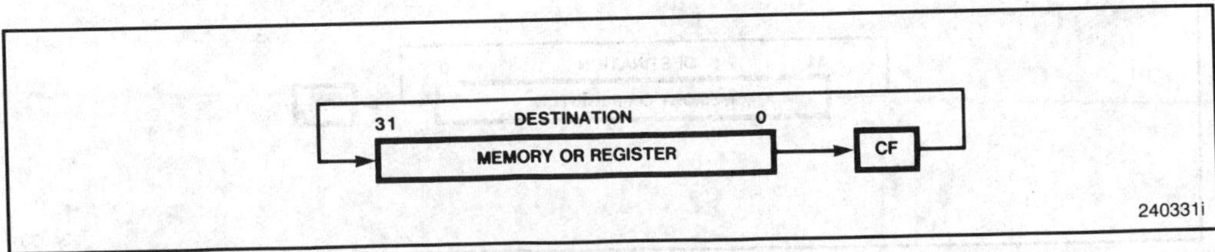

Figure 3-14. RCR Instruction

This loop is simple, yet allows the data to be moved in 32-bit chunks for the highest possible performance. Without a double shift, the best which can be achieved is 16 bits per loop iteration by using a 32-bit shift, and replacing the XCHG instruction with a ROR instruction by 16 to swap the high and low words of registers. A more general loop than shown above would require some extra masking on the first doubleword moved (before the main loop), and on the last doubleword moved (after the main loop), but would have the same 32-bits per loop iteration as the code above.

3.4.4.5 FAST BIT STRING INSERT AND EXTRACT

The double shift instructions also make possible:

- Fast insertion of a bit string from a register into an arbitrary bit location in a larger bit string in memory, without disturbing the bits on either side of the inserted bits
- Fast extraction of a bit string into a register from an arbitrary bit location in a larger bit string in memory, without disturbing the bits on either side of the extracted bits

The following coded examples illustrate bit insertion and extraction under various conditions:

1. Bit String Insertion into Memory (when the bit string is 1-25 bits long, i.e., spans four bytes or less):

```
; Insert a right-justified bit string from a register into
; a bit string in memory.
;
;
Assumptions:
; 1. The base of the string array is doubleword aligned.
; 2. The length of the bit string is an immediate value
;    and the bit offset is held in a register.
;
; The ESI register holds the right-justified bit string
; to be inserted.
; The EDI register holds the bit offset of the start of the
; substring.
; The EAX register and ECX are also used.
;
MOV   ECX,EDI                  ; save original offset
SHR   EDI,3                    ; divide offset by 8 (byte addr)
AND   CL,7H                    ; get low three bits of offset
MOV   EAX,[EDI]strg_base       ; move string dword into EAX
ROR   EAX,CL                   ; right justify old bit field
SHRD  EAX,ESI,length           ; bring in new bits
ROL   EAX,length               ; right justify new bit field
ROL   EAX,CL                   ; bring to final position
MOV[EDI]strg_base,EAX          ; replace doubleword in memory
```

2. Bit String Insertion into Memory (when the bit string is 1–31 bits long, i.e., spans five bytes or less):

```
; Insert a right-justified bit string from a register into
; a bit string in memory.
;
; Assumptions:
; 1. The base of the string array is doubleword aligned.
; 2. The length of the bit string is an immediate value
;    and the bit offset is held in a register.
;
; The ESI register holds the right-justified bit string
; to be inserted.
; The EDI register holds the bit offset of the start of the
; substring.
; The EAX, EBX, ECX, and EDI registers also are used.
;
MOV   ECX,EDI                 ; temp storage for offset
SHR   EDI,5                   ; divide offset by 32 (dwords)
SHL   EDI,2                   ; multiply by 4 (byte address)
AND   CL,1FH                  ; get low five bits of offset
MOV   EAX,[EDI]strg_base      ; move low string dword into EAX
MOV   EDX,[EDI]strg_base+4    ; other string dword into EDX
MOV   EBX,EAX                 ; temp storage for part of string
SHRD  EAX,EDX,CL              ; shift by offset within dword
SHRD  EAX,EBX,CL              ; shift by offset within dword
SHRD  EAX,ESI,length          ; bring in new bits
ROL   EAX,length              ; right justify new bit field
MOV   EBX,EAX                 ; temp storage for string
SHLD  EAX,EDX,CL              ; shift by offset within word
SHLD  EDX,EBX,CL              ; shift by offset within word
MOV   [EDI]strg_base,EAX      ; replace dword in memory
MOV   [EDI]strg_base+4,EDX    ; replace dword in memory
```

3. Bit String Insertion into Memory (when the bit string is exactly 32 bits long, i.e., spans four or five bytes):

```
; Insert right-justified bit string from a register into
; a bit string in memory.
;
; Assumptions:
; 1. The base of the string array is doubleword aligned.
; 2. The length of the bit string is 32 bits
;    and the bit offset is held in a register.
;
; The ESI register holds the 32-bit string to be inserted.
; The EDI register holds the bit offset to the start of the
; substring.
; The EAX, EBX, ECX, and EDI registers also are used.
;
MOV   EDX,EDI                 ; save original offset
```

```
SHR    EDI,5                       ; divide offset by 32 (dwords)
SHL    EDI,2                       ; multiply by 4 (byte address)
AND    CL,1FH                      ; isolate low five bits of offset
MOV    EAX,[EDI]strg_base          ; move low string dword into EAX
MOV    EDX,[EDI]strg_base+4        ; other string dword into EDX
MOV    EBX,EAX                     ; temp storage for part of string
SHRD   EAX,EDX                     ; shift by offset within dword
SHRD   EDX,EBX                     ; shift by offset within dword
MOV    EAX,ESI                     ; move 32-bit field into position
MOV    EBX,EAX                     ; temp storage for part of string
SHLD   EAX,EDX                     ; shift by offset within word
SHLD   EDX,EBX                     ; shift by offset within word
MOV    [EDI]strg_base,EAX          ; replace dword in memory
MOV    [EDI]strg_base,+4,EDX       ; replace dword in memory
```

4. Bit String Extraction from Memory (when the bit string is 1-25 bits long, i.e., spans four bytes or less):

```
; Extract a right-justified bit string into a register from
; a bit string in memory.
;
; Assumptions:
; 1) The base of the string array is doubleword aligned.
; 2) The length of the bit string is an immediate value
;    and the bit offset is held in a register.
;
; The EAX register hold the right-justified, zero-padded
; bit string that was extracted.
; The EDI register holds the bit offset of the start of the
; substring.
; The EDI, and ECX registers also are used.
;
MOV    ECX,EDI                     ; temp storage for offset
SHR    EDI,3                       ; divide offset by 8 (byte addr)
AND    CL,7H                       ; get low three bits of offset
MOV    EAX,[EDI]strg_base          ; move string dword into EAX
SHR    EAX,CL                      ; shift by offset within dword
AND    EAX,mask                    ; extracted bit field in EAX
```

5. Bit String Extraction from Memory (when bit string is 1-32 bits long, i.e., spans five bytes or less):

```
; Extract a right-justified bit string into a register from a
; bit string in memory.
;
; Assumptions:
; 1) The base of the string array is doubleword aligned.
; 2) The length of the bit string is an immediate
;    value and the bit offset is held in a register.
;
; The EAX register holds the right-justified, zero-padded
; bit string that was extracted.
```

```
; The EDI register holds the bit offset of the start of the
; substring.
; The EAX, EBX, and ECX registers also are used.
;
MOV   ECX,EDI                  ; temp storage for offset
SHR   EDI,5                    ; divide offset by 32 (dwords)
SHL   EDI,2                    ; multiply by 4 (byte address)
AND   CL,1FH                   ; get low five bits of offset in
MOV   EAX,[EDI]strg_base       ; move low string dword into EAX
MOV   EDX,[EDI]strg_base +4    ; other string dword into EDX
SHRD  EAX,EDX,CL               ; shift right by offset in dword
AND   EAX,mask                 ; extracted bit field in EAX
```

3.4.5 Byte-Set-On-Condition Instructions

This group of instructions sets a byte to the value of zero or one, depending on any of the 16 conditions defined by the status flags. The byte may be in a register or in memory. These instructions are especially useful for implementing Boolean expressions in high-level languages such as Pascal.

Some languages represent a logical one as an integer with all bits set. This can be done by using the SET*cc* instruction with the mutually exclusive condition, then decrementing the result.

SET*cc* (Set Byte on Condition *cc*) loads the value 1 into a byte if condition *cc* is true; clears the byte otherwise. See Appendix D for a definition of the possible conditions.

3.4.6 Test Instruction

TEST (Test) performs the logical "and" of the two operands, clears the OF and CF flags, leaves the AF flag undefined, and updates the SF, ZF, and PF flags. The flags can be tested by conditional control transfer instructions or the byte-set-on-condition instructions. The operands may be bytes, words, or doublewords.

The difference between the TEST and AND instructions is the TEST instruction does not alter the destination operand. The difference between the TEST and BT instructions is the TEST instruction can test the value of multiple bits in one operation, while the BT instruction tests a single bit.

3.5 CONTROL TRANSFER INSTRUCTIONS

The 386 DX microprocessor provides both conditional and unconditional control transfer instructions to direct the flow of execution. Conditional transfers are executed only for certain combinations of the state of the flags. Unconditional control transfers are always executed.

3.5.1 Unconditional Transfer Instructions

The JMP, CALL, RET, INT and IRET instructions transfer execution to a destination in a code segment. The destination can be within the same code segment (*near* transfer) or in a different code segment (*far* transfer). The forms of these instructions which transfer execution to other segments are discussed in a later section of this chapter. If the model of memory organization used in a particular application does not make segments visible to application programmers, far transfers will not be used.

3.5.1.1 JUMP INSTRUCTION

JMP (Jump) unconditionally transfers execution to the destination. The JMP instruction is a one-way transfer of execution; it does not save a return address on the stack.

The JMP instruction transfers execution from the current routine to a different routine. The address of the routine is specified in the instruction, in a register, or in memory. The location of the address determines whether it is interpreted as a relative address or an absolute address.

Relative Address. A relative jump uses a displacement (immediate mode constant used for address calculation) held in the instruction. The displacement is signed and variable-length (byte or doubleword). The destination address is formed by adding the displacement to the address held in the EIP register. The EIP register then contains the address of the next instruction to be executed.

Absolute Address. An absolute jump is used with a 32-bit segment offset in either of the following ways:

1. The program can jump to an address in a general register. This 32-bit value is copied into the EIP register and execution continues.
2. The destination address can be a memory operand specified using the standard addressing modes. The operand is copied into the EIP register and execution continues.

3.5.1.2 CALL INSTRUCTIONS

CALL (Call Procedure) transfers execution and saves the address of the instruction following the CALL instruction for later use by a RET (Return) instruction. CALL pushes the current contents of the EIP register on the stack. The RET instruction in the called procedure uses this address to transfer execution back to the calling program.

CALL instructions, like JMP instructions, have relative and absolute forms.

Indirect CALL instructions specify an absolute address in one of the following ways:

1. The program can jump to an address in a general register. This 32-bit value is copied into the EIP register, the return address is pushed on the stack, and execution continues.

2. The destination address can be a memory operand specified using the standard addressing modes. The operand is copied into the EIP register, the return address is pushed on the stack, and execution continues.

3.5.1.3 RETURN AND RETURN-FROM-INTERRUPT INSTRUCTIONS

RET (Return From Procedure) terminates a procedure and transfers execution to the instruction following the CALL instruction which originally invoked the procedure. The RET instruction restores the contents of the EIP register which were pushed on the stack when the procedure was called.

The RET instructions have an optional immediate operand. When present, this constant is added to the contents of the ESP register, which has the effect of removing any parameters pushed on the stack before the procedure call.

IRET (Return From Interrupt) returns control to an interrupted procedure. The IRET instruction differs from the RET instruction in that it also restores the EFLAGS register from the stack. The contents of the EFLAGS register are stored on the stack when an interrupt occurs.

3.5.2 Conditional Transfer Instructions

The conditional transfer instructions are jumps which transfer execution if the states in the EFLAGS register match conditions specified in the instruction.

3.5.2.1 CONDITIONAL JUMP INSTRUCTIONS

Table 3-3 shows the mnemonics for the jump instructions. The instructions listed as pairs are alternate names for the same instruction. The assembler provides these names for greater clarity in program listings.

A form of the conditional jump instructions is available which uses a displacement added to the contents of the EIP register if the specified condition is true. The displacement may be a byte or doubleword. The displacement is signed; it can be used to jump forward or backward.

3.5.2.2 LOOP INSTRUCTIONS

The loop instructions are conditional jumps which use a value placed in the ECX register as a count for the number of times to run a loop. All loop instructions decrement the contents of the ECX register on each repetition and terminate when zero is reached. Four of the five loop instructions accept the ZF flag as a condition for terminating the loop before the count reaches zero.

Table 3-3. Conditional Jump Instructions

Mnemonic	Flag States	Description
Unsigned Conditional Jumps		
JA/JNBE	(CF or ZF) = 0	above/not below nor equal
JAE/JNB	CF = 0	above or equal/not below
JB/JNAE	CF = 1	below/not above nor equal
JBE/JNA	(CF or ZF) = 1	below or equal/not above
JC	CF = 1	carry
JE/JZ	ZF = 1	equal/zero
JNC	CF = 0	not carry
JNE/JNZ	ZF = 0	not equal/not zero
JNP/JPO	PF = 0	not parity/parity odd
JP/JPE	PF = 1	parity/parity even
Signed Conditional Jumps		
JG/JNLE	((SF xor OF) or ZF) = 0	greater/not less nor equal
JGE/JNL	(SF xor OF) = 0	greater or equal/not less
JL/JNGE	(SF xor OF) = 1	less/not greater nor equal
JLE/JNG	((SF xor OF) or ZF) = 1	less or equal/not greater
JNO	OF = 0	not overflow
JNS	SF = 0	not sign (non-negative)
JO	OF = 1	overflow
JS	SF = 1	sign (negative)

LOOP (Loop While ECX Not Zero) is a conditional jump instruction which decrements the contents of the ECX register before testing for the loop-terminating condition. If contents of the ECX register are non-zero, the program jumps to the destination specified in thc instruction. The LOOP instruction causes the execution of a block of code to be repeated until the count reaches zero. When zero is reached, execution is transferred to the instruction immediately following the LOOP instruction. If the value in the ECX register is zero when the instruction is first called, the count is predecremented to 0FFFFFFFFH and the LOOP runs 2^{32} times.

LOOPE (Loop While Equal) and **LOOPZ (Loop While Zero)** are synonyms for the same instruction. These instructions are conditional jumps which decrement the contents of the ECX register before testing for the loop-terminating condition. If the contents of the ECX register are non-zero and the ZF flag is set, the program jumps to the destination specified in the instruction. When zero is reached or the ZF flag is clear, execution is transferred to the instruction immediately following the LOOPE/LOOPZ instruction.

LOOPNE (Loop While Not Equal) and **LOOPNZ (Loop While Not Zero)** are synonyms for the same instruction. These instructions are conditional jumps which decrement the contents of the ECX register before testing for the loop-terminating condition. If the contents of the ECX register are non-zero and the ZF flag is clear, the program jumps to the destination specified in the instruction. When zero is reached or the ZF flag is set, execution is transferred to the instruction immediately following the LOOPE/LOOPZ instruction.

3.5.2.3 EXECUTING A LOOP OR REPEAT ZERO TIMES

JECXZ (Jump if ECX Zero) jumps to the destination specified in the instruction if the ECX register holds a value of zero. The JECXZ instruction is used in combination with the LOOP instruction and with the string scan and compare instructions. Because these instructions decrement the contents of the ECX register before testing for zero, a loop will run 2^{32} times if the loop is entered with a zero value in the ECX register. The JECXZ instruction is used to create loops which fall through without executing when the initial value is zero. A JECXZ instruction at the beginning of a loop can be used to jump out of the loop if the count is zero. When used with repeated string scan and compare instructions, the JECXZ instruction can determine whether the loop terminated due to the count or due to satisfaction of the scan or compare conditions.

3.5.3 Software Interrupts

The INT, INTO, and BOUND instructions allow the programmer to specify a transfer of execution to an exception or interrupt handler.

INT*n* (Software Interrupt) calls the handler specified by an interrupt vector encoded in the instruction. The INT instruction may specify any interrupt type. This instruction is used to support multiple types of software interrupts or to test the operation of interrupt service routines. The interrupt service routine terminates with an IRET instruction, which returns execution to the instruction following the INT instruction.

INTO (Interrupt on Overflow) calls the handler for the overflow exception, if the OF flag is set. If the flag is clear, execution continues without calling the handler. The OF flag is set by arithmetic, logical, and string instructions. This instruction supports the use of software interrupts for handling error conditions, such as arithmetic overflow.

BOUND (Detect Value Out of Range) compares the signed value held in a general register against an upper and lower limit. The handler for the bounds-check exception is called if the value held in the register is less than the lower bound or greater than the upper bound. This instruction supports the use of software interrupts for bounds checking, such as checking an array index to make sure it falls within the range defined for the array.

The BOUND instruction has two operands. The first operand specifies the general register being tested. The second operand is the base address of two words or doublewords at adjacent locations in memory. The lower limit is the word or doubleword with the lower address; the upper limit has the higher address. The BOUND instruction assumes that the upper limit and lower limit are in adjacent memory locations. These limit values cannot be register operands; if they are, an invalid-opcode exception occurs.

The upper and lower limits of an array can reside just before the array itself. This puts the array bounds at a constant offset from the beginning of the array. Because the address of the array already will be present in a register, this practice avoids extra bus cycles to obtain the effective address of the array bounds.

3.6 STRING OPERATIONS

String operations manipulate large data structures in memory, such as alphanumeric character strings. See also the section on I/O for information about the string I/O instructions (also known as block I/O instructions).

The string operations are made by putting string instructions (which execute only one iteration of an operation) together with other features of the Intel386 architecture, such as repeat prefixes. The string instructions are:

MOVS – Move String
CMPS – Compare string
SCAS – Scan string
LODS – Load string
STOS – Store string

After a string instruction executes, the string source and destination registers point to the next elements in their strings. These registers automatically increment or decrement their contents by the number of bytes occupied by each string element. A string element can be a byte, word, or doubleword. The string registers are:

ESI – Source index register
EDI – Destination index register

String operations can begin at higher addresses and work toward lower ones, or they can begin at lower addresses and work toward higher ones. The direction is controlled by:

DF – Direction flag

If the DF flag is clear, the registers are incremented. If the flag is set, the registers are decremented. These instructions set and clear the flag:

STD – Set direction flag instruction
CLD – Clear direction flag instruction

To operate on more than one element of a string, a repeat prefix must be used, such as:

REP – Repeat while the ECX register not zero
REPE/REPZ – Repeat while the ECX register not zero and the ZF flag is set
REPNE/REPNZ – Repeat while the ECX register not zero and the ZF flag is clear

Exceptions or interrupts which occur during a string instruction leave the registers in a state which allows the string instruction to be restarted. The source and destination registers point to the next string elements, the EIP register points to the string instruction, and the ECX register has the value it held following the last successful iteration. All that is necessary to restart the operation is to service the interrupt or fix the source of the exception, then execute an IRET instruction.

3.6.1 Repeat Prefixes

The repeat prefixes **REP (Repeat While ECX Not Zero)**, **REPE/REPZ (Repeat While Equal/Zero)**, and **REPNE/REPNZ (Repeat While Not Equal/Not Zero)** specify repeated operation of a string instruction. This form of iteration allows string operations to proceed much faster than would be possible with a software loop.

When a string instruction has a repeat prefix, the operation executes until one of the termination conditions specified by the prefix is satisfied.

For each repetition of the instruction, the string operation may be suspended by an exception or interrupt. After the exception or interrupt has been serviced, the string operation can restart where it left off. This mechanism allows long string operations to proceed without affecting the interrupt response time of the system.

All three prefixes shown in Table 3-4 cause the instruction to repeat until the ECX register is decremented to zero, if no other termination condition is satisfied. The repeat prefixes differ in their other termination condition. The REP prefix has no other termination condition. The REPE/REPZ and REPNE/REPNZ prefixes are used exclusively with the SCAS (Scan String) and CMPS (Compare String) instructions. The REPE/REPZ prefix terminates if the ZF flag is clear. The REPNE/REPNZ prefix terminates if the ZF flag is set. The ZF flag does not require initialization before execution of a repeated string instruction, because both the SCAS and CMPS instructions affect the ZF flag according to the results of the comparisons they make.

3.6.2 Indexing and Direction Flag Control

Although the general registers are completely interchangable under most conditions, the string instructions require the use of two specific registers. The source and destination strings are in memory addressed by the ESI and EDI registers. The ESI register points to source operands. By default, the ESI register is used with the DS segment register. A segment-override prefix allows the ESI register to be used with the CS, SS, ES, FS, or GS segment registers. The EDI register points to destination operands. It uses the segment indicated by the ES segment register; no segment override is allowed. The use of two different segment registers in one instruction permits operations between strings in different segments.

When ESI and EDI are used in string instructions, they automatically are incremented or decremented after each iteration. String operations can begin at higher addresses and work toward lower ones, or they can begin at lower addresses and work toward higher ones. The direction is controlled by the DF flag. If the flag is clear, the registers are

Table 3-4. Repeat Instructions

Repeat Prefix	Termination Condition 1	Termination Condition 2
REP	ECX=0	none
REPE/REPZ	ECX=0	ZF=0
REPNE/REPNZ	ECX=0	ZF=1

incremented. If the flag is set, the registers are decremented. The STD and CLD instructions set and clear this flag. Programmers should always put a known value in the DF flag before using a string instruction.

3.6.3 String Instructions

MOVS (Move String) moves the string element addressed by the ESI register to the location addressed by the EDI register. The MOVSB instruction moves bytes, the MOVSW instruction moves words, and the MOVSD instruction moves doublewords. The MOVS instruction, when accompanied by the REP prefix, operates as a memory-to-memory block transfer. To set up this operation, the program must initialize the ECX, ESI, and EDI registers. The ECX register specifies the number of elements in the block.

CMPS (Compare Strings) subtracts the destination string element from the source string element and updates the AF, SF, PF, CF and OF flags. Neither string element is written back to memory. If the string elements are equal, the ZF flag is set; otherwise, it is cleared. CMPSB compares bytes, CMPSW compares words, and CMPSD compares doublewords.

SCAS (Scan String) subtracts the destination string element from the EAX, AX, or AL register (depending on operand length) and updates the AF, SF, ZF, PF, CF and OF flags. The string and the register are not modified. If the values are equal, the ZF flag is set; otherwise, it is cleared. The SCASB instruction scans bytes; the SCASW instruction scans words; the SCASD instruction scans doublewords.

When the REPE/REPZ or REPNE/REPNZ prefix modifies either the SCAS or CMPS instructions, the loop which is formed is terminated by the loop counter or the effect the SCAS or CMPS instruction has on the ZF flag.

LODS (Load String) places the source string element addressed by the ESI register into the EAX register for doubleword strings, into the AX register for word strings, or into the AL register for byte strings. This instruction usually is used in a loop, where other instructions process each element of the string as they appear in the register.

STOS (Store String) places the source string element from the EAX, AX, or AL register into the string addressed by the EDI register. This instruction usually is used in a loop, where it writes to memory the result of processing a string element read from memory with the LODS instruction. A REP STOS instruction is the fastest way to initialize a large block of memory.

3.7 INSTRUCTIONS FOR BLOCK-STRUCTURED LANGUAGES

These instructions provide machine-language support for implementing block-structured languages, such as C and Pascal. They include ENTER and LEAVE, which simplify procedure entry and exit in compiler-generated code. They support a structure of pointers and local variables on the stack called a *stack frame*.

ENTER (Enter Procedure) creates a stack frame compatible with the scope rules of block-structured languages. In these languages, a procedure has access to its own variables and some number of other variables defined elsewhere in the program. The scope of a procedure is the set of variables to which it has access. The rules for scope vary among languages; they may be based on the nesting of procedures, the division of the program into separately-compiled files, or some other modularization scheme.

The ENTER instruction has two operands. The first specifies the number of bytes to be reserved on the stack for dynamic storage in the procedure being entered. Dynamic storage is the memory allocated for variables created when the procedure is called, also known as automatic variables. The second parameter is the lexical nesting level (from 0 to 31) of the procedure. The nesting level is the depth of a procedure in the heirarchy of a block-structured program. The lexical level has no particular relationship to either the protection privilege level or to the I/O privilege level.

The lexical nesting level determines the number of stack frame pointers to copy into the new stack frame from the preceding frame. A stack frame pointer is a doubleword used to access the variables of a procedure. The set of stack frame pointers used by a procedure to access the variables of other procedures is called the *display*. The first doubleword in the display is a pointer to the previous stack frame. This pointer is used by a LEAVE instruction to undo the effect of an ENTER instruction by discarding the current stack frame.

Example: `ENTER 2048,3`

Allocates 2K bytes of dynamic storage on the stack and sets up pointers to two previous stack frames in the stack frame for this procedure.

After the ENTER instruction creates the display for a procedure, it allocates the dynamic (automatic) local variables for the procedure by decrementing the contents of the ESP register by the number of bytes specified in the first parameter. This new value in the ESP register serves as the initial top-of-stack for all PUSH and POP operations within the procedure.

To allow a procedure to address its display, the ENTER instruction leaves the EBP register pointing to the first doubleword in the display. Because stacks grow down, this is actually the doubleword with the highest address in the display. Data manipulation instructions which specify the EBP register as a base register automatically address locations within the stack segment instead of the data segment.

The ENTER instruction can be used in two ways: nested and non-nested. If the lexical level is 0, the non-nested form is used. The non-nested form pushes the contents of the EBP register on the stack, copies the contents of the ESP register into the EBP register, and subtracts the first operand from the contents of the ESP register to allocate dynamic storage. The non-nested form differs from the nested form in that no stack frame pointers are copied. The nested form of the ENTER instruction occurs when the second parameter (lexical level) is not zero.

Figure 3-15 shows the formal definition of the ENTER instruction. STORAGE is the number of bytes of dynamic storage to allocate for local variables, and LEVEL is the lexical nesting level.

The main procedure (in which all other procedures are nested) operates at the highest lexical level, level 1. The first procedure it calls operates at the next deeper lexical level, level 2. A level 2 procedure can access the variables of the main program, which are at fixed locations specified by the compiler. In the case of level 1, the ENTER instruction allocates only the requested dynamic storage on the stack because there is no previous display to copy.

A procedure which calls another procedure at a lower lexical level gives the called procedure access to the variables of the caller. The ENTER instruction provides this access by placing a pointer to the calling procedure's stack frame in the display.

A procedure which calls another procedure at the same lexical level should not give access to its variables. In this case, the ENTER instruction copies only that part of the display from the calling procedure which refers to previously nested procedures operating at higher lexical levels. The new stack frame does not include the pointer for addressing the calling procedure's stack frame.

The ENTER instruction treats a re-entrant procedure as a call to a procedure at the same lexical level. In this case, each succeeding iteration of the re-entrant procedure can address only its own variables and the variables of the procedures within which it is nested. A re-entrant procedure always can address its own variables; it does not require pointers to the stack frames of previous iterations.

By copying only the stack frame pointers of procedures at higher lexical levels, the ENTER instruction makes certain that procedures access only those variables of higher lexical levels, not those at parallel lexical levels (see Figure 3-16).

Block-structured languages can use the lexical levels defined by ENTER to control access to the variables of nested procedures. In the figure, for example, if PROCEDURE A calls PROCEDURE B which, in turn, calls PROCEDURE C, then PROCEDURE C

```
Push EBP
Set a temporary value FRAME_PTR := ESP
If LEVEL > 0 then
    Repeat (LEVEL-1) times:
        EBP := EBP -4
        Push the doubleword pointed to by EBP
    End repeat
    Push FRAME_PTR
End if
EBP := FRAME_PTR
ESP := ESP - STORAGE
```

Figure 3-15. Formal Definition of the ENTER Instruction

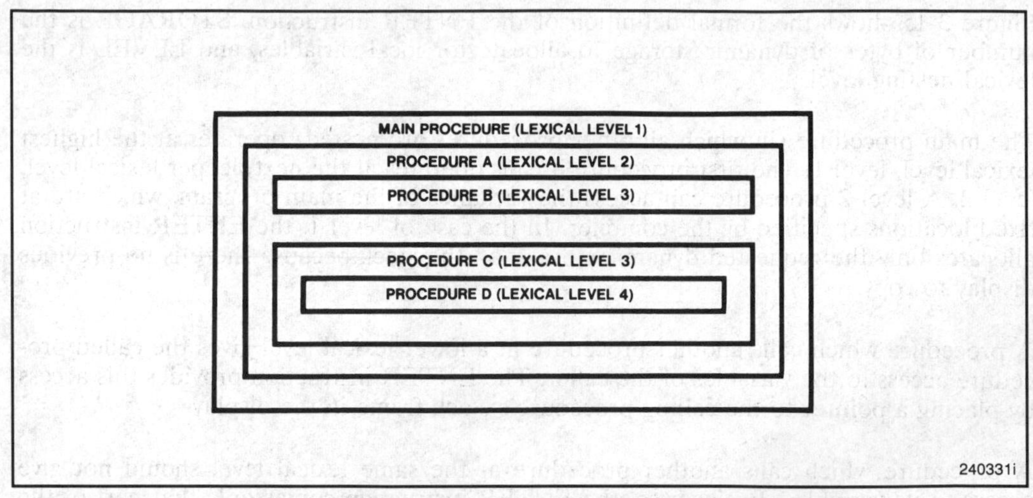

Figure 3-16. Nested Procedures

will have access to the variables of MAIN and PROCEDURE A, but not those of PROCEDURE B because they are at the same lexical level. The following definition describes the access to variables for the nested procedures in the figure.

1. MAIN has variables at fixed locations.
2. PROCEDURE A can access only the variables of MAIN.
3. PROCEDURE B can access only the variables of PROCEDURE A and MAIN. PROCEDURE B cannot access the variables of PROCEDURE C or PROCEDURE D.
4. PROCEDURE C can access only the variables of PROCEDURE A and MAIN. PROCEDURE C cannot access the variables of PROCEDURE B or PROCEDURE D.
5. PROCEDURE D can access the variables of PROCEDURE C, PROCEDURE A, and MAIN. PROCEDURE D cannot access the variables of PROCEDURE B.

In the following diagram, an ENTER instruction at the beginning of the MAIN program creates three doublewords of dynamic storage for MAIN, but copies no pointers from other stack frames (See Figure 3-17). The first doubleword in the display holds a copy of the last value in the EBP register before the ENTER instruction was executed. The second doubleword (which, because stacks grow down, is stored at a lower address) holds a copy of the contents of the EBP register following the ENTER instruction. After the instruction is executed, the EBP register points to the first doubleword pushed on the stack, and the ESP register points to the last doubleword in the stack frame.

When MAIN calls PROCEDURE A, the ENTER instruction creates a new display (See Figure 3-18). The first doubleword is the last value held in MAIN's EBP register. The second doubleword is a pointer to MAIN's stack frame which is copied from the second doubleword in MAIN's display. This happens to be another copy of the last value held in

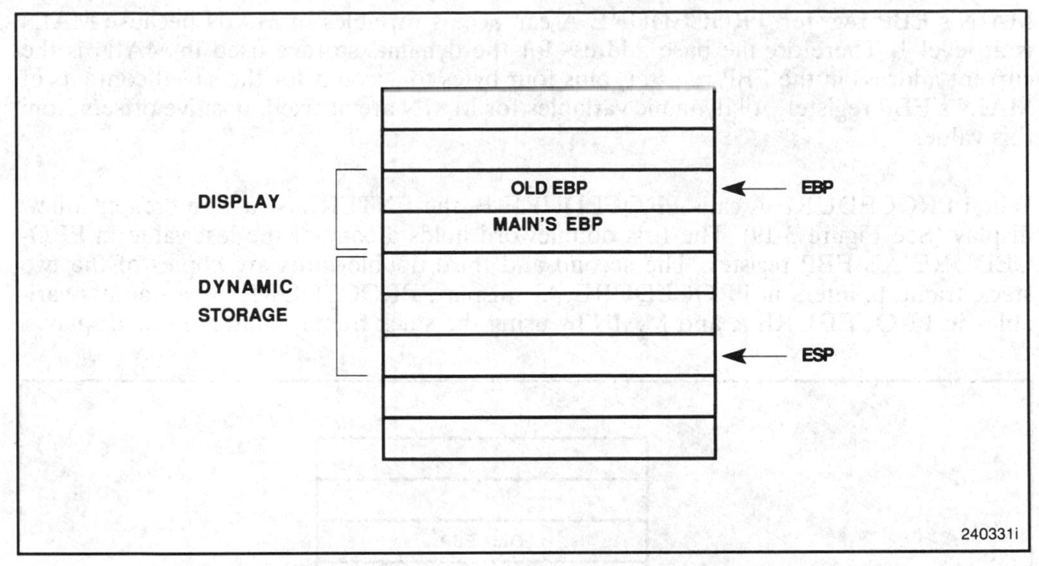

Figure 3-17. Stack Frame After Entering MAIN

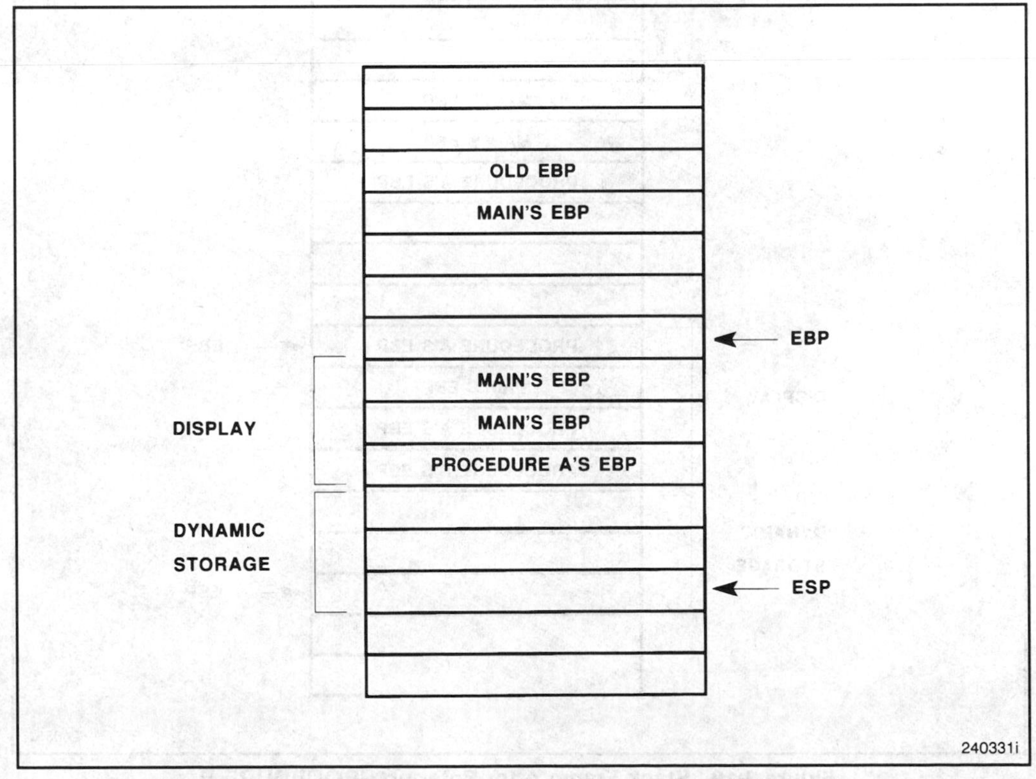

Figure 3-18. Stack Frame After Entering PROCEDURE A

MAIN's EBP register. PROCEDURE A can access variables in MAIN because MAIN is at level 1. Therefore the base address for the dynamic storage used in MAIN is the current address in the EBP register, plus four bytes to account for the saved contents of MAIN's EBP register. All dynamic variables for MAIN are at fixed, positive offsets from this value.

When PROCEDURE A calls PROCEDURE B, the ENTER instruction creates a new display (See Figure 3-19). The first doubleword holds a copy of the last value in PROCEDURE A's EBP register. The second and third doublewords are copies of the two stack frame pointers in PROCEDURE A's display. PROCEDURE B can access variables in PROCEDURE A and MAIN by using the stack frame pointers in its display.

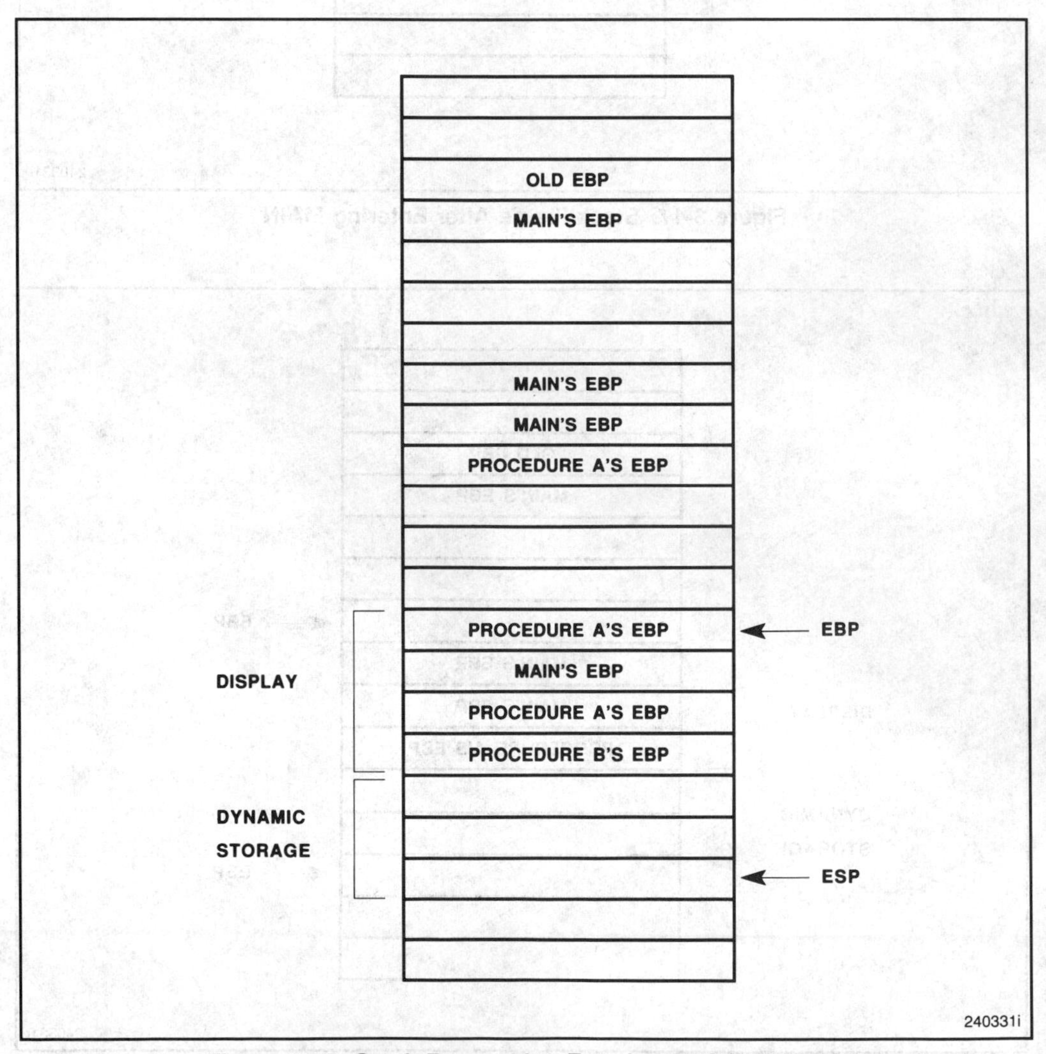

Figure 3-19. Stack Frame After Entering PROCEDURE B

When PROCEDURE B calls PROCEDURE C, the ENTER instruction creates a new display for PROCEDURE C (See Figure 3-20). The first doubleword holds a copy of the last value in PROCEDURE B's EBP register. This is used by the LEAVE instruction to restore PROCEDURE B's stack frame. The second and third doublewords are copies of the two stack frame pointers in PROCEDURE A's display. If PROCEDURE C were at the next deeper lexical level from PROCEDURE B, a fourth doubleword would be copied, which would be the stack frame pointer to PROCEDURE B's local variables.

Note that PROCEDURE B and PROCEDURE C are at the same level, so PROCEDURE C is not intended to access PROCEDURE B's variables. This does not mean that PROCEDURE C is completely isolated from PROCEDURE B; PROCEDURE C is called by PROCEDURE B, so the pointer to the returning stack frame is a pointer to PROCEDURE B's stack frame. In addition, PROCEDURE B can pass parameters to PROCEDURE C either on the stack or through variables global to both procedures (i.e., variables in the scope of both procedures).

LEAVE (Leave Procedure) reverses the action of the previous ENTER instruction. The LEAVE instruction does not have any operands. The LEAVE instruction copies the contents of the EBP register into the ESP register to release all stack space allocated to the procedure. Then the LEAVE instruction restores the old value of the EBP register from the stack. This simultaneously restores the ESP register to its original value. A subsequent RET instruction then can remove any arguments and the return address pushed on the stack by the calling program for use by the procedure.

3.8 FLAG CONTROL INSTRUCTIONS

The flag control instructions change the state of bits in the EFLAGS register, as shown in Table 3-5.

3.8.1 Carry and Direction Flag Control Instructions

The carry flag instructions are useful with instructions like the rotate-with-carry instructions RCL and RCR. They can initialize the carry flag, CF, to a known state before execution of an instruction which copies the flag into an operand.

The direction flag control instructions set or clear the direction flag, DF, which controls the direction of string processing. If the DF flag is clear, the processor increments the string index registers, ESI and EDI, after each iteration of a string instruction. If the DF flag is set, the processor decrements these index registers.

3.8.2 Flag Transfer Instructions

Though specific instructions exist to alter the CF and DF flags, there is no direct method of altering the other application-oriented flags. The flag transfer instructions allow a program to change the state of the other flag bits using the bit manipulation instructions once these flags have been moved to the stack or the AH register.

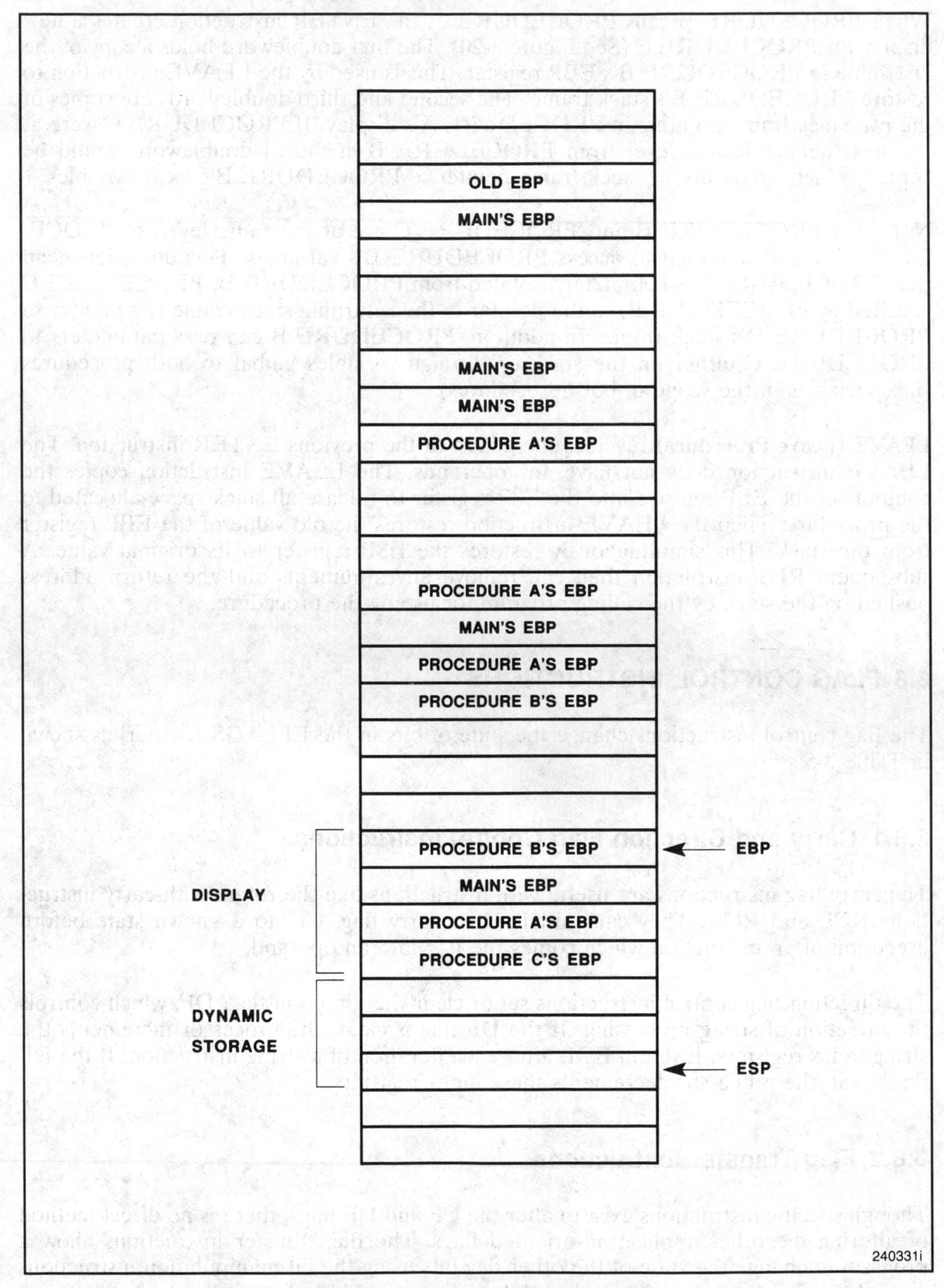

Figure 3-20. Stack Frame After Entering PROCEDURE C

Table 3-5. Flag Control Instructions

Instruction	Effect
STC (Set Carry Flag)	CF ← 1
CLC (Clear Carry Flag)	CF ← 0
CMC (Complement Carry Flag)	CF ← - (CF)
CLD (Clear Direction Flag)	DF ← 0
STD (Set Direction Flag)	DF ← 1

The LAHF and SAHF instructions deal with five of the status flags, which are used primarily by the arithmetic and logical instructions.

LAHF (Load AH from Flags) copies the SF, ZF, AF, PF, and CF flags to the AH register bits 7, 6, 4, 2, and 0, respectively (see Figure 3-21). The contents of the remaining bits 5, 3, and 1 are left undefined. The contents of the EFLAGS register remain unchanged.

SAHF (Store AH into Flags) copies bits 7, 6, 4, 2, and 0 from the AH register into the SF, ZF, AF, PF, and CF flags, respectively (see Figure 3-21).

The PUSHF and POPF instructions are not only useful for storing the flags in memory where they can be examined and modified, but also are useful for preserving the state of the EFLAGS register while executing a subroutine.

PUSHF (Push Flags) pushes the lower word of the EFLAGS register onto the stack (see Figure 3-22). The PUSHFD instruction pushes the entire EFLAGS register onto the stack (the RF flag reads as clear, however).

POPF (Pop Flags) pops a word from the stack into the EFLAGS register. Only bits 14, 11, 10, 8, 7, 6, 4, 2, and 0 are affected with all uses of this instruction. If the privilege level of the current code segment is 0 (most privileged), the IOPL bits (bits 13 and 12)

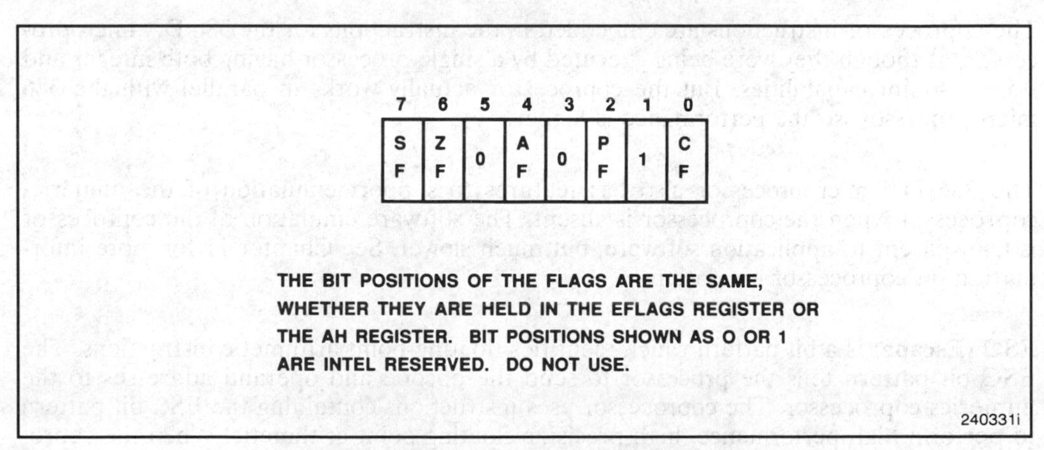
7 6 5 4 3 2 1 0
SF ZF 0 AF 0 PF 1 CF
THE BIT POSITIONS OF THE FLAGS ARE THE SAME, WHETHER THEY ARE HELD IN THE EFLAGS REGISTER OR THE AH REGISTER. BIT POSITIONS SHOWN AS 0 OR 1 ARE INTEL RESERVED. DO NOT USE.
240331i

Figure 3-21. Low Byte of EFLAGS Register

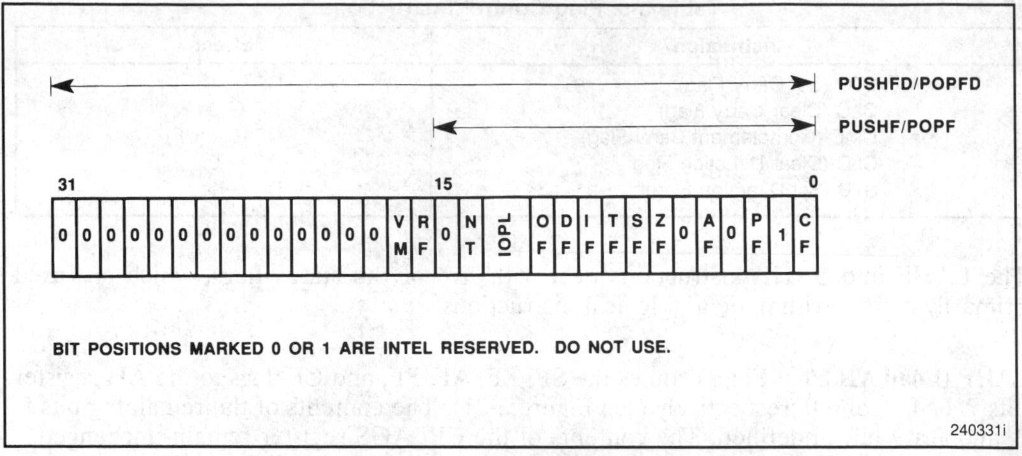

Figure 3-22. Flags Used with PUSHF and POPF

also are affected. If the I/O privilege level (IOPL) is 0, the IF flag (bit 9) also is affected. The POPFD instruction pops a doubleword into the EFLAGS register, but it only can change the state of the same bits affected by a POPF instruction.

3.9 COPROCESSOR INTERFACE INSTRUCTIONS

The 387 DX Numerics Coprocessor provides an extension to the instruction set of the base architecture. The coprocessor extends the instruction set of the 386 DX microprocessor to support high-precision integer and floating-point calculations. These extensions include arithmetic, comparison, transcendental, and data transfer instructions. The coprocessor also contains frequently-used constants, to enhance the speed of numeric calculations.

The coprocessor instructions are embedded in the instructions for the 386 DX microprocessor, as though they were being executed by a single processor having both integer and floating-point capabilities. But the coprocessor actually works in parallel with the 386 microprocessor, so the performance is higher.

The 386 DX microprocessor also has features to support emulation of the numerics coprocessor when the coprocessor is absent. The software emulation of the coprocessor is transparent to application software, but much slower. See Chapter 11 for more information on coprocessor emulation.

ESC (Escape) is a bit pattern which identifies floating-point arithmetic instructions. The ESC bit pattern tells the processor to send the opcode and operand addresses to the numerics coprocessor. The coprocessor uses instructions containing the ESC bit pattern to perform high-performance, high-precision floating point arithmetic. When the coprocessor is not present, these instructions generate coprocessor-not-available exceptions.

WAIT (Wait) is an instruction which suspends program execution while the BUSY# pin is active. The signal on this pin indicates that the coprocessor has not completed an operation. When the operation completes, the processor resumes execution and can read the result. The WAIT instruction is used to synchronize the processor with the coprocessor. Typically, a coprocessor instruction is launched, a WAIT instruction is executed, then the results of the coprocessor instruction are read. Between the coprocessor instruction and the WAIT instruction, there is an opportunity to execute some number of non-coprocessor instructions in parallel with the coprocessor instruction.

3.10 SEGMENT REGISTER INSTRUCTIONS

There are several distinct types of instructions which use segment registers. They are grouped together here because, if system designers choose an unsegmented model of memory organization, none of these instructions are used. The instructions which deal with segment registers are:

1. Segment-register transfer instructions.

```
MOV  SegReg, ...
MOV  ..., SegReg
PUSH SegReg
POP  SegReg
```

2. Control transfers to another executable segment.

```
JMP  far
CALL far
RET  far
```

3. Data pointer instructions.

```
LDS reg, 48-bit memory operand
LES reg, 48-bit memory operand
LFS reg, 48-bit memory operand
LGS reg, 48-bit memory operand
LSS reg, 48-bit memory operand
```

4. Note that the following interrupt-related instructions also are used in unsegmented systems. Although they can transfer execution between segments when segmentation is used, this is transparent to the application programmer.

```
INT n
INTO
BOUND
IRET
```

3.10.1 Segment-Register Transfer Instructions

Forms of the MOV, POP, and PUSH instructions also are used to load and store segment registers. These forms operate like the general-register forms, except that one operand is a segment register. The MOV instruction cannot copy the contents of a segment register into another segment register.

The POP and MOV instructions cannot place a value in the CS register (code segment); only the far control-transfer instructions affect the CS register. When the destination is the SS register (stack segment), interrupts are disabled until after the next instruction.

When a segment register is loaded, the signal on the LOCK# pin of the processor is asserted. This prevents other bus masters from modifying a segment descriptor while it is being read.

No 16-bit operand size prefix is needed when transferring data between a segment register and a 32-bit general register.

3.10.2 Far Control Transfer Instructions

The far control-transfer instructions transfer execution to a destination in another segment by replacing the contents of the CS register. The destination is specified by a far pointer, which is a 16-bit segment selector and a 32-bit offset into the segment. The far pointer can be an immediate operand or an operand in memory.

Far CALL. An intersegment CALL instruction places the values held in the EIP and CS registers on the stack.

Far RET. An intersegment RET instruction restores the values of the CS and EIP registers from the stack.

3.10.3 Data Pointer Instructions

The data pointer instructions load a far pointer into the processor registers. A far pointer consists of a 16-bit segment selector, which is loaded into a segment register, and a 32-bit offset into the segment, which is loaded into a general register.

LDS (Load Pointer Using DS) copies a far pointer from the source operand into the DS register and a general register. The source operand must be a memory operand, and the destination operand must be a general register.

Example: `LDS ESI, STRING_X`

Loads the DS register with the segment selector for the segment addressed by STRING_X, and loads the offset within the segment to STRING_X into the ESI register. Specifying the ESI register as the destination operand is a convenient way to prepare for a string operation, when the source string is not in the current data segment.

LES (Load Pointer Using ES) has the same effect as the LDS instruction, except the segment selector is loaded into the ES register rather than the DS register.

Example: `LES EDI, DESTINATION_X`

Loads the ES register with the segment selector for the segment addressed by DESTINATION_X, and loads the offset within the segment to DESTINATION_X into the EDI register. This instruction is a convenient way to select a destination for a string operation if the desired location is not in the current E-data segment.

LFS (Load Pointer Using FS) has the same effect as the LDS instruction, except the FS register receives the segment selector rather than the DS register.

LGS (Load Pointer Using GS) has the same effect as the LDS instruction, except the GS register receives the segment selector rather than the DS register.

LSS (Load Pointer Using SS) has the same effect as the LDS instruction, except the SS register receives the segment selector rather than the DS register. This instruction is especially important, because it allows the two registers which identify the stack (the SS and ESP registers) to be changed in one uninterruptible operation. Unlike the other instructions which can load the SS register, interrupts are not inhibited at the end of the LSS instruction. The other instructions, such as POP SS, turn off interrupts to permit the following instruction to load the ESP register without an intervening interrupt. Since both the SS and ESP registers can be loaded by the LSS instruction, there is no need to disable or re-enable interrupts.

3.11 MISCELLANEOUS INSTRUCTIONS

The following instructions do not fit in any of the previous categories, but are no less important.

3.11.1 Address Calculation Instruction

LEA (Load Effective Address) puts the 32-bit offset to a source operand in memory (rather than its contents) into the destination operand. The source operand must be in memory, and the destination operand must be a general register. This instruction is especially useful for initializing the ESI or EDI registers before the execution of string instructions or initializing thc EBX register before an XLAT instruction. The LEA instruction can perform any indexing or scaling which may be needed.

Example: `LEA EBX, EBCDIC_TABLE`

Causes the processor to place the address of the starting location of the table labeled EBCDIC_TABLE into EBX.

3.11.2 No-Operation Instruction

NOP (No Operation) occupies a byte of code space. When executed, it increments the EIP register to point at the next instruction, but affects nothing else.

3.11.3 Translate Instruction

XLATB (Translate) replaces the contents of the AL register with a byte read from a translation table in memory. The contents of the AL register are interpreted as an unsigned index into this table, with the contents of the EBX register used as the base address. The XLAT instruction does the same operation and loads its result into the same register, but it gets the byte operand from memory. This function is used to convert character codes from one alphabet into another. For example, an ASCII code could be used to look up its EBCDIC equivalent.

3.12 USAGE GUIDELINES

The instruction set of the 386 DX microprocessor has been designed with certain programming practices in mind. These practices are particularly relevant to assembly language programmers, but may be of interest to compiler designers as well.

- Use the EAX register when possible. Many instructions are one byte shorter when the EAX register is used, such as loads and stores to memory when absolute addresses are used, transfers to other registers using the XCHG instruction, and operations using immediate operands.
- Use the D-data segment when possible. Instructions which deal with the D-space are one byte shorter than instructions which use the other data segments, because of the lack of a segment-override prefix.
- Emphasize short one-, two-, and three-byte instructions. Because instructions for the 386 DX microprocessor begin and end on byte boundaries, it has been possible to provide many instruction encodings which are more compact than those for processors with word-aligned instruction sets. An instruction in a word-aligned instruction set must be either two or four bytes long (or longer). Byte alignment reduces code size and increases execution speed.
- Access 16-bit data with the MOVSX and MOVZX instructions. These instructions sign-extend and zero-extend word operands to doubleword length. This eliminates the need for an extra instruction to initialize the high word.
- For fastest interrupt response, use the NMI interrupt when possible.
- In place of using an ENTER instruction at lexical level 0, use a code sequence like:

  ```
  PUSH EBP
  MOV EBP, ESP
  SUB ESP, BYTE_COUNT
  ```

  This executes in six clock cycles, rather than ten.

The following techniques may be applied as optimizations to enhance the speed of a system after its basic functions have been implemented:

- The jump instructions come in two forms: one form has an eight-bit immediate for relative jumps in the range from 128 bytes back to 127 bytes forward, the other form has a full 32-bit displacement. Many assemblers use the long form in situations where the short form can be used. When it is clear that the short form may be used, explicitly specify the destination operand as being byte length. This tells the assembler to use the short form. If the assembler does not support this function, it will generate an error. Note that some assemblers perform this optimization automatically.

- Use the ESP register to reference the stack in the deepest level of subroutines. Don't bother setting up the EBP register and stack frame.
- For fastest task switching, perform task switching in software. This allows a smaller processor state to be saved and restored. See Chapter 7 for a discussion of multitasking.
- Use the LEA instruction for adding registers together. When a base register and index register are used with the LEA instruction, the destination is loaded with their sum. The contents of the index register may be scaled by 2, 4, or 8.
- Use the LEA instruction for adding a constant to a register. When a base register and a displacement are used with the LEA instruction, the destination is loaded with their sum. The LEA instruction can be used with a base register, index register, scale factor, and displacement.
- Use integer move instructions to transfer floating-point data.
- Use the form of the RET instruction which takes an immediate value for byte-count. This is a faster way to remove parameters from the stack than an ADD ESP instruction. It saves three clock cycles on every subroutine return, and 10% in code size.
- When several references are made to a variable addressed with a displacement, load the displacement into a register.

Part II
Systems Programming

System Architecture 4

CHAPTER 4
SYSTEM ARCHITECTURE

Many of the architectural features of the 386™ DX microprocessor are used only by system programmers. This chapter presents an overview of these features. Application programmers may need to read this chapter, and the following chapters which describe the use of these features, in order to understand the hardware facilities used by system programmers to create a reliable and secure environment for application programs. The system-level architecture also supports powerful debugging features which application programmers may wish to use during program development.

The system-level features of the Intel386™ architecture include:

Memory Management
Protection
Multitasking
Input/Output
Exceptions and Interrupts
Initialization
Coprocessing and Multiprocessing
Debugging

These features are supported by registers and instructions, all of which are introduced in the following sections. The purpose of this chapter is not to explain each feature in detail, but rather to place the remaining chapters of Part II in perspective. When a register or instruction is mentioned, it is accompanied by an explanation or a reference to a following chapter.

4.1 SYSTEM REGISTERS

The registers intended for use by system programmers fall into these categories:

EFLAGS Register
Memory-Management Registers
Control Registers
Debug Registers
Test Registers

The system registers control the execution environment of application programs. Most systems restrict access to these facilities by application programs (although systems can be built where all programs run at the most privileged level, in which case application programs are allowed to modify these facilities).

4.1.1 System Flags

The system flags of the EFLAGS register control I/O, maskable interrupts, debugging, task switching, and the virtual-8086 mode. An application program should ignore these flags. An application program should not attempt to change their state. In most systems, an attempt to change the state of a system flag by an application program results in an exception. The 386 DX microprocessor makes use of some of the bit positions which are reserved on the 386 DX microprocessor. A 386 DX program should not attempt to change the state of these bits. These flags are shown in Figure 4-1.

VM (Virtual-8086 Mode, bit 17)

Setting the VM flag places the processor in virtual-8086 mode. This is an emulation of the programming environment of an 8086 processor. See Chapter 15 for more information.

RF (Resume Flag, bit 16)

The RF flag temporarily disables debug exceptions so that an instruction can be restarted after a debug exception without immediately causing another debug exception. When the debugger is entered, this flag allows it to run normally (rather than recursively calling itself until the stack overflows). The RF flag is not affected by the

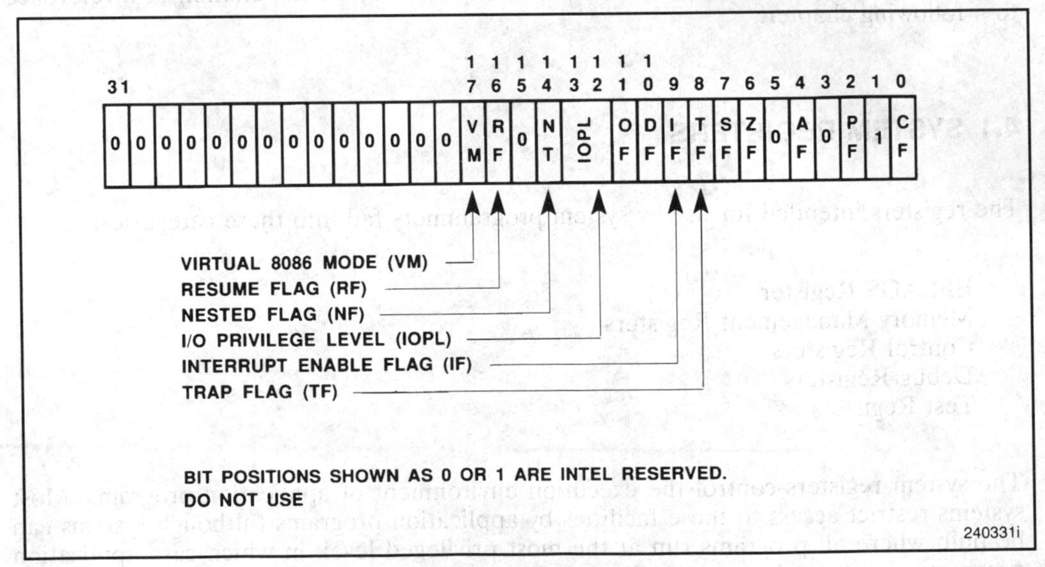

Figure 4-1. System Flags

POPF instruction, but it is affected by the POPFD and IRET instructions. See Chapter 12 for details.

NT (Nested Task, bit 14)

The processor uses the nested task flag to control chaining of interrupted and called tasks. The NT flag affects the operation of the IRET instruction. The NT flag is affected by the POPF, POPFD, and IRET instructions. Improper changes to the state of this flag can generate unexpected exceptions in application programs. See Chapter 7 and Chapter 9 for more information on nested tasks.

IOPL (I/O Privilege Level, bits 12 and 13)

The I/O privilege level is used by the protection mechanism to control access to the I/O address space. The privilege level of the code segment currently executing (CPL) and the IOPL determine whether this field can be modified by the POPF, POPFD, and IRET instructions. See Chapter 8 for more information.

IF (Interrupt-Enable Flag, bit 9)

Setting the IF flag puts the processor in a mode in which it responds to maskable interrupt requests (INTR interrupts). Clearing the IF flag disables these interrupts. The IF flag has no effect on either exceptions or nonmaskable interrupts (NMI interrupts). The CPL and IOPL determine whether this field can be modified by the CLI, STI, POPF, POPFD, and IRET instructions. See Chapter 9 for more details about interrupts.

TF (Trap Flag, bit 8)

Setting the TF flag puts the processor into single-step mode for debugging. In this mode, the processor generates a debug exception after each instruction, which allows a program to be inspected as it executes each instruction. Single-stepping is just one of several debugging features of the 386 DX microprocessor. If an application program sets the TF flag using the POPF, POPFD, or IRET instructions, a debug exception is generated. See Chapter 12 for more information.

4.1.2 Memory-Management Registers

Four registers of the 386 DX microprocessor specify the location of the data structures which control segmented memory management, as shown in Figure 4-2. Special instructions are provided for loading and storing these registers. The GDTR and IDTR registers may be loaded with instructions which get a six-byte block of data from memory. The LDTR and TR registers may be loaded with instructions which take a 16-bit segment selector as an operand. The remaining bytes of these registers are then loaded automatically by the processor from the descriptor referenced by the operand.

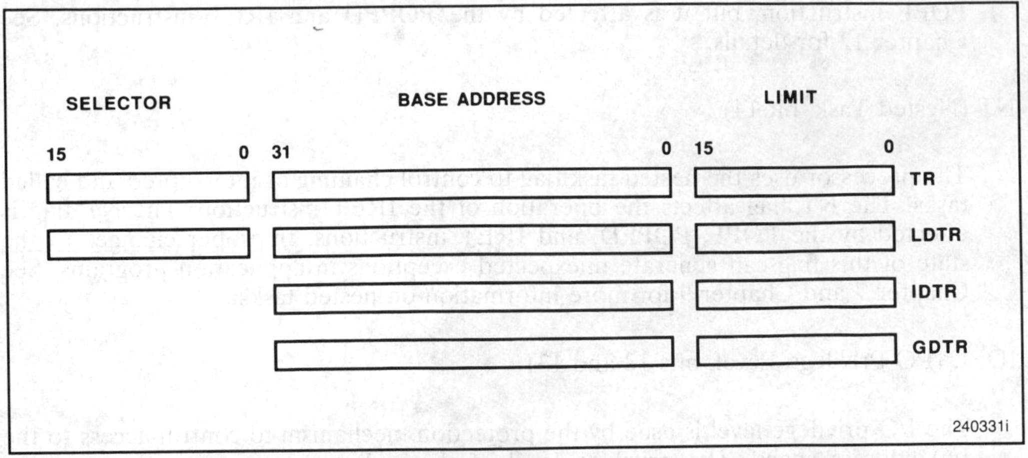

Figure 4-2. Memory Management Registers

Most systems will protect the instructions which load memory-management registers from use by application programs (although a system in which no protection is used is possible).

GDTR Global Descriptor Table Register

This register holds the 32-bit base address and 16-bit segment limit for the global descriptor table (GDT). When a reference is made to data in memory, a segment selector is used to find a segment descriptor in the GDT or LDT. A segment descriptor contains the base address for a segment. See Chapter 5 for an explanation of segmentation.

LDTR Local Descriptor Table Register

This register holds the 32-bit base address, 16-bit segment limit, and 16-bit segment selector for the local descriptor table (LDT). The segment which contains the LDT has a segment descriptor in the GDT. There is no segment descriptor for the GDT. When a reference is made to data in memory, a segment selector is used to find a segment descriptor in the GDT or LDT. A segment descriptor contains the base address for a segment. See Chapter 5 for an explanation of segmentation.

IDTR Interrupt Descriptor Table Register

This register holds the 32-bit base address and 16-bit segment limit for the interrupt descriptor table (IDT). When an interrupt occurs, the interrupt vector is used as an index to get a gate descriptor from this table. The gate descriptor contains a far pointer used to start up the interrupt handler. See Chapter 9 for details of the interrupt mechanism.

TR Task Register

This register holds the 32-bit base address, 16-bit segment limit, and 16-bit segment selector for the task currently being executed. It references a task state segment (TSS) descriptor in the global descriptor table. See Chapter 7 for a description of the multitasking features of the 386 DX microprocessor.

4.1.3 Control Registers

Figure 4-3 shows the format of the control registers CR0, CR1, CR2, and CR3. Most systems prevent application programs from loading the control registers (although an unprotected system would allow this). Application programs can read this register to determine if a numerics coprocessor is present. Forms of the MOV instruction allow the register to be loaded from or stored in general registers. For example:

```
MOV  EAX,  CR0
MOV  CR3,  EBX
```

The CR0 register contains system control flags, which control modes or indicate states which apply generally to the processor, rather than to the execution of an individual task. A program should not attempt to change any of the reserved bit positions.

PG (Paging, bit 31)

This bit enables paging when set, and disables paging when clear. See Chapter 5 for more information about paging. See Chapter 10 for information on how to enable paging.

R (Reserved, bit 4)

This bit is reserved by Intel. When loading CR0, care should be taken not to alter the value of this bit.

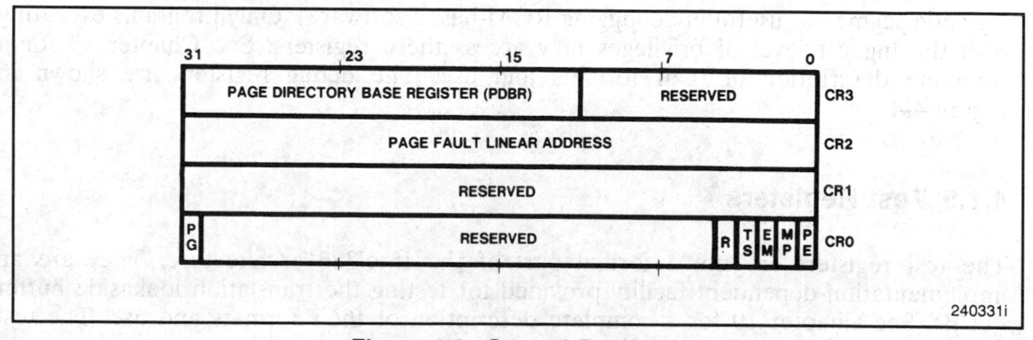

Figure 4-3. Control Registers

TS (Task Switched, bit 3)

The processor sets the TS bit with every task switch and tests it when interpreting coprocessor instructions. See Chapter 11 for more information.

EM (Emulation, bit 2)

When set, the EM bit indicates coprocessor functions are to be emulated in software. See Chapter 11 for more information.

MP (Math Present, bit 1)

The MP bit controls the function of the WAIT instruction, which is used to synchronize with a coprocessor. See Chapter 11 for more information.

PE (Protection Enable, bit 0)

Setting the PE bit enables protection of segments and pages. See Chapter 6 for more information about protection. See Chapter 10 and Chapter 14 for information on how to enable paging.

When an exception is generated during paging, the CR2 register has the 32-bit linear address which caused the exception. See Chapter 9 for more information about handling exceptions generated during paging (page faults).

When paging is used, the CR3 register has the 20 most-significant bits of the address of the page directory (the first-level page table). Note that the page directory must be aligned to a page boundary, so the low 12 bits of the register must be kept clear. The CR3 register is also known as the page-directory base register (PDBR).

4.1.4 Debug Registers

The debug registers bring advanced debugging abilities to the 386 DX microprocessor, including data breakpoints and the ability to set instruction breakpoints without modifying code segments (useful in debugging ROM-based software). Only programs executing with the highest level of privileges may access these registers. See Chapter 12 for a complete description of their formats and use. The debug registers are shown in Figure 4-4.

4.1.5 Test Registers

The test registers are not a formal part of the Intel386 architecture. They are an implementation-dependent facility provided for testing the translation lookaside buffer (TLB). See Chapter 10 for a complete description of their formats and use. The test registers are shown in Figure 4-5.

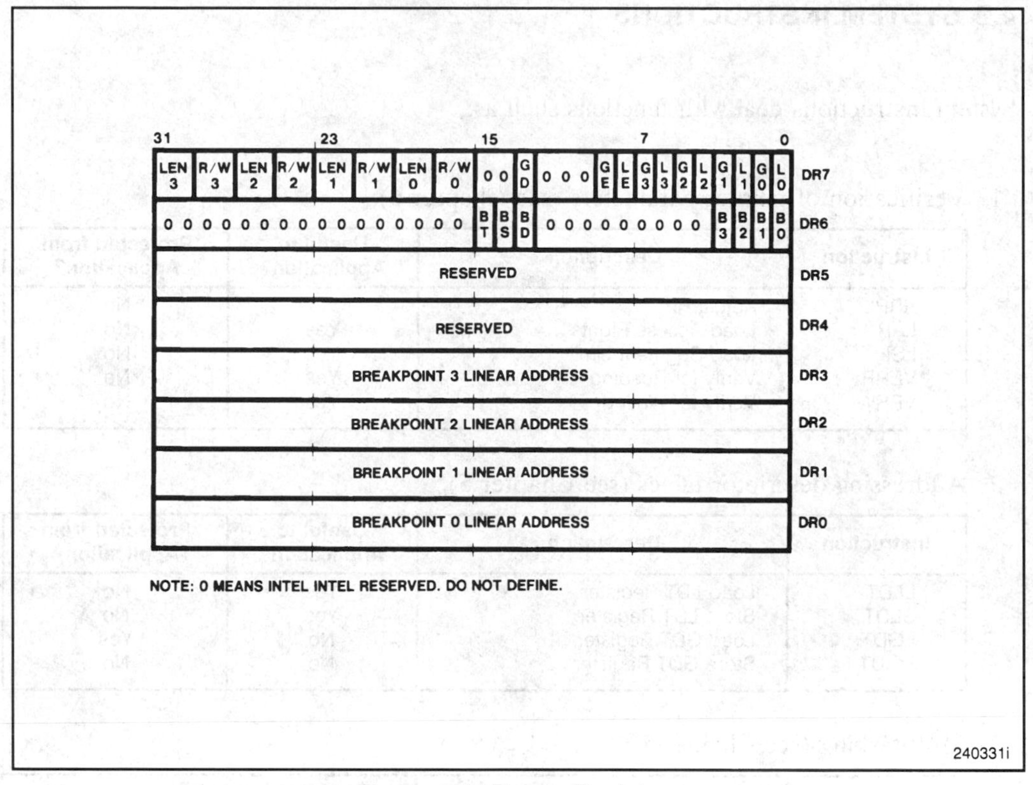

Figure 4-4. Debug Registers

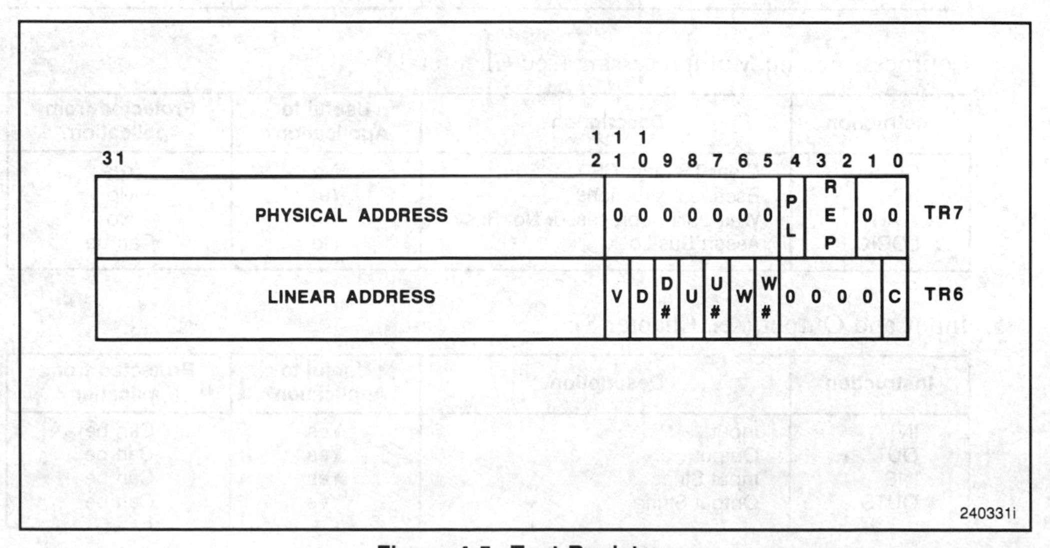

Figure 4-5. Test Registers

4.2 SYSTEM INSTRUCTIONS

System instructions deal with functions such as:

1. Verification of pointer parameters (see Chapter 6):

Instruction	Description	Useful to Application?	Protected from Application?
ARPL	Adjust RPL	No	No
LAR	Load Access Rights	Yes	No
LSL	Load Segment Limit	Yes	No
VERR	Verify for Reading	Yes	No
VERW	Verify for Writing	Yes	No

2. Addressing descriptor tables (see Chapter 5):

Instruction	Description	Useful to Application?	Protected from Application?
LLDT	Load LDT Register	Yes	No
SLDT	Store LDT Register	Yes	No
LGDT	Load GDT Register	No	Yes
SGDT	Store GDT Register	No	No

3. Multitasking (see Chapter 7):

Instruction	Description	Useful to Application?	Protected from Application?
LTR	Load Task Register	No	Yes
STR	Store Task Register	Yes	No

4. Coprocessing and Multiprocessing (see Chapter 11):

Instruction	Description	Useful to Application?	Protected from Application?
CLTS	Clear TS bit in CR0	No	Yes
ESC	Escape Instructions	Yes	No
WAIT	Wait Until Coprocessor Not Busy	Yes	No
LOCK	Assert Bus-Lock	No	Can be

5. Input and Output (see Chapter 8):

Instruction	Description	Useful to Application?	Protected from Application?
IN	Input	Yes	Can be
OUT	Output	Yes	Can be
INS	Input String	Yes	Can be
OUTS	Output String	Yes	Can be

6. Interrupt control (see Chapter 9):

Instruction	Description	Useful to Application?	Protected from Application?
CLI	Clear IF flag	Can Be	Can be
STI	Store IF flag	Can be	Can be
LIDT	Load IDT Register	No	Yes
SIDT	Store IDT Register	No	No

7. Debugging (see Chapter 10):

Instruction	Description	Useful to Application?	Protected from Application?
MOV	LOAD and store debug registers	No	Yes

8. System Control:

Instruction	Description	Useful to Application?	Protected from Application?
SMSW	Store MSW	No	No
LMSW	Load MSW	No	Yes
MOV	Load and Store CR0	No	Yes
HLT	Halt Processor	No	Yes

The SMSW and LMSW instructions are provided for compatibility with the 80286 processor. A program for the 386 DX microprocessor should not use these instructions. A program should access the CR0 register using forms of the MOV instruction. The LMSW instruction does not affect the PG bit, and it cannot be used to clear the PE bit.

The HLT instruction stops the processor until an enabled interrupt or RESET# signal is received. (Note that the NMI interrupt is always enabled.) A special bus cycle is generated by the processor to indicate halt mode has been entered. Hardware may respond to this signal in a number of ways. An indicator light on the front panel may be turned on. An NMI interrupt for recording diagnostic information may be generated. Reset initialization may be invoked. Software designers may need to be aware of the response of hardware to halt mode.

In addition to the chapters mentioned above, detailed information about each of these instructions can be found in the instruction reference chapter, Chapter 17.

Memory Management 5

CHAPTER 5
MEMORY MANAGEMENT

Memory management is a hardware mechanism which lets operating systems create simplified environments for running programs. For example, when several programs are running at the same time, they must each be given an independent address space. If they all had to share the same address space, each would have to perform difficult and time-consuming checks to avoid interfering with the others.

Memory management consists of segmentation and paging. Segmentation is used to give each program several independent, protected address spaces. Paging is used to support an environment where large address spaces are simulated using a small amount of RAM and some disk storage. System designers may choose to use either or both of these mechanisms. When several programs are running at the same time, either mechanism can be used to protect programs against interference from other programs.

Segmentation allows memory to be completely unstructured and simple, like the memory model of an 8-bit processor, or highly structured with address translation and protection. The memory management features apply to units called *segments*. Each segment is an independent, protected address space. Access to segments is controlled by data which describes its size, the privilege level required to access it, the kinds of memory references which can be made to it (instruction fetch, stack push or pop, read operation, write operation, etc.), and whether it is present in memory.

Segmentation is used to control memory access, which is useful for catching bugs during program development and for increasing the reliability of the final product. It also is used to simplify the linkage of object code modules. There is no reason to write position-independent code when full use is made of the segmentation mechanism, because all memory references can be made relative to the base addresses of a module's code and data segments. Segmentation can be used to create ROM-based software modules, in which fixed addresses (fixed, in the sense that they cannot be changed) are offsets from a segment's base address. Different software systems can have the ROM modules at different physical addresses because the segmentation mechanism will direct all memory references to the right place.

In a simple memory architecture, all addresses refer to the same address space. This is the memory model used by 8-bit microprocessors, such as the 8080 processor, where the logical address is the physical address. The 386™ DX microprocessor can be used in this way by mapping all segments into the same address space and keeping paging disabled. This might be done where an older design is being updated to 32-bit technology without also adopting the new architectural features.

An application also could make partial use of segmentation. A frequent cause of software failures is the growth of the stack into the instruction code or data of a program. Segmentation can be used to prevent this. The stack can be put in an address space separate from the address space for either code or data. Stack addresses always would refer to the memory in the stack segment, while data addresses always would refer to memory in the data segment. The stack segment would have a maximum size enforced by hardware. Any attempt to grow the stack beyond this size would generate an exception.

A complex system of programs may make full use of segmentation. For example, a system in which programs share data in real time can have precise control of access to that data. Program bugs would appear as exceptions generated when a program makes improper access. This would be useful as an aid to debugging during program development, and it also may be used to trigger error-recovery procedures in systems delivered to the end-user.

Segmentation hardware translates a segmented (logical) address into an address for a continuous, unsegmented address space, called a linear address. If paging is enabled, paging hardware translates a linear address into a physical address. If paging is not enabled, the linear address is used as the physical address. The physical address appears on the address bus coming out of the processor.

Paging is a mechanism used to simulate a large, unsegmented address space using a small, fragmented address space and some disk storage. Paging provides access to data structures larger than the available memory space by keeping them partly in memory and partly on disk.

Paging is applied to units of 4K bytes called *pages*. When a program attempts to access a page which is on disk, the program is interrupted in a special way. Unlike other exceptions and interrupts, an exception generated due to address translation restores the contents of the processor registers to values which allow the exception-generating instruction to be re-executed. This special treatment is called *instruction restart*. It allows the operating system to read the page from disk, update the mapping of linear addresses to physical addresses for that page, and restart the program. This process is transparent to the program.

If an operating system never sets bit 31 of the CR0 register (the PG bit), the paging mechanism is not enabled. Linear addresses are used as physical addresses. This might be done where a design using a 16-bit processor is being updated to use a 32-bit processor. An operating system written for a 16-bit processor does not use paging because the size of its address space is so small (64K bytes) that it is more efficient to swap entire segments between RAM and disk, rather than individual pages.

Paging would be enabled for operating systems which can support demand-paged virtual memory, such as UNIX. Paging is transparent to application software, so an operating system intended to support application programs written for 16-bit processors may run those programs with paging enabled. Unlike paging, segmentation is not transparent to application programs. Programs which use segmentation must be run with the segments they were designed to use.

5.1 SELECTING A SEGMENTATION MODEL

A model for the segmentation of memory is chosen on the basis of reliability and performance. For example, a system which has several programs sharing data in real-time would get maximum performance from a model which checks memory references in hardware. This would be a multi-segment model.

At the other extreme, a system which has just one program may get higher performance from an unsegmented or "flat" model. The elimination of "far" pointers and segment-override prefixes reduces code size and increases execution speed. Context switching is faster, because the contents of the segment registers no longer have to be saved or restored.

Some of the benefits of segmentation also can be provided by paging. For example, data can be shared by mapping the same page into the address space of each program.

5.1.1 Flat Model

The simplest model is the flat model. In this model, all segments are mapped to the entire physical address space. To the greatest extent possible, this model removes the segmentation mechanism from the architecture seen by either the system designer or the application programmer. This might be done for a programming environment like UNIX, which supports paging but does not support segmentation.

A segment is defined by a segment descriptor. At least two segment descriptors must be created for a flat model, one for code references and one for data references. The segment selector for the stack segment may be mapped to the data-segment descriptor. Whenever memory is accessed, the contents of one of the segment registers are used to select a segment descriptor. The segment descriptor provides the base address of the segment and its limit, as well as access control information (see Figure 5-1).

ROM usually is put at the top of the physical address space, because the processor begins execution at 0FFFFFFF0H. RAM is placed at the bottom of the address space because the initial base address for the DS data segment after reset initialization is 0.

For a flat model, each descriptor has a base address of 0 and a segment limit of 4 gigabytes. By setting the segment limit to 4 gigabytes, the segmentation mechanism is kept from generating exceptions for memory references which fall outside of a segment. Exceptions could still be generated by the paging or protection mechanisms, but these also can be removed from the memory model.

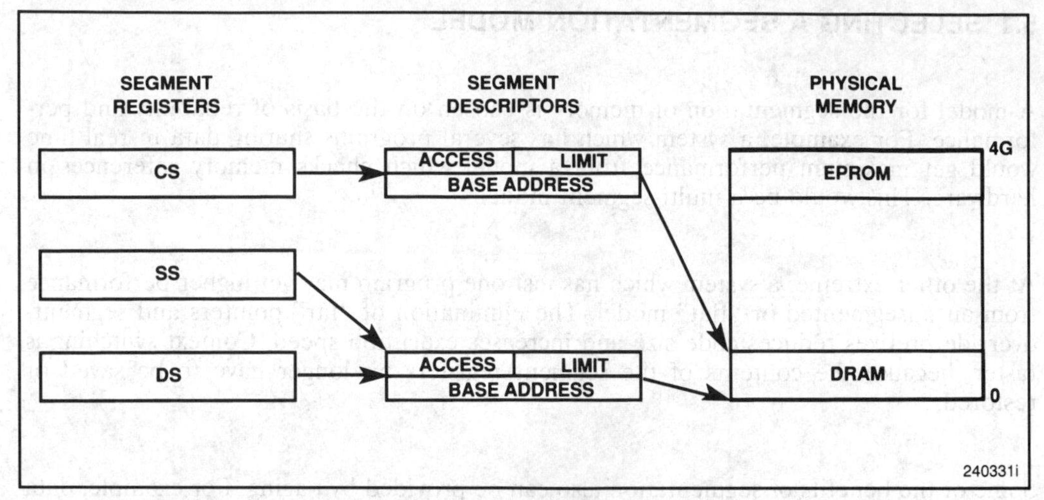

Figure 5-1. Flat Model

5.1.2 Protected Flat Model

The protected flat model is like the flat model, except the segment limits are set to include only the range of addresses for which memory actually exists. A general-protection exception will be generated on any attempt to access unimplemented memory. This might be used for systems in which the paging mechanism is disabled, because it provides a minimum level of hardware protection against some kinds of program bugs.

In this model, the segmentation hardware prevents programs from addressing non-existent memory locations. The consequences of being allowed access to these memory locations are hardware-dependent. For example, if the processor does not receive a READY# signal (the signal used to acknowledge and terminate a bus cycle), the bus cycle does not terminate and program execution stops.

Although no program should make an attempt to access these memory locations, an attempt may occur as a result of program bugs. Without hardware checking of addresses, it is possible that a bug could suddenly stop program execution. With hardware checking, programs fail in a controlled way. A diagnostic message can appear, and recovery procedures can be attempted.

An example of a protected flat model is shown in Figure 5-2. Here, segment descriptors have been set up to cover only those ranges of memory which exist. A code and a data segment cover the EPROM and DRAM of physical memory. A second data segment has been created to cover EPROM. This allows EPROM to be referenced as data. This would be done, for example, to access constants stored with the instruction code in ROM.

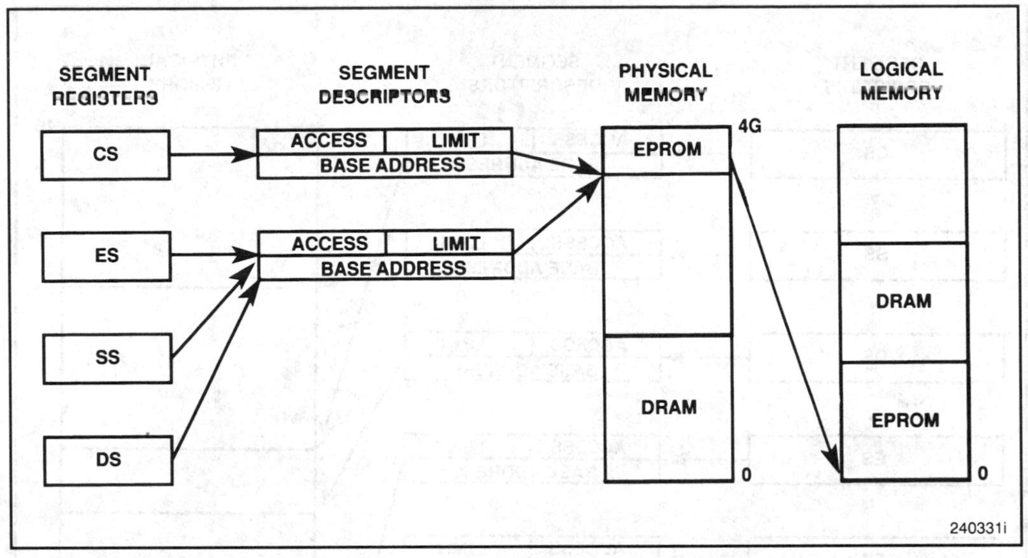

Figure 5-2. Protected Flat Model

5.1.3 Multi-Segment Model

The most sophisticated model is the multi-segment model. Here, the full capabilities of the segmentation mechanism are used. Each program is given its own table of segment descriptors, and its own segments. The segments can be completely private to the program, or they can be shared with specific other programs. Access between programs and particular segments can be individually controlled.

Up to six segments can be ready for immediate use. These are the segments which have segment selectors loaded in the segment registers. Other segments are accessed by loading their segment selectors into the segment registers (see Figure 5-3).

Each segment is a separate address space. Even though they may be placed in adjacent blocks of physical memory, the segmentation mechanism prevents access to the contents of one segment by reading beyond the end of another. Every memory operation is checked against the limit specified for the segment it uses. An attempt to address memory beyond the end of the segment generates a general-protection exception.

The segmentation mechanism only enforces the address range specified in the segment descriptor. It is the responsibility of the operating system to allocate separate address ranges to each segment. There may be situations in which it is desirable to have segments which share the same range of addresses. For example, a system may have both code and data stored in a ROM. A code segment descriptor would be used when the ROM is accessed for instruction fetches. A data segment descriptor would be used when the ROM is accessed as data.

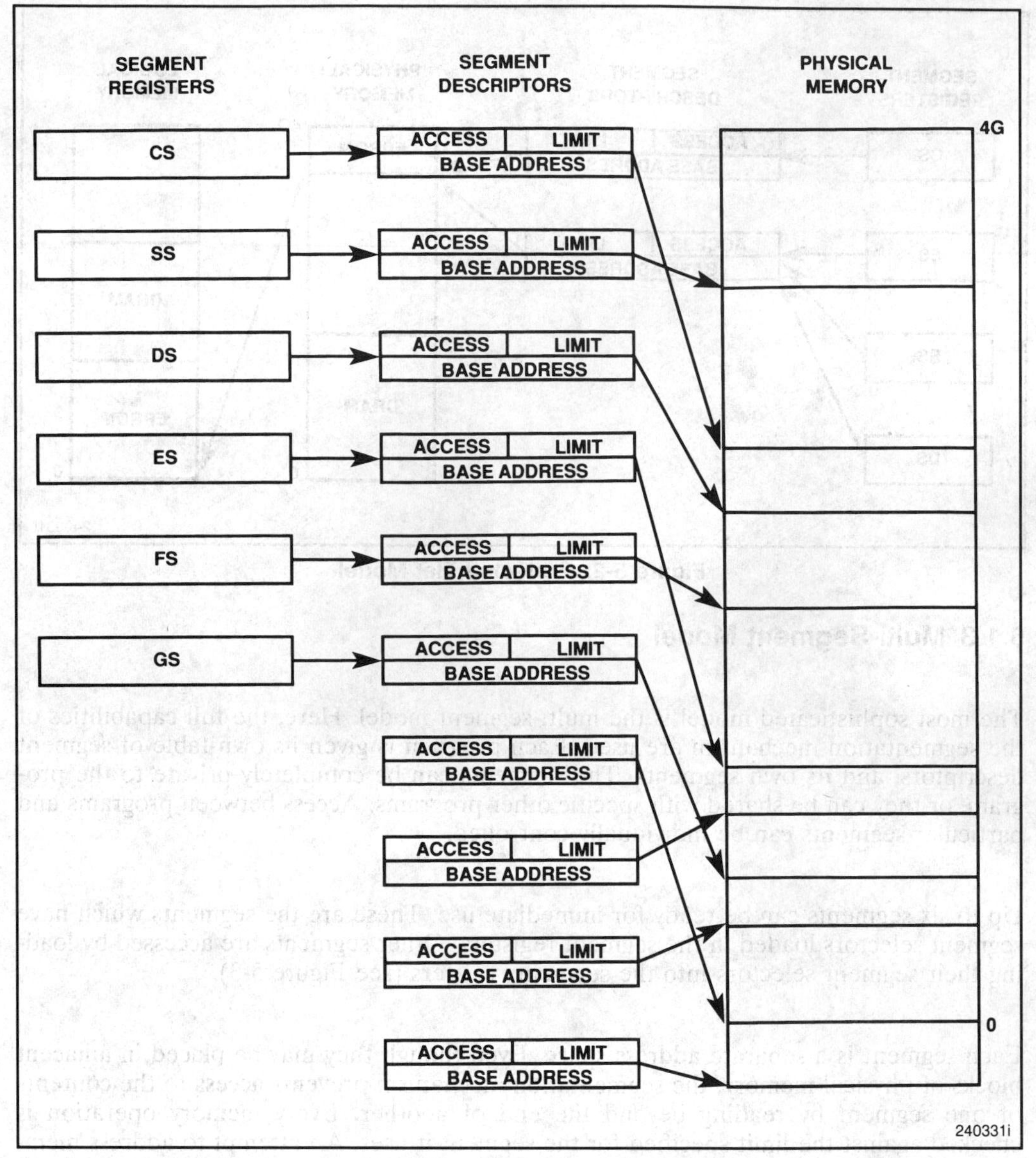

Figure 5-3. Multi-Segment Model

5.2 SEGMENT TRANSLATION

A logical address consists of the 16-bit segment selector for its segment and a 32-bit offset into the segment. A logical address is translated into a linear address by adding the offset to the base address of the segment. The base address comes from the *segment descriptor*, a data structure in memory which provides the size and location of a segment, as well as access control information. The segment descriptor comes from one of two tables, the global descriptor table (GDT) or the local descriptor table (LDT). There is one GDT for all programs in the system, and one LDT for each separate program being run. If the operating system allows, different programs can share the same LDT. The system also may be set up with no LDTs; all programs may use the GDT.

Every logical address is associated with a segment (even if the system maps all segments into the same linear address space). Although a program may have thousands of segments, only six may be available for immediate use. These are the six segments whose segment selectors are loaded in the processor. The segment selector holds information used to translate the logical address into the corresponding linear address.

Separate *segment registers* exist in the processor for each kind of memory reference (code space, stack space, and data spaces). They hold the segment selectors for the segments currently in use. Access to other segments requires loading a segment register using a form of the MOV instruction. Up to four data spaces may be available at the same time, so there are a total of six segment registers.

When a segment selector is loaded, the base address, segment limit, and access control information also are loaded into the segment register. The processor does not reference the descriptor tables again until another segment selector is loaded. The information saved in the processor allows it to translate addresses without making extra bus cycles. In systems in which multiple processors have access to the same descriptor tables, it is the responsibility of software to reload the segment registers when the descriptor tables are modified. If this is not done, an old segment descriptor cached in a segment register might be used after its memory-resident version has been modified.

The segment selector contains a 13-bit index into one of the descriptor tables. The index is scaled by eight (the number of bytes in a segment descriptor) and added to the 32-bit base address of the descriptor table. The base address comes from either the global descriptor table register (GDTR) or the local descriptor table register (LDTR). These registers hold the linear address of the beginning of the descriptor tables. A bit in the segment selector specifies which table to use, as shown in Figure 5-4.

The translated address is the linear address, as shown in Figure 5-5. If paging is not used, it also is the physical address. If paging is used, a second level of address translation produces the physical address. This translation is described in Section 5.3.

5.2.1 Segment Registers

Each kind of memory reference is associated with a segment register. Code, data, and stack references each access the segments specified by the contents of their segment registers. More segments can be made available by loading their segment selectors into these registers during program execution.

Every segment register has a "visible" part and an "invisible" part, as shown in Figure 5-6. There are forms of the MOV instruction to access the visible part of these segment registers. The invisible part is maintained by the processor.

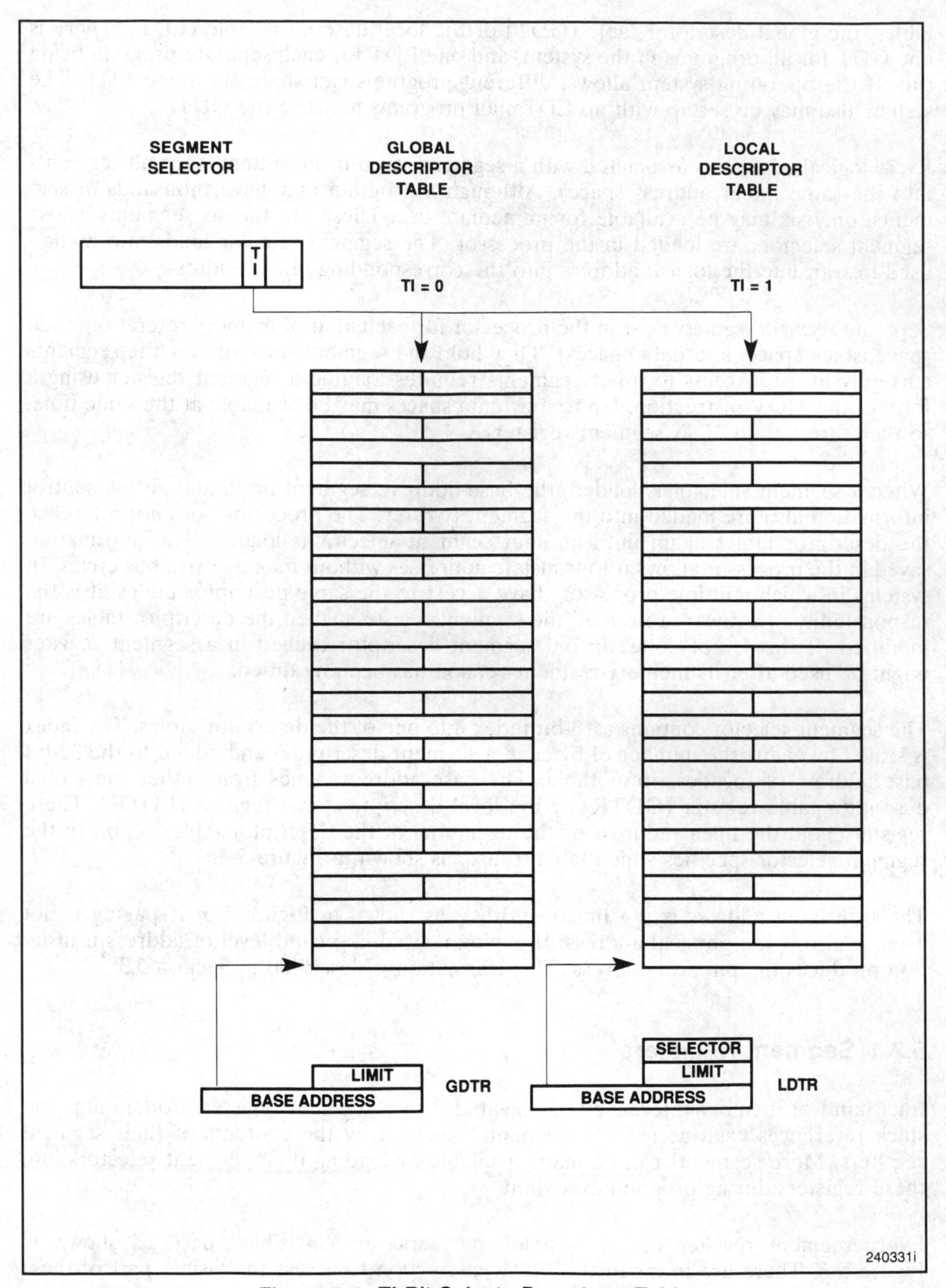

Figure 5-4. TI Bit Selects Descriptor Table

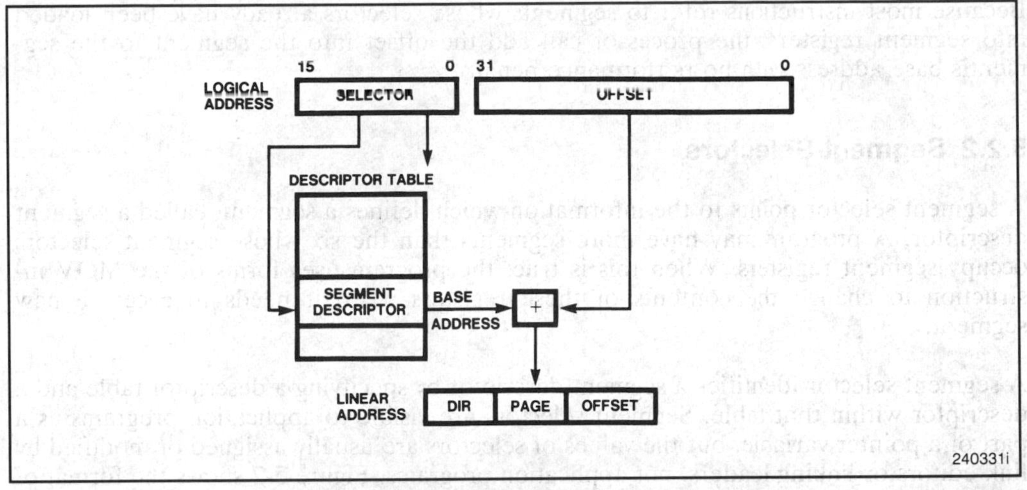

Figure 5-5. Segment Registers

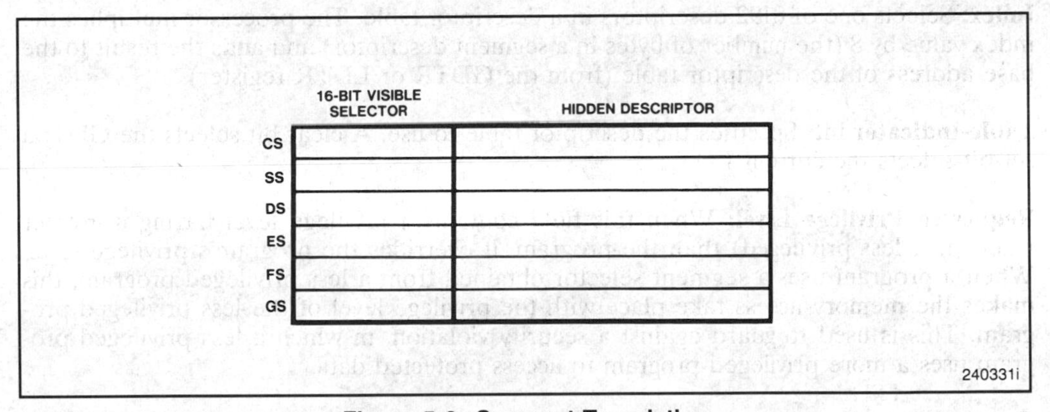

Figure 5-6. Segment Translation

The operations which load these registers are instructions for application programs (described in Chapter 3). There are two kinds of these instructions:

1. Direct load instructions such as the MOV, POP, LDS, LSS, LGS, and LFS instructions. These instructions explicitly reference the segment registers.

2. Implied load instructions such as the far pointer versions of the CALL and JMP instructions. These instructions change the contents of the CS register as an incidental part of their function.

When these instructions are used, the visible part of the segment register is loaded with a segment selector. The processor automatically fetches the base address, limit, type, and other information from the descriptor table and loads the invisible part of the segment register.

Because most instructions refer to segments whose selectors already have been loaded into segment registers, the processor can add the offset into the segment to the segment's base address with no performance penalty.

5.2.2 Segment Selectors

A segment selector points to the information which defines a segment, called a segment descriptor. A program may have more segments than the six whose segment selectors occupy segment registers. When this is true, the program uses forms of the MOV instruction to change the contents of these registers when it needs to access a new segment.

A segment selector identifies a segment descriptor by specifying a descriptor table and a descriptor within that table. Segment selectors are visible to application programs as a part of a pointer variable, but the values of selectors are usually assigned or modified by link editors or linking loaders, not application programs. Figure 5-7 shows the format of a segment selector.

Index: Selects one of 8192 descriptors in a descriptor table. The processor multiplies the index value by 8 (the number of bytes in a segment descriptor) and adds the result to the base address of the descriptor table (from the GDTR or LDTR register).

Table-Indicator bit: Specifies the descriptor table to use. A clear bit selects the GDT; a set bit selects the current LDT.

Requested Privilege Level: When this field contains a privilege level having a greater value (i.e., less privileged) than the program, it overrides the program's privilege level. When a program uses a segment selector obtained from a less privileged program, this makes the memory access take place with the privilege level of the less privileged program. This is used to guard against a security violation, in which a less privileged program uses a more privileged program to access protected data.

For example, system utilities or device drivers must run with a high level of privilege in order to access protected facilities, such as the control registers of peripheral interfaces. But they must not interfere with other protected facilities, even if a request to do so is

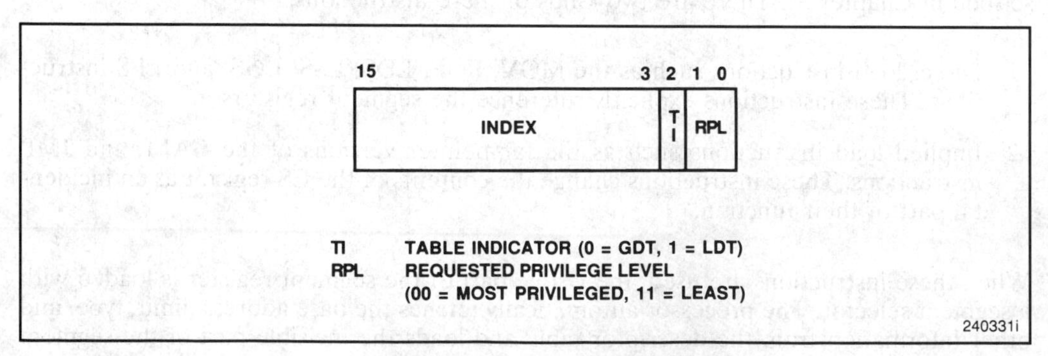

Figure 5-7. Segment Selector

received from a less privileged program. If a program requested reading a sector of disk into memory occupied by a more privileged program, such as the operating system, the RPL can be used to generate a general-protection exception when the segment selector obtained from the less privileged program is used. This exception occurs even though the program using the segment selector would have a sufficient privilege level to perform the operation on its own.

Because the first entry of the GDT is not used by the processor, a selector which has an index of 0 and a table indicator of 0 (i.e., a selector which points to the first entry of the GDT) is used as a "null selector." The processor does not generate an exception when a segment register (other than the CS or SS registers) is loaded with a null selector. It does, however, generate an exception when a segment register holding a null selector is used to access memory. This feature can be used to initialize unused segment registers.

5.2.3 Segment Descriptors

A segment descriptor is a data structure in memory which provides the processor with the size and location of a segment, as well as control and status information. Descriptors typically are created by compilers, linkers, loaders, or the operating system, but not application programs. Figure 5-8 illustrates the two general descriptor formats. The system segment descriptor is described more fully in Chapter 6. All types of segment descriptors take one of these formats.

Base: Defines the location of the segment within the 4 gigabyte physical address space. The processor puts together the three base address fields to form a single 32-bit value.

Granularity bit: Turns on scaling of the Limit field by a factor of 4096 (2^{12}). When the bit is clear, the segment limit is interpreted in units of one byte; when set, the segment limit is interpreted in units of 4K bytes (one page). Note that the twelve least significant bits of the address are not tested when scaling is used. For example, a limit of 0 with the Granularity bit set results in valid offsets from 0 to 4095. Also note that only the Limit field is affected. The base address remains byte granular.

Limit: Defines the size of the segment. The processor puts together the two limit fields to form a 20-bit value. The processor interprets the limit in one of two ways, depending on the setting of the Granularity bit:

1. If the Granularity bit is clear, the Limit has a value from 1 byte to 1 megabyte, in increments of 1 byte.
2. If the Granularity bit is set, the Limit has a value from 4 kilobytes to 4 gigabytes, in increments of 4K bytes.

For most segments, a logical address may have an offset ranging from 0 to the limit. Other offsets generate exceptions. Expand-down segments reverse the sense of the Limit field; they may be addressed with any offset except those from 0 to the limit (see the Type field, below). This is done to allow segments to be created in which increasing the value held in the Limit field allocates new memory at the bottom of the segment's

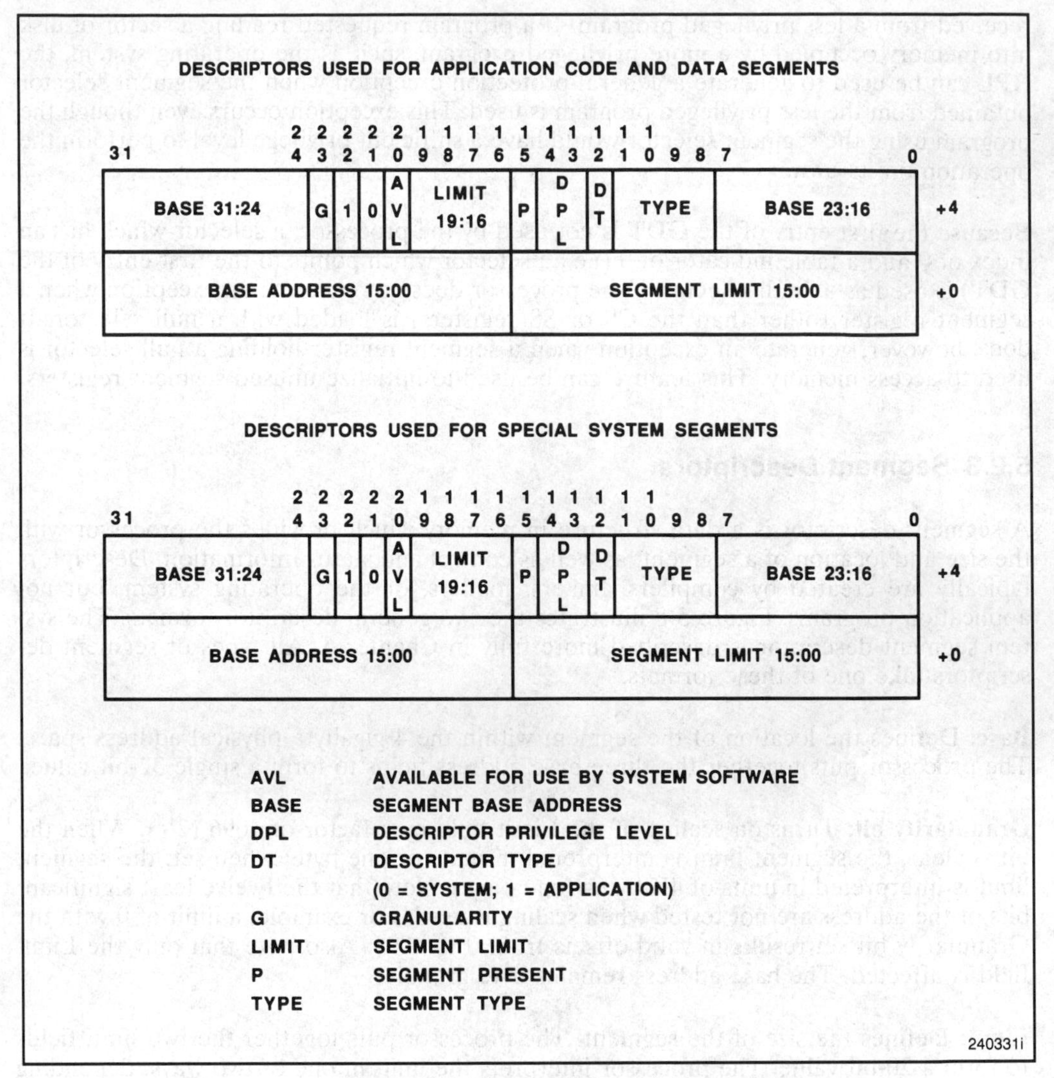

Figure 5-8. Segment Descriptors

address space, rather than at the top. Expand-down segments are intended to hold stacks, but it is not necessary to use them. If a stack is going to be put in a segment which does not need to change size, it can be a normal data segment.

DT field: The descriptors for application segments have this bit set. This bit is clear for system segments and gates.

Type: The interpretation of this field depends on whether the segment descriptor is for an application segment or a system segment. System segments have a slightly different descriptor format, discussed in Chapter 6. The Type field of a memory descriptor specifies the kind of access which may be made to a segment, and its direction of growth (see Table 5-1).

For data segments, the three lowest bits of the type field can be interpreted as expand-down (E), write enable (W), and accessed (A). For code segments, the three lowest bits of the type field can be interpreted as conforming (C), read enable (R), and accessed (A).

Data segments can be read-only or read/write. Stack segments are data segments which must be read/write. Loading the SS register with a segment selector for any other type of segment generates a general-protection exception. If the stack segment needs to be able to change size, it can be an expand-down data segment. The meaning of the segment limit is reversed for an expand-down segment. While an offset in the range from 0 to the segment limit is valid for other kinds of segments (outside this range a general-protection exception is generated), in an expand-down segment these offsets are the ones which generate exceptions. The valid offsets in an expand-down segment are those which generate exceptions in the other kinds of segments. Other segments must be addressed by offsets which are equal or less than the segment limit. Offsets into expand-down segments always must be greater than the segment limit. This interpretation of the segment limit causes memory space to be allocated at the bottom of the segment when the segment limit is increased, which is correct for stack segments because they grow toward lower addresses. If the stack is given a segment which does not change size, it does not need to be an expand-down segment.

Code segments can be execute-only or execute/read. An execute/read segment might be used, for example, when constants have been placed with instruction code in a ROM. In

Table 5-1. Application Segment Types

Number	E	W	A	Type	Description
0	0	0	0	Data	Read-Only
1	0	0	1	Data	Read-Only, accessed
2	0	1	0	Data	Read/Write
3	0	1	1	Data	Read/Write, accessed
4	1	0	0	Data	Read-Only, expand-down
5	1	0	1	Data	Read-Only, expand-down, accessed
6	1	1	0	Data	Read/Write, expand-down
7	1	1	1	Data	Read/Write, expand-down, accessed
Number	**C**	**R**	**A**	**Type**	**Description**
8	0	0	0	Code	Execute-Only
9	0	0	1	Code	Execute-Only, accessed
10	0	1	0	Code	Execute/Read
11	0	1	1	Code	Execute/Read, accessed
12	0	0	0	Code	Execute-Only, conforming
13	0	0	1	Code	Execute-Only, conforming, accessed
14	0	1	0	Code	Execute/Read-Only, conforming
15	0	1	1	Code	Execute/Read-Only, conforming, accessed

this case, the constants can be read either by using an instruction with a CS override prefix or by placing a segment selector for the code segment in a segment register for a data segment.

Code segments can be either conforming or non-conforming. A transfer of execution into a more privileged conforming segment keeps the current privilege level. A transfer into a non-conforming segment at a different privilege level results in a general-protection exception, unless a task gate is used (see Chapter 6 for a discussion of multi-tasking). System utilities which do not access protected facilities, such as data-conversion functions (e.g., EBCDIC/ASCII translation, Huffman encoding/decoding, math library) and some types of exceptions (e.g., Divide Error, INTO-detected overflow, and BOUND range exceeded) may be loaded in conforming code segments.

The Type field also reports whether the segment has been accessed. Segment descriptors initially report a segment as having been accessed. If the Type field then is set to a value for a segment which has not been accessed, the processor restores the value if the segment is accessed. By clearing and testing the low bit of the Type field, software can monitor segment usage (the low bit of the Type field also is called the Accessed bit).

For example, a program development system might clear all of the Accessed bits for the segments of an application. If the application crashes, the states of these bits can be used to generate a map of all the segments accessed by the application. Unlike the break-points provided by the debugging mechanism (Chapter 12), the usage information applies to segments rather than physical addresses.

Note that the processor updates the Type field when a segment is accessed, even if the access is a read cycle. If the descriptor tables have been put in ROM, it is necessary for the hardware designer to prevent the ROM from being enabled onto the data bus during a write cycle. It also is necessary to return the READY# signal to the processor when a write cycle to ROM occurs, otherwise the cycle does not terminate.

DPL (Descriptor Privilege Level): Defines the privilege level of the segment. This is used to control access to the segment, using the protection mechanism described in Chapter 6.

Segment-Present bit: If this bit is clear, the processor generates a segment-not-present exception when a selector for the descriptor is loaded into a segment register. This is used to detect access to segments which have become unavailable. A segment can become unavailable when the system needs to create free memory. Items in memory, such as character fonts or device drivers, which currently are not being used are de-allocated. An item is de-allocated by marking the segment "not present" (this is done by clearing the Segment-Present bit). The memory occupied by the segment then can be put to another use. The next time the de-allocated item is needed, the segment-not-present exception will indicate the segment needs to be loaded into memory. When this kind of memory management is provided in a manner invisible to application programs, it is called *virtual memory*. A system may maintain a total amount of virtual memory far larger than physical memory by keeping only a few segments present in physical memory at any one time.

Figure 5-9 shows the format of a descriptor when the Segment-Present bit is clear. When this bit is clear, the operating system is free to use the locations marked Available to store its own data, such as information regarding the whereabouts of the missing segment.

5.2.4 Segment Descriptor Tables

A segment descriptor table is an array of segment descriptors. There are two kinds of descriptor tables:

- The global descriptor table (GDT)
- The local descriptor tables (LDT)

There is one GDT for all tasks, and an LDT for each task being run. A descriptor table is an array of segment descriptors, as shown in Figure 5-10. A descriptor table is variable in length and may contain up to 8192 (2^{13}) descriptors. The first descriptor in the GDT is not used by the processor. A segment selector to this "null descriptor" does not generate an exception when loaded into a segment register, but it always generates an exception when an attempt is made to access memory using the descriptor. By initializing the segment registers with this segment selector, accidental reference to unused segment registers can be guaranteed to generate an exception.

5.2.5 Descriptor Table Base Registers

The processor finds the global descriptor table (GDT) and interrupt descriptor table (IDT) using the GDTR and IDTR registers. These registers hold descriptors for tables in the physical address space. They also hold limit values for the size of these tables (see Figure 5-11).

The limit value is expressed in bytes. As with segments, the limit value is added to the base address to get the address of the last valid byte. A limit value of 0 results in exactly one valid byte. Because segment descriptors are always eight bytes, the limit should

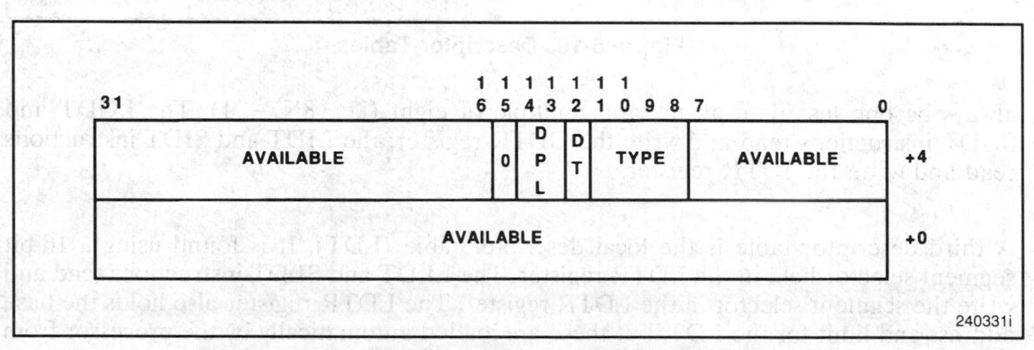

Figure 5-9. Segment Descriptor (Segment Not Present)

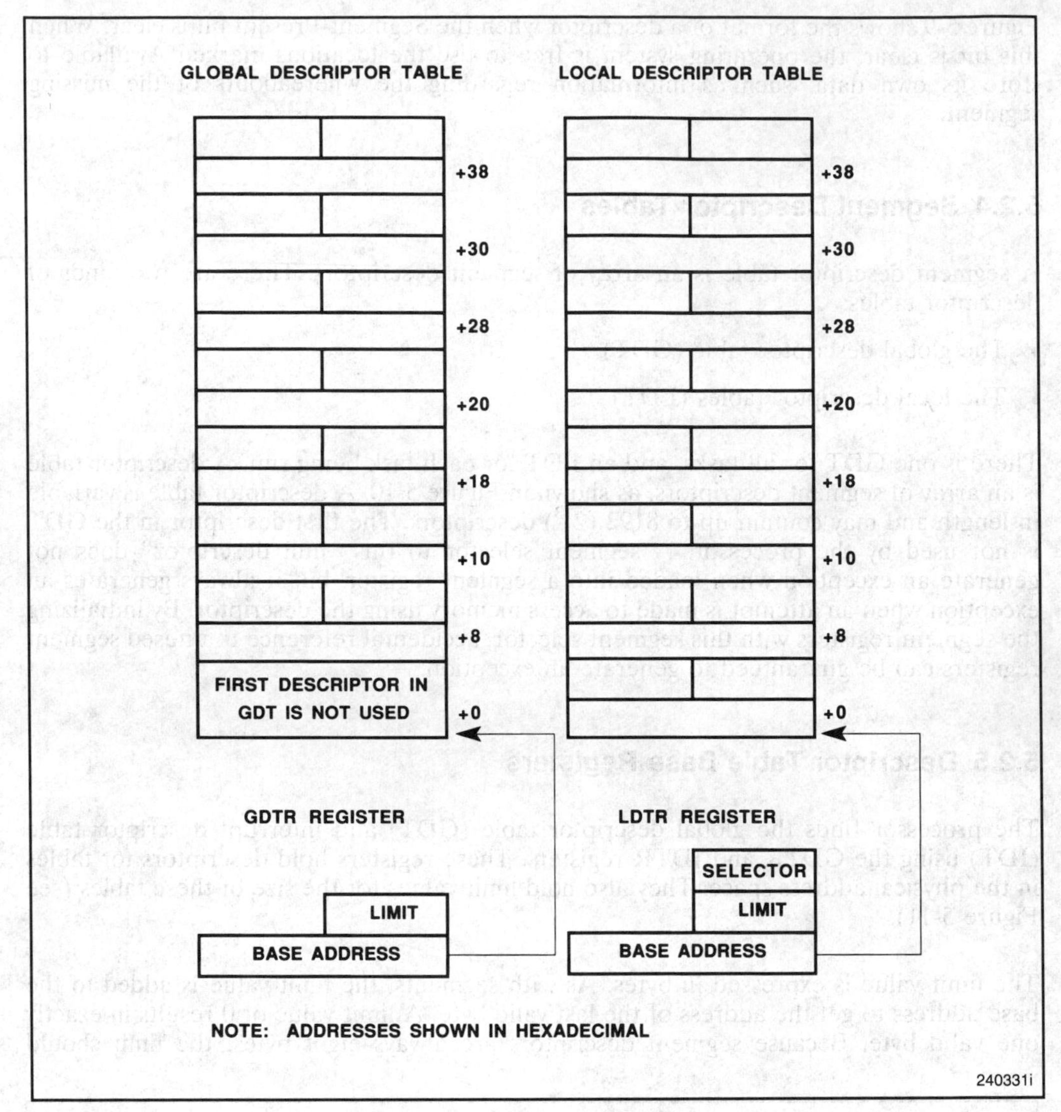

Figure 5-10. Descriptor Tables

always be one less than an integral multiple of eight (i.e., 8N − 1). The LGDT and SGDT instructions read and write the GDTR register; the LIDT and SIDT instructions read and write the IDTR register.

A third descriptor table is the local descriptor table (LDT). It is found using a 16-bit segment selector held in the LDTR register. The LLDT and SLDT instructions read and write the segment selector in the LDTR register. The LDTR register also holds the base address and limit for the LDT, but these are loaded automatically by the processor from the segment descriptor for the LDT.

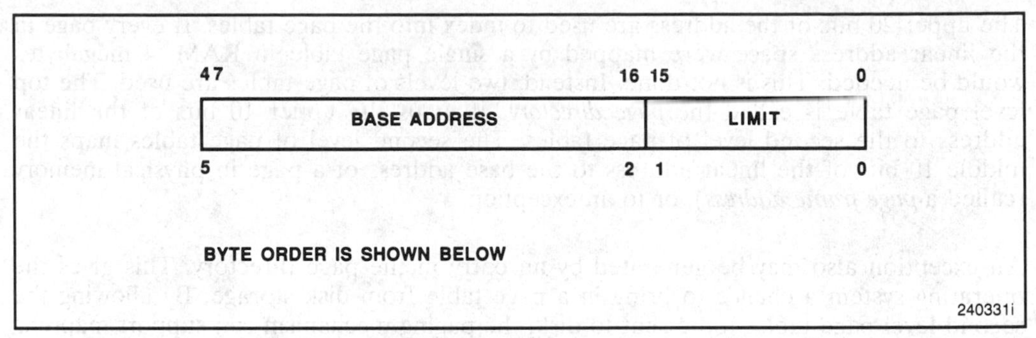

Figure 5-11. Descriptor Table Base Register

5.3 PAGE TRANSLATION

A linear address is a 32-bit address into a uniform, unsegmented address space. This address space may be a large physical address space (i.e., an address space composed of 4 gigabytes of RAM), or paging may be used to simulate this address space using a small amount of RAM and some disk storage. When paging is used, a linear address is translated into its corresponding physical address, or an exception is generated. The exception gives the operating system a chance to read the page from disk (perhaps sending a different page out to disk in the process), then restart the program which generated the exception.

Paging is different from segmentation through its use of small, fixed-size pages. Unlike segments, which usually are the same size as the data structures they hold, on the 386 DX microprocessor, pages are always 4K bytes. If segmentation is the only form of address translation which is used, a data structure which is present in physical memory will have all of its parts in memory. If paging is used, a data structure may be partly in memory and partly in disk storage.

The information which maps linear addresses into physical addresses and exceptions is held in data structures in memory, called *page tables*. As with segmentation, this information is cached in processor registers to minimize the number of bus cycles required for address translation. Unlike segmentation, these processor registers are completely invisible to application programs. (For testing purposes, these registers are visible to programs running with maximum privileges; see Chapter 10 for details.)

The paging mechanism treats the 32-bit linear address as having three parts, two 10-bit indexes into the page tables and a 12-bit offset into the page addressed by the page tables. Because both the virtual pages in the linear address space and the physical pages of memory are aligned to 4K-byte page boundaries, there is no need to modify the low 12 bits of the address. These 12 bits pass straight through the paging hardware, whether paging is enabled or not. Note that this is different from segmentation, because segments can start at any byte address.

The upper 20 bits of the address are used to index into the page tables. If every page in the linear address space were mapped by a single page table in RAM, 4 megabytes would be needed. This is not done. Instead, two levels of page tables are used. The top level page table is called the *page directory*. It maps the upper 10 bits of the linear address to the second level of page tables. The second level of page tables maps the middle 10 bits of the linear address to the base address of a page in physical memory (called a *page frame address*), or to an exception.

An exception also may be generated by an entry in the page directory. This gives the operating system a chance to bring in a page table from disk storage. By allowing the second-level page tables to be sent to disk, the paging mechanism can support mapping of the entire linear address space using only a few pages in memory.

The CR3 register holds the page frame address of the page directory. For this reason, it also is called the page directory base register or PDBR. The upper 10 bits of the linear address are scaled by four (the number of bytes in a page table entry) and added to the value in the PDBR register to get the physical address of an entry in the page directory. Because the page frame address is always clear in its lowest 12 bits, this addition is performed by concatenation (replacement of the low 12 bits with the scaled index).

When the entry in the page directory is accessed, a number of checks are performed. Exceptions may be generated if the page is protected or is not present in memory. If no exception is generated, the upper 20 bits of the page table entry are used as the page-frame address of a second-level page table. The middle 10 bits of the linear address are scaled by four (again, the size of a page table entry) and concatenated with the page frame address to get the physical address of an entry in the second-level page table.

Again, access checks are performed, and exceptions may be generated. If no exception occurs, the upper 20 bits of the second-level page table entry are concatenated with the lowest 12 bits of the linear address to form the physical address of the operand (data) in memory.

Although this process may seem complex, it all takes place with very little overhead. The processor has a cache for page table entries called the translation lookaside buffer (TLB). The TLB satisfies most requests for reading the page tables. Extra bus cycles occur only when a new page is accessed. The page size (4K bytes) is large enough so that very few bus cycles are made to the page tables, compared to the number of bus cycles made to instructions and data. At the same time, the page size is small enough to make efficient use of memory. (No matter how small a data structure is, it occupies at least one page of memory; page sizes larger than 4K bytes waste memory.)

5.3.1 PG Bit Enables Paging

If paging is enabled, a second stage of address translation is used to generate the physical address from the linear address. If paging is not enabled, the linear address is used as the physical address.

Paging is enabled when bit 31 (the PG bit) of the CR0 register is set. This bit usually is set by the operating system during software initialization. The PG bit must be set if the operating system is running more than one program in virtual-8086 mode or if demand-paged virtual memory is used.

5.3.2 Linear Address

A linear address is mapped to a physical address by specifying a page table, a page within that table, and an offset within that page. Figure 5-12 shows the format of a linear address.

Figure 5-13 shows how the processor translates the DIR, PAGE, and OFFSET fields of a linear address into the physical address using two levels of page tables. The addressing mechanism uses the DIR field as an index into a page directory, uses the PAGE field as an index into the page table determined by the page directory, and uses the OFFSET field to address an operand within the page specified by the page table.

5.3.3 Page Tables

A page table is an array of 32-bit entries. A page table is itself a page, and contains 4096 bytes of memory or, at most, 1K 32-bit entries.

Two levels of tables are used to address a page of memory. The top level is called the page directory. It addresses up to 1K page tables in the second level. A page table in the second level addresses up to 1K pages in physical memory. All the tables addressed by one page directory, therefore, can address 1M or 2^{20} pages. Because each page contains 4K or 2^{12} bytes, the tables of one page directory can span the entire linear address space of the 386 DX microprocessor ($2^{20} \times 2^{12} = 2^{32}$).

The physical address of the current page directory is stored in the CR3 register, also called the page directory base register (PDBR). Memory management software has the option of using one page directory for all tasks, one page directory for each task, or some combination of the two. See Chapter 10 for information on initialization of the CR3 register. See Chapter 7 for how the contents of the CR3 register can change for each task.

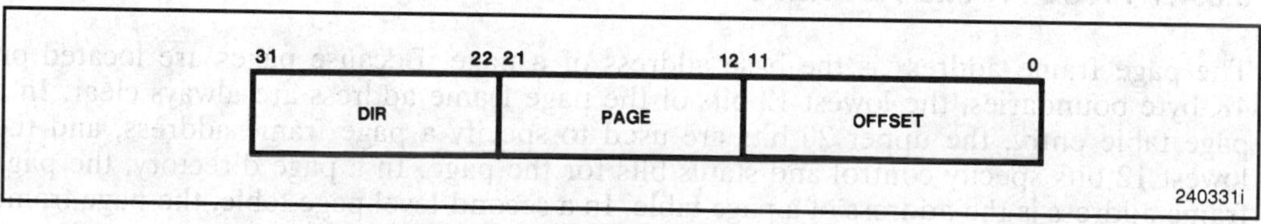

Figure 5-12. Format of a Linear Address

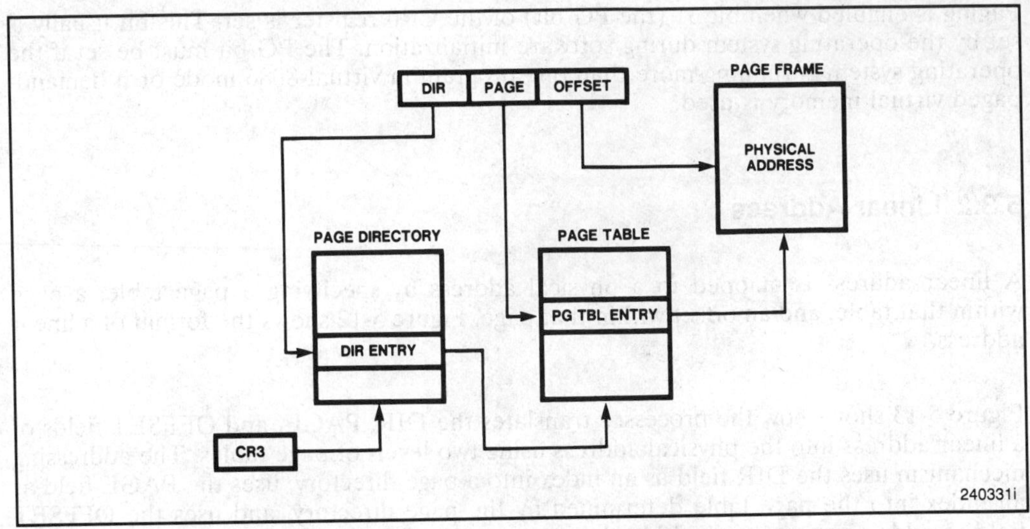

Figure 5-13. Page Translation

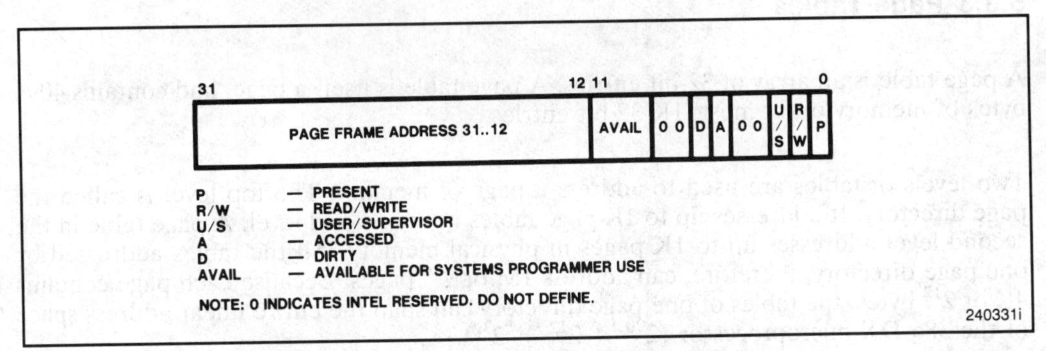

Figure 5-14. Format of a Page Table Entry

5.3.4 Page-Table Entries

Entries in either level of page tables have the same format. Figure 5-14 illustrates this format.

5.3.4.1 PAGE FRAME ADDRESS

The page frame address is the base address of a page. Because pages are located on 4K-byte boundaries, the lowest 12 bits of the page frame address are always clear. In a page table entry, the upper 20 bits are used to specify a page frame address, and the lowest 12 bits specify control and status bits for the page. In a page directory, the page frame address is the address of a page table. In a second-level page table, the page frame address is the address of a page containing instructions or data.

5.3.4.2 PRESENT BIT

The Present bit indicates whether the page frame address in a page table entry maps to a page in physical memory. When set, the page is in memory.

When the Present bit is clear, the page is not in memory, and the rest of the page table entry is available for the operating system, for example, to store information regarding the whereabouts of the missing page. Figure 5-15 illustrates the format of a page table entry when the Present bit is clear.

If the Present bit is clear in either level of page tables when an attempt is made to use a page table entry for address translation, a page-fault exception is generated. In systems which support demand-paged virtual memory, the following sequence of events then occurs:

1. The operating system copies the page from disk storage into physical memory.
2. The operating system loads the page frame address into the page table entry and sets its Present bit. Other bits, such as the R/W bit, may be set, too.
3. Because a copy of the old page table entry may still exist in the translation lookaside buffer (TLB), the operating system empties it. See Section 5.3.5 for a discussion of the TLB and how to empty it.
4. The program which caused the exception is then restarted.

Note that there is no Present bit for the page directory. Although the page directory may be in disk storage while the tasks which use it are suspended, it must be brought into memory before any of these tasks may be run.

5.3.4.3 ACCESSED AND DIRTY BITS

These bits provide data about page usage in both levels of page tables. The Accessed bit is used to report read or write access to a page or second-level page table. The Dirty bit is used to report write access to a page.

With the exception of the Dirty bit in a page directory entry, these bits are set by the hardware; however, the processor does not clear either of these bits. The processor sets the Accessed bits in both levels of page tables before a read or write operation to a page. The processor sets the Dirty bit in the second-level page table before a write operation to an address mapped by that page table entry. The Dirty bit in directory entries is undefined.

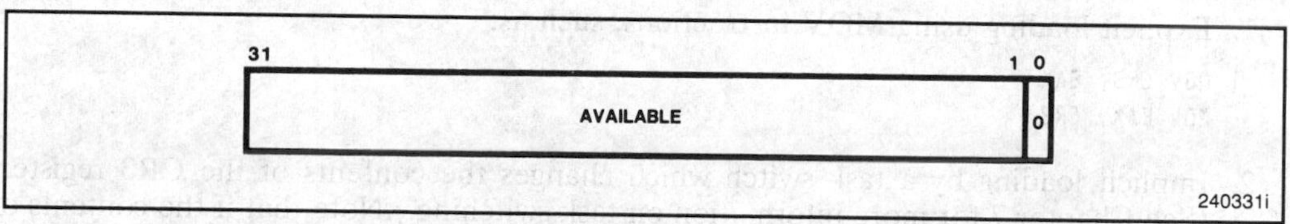

Figure 5-15. Format of a Page Table Entry for a Not-Present Page

The operating system may use the Accessed bit when it needs to create some free memory by sending a page or second-level page table to disk storage. By periodically clearing the Accessed bits in the page tables, it can see which pages have been used recently. Pages which have not been used are candidates for sending out to disk.

The operating system may use the Dirty bit when a page is sent back to disk. By clearing the Dirty bit when the page is brought into memory, the operating system can see if it has received any write access. If there is a copy of the page on disk, and the copy in memory has not received any writes, there is no need to update disk from memory.

See Chapter 11 for how the 386 DX microprocessor updates the Accessed and Dirty bits in multiprocessor systems.

5.3.4.4 READ/WRITE AND USER/SUPERVISOR BITS

The Read/Write and User/Supervisor bits are used for protection checks applied to pages, which the processor performs at the same time as address translation. See Chapter 6 for more information.

5.3.5 Translation Lookaside Buffer

The processor stores the most recently used page table entries in an on-chip cache, called the translation lookaside buffer or TLB. Most paging is performed using the contents of the TLB. Bus cycles to the page tables are performed only when a new page is used.

The TLB is invisible to application programs, but not to operating systems. Operating-system programmers must flush the TLB (dispose of its page table entries) when entries in the page tables are changed. If this is not done, old data which has not received the changes might get used for address translation. A change to an entry for a page which is not present in memory does not require flushing the TLB, because entries for not-present pages are not cached.

The TLB is flushed when the CR3 register is loaded. The CR3 register can be loaded in either of two ways:

1. Explicit loading using MOV instructions, such as:

```
MOV CR3, EAX
MOV EAX, CR3
```

2. Implicit loading by a task switch which changes the contents of the CR3 register. (See Chapter 7 for more information on task switching.) Note that if the contents of the CR3 register do not change during a task switch, the TLB is not flushed.

5.4 COMBINING SEGMENT AND PAGE TRANSLATION

Figure 5-16 combines Figure 5-2 and Figure 5-9 to summarize both stages of translation from a logical address to a physical address when paging is enabled. Options available in both stages of address translation can be used to support several different styles of memory management.

5.4.1 Flat Model

When the 386 DX microprocessor is used to run software written without segments, it may be desirable to remove the segmentation features of the 386 DX microprocessor. The 386 DX microprocessor does not have a mode bit for disabling segmentation, but the same effect can be achieved by mapping the stack, code, and data spaces to the same range of linear addresses. The 32-bit offsets used by 386 DX microprocessor instructions can cover the entire linear address space.

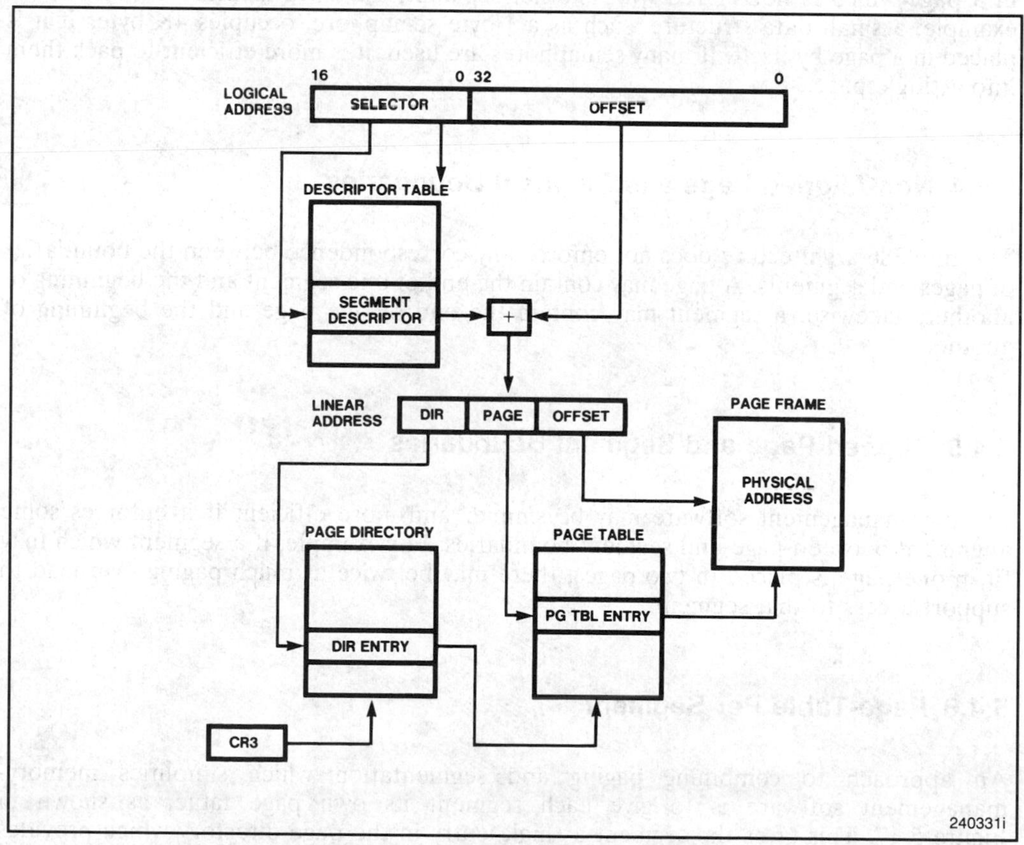

Figure 5-16. Combined Segment and Page Address Translation

When paging is used, the segments can be mapped to the entire linear address space. If more than one program is being run at the same time, the paging mechanism can be used to give each program a separate address space.

5.4.2 Segments Spanning Several Pages

The Intel386™ architecture allows segments which are larger the size of a page (4K bytes). For example, a large data structure may span thousands of pages. If paging were not used, access to any part of the data structure would require the entire data structure to be present in physical memory. With paging, only the page containing the part being accessed needs to be in memory.

5.4.3 Pages Spanning Several Segments

Segments also may be smaller than the size of a page. If one of these segments is placed in a page which is not shared with another segment, the extra memory is wasted. For example, a small data structure, such as a 1-byte semaphore, occupies 4K bytes if it is placed in a page by itself. If many semaphores are used, it is more efficient to pack them into a single page.

5.4.4 Non-Aligned Page and Segment Boundaries

The Intel386 architecture does not enforce any correspondence between the boundaries of pages and segments. A page may contain the end of one segment and the beginning of another. Likewise, a segment may contain the end of one page and the beginning of another.

5.4.5 Aligned Page and Segment Boundaries

Memory-management software may be simpler and more efficient if it enforces some alignment between page and segment boundaries. For example, if a segment which may fit in one page is placed in two pages, there may be twice as much paging overhead to support access to that segment.

5.4.6 Page-Table Per Segment

An approach to combining paging and segmentation which simplifies memory-management software is to give each segment its own page table, as shown in Figure 5-17. This gives the segment a single entry in the page directory which provides the access control information for paging the segment.

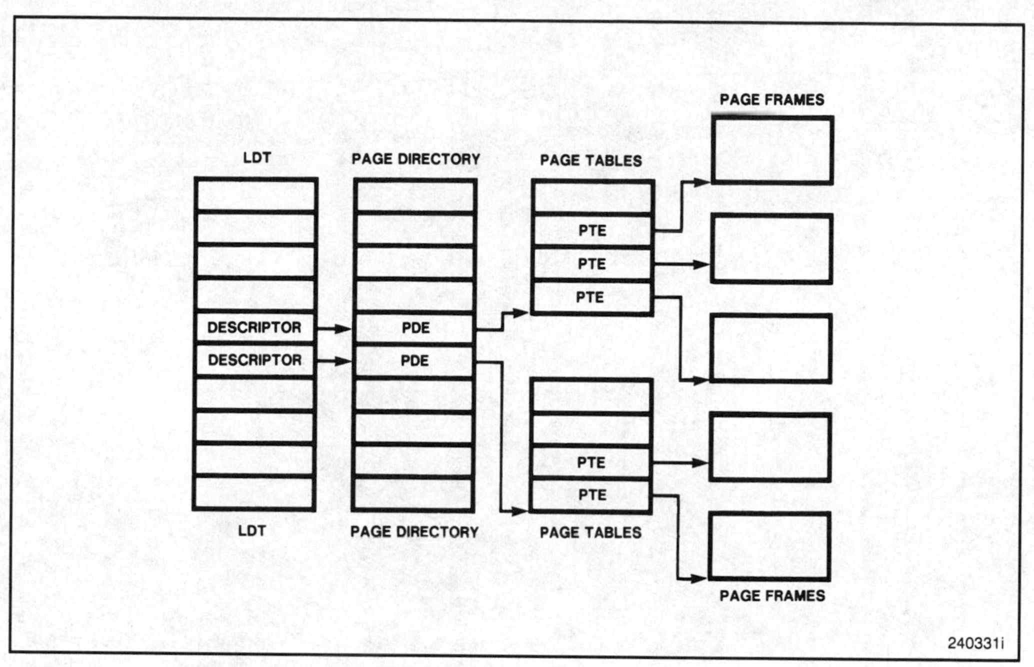

Figure 5-17. Each Segment Can Have Its Own Page Table

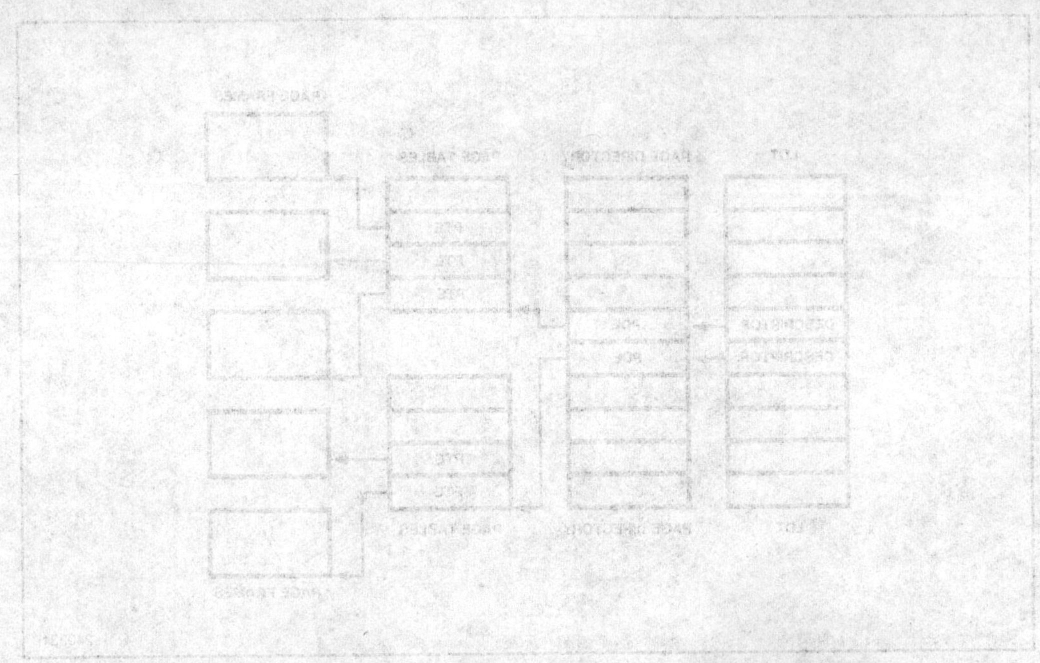

Protection 6

CHAPTER 6
PROTECTION

Protection is necessary for reliable multitasking. Protection can be used to prevent tasks from interfering with each other. For example, protection can keep one task from overwriting the instructions or data of another task.

During program development, the protection mechanism can give a clearer picture of program bugs. When a program makes an unexpected reference to the wrong memory space, the protection mechanism can block the event and report its occurrence.

In end-user systems, the protection mechanism can guard against the possibility of software failures caused by undetected program bugs. If a program fails, its effects can be confined to a limited domain. The operating system can be protected against damage, so diagnostic information can be recorded and automatic recovery may be attempted.

Protection may be applied to segments and pages. Two bits in a processor register define the privilege level of the program currently running (called the current privilege level or CPL). The CPL is checked during address translation for segmentation and paging.

Although there is no control register or mode bit for turning off the protection mechanism, the same effect can be achieved by assigning privilege level 0 (the highest level of privilege) to all segment selectors, segment descriptors, and page table entries.

6.1 SEGMENT-LEVEL PROTECTION

Protection provides the ability to limit the amount of interference a malfunctioning program can inflict on other programs and their data. Protection is a valuable aid in software development because it allows software tools (operating system, debugger, etc.) to survive in memory undamaged. When an application program fails, the software is available to report diagnostic messages, and the debugger is available for post-mortem analysis of memory and registers. In production, protection can make software more reliable by giving the system an opportunity to initiate recovery procedures.

Each memory reference is checked to verify that it satisfies the protection checks. All checks are made before the memory cycle is started; any violation prevents the cycle from starting and results in an exception. Because checks are performed in parallel with address translation, there is no performance penalty. There are five protection checks:

1. Type check
2. Limit check
3. Restriction of addressable domain
4. Restriction of procedure entry points
5. Restriction of instruction set

A protection violation results in an exception. See Chapter 9 for an explanation of the exception mechanism. This chapter describes the protection violations which lead to exceptions.

6.2 SEGMENT DESCRIPTORS AND PROTECTION

Figure 6-1 shows the fields of a segment descriptor which are used by the protection mechanism. Individual bits in the Type field also are referred to by the names of their functions.

Protection parameters are placed in the descriptor when it is created. In general, application programmers do not need to be concerned about protection parameters.

When a program loads a segment selector into a segment register, the processor loads both the base address of the segment and the protection information. The invisible part of each segment register has storage for the base, limit, type, and privilege level. While this information is resident in the segment register, subsequent protection checks on the same segment can be performed with no performance penalty.

6.2.1 Type Checking

In addition to the descriptors for application code and data segments, the 386™ DX microprocessor has descriptors for system segments and gates. These are data structures used for managing tasks (Chapter 7) and exceptions and interrupts (Chapter 9). Table 6-1 lists all the types defined for system segments and gates. Note that not all descriptors define segments; gate descriptors hold pointers to procedure entry points.

Table 6-1. System Segment and Gate Types

Type	Description
0	reserved
1	Available 80286 TSS
2	LDT
3	Busy 80286 TSS
4	Call Gate
5	Task Gate
6	80286 Interrupt Gate
7	80286 Trap Gate
8	reserved
9	Available 386™ DX TSS
10	reserved
11	Busy 386 DX TSS
12	386 DX Call Gate
13	reserved
14	386 DX Interrupt Gate
15	386 DX Task Gate

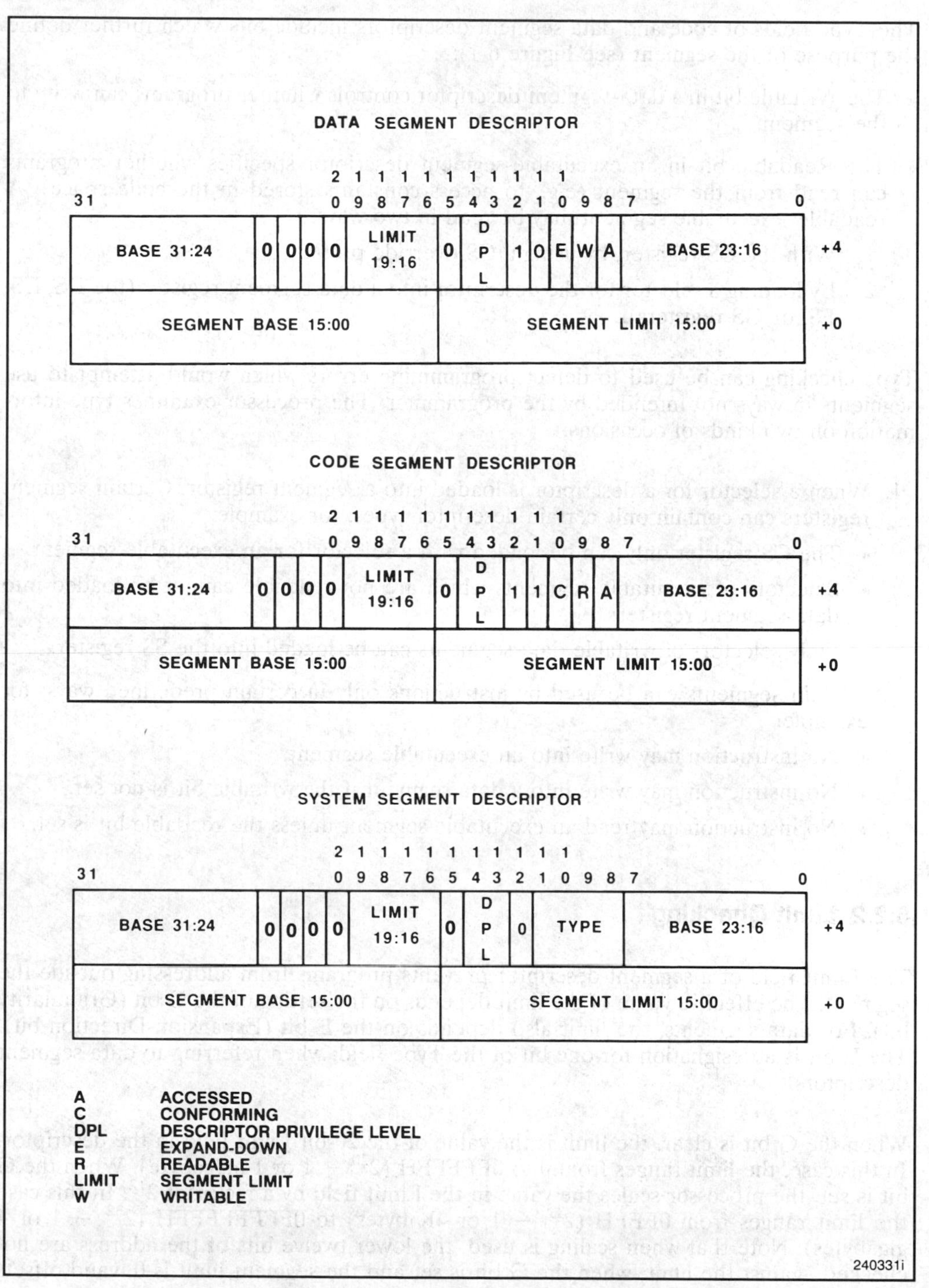

Figure 6-1. Descriptor Fields Used for Protection

The Type fields of code and data segment descriptors include bits which further define the purpose of the segment (see Figure 6-1):

- The Writable bit in a data-segment descriptor controls whether programs can write to the segment.
- The Readable bit in an executable-segment descriptor specifies whether programs can read from the segment (e.g., to access constants stored in the code space). A readable, executable segment may be read in two ways:
  1. With the CS register, by using a CS override prefix.
  2. By loading a selector for the descriptor into a data-segment register (the DS, ES, FS, or GS registers).

Type checking can be used to detect programming errors which would attempt to use segments in ways not intended by the programmer. The processor examines type information on two kinds of occasions:

1. When a selector for a descriptor is loaded into a segment register. Certain segment registers can contain only certain descriptor types; for example:
   - The CS register only can be loaded with a selector for an executable segment.
   - Selectors of executable segments which are not readable cannot be loaded into data-segment registers.
   - Only selectors of writable data segments can be loaded into the SS register.
2. Certain segments can be used by instructions only in certain predefined ways; for example:
   - No instruction may write into an executable segment.
   - No instruction may write into a data segment if the writable bit is not set.
   - No instruction may read an executable segment unless the readable bit is set.

6.2.2 Limit Checking

The Limit field of a segment descriptor prevents programs from addressing outside the segment. The effective value of the limit depends on the setting of the G bit (Granularity bit). For data segments, the limit also depends on the E bit (Expansion-Direction bit). The E bit is a designation for one bit of the Type field, when referring to data segment descriptors.

When the G bit is clear, the limit is the value of the 20-bit Limit field in the descriptor. In this case, the limit ranges from 0 to 0FFFFFH ($2^{20} - 1$ or 1 megabyte). When the G bit is set, the processor scales the value in the Limit field by a factor of 2^{12}. In this case the limit ranges from 0FFFH ($2^{12} - 1$ or 4K bytes) to 0FFFFFFFFH ($2^{32} - 1$ or 4 gigabytes). Note that when scaling is used, the lower twelve bits of the address are not checked against the limit; when the G bit is set and the segment limit is 0, valid offsets within the segment are 0 through 4095.

For all types of segments except expand-down data segments (stack segments), the value of the limit is one less than the size, in bytes, of the segment. The processor causes a general-protection exception in any of these cases:

- Attempt to access a memory byte at an address > limit
- Attempt to access a memory word at an address > (limit − 1)
- Attempt to access a memory doubleword at an address > (limit − 3)

For expand-down data segments, the limit has the same function but is interpreted differently. In these cases the range of valid offsets is from (limit + 1) to $2^{32} - 1$. An expand-down segment has maximum size when the segment limit is 0.

Limit checking catches programming errors such as runaway subscripts and invalid pointer calculations. These errors are detected when they occur, so identification of the cause is easier. Without limit checking, these errors could overwrite critical memory in another module, and the existence of these errors would not be discovered until the damaged module crashed, an event which may occur long after the actual error. Protection can block these errors and report their source.

In addition to limit checking on segments, there is limit checking on the descriptor tables. The GDTR and LDTR registers contain a 16-bit limit value. It is used by the processor to prevent programs from selecting a segment descriptor outside the descriptor table. The limit of a descriptor table identifies the last valid byte of the table. Because each descriptor is eight bytes long, a table which contains up to N descriptors should have a limit of 8N − 1.

A descriptor may be given a zero value. This refers to the first descriptor in the GDT, which is not used. Although this descriptor may be loaded into a segment register, any attempt to reference memory using this descriptor will generate a general-protection exception.

6.2.3 Privilege Levels

The protection mechanism recognizes four privilege levels, numbered from 0 to 3. The greater numbers mean lesser privileges. If all other protection checks are satisfied, a general-protection exception is generated if a program attempts to access a segment using a less privileged level (greater privilege number) than that applied to the segment.

Although no control register or mode bit is provided for turning off the protection mechanism, the same effect can be achieved by assigning all privilege levels the value of 0. (The PE bit in the CR0 register is not an enabling bit for the protection mechanism alone; it is used to enable "protected mode," the mode of program execution in which the full 32-bit architecture is available. When protected mode is disabled, the processor operates in "real-address mode," where it appears as a fast, enhanced 8086 processor.)

Privilege levels can be used to improve the reliability of operating systems. By giving the operating system the highest privilege level, it is protected from damage by bugs in other programs. If a program crashes, the operating system has a chance to generate a diagnostic message and attempt recovery procedures.

Another level of privilege can be established for other parts of the system software, such as the programs which handle peripheral devices, called *device drivers*. If a device driver crashes, the operating system should be able to report a diagnostic message, so it makes sense to protect the operating system against bugs in device drivers. A device driver, however, may service an important peripheral such as a disk drive. If the application program crashed, the device driver should not corrupt the directory structure of the disk, so it makes sense to protect device drivers against bugs in applications. Device drivers should be given an intermediate privilege level between the operating system and the application programs. Application programs are given the lowest privilege level.

Figure 6-2 shows how these levels of privilege can be interpreted as rings of protection. The center is for the segments containing the most critical software, usually the kernel of an operating system. Outer rings are for less critical software.

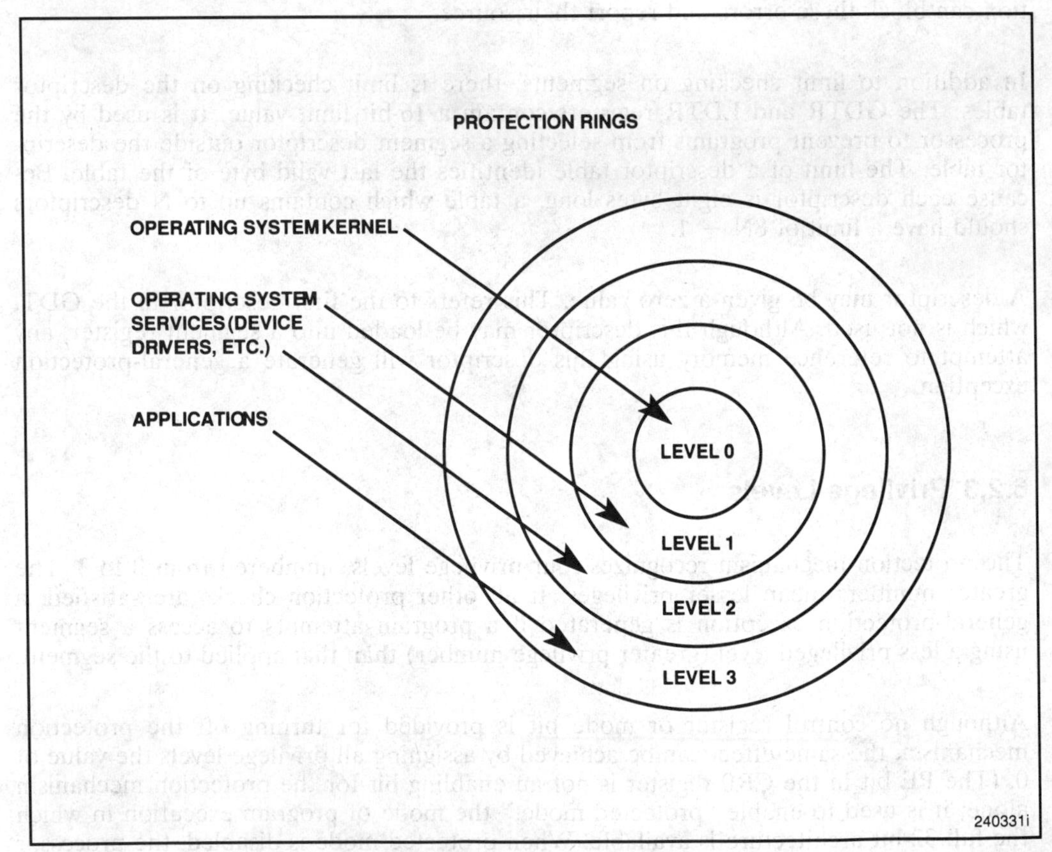

Figure 6-2. Protection Flags

The following data structures contain privilege levels:

- The lowest two bits of the CS segment register hold the *current privilege level (CPL)*. This is the privilege level of the program being run. The lowest two bits of the SS register also hold a copy of the CPL. Normally, the CPL is equal to the privilege level of the code segment from which instructions are being fetched. The CPL changes when control is transferred to a code segment with a different privilege level.
- Segment descriptors contain a field called the *descriptor privilege level (DPL)*. The DPL is the privilege level applied to a segment.
- Segment selectors contain a field called the *requested privilege level (RPL)*. The RPL is intended to represent the privilege level of the procedure which created the selector. If the RPL is a less privileged level than the CPL, it overrides the CPL. When a more privileged program receives a segment selector from a less privileged program, the RPL causes the memory access take place at the less privileged level.

Privilege levels are checked when the selector of a descriptor is loaded into a segment register. The checks used for data access differ from those used for transfers of execution among executable segments; therefore, the two types of access are considered separately in the following sections.

6.3 RESTRICTING ACCESS TO DATA

To address operands in memory, a segment selector for a data segment must be loaded into a data-segment register (the DS, ES, FS, GS, or SS registers). The processor checks the segment's privilege levels. The check is performed when the segment selector is loaded. As Figure 6-3 shows, three different privilege levels enter into this type of privilege check.

The three privilege levels which are checked are:

1. The CPL (current privilege level) of the program. This is held in the two least-significant bit positions of the CS register.
2. The DPL (descriptor privilege level) of the segment descriptor of the segment containing the operand.
3. The RPL (requestor's privilege level) of the selector used to specify the segment containing the operand. This is held in the two lowest bit positions of the segment register used to access the operand (the SS, DS, ES, FS, or GS registers). If the operand is in the stack segment, the RPL is the same as the CPL.

Instructions may load a segment register only if the DPL of the segment is the same or a less privileged level (greater privilege number) than the less privileged of the CPL and the selector's RPL.

The addressable domain of a task varies as its CPL changes. When the CPL is 0, data segments at all privilege levels are accessible; when the CPL is 1, only data segments at privilege levels 1 through 3 are accessible; when the CPL is 3, only data segments at privilege level 3 are accessible.

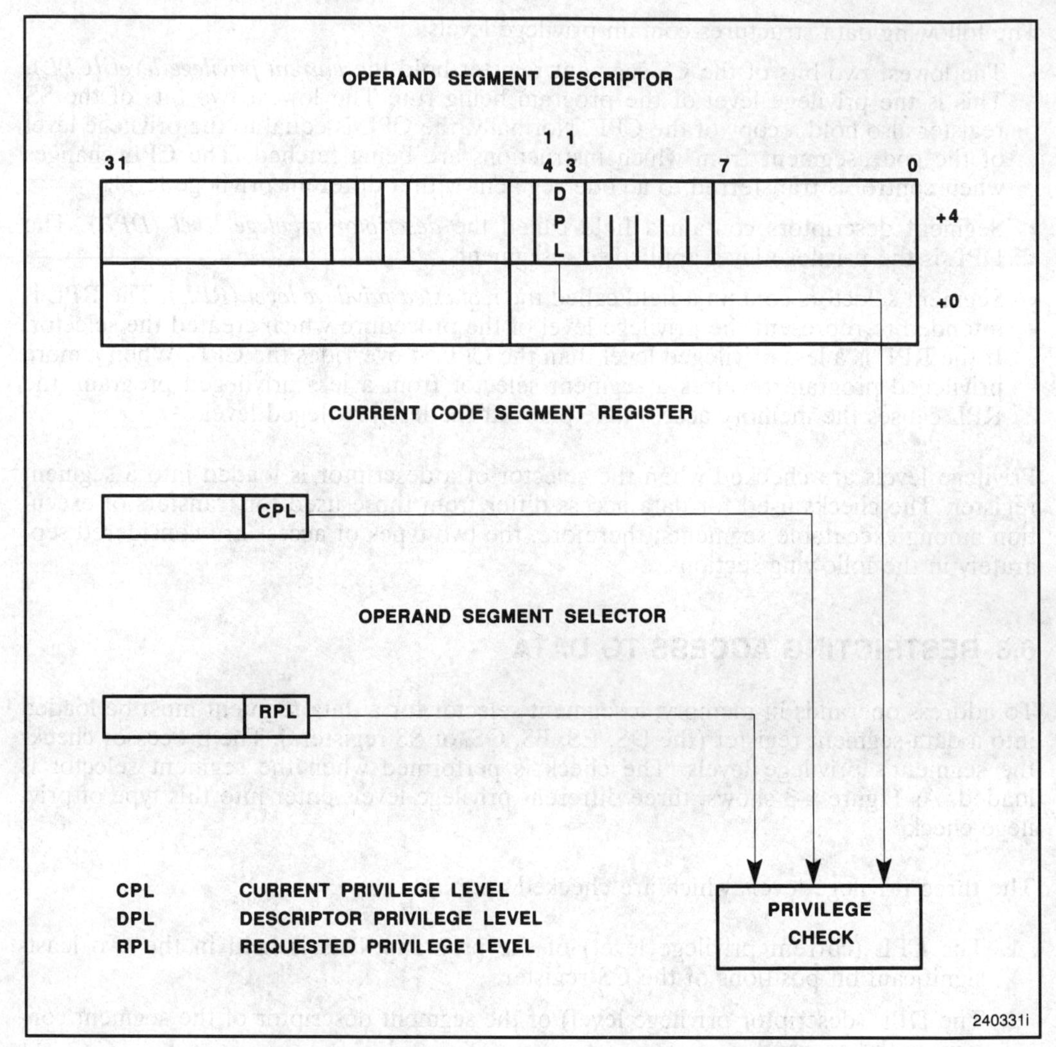

Figure 6-3. Privilege Check for Data Access

6.3.1 Accessing Data in Code Segments

It may be desirable to store data in a code segment, for example, when both code and data are provided in ROM. Code segments may legitimately hold constants; it is not possible to write to a segment defined as a code segment, unless a data segment is mapped to the same address space. The following methods of accessing data in code segments are possible:

1. Load a data-segment register with a segment selector for a nonconforming, readable, executable segment.

2. Load a data-segment register with a segment selector for a conforming, readable, executable segment.
3. Use a code-segment override prefix to read a readable, executable segment whose selector already is loaded in the CS register.

The same rules for access to data segments apply to case 1. Case 2 is always valid because the privilege level of a code segment with a set Conforming bit is effectively the same as the CPL, regardless of its DPL. Case 3 is always valid because the DPL of the code segment selected by the CS register is the CPL.

6.4 RESTRICTING CONTROL TRANSFERS

With the 386 DX microprocessor, control transfers are provided by the JMP, CALL, RET, INT, and IRET instructions, as well as by the exception and interrupt mechanisms. Exceptions and interrupts are special cases discussed in Chapter 9. This chapter discusses only the JMP, CALL, and RET instructions.

The "near" forms of the JMP, CALL, and RET instructions transfer program control within the current code segment, and therefore are subject only to limit checking. The processor checks that the destination of the JMP, CALL, or RET instruction does not exceed the limit of the current code segment. This limit is cached in the CS register, so protection checks for near transfers require no performance penalty.

The operands of the "far" forms of the JMP and CALL instruction refer to other segments, so the processor performs privilege checking. There are two ways a JMP or CALL instruction can refer to another segment:

1. The operand selects the descriptor of another executable segment.
2. The operand selects a call gate descriptor. This gated form of transfer is discussed in Chapter 7.

As Figure 6-4 shows, two different privilege levels enter into a privilege check for a control transfer which does not use a call gate:

1. The CPL (current privilege level).
2. The DPL of the descriptor of the destination code segment.

Normally the CPL is equal to the DPL of the segment which the processor is currently executing. The CPL may, however, be greater (less privileged) than the DPL if the current code segment is a *conforming segment* (as indicated by the Type field of its segment descriptor). A conforming segment runs at the privilege level of the calling procedure. The processor keeps a record of the CPL cached in the CS register; this value can be different from the DPL in the segment descriptor of the current code segment.

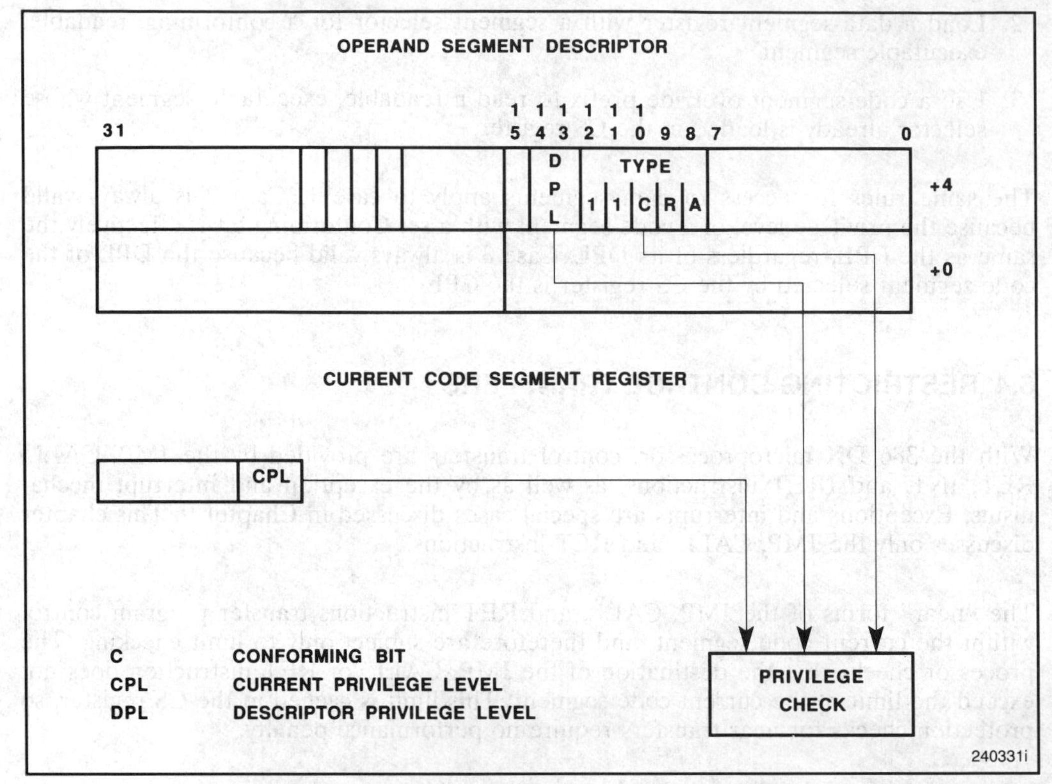

Figure 6-4. Privilege Check for Control Transfer without Gate

The processor only permits a JMP or CALL instruction directly into another segment if one of the following privilege rules is satisfied:

- The DPL of the segment is equal to the current CPL.
- The segment is a conforming code segment, and its DPL is less (more privileged) than the current CPL.

Conforming segments are used for programs, such as math libraries and some kinds of exception handlers, which support applications but do not require access to protected system facilities. When control is transferred to a conforming segment, the CPL does not change, even if the selector used to address the segment has a different RPL. This is the only condition in which the CPL may be different from the DPL of the current code segment.

Most code segments are not conforming. For these segments, control can be transferred without a gate only to other code segments at the same level of privilege. It is sometimes necessary, however, to transfer control to higher privilege levels. This is accomplished with the CALL instruction using call-gate descriptors, which is explained in Chapter 7. The JMP instruction may never transfer control to a nonconforming segment whose DPL does not equal the CPL.

6.5 GATE DESCRIPTORS

To provide protection for control transfers among executable segments at different privilege levels, the 386 DX microprocessor uses *gate descriptors*. There are four kinds of gate descriptors:

- Call gates
- Trap gates
- Interrupt gates
- Task gates

Task gates are used for task switching and are discussed in Chapter 7. Chapter 9 explains how trap gates and interrupt gates are used by exceptions and interrupts. This chapter is concerned only with call gates. Call gates are a form of protected control transfer. They are used for control transfers between different privilege levels. They only need to be used in systems in which more than one privilege level is used. Figure 6-5 illustrates the format of a call gate.

A call gate has two main functions:

1. To define an entry point of a procedure.
2. To specify the privilege level required to enter a procedure.

Call gate descriptors are used by CALL and JUMP instructions in the same manner as code segment descriptors. When the hardware recognizes that the segment selector for the destination refers to a gate descriptor, the operation of the instruction is determined by the contents of the call gate. A call gate descriptor may reside in the GDT or in an LDT, but not in the interrupt descriptor table (IDT).

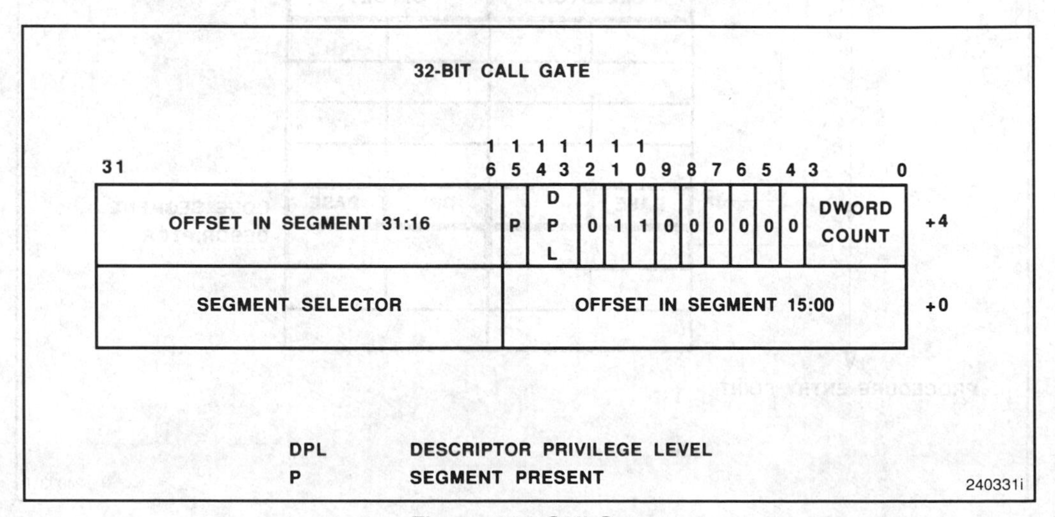

Figure 6-5. Call Gate

The selector and offset fields of a gate form a pointer to the entry point of a procedure. A call gate guarantees that all control transfers to other segments go to a valid entry point, rather than to the middle of a procedure (or worse, to the middle of an instruction). The operand of the control transfer instruction is not the segment selector and offset within the segment to the procedure's entry point. Instead, the segment selector points to a gate descriptor, and the offset is not used. Figure 6-6 shows this form of addressing.

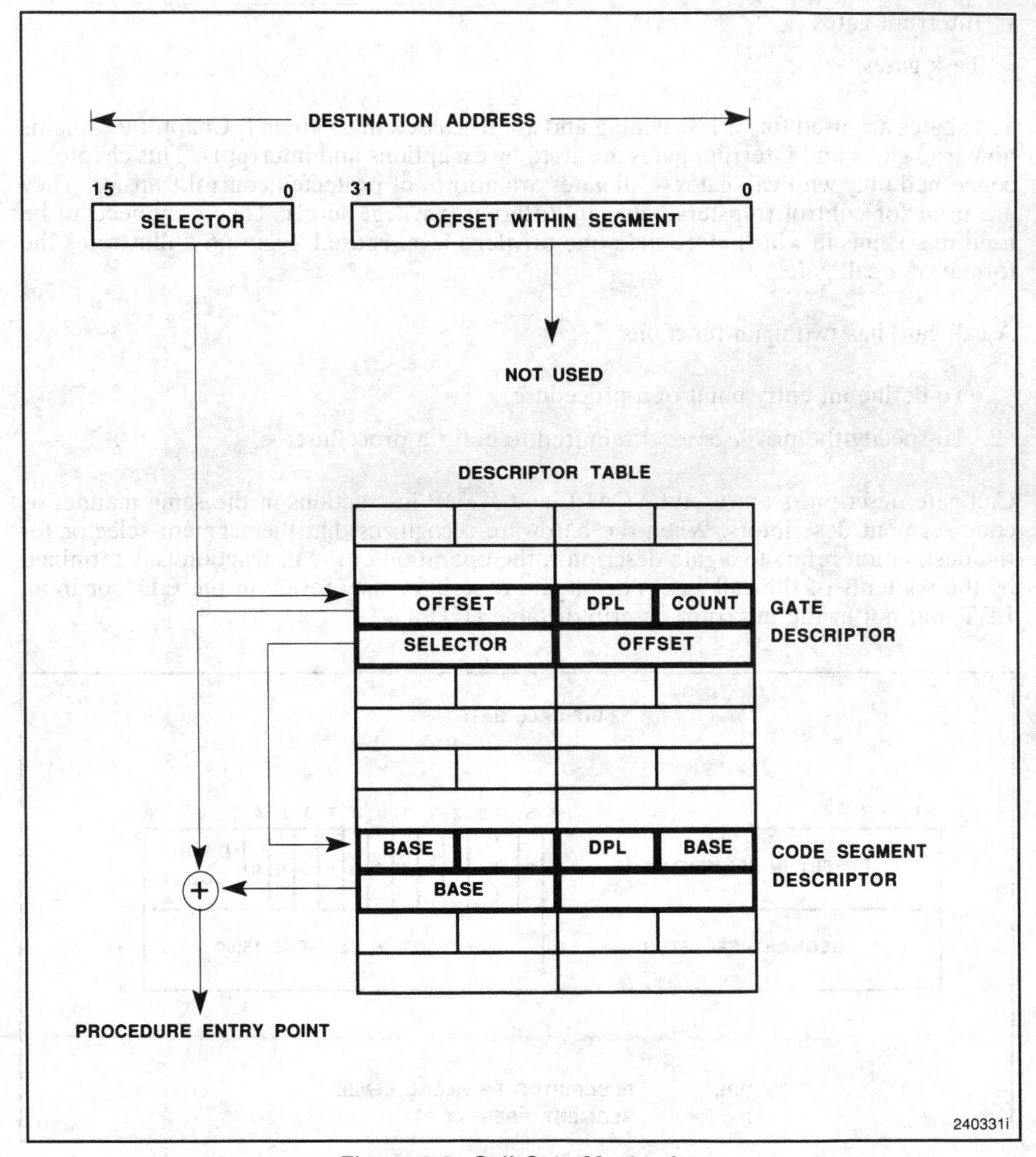

Figure 6-6. Call Gate Mechanism

As shown in Figure 6-7, four different privilege levels are used to check the validity of a control transfer through a call gate.

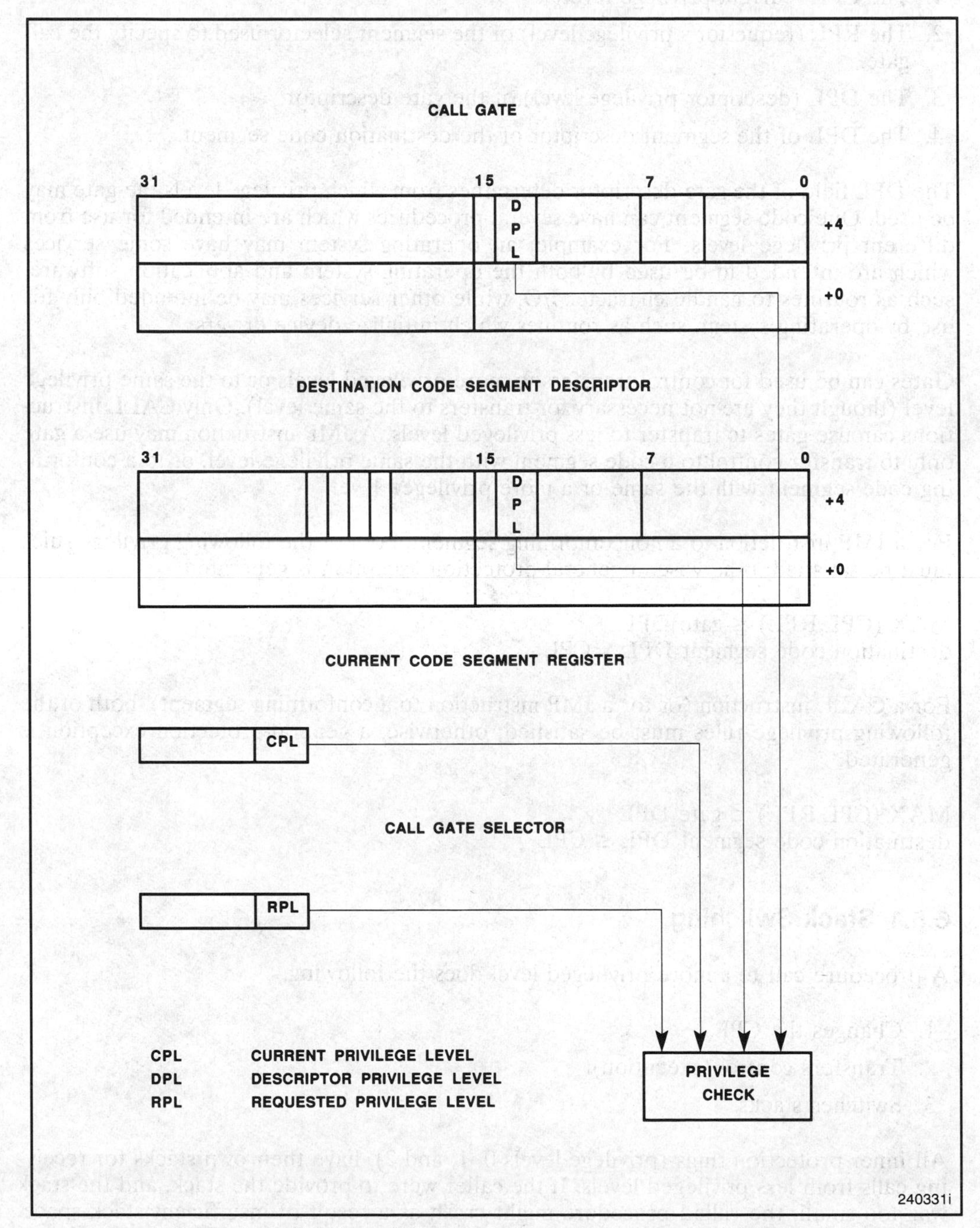

Figure 6-7. Privilege Check for Control Transfer with Call Gate

The privilege levels checked during a transfer of execution through a call gate are:

1. The CPL (current privilege level).
2. The RPL (requestor's privilege level) of the segment selector used to specify the call gate.
3. The DPL (descriptor privilege level) of the gate descriptor.
4. The DPL of the segment descriptor of the destination code segment.

The DPL field of the gate descriptor determines from which privilege levels the gate may be used. One code segment can have several procedures which are intended for use from different privilege levels. For example, an operating system may have some services which are intended to be used by both the operating system and application software, such as routines to handle character I/O, while other services may be intended only for use by operating system, such as routines which initialize device drivers.

Gates can be used for control transfers to more privileged levels or to the same privilege level (though they are not necessary for transfers to the same level). Only CALL instructions can use gates to transfer to less privileged levels. A JMP instruction may use a gate only to transfer control to a code segment with the same privilege level, or to a conforming code segment with the same or a more privileged level.

For a JMP instruction to a nonconforming segment, both of the following privilege rules must be satisfied; otherwise, a general-protection exception is generated.

MAX (CPL,RPL) ≤ gate DPL
destination code segment DPL = CPL

For a CALL instruction (or for a JMP instruction to a conforming segment), both of the following privilege rules must be satisfied; otherwise, a general-protection exception is generated.

MAX (CPL,RPL) ≤ gate DPL
destination code segment DPL ≤ CPL

6.5.1 Stack Switching

A procedure call to a more privileged level does the following:

1. Changes the CPL.
2. Transfers control (execution).
3. Switches stacks.

All inner protection rings (privilege levels 0, 1, and 2), have their own stacks for receiving calls from less privileged levels. If the caller were to provide the stack, and the stack was too small, the called procedure might crash as a result of insufficient stack space. Instead, less privileged programs are prevented from crashing more privileged programs by creating a new stack when a call is made to a more privileged level. The new stack is created, parameters are copied from the old stack, the contents of registers are saved, and execution proceeds normally. When the procedure returns, the contents of the saved registers restore the original stack. A complete description of the task switching mechanism is provided in Chapter 7.

The processor finds the space to create new stacks using the task state segment (TSS), as shown in Figure 6-8. Each task has its own TSS. The TSS contains initial stack pointers for the inner protection rings. The operating system is responsible for creating each TSS and initializing its stack pointers. An initial stack pointer consists of a segment selector and an initial value for the ESP register (an initial offset into the segment). The initial stack pointers are strictly read-only values. The processor does not change them while the task runs. These stack pointers are used only to create new stacks when calls are made to more privileged levels. These stacks disappear when the called procedure returns. The next time the procedure is called, a new stack is created using the initial stack pointer.

When a call gate is used to change privilege levels, a new stack is created by loading an address from the TSS. The processor uses the DPL of the destination code segment (the new CPL) to select the initial stack pointer for privilege level 0, 1, or 2.

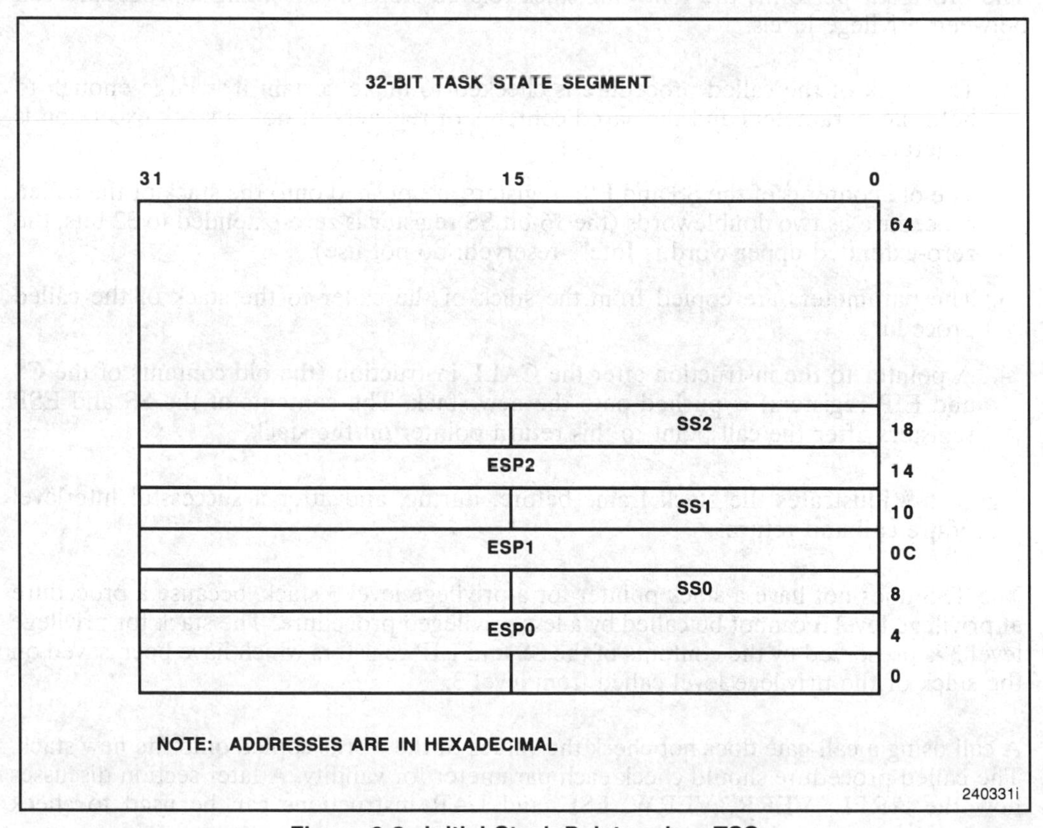

Figure 6-8. Initial Stack Pointers in a TSS

The DPL of the new stack segment must equal the new CPL; if not, a stack-fault exception is generated. It is the responsibility of the operating system to create stacks and stack-segment descriptors for all privilege levels which are used. The stacks must be read/write as specified in the Type field of their segment descriptors. They must contain enough space, as specified in the Limit field, to hold the contents of the SS and ESP registers, the return address, and the parameters and temporary variables required by the called procedure.

As with calls within a privilege level, parameters for the procedure are placed on the stack. The parameters are copied to the new stack. The parameters can be accessed within the called procedure using the same relative addresses which would have been used if no stack switching had occurred. The count field of a call gate tells the processor how many doublewords (up to 31) to copy from the caller's stack to the stack of the called procedure. If the count is 0, no parameters are copied.

If more than 31 doublewords of data need to be passed to the called procedure, one of the parameters can be a pointer to a data structure, or the saved contents of the SS and ESP registers may be used to access parameters in the old stack space.

The processor performs the following stack-related steps in executing a procedure call between privilege levels.

1. The stack of the called procedure is checked to make certain it is large enough to hold the parameters and the saved contents of registers; if not, a stack exception is generated.
2. The old contents of the SS and ESP registers are pushed onto the stack of the called procedure as two doublewords (the 16-bit SS register is zero-extended to 32 bits; the zero-extended upper word is Intel® reserved; do not use).
3. The parameters are copied from the stack of the caller to the stack of the called procedure.
4. A pointer to the instruction after the CALL instruction (the old contents of the CS and EIP registers) is pushed onto the new stack. The contents of the SS and ESP registers after the call point to this return pointer on the stack.

Figure 6-9 illustrates the stack frame before, during, and after a successful interlevel procedure call and return.

The TSS does not have a stack pointer for a privilege level 3 stack, because a procedure at privilege level 3 cannot be called by a less privileged procedure. The stack for privilege level 3 is preserved by the contents of the SS and EIP registers which have been saved on the stack of the privilege level called from level 3.

A call using a call gate does not check the values of the words copied onto the new stack. The called procedure should check each parameter for validity. A later section discusses how the ARPL, VERR, VERW, LSL, and LAR instructions can be used to check pointer values.

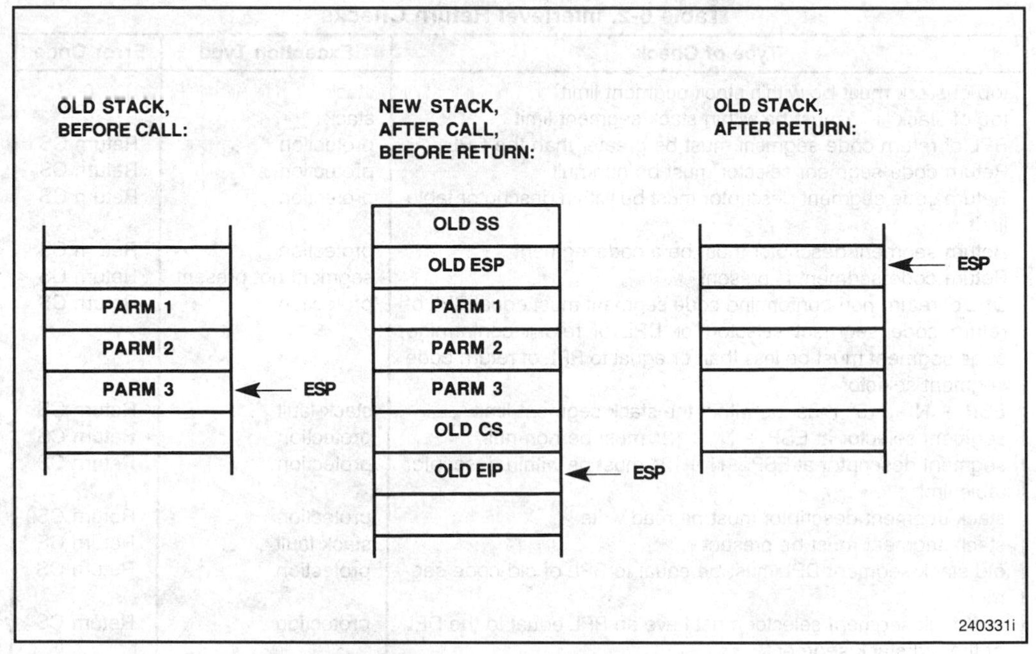

Figure 6-9. Stack Frame during Interlevel Call

6.5.2 Returning from a Procedure

The "near" forms of the RET instruction only transfer control within the current code segment, therefore are subject only to limit checking. The offset to the instruction following the CALL instruction is popped from the stack into the EIP register. The processor checks that this offset does not exceed the limit of the current code segment.

The "far" form of the RET instruction pops the return address which was pushed onto the stack by an earlier far CALL instruction. Under normal conditions, the return pointer is valid, because it was generated by a CALL or INT instruction. Nevertheless, the processor performs privilege checking because of the possibility that the current procedure altered the pointer or failed to maintain the stack properly. The RPL of the code-segment selector popped off the stack by the return instruction should have the privilege level of the calling procedure.

A return to another segment can change privilege levels, but only toward less privileged levels. When a RET instruction encounters a saved CS value whose RPL is numerically greater than the CPL (less privileged level), a return across privilege levels occurs. A return of this kind performs these steps:

1. The checks shown in Table 6-2 are made, and the CS, EIP, SS, and ESP registers are loaded with their former values, which were saved on the stack.

Table 6-2. Interlevel Return Checks

Type of Check	Exception Type	Error Code
top-of-stack must be within stack segment limit	stack	0
top-of-stack + 7 must be within stack segment limit	stack	0
RPL of return code segment must be greater than the CPL	protection	Return CS
Return code segment selector must be non-null	protection	Return CS
Return code segment descriptor must be within descriptor table limit	protection	Return CS
Return segment descriptor must be a codesegment	protection	Return CS
Return code segment is present	segment not present	Return CS
DPL of return non-conforming code segment must equal RPL of return code segment selector, or DPL of return conforming code segment must be less than or equal to RPL of return code segment selector	protection	Return CS
ESP + N + 15* must be within the stack segment limit	stack fault	Return CS
segment selector at ESP + N + 12* must be non-null	protection	Return CS
segment descriptor at ESP +N +12* must be within descriptor table limit	protection	Return CS
stack segment descriptor must be read/write	protection	Return CS
stack segment must be present	stack fault	Return CS
old stack segment DPL must be equal to RPL of old code segment	protection	Return CS
old stack segment selector must have an RPL equal to the DPL of the old stack segment	protection	Return CS

*N is the value of the immediate operand supplied with the RET instruction.

2. The old contents of the SS and ESP registers (from the top of the current stack) are adjusted by the number of bytes indicated in the RET instruction. The resulting ESP value is not checked against the limit of the stack segment. If the ESP value is beyond the limit, that fact is not recognized until the next stack operation. (The contents of the SS and ESP registers for the returning procedure are not preserved; normally, their values are the same as those contained in the TSS.)

3. The contents of the DS, ES, FS, and GS segment registers are checked. If any of these registers refer to segments whose DPL is less than the new CPL (excluding conforming code segments), the segment register is loaded with the null selector (Index = 0, TI = 0). The RET instruction itself does not signal exceptions in these cases; however, any subsequent memory reference using a segment register containing the null selector will cause a general-protection exception. This prevents less privileged code from accessing more privileged segments using selectors left in the segment registers by a more privileged procedure.

6.5.3 Mixing 16 and 32-Bit Stacks

When 80286 code is ported to the 386 DX microprocessor through system calls to level 0, there is 16-bit software at a user level (level 3) and 32-bit system software at the system level (level 0). To support the level transitions, there may be different mixes of stack frames (16 or 32 bit) at these two levels. In addition, such calls have to go through call gates which may either be 16-bit or 32-bit call gates. Proper ESP update during CALLs and RETurns is necessary. ESP updates in cases involving 16-bit and 32-bit mixes are as follows:

CALL From (Level 3)	Using	RET From (Level 0)	ESP most significant 16-bits After CALL	After RET
16-bit SS	16-bit Gate	16-bit SS	Unchanged	Unchanged
16-bit SS	16-bit Gate	32-bit SS	Correct	Unchanged
16-bit SS	32-bit Gate	16-bit SS	Unchanged	Unchanged
16-bit SS	32-bit Gate	32-bit SS	Correct	Unchanged
32-bit SS	16-bit Gate	16-bit SS	Unchanged	Not Reliable
32-bit SS	16-bit Gate	32-bit SS	Correct	Not Reliable
32-bit SS	32-bit Gate	16-bit SS	Unchanged	Correct
32-bit SS	32-bit Gate	32-bit SS	Correct	Correct

NOTES:

1. Level 3 code is always 16-bit and Level 0 code is always 32-bit.
2. The current TSS is used to obtain the higher privilege level SS and (E)SP values. If the destination stack (the level 0 stack in this case) is 32-bit, then the current TSS should also be 32-bit, so that the correct 32-bit ESP is read to form the address for the pushes on the new (level 0) stack. In this case, the 16-bit code at level 3 should have 32-bit TSS, when the stack frame at the called level is 32-bit.
3. If there is a call from a 32-bit SS using a 16-bit gate, then the upper 16-bits of ESP on RET are not reliable. This is because the *gate size* determines the length of the operands to be pushed on the return stack during the call. During RET, the same 16-bits of SP are read, but since the source stack is 32-bits the entire ESP is updated, not just ESP.

6.6 INSTRUCTIONS RESERVED FOR THE OPERATING SYSTEM

Instructions which can affect the protection mechanism or influence general system performance can only be executed by trusted procedures. The 386 DX microprocessor has two classes of such instructions:

1. Privileged instructions—those used for system control.
2. Sensitive instructions—those used for I/O and I/O-related activities.

6.6.1 Privileged Instructions

The instructions which affect protected facilities can be executed only when the CPL is 0 (most privileged). If one of these instructions is executed when the CPL is not 0, a general-protection exception is generated. These instructions include:

CLTS —Clear Task-Switched Flag
HLT —Halt Processor
LGDT —Load GDT Register
LIDT —Load IDT Register
LLDT —Load LDT Register
LMSW —Load Machine Status Word
LTR —Load Task Register

MOV to/from CR0 – Move to Control Register 0
MOV to/from DRn – Move to Debug Register n
MOV to/from TRn – Move to Test Register n

6.6.2 Sensitive Instructions

Instructions which deal with I/O need to be protected, but they also need to be used by procedures executing at privilege levels other than 0 (the most privileged level). The mechanisms for protection of I/O operations are covered in detail in Chapter 8.

6.7 INSTRUCTIONS FOR POINTER VALIDATION

Pointer validation is necessary for maintaining isolation between privilege levels. It consists of the following steps:

1. Check if the supplier of the pointer is allowed to access the segment.
2. Check if the segment type is compatible with its use.
3. Check if the pointer offset exceeds the segment limit.

Although the 386 DX microprocessor automatically performs checks 2 and 3 during instruction execution, software must assist in performing the first check. The ARPL instruction is provided for this purpose. Software also can use steps 2 and 3 to check for potential violations, rather than waiting for an exception to be generated. The LAR, LSL, VERR, and VERW instructions are provided for this purpose.

LAR (Load Access Rights) is used to verify that a pointer refers to a segment of a compatible privilege level and type. The LAR instruction has one operand – a segment selector for a descriptor whose access rights are to be checked. The segment descriptor must be readable at a privilege level which is numerically greater (less privileged) than the CPL and the selector's RPL. If the descriptor is readable, the LAR instruction gets the second doubleword of the descriptor, masks this value with 00FxFF00H, stores the result into the specified 32-bit destination register, and sets the ZF flag. (The x indicates that the corresponding four bits of the stored value are undefined.) Once loaded, the access rights can be tested. All valid descriptor types can be tested by the LAR instruction. If the RPL or CPL is greater than the DPL, or if the segment selector would exceed the limit for the descriptor table, no access rights are returned, and the ZF flag is cleared. Conforming code segments may be accessed from any privilege level.

LSL (Load Segment Limit) allows software to test the limit of a segment descriptor. If the descriptor referenced by the segment selector (in memory or a register) is readable at the CPL, the LSL instruction loads the specified 32-bit register with a 32-bit, byte granular limit calculated from the concatenated limit fields and the G bit of the descriptor. This only can be done for descriptors which describe segments (data, code, task state, and local descriptor tables); gate descriptors are inaccessible. (Table 6-3 lists in detail which types are valid and which are not.) Interpreting the limit is a function of the

Table 6-3. Valid Descriptor Types for LSL Instruction

Type Code	Descriptor Type	Valid?
0	Reserved	no
1	reserved	no
2	LDT	yes
3	reserved	no
4	reserved	no
5	Task Gate	no
6	reserved	no
7	reserved	no
8	reserved	no
9	Available 386™ DX TSS	yes
A	reserved	no
B	Busy 386 DX TSS	yes
C	386 DX Call Gate	no
D	reserved	no
E	386 DX Interrupt Gate	no
F	386 DX Trap Gate	no

segment type. For example, downward-expandable data segments (stack segments) treat the limit differently than other kinds of segments. For both the LAR and LSL instructions, the ZF flag is set if the load was successful; otherwise, the ZF flag is cleared.

6.7.1 Descriptor Validation

The 386 DX microprocessor has two instructions, VERR and VERW, which determine whether a segment selector points to a segment which can be read or written using the CPL. Neither instruction causes a protection fault if the segment cannot be accessed.

VERR (Verify for Reading) verifies a segment for reading and sets the ZF flag if that segment is readable using the CPL. The VERR instruction checks the following:

- The segment selector points to a segment descriptor within the bounds of the GDT or an LDT.
- The segment selector indexes to a code or data segment descriptor.
- The segment is readable and has a compatible privilege level.

The privilege check for data segments and nonconforming code segments verifies that the DPL must be a less privileged level than either the CPL or the selector's RPL. Conforming segments are not checked for privilege level.

VERW (Verify for Writing) provides the same capability as the VERR instruction for verifying writability. Like the VERR instruction, the VERW instruction sets the ZF flag if the segment can be written. The instruction verifies the descriptor is within bounds, is a segment descriptor, is writable, and has a DPL which is a less privileged level than either the CPL or the selector's RPL. Code segments are never writable, whether conforming or not.

6.7.2 Pointer Integrity and RPL

The requested privilege level (RPL) can prevent accidental use of pointers which crash more privileged code from a less privileged level.

A common example is a file system procedure, FREAD (file_id, n_bytes, buffer_ptr). This hypothetical procedure reads data from a disk file into a buffer, overwriting whatever is already there. It services requests from programs operating at the application level, but it must run in a privileged mode in order to read from the system I/O buffer. If the application program passed this procedure a bad buffer pointer, one which pointed at critical code or data in a privileged address space, the procedure could cause damage which would crash the system.

Use of the RPL can avoid this problem. The RPL allows a privilege override to be assigned to a selector. This privilege override is intended to be the privilege level of the code segment which generated the segment selector. In the above example, the RPL would be the CPL of the application program which called the system level procedure. The 386 DX microprocessor automatically checks any segment selector loaded into a segment register to determine whether its RPL allows access.

To take advantage of the processor's checking of the RPL, the called procedure need only check that all segment selectors passed to it have an RPL for the same or a less privileged level as the original caller's CPL. This guarantees that the segment selectors are not more privileged than their source. If a selector is used to access a segment which the source would not be able to access directly, i.e., the RPL is less privileged than the segment's DPL, a general-protection exception is generated when the selector is loaded into a segment register.

ARPL (Adjust Requested Privilege Level) adjusts the RPL field of a segment selector to be the larger (less privileged) of its original value and the value of the RPL field for a segment selector stored in a general register. The RPL fields are the two least significant bits of the segment selector and the register. The latter normally is a copy of the caller's CS register on the stack. If the adjustment changes the selector's RPL, the ZF flag is set; otherwise, the ZF flag is cleared.

6.8 PAGE-LEVEL PROTECTION

Protection applies to both segments and pages. When the flat model for memory segmentation has been used, page-level protection prevents programs from interfering with each other.

Each memory reference is checked to verify that it satisfies the protection checks. All checks are made before the memory cycle is started; any violation prevents the cycle from starting and results in an exception. Because checks are performed in parallel with address translation, there is no performance penalty. There are two page-level protection checks:

1. Restriction of addressable domain
2. Type checking

A protection violation results in an exception. See Chapter 9 for an explanation of the exception mechanism. This chapter describes the protection violations which lead to exceptions.

6.8.1 Page-Table Entries Hold Protection Parameters

Figure 6-10 highlights the fields of a page table entry which control access to pages. The protection checks are applied for both first- and second-level page tables.

6.8.1.1 RESTRICTING ADDRESSABLE DOMAIN

Privilege is interpreted differently for pages and segments. With segments, there are four privilege levels, ranging from 0 (most privileged) to 3 (least privileged). With pages, there are two levels of privilege:

1. Supervisor level (U/S=0)—for the operating system, other system software (such as device drivers), and protected system data (such as page tables).
2. User level (U/S=1)—for application code and data.

The privilege levels used for segmentation are mapped into the privilege levels used for paging. If the CPL is 0, 1, or 2, the processor is running at supervisor level. If the CPL is 3, the processor is running at user level.

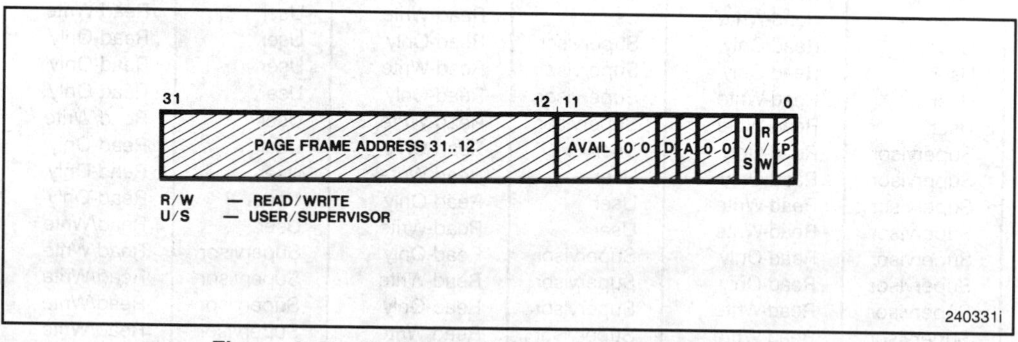

Figure 6-10. Protection Fields of a Page Table Entry

When the processor is running at supervisor level, all pages are accessible. When the processor is running at user level, only pages from the user level are accessible.

6.8.1.2 TYPE CHECKING

Only two types of pages are recognized by the protection mechanism:

1. Read-only access (R/W=0)

2. Read/write access (R/W=1)

When the processor is running at supervisor level, all pages are both readable and writable (write-protection is ignored). When the processor is running at user level, only pages which belong to user level and are marked for read/write access are writable. User-level pages which are read/write or read-only are readable. Pages from the supervisor level are neither readable nor writable from user level. A general-protection exception is generated on any attempt to violate the protection rules.

6.8.2 Combining Protection of Both Levels of Page Tables

For any one page, the protection attributes of its page directory entry (first-level page table) may differ from those of its second-level page table entry. The 386 DX microprocessor checks the protection for a page by examining the protection specified in both the page directory (first-level page table) and the second-level page table. Table 6-4 shows the protection provided by the possible combinations of protection attributes.

Table 6-4. Combined Page Directory and Page Table Protection

Page Directory Entry		Page Table Entry		Combined Effect	
Privilege	**Access Type**	**Privilege**	**Access Type**	**Privilege**	**Access Type**
User	Read-Only	User	Read-Only	User	Read-Only
User	Read-Only	User	Read-Write	User	Read-Only
User	Read-Write	User	Read-Only	User	Read-Only
User	Read-Write	User	Read-Write	User	Read/Write
User	Read-Only	Supervisor	Read-Only	User	Read-Only
User	Read-Only	Supervisor	Read-Write	User	Read-Only
User	Read-Write	Supervisor	Read-Only	User	Read-Only
User	Read-Write	Supervisor	Read-Write	User	Read/Write
Supervisor	Read-Only	User	Read-Only	User	Read-Only
Supervisor	Read-Only	User	Read-Write	User	Read-Only
Supervisor	Read-Write	User	Read-Only	User	Read-Only
Supervisor	Read-Write	User	Read-Write	User	Read/Write
Supervisor	Read-Only	Supervisor	Read-Only	Supervisor	Read/Write
Supervisor	Read-Only	Supervisor	Read-Write	Supervisor	Read/Write
Supervisor	Read-Write	Supervisor	Read-Only	Supervisor	Read/Write
Supervisor	Read-Write	Supervisor	Read-Write	Supervisor	Read/Write

6.8.3 Overrides to Page Protection

Certain accesses are checked as if they are privilege-level 0 accesses, for any value of CPL:

- Access to segment descriptors (LDT, GDT, TSS and IDT).
- Access to inner stack during a CALL instruction, or exceptions and interrupts, when a change of privilege level occurs.

6.9 COMBINING PAGE AND SEGMENT PROTECTION

When paging is enabled, the 386 DX microprocessor first evaluates segment protection, then evaluates page protection. If the processor detects a protection violation at either the segment level or the page level, the operation does not go through; an exception occurs instead. If an exception is generated by segmentation, no paging exception is generated for the operation.

For example, it is possible to define a large data segment which has some parts which are read-only and other parts which are read-write. In this case, the page directory (or page table) entries for the read-only parts would have the U/S and R/W bits specifying no write access for all the pages described by that directory entry (or for individual pages specified in the second-level page tables). This technique might be used, for example, to define a large data segment, part of which is read-only (for shared data or ROMmed constants). This defines a "flat" data space as one large segment, with "flat" pointers used to access this "flat" space, while protecting shared data, shared files mapped into the virtual space, and supervisor areas.

Multitasking 7

CHAPTER 7
MULTITASKING

The 386™ DX microprocessor provides hardware support for multitasking. A *task* is a program which is running, or waiting to run while another program is running. A task is invoked by an interrupt, exception, jump, or call. When one of these forms of transferring execution is used with a destination specified by an entry in one of the descriptor tables, this descriptor can be a type which causes a new task to begin execution after saving the state of the current task. There are two types of task-related descriptors which can occur in a descriptor table: task state segment descriptors and task gates. When execution is passed to either kind of descriptor, a *task switch* occurs.

A task switch is like a procedure call, but it saves more processor state information. A procedure call only saves the contents of the general registers, and it might save the contents of only one register (the EIP register). A procedure call pushes the contents of the saved registers on the stack, in order that a procedure may call itself. When a procedure calls itself, it is said to be *re-entrant*.

A task switch transfers execution to a completely new environment, the environment of a task. This requires saving the contents of nearly all the processor registers, such as the EFLAGS register. Unlike procedures, tasks are not re-entrant. A task switch does not push anything on the stack. The processor state information is saved in a data structure in memory, called a *task state segment*.

The registers and data structures which support multitasking are:

- Task state segment
- Task state segment descriptor
- Task register
- Task gate descriptor

With these structures, the 386 DX microprocessor can switch execution from one task to another, with the context of the original task saved to allow the task to be restarted. In addition to the simple task switch, the 386 DX microprocessor offers two other task-management features:

1. Interrupts and exceptions can cause task switches (if needed in the system design). The processor not only performs a task switch to handle the interrupt or exception, but it automatically switches back when the interrupt or exception returns. Interrupts may occur during interrupt tasks.
2. With each switch to another task, the 386 DX microprocessor also can switch to another LDT. This can be used to give each task a different logical-to-physical address mapping. This is an additional protection feature, because tasks can be isolated and prevented from interfering with one another. The PDBR register also is reloaded. This allows the paging mechanism to be used to enforce the isolation between tasks.

Use of the multitasking mechanism is optional. In some applications, it may not be the best way to manage program execution. Where extremely fast response to interrupts is needed, the time required to save the processor state may be too great. A possible compromise in these situations is to use the task-related data structures, but perform task switching in software. This allows a smaller processor state to be saved. This technique can be one of the optimizations used to enhance system performance after the basic functions of a system have been implemented.

7.1 TASK STATE SEGMENT

The processor state information needed to restore a task is saved in a type of segment, called a *task state segment* or TSS. Figure 7-1 shows the format of a TSS for a 386 DX CPU (compatibility with 80286 tasks is provided by a different kind of TSS; see Chapter 13). The fields of a TSS are divided into two main categories:

1. Dynamic fields the processor updates with each task switch. These fields store:
   - The general registers (EAX, ECX, EDX, EBX, ESP, EBP, ESI, and EDI).
   - The segment registers (ES, CS, SS, DS, FS, and GS).
   - The flags register (EFLAGS).
   - The instruction pointer (EIP).
   - The selector for the TSS of the previous task (updated only when a return is expected).
2. Static fields the processor reads, but does not change. These fields are set up when a task is created. These fields store:
   - The selector for the task's LDT.
   - The logical address of the stacks for privilege levels 0, 1, and 2.
   - The T-bit (debug trap bit) which, when set, causes the processor to raise a debug exception when a task switch occurs. (See Chapter 12 for more information on debugging.)
   - The base address for the I/O permission bit map. If present, this map is stored in the TSS at higher addresses. The base address points to the beginning of the map. (See Chapter 8 for more information about the I/O permission bit map.)

If paging is used, it is important to avoid placing a page boundary within the part of the TSS which is read by the processor during a task switch (the first 108 bytes). If a page boundary is placed within this part of the TSS, the pages on either side of the boundary must be present at the same time. It is an unrecoverable error to receive a page fault or general-protection exception after the processor has started to read the TSS.

7.2 TSS DESCRIPTOR

The task state segment, like all other segments, is defined by a descriptor. Figure 7-2 shows the format of a TSS descriptor.

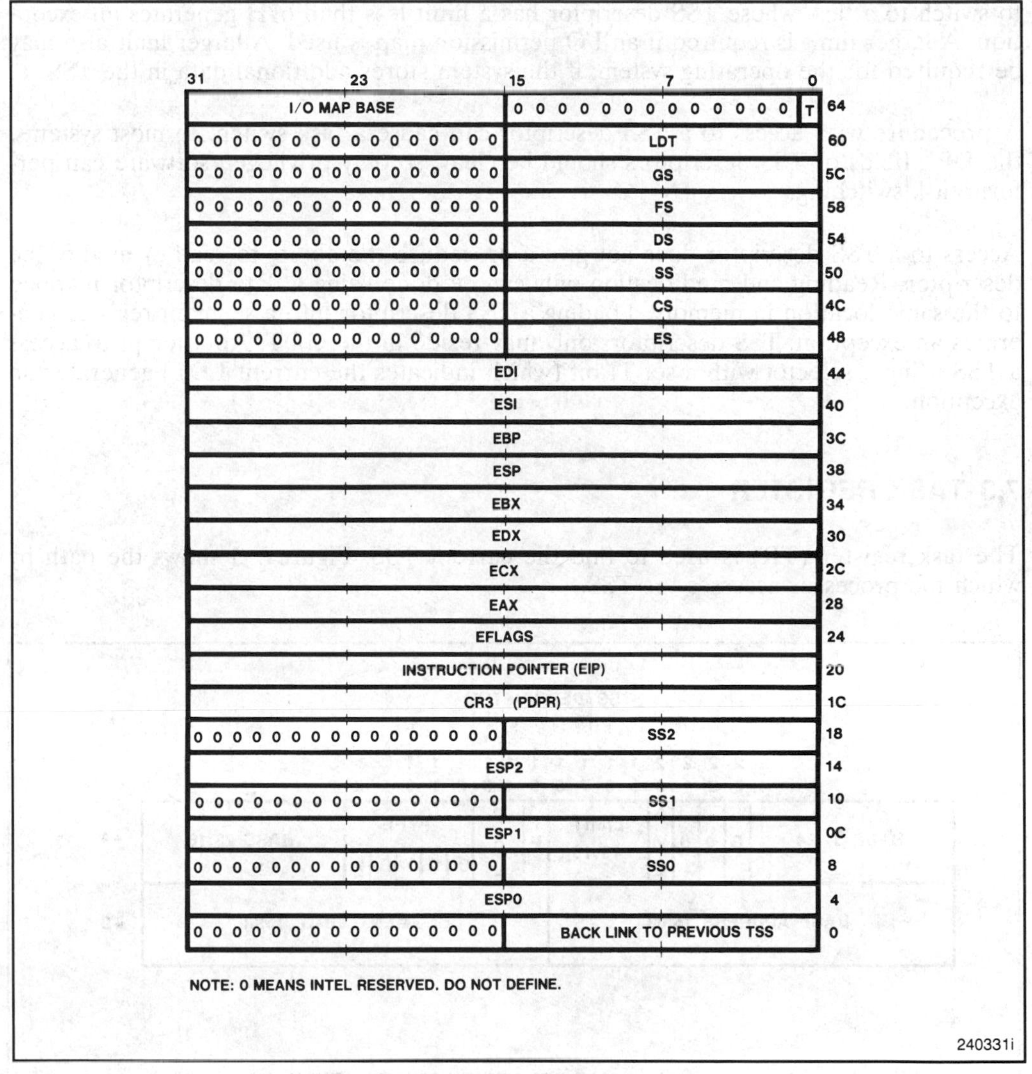

Figure 7-1. Task State Segment

The Busy bit in the Type field indicates whether the task is busy. A busy task is currently running or waiting to run. A Type field with a value of 9 indicates an inactive task; a value of 11 (decimal) indicates a busy task. Tasks are not re-entrant. The 386 DX microprocessor uses the Busy bit to detect an attempt to call a task whose execution has been interrupted.

The Base, Limit, and DPL fields and the Granularity bit and Present bit have functions similar to their use in data-segment descriptors. The Limit field must have a value equal to or greater than 67H, one byte less than the minimum size of a task state. An attempt to switch to a task whose TSS descriptor has a limit less than 67H generates an exception. A larger limit is required if an I/O permission map is used. A larger limit also may be required for the operating system, if the system stores additional data in the TSS.

A procedure with access to a TSS descriptor can cause a task switch. In most systems, the DPL fields of TSS descriptors should be clear, so only privileged software can perform task switching.

Access to a TSS descriptor does not give a procedure the ability to read or modify the descriptor. Reading and modification only can be done using a data descriptor mapped to the same location in memory. Loading a TSS descriptor into a segment register generates an exception. TSS descriptors only may reside in the GDT. An attempt to access a TSS using a selector with a set TI bit (which indicates the current LDT) generates an exception.

7.3 TASK REGISTER

The task register (TR) is used to find the current TSS. Figure 7-3 shows the path by which the processor accesses the TSS.

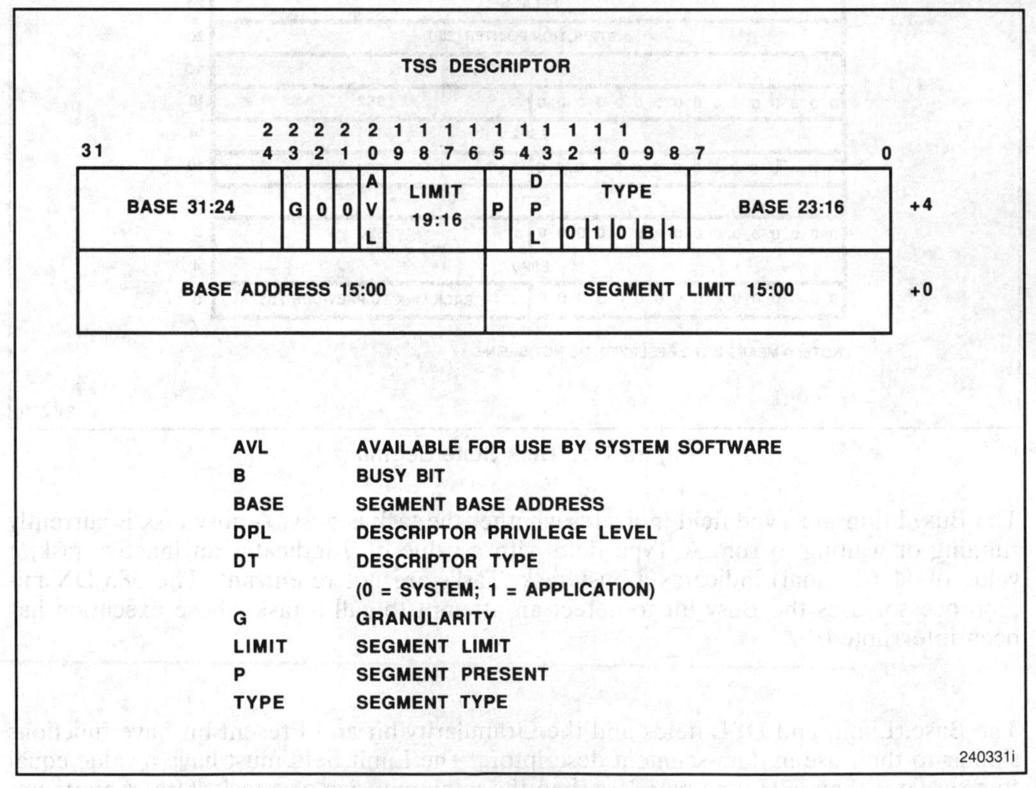

Figure 7-2. TSS Descriptor

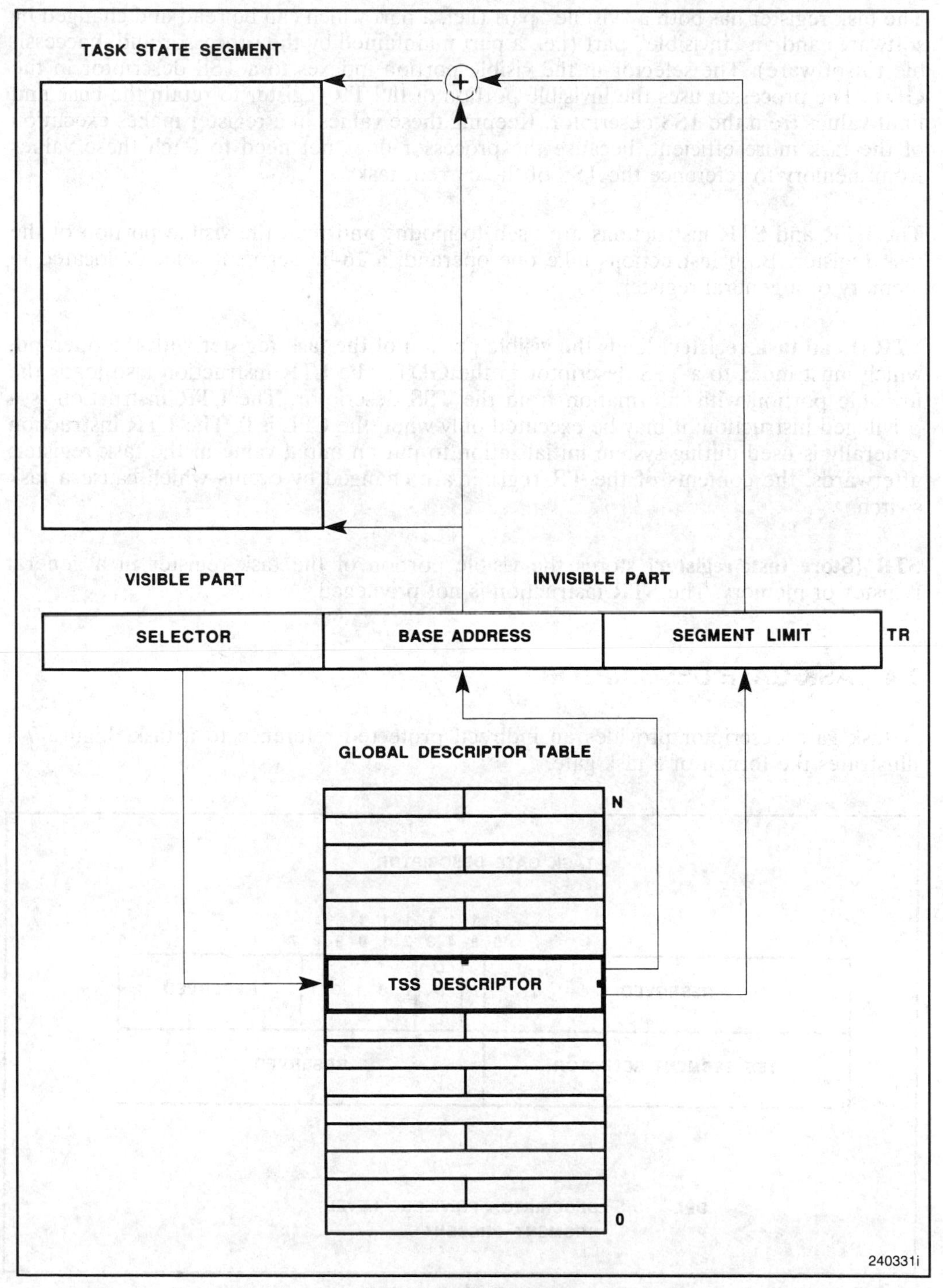

Figure 7-3. TR Register

The task register has both a "visible" part (i.e., a part which can be read and changed by software) and an "invisible" part (i.e., a part maintained by the processor and inaccessible to software). The selector in the visible portion indexes to a TSS descriptor in the GDT. The processor uses the invisible portion of the TR register to retain the base and limit values from the TSS descriptor. Keeping these values in a register makes execution of the task more efficient, because the processor does not need to fetch these values from memory to reference the TSS of the current task.

The LTR and STR instructions are used to modify and read the visible portion of the task register. Both instructions take one operand, a 16-bit segment selector located in memory or a general register.

LTR (Load task register) loads the visible portion of the task register with the operand, which must index to a TSS descriptor in the GDT. The LTR instruction also loads the invisible portion with information from the TSS descriptor. The LTR instruction is a privileged instruction; it may be executed only when the CPL is 0. The LTR instruction generally is used during system initialization to put an initial value in the task register; afterwards, the contents of the TR register are changed by events which cause a task switch.

STR (Store task register) stores the visible portion of the task register in a general register or memory. The STR instruction is not privileged.

7.4 TASK GATE DESCRIPTOR

A task gate descriptor provides an indirect, protected reference to a task. Figure 7-4 illustrates the format of a task gate.

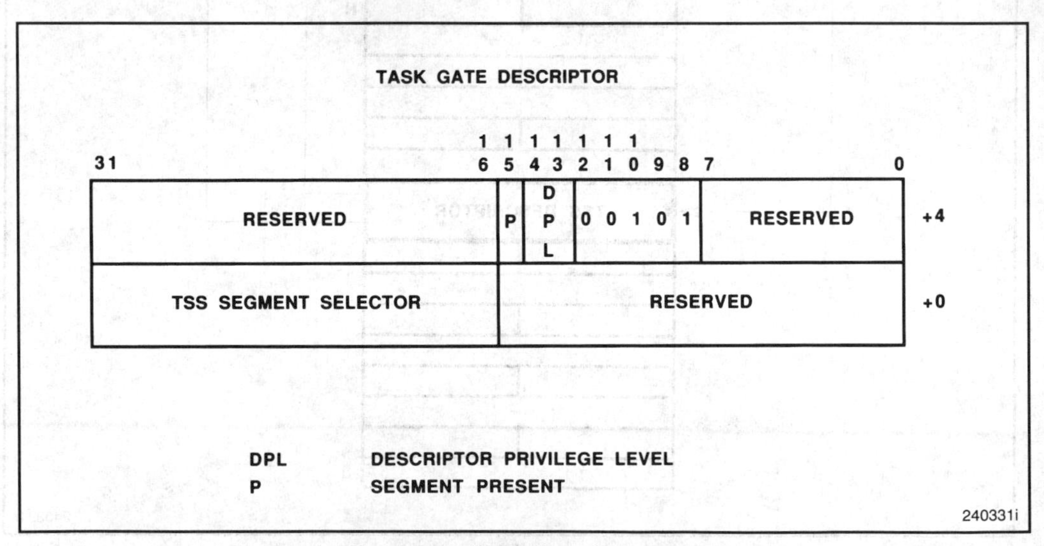

Figure 7-4. Task Gate Descriptor

The Selector field of a task gate indexes to a TSS descriptor. The RPL in this selector is not used.

The DPL of a task gate controls access to the descriptor for a task switch. A procedure may not select a task gate descriptor unless the selector's RPL and the CPL of the procedure are numerically less than or equal to the DPL of the descriptor. This prevents less privileged procedures from causing a task switch. (Note that when a task gate is used, the DPL of the destination TSS descriptor is not used.)

A procedure with access to a task gate can cause a task switch, as can a procedure with access to a TSS descriptor. Both task gates and TSS descriptors are provided to satisfy three needs:

1. The need for a task to have only one Busy bit. Because the Busy bit is stored in the TSS descriptor, each task should have only one such descriptor. There may, however, be several task gates which select a single TSS descriptor.
2. The need to provide selective access to tasks. Task gates fill this need, because they can reside in an LDT and can have a DPL which is different from the TSS descriptor's DPL. A procedure which does not have sufficient privilege to use the TSS descriptor in the GDT (which usually has a DPL of 0) can still call another task if it has access to a task gate in its LDT. With task gates, the operating system can limit task switching to specific tasks.
3. The need for an interrupt or exception to cause a task switch. Task gates also may reside in the IDT, which allows interrupts and exceptions to cause task switching. When an interrupt or exception supplies a vector to a task gate, the 386 DX microprocessor switches to the indicated task.

Figure 7-5 illustrates how both a task gate in an LDT and a task gate in the IDT can identify the same task.

7.5 TASK SWITCHING

The 386 DX microprocessor transfers execution to another task in any of four cases:

1. The current task executes a JMP or CALL to a TSS descriptor.
2. The current task executes a JMP or CALL to a task gate.
3. An interrupt or exception indexes to a task gate in the IDT.
4. The current task executes an IRET when the NT flag is set.

The JMP, CALL, and IRET instructions, as well as interrupts and exceptions, are all ordinary mechanisms of the 386 DX microprocessor which can be used in circumstances in which no task switch occurs. The descriptor type (when a task is called) or the NT flag (when the task returns) make the difference between the standard mechanism and the form which causes a task switch.

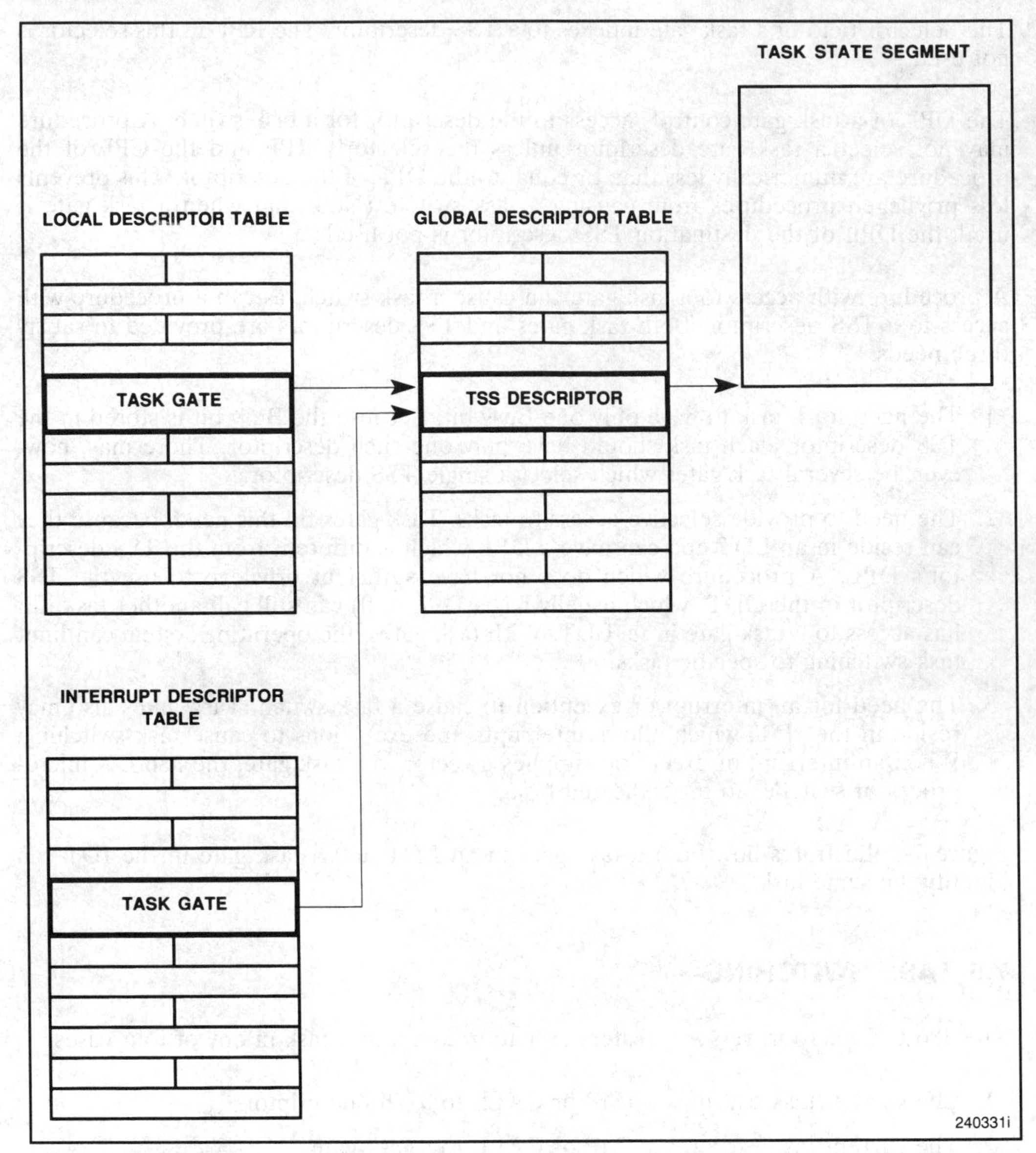

Figure 7-5. Task Gates Reference Tasks

To cause a task switch, a JMP or CALL instruction can transfer execution to either a TSS descriptor or a task gate. The effect is the same in either case: the 386 DX microprocessor transfers execution to the specified task.

An exception or interrupt causes a task switch when it indexes to a task gate in the IDT. If it indexes to an interrupt or trap gate in the IDT, a task switch does not occur. See Chapter 9 for more information on the interrupt mechanism.

An interrupt service routine always returns execution to the interrupted procedure, which may be in another task. If the NT flag is clear, a normal return occurs. If the NT flag is set, a task switch occurs. The task receiving the task switch is specified by the TSS selector in the TSS of the interrupt service routine.

A task switch has these steps:

1. Check that the current task is allowed to switch to the new task. Data-access privilege rules apply to JMP and CALL instructions. The DPL of the TSS descriptor and the task gate must be greater than or equal to both the CPL and the RPL of the gate selector. Exceptions, interrupts, and IRET instructions are permitted to switch tasks regardless of the DPL of the destination task gate or TSS descriptor.
2. Check that the TSS descriptor of the new task is marked present and has a valid limit (greater than or equal to 67H). Any errors up to this point occur in the context of the current task. These errors restore any changes made in the processor state when an attempt is made to exercute the error-generating instruction. This lets the return address for the exception handler point to the error-generating instruction, rather than the instruction following the error-generating instruction. The exception handler can fix the condition which caused the error, and restart the task. The intervention of the exception handler can be completely transparent to the application program.
3. Save the state of the current task. The processor finds the base address of the current TSS in the task register. The processor registers are copied into the current TSS (the EAX, ECX, EDX, EBX, ESP, EBP, ESI, EDI, ES, CS, SS, DS, FS, GS, and EFLAGS registers).
4. Load the TR register with the selector to the new task's TSS descriptor, set the new task's Busy bit, and set the TS bit in the CR0 register. The selector is either the operand of a JMP or CALL instruction, or it is taken from a task gate.
5. Load the new task's state from its TSS and continue execution. The registers loaded are the LDTR register; the EFLAGS register; the general registers EIP, EAX, ECX, EDX, EBX, ESP, EBP, ESI, EDI; and the segment registers ES, CS, SS, DS, FS, and GS. Any errors detected in this step occur in the context of the new task. To an exception handler, the first instruction of the new task appears not to have executed.

Note that the state of the old task is always saved when a task switch occurs. If the task is resumed, execution starts with the instruction which normally would have been next. The registers are restored to the values they held when the task stopped running.

Every task switch sets the TS (task switched) bit in the CR0 register. The TS bit is useful to system software when a coprocessor (such as a numerics coprocessor) is present. The TS bit indicates that the context of the coprocessor may be different from that of the current task. Chapter 11 discusses the TS bit and coprocessors in more detail.

Exception service routines for exceptions caused by task switching (exceptions resulting from steps 5 through 17 shown in Table 7-1) may be subject to recursive calls if they attempt to reload the segment selector which generated the exception. The cause of the exception (or the first of multiple causes) should be fixed before reloading the selector.

Table 7-1. Checks Made during a Task Switch

Step	Condition Checked	Exception[1]	Error Code Reference
1	TSS descriptor is present in memory	NP	New Task's TSS
2	TSS descriptor is not busy	GP	New Task's TSS
3	TSS segment limit greater than or equal to 103	TS	New Task's TSS
4	Registers are loaded from the values in the TSS		
5	LDT selector of new task is valid[2]	TS	New Task's TSS
6	Code segment DPL matches selector RPL	TS	New Code Segment
7	SS selector is valid[2]	TS	New Stack Segment
8	Stack segment is present in memory	SF	New Stack Segment
9	Stack segment DPL matches CPL	TS	New Stack Segment
10	LDT of new task is present in memory	TS	New Task's TSS
11	CS selector is valid[2]	TS	New Code Segment
12	Code segment is present in memory	NP	New Code Segment
13	Stack segment DPL matches selector RPL	TS	New Stack Segment
14	DS, ES, FS, and GS selectors are valid[2]	TS	New Data Segment
15	DS, ES, FS, and GS segments are readable	TS	New Data Segment
16	DS, ES, FS, and GS segments are present in memory	NP	New Data Segment
17	DS, ES, FS, and GS segment DPL greater than or equal to CPL (unless these are conforming segments)	TS	New Data Segment

1. NP = Segment-not-present exception, GP = General-protection exception, TS = Invalid-TSS exception, SF = Stack exception.
2. A selector is valid if it is in the compatible type of table (e.g., an LDT selector may not be in any table except the GDT), occupies an address within the table's segment limit, and refers to a compatible type of descriptor (e.g. a selector in the CS register only is valid when it indexes to a descriptor for a code segment; the descriptor type is specified in its Type field).

The privilege level at which the old task was running has no relation to the privilege level of the new task. Because the tasks are isolated by their separate address spaces and task state segments, and because privilege rules control access to a TSS, no privilege checks are needed to perform a task switch. The new task begins executing at the privilege level indicated by the RPL of new contents of the CS register, which are loaded from the TSS.

7.6 TASK LINKING

The Link field of the TSS and the NT flag are used to return execution to the previous task. The NT flag indicates whether the currently executing task is nested within the execution of another task, and the Link field of the current task's TSS holds the TSS selector for the higher-level task, if there is one (see Figure 7-6).

When an interrupt, exception, jump, or call causes a task switch, the 386 DX microprocessor copies the segment selector for the current task state segment into the TSS for the new task and sets the NT flag. The NT flag indicates the Link field of the TSS has been loaded with a saved TSS selector. The new task releases control by executing an IRET instruction. When an IRET instruction is executed, the NT flag is checked. If it is set, the processor does a task switch to the previous task. Table 7-2 summarizes the uses of the fields in a TSS which are affected by task switching.

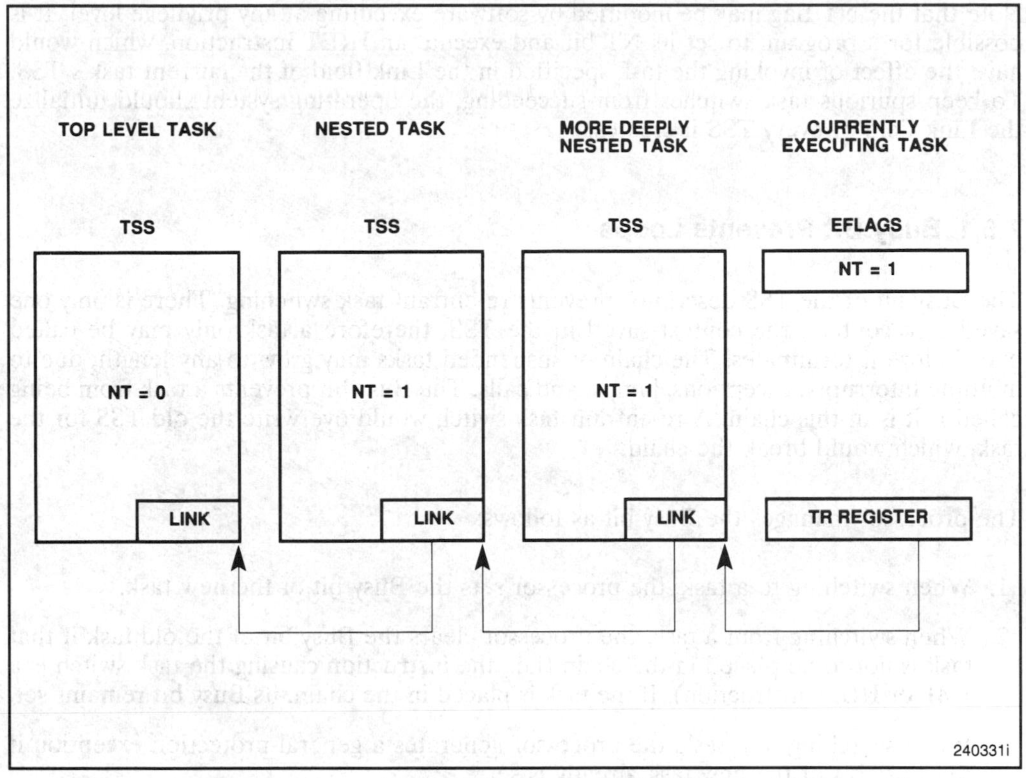

Figure 7-6. Nested Tasks

Table 7-2. Effect of a Task Switch on Busy, NT, and Link Fields

Field	Effect of Jump	Effect of CALL Instruction or Interrupt	Effect of IRET Instruction
Busy bit of new task	Bit is set. Must have been clear before.	Bit is set. Must have been clear before.	No change. Must be set.
Busy bit of old task	Bit is cleared.	No change. Bit is currently set.	Bit is cleared.
NT flag of new task	Flag is cleared.	Flag is set.	No change.
NT flag of old task	No change.	No change.	Flag is cleared.
Link field of new task.	No change.	Loaded with selector for old task's TSS.	No change.
Link field of old task.	No change.	No change.	No change.

Note that the NT flag may be modified by software executing at any privilege level. It is possible for a program to set its NT bit and execute an IRET instruction, which would have the effect of invoking the task specified in the Link field of the current task's TSS. To keep spurious task switches from succeeding, the operating system should initialize the Link field of every TSS it creates.

7.6.1 Busy Bit Prevents Loops

The Busy bit of the TSS descriptor prevents re-entrant task switching. There is only one saved task context, the context saved in the TSS, therefore a task only may be called once before it terminates. The chain of suspended tasks may grow to any length, due to multiple interrupts, exceptions, jumps, and calls. The Busy bit prevents a task from being called if it is in this chain. A re-entrant task switch would overwrite the old TSS for the task, which would break the chain.

The processor manages the Busy bit as follows:

1. When switching to a task, the processor sets the Busy bit of the new task.
2. When switching from a task, the processor clears the Busy bit of the old task if that task is not to be placed in the chain (i.e., the instruction causing the task switch is a JMP or IRET instruction). If the task is placed in the chain, its Busy bit remains set.
3. When switching to a task, the processor generates a general-protection exception if the Busy bit of the new task already is set.

In this way, the processor prevents a task from switching to itself or to any task in the chain, which prevents re-entrant task switching.

The Busy bit may be used in multiprocessor configurations, because the processor asserts a bus lock when it sets or clears the Busy bit. This keeps two processors from invoking the same task at the same time. (See Chapter 11 for more information on multiprocessing.)

7.6.2 Modifying Task Linkages

Modification of the chain of suspended tasks may be needed to resume an interrupted task before the task which interrupted it. A reliable way to do this is:

1. Disable interrupts.
2. First change the Link field in the TSS of the interrupting task, then clear the Busy bit in the TSS descriptor of the task being removed from the chain.
3. Re-enable interrupts.

7.7 TASK ADDRESS SPACE

The LDT selector and PDBR (CR3) field of the TSS can be used to give each task its own LDT and page tables. Because segment descriptors in the LDTs are the connections between tasks and segments, separate LDTs for each task can be used to set up individual control over these connections. Access to any particular segment can be given to any particular task by placing a segment descriptor for that segment in the LDT for that task. If paging is enabled, each task can have its own set of page tables for mapping linear addresses to physical addresses.

It also is possible for tasks to have the same LDT. This is a simple and memory-efficient way to allow some tasks to communicate with or control each other, without dropping the protection barriers for the entire system.

Because all tasks have access to the GDT, it also is possible to create shared segments accessed through segment descriptors in this table.

7.7.1 Task Linear-to-Physical Space Mapping

The choices for arranging the linear-to-physical mappings of tasks fall into two general classes:

1. One linear-to-physical mapping shared among all tasks. When paging is not enabled, this is the only choice. Without paging, all linear addresses map to the same physical addresses. When paging is enabled, this form of linear-to-physical mapping is obtained by using one page directory for all tasks. The linear space may exceed the available physical space if demand-paged virtual memory is supported.

2. Independent linear-to-physical mappings for each task. This form of mapping comes from using a different page directory for each task. Because the PDBR (page directory base register) is loaded from the TSS with each task switch, each task may have a different page directory.

The linear address spaces of different tasks may map to completely distinct physical addresses. If the entries of different page directories point to different page tables and the page tables point to different pages of physical memory, then the tasks do not share any physical addresses.

The task state segments must lie in a space accessible to all tasks so that the mapping of TSS addresses does not change while the processor is reading and updating the TSSs during a task switch. The linear space mapped by the GDT also should be mapped to a shared physical space; otherwise, the purpose of the GDT is defeated. Figure 7-7 shows how the linear spaces of two tasks can overlap in the physical space by sharing page tables.

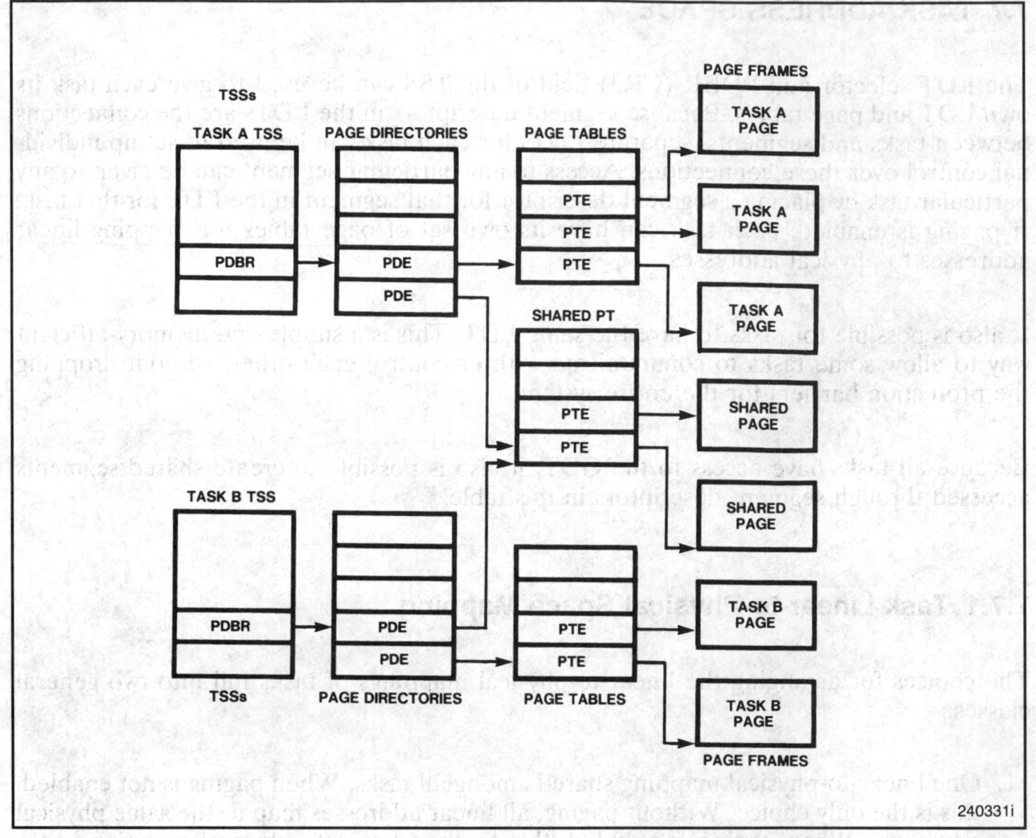

Figure 7-7. Overlapping Linear-to-Physical Mappings

7.7.2 Task Logical Address Space

By itself, an overlapping linear-to-physical space mapping does not allow sharing of data among tasks. To share data, tasks must also have a common logical-to-linear space mapping; i.e., they also must have access to descriptors which point into a shared linear address space. There are three ways to create shared logical-to-physical address-space mappings:

1. Through the segment descriptors in the GDT. All tasks have access to the descriptors in the GDT. If those descriptors point into a linear-address space which is mapped to a common physical-address space for all tasks, then the tasks can share data and instructions.

2. Through shared LDTs. Two or more tasks can use the same LDT if the LDT selectors in their TSSs select the same LDT for use in address translation. Segment descriptors in the LDT addressing linear space mapped to overlapping physical

space provide shared physical memory. This method of sharing is more selective than sharing by the GDT; the sharing can be limited to specific tasks. Other tasks in the system may have different LDTs which do not give them access to the shared areas.

3. Through segment descriptors in the LDTs which map to the same linear address space. If the linear address space is mapped to the same physical space by the page mapping of the tasks involved, these descriptors permit the tasks to share space. Such descriptors are commonly called "aliases." This method of sharing is even more selective than those listed above; other descriptors in the LDTs may point to independent linear addresses which are not shared.

space provide shared physical memory. This method of sharing is more selective than sharing by the GDT; the sharing can be limited to specific tasks. Other tasks in the system may have different LDTs which do not give them access to the shared areas.

Through segment descriptors in the LDTs which map to the same linear address space. If the linear address space is mapped to the same physical space by the page mapping of the tasks involved, these descriptors permit the tasks to share space. Such descriptors are commonly called "aliases." This method of sharing is even more selective than those listed above; other descriptors in the LDTs may point to independent linear addresses which are not shared.

Input/Output 8

CHAPTER 8
INPUT/OUTPUT

This chapter explains the input/output architecture of the 386™ DX microprocessor. Input/output is accomplished through I/O ports, which are registers connected to peripheral devices. An I/O port can be an input port, an output port, or a bidirectional port. Some I/O ports are used for carrying data, such as the transmit and receive registers of a serial interface. Other I/O ports are used to control peripheral devices, such as the control registers of a disk controller.

The input/output architecture is the programmer's model of how these ports are accessed. The discussion of this model includes:

- Methods of addressing I/O ports.
- Instructions which perform I/O operations.
- The I/O protection mechanism.

8.1 I/O ADDRESSING

The 386 DX microprocessor allows I/O ports to be addressed in either of two ways:

- Through a separate I/O address space accessed using I/O instructions.
- Through memory-mapped I/O, where I/O ports appear in the address space of physical memory.

The use of a separate I/O address space is supported by special instructions and a hardware protection mechanism. When memory-mapped I/O is used, the general-purpose instruction set can be used to access I/O ports, and protection is provided using segmentation or paging. Some system designers may prefer to use the I/O facilities built into the processor, while others may prefer the simplicity of a single physical address space.

If segmentation or paging is used for protection of the I/O address space, the AVL fields in segment descriptors or page table entries may be used to mark pages containing I/O as unrelocatable and unswappable. The AVL fields are provided for this kind of use, where a system programmer needs to make an extension to the address translation and protection mechanisms.

Hardware designers use these ways of mapping I/O ports into the address space when they design the address decoding circuits of a system. I/O ports can be mapped twice, so that they appear in both the I/O address space and the address space of physical memory. System programmers may wish to tell the hardware designers what kind of I/O addressing they would like to have.

8.1.1 I/O Address Space

The 386 DX microprocessor provides a separate I/O address space, distinct from the address space for physical memory, where I/O ports can be placed. The I/O address space consists of 2^{16} (64K) individually addressable 8-bit ports; any two consecutive 8-bit ports can be treated as a 16-bit port, and any four consecutive ports can be a 32-bit port. Extra bus cycles are required if a port crosses the boundary between two doublewords in physical memory.

The M/IO# pin on the 386 DX microprocessor indicates when a bus cycle to the I/O address space occurs. When a separate I/O address space is used, it is the responsibility of the hardware designer to make use of this signal to select I/O ports rather than memory. In fact, the use of the separate I/O address space simplifies the hardware design because these ports can be selected by a single signal; unlike other processors, it is not necessary to decode a number of upper address lines in order to set up a separate I/O address space.

A program can specify the address of a port in two ways. With an immediate byte constant, the program can specify:

- 256 8-bit ports numbered 0 through 255.
- 128 16-bit ports numbered 0, 2, 4, . . . , 252, 254.
- 64 32-bit ports numbered 0, 4, 8, . . . , 248, 252.

Using a value in the DX register, the program can specify:

- 8-bit ports numbered 0 through 65535.
- 16-bit ports numbered 0, 2, 4, . . . , 65532, 65534.
- 32-bit ports numbered 0, 4, 8, . . . , 65528, 65532.

The 386 DX microprocessor can transfer 8, 16, or 32 bits to a device in the I/O space. Like words in memory, 16-bit ports should be aligned to even addresses so that all 16 bits can be transferred in a single bus cycle. Like doublewords in memory, 32-bit ports should be aligned to addresses which are multiples of four. The processor supports data transfers to unaligned ports, but there is a performance penalty because an extra bus cycle must be used.

The IN and OUT instructions move data between a register and a port in the I/O address space. The instructions INS and OUTS move strings of data between the memory address space and ports in the I/O address space.

Note that I/O port addresses 0F8H through 0FFH are reserved for use by Intel. Do not assign I/O ports to these addresses. Also note that the processor performs bus cycles to I/O addresses 800000F8H and 800000FCH as part of the coprocessor interface (these addresses are beyond the defined range of the I/O address space).

8.1.2 Memory-Mapped I/O

I/O devices may be placed in the address space for physical memory. This is called memory-mapped I/O. As long as the devices respond like memory components, they can be used with memory-mapped I/O.

Memory-mapped I/O provides additional programming flexibility. Any instruction which references memory may be used to access an I/O port located in the memory space. For example, the MOV instruction can transfer data between any register and a port. The AND, OR, and TEST instructions may be used to manipulate bits in the control and status registers of peripheral devices (see Figure 8-1). Memory-mapped I/O can use the full instruction set and the full complement of addressing modes to address I/O ports.

Memory-mapped I/O, like any other memory reference, is subject to access protection and control. See Chapter 6 for a discussion of memory protection.

8.2 I/O INSTRUCTIONS

The I/O instructions of the 386 DX microprocessor provide access to the processor's I/O ports for the transfer of data. These instructions have the address of a port in the I/O address space as an operand. There are two kinds of I/O instructions:

1. Those which transfer a single item (byte, word, or doubleword) to or from a register.

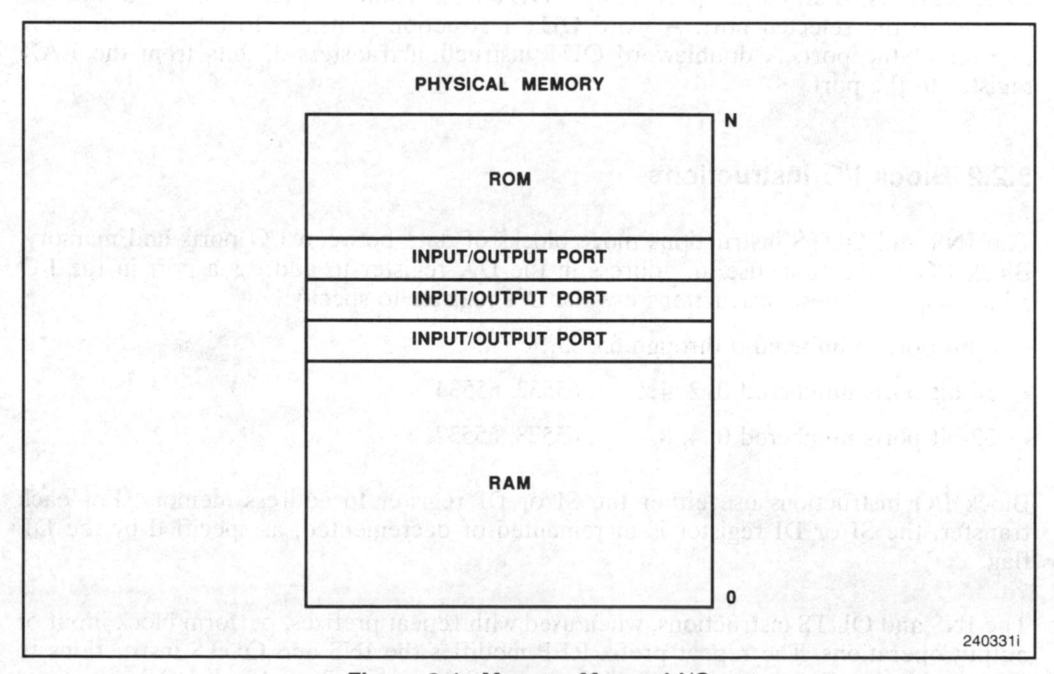

Figure 8-1. Memory-Mapped I/O

2. Those which transfer strings of items (strings of bytes, words, or doublewords) located in memory. These are known as "string I/O instructions" or "block I/O instructions."

These instructions cause the M/IO# signal to be driven low (logic 0) during a bus cycle, which indicates to external hardware that access to the I/O address space is taking place. If memory-mapped I/O is used, there is no reason to use I/O instructions.

8.2.1 Register I/O Instructions

The I/O instructions IN and OUT move data between I/O ports and the EAX register (32-bit I/O), the AX register (16-bit I/O), or the AL (8-bit I/O) register. The IN and OUT instructions address I/O ports either directly, with the address of one of 256 port addresses coded in the instruction, or indirectly using an address in the DX register to select one of 64K port addresses.

IN (Input from Port) transfers a byte, word, or doubleword from an input port to the AL, AX, or EAX registers. A byte IN instruction transfers 8 bits from the selected port to the AL register. A word IN instruction transfers 16 bits from the port to the AX register. A doubleword IN instruction transfers 32 bits from the port to the EAX register.

OUT (Output from Port) transfers a byte, word, or doubleword from the AL, AX, or EAX registers to an output port. A byte OUT instruction transfers 8 bits from the AL register to the selected port. A word OUT instruction transfers 16 bits from the AX register to the port. A doubleword OUT instruction transfers 32 bits from the EAX register to the port.

8.2.2 Block I/O Instructions

The INS and OUTS instructions move blocks of data between I/O ports and memory. Block I/O instructions use an address in the DX register to address a port in the I/O address space. These instructions use the DX register to specify:

- 8-bit ports numbered 0 through 65535.
- 16-bit ports numbered 0, 2, 4, . . . , 65532, 65534.
- 32-bit ports numbered 0, 4, 8, . . . , 65528, 65532.

Block I/O instructions use either the SI or DI register to address memory. For each transfer, the SI or DI register is incremented or decremented, as specified by the DF flag.

The INS and OUTS instructions, when used with repeat prefixes, perform block input or output operations. The repeat prefix REP modifies the INS and OUTS instructions to transfer blocks of data between an I/O port and memory. These block I/O instructions are string instructions (see Chapter 3 for more on string instructions). They simplify programming and increase the speed of data transfer by eliminating the need to use a separate LOOP instruction or an intermediate register to hold the data.

The string I/O instructions operate on byte strings, word strings, or doubleword strings. After each transfer, the memory address in the ESI or EDI registers is incremented or decremented by 1 for byte operands, by 2 for word operands, or by 4 for doubleword operands. The DF flag controls whether the register is incremented (the DF flag is clear) or decremented (the DF flag is set).

INS (Input String from Port) transfers a byte, word, or doubleword string element from an input port to memory. The INSB instruction transfers a byte from the selected port to the memory location addressed by the ES and EDI registers. The INSW instruction transfers a word. The INSD instruction transfers a doubleword. A segment override prefix cannot be used to specify an alternate destination segment. Combined with a REP prefix, an INS instruction makes repeated read cycles to the port, and puts the data into consecutive locations in memory.

OUTS (Output String from Port) transfers a byte, word, or doubleword string element from memory to an output port. The OUTSB instruction transfers a byte from the memory location addressed by the ES and EDI registers to the selected port. The OUTSW instruction transfers a word. The OUTSD instruction transfers a doubleword. A segment override prefix cannot be used to specify an alternate source segment. Combined with a REP prefix, an OUTS instruction reads consecutive locations in memory, and writes the data to an output port.

8.3 PROTECTION AND I/O

The I/O architecture has two protection mechanisms:

1. The IOPL field in the EFLAGS register controls access to the I/O instructions.
2. The I/O permission bit map of a TSS segment controls access to individual ports in the I/O address space.

These protection mechanisms are available only when a separate I/O address space is used. When memory-mapped I/O is used, protection is provided using segmentation or paging.

8.3.1 I/O Privilege Level

In systems where I/O protection is used, access to I/O instructions is controlled by the IOPL field in the EFLAGS register. This permits the operating system to adjust the privilege level needed to perform I/O. In a typical protection ring model, privilege levels 0 and 1 have access to the I/O instructions. This lets the operating system and the device drivers perform I/O, but keeps applications and less privileged device drivers from accessing the I/O address space. Applications access I/O through the operating system.

The following instructions can be executed only if CPL ≤ IOPL:

IN – Input
INS – Input String
OUT – Output
OUTS – Output String
CLI – Clear Interrupt-Enable Flag
STI – Set Interrupt-Enable Flag

These instructions are called "sensitive" instructions, because they are sensitive to the IOPL field. In virtual-8086 mode, IOPL is not used; only the I/O permission bit map limits access to I/O ports (see Chapter 15).

To use sensitive instructions, a procedure must run at a privilege level at least as privileged as that specified by the IOPL field. Any attempt by a less privileged procedure to use a sensitive instruction results in a general-protection exception. Because each task has its own copy of the EFLAGS register, each task can have a different IOPL.

A task can change IOPL only with the POPF instruction; however, such changes are privileged. No procedure may changer its IOPL unless it is running at privilege level 0. An attempt by a less privileged procedure to change the IOPL does not result in an exception; the IOPL simply remains unchanged.

The POPF instruction also may be used to change the state of the IF flag (as can the CLI and STI instructions); however, changes to the IF flag using the POPF instruction are IOPL-sensitive. A procedure may change the setting of the IF flag with a POPF instruction only if it runs with a CPL at least as privileged as the IOPL. An attempt by a less privileged procedure to change the IF flag does not result in an exception; the IF flag simply remains unchanged.

8.3.2 I/O Permission Bit Map

The 386 DX microprocessor can generate exceptions for references to specific I/O addresses. These addresses are specified in the I/O permission bit map in the TSS (see Figure 8-2). The size of the map and its location in the TSS are variable. The processor finds the I/O permission bit map with the I/O map base address in the TSS. The base address is a 16-bit offset into the TSS. This is an offset to the beginning of the bit map. The limit of the TSS is the limit on the size of the I/O permission bit map.

Because each task has its own TSS, each task has its own I/O permission bit map. Access to individual I/O ports can be granted to individual tasks.

If the CPL and IOPL allow I/O instructions to execute, the processor checks the I/O permission bit map. Each bit in the map corresponds to an I/O port byte address; for example, the control bit for address 41 (decimal) in the I/O address space is found at bit position 1 of the sixth byte in the bit map. The processor tests all the bits corresponding

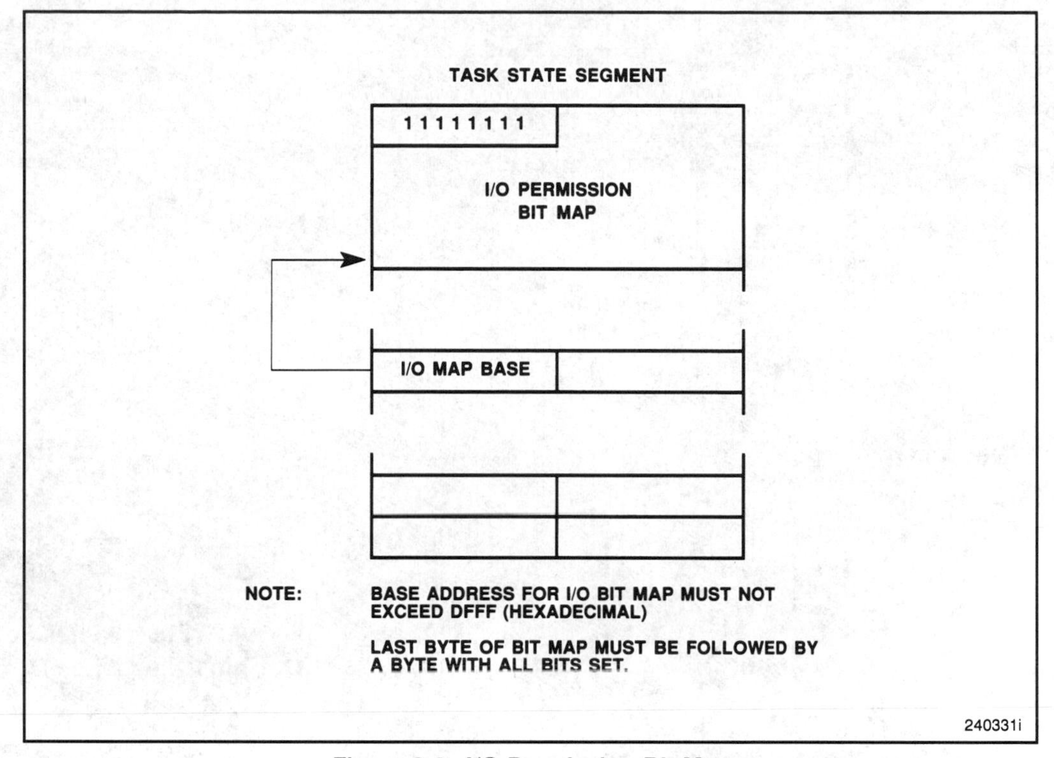

Figure 8-2. I/O Permission Bit Map

to the I/O port being addressed; for example, a doubleword operation tests four bits corresponding to four adjacent byte addresses. If any tested bit is set, a general-protection exception is generated. If all tested bits are clear, the I/O operation proceeds.

Because I/O ports which are not aligned to word and doubleword boundaries are permitted, it is possible that the processor may need to access two bytes in the bit map when I/O permission is checked. For maximum speed, the processor has been designed to read two bytes for every access to an I/O port. To prevent exceptions from being generated when the ports with the highest addresses are accessed, an extra byte needs to come after the table. This byte must have all of its bits set, and it must be within the segment limit.

It is not necessary for the I/O permission bit map to represent all the I/O addresses. I/O addresses not spanned by the map are treated as if they had set bits in the map. For example, if the TSS segment limit is 10 bytes past the bit map base address, the map has 11 bytes and the first 80 I/O ports are mapped. Higher addresses in the I/O address space generate exceptions.

If the I/O bit map base address is greater than or equal to the TSS segment limit, there is no I/O permission map, and all I/O instructions generate exceptions. The base address must be less than or equal to 0DFFFH.

Figure 8-2. I/O Permission Bit Map

for the I/O port being addressed; for example, a doubleword operation tests four bits corresponding to four adjacent byte addresses. If any tested bit is set, a general-protection exception is generated. If all tested bits are clear, the I/O operation proceeds.

Because I/O ports which are not aligned to word and doubleword boundaries are permitted, it is possible that the processor may need to access two bytes in the bit map when I/O permission is checked. For maximum speed, the processor has been designed to read two bytes for every access to an I/O port. To prevent exceptions from being generated when the ports with the highest addresses are accessed, an extra byte needs to come after the table. This byte must have all of its bits set, and it must be within the segment limit.

It is not necessary for the I/O permission bit map to represent all the I/O addresses. I/O addresses not spanned by the map are treated as if they had set bits in the map. For example, if the TSS segment limit is 10 bytes past the bit map base address, the map has 11 bytes and the first 80 I/O ports are mapped. Higher addresses in the I/O address space generate exceptions.

If the I/O bit map base address is greater than or equal to the TSS segment limit, there is no I/O permission map, and all I/O instructions generate exceptions. The base address must be less than or equal to 0DFFFH.

Exceptions and Interrupts 9

CHAPTER 9
EXCEPTIONS AND INTERRUPTS

Exceptions and interrupts are forced transfers of execution to a task or a procedure. The task or procedure is called a *handler*. Interrupts occur at random times during the execution of a program, in response to signals from hardware. Exceptions occur when instructions are executed which provoke exceptions. Usually, the servicing of interrupts and exceptions is performed in a manner transparent to application programs. Interrupts are used to handle events external to the processor, such as requests to service peripheral devices. Exceptions handle conditions detected by the processor in the course of executing instructions, such division by 0.

There two sources for interrupts and two sources for exceptions:

1. Interrupts
   - Maskable interrupts, which are received on the INTR input of the 386™ DX microprocessor. Maskable interrupts do not occur unless the interrupt-enable flag (IF) is set.
   - Nonmaskable interrupts, which are received on the NMI (Non-Maskable Interrupt) input of the processor. The processor does not provide a mechanism to prevent nonmaskable interrupts.
2. Exceptions
   - Processor-detected exceptions. These are further classified as *faults*, *traps*, and *aborts.*
   - Programmed exceptions. The INTO, INT 3, INT *n*, and BOUND instructions may trigger exceptions. These instructions often are called "software interrupts," but the processor handles them as exceptions.

This chapter explains the features of the 386 DX microprocessor which control and respond to interrupts.

9.1 EXCEPTION AND INTERRUPT VECTORS

The processor associates an identifying number with each different type of interrupt or exception. This number is called a *vector*.

The NMI interrupt and the exceptions are assigned vectors in the range 0 through 31. Not all of these vectors are currently used in the Intel386™ architecture; unassigned vectors in this range are reserved for possible future uses. Do not use unassigned vectors.

The vectors for maskable interrupts are determined by hardware. External interrupt controllers (such as Intel's 8259A Programmable Interrupt Controller) put the vector on the bus of the 386 DX microprocessor during its interrupt-acknowledge cycle. Any vectors in the range 32 through 255 can be used. Table 9-1 shows the assignment of exception and interrupt vectors.

Table 9-1. Exception and Interrupt Vectors

Vector Number	Description
0	Divide Error
1	Debug Exception
2	NMI Interrupt
3	Breakpoint
4	INTO-detected Overflow
5	BOUND Range Exceeded
6	Invalid Opcode
7	Coprocessor Not Available
8	Double Fault
9	Coprocessor Segment Overrun
10	Invalid Task State Segment
11	Segment Not Present
12	Stack Fault
13	General Protection
14	Page Fault
15	(Intel® reserved. Do not use.)
16	Coprocessor Error
17-31	(Intel reserved. Do not use.)
32-255	Maskable Interrupts

Exceptions are classified as *faults*, *traps*, or *aborts* depending on the way they are reported and whether restart of the instruction which caused the exception is supported.

Faults A fault is an exception which is reported at the instruction boundary prior to the instruction in which the exception was detected. The fault is reported with the machine restored to a state which permits the instruction to be restarted. The return address for the fault handler points to the instruction which generated the fault, rather than the instruction following the faulting instruction.

Traps A trap is an exception which is reported at the instruction boundary immediately after the instruction in which the exception was detected.

Aborts An abort is an exception which does not always report the location of the instruction causing the exception and does not allow restart of the program which caused the exception. Aborts are used to report severe errors, such as hardware errors and inconsistent or illegal values in system tables.

9.2 INSTRUCTION RESTART

For most exceptions and interrupts, transfer of execution does not take place until the end of the current instruction. This leaves the EIP register pointing at the instruction which comes after the instruction which was being executed when the exception or interrupt occurred. If the instruction has a repeat prefix, transfer takes place at the end of the current iteration with the registers set to execute the next iteration. But if the exception is a fault, the processor registers are restored to the state they held before execution of the instruction began. This permits *instruction restart*.

Instruction restart is used to handle exceptions which block access to operands. For example, an application program could make reference to data in a segment which is not present in memory. When the exception occurs, the exception handler must load the segment (probably from a hard disk) and resume execution beginning with the instruction which caused the exception. At the time the exception occurs, the instruction may have altered the contents of some of the processor registers. If the instruction read an operand from the stack, it is necessary to restore the stack pointer to its previous value. All of these restoring operations are performed by the processor in a manner completely transparent to the application program.

When a fault occurs, the EIP register is restored to point to the instruction which received the exception. When the exception handler returns, execution resumes with this instruction.

9.3 ENABLING AND DISABLING INTERRUPTS

Certain conditions and flag settings cause the processor to inhibit certain kinds of interrupts and exceptions.

9.3.1 NMI Masks Further NMIs

While an NMI interrupt handler is executing, the processor disables additional calls to the procedure or task which handles the interrupt until the next IRET instruction is executed. This prevents stacking up calls to the interrupt handler.

9.3.2 IF Masks INTR

The IF flag can turn off servicing of interrupts received on the INTR pin of the processor. When the IF flag is clear, INTR interrupts are ignored; when the IF flag is set, INTR interrupts are serviced. As with the other flag bits, the processor clears the IF flag in response to a RESET signal. The STI and CLI instructions set and clear the IF flag.

CLI (Clear Interrupt-Enable Flag) and **STI (Set Interrupt-Enable Flag)** put the IF flag (bit 9 in the EFLAGS register) in a known state. These instructions may be executed only if the CPL is an equal or more privileged level than the IOPL. A general-protection exception is generated if they are executed with a lesser privileged level.

The IF flag also is affected by the following operations:

- The PUSHF instruction stores all flags on the stack, where they can be examined and modified. The POPF instruction can be used to load the modified form back into the EFLAGS register.

- Task switches and the POPF and IRET instructions load the EFLAGS register; therefore, they can be used to modify the setting of the IF flag.
- Interrupts through interrupt gates automatically clear the IF flag, which disables interrupts. (Interrupt gates are explained later in this chapter.)

9.3.3 RF Masks Debug Faults

The RF flag in the EFLAGS register can be used to turn off servicing of debug faults. If it is clear, debug faults are serviced; if it is set, they are ignored. This is used to suppress multiple calls to the debug exception handler when a breakpoint occurs.

For example, an instruction breakpoint may have been set for an instruction which references data in a segment which is not present in memory. When the instruction is executed for the first time, the breakpoint generates a debug exception. Before the debug handler returns, it should set the RF flag in the copy of the EFLAGS register saved on the stack. This allows the segment-not-present fault to be reported after the debug exception handler transfers execution back to the instruction. If the flag is not set, another debug exception occurs after the debug exception handler returns.

The processor sets the RF bit in the saved contents of the EFLAGS register when the other faults occur, so multiple debug exceptions are not generated when the instruction is restarted due to the segment-not-present fault. The processor clears its RF flag when the execution of the faulting instruction completes. This allows an instruction breakpoint to be generated for the following instruction. (See Chapter 12 for more information on debugging.)

9.3.4 MOV or POP to SS Masks Some Exceptions and Interrupts

Software which needs to change stack segments often uses a pair of instructions; for example:

```
MOV   SS,   AX
MOV   ESP, StackTop
```

If an interrupt or exception occurs after the segment selector has been loaded but before the ESP register has been loaded, these two parts of the logical address into the stack space are inconsistent for the duration of the interrupt or exception handler.

To prevent this situation, the 386 DX microprocessor inhibits interrupts, debug exceptions, and single-step trap exceptions after either a MOV to SS instruction or a POP to SS instruction, until the instruction boundary following the next instruction is reached. General-protection faults may still be generated. If the LSS instruction is used to modify the contents of the SS register, the problem does not occur.

9.4 PRIORITY AMONG SIMULTANEOUS EXCEPTIONS AND INTERRUPTS

If more than one exception or interrupt is pending at an instruction boundary, the processor services them in a predictable order. The priority among classes of exception and interrupt sources is shown in Table 9-2. The processor first services a pending exception or interrupt from the class which has the highest priority, transferring execution to the first instruction of the handler. Lower priority exceptions are discarded; lower priority interrupts are held pending. Discarded exceptions are re-issued when the interrupt handler returns execution to the point of interruption.

9.5 INTERRUPT DESCRIPTOR TABLE

The interrupt descriptor table (IDT) associates each exception or interrupt vector with a descriptor for the procedure or task which services the associated event. Like the GDT and LDTs, the IDT is an array of 8-byte descriptors. Unlike the GDT, the first entry of the IDT may contain a descriptor. To form an index into the IDT, the processor scales the exception or interrupt vector by eight, the number of bytes in a descriptor. Because there are only 256 vectors, the IDT need not contain more than 256 descriptors. It can contain fewer than 256 descriptors; descriptors are required only for the interrupt vectors which may occur.

The IDT may reside anywhere in physical memory. As Figure 9-1 shows, the processor locates the IDT using the IDTR register. This register holds both a 32-bit base address and 16-bit limit for the IDT. The LIDT and SIDT instructions load and store the contents of the IDTR register. Both instructions have one operand, which is the address of six bytes in memory.

If a vector references a descriptor beyond the limit, the processor enters shutdown mode. In this mode, the processor stops executing instructions until an NMI interrupt is received or reset initialization is invoked. The processor generates a special bus cycle to indicate it has entered shutdown mode. Software designers may need to be aware of the response of hardware to receiving this signal. For example, hardware may turn on an indicator light on the front panel, generate an NMI interrupt to record diagnostic information, or invoke reset initialization.

Table 9-2. Priority Among Simultaneous Exceptions and Interrupts

Priority	Description
Highest	Faults except debug faults
	Trap instructions INTO, INT *n*, INT 3
	Debug traps for this instruction
	Debug traps for next instruction
	NMI interrupt
Lowest	INTR interrupt

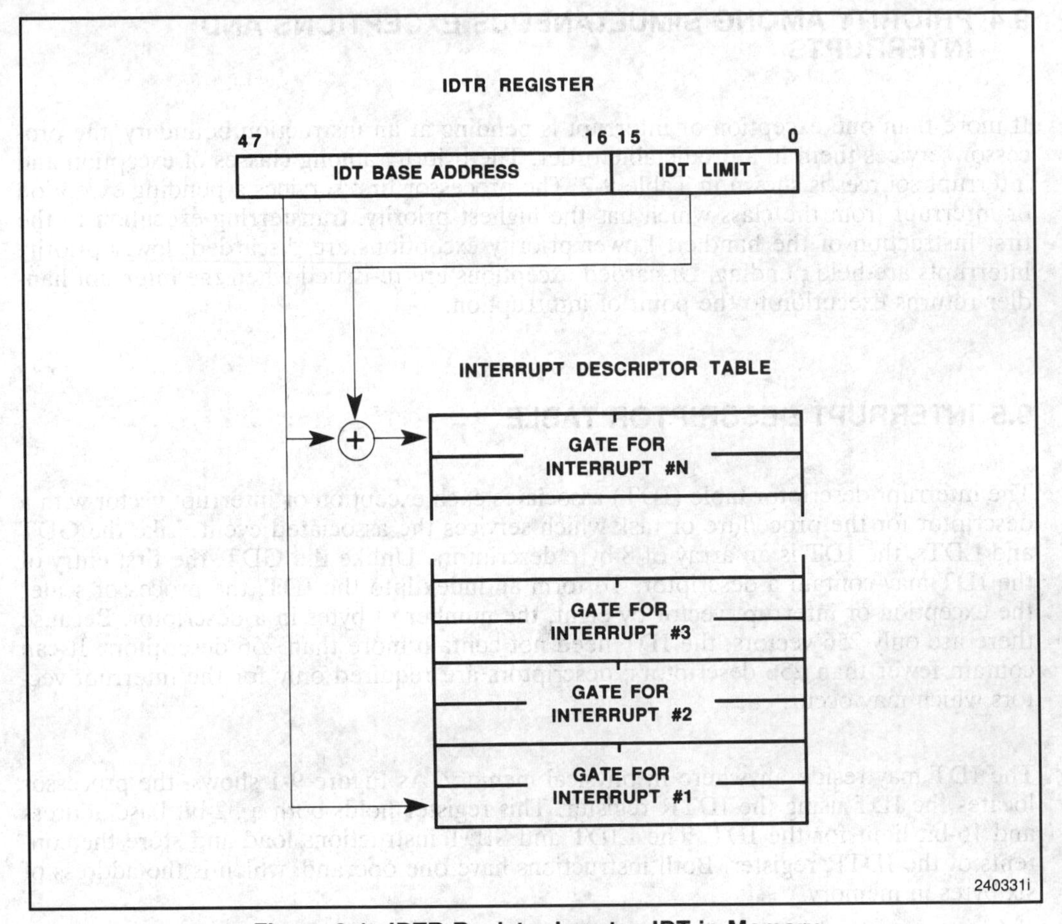

Figure 9-1. IDTR Register Locates IDT in Memory

LIDT (Load IDT register) loads the IDTR register with the base address and limit held in the memory operand. This instruction can be executed only when the CPL is 0. It normally is used by the initialization code of an operating system when creating an IDT. An operating system also may use it to change from one IDT to another.

SIDT (Store IDT register) copies the base and limit value stored in IDTR to memory. This instruction can be executed at any privilege level.

9.6 IDT DESCRIPTORS

The IDT may contain any of three kinds of descriptors:

- Task gates
- Interrupt gates
- Trap gates

Figure 9-2 shows the format of task gates, interrupt gates, and trap gates. (The task gate in an IDT is the same as the task gatc in the GDT or an LDT already discussed in Chapter 7.)

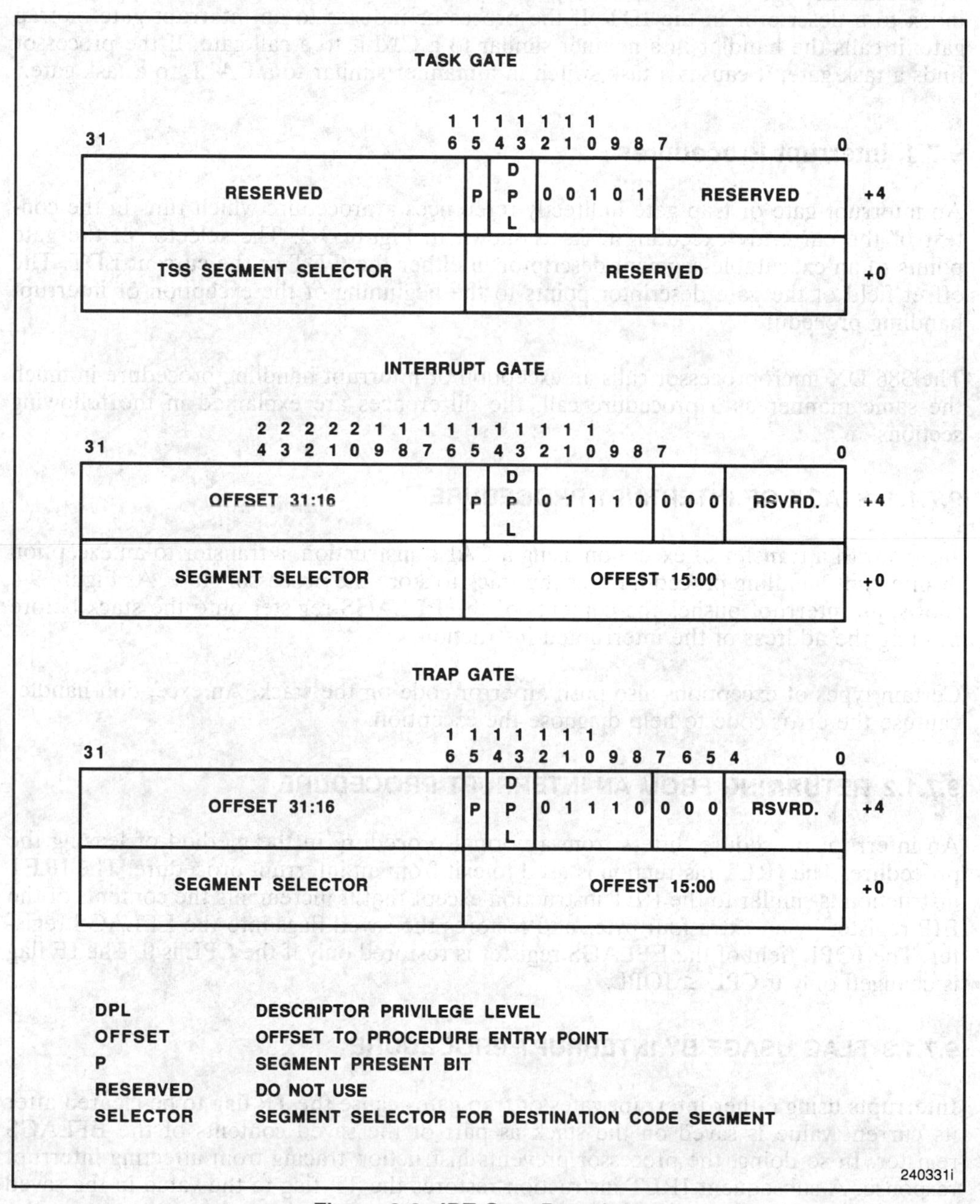

Figure 9-2. IDT Gate Descriptors

9.7 INTERRUPT TASKS AND INTERRUPT PROCEDURES

Just as a CALL instruction can call either a procedure or a task, so an exception or interrupt can "call" an interrupt handler as either a procedure or a task. When responding to an exception or interrupt, the processor uses the exception or interrupt vector to index to a descriptor in the IDT. If the processor indexes to an interrupt gate or trap gate, it calls the handler in a manner similar to a CALL to a call gate. If the processor finds a task gate, it causes a task switch in a manner similar to a CALL to a task gate.

9.7.1 Interrupt Procedures

An interrupt gate or trap gate indirectly references a procedure which runs in the context of the currently executing task, as shown in Figure 9-3. The selector of the gate points to an executable-segment descriptor in either the GDT or the current LDT. The offset field of the gate descriptor points to the beginning of the exception or interrupt handling procedure.

The 386 DX microprocessor calls an exception or interrupt handling procedure in much the same manner as a procedure call; the differences are explained in the following sections.

9.7.1.1 STACK OF INTERRUPT PROCEDURE

Just as with a transfer of execution using a CALL instruction, a transfer to an exception or interrupt handling procedure uses the stack to store the processor state. As Figure 9-4 shows, an interrupt pushes the contents of the EFLAGS register onto the stack before pushing the address of the interrupted instruction.

Certain types of exceptions also push an error code on the stack. An exception handler can use the error code to help diagnose the exception.

9.7.1.2 RETURNING FROM AN INTERRUPT PROCEDURE

An interrupt procedure differs from a normal procedure in the method of leaving the procedure. The IRET instruction is used to exit from an interrupt procedure. The IRET instruction is similar to the RET instruction except that it increments the contents of the EIP register by an extra four bytes and restores the saved flags into the EFLAGS register. The IOPL field of the EFLAGS register is restored only if the CPL is 0. The IF flag is changed only if CPL $\leq$ IOPL.

9.7.1.3 FLAG USAGE BY INTERRUPT PROCEDURE

Interrupts using either interrupt gates or trap gates cause the TF flag to be cleared after its current value is saved on the stack as part of the saved contents of the EFLAGS register. In so doing, the processor prevents instruction tracing from affecting interrupt response. A subsequent IRET instruction restores the TF flag to the value in the saved contents of the EFLAGS register on the stack.

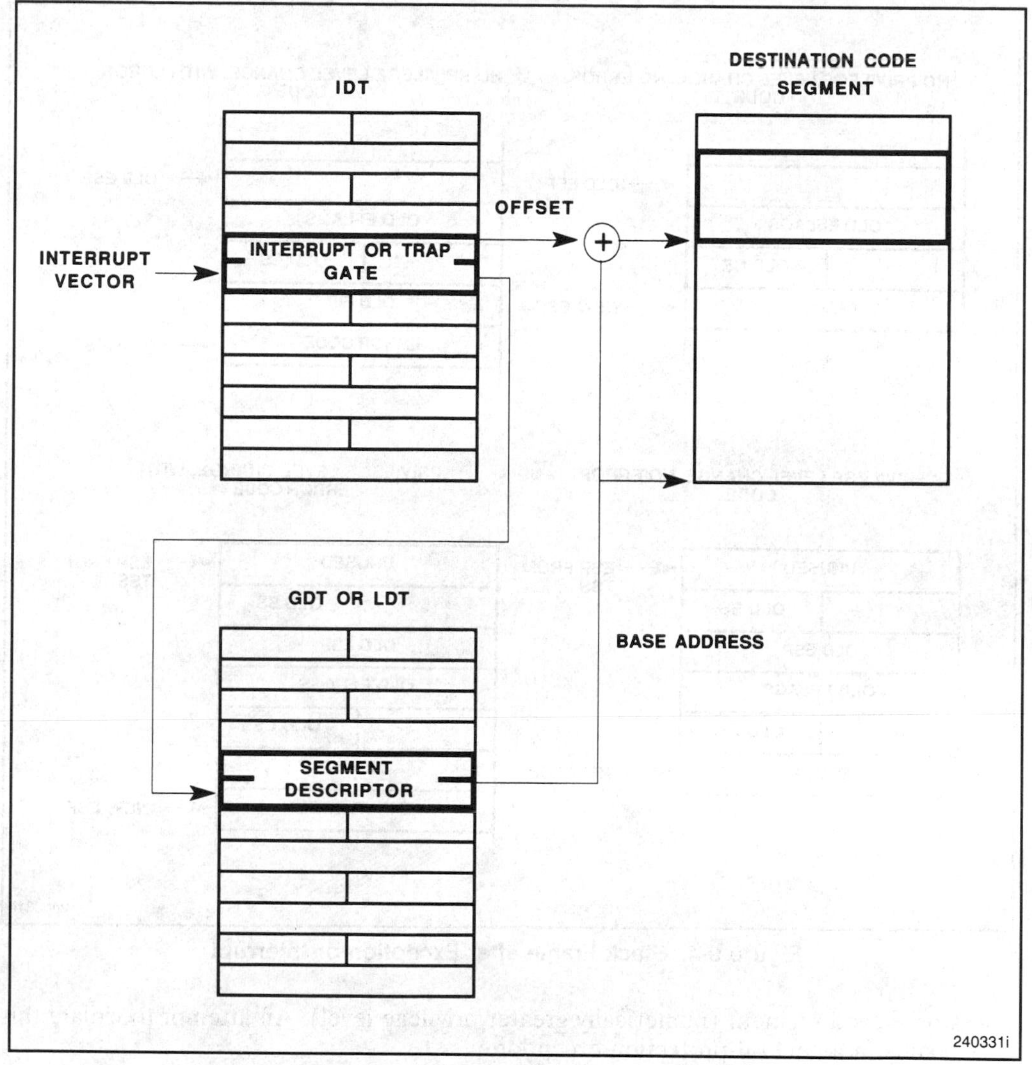

Figure 9-3. Interrupt Procedure Call

The difference between an interrupt gate and a trap gate is its effect on the IF flag. An interrupt which uses an interrupt gate clears the IF flag, which prevents other interrupts from interfering with the current interrupt handler. A subsequent IRET instruction restores the IF flag to the value in the saved contents of the EFLAGS register on the stack. An interrupt through a trap gate does not change the IF flag.

9.7.1.4 PROTECTION IN INTERRUPT PROCEDURES

The privilege rule which governs interrupt procedures is similar to that for procedure calls: the processor does not permit an interrupt to transfer execution to a procedure in

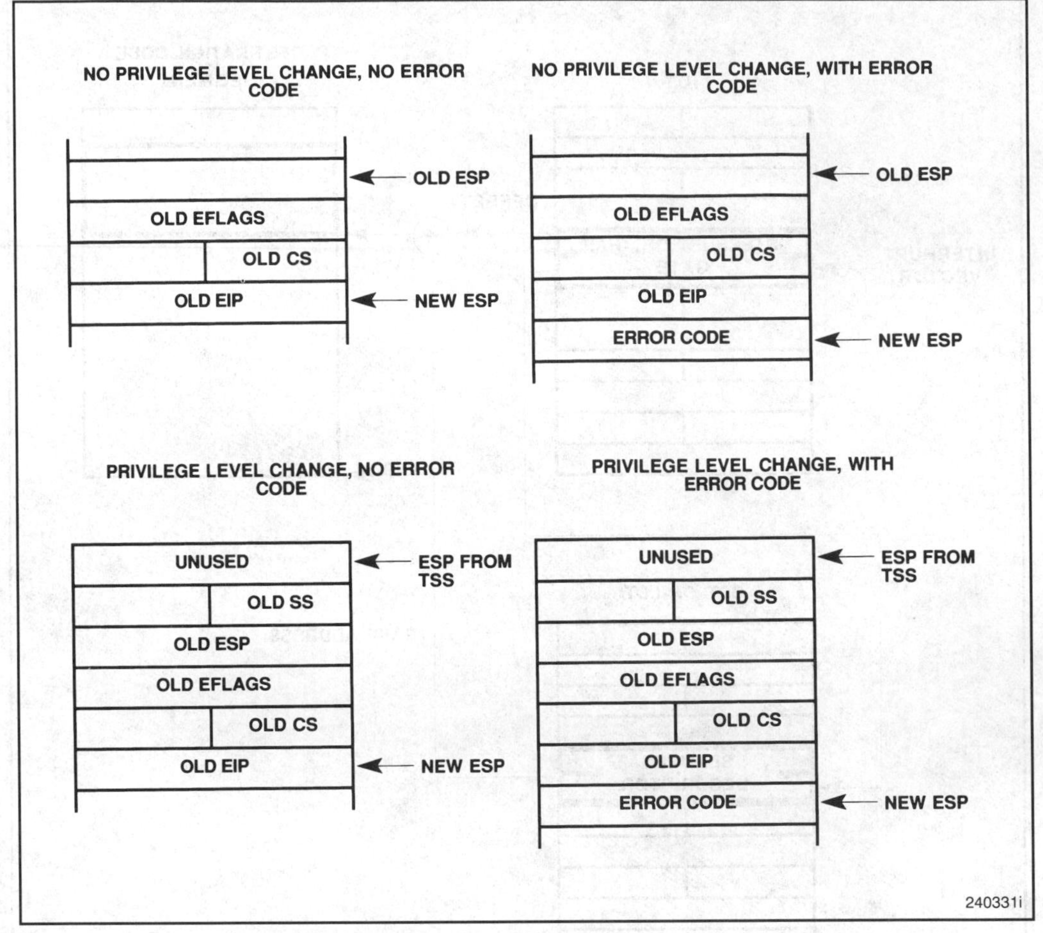

Figure 9-4. Stack Frame after Exception or Interrupt

a less privileged segment (numerically greater privilege level). An attempt to violate this rule results in a general-protection exception.

Because interrupts generally do not occur at predictable times, this privilege rule effectively imposes restrictions on the privilege levels at which exception and interrupt handling procedures can run. Either of the following techniques can be used to keep the privilege rule from being violated.

- The exception or interrupt handler can be placed in a conforming code segment. This technique can be used by handlers for certain exceptions (divide error, for example). These handlers must use only the data available on the stack. If the handler needs data from a data segment, the data segment would have to have privilege level 3, which would make it unprotected.
- The handler can be placed in a code segment with privilege level 0. This handler would always run, no matter what CPL the program has.

9.7.2 Interrupt Tasks

A task gate in the IDT indirectly references a task, as Figure 9-5 illustrates. The segment selector in the task gate addresses a TSS descriptor in the GDT.

When an exception or interrupt calls a task gate in the IDT, a task switch results. Handling an interrupt with a separate task offers two advantages:

- The entire context is saved automatically.
- The interrupt handler can be isolated from other tasks by giving it a separate address space. This is done by giving it a separate LDT.

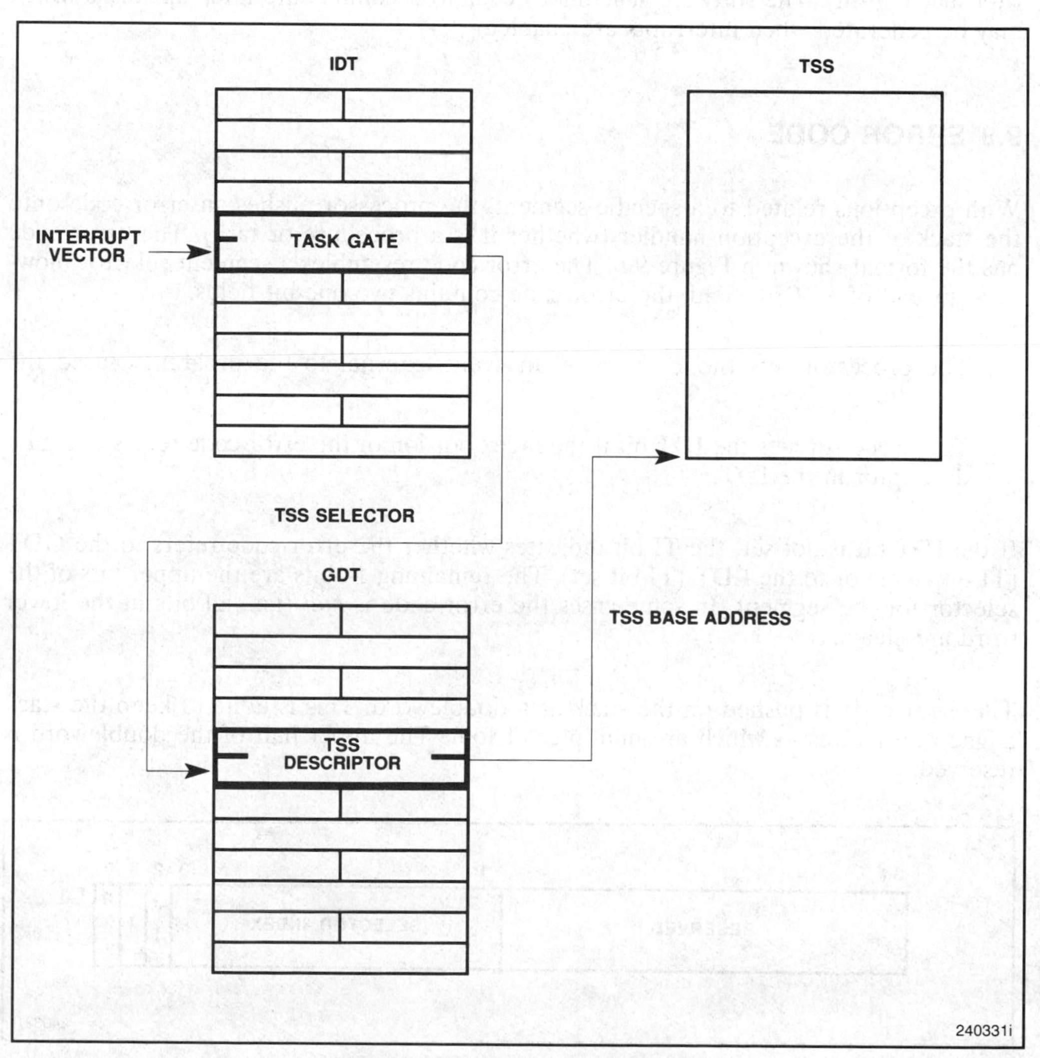

Figure 9-5. Interrupt Task Switch

A task switch caused by an interrupt operates in the same manner as the other task switches described in Chapter 7. The interrupt task returns to the interrupted task by executing an IRET instruction.

Some exceptions return an error code. If the task switch is caused by one of these, the processor pushes the code onto the stack corresponding to the privilege level of the interrupt handler.

When interrupt tasks are used in an operating system for the 386 DX microprocessor, there are actually two mechanisms which can create new tasks: the software scheduler (part of the operating system) and the hardware scheduler (part of the processor's interrupt mechanism). The software scheduler needs to accommodate interrupt tasks which may be generated when interrupts are enabled.

9.8 ERROR CODE

With exceptions related to a specific segment, the processor pushes an error code onto the stack of the exception handler (whether it is a procedure or task). The error code has the format shown in Figure 9-6. The error code resembles a segment selector; however instead of an RPL field, the error code contains two one-bit fields:

1. The processor sets the EXT bit if an event external to the program caused the exception.

2. The processor sets the IDT bit if the index portion of the error code refers to a gate descriptor in the IDT.

If the IDT bit is not set, the TI bit indicates whether the error code refers to the GDT (TI bit clear) or to the LDT (TI bit set). The remaining 14 bits are the upper bits of the selector for the segment. In some cases the error code is *null* (i.e., all bits in the lower word are clear).

The error code is pushed on the stack as a doubleword. This is done to keep the stack aligned on addresses which are multiples of four. The upper half of the doubleword is reserved.

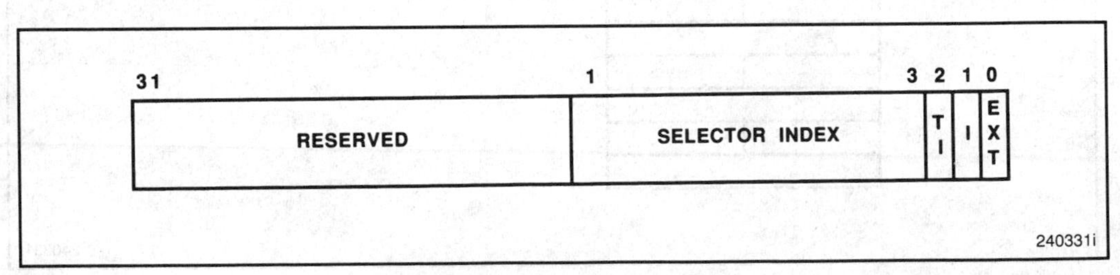

Figure 9-6. Error Code

9.9 EXCEPTION CONDITIONS

The following sections describe conditions which generate exceptions. Each description classifies the exception as a *fault*, *trap*, or *abort*. This classification provides information needed by system programmers for restarting the procedure in which the exception occurred:

Faults — The saved contents of the CS and EIP registers point to the instruction which generated the fault.

Traps — The saved contents of the CS and EIP registers stored when the trap occurs point to the instruction to be executed after the instruction which generated the trap. If a trap is detected during an instruction which transfers execution, the saved contents of the CS and EIP registers reflect the transfer. For example, if a trap is detected in a JMP instruction, the saved contents of the CS and EIP registers point to the destination of the JMP instruction, not to the instruction at the next address above the JMP instruction.

Aborts — An abort is an exception which permits neither precise location of the instruction causing the exception nor restart of the program which caused the exception. Aborts are used to report severe errors, such as hardware errors and inconsistent or illegal values in system tables.

9.9.1 Interrupt 0—Divide Error

The divide-error fault occurs during a DIV or an IDIV instruction when the divisor is 0.

9.9.2 Interrupt 1—Debug Exceptions

The processor generates a debug exception for a number of conditions; whether the exception is a fault or a trap depends on the condition, as shown below:

- Instruction address breakpoint fault
- Data address breakpoint trap
- General detect fault
- Single-step trap
- Task-switch breakpoint trap

The processor does not push an error code for this exception. An exception handler can examine the debug registers to determine which condition caused the exception. See Chapter 12 for more detailed information about debugging and the debug registers.

9.9.3 Interrupt 3 — Breakpoint

The INT 3 instruction generates a breakpoint trap. The INT 3 instruction is one byte long, which makes it easy to replace an opcode in a code segment in RAM with the breakpoint opcode. The operating system or a debugging tool can use a data segment mapped to the same physical address space as the code segment to place an INT 3 instruction in places where it is desired to call the debugger. Debuggers use breakpoints as a way to suspend program execution in order to examine registers, variables, etc.

The saved contents of the CS and EIP registers point to the byte following the breakpoint. If a debugger allows the suspended program to resume execution, it replaces the INT 3 instruction with the original opcode at the location of the breakpoint, and it decrements the saved contents of the EIP register before returning. See Chapter 12 for more information on debugging.

9.9.4 Interrupt 4 — Overflow

The overflow trap occurs when the processor executes an INTO instruction with the OF flag set. Because signed and unsigned arithmetic both use some of the same instructions, the processor cannot determine when overflow actually occurs. Instead, it sets the OF flag when the results, if interpreted as signed numbers, would be out of range. When doing arithmetic on signed operands, the OF flag can be tested directly or the INTO instruction can be used.

9.9.5 Interrupt 5 — Bounds Check

The bounds-check fault is generated when the processor, while executing a BOUND instruction, finds that the operand exceeds the specified limits. A program can use the BOUND instruction to check a signed array index against signed limits defined in a block of memory.

9.9.6 Interrupt 6 — Invalid Opcode

The invalid-opcode fault is generated when an unreserved invalid opcode is detected by the execution unit. (The exception is not detected until an attempt is made to execute the invalid opcode; i.e., prefetching an invalid opcode does not cause this exception.) No error code is pushed on the stack. The exception can be handled within the same task.

This exception also occurs when the type of operand is invalid for the given opcode. Examples include an intersegment JMP instruction using a register operand, or an LES instruction with a register source operand.

A third condition which generates this exception is the use of the LOCK prefix with an instruction which may not be locked. Only certain instructions may be used with bus locking, and only forms of these instructions which write to a destination in memory may be used. All other uses of the LOCK prefix generate an invalid-opcode exception.

The following is a list of undefined opcodes that are reserved by Intel. These opcodes do not generate interrupt 6.

Intel reserved opcodes (single byte)
82
D6
F1

Intel reserved opcodes (two byte)
0F 07
0F 10
0F 11
0F 12
0F 13
F6 XX
F7 XX

C0 XX
C1 XX
D0 XX
D1 XX
D2 XX
D3 XX

9.9.7 Interrupt 7 — Coprocessor Not Available

The coprocessor-not-available fault is generated by either of two conditions:

- The processor executes an ESC instruction, and the EM bit of the CR0 register is set.
- The processor executes a WAIT instruction or an ESC instruction, and both the MP bit and the TS bit of the CR0 register are set.

See Chapter 11 for more information about the coprocessor interface.

9.9.8 Interrupt 8 — Double Fault

Normally, when the processor detects an exception while trying to call the handler for a prior exception, the two exceptions can be handled serially. If, however, the processor cannot handle them serially, it signals the double-fault exception instead. To determine when two faults are to be signalled as a double fault, the 386 DX microprocessor divides the exceptions into three classes: benign exceptions, contributory exceptions, and page faults. Table 9-3 shows this classification.

Table 9-3. Interrupt and Exception Classes

Class	Vector Number	Description
Benign Exceptions and Interrupts	1 2 3 4 5 6 7 16	Debug Exceptions NMI Interrupt Breakpoint Overflow Bounds Check Invalid Opcode Coprocessor Not Available Coprocessor Error
Contributory Exceptions	0 9 10 11 12 13	Divide Error Coprocessor Segment Overrun Invalid TSS Segment Not Present Stack Fault General Protection
Page Faults	14	Page Fault

When two benign exceptions or interrupts occur, or one benign and one contributory, the two events can be handled in succession. When two contributory events occur, they cannot be handled, and a double-fault exception is generated.

If a benign or contributory exception is followed by a page fault, the two events can be handled in succession. This is also true if a page fault is followed by a benign exception. However if a page fault is followed by a contributory exception or another page fault, a double-fault abort is generated.

The processor always pushes an error code onto the stack of the double-fault handler; however, the error code is always 0. The faulting instruction may not be restarted. If any other exception occurs while attempting to call the double-fault handler, the processor enters shutdown mode. This mode is similar to the state following execution of a HLT instruction. No instructions are executed until an NMI interrupt or a RESET signal is received. The processor generates a special bus cycle to indicate it has entered shutdown mode.

9.9.9 Interrupt 9 – Coprocessor Segment Overrun

The coprocessor-segment overrun abort is generated if the middle portion of a coprocessor operand is protected or not-present. This exception can be avoided. See Chapter 11 for more information about the coprocessor interface.

9.9.10 Interrupt 10 – Invalid TSS

An invalid-TSS fault is generated if a task switch to a segment with an invalid TSS is attempted. A TSS is invalid in the cases shown in Table 9-4. An error code is pushed

Table 9-4. Invalid TSS Conditions

Error Code Index	Description
TSS segment	TSS segment limit less than 67H
LDT segment	Invalid LDT or LDT not present
Stack segment	Stack segment selector exceeds descriptor table limit
Stack segment	Stack segment is not writable
Stack segment	Stack segment DPL not compatible with CPL
Stack segment	Stack segment selector RPL not compatible with CPL
Code segment	Code segment selector exceeds descriptor table limit
Code segment	Code segment is not executable
Code segment	Non-conforming code segment DPL not equal to CPL
Code segment	Conforming code segment DPL greater than CPL
Data segment	Data segment selector exceeds descriptor table limit
Data segment	Data segment not readable

onto the stack of the exception handler to help identify the cause of the fault. The EXT bit indicates whether the exception was caused by a condition outside the control of the program (e.g., if an external interrupt using a task gate attempted a task switch to an invalid TSS).

This fault can occur either in the context of the original task or in the context of the new task. Until the processor has completely verified the presence of the new TSS, the exception occurs in the context of the original task. Once the existence of the new TSS is verified, the task switch is considered complete; i.e., the TR register is loaded with a selector for the new TSS and, if the switch is due to a CALL or interrupt, the Link field of the new TSS references the old TSS. Any errors discovered by the processor after this point are handled in the context of the new task.

To ensure a TSS is available to process the exception, the handler for an invalid-TSS exception must be a task called using a task gate.

9.9.11 Interrupt 11 – Segment Not Present

The segment-not-present fault is generated when the processor detects that the present bit of a descriptor is clear. The processor can generate this fault in any of these cases:

- While attempting to load the CS, DS, ES, FS, or GS registers; loading the SS register, however, causes a stack fault.
- While attempting to load the LDT register using an LLDT instruction; loading the LDT register during a task switch operation, however, causes an invalid-TSS exception.
- While attempting to use a gate descriptor which is marked segment-not-present.

This fault is restartable. If the exception handler loads the segment and returns, the interrupted program resumes execution.

If a segment-not-present exception occurs during a task switch, not all the steps of the task switch are complete. During a task switch, the processor first loads all the segment registers, then checks their contents for validity. If a segment-not-present exception is discovered, the remaining segment registers have not been checked and therefore may not be usable for referencing memory. The segment-not-present handler should not rely on being able to use the segment selectors found in the CS, SS, DS, ES, FS, and GS registers without causing another exception. The exception handler should check all segment registers before trying to resume the new task; otherwise, general protection faults may result later under conditions which make diagnosis more difficult. There are three ways to handle this case:

1. Handle the segment-not-present fault with a task. The task switch back to the interrupted task causes the processor to check the registers as it loads them from the TSS.

2. Use the PUSH and POP instructions on all segment registers. Each POP instruction causes the processor to check the new contents of the segment register.

3. Check the saved contents of each segment register in the TSS, simulating the test which the processor makes when it loads a segment register.

This exception pushes an error code onto the stack. The EXT bit of the error code is set if an event external to the program caused an interrupt which subsequently referenced a not-present segment. The IDT bit is set if the error code refers to an IDT entry (e.g., an INT instruction referencing a not-present gate).

An operating system typically uses the segment-not-present exception to implement virtual memory at the segment level. A not-present indication in a gate descriptor, however, usually does not indicate that a segment is not present (because gates do not necessarily correspond to segments). Not-present gates may be used by an operating system to trigger exceptions of special significance to the operating system.

9.9.12 Interrupt 12—Stack Exception

A stack fault is generated under two conditions:

- As a result of a limit violation in any operation which refers to the SS register. This includes stack-oriented instructions such as POP, PUSH, ENTER, and LEAVE, as well as other memory references which implicitly use the stack (for example, MOV AX, [BP+6]). The ENTER instruction generates this exception when there is too little space for allocating local variables.

- When attempting to load the SS register with a descriptor which is marked segment-not-present but is otherwise valid. This can occur in a task switch, a CALL instruction to a different privilege level, a return to a different privilege level, an LSS instruction, or a MOV or POP instruction to the SS register.

When the processor detects a stack exception, it pushes an error code onto the stack of the exception handler. If the exception is due to a not-present stack segment or to overflow of the new stack during an interlevel CALL, the error code contains a selector to the segment which caused the exception (the exception handler can test the present bit in the descriptor to determine which exception occurred); otherwise, the error code is 0.

An instruction generating this fault is restartable in all cases. The return address pushed onto the exception handler's stack points to the instruction which needs to be restarted. This instruction usually is the one which caused the exception; however, in the case of a stack exception from loading a not-present stack-segment descriptor during a task switch, the indicated instruction is the first instruction of the new task.

When a stack exception occurs during a task switch, the segment registers may not be usable for addressing memory. During a task switch, the selector values are loaded before the descriptors are checked. If a stack exception is generated, the remaining segment registers have not been checked and may cause exceptions if they are used. The stack fault handler should not expect to use the segment selectors found in the CS, SS, DS, ES, FS, and GS registers without causing another exception. The exception handler should check all segment registers before trying to resume the new task; otherwise, general protection faults may result later under conditions where diagnosis is more difficult.

9.9.13 Interrupt 13—General Protection

All protection violations which do not cause another exception cause a general-protection exception. This includes (but is not limited to):

- Exceeding the segment limit when using the CS, DS, ES, FS, or GS segments.
- Exceeding the segment limit when referencing a descriptor table.
- Transferring execution to a segment which is not executable.
- Writing to a read-only data segment or a code segment.
- Reading from an execute-only code segment.
- Loading the SS register with a selector for a read-only segment (unless the selector comes from a TSS during a task switch, in which case an invalid-TSS exception occurs).
- Loading the SS, DS, ES, FS, or GS register with a selector for a system segment.
- Loading the DS, ES, FS, or GS register with a selector for an execute-only code segment.
- Loading the SS register with the selector of an executable segment.
- Accessing memory using the DS, ES, FS, or GS register when it contains a null selector.
- Switching to a busy task.
- Violating privilege rules.

- Exceeding the instruction length limit of 15 bytes (this only can occur when redundant prefixes are placed before an instruction).
- Loading the CR0 register with a set PG bit (paging enabled) and a clear PE bit (protection disabled).
- Interrupt or exception through an interrupt or trap gate from virtual-8086 mode to a handler at a privilege level other than 0.

The general-protection exception is a fault. In response to a general-protection exception, the processor pushes an error code onto the exception handler's stack. If loading a descriptor causes the exception, the error code contains a selector to the descriptor; otherwise, the error code is null. The source of the selector in an error code may be any of the following:

1. An operand of the instruction.
2. A selector from a gate which is the operand of the instruction.
3. A selector from a TSS involved in a task switch.

9.9.14 Interrupt 14 – Page Fault

A page fault occurs when paging is enabled (the PG bit in the CR0 register is set) and the processor detects one of the following conditions while translating a linear address to a physical address:

- The page-directory or page-table entry needed for the address translation has a clear Present bit, which indicates that a page table or the page containing the operand is not present in physical memory.
- The procedure does not have sufficient privilege to access the indicated page.

The processor provides the page fault handler two items of information which aid in diagnosing the exception and recovering from it:

- An error code on the stack. The error code for a page fault has a format different from that for other exceptions (see Figure 9-7). The error code tells the exception handler three things:
    1. Whether the exception was due to a not-present page or to an access rights violation.
    2. Whether the processor was executing at user or supervisor level at the time of the exception.
    3. Whether the memory access which caused the exception was a read or write.
- The contents of the CR2 register. The processor loads the CR2 register with the 32-bit linear address which generated the exception. The exception handler can use this address to locate the corresponding page directory and page table entries. If another page fault can occur during execution of the page fault handler, the handler should push the contents of the CR2 register onto the stack.

Field	Value	Description
U/S	0	The access causing the fault originated when the processor was executing in supervisor mode.
	1	The access causing the fault originated when the processor was executing in user mode.
W/R	0	The access causing the fault was a read.
	1	The access causing the fault was a write.
P	0	The fault was caused by a not-present page.
	1	The fault was caused by a page-level protection violation.

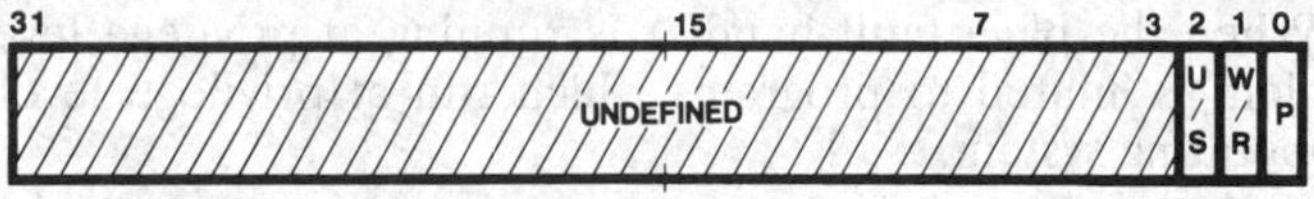

31–3	2	1	0
UNDEFINED	U/S	W/R	P

240331i

Figure 9-7. Page Fault Error Code

9.9.14.1 PAGE FAULT DURING TASK SWITCH

These operations during a task switch cause access to memory:

1. Write the state of the original task in the TSS of that task.
2. Read the GDT to locate the TSS descriptor of the new task.
3. Read the TSS of the new task to check the types of segment descriptors from the TSS.
4. May read the LDT of the new task in order to verify the segment registers stored in the new TSS.

A page fault can result from accessing any of these operations. In the last two cases the exception occurs in the context of the new task. The instruction pointer refers to the next instruction of the new task, not to the instruction which caused the task switch (or the last instruction to be executed, in the case of an interrupt). If the design of the operating system permits page faults to occur during task-switches, the page-fault handler should be called through a task gate.

9.9.14.2 PAGE FAULT WITH INCONSISTENT STACK POINTER

Special care should be taken to ensure that a page fault does not cause the processor to use an invalid stack pointer (SS:ESP). Software written for Intel® 16-bit processors often uses a pair of instructions to change to a new stack; for example:

```
MOV SS, AX
MOV SP, StackTop
```

With the 386 DX microprocessor, because the second instruction accesses memory, it is possible to get a page fault after the selector in the SS segment register has been changed but before the contents of the SP register have received the corresponding change. At this point, the two parts of the stack pointer SS:SP (or, for 32-bit programs, SS:ESP) are inconsistent. The new stack segment is being used with the old stack pointer.

The processor does not use the inconsistent stack pointer if the handling of the page fault causes a stack switch to a well defined stack (i.e., the handler is a task or a more privileged procedure). However, if the page fault handler is called by a trap or interrupt gate and the page fault occurs at the same privilege level as the page fault handler, the processor will attempt to use the stack indicated by the inconsistent stack pointer.

In systems which use paging and handle page faults within the faulting task (with trap or interrupt gates), software executing at the same privilege level as the page fault handler should initialize a new stack by using the LSS instruction rather than an instruction pair shown above. When the page fault handler is running at privilege level 0 (the normal case), the problem is limited to programs which run at privilege level 0, typically the kernel of the operating system.

9.9.15 Interrupt 16 — Coprocessor Error

A coprocessor-error fault is generated when the processor detects a signal from the 387™ DX numerics coprocessor on the ERROR# pin. If the EM bit of the CR0 register is clear (no emulation), the processor tests this pin at the beginning of certain ESC instructions or when it executes a WAIT instruction. See Chapter 11 for more information on the coprocessor interface.

9.10 EXCEPTION SUMMARY

Table 9-5 summarizes the exceptions recognized by the 386 DX microprocessor.

Table 9-5. Exception Summary

Description	Vector Number	Return Address Points to Faulting Instruction?	Exception Type	Source of the Exception
Division by Zero	0	Yes	FAULT	DIV and IDIV instructions
Debug Exceptions	1	[1]	[1]	Any code or data reference
Breakpoint	3	No	TRAP	INT 3 instruction
Overflow	4	No	TRAP	INTO instruction
Bounds Check	5	Yes	FAULT	BOUND instruction
Invalid Opcode	6	Yes	FAULT	Reserved Opcodes
Coprocessor Not Available	7	Yes	FAULT	ESC and WAIT instructions
Double Fault	8	Yes	ABORT	Any instruction
Coprocessor Segment Overrun	9	No	ABORT	ESC instructions
Invalid TSS	10	Yes	FAULT[2]	JMP, CALL, IRET instructions, interrupts, and exceptions
Segment Not Present	11	Yes	FAULT	Any instruction which changes segments
Stack Fault	12	Yes	FAULT	Stack operations
General Protection	13	Yes	FAULT/TRAP[3]	Any code or data reference
Page Fault	14	Yes	FAULT	Any code or data reference
Coprocessor Error	16	Yes	FAULT[4]	ESC and WAIT instructions
Software Interrupt	0 to 255	No	TRAP	INT n instructions

1. Debug exceptions are either traps or faults. The exception handler can distinguish between traps and faults by examining the contents of the DR6 register.
2. An invalid-TSS exception cannot be restarted if it occurs within a handler.
3. All general-protection faults are restartable. If the fault occurs while attempting to call the handler, the interrupted program is restartable, but the interrupt may be lost.
4. Coprocessor errors are not reported until the first ESC or WAIT instruction following the ESC instruction which generated the error.

Initialization 10

CHAPTER 10
INITIALIZATION

The 386™ DX microprocessor has an input, called the RESET# pin, which invokes reset initialization. After asserting the signal on the RESET# pin, some registers of the 386 DX microprocessor are set to known states. These known states, such as the contents of the EIP register, are sufficient to allow software to begin execution. Software then can build the data structures in memory, such as the GDT and IDT tables, which are used by system and application software.

Hardware asserts the RESET# signal at power-up. Hardware may assert this signal at other times. For example, a button may be provided for manually invoking reset initialization. Reset also may be the response of hardware to receiving a halt or shutdown indication.

After reset initialization, the DH register holds a number which identifies the processor type. Binary object code can be made compatible with other Intel® processors by using this number to select the correct initialization software. Note the 386 DX microprocessor has several processing modes. It begins execution in a mode which emulates an 8086 processor, called real-address mode. If protected mode is to be used (the mode in which the 32-bit instruction set is available), the initialization software changes the setting of a mode bit in the CR0 register.

10.1 PROCESSOR STATE AFTER RESET

A self-test may be requested at power-up. The self-test is requested by asserting the signal on the BUSY# pin during the falling edge of the RESET# signal. It is the responsibility of the hardware designer to provide the request for self-test, if desired. Reset initialization takes 350 to 450 CLK2 clock periods. If the self-test is selected, it takes about 2^{20} clock periods (Intel reserves the right to change the exact number of periods without notification). For a 16 MHz processor, this takes about 33 milliseconds. (Note that chips are graded by their CLK frequency, which is half the frequency of CLK2.)

The EAX register is clear if the 386 DX microprocessor passed the test. A non-zero value in the EAX register after self-test indicates the processor is faulty. If the self-test is not requested, the contents of the EAX register after reset initialization are undefined (possibly non-zero). The DX register holds a component identifier and revision number after reset initialization, as shown in Figure 10-1. The DH register contains the value 3, which indicates a 386 DX microprocessor. The DL register contains a unique identifier of the revision level.

The state of the CR0 register following power-up is shown in Figure 10-2. These states put the processor into real-address mode with paging disabled.

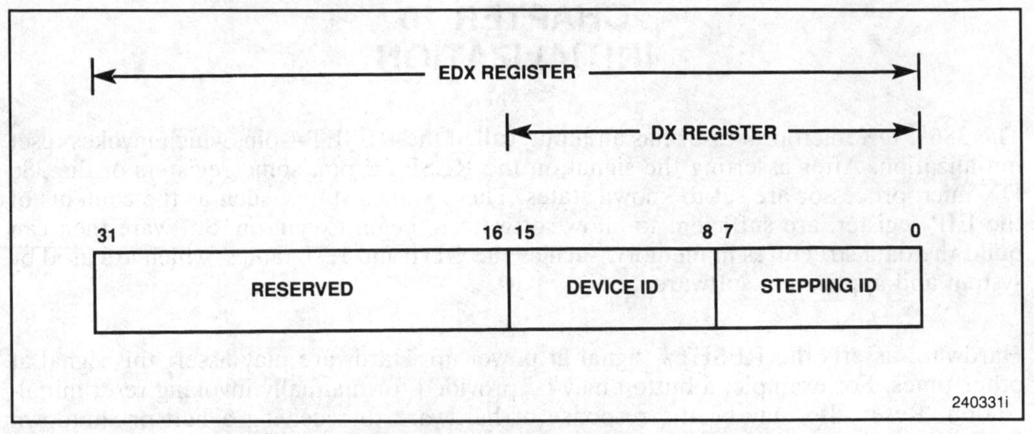

Figure 10-1. Contents of the EDX Register after Reset

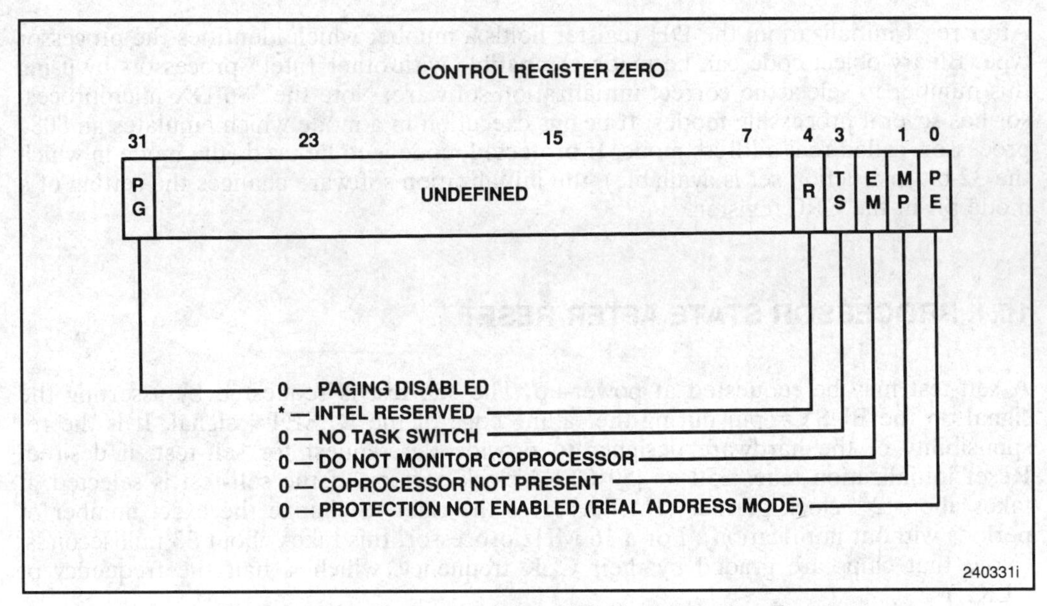

Figure 10-2. Contents of the CR0 Register after Reset

The state of the EBX, ECX, ESI, EDI, EBP, ESP, GDTR, LDTR, TR, and debug registers is undefined following power-up. Software should not depend on any undefined states. The state of the flags and other registers following power-up is shown in Table 10-1.

Note that the invisible parts of the CS and DS segment registers are initialized to values which allow execution to begin, even though segments have not been defined. The base address for the code segment is set to 64K below the top of the physical address space, which allows room for a ROM to hold the initialization software. The base address for the data segments are set to the bottom of the physical address space (address 0), where

Table 10-1. Processor State Following Power-Up

Register	State (hexadecimal)
EFLAGS	XXXX0002H[1]
EIP	0000FFF0H
CS	0F000H[2]
DS	0000H[3]
SS	0000H
ES	0000H[3]
PS	0000H
GS	0000H
IDTR (base)	00000000H
IDTR (limit)	03FFH
DR7	0000H

1. The high fourteen bits of the EFLAGS register are undefined following power-up. All of the flags are clear.
2. The invisible part of the CS register holds a base address of 0FFFF0000H and a limit of 0FFFFH.
3. The invisible parts of the DS and ES registers hold a base address of 0 and a limit of 0FFFFH.

RAM is expected to be. To preserve these addresses, no instruction which loads the segment registers should be executed until a descriptor table has been defined and its base address and limit have been loaded into the GDTR register.

10.2 SOFTWARE INITIALIZATION IN REAL-ADDRESS MODE

After reset initialization, software sets up data structures needed for the processor to perform basic system functions, such as handling interrupts. If the processor remains in real-address mode, software sets up data structures in the form used by the 8086 processor. If the processor is going to operate in protected mode, software sets up data structures in the form used by the 80286 and 386 DX microprocessors, then switches modes.

10.2.1 System Tables

In real-address mode, no descriptor tables are used. The interrupt vector table, which starts at address 0, needs to be loaded with pointers to exception and interrupt handlers before interrupts can be enabled. The NMI interrupt is always enabled. If the interrupt vector table and the NMI interrupt handler need to be loaded into RAM, there will be a period of time following reset initialization when an NMI interrupt cannot be handled.

10.2.2 NMI Interrupt

Hardware must provide a mechanism to prevent an NMI interrupt from being generated while software is unable to handle it. For example, the interrupt vector table and NMI interrupt handler can be provided in ROM. This allows an NMI interrupt to be handled immediately after reset initialization. Another solution would be to provide a mechanism which passes the NMI signal through an AND gate controlled by a bit in an I/O port.

Hardware can clear the bit when the processor is reset, and software can set the bit when it is ready to handle NMI interrupts. System software designers should be aware of the mechanism used by hardware to protect software from NMI interrupts following reset.

10.2.3 First Instruction

Execution begins with the instruction addressed by the initial contents of the CS and IP registers. To allow the initialization software to be placed in a ROM at the top of the address space, the high 12 bits of addresses issued for the code segment are set, until the first instruction which loads the CS register, such as a far jump or call. As a result, instruction fetching begins from address 0FFFFFFF0H. Because the size of the ROM is unknown, the first instruction is intended to be a jump to the beginning of the initialization software. Only near jumps may be performed within the ROM-based software. After a far jump is executed, addresses issued for the code segment are clear in their high 12 bits.

10.3 SWITCHING TO PROTECTED MODE

Before switching to protected mode, a minimum set of system data structures must be created, and a minimum number of registers must be initialized.

10.3.1 System Tables

To allow protected mode software to access programs and data, at least one descriptor table, the GDT, and two descriptors must be created. Descriptors are needed for a code segment and a data segment. The stack can be be placed in a normal read/write data segment, so no descriptor for the stack is required. Before the GDT can be used, the base address and limit for the GDT must be loaded into the GDTR register using an LGDT instruction.

10.3.2 NMI Interrupt

If hardware allows NMI interrupts to be generated, the IDT and a gate for the NMI interrupt handler need to be created. Before the IDT can be used, the base address and limit for the IDT must be loaded into the IDTR register using an LIDT instruction.

10.3.3 PE Bit

Protected mode is entered by setting the PE bit in the CR0 register. Either an LMSW or MOV CR0 instruction may be used to set this bit (the MSW register is part of the CR0 register). (Note: When writing to CR0, do not alter the value of undefined bits. Read CR0, change bits necessary and then write CR0.) Because the processor overlaps the interpretation of several instructions, it is necessary to discard the instructions which already have been read into the processor. A JMP instruction immediately after the LMSW instruction changes the flow of execution, so it has the effect of emptying the processor of instructions which have been fetched or decoded.

After entering protected mode, the segment registers continue to hold the contents they had in real-address mode. Software should reload all the segment registers. Execution in protected mode begins with a CPL of 0.

10.4 SOFTWARE INITIALIZATION IN PROTECTED MODE

The data structures needed in protected mode are determined by the memory-management features which are used. The processor supports segmentation models which range from a single, uniform address space (flat model) to a highly structured model with several independent, protected address spaces for each task (multisegmented model). Paging can be enabled for allowing access to large data structures which are partly in memory and partly on disk. Both of these forms of address translation require data structures which are set up by the operating system and used by the memory-management hardware.

10.4.1 Segmentation

A flat model without paging only requires a GDT with one code and one data segment descriptor. A flat model with paging requires code and data descriptors for supervisor mode and another set of code and data descriptors for user mode. In addition, it requires a page directory and at least one second-level page table.

A multisegmented model may require additional segments for the operating system, as well as segments and LDTs for each application program. LDTs require segment descriptors in the GDT. Most operating systems, such as OS/2, allocate new segments and LDTs as they are needed. This provides maximum flexibility for handling a dynamic programming environment, such as an engineering workstation. An embedded system, such as a process controller, might pre-allocate a fixed number of segments and LDTs for a fixed number of application programs. This would be a simple and efficient way to structure the software environment of a system which requires fast real-time performance.

10.4.2 Paging

Unlike segmentation, paging is controlled by a mode bit. If the PG bit in the CR0 register is clear (its state following reset initialization), the paging mechanism is completely absent from the processor architecture seen by programmers.

If the PG bit is set, paging is enabled. The bit may be set using a MOV CR0 instruction. Before setting the PG bit, the following conditions must be true:

- Software has created at least two page tables, the page directory and at least one second-level page table.

- The PDBR register (same as the CR3 register) is loaded with the base address of the page directory.
- The processor is in protected mode (paging is not available in real-address mode). If all other restrictions are met, the PG and PE bits can be set at the same time.

As with the PE bit, setting the PG bit must be followed immediately with a JMP instruction. (Alternatively, the code which sets the PG bit can come from a page which has the same physical address after paging is enabled.)

10.4.3 Tasks

If the multitasking mechanism is not used, it is unnecessary to initialize the TR register.

If the multitasking mechanism is used, a TSS and a TSS descriptor for the initialization software must be created. TSS descriptors must not be marked as busy when they are created; TSS descriptors should be marked as busy only as a side-effect of performing a task switch. As with descriptors for LDTs, TSS descriptors reside in the GDT. The LTR instruction is used to load a selector for the TSS descriptor of the initialization software into the TR register. This instruction marks the TSS descriptor as busy, but does not perform a task switch. The selector must be loaded before performing the first task switch, because a task switch copies the current task state into the TSS. After the LTR instruction has been used, further operations on the TR register are performed by task switching. As with segments and LDTs, TSSs and TSS descriptors can be either preallocated or allocated as needed.

10.5 TLB TESTING

The 386 DX microprocessor provides a mechanism for testing the translation lookaside buffer (TLB), the cache used for translating linear addresses to physical addresses. Although failure of the TLB hardware is extremely unlikely, users may wish to include TLB confidence tests among other power-up tests for the 386 DX microprocessor.

NOTE

This TLB testing mechanism is unique to the 386 DX microprocessor and may not be continued in the same way in future processors. Software which uses this mechanism may be incompatible with future processors.

When testing the TLB, turn off paging to avoid interference with the test data written to the TLB.

10.5.1 Structure of the TLB

The TLB is a four-way set-associative memory. Figure 10-3 illustrates the structure of the TLB. There are four sets of eight entries each. Each entry consists of a tag and data. Tags are 24 bits wide. They contain the high-order 20 bits of the linear address, the valid bit, and three attribute bits. The data portion of each entry contains the upper 12 bits of the physical address.

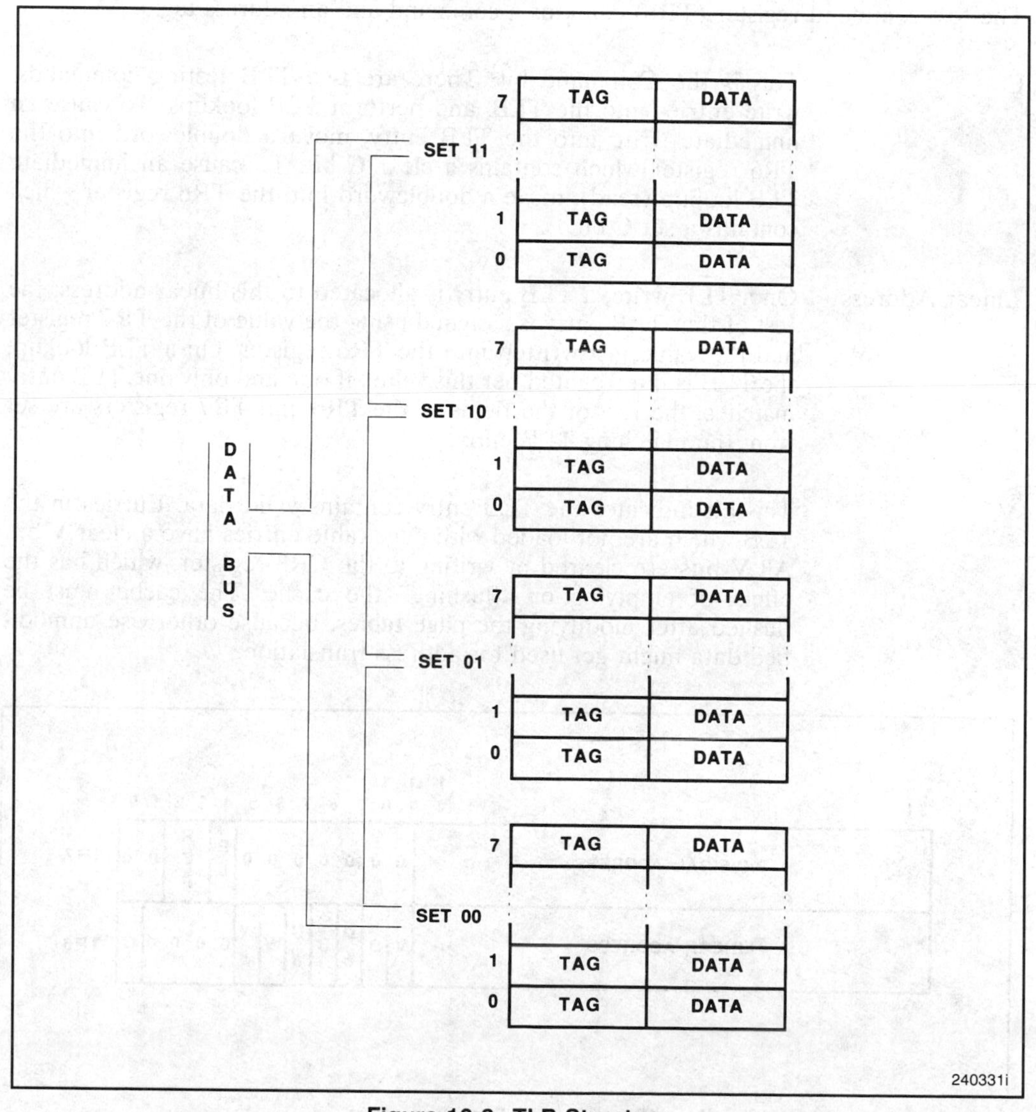

Figure 10-3. TLB Structure

10.5.2 Test Registers

Two test registers, shown in Figure 10-4, are provided for the purpose of testing. The TR6 register is the test command register, and the TR7 register is the test data register. These registers are accessed by variants of the MOV instruction. The MOV instructions are defined in both real-address mode and protected mode. The test registers are privileged resources; in protected mode, the MOV instructions which access them can be executed only at privilege level 0 (most privileged). An attempt to read or write the test registers from any other privilege level causes a general-protection exception.

The test command register (TR6) contains a command and an address tag:

C — This is the Command bit. There are two TLB testing commands: write entries into the TLB, and perform TLB lookups. To cause an immediate write into the TLB entry, move a doubleword into the TR6 register which contains a clear C bit. To cause an immediate TLB lookup (read), move a doubleword into the TR6 register which contains a set C bit.

Linear Address — On a TLB write, a TLB entry is allocated to this linear address; the rest of that TLB entry is assigned using the value of the TR7 register and the value just written into the TR6 register. On a TLB lookup, the TLB is interrogated per this value; if one and only one TLB entry matches, the rest of the fields of the TR6 and TR7 registers are set from the matching TLB entry.

V — This bit indicates the TLB entry contains valid data. Entries in the TLB which are not loaded with page table entries have a clear V bit. All V bits are cleared by writing to the CR3 register, which has the effect of emptying or "flushing" the cache. The cache must be flushed after modifying the page tables, because otherwise unmodified data might get used for address translation.

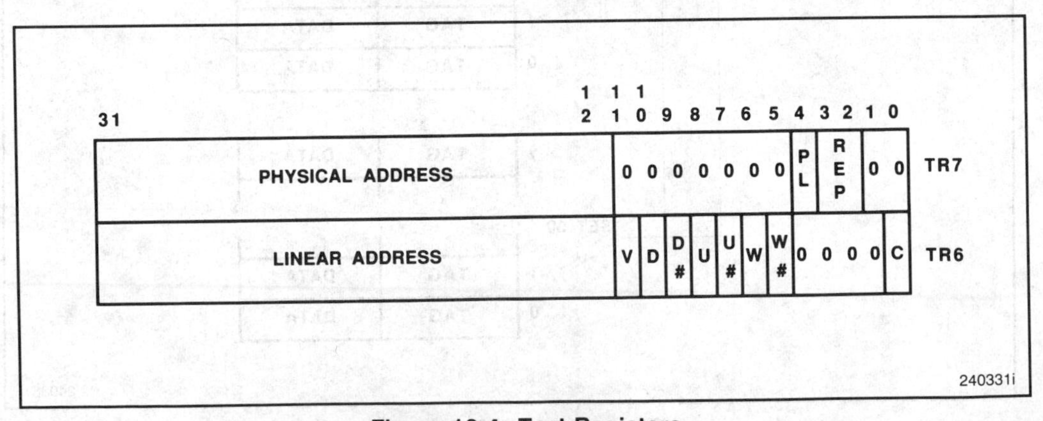

Figure 10-4. Test Registers

D, D# The D bit (and its complement).

U, U# The U/S bit (and its complement).

W, W# The R/W bit (and its complement).

The meaning of these pairs of bits is given in Table 10-2.

The test data register (TR7) holds data read from or data to be written to the TLB.

Physical Address This is the data field of the TLB. On a write to the TLB, the TLB entry allocated to the linear address in the TR6 register is set to this value. On a TLB lookup (read), the data field (physical address) from the TLB is loaded into this field.

PL On a TLB write, a set PL bit causes the REP field of the TR7 register to be used for selecting which of four associative blocks of the TLB entry is loaded. If the PL bit is clear, the internal pointer of the paging unit is used to select the block. On a TLB lookup (read), the PL bit indicates whether the read was a hit (the PL bit is set) or a miss (the PL bit is clear).

REP For a TLB write, selects which of four associative blocks of the TLB is to be written. For a TLB read, if the PL bit is set, REP reports in which of the four associative blocks the tag was found; if the PL bit is clear, the contents of this field are undefined.

10.5.3 Test Operations

To write a TLB entry:

1. Move a doubleword to the TR7 register which contains the desired physical address, PL, and REP values. The PL bit must be set. The REP field must point to the associative block in which to place the entry.
2. Move a doubleword to the TR6 register which contains the appropriate linear address, and values for the V, D, U, and W bits. The C bit must be set.

Do not write duplicate tags; the results of doing so are undefined.

Table 10-2. Meaning of Bit Pairs in the TR6 Register

Bit	Bit#	Effect during TLB Lookup	Value after TLB Write
0	0	Miss all	Bit is undefined
0	1	Match if the bit is clear	Bit is clear
1	0	Match if the bit is clear	Bit is set
1	1	Match all	Bit is undefined

To lookup (read) a TLB entry:

1. Move a doubleword to the TR6 register which contains the appropriate linear address and attributes. The C bit must be set.
2. Read the TR7 register. If the PL bit in the TR7 register is set, then the rest of the register contents report the TLB contents. If the PL bit is clear, then the other values in the TR7 register are indeterminate.

For the purposes of testing, the V bit functions as another bit of addresss. The V bit for a lookup request should usually be set, so that uninitialized tags do not match. Lookups with the V bit clear are unpredictable if any tags are unitialized.

10.6 INITIALIZATION EXAMPLE

```
; ***********************************************************************
;
; This is an example of startup code to put either 80386/80376
; into flat mode. All of memory is treated as simple, linear
; RAM. There are no interrupt routines. The Builder creates the
; GDT-alias and IDT-alias and places them, by default, in GDT[1]
; and GDT[2]. Other entries in the GDT are speicifed in the
; Build file. After initialization it jumps to a C startup
; routine. To use this template, change this jmp address to that
; of your code, or make the label of your code "c_startup".
;
; ***********************************************************************

NAME FLAT                 ; name of object module
EXTRN    c_startup:near ; this is the label jmped to after init

pe_flag        equ 1
data_sec       equ 20h    ; assume code is GDT[3], data GDT[4]

INIT_CODE    SEGMENT ER PUBLIC USE32     ; Segment base at 0ffffff80h

PUBLIC GDT_DESC

gdt_desc    dq  ?

PUBLIC    START

start:
    cld                         ; clear direction flag
    smsw bx                     ; check for processor (80376) at reset
    test bl,1                   ; use SMSW ratherthan MOV for speed
    jnz pestart
realstart:                      ; is an 80386 and in real mode
    db 66h                      ; force the next operand into 32-bit mode.
    mov eax,offset gdt_desc     ; move address of the GDT descriptor into eax
    xor ebx,ebx                 ; clear ebx
    mov bh,ah                   ; load 8 bits of address into bh
    mov bl,al                   ; load 8 bitsof address into bl
    db 67h
    db 66h                      ; use the 32-bit form of LGDT to load
    lgdt cs:[ebx]               ; the 32-bits of address into the GDTR
    smsw ax                     ; go into protected mode (set PE bit)
    or al,pe_flag               ; only change the PE bit, leave other bits unchanged
    lmsw ax
    jmp next                    ; flush prefetch queue
```

```
pestart:
    mov edx,eax
    mov ebx,offset gdt_desc
    xor eax,eax
    mov ax,bx                    ; lowerportion of address only
    lgdt cs:[eax]
    xor ebx,ebx                  ; initialize data selectors
    mov bl,data_selc             ; GDT[3]
    mov ds,bx
    mov ss,bx
    mov es,bx
    mov fs,bx
    mov gs,bx
    jmp pejump
next:
    xor ebx,ebx                  ; initialize data selectors
    mov bl,data_selc             ; GDT[3]
    mov ds,bx
    mov ss,bx
    mov es, bx
    mov fx,bx
    mov gs,bx
    db 66h                       ; forthe 80386, need to make a 32-bit jump
pejump:
    jmp far ptr c_startup        ; but the 80376 is already 32-bit.

    org 70h                      ; only if segment base is at0ffffff80h
    jmp short start
INIT_CODE ENDS
END
```

This code should be linked with the application for boot loadable code. The following code illustrates a dummy application.

```
$title("Example Startup Code,Copyright 1989, Intel Corporation")

        name    dummy_application;

data    segment rw publich use32

dontworry   db      8 dup (?)
behappy     db      4ah, 69h,6dh, 20h, 4bh, 26h, 52h

data    ends


code32  segment er public use32
        assume  ds:data, es:data

        public  int0,int1_3,int2,int4,int5,int6,int7,int8,int9
        public  int10,int11,int12,int13,int14,int16
        public  c_startup

data_vers   db  ' 5/3/89', ' Ver 1.00'
            db ' IntelCorporation '

c_startup:
        hlt

; ************************************************************************
;       Int0 routine
; ************************************************************************

int0    proc    far
        hlt
int0    endp
```

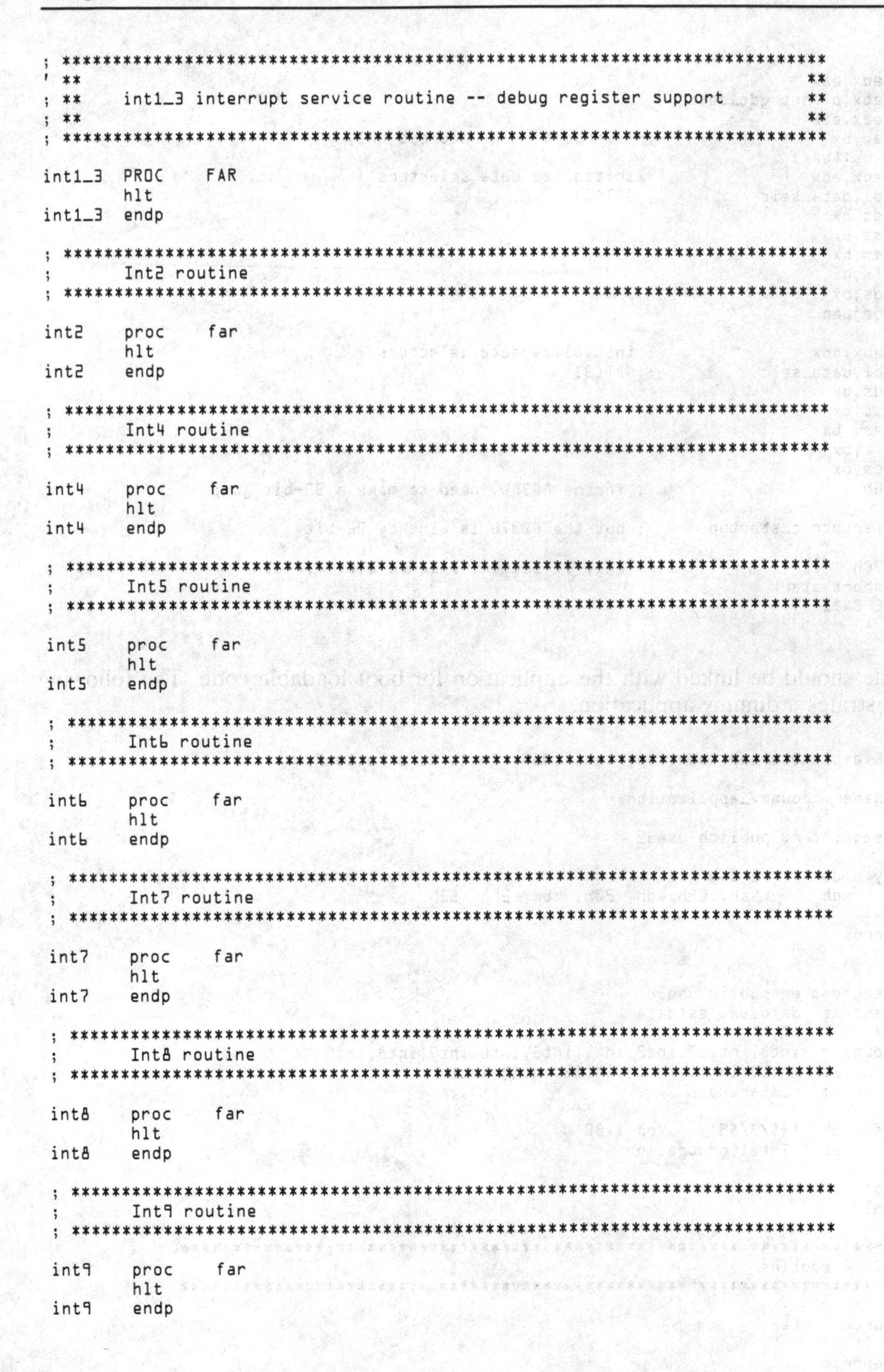

```
; **********************************************************************
' **                                                                  **
; **    int1_3 interrupt service routine -- debug register support    **
; **                                                                  **
; **********************************************************************

int1_3  PROC     FAR
        hlt
int1_3  endp

; **********************************************************************
;       Int2 routine
; **********************************************************************

int2    proc     far
        hlt
int2    endp

; **********************************************************************
;       Int4 routine
; **********************************************************************

int4    proc     far
        hlt
int4    endp

; **********************************************************************
;       Int5 routine
; **********************************************************************

int5    proc     far
        hlt
int5    endp

; **********************************************************************
;       Int6 routine
; **********************************************************************

int6    proc     far
        hlt
int6    endp

; **********************************************************************
;       Int7 routine
; **********************************************************************

int7    proc     far
        hlt
int7    endp

; **********************************************************************
;       Int8 routine
; **********************************************************************

int8    proc     far
        hlt
int8    endp

; **********************************************************************
;       Int9 routine
; **********************************************************************

int9    proc     far
        hlt
int9    endp
```

```
; ***********************************************************************
;        Int10 routine
; ***********************************************************************

int10    proc     far
         hlt
int10    endp

; ***********************************************************************
;        Int11 routine
; ***********************************************************************

int11    proc     far
         hlt
int11    endp

; ***********************************************************************
;        Int12 routine
; ***********************************************************************
int12    proc     far
         hlt
int12    endp

; ***********************************************************************
;        Get controlfrom interrupt 13
; ***********************************************************************

int13    proc     far
         hlt
int13    endp

; ***********************************************************************
;        Int14 routine
; ***********************************************************************

int14    proc     far
         hlt
int14    endp

; ***********************************************************************
;        Int16 routine
; ***********************************************************************

int16    proc     far
         hlt
int16    endp

code32   ends
         end
```

The following build file illustrates how to link these two pieces of code.

```
FLAT; -- build program id

SEGMENT
   *segments (dpl=0),                -- Give all user segments a DPL of 0.
   _phantom_code_ (dpl=0,ra),        -- These two segments are created by
   _phantom_data_ (dpl=0),           -- the builder when the FLAT control is used.
    init_code (base=0ffffff80h,ra), -- Put startup code at the reset vector
    code32 (base = 0ffffef00h,ra),
    data (base = 0h);
```

```
TASK
    MAIN_TASK                          -- Dummy initialized task segment
        (
        CODE = c_startup,              -- Entry point is main, which
                                       -- must be a public id.
        DPL = 0,                       -- Task privilege level is 0.
        DATA = DATA,                   -- Points to a segment that
                                       -- indicates initial DS value.
        STACKS = (DATA),               -- Segment id points to stack
                                       -- segment. Sets the intial SS:ESP.
        NO INTENABLED.                 -- Disable interrupts.
        PRESENT                        -- Present bit in TSS set to 1.
        );
GATE                                         -- Define intial interrupts/faults
     i0 (entry=int0, dpl=0, trap),           -- Divide by zero trap
     i1 (entry=int1_3,dpl=0, trap),          -- Debug/trap register support
     i2 (entry=int2, dpl=0, trap),           -- NMI interrupt
     i3 (entry=int1_3, dpl=0, trap),         -- interrupt 3 debug support
     i4 (entry=int4, dpl=0, trap),           -- Overflow Exception
     i5 (entry=int5, dpl=0, trap),           -- Bounds Check Exception
     i6 (entry=int6, dpl=0, trap),           -- Invalid Opcode Exception
     i7 (entry=int7, dpl=0, trap),           -- Coprocessor not avaiable
     i8 (entry=int8,dpl=0, trap),            -- Double fault
     i9 (entry=int9, dpl=0, trap),           -- Coprocessor Segment Overrun
     i10 (entry=int10, dpl=0, trap),         -- invalid TSS exception
     i11 (entry=int11, dpl=0, trap),         -- segmentnot present exception
     i12 (entry=int12, dpl=0, trap),         -- stack exception
     i13 (entry=int13, dpl=0, trap),         -- trap gate disables interrupts
     i14 (entry=int14, dpl=0, trap),         -- page fault
     i16 (entry=int16, dpl=0, trap),         -- coprocessor error
TABLE
    GDT                                   -- create GDT
        (LOCATION = GDT_DESC,             -- In a buffer starting at GDT_DESC[
                                          -- BLD386 places the GDT base and
                                          -- GDT limit values. Buffer must be
                                          -- 6 bytes long.The base and limit
                                          -- values are places in this buffer
                                          -- as two bytes of limit plus
                                          -- four bytes of basein the format
                                          -- required for use by the LGDT
                                          -- instruction.

        ENTRY = (3:_phantom_ocde_,              -- Explicitly place segment
                 4:_phantom_data_,              -- entries into the GDT
                 5:main_task
                 )
        ),

    IDT
        (BASE = 0ffff8000h,
         ENTRY=( 0:i0,
                 1:i1,
                 2:i2,
                 3:i3,
                 4:i4,
                 5:i5,
                 6:i6,
                 7:i7,
                 8:i8,
                 9:i9,
                10:i10,
                11:i11,
                12:i12,
                13:i13,
                14:i14,
                16:i16)
        ),
```

```
    dummyldt
        (ENTRY=( 1:code32,
                 2:data,
                 3:int_code)
        );

MEMORY
    (RANGE = (EPROM = ROM(0ffff8000h..0ffffffffh),
              DRAM = RAM(0..0ffffh)),
    ALLOCATE = (MAIN_TASK)));

END
```

The commands to assemble and build a boot loadable application named "init" are contained in the following batch file. "Init.asm" is the code to put the 386 CPU in flat mode and "startup.asm" is the dummy application code.

```
asm386 init.asm debug
asm386 startup.asm debug
bnd386 startup.obj,init.obj nolo debug oj (init.bnd)
bld386 init.bnd bf (init.bld) bl flat
map386 init
```

This batch file used version 3.0 of the Intel RLL utilities and Intel 386ASM assembler to assemble and build the code.

11 Coprocessing and Multiprocessing

CHAPTER 11
COPROCESSING AND MULTIPROCESSING

A common method of increasing system performance is to use multiple processors. The Intel386™ architecture supports two kinds of multiprocessing:

- An interface for specific, performance-enhancing processors called *coprocessors*. These processors extend the instruction set of the 386™ DX microprocessor to include groups of closely-related instructions which are executed, in parallel with the original instruction set, by dedicated hardware. These extensions include IEEE-format floating-point arithmetic and raster-scan computer graphics.
- An interface for other processors. Other processors could be an 80286 processor, another 386 DX microprocessor, or an 8086 or 8088 processor in a PC or workstation. Several 386 DX microprocessors could be in the same system to control multiple peripheral devices or to provide additional computational power.

11.1 COPROCESSING

The features of the Intel386 architecture which are the coprocessor interface include:

- ESC and WAIT instructions
- TS, EM, and MP bits of the CR0 register
- Coprocessor Exceptions

11.1.1 Software Recognition of the Numeric Coprocessor

Figure 11-1 shows an example of a recognition routine that determines whether or not a math coprocessor is present. This routine can be executed on any 386 DX, 386 SX, 80286 or 8086 microprocessor hardware configuration that has a coprocessor socket.

The example guards against the possibility of accidentally reading an expected value from a floating data bus when no numeric coprocessor is present. Data read from a floating bus is undefined. By expecting to read a specific bit pattern from the numeric coprocessor, the routine protects itself from the indeterminate state of the bus. The example also avoids depending on any values in reserved bits, thereby maintaining compatibility with future numerics coprocessors.

11.1.2 The ESC and WAIT Instructions

The 386 DX microprocessor interprets the bit pattern 11011 (binary) in the highest five bits of the first byte of an instruction as an opcode intended for a coprocessor. Instructions which start with this bit pattern are called ESCAPE or ESC instructions. The processor performs the following functions before sending these instructions to the coprocessor:

- Test the EM bit to determine whether coprocessor functions are to be emulated by software.

```
8086/87/88/186 MACRO ASSEMBLER   Test for presence of a Numerics Chip, Revision 1.0                    PAGE 1

DOS 3.20 (033-N) 8086/87/88/186 MACRO ASSEMBLER V2.0 ASSEMBLY OF MODULE TEST_NPX
OBJECT MODULE PLACED IN FINDNPX.OBJ

LOC  OBJ              LINE    SOURCE

                         1 +1 $title('Test for presence of a Numerics Chip, Revision 1.0')
                         2
                         3            name    Test_NPX
                         4
----                     5    stack   segment stack 'stack'
0000 (100                6            dw      100 dup (?)
     ????
     )
00C8 ????                7    sst     dw          ?
----                     8    stack   ends
                         9
                        10    data    segment public 'data'
----
0000 0000               11    temp    dw      0h
----                    12    data    ends
                        13
                        14    dgroup  group   data,stack
                        15    cgroup  group   code
                        16
----                    17    code    segment public 'code'
                        18            assume  cs:cgroup, ds:dgroup
                        19
0000                    20    start:
                        21    ;
                        22    ;       Look for an 8087, 80287, 387 SX or 387 DX NPX
                        23    ;       Note that we cannot execute WAIT on 8086/88 if no 8087 is present.
                        24    ;
0000                    25    test_npx:
0000 90DBE3             26            fninit                  ; Must use non-wait form
0003 BE0000        R    27            mov     si,offset dgroup:temp
0006 C7045A5A           28            mov     word ptr [si],5A5AH ; Initialize temp to non-zero value
000A 90DD3C             29            fnstsw  [si]            ; Must use non-wait form of fstsw
                        30                                    ; It is not necessary to use a WAIT instruction
                        31                                    ; after fnstsw or fnstcw. Do not use one here.
000D 803C00             32            cmp     byte ptr [si],0 ; See if correct status with zeroes was read
0010 752A               33            jne     no_npx          ; Jump if not a valid status word, meaning no NPX
                        34    ;
                        35    ;       Now see if ones can be correctly written from the control word.
                        36    ;
0012 90D93C             37            fnstcw  [si]            ; Look at the control word; do not use WAIT form
                        38                                    ; Do not use a WAIT instruction here!
0015 8B04               39            mov     ax,[si]         ; See if ones can be written by NPX
0017 253F10             40            and     ax,103fh        ; See if selected parts of control word look OK
001A 3D3F00             41            cmp     ax,3fh          ; Check that ones and zeroes were corretly read
001D 751D               42            jne     no_npx          ; Jump if no NPX is installed
                        43    ;
                        44    ;       Some numerics chip is installed. NPX instructions and WAIT are now safe.
                        45    ;       See if the NPX is an 8087, 80287, 387 SX or 387 DX
                        46    ;       This code is necessary if a denormal exception handler is used or the
                        47    ;       new 387 instructions will be used.
                        48    ;
001F 9BD9E8             49            fld1                    ; Must use default control word from FNINIT
0022 9BD9EE             50            fldz                    ; Form infinity
0025 9BDEF9             51            fdiv                    ; 8087/287 says + inf = -inf
0028 9BD9C0             52            fld     st              ; Form negative infinity
002B 9BD9E0             53            fchs                    ; 387 SX/DX says + inf <> -inf
002E 9BDED9             54            fcompp                  ; See if they are the same and remove them
0031 9BDD3C             55            fstsw   [si]            ; Look at status from FCOMPP
0034 8B04               56            mov     ax,[si]
0036 9E                 57            sahf                    ; See if the infinities matched
0037 7406               58            je      found_87_287    ; Jump if 8087/287 is present
                        59    ;
                        60    ;       A 387 SX/DX is present. If denormal exceptions are used for an 8087/287,
                        61    ;       they must be masked. The 387 SX/DX will automatically normalize denormal
                        62    ;       operands faster than an exception handler can.
                        63    ;
```

Figure 11-1. Software Routine to Recognize a Math Coprocessor

```
8086/87/88/186 MACRO ASSEMBLER   Test for presence of a Numerics Chip, Revision 1.0                  PAGE 2

LOC  OBJ                 LINE    SOURCE

0039 EB0790               64              jmp       found_387 SX_DX
003C                      65     no_npx:
                          66     ;        set up for no NPX
                          67     ;              ...
                          68     ;
003C EB0490               69              jmp exit
003F                      70     found_87_287:
                          71     ;        set up for 87/287
                          72     ;              ...
                          73     ;
003F EB0190               74              jmp exit
0042                      75     found_387 SX_DX
                          76     ;        set up for 387 SX/DX
                          77     ;              ...
                          78     ;
0042                      79     exit;
----                      80     code     ends
                          81     end      start,ds:dgroup,ss:dgroup:sst

ASSEMBLY COMPLETE, NO ERRORS FOUND
```

Figure 11-1. Software Routine to Recognize a Math Coprocessor (contd.)

- Test the TS bit to determine whether there has been a context switch since the last ESC instruction.
- For some ESC instructions, test the signal on the ERROR# pin to determine whether the coprocessor produced an error in the previous ESC instruction.

The WAIT instruction is not an ESC instruction, but it causes the processor to perform some of the tests which are performed for an ESC instruction. The processor performs the following actions for a WAIT instruction:

- Wait until the coprocessor no longer asserts the BUSY# pin.
- Test the signal on the ERROR# pin (after the signal on the BUSY# pin is deasserted). If the signal on the ERROR# pin is asserted, the 386 DX microprocessor generates the coprocessor-error exception, which indicates that the coprocessor produced an error in the previous ESC instruction.

The WAIT instruction can be used to generate a coprocessor-error exception if an error is pending from a previous ESC instruction.

11.1.3 The EM and MP Bits

The EM and MP bits of the CR0 register affect the operations which are performed in response to coprocessor instructions.

The EM bit determines whether coprocessor functions are to be emulated. If the EM bit is set when an ESC instruction is executed, the coprocessor-not-available exception is generated. The exception handler then can emulate the coprocessor instruction. This mechanism is used to create software which adapts to the hardware environment; installing a coprocessor for performance enhancement can be as simple as plugging in a chip.

The MP bit controls whether the processor monitors the signals from the coprocessor. This bit is an enabling signal for the hardware interface to the coprocessor. The MP bit affects the operations performed for the WAIT instruction. If the MP bit is set when a WAIT instruction is executed, then the TS bit is tested; otherwise, it is not. If the TS bit is set under these conditions, the coprocessor-not-available exception is generated.

The states of the EM and MP bits can be modified using a MOV instruction with the CR0 register as the destination operand. The states can be read using a MOV instruction with the CR0 register as the source operand. These forms of the MOV instruction can be executed only with privilege level 0 (most privileged).

11.1.4 The TS Bit

The TS bit of the CR0 register indicates that the context of the coprocessor does not match that of the task being run on the 386 DX microprocessor. The 386 DX microprocessor sets the TS bit each time it performs a task switch (whether triggered by software or by a hardware interrupt). If the TS bit is set while an ESC instruction is executed, a coprocessor-not-available exception is generated. The WAIT instruction also generates this exception, if both the TS and MP bits are set. This exception gives software the opportunity to switch the context of the coprocessor to correspond to the current task.

The CLTS instruction (legal only at privilege level 0) clears the TS bit.

11.1.5 Coprocessor Exceptions

Three exceptions are used by the coprocessor interface: interrupt 7 (coprocessor not available), interrupt 9 (coprocessor segment overrun), and interrupt 16 (coprocessor error).

11.1.5.1 INTERRUPT 7—COPROCESSOR NOT AVAILABLE

This exception occurs in either of two conditions:

- The processor executes an ESC instruction while the EM bit is set. In this case, the exception handler should emulate the instruction which caused the exception. The TS bit also may be set.
- The processor executes either the WAIT instruction or an ESC instruction when both the MP and TS bits are set. In this case, the exception handler should update the state of the coprocessor, if necessary.

11.1.5.2 INTERRUPT 9—COPROCESSOR SEGMENT OVERRUN

A coprocessor operand may cross the address limit. The address limit is the point at which the address space wraps around. For segments with 32-bit addressing, the address limit is 0FFFFFFFFH; for segments with 16-bit addressing, the address limit is 0FFFFH; for expand-down segments, the address limit is 0.

The processor checks only the first and last bytes of a coprocessor operand before performing an operation on the operand. If the first and last bytes of the operand are in the segment, but on different sides of the address limit, it is possible for the middle part of the operand to be in memory which is outside of the segment, write-protected, or not-present. For example, a 64-bit operand at address 0FFFCH in a segment with 16-bit addressing occupies the bytes from 0FFFCH to 0FFFFH and from 0 to 3. If the segment limit is set to 0FFFDH, the second, third, and fourth bytes of the operand are outside of the segment. If a new page starts at 0FFFDH, the second, third, and fourth bytes of the operand may be write-protected or not-present. Any of these cases will generate a coprocessor-segment-overrun exception.

The addresses of the failed numeric instruction and its operand may be lost; a FSTENV instruction does not return reliable numeric coprocessor state information. The coprocessor-segment-overrun exception should be handled by executing a FNINIT instruction (i.e., a FINIT instruction without a preceding WAIT instruction). The return address on the stack might not point to either the failed numeric instruction or the instruction following the failed numeric instruction. The failed numeric instruction is not restartable; however, the interrupted task may be restartable if it did not contain the failed numeric instruction.

For the 387™ DX math coprocessor, the address limit can be avoided by keeping coprocessor operands at least 108 bytes away from the limit (108 bytes is the largest number of bytes affected by a floating-point arithmetic instruction, the FSTORE instruction).

11.1.5.3 INTERRUPT 16—COPROCESSOR ERROR

The 387 DX math coprocessor can generate a coprocessor-error exception in response to six different exception conditions. If the exception condition is not masked by a bit in the control register of the coprocessor, it appears as a signal at the ERROR# input of the processor. The processor generates a coprocessor-error exception the next time the signal on the ERROR# input is sampled, which is only at the beginning of the next WAIT instruction or certain ESC instructions. If the exception is masked, the coprocessor handles the exception itself; it does not assert the signal on the ERROR# input in this case.

11.2 GENERAL-PURPOSE MULTIPROCESSING

The 386 DX microprocessor has the basic features needed to implement a general-purpose multiprocessing system. While the system architecture of multiprocessor systems varies greatly, they generally have a need for reliable communications with memory. A processor in the process of reading a segment descriptor, for example, should reject attempts to update the descriptor until the read operation is complete.

It also is necessary to have reliable communications with other processors. Bus masters need to exchange data in a reliable way. For example, a bit in memory may be shared by several bus masters for use as a signal that some resource, such as a peripheral device, is idle. A bus master may test this bit, see that the resource is free, and change the state of the bit. The state would indicate to other potential bus masters that the resource is in use. A problem could arise if another bus master reads the bit between the time the first bus master reads the bit and the time the state of the bit is changed. This condition would indicate to both potential bus masters that the resource is free. They may interfere with each other as they both attempt to use the resource. The processor prevents this problem through support of locked bus cycles; requests for control of the bus are ignored during locked cycles.

The 386 DX microprocessor protects the integrity of critical memory operations by asserting a signal called LOCK#. It is the responsibility of the hardware designer to use this signal for blocking memory access between processors when this signal is asserted.

The processor automatically asserts this signal for some critical memory operations. Software can specify which other memory operations also need to have this signal asserted.

The features of the general-purpose multiprocessing interface include:

- The LOCK# signal, which appears on a pin of the processor.
- The LOCK instruction prefix, which allows software to assert the LOCK# signal.
- Automatic assertion of the LOCK# signal; for some kinds of memory operations.

11.2.1 LOCK Prefix and the LOCK# Signal

The LOCK prefix and its bus signal only should be used to prevent other bus masters from interrupting a data movement operation. The LOCK prefix only may be used with the following 386 DX CPU instructions when they modify memory. An invalid-opcode exception results from using the LOCK prefix before any other instruction, or with these instructions when no write operation is made to memory (i.e., when the destination operand is in a register).

- Bit test and change: the BTS, BTR, and BTC instructions.
- Exchange: the XCHG instruction.
- One-operand arithmetic and logical: the INC, DEC, NOT, NEG instructions.
- Two-operand arithmetic and logical: the ADD, ADC, SUB, SBB, AND, OR, and XOR instructions.

A locked instruction is guaranteed to lock only the area of memory defined by the destination operand, but may lock a larger memory area. For example, typical 8086 and 80286 configurations lock the entire physical memory space.

Semaphores (shared memory used for signalling between multiple processors) should be accessed using identical address and length. For example, if one processor accesses a semaphore using word access, other processors should not access the semaphore using byte access.

The integrity of the lock is not affected by the alignment of the memory field. The LOCK# signal is asserted for as many bus cycles as necessary to update the entire operand.

11.2.2 Automatic Locking

There are some critical memory operations for which the processor automatically asserts the LOCK# signal. These operations are:

- Acknowledging interrupts.

  After an interrupt request, the interrupt controller uses the data bus to send the interrupt vector of the source of the interrupt to the processor. The processor asserts LOCK# to ensure no other data appears on the data bus during this time.

- Setting the Busy bit of a TSS descriptor.

  The processor tests and sets the Busy bit in the Type field of the TSS descriptor when switching to a task. To ensure two different processors do not switch to the same task simultaneously, the processor asserts the LOCK# signal while testing and setting this bit.

- Loading of segment descriptors.

  While copying the contents of a segment descriptor from a descriptor table to a segment register, the processor asserts LOCK# so the descriptor will not be modified by another processor while it is being loaded. For this action to be effective, operating-system procedures which update descriptors should use the following steps:

  - Use a locked operation when updating the access-rights byte to mark the descriptor not-present, and specify a value for the Type field which indicates the descriptor is being updated.
  - Update the fields of the descriptor. (This may require several memory accesses; therefore, LOCK cannot be used.)
  - Use a locked operation when updating the access-rights byte to mark the descriptor as valid and present.

- Executing an XCHG instruction.

  The 386 DX microprocessor always asserts LOCK# during an XCHG instruction which references memory (even if the LOCK prefix is not used).

11.2.3 Stale Data

Multiprocessor systems are subject to conditions under which updates to data in one processor are not applied to copies of the data in other processors. This can occur with the 386 DX microprocessor when segment descriptors are updated.

If multiple processors are sharing segment descriptors and one processor updates a segment descriptor, the other processors may retain old copies of the descriptor in the invisible part of their segment registers.

An interrupt sent from one processor to another can handle this problem. When one processor changes data which may be held in other processors, it can send an interrupt signal to them. If the interrupt is serviced by an interrupt task, the task switch automatically discards the data in the invisible part of the segment registers. When the task returns, the data is updated from the descriptor tables in memory.

In multiprocessor systems which need a cachability signal from the processor, it is recommended that physical address pin A31 be used to indicate cachability. Segment descriptors or page table entries may be used to control this bit from software. The system then can possess up to 2 gigabytes of physical memory (half the address space is sacrificed).

Debugging 12

CHAPTER 12
DEBUGGING

The 386™ DX microprocessor has advanced debugging facilities which are particularly important for sophisticated software systems, such as multitasking operating systems. The failure conditions for these software systems can be very complex and time-dependent. The debugging features of the 386 DX microprocessor give the system programmer valuable tools for looking at the dynamic state of the processor.

The debugging support is accessed through the debug registers. They hold the addresses of memory locations, called *breakpoints*, which invoke debugging software. An exception is generated when a memory operation is made to one of these addresses. A breakpoint is specified for a particular form of memory access, such as an instruction fetch or a doubleword write operation. The debug registers support both instruction breakpoints and data breakpoints.

With other processors, instruction breakpoints are set by replacing normal instructions with breakpoint instructions. When the breakpoint instruction is executed, the debugger is called. But with the debug registers of the 386 DX microprocessor, this is not necessary. By eliminating the need to write into the code space, the debugging process is simplified (there is no need to set up a data segment mapped to the same memory as the code segment) and breakpoints can be set in ROM-based software. In addition, breakpoints can be set on reads and writes to data which allows real-time monitoring of variables.

12.1 DEBUGGING SUPPORT

The features of the Intel386™ architecture which support debugging are:

Reserved debug interrupt vector

Specifies a procedure or task to be called when an event for the debugger occurs.

Debug address registers

Specifies the addresses of up to four breakpoints.

Debug control register

Specifies the forms of memory access for the breakpoints.

Debug status register

Reports conditions which were in effect at the time of the exception.

Trap bit of TSS (T-bit)

Generates a debug exception when an attempt is made to perform a task switch to a task with this bit set in its TSS.

Resume flag (RF)

Suppresses multiple exceptions to the same instruction.

Trap flag (TF)

Generates a debug exception after every execution of an instruction.

Breakpoint instruction

Calls the debugger (generates a debug exception). This instruction is an alternative way to set code breakpoints. It is especially useful when more than four breakpoints are desired, or when breakpoints are being placed in the source code.

Reserved interrupt vector for breakpoint exception

Calls a procedure or task when a breakpoint instruction is executed.

These features allow a debugger to be called either as a separate task or as a procedure in the context of the current task. The following conditions can be used to call the debugger:

- Task switch to a specific task.
- Execution of the breakpoint instruction.
- Execution of any instruction.
- Execution of an instruction at a specified address.
- Read or write of a byte, word, or doubleword at a specified address.
- Write to a byte, word, or doubleword at a specified address.
- Attempt to change the contents of a debug register.

12.2 DEBUG REGISTERS

Six registers are used to control debugging. These registers are accessed by forms of the MOV instruction. A debug register may be the source or destination operand for one of these instructions. The debug registers are privileged resources; the MOV instructions which access them may be executed only at privilege level 0. An attempt to read or write the debug registers from any other privilege level generates a general-protection exception. Figure 12-1 shows the format of the debug registers.

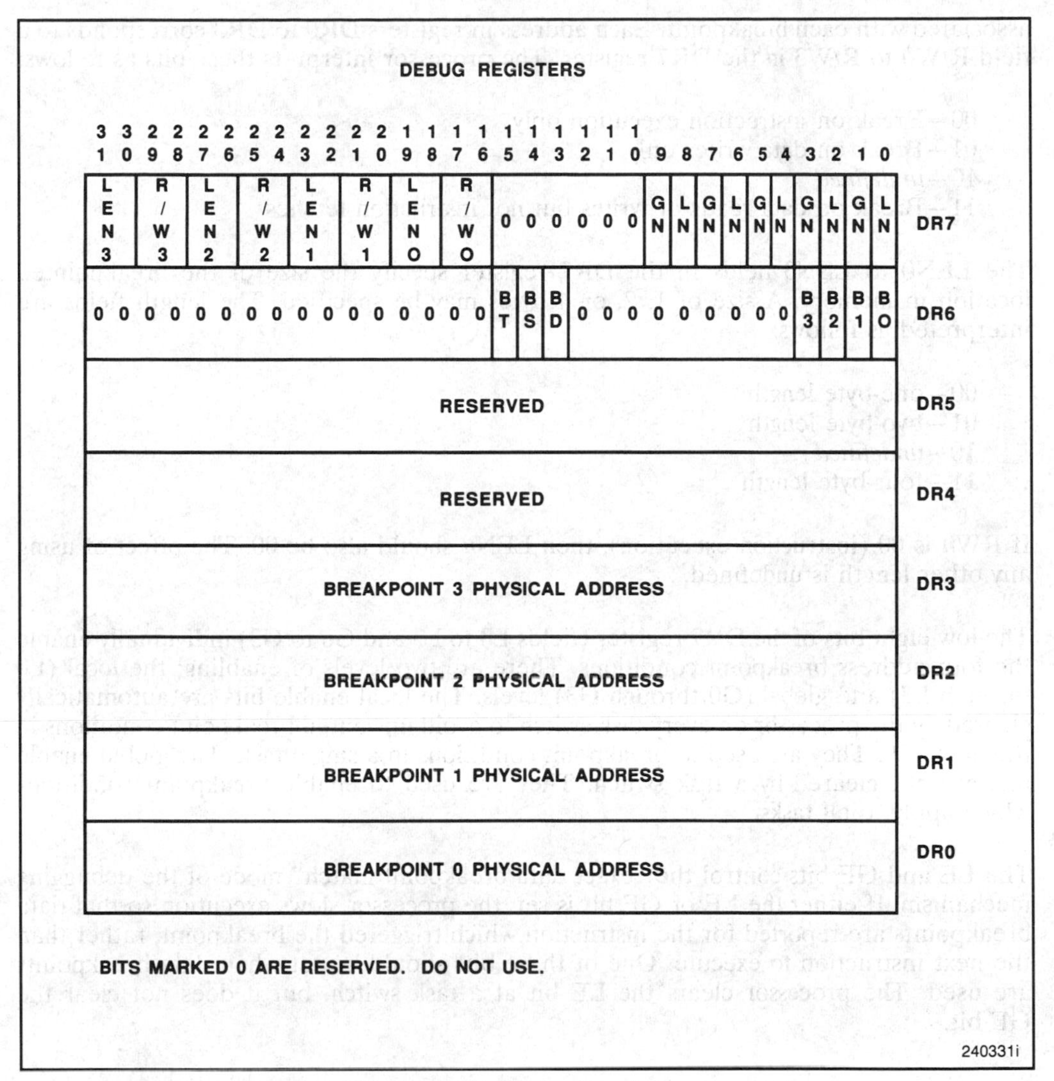

Figure 12-1. Debug Registers

12.2.1 Debug Address Registers (DR0-DR3)

Each of these registers holds the linear address for one of the four breakpoints. If paging is enabled, these addresses are translated to physical addresses by the paging algorithm. Each breakpoint condition is specified further by the contents of the DR7 register.

12.2.2 Debug Control Register (DR7)

The debug control register shown in Figure 12-1 specifies the sort of memory access associated with each breakpoint. Each address in registers DR0 to DR3 corresponds to a field R/W0 to R/W3 in the DR7 register. The processor interprets these bits as follows:

00 – Break on instruction execution only
01 – Break on data writes only
10 – *undefined*
11 – Break on data reads or writes but not instruction fetches

The LEN0 to LEN3 fields in the DR7 register specify the size of the breakpointed location in memory. A size of 1, 2, or 4 bytes may be specified. The length fields are interpreted as follows:

00 – one-byte length
01 – two-byte length
10 – *undefined*
11 – four-byte length

If RW*n* is 00 (instruction execution), then LEN*n* should also be 00. The effect of using any other length is undefined.

The low eight bits of the DR7 register (fields L0 to L3 and G0 to G3) individually enable the four address breakpoint conditions. There are two levels of enabling: the local (L0 through L3) and global (G0 through G3) levels. The local enable bits are automatically cleared by the processor on every task switch to avoid unwanted breakpoint conditions in the new task. They are used to breakpoint conditions in a single task. The global enable bits are not cleared by a task switch. They are used to enable breakpoint conditions which apply to all tasks.

The LE and GE bits control the "exact data breakpoint match" mode of the debugging mechanism. If either the LE or GE bit is set, the processor slows execution so that data breakpoints are reported for the instruction which triggered the breakpoint, rather than the next instruction to execute. One of these bits should be set when data breakpoints are used. The processor clears the LE bit at a task switch, but it does not clear the GE bit.

12.2.3 Debug Status Register (DR6)

The debug status register shown in Figure 12-1 reports conditions sampled at the time the debug exception was generated. Among other information, it reports which breakpoint triggered the exception.

When an enabled breakpoint generates a debug exception, it loads the low four bits of this register (B0 through B3) before entering the debug exception handler. The B bit is set if the condition described by the DR, LEN, and R/W bits is true, even if the breakpoint is not enabled by the L and G bits. The processor sets the B bits for all breakpoints which match the conditions present at the time the debug exception is generated, whether or not they are enabled.

The BT bit is associated with the T bit (debug trap bit) of the TSS (see Chapter 6 for the format of a TSS). The processor sets the BT bit before entering the debug handler if a task switch has occurred to a task with a set T bit in its TSS. There is no bit in the DR7 register to enable or disable this exception; the T bit of the TSS is the only enabling bit.

The BS bit is associated with the TF flag. The BS bit is set if the debug exception was triggered by the single-step execution mode (TF flag set). The single-step mode is the highest-priority debug exception; when the BS bit is set, any of the other debug status bits also may be set.

The BD bit is set if the next instruction will read or write one of the eight debug registers while they are being used by in-circuit emulation.

Note that the contents of the DR6 register are never cleared by the processor. To avoid any confusion in identifying debug exceptions, the debug handler should clear the register before returning.

12.2.4 Breakpoint Field Recognition

The address and LEN bits for each of the four breakpoint conditions define a range of sequential byte addresses for a data breakpoint. The LEN bits permit specification of a one-, two-, or four-byte range. Two-byte ranges must be aligned on word boundaries (addresses which are multiples of two) and four-byte ranges must be aligned on doubleword boundaries (addresses which are multiples of four). These requirements are enforced by the processor; it uses the LEN bits to mask the lower address bits in the debug registers. Unaligned code or data breakpoint addresses do not yield the expected results.

A data breakpoint for reading or writing is triggered if any of the bytes participating in a memory access is within the range defined by a breakpoint address register and its LEN bits. Table 12-1 gives some examples of combinations of addresses and fields with memory references which do and do not cause traps.

A data breakpoint for an unaligned operand can be made from two sets of entries in the breakpoint registers where each entry is byte-aligned, and the two entries together cover the operand. This breakpoint generates exceptions only for the operand, not for any neighboring bytes.

Instruction breakpoint addresses must have a length specification of one byte (LEN = 00); the behavior of code breakpoints for other operand sizes is undefined. The processor recognizes an instruction breakpoint address only when it points to the first byte of an instruction. If the instruction has any prefixes, the breakpoint address must point to the first prefix.

Table 12-1. Breakpointing Examples

Comment		Address (hex)	Length (in bytes)
Register Contents	DR0	A0001	1 (LEN0 = 00)
Register Contents	DR1	A0002	1 (LEN0 = 00)
Register Contents	DR2	B0002	2 (LEN0 = 01)
Register Contents	DR3	C0000	4 (LEN0 = 11)
Memory Operations Which Trap		A0001	1
		A0002	1
		A0001	2
		A0002	2
		B0002	2
		B0001	4
		C0000	4
		C0001	2
		C0003	1
Memory Operations Which Don't Trap		A0000	1
		A0003	4
		B0000	2
		C0004	4

12.3 DEBUG EXCEPTIONS

Two of the interrupt vectors of the 386 DX microprocessor are reserved for debug exceptions. The debug exception is the usual way to invoke debuggers designed for the 386 DX microprocessor; the breakpoint exception is intended for putting breakpoints in debuggers.

12.3.1 Interrupt 1 — Debug Exceptions

The handler for this exception usually is a debugger or part of a debugging system. The processor generates a debug exception for any of several conditions. The debugger can check flags in the DR6 and DR7 registers to determine which condition caused the exception and which other conditions also might apply. Table 12-2 shows the states of these bits for each kind of breakpoint condition.

Table 12-2. Debug Exception Conditions

Flags Tested	Description
BS = 1	Single-step trap
B0 = 1 and (GE0 = 1 or LE0 = 1)	Breakpoint defined by DR0, LEN0, and R/W0
B1 = 1 and (GE1 = 1 or LE1 = 1)	Breakpoint defined by DR1, LEN1, and R/W1
B2 = 1 and (GE2 = 1 or LE2 = 1)	Breakpoint defined by DR2, LEN2, and R/W2
B3 = 1 and (GE3 = 1 or LE3 = 1)	Breakpoint defined by DR3, LEN3, and R/W3
BD = 1	Debug registers in use for in-circuit emulation
BT = 1	Task switch

Instruction breakpoints are faults; other debug exceptions are traps. The debug exception may report either or both at one time. The following sections present details for each class of debug exception.

12.3.1.1 INSTRUCTION-BREAKPOINT FAULT

The processor reports an instruction breakpoint before it executes the breakpointed instruction (i.e., a debug exception caused by an instruction breakpoint is a fault).

The RF flag permits the debug exception handler to restart instructions which cause faults other than debug faults. When one of these faults occurs, the system software writer must set the RF bit in the copy of the EFLAGS register which is pushed on the stack in the debug exception handler routine. This bit is set in preparation of resuming the program's execution at the breakpoint address without generating another breakpoint fault on the same instruction. (Note: the RF bit does not cause breakpoint traps or other kinds of faults to be ignored.)

The processor clears the RF flag at the successful completion of every instruction except after the IRET instruction, the POPF instruction, and JMP, CALL, or INT instructions which cause a task switch. These instructions set the RF flag to the value specified by the the saved copy of the EFLAGS register.

The proccssor sets the RF flag in the copy of the EFLAGS register pushed on the stack before entry into any fault handler. When the fault handler is entered for instruction breakpoints, for example, the RF flag is set in the copy of the EFLAGS register pushed on the stack; therefore, the IRET instruction which returns control from the exception handler will set the RF flag in the EFLAGS register, and execution will resume at the breakpointed instruction without generating another breakpoint for the same instruction.

If, after a debug fault, the RF flag is set and the debug handler retries the faulting instruction, it is possible that retrying the instruction will generate other faults. The restart of the instruction after these faults also occurs with the RF flag set, so repeated debug faults continue to be suppressed. The processor clears the RF flag only after *successful* completion of the instruction.

12.3.1.2 DATA-BREAKPOINT TRAP

A data-breakpoint exception is a trap; i.e., the processor generates an exception for a data breakpoint after executing the instruction which accesses the breakpointed memory location.

When using data breakpoints, it is recommended either the LE or GE bits of the DR7 register also be set. If either the LE or GE bits are set, any data breakpoint trap is reported immediately after completion of the instruction which accessed the breakpointed memory location. This immediate reporting is done by forcing the 386 DX microprocessor execution unit to wait for completion of data operand transfers before beginning execution of the next instruction. If neither bit is set, data breakpoints may not be generated until one instruction after the data is accessed, or they may not be generated at all. This is because instruction execution normally is overlapped with memory transfers. Execution of the next instruction may begin before the memory operations of the previous instruction are completed.

If a debugger needs to save the contents of a write breakpoint location, it should save the original contents before setting the breakpoint. Because data breakpoints are traps, the original data is overwritten before the trap exception is generated. The handler can report the saved value after the breakpoint is triggered. The data in the debug registers can be used to address the new value stored by the instruction which triggered the breakpoint.

12.3.1.3 GENERAL-DETECT FAULT

The general-detect fault occurs when an attempt is made to use the debug registers at the same time they are being used by in-circuit emulation. This additional protection feature is provided to guarantee emulators can have full control over the debug registers when required. The exception handler can detect this condition by checking the state of the BD bit of the DR6 register.

12.3.1.4 SINGLE-STEP TRAP

This trap occurs after an instruction is executed if the TF flag was set before the instruction was executed. Note the exception does not occur after an instruction which sets the TF flag. For example, if the POPF instruction is used to set the TF flag, a single-step trap does not occur until after the instruction following the POPF instruction.

The processor clears the TF flag before calling the exception handler. If the TF flag was set in a TSS at the time of a task switch, the exception occurs after the first instruction is executed in the new task.

The single-step flag normally is not cleared by privilege changes inside a task. The INT instructions, however, do clear the TF flag. Therefore, software debuggers which single-step code must recognize and emulate INT*n* or INTO instructions rather than executing them directly.

To maintain protection, the operating system should check the current execution privilege level after any single-step trap to see if single stepping should continue at the current privilege level.

The interrupt priorities guarantee that if an external interrupt occurs, single stepping stops. When both an external interrupt and a single step interrupt occur together, the single step interrupt is processed first. This clears the TF flag. After saving the return address or switching tasks, the external interrupt input is examined before the first instruction of the single step handler executes. If the external interrupt is still pending, then it is serviced. The external interrupt handler does not run in single-step mode. To single step an interrupt handler, single step an INT*n* instruction which calls the interrupt handler.

12.3.1.5 TASK-SWITCH TRAP

The debug exception also occurs after a task switch if the T bit of the new task's TSS is set. The exception occurs after control has passed to the new task, but before the first instruction of that task is executed. The exception handler can detect this condition by examining the BT bit of the DR6 register.

Note that if the debug exception handler is a task, the T bit of its TSS should not be set. Failure to observe this rule will put the processor in a loop.

12.3.2 Interrupt 3 – Breakpoint Instruction

The breakpoint trap is caused by execution of the INT 3 instruction. Typically, a debugger prepares a breakpoint by replacing the first opcode byte of an instruction with the opcode for the breakpoint instruction. When execution of the INT 3 instruction calls the exception handler, the return address points to the first byte of the instruction following the INT 3 instruction.

With older processors, this feature is used extensively for setting instruction breakpoints. With the 386 DX microprocessor, this use is more easily handled using the debug registers. However, the breakpoint exception still is useful for breakpointing debuggers, because the breakpoint exception can call an exception handler other than itself. The breakpoint exception also can be useful when it is necessary to set a greater number of breakpoints than permitted by the debug registers, or when breakpoints are being placed in the source code of a program under development.

12.3.1.5 TASK-SWITCH TRAP

The debug exception also occurs after a task switch if the T bit of the new task's TSS is set. The exception occurs after control has passed to the new task, but before the first instruction of that task is executed. The exception handler can detect this condition by examining the BT bit of the DR6 register.

Note that if the debug exception handler is a task, the T bit of its TSS should not be set. Failure to observe this rule will put the processor in a loop.

12.3.2 Interrupt 3—Breakpoint Instruction

The breakpoint trap is caused by execution of the INT 3 instruction. Typically, a debugger prepares a breakpoint by replacing the first opcode byte of an instruction with the opcode for the breakpoint instruction. When execution of the INT 3 instruction calls the exception handler, the return address points to the first byte of the instruction following the INT 3 instruction.

With older processors, this feature is used extensively for setting instruction breakpoints. With the 386 DX microprocessor, this use is more easily handled using the debug registers. However, the breakpoint exception still is useful for breakpointing debuggers, because the breakpoint exception can call an exception handler other than itself. The breakpoint exception also can be useful when it is necessary to set a greater number of breakpoints than permitted by the debug registers, or when breakpoints are being placed in the source code of a program under development.

Part III
Compatibility

Executing 80286 Programs 13

CHAPTER 13
EXECUTING 80286 PROGRAMS

In general, programs written for protected mode on an 80286 processor run without modification on the 386™ DX microprocessor, because the features of the 80286 processor are an object-code compatible subset of those of the 386 DX microprocessor. The Default bit in segment descriptors indicates whether the processor is to treat a code, data, or stack segment as an 80286 or 386 DX CPU segment.

The segment descriptors used by the 80286 processor are supported by the 386 DX microprocessor if the Intel®-reserved word (highest word) of the descriptor is clear. On the 386 DX microprocessor, this word includes the upper bits of the base address and the segment limit.

The segment descriptors for data segments, code segments, local descriptor tables (there are no descriptors for global descriptor tables), and task gates are the same for both the 80286 and 386 DX microprocessors. Other 80286 descriptors, TSS segment, call gate, interrupt gate, and trap gate, are supported by the 386 DX microprocessor. The 386 DX microprocessor also has new versions of descriptors for TSS segment, call gate, interrupt gate, and trap gate which support the 32-bit architecture of the 386 DX microprocessor. Both kinds of descriptors can be used in the same system.

For those segment descriptors common to both the 80286 and 386 DX microprocessors, clear bits in the reserved word cause the 386 DX microprocessor to interpret these descriptors exactly as the 80286 processor does; for example:

Base Address — The upper eight bits of the 32-bit base address are clear, which limits base addresses to 24 bits.

Limit — The upper four bits of the limit field are clear, restricting the value of the limit field to 64K bytes.

Granularity bit — The Granularity bit is clear, indicating the value of the 16-bit limit is interpreted in units of 1 byte.

Big bit — In a data-segment descriptor, the B bit is clear, indicating the segment is no larger than 64 Kbytes.

Default bit — In an code-segment descriptor, the D bit is clear, indicating 16-bit addressing and operands are the default. In a stack-segment descriptor, the D bit is clear, indicating use of the SP register (instead of the ESP register) and a 64K byte maximum segment limit.

For formats of these descriptors and documentation of their use see the *iAPX 80286 Programmer's Reference Manual*.

13.1 TWO WAYS TO RUN 80286 TASKS

When porting 80286 programs to the 386 DX microprocessor, there are two approaches to consider:

1. Porting an entire 80286 software system to the 386 DX microprocessor, complete with the old operating system, loader, and system builder.

   In this case, all tasks will have 80286 TSSs. The 386 DX microprocessor is being used as if it were a faster version of the 80286 processor.

2. Porting selected 80286 applications to run in a 386 DX microprocessor environment with a 386 DX microprocessor operating system, loader, and system builder.

   In this case, the TSSs used to represent 80286 tasks should be changed to 386 DX processor TSSs. It is possible to mix 80286 and 386 DX processor TSSs, but the benefits are small and the problems are great. All tasks in a 386 DX microprocessor software system should have 386 DX processor TSSs. It is not necessary to change the 80286 object modules themselves; TSSs are usually constructed by the operating system, by the loader, or by the system builder. See Chapter 16 for more discussion of the interface between 16-bit and 32-bit code.

13.2 DIFFERENCES FROM 80286 PROCESSOR

The few differences between the 80286 and 386 DX microprocessors affect operating systems more than application programs.

13.2.1 Wraparound of 80286 Processor 24-Bit Physical Address Space

With the 80286 processor, any base and offset combination which addresses beyond 16 megabytes wraps around to the first megabyte of the address space. With the 386 DX microprocessor, because it has a greater physical address space, any such address maps to the 17th megabyte. In the unlikely event that any software depends on address wraparound, the same effect can be simulated on the 386 DX microprocessor by using paging to map the first 64K bytes past the top of the 16 megabyte address space to the bottom 64K bytes of the segment.

13.2.2 Reserved Word of Segment Descriptor

Because the 386 DX microprocessor uses the contents of the reserved word of 80286 segment descriptors, 80286 programs which place values in this word may not run correctly on the 386 DX microprocessor.

13.2.3 New Segment Descriptor Type Codes

Operating-system code which manages space in descriptor tables often uses an invalid value in the access-rights field of descriptor-table entries to identify unused entries. Access rights values of 80H and 00H remain invalid for both the 80286 and 386 DX microprocessors. Other values which were invalid on the 80286 processor may be valid on the 386 DX microprocessor because uses for these bits are defined for the 386 DX microprocessor.

13.2.4 Restricted Semantics of LOCK Prefix

The 80286 processor performs the bus lock function differently than the 386 DX microprocessor. Programs which use forms of memory locking specific to the 80286 processor may not run properly when run on the 386 DX microprocessor.

The LOCK prefix and its bus signal only should be used to prevent other bus masters from interrupting a data movement operation. The LOCK prefix only may be used with the following 386 DX microprocessor instructions when they modify memory. An invalid-opcode exception results from using the LOCK prefix before any other instruction, or with these instructions when no write operation is made to memory (i.e., when the destination operand is in a register).

- Bit test and change: the BTS, BTR, and BTC instructions.
- Exchange: the XCHG instruction.
- One-operand arithmetic and logical: the INC, DEC, NOT, NEG instructions.
- Two-operand arithmetic and logical: the ADD, ADC, SUB, SBB, AND, OR, and XOR instructions.

A locked instruction is guaranteed to lock only the area of memory defined by the destination operand, but may lock a larger memory area. For example, typical 8086 and 80286 processor configurations lock the entire physical memory space.

On the 80286 processor, the LOCK prefix is sensitive to IOPL; if CPL is less privileged than the IOPL, a general protection exception is generated. On the 386 DX microprocessor, no check against IOPL is performed.

13.2.5 Additional Exceptions

The 386 DX microprocessor defines new exceptions which can occur even in systems designed for the 80286 proccssor.

- Exception #6 – invalid opcode

  This exception can result from improper use of the LOCK instruction prefix.

- Exception #14 – page fault

  This exception may occur in an 80286 program if the operating system enables paging. Paging can be used in a system with 80286 tasks if all tasks use the same page directory. Because there is no place in an 80286 TSS to store the PDBR register, switching to an 80286 task does not change the value of the PDBR register. Tasks ported from the 80286 processor should be given 386 DX processor's TSSs so they can make full use of paging.

microprocessors. Other values which were invalid on the 80286 processor may be valid on the 386 DX microprocessor because uses for these bits are defined for the 386 DX microprocessor.

13.2.4 Restricted Semantics of LOCK Prefix

The 80286 processor performs the bus lock function differently than the 386 DX microprocessor. Programs which use forms of memory locking specific to the 80286 processor may not run properly when run on the 386 DX microprocessor.

The LOCK prefix and its bus signal only should be used to prevent other bus masters from interrupting a data movement operation. The LOCK prefix only may be used with the following 386 DX microprocessor instructions when they modify memory. An invalid-opcode exception results from using the LOCK prefix before any other instruction, or with these instructions when no write operation is made to memory (i.e., when the destination operand is in a register).

- Bit test and change: the BTS, BTR, and BTC instructions.
- Exchange: the XCHG instruction.
- One-operand arithmetic and logical: the INC, DEC, NOT, NEG instructions.
- Two-operand arithmetic and logical: the ADD, ADC, SUB, SBB, AND, OR, and XOR instructions.

A locked instruction is guaranteed to lock only the area of memory defined by the destination operand, but may lock a larger memory area. For example, typical 8086 and 80286 processor configurations lock the entire physical memory space.

On the 80286 processor, the LOCK prefix is sensitive to IOPL; if CPL is less privileged than the IOPL, a general-protection exception is generated. On the 386 DX microprocessor, no check against IOPL is performed.

13.2.5 Additional Exceptions

The 386 DX microprocessor defines new exceptions which can occur even in systems designed for the 80286 processor.

- Exception #6—invalid opcode

  This exception can result from improper use of the LOCK instruction prefix.

- Exception #14—page fault

  This exception may occur in an 80286 program if the operating system enables paging. Paging can be used in a system with 80286 tasks as long as all tasks use the same page tables. Because there is no place in an 80286 TSS to store the PDBR register, switching to an 80286 task does not change the value of the PDBR register. Tasks ported from the 80286 processor should be given 386 DX processor TSSs so they can make full use of paging.

386™ DX Microprocessor Real-Address Mode

14

CHAPTER 14
386™ DX MICROPROCESSOR REAL-ADDRESS MODE

The real-address mode of the 386™ DX microprocessor runs programs written for the 8086, 8088, 80186, or 80188 processors, or for the real-address mode of an 80286 processor.

The architecture of the 386 DX microprocessor in this mode is almost identical to that of the 8086, 8088, 80186, and 80188 processors. To a programmer, a 386 DX microprocessor in real-address mode appears as a high-speed 8086 processor with extensions to the instruction set and registers. The principal features of this architecture are defined in Chapters 2 and 3.

This chapter discusses certain additional topics which complete the system programmer's view of the 386 DX microprocessor in real-address mode:

- Address formation.
- Extensions to registers and instructions.
- Interrupt and exception handling.
- Entering and leaving real-address mode.
- Real-address mode exceptions.
- Differences from 8086 processor.
- Differences from 80286 processor in real-address mode.

14.1 ADDRESS TRANSLATION

In real-address mode, the 386 DX microprocessor does not interpret 8086 selectors by referring to descriptors; instead, it forms linear addresses as an 8086 processor would. It shifts the selector left by four bits to form a 20-bit base address. The effective address is extended with four clear bits in the upper bit positions and added to the base address to create a linear address, as shown in Figure 14-1.

Because of the possibility of a carry, the resulting linear address may have as many as 21 significant bits. An 8086 program may generate linear addresses anywhere in the range 0 to 10FFEFH (1 megabyte plus approximately 64K bytes) of the linear address space. Because paging is not available in real-address mode, the linear address is used as the physical address.

Unlike the 8086 and 80286 processors, the 386 DX microprocessor can generate 32-bit effective addresses using an address override prefix; however in real-address mode, the value of a 32-bit address may not exceed 65,535 without causing an exception. For full compatibility with 80286 real-address mode, pseudo-protection faults (interrupt 12 or 13 with no error code) occur if an effective address is generated outside the range 0 through 65,535.

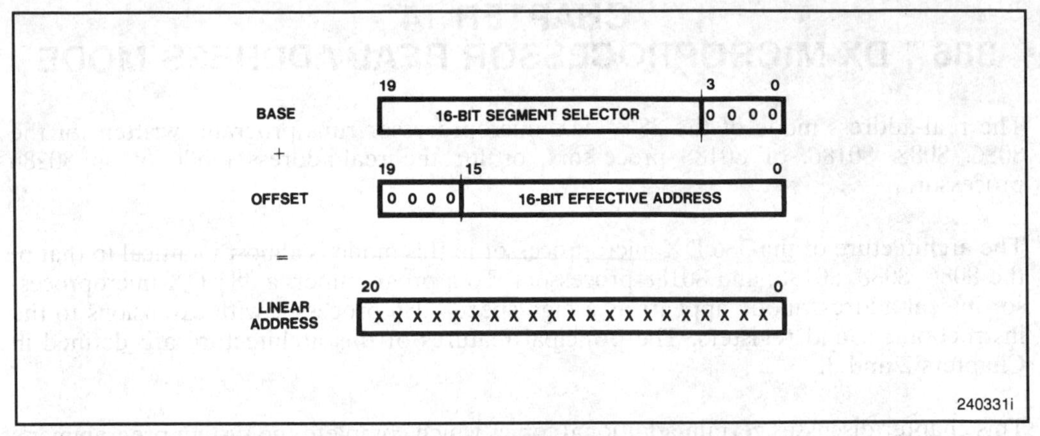

Figure 14-1. 8086 Address Translation

14.2 REGISTERS AND INSTRUCTIONS

The register set available in real-address mode includes all the registers defined for the 8086 processor plus the new registers introduced with the 386 DX microprocessor: FS, GS, debug registers, control registers, and test registers. New instructions which explicitly operate on the segment registers FS and GS are available, and the new segment-override prefixes can be used to cause instructions to use the FS and GS registers for address calculations.

The instruction codes which generate invalid-opcode exceptions include instructions from protected mode which move or test 386 DX microprocessor segment selectors and segment descriptors, i.e., the VERR, VERW, LAR, LSL, LTR, STR, LLDT, and SLDT instructions. Programs executing in real-address mode are able to take advantage of the new application-oriented instructions added to the architecture with the introduction of the 80186, 80188, 80286, and 386 DX microprocessors:

- New instructions introduced on the 80186, 80188, and 80286 processors.
  - PUSH immediate data
  - Push all and pop all (PUSHA and POPA)
  - Multiply immediate data
  - Shift and rotate by immediate count
  - String I/O
  - ENTER and LEAVE instructions
  - BOUND instruction
- New instructions introduced on the 386 DX microprocessor.
  - LSS, LFS, LGS instructions
  - Long-displacement conditional jumps
  - Single-bit instructions

- Bit scan instructions
- Double-shift instructions
- Byte set on condition instruction
- Move with sign/zero extension
- Generalized multiply instruction
- MOV to and from control registers
- MOV to and from test registers
- MOV to and from debug registers

14.3 INTERRUPT AND EXCEPTION HANDLING

Interrupts and exceptions in 386 DX microprocessor real-address mode work much as they do on an 8086 processor. Interrupts and exceptions call interrupt procedures through an interrupt table. The processor scales the interrupt or exception identifier by four to obtain an index into the interrupt table. The entries of the interrupt table are far pointers to the entry points of interrupt or exception handler procedures. When an interrupt occurs, the processor pushes the current values of the CS and IP registers onto the stack, disables interrupts, clears the TF flag, and transfers control to the location specified in the interrupt table. An IRET instruction at the end of the handler procedure reverses these steps before returning control to the interrupted procedure. Exceptions do not return error codes in real-address mode.

The primary difference in the interrupt handling of the 386 DX microprocessor compared to the 8086 processor is the location and size of the interrupt table depend on the contents of the IDTR register. Ordinarily, this fact is not apparent to programmers, because, after reset initialization, the IDTR register contains a base address of 0 and a limit of 3FFH, which is compatible with the 8086 processor. However, the LIDT instruction can be used in real-address mode to change the base and limit values in the IDTR register. See Chapter 9 for details on the IDTR register, and the LIDT and SIDT instructions. If an interrupt occurs and its entry in the interrupt table is beyond the limit stored in the IDTR register, a double-fault exception is generated.

14.4 ENTERING AND LEAVING REAL-ADDRESS MODE

Real-address mode is in effect after reset initialization. Even if the system is going to run in protected mode, the start-up program runs in real-address mode while preparing to switch to protected mode.

14.4.1 Switching to Protected Mode

The only way to leave real-address mode is to switch to protected mode. The processor enters protected mode when a MOV to CR0 instruction sets the PE (protection enable) bit in the CR0 register. (For compatibility with the 80286 processor, the LMSW instruction also may be used to set the PE bit.)

See Chapter 10 "Initialization" for other aspects of switching to protected mode.

14.5 SWITCHING BACK TO REAL-ADDRESS MODE

The processor re-enters real-address mode if software clears the PE bit in the CR0 register with a MOV CR0 instruction (for compatibility with the 80286 processor, the LMSW instruction can set the PE bit, but cannot clear it). A procedure which re-enters real-address mode should proceed as follows:

1. If paging is enabled, perform the following sequence:
   - Transfer control to linear addresses which have an identity mapping; i.e., linear addresses equal physical addresses.
   - Clear the PG bit in the CR0 register.
   - Move a 0 into the CR3 register to flush the TLB.
2. Transfer control to a segment which has a limit of 64K (0FFFFH). This loads the CS register with the segment limit it needs to have in real mode.
3. Load segment registers SS, DS, ES, FS, and GS with a selector for a descriptor containing the following values, which are appropriate for real mode:
   - Limit = 64K (0FFFFH)
   - Byte granular (G = 0)
   - Expand up (E = 0)
   - Writable (W = 1)
   - Present (P = 1)
   - Base = any value

   Note that if the segment registers are not reloaded, execution continues using the descriptors loaded during protected mode.
4. Disable interrupts. A CLI instruction disables INTR interrupts. NMI interrupts can be disabled with external circuitry.
5. Clear the PE bit in the CR0 register.
6. Jump to the real mode program using a far JMP instruction. This flushes the instruction queue and puts appropriate values in the access rights of the CS register.
7. Use the LIDT instruction to load the base and limit of the real-mode interrupt vector table.
8. Enable interrupts.
9. Load the segment registers as needed by the real-mode code.

14.6 REAL-ADDRESS MODE EXCEPTIONS

The 386 DX microprocessor reports some exceptions differently when executing in real-address mode than when executing in protected mode. Table 14-1 details the real-address-mode exceptions.

Table 14-1. Exceptions and Interrupts

Description	Vector	Source of the Exoeption	Does the Return Address Point to the Instruction Which Caused the Exception?
Divide Error	0	DIV and IDIV instructions	yes
Debug	1	any	[1]
Breakpoint	3	INT instruction	no
Overflow	4	INTO instruction	no
Bounds Check	5	BOUND instruction	yes
Invalid Opcode	6	reserved opcodes and improper use of LOCK prefix	yes
Coprocessor Not Available	7	ESC or WAIT	yes
IDT limit too small	8	any	yes
Reserved	9 to 11		
Stack Exception	12	stack operation crosses address limit	yes
Protection	13	operand crosses address limit, instruction crosses address limit, or instruction exceeds 15 bytes	yes
Reserved	14 and 15		
Coprocessor Error	16	ESC or WAIT instructions	yes[2]
Software Interrupt	0 to 255	INT *n* instructions	no

1. Some debug exceptions point to the faulting instruction, others point to the following instruction. The exception handler can test the DR6 register to determine which has occurred.
2. Coprocessor errors are reported on the first ESC or WAIT instruction after the ESC instruction which generated the error.

14.7 DIFFERENCES FROM 8086 PROCESSOR

In general, the 386 DX microprocessor in real-address mode will correctly run ROM-based software designed for the 8086, 8088, 80186, and 80188 processors. Following is a list of the minor differences between program execution on the 8086 and 386 DX microprocessors.

1. Instruction clock counts.

   The 386 DX microprocessor takes fewer clocks for most instructions than the 8086 processor. The areas most likely to be affected are:

   - Delays required by I/O devices between I/O operations.
   - Assumed delays with 8086 processor operating in parallel with an 8087.

2. Divide-error exceptions point to the DIV instruction.

   Divide-error exceptions on the 386 DX microprocessor always leave the saved CS:IP value pointing to the instruction which failed. On the 8086 processor, the CS:IP value points to the next instruction.

3. Undefined 8086 processor opcodes.

   Opcodes which were not defined for the 8086 processor generate an invalid-opcode exception or execute one of the new instructions introduced with the 80286 or 386 DX microprocessors.

4. Value written by PUSH SP.

   The 386 DX microprocessor pushes a different value on the stack for a PUSH SP instruction than the 8086 processor. The 386 DX microprocessor pushes the value of the SP register before it is incremented as part of the push operation; the 8086 processor pushes the value of the SP register after it is incremented. If the value pushed is important, replace PUSH SP instructions with the following three instructions:

```
PUSH  BP
MOV   BP, SP
XCHG  BP, [BP]
```

   This code functions as the 8086 processor PUSH SP instruction on the 386 DX microprocessor.

5. Shift or rotate by more than 31 bits.

   The 386 DX microprocessor masks all shift and rotate counts to the lowest five bits. This MOD 32 operation limits the count to a maximum of 31 bits, which limits the amount of time that interrupt response may be delayed while the instruction is executing.

6. Redundant prefixes.

   The 386 DX microprocessor sets a limit of 15 bytes on instruction length. The only way to violate this limit is by putting redundant prefixes before an instruction. A general-protection exception is generated if the limit on instruction length is violated. The 8086 processor has no instruction length limit.

7. Operand crossing offset 0 or 65,535.

   On the 8086 processor, an attempt to access a memory operand which crosses offset 65,535 (e.g., MOV a word to offset 65,535) or offset 0 (e.g., PUSH a word when SP = 1) causes the offset to wrap around modulo 65,536. The 386 DX microprocessor generates an exception in these cases: a general-protection exception if the segment is a data segment (i.e., if the CS, DS, ES, FS, or GS register is being used to address the segment) or a stack exception if the segment is a stack segment (i.e., if the SS register is being used).

8. Sequential execution across offset 65,535.

   On the 8086 processor, if sequential execution of instructions proceeds past offset 65,535, the processor fetches the next instruction byte from offset 0 of the same segment. On the 386 DX microprocessor, the processor generates a general-protection exception in such a case.

9. LOCK is restricted to certain instructions.

   The LOCK prefix and its output signal should only be used to prevent other bus masters from interrupting a data movement operation. The LOCK prefix only may be used with the following 386 DX microprocessors instructions when they modify memory. An invalid-opcode exception results from using LOCK before any other instruction, or with these instructions when no write operation is made to memory.

   - Bit test and change: the BTS, BTR, and BTC instructions.
   - Exchange: the XCHG instruction.
   - One-operand arithmetic and logical: the INC, DEC, NOT, NEG instructions.
   - Two-operand arithmetic and logical: the ADD, ADC, SUB, SBB, AND, OR, and XOR instructions.

10. Single-stepping external interrupt handlers.

    The priority of the 386 DX microprocessor single-step exception is different from the 8086 processor. The change prevents an external interrupt handler from being single-stepped if the interrupt occurs while a program is being single-stepped. The 386 DX microprocessor single-step exception has higher priority than any external interrupt. The 386 DX microprocessor still may single-step through an interrupt handler called by the INT instructions or by an exception.

11. IDIV exceptions for quotients of 80H or 8000H.

    The 386 DX microprocessor can generate the largest negative number as a quotient for the IDIV instruction. The 8086 processor generates a divide-error exception instead.

12. Flags in stack.

    The setting of the flags stored by the PUSHF instruction, by interrupts, and by exceptions is different from that stored by the 8086 processor in bit positions 12 through 15. On the 8086 processor these bits are set, but in the 386 DX real-address mode, bit 15 is always clear, and bits 14 through 12 have the last value loaded into them.

13. NMI interrupting NMI handlers.

    After an NMI interrupt is recognized by the 386 DX microprocessor, the NMI interrupt is masked until an IRET instruction is executed.

14. Coprocessor errors call the coprocessor-error exception.

    Any 386 DX microprocessor with a coprocessor must use the coprocessor-error exception. If an 8086 processor uses another exception for the 8087 interrupt, both exception vectors should call the coprocessor-error exception handler.

15. Numeric exception handlers should allow prefixes.

    On the 386 DX microprocessor, the value of the CS and IP registers saved for coprocessor-error exceptions points at any prefixes which come before the ESC instruction. On the 8086 processor, the saved CS:IP points to the ESC instruction.

16. Coprocessor does not use interrupt controller.

    The coprocessor-error signal to the 386 DX microprocessor does not pass through an interrupt controller (an INT signal from 8087 coprocessor does). Some instructions in a coprocessor-error exception handler may need to be deleted if they use the interrupt controller.

17. One megabyte wraparound.

    The address space of the 386 DX microprocessor does not wraparound at 1 megabyte in real-address mode. On members of the 8086 family, it is possible to specify addresses greater than 1 megabyte. For example, with a selector value 0FFFFH and an offset of 0FFFFH, the effective address would be 10FFEFH (1 megabyte + 65519 bytes). The 8086 processor, which can form addresses up to 20 bits long, truncates the uppermost bit, which "wraps" this address to 0FFEFH. However, the 386 DX microprocessor, which can form addresses up to 32 bits long, does not truncate this bit.

18. Response to bus hold.

    Unlike the 8086 and 80286 processors, the 386 DX microprocessor responds to requests for control of the bus from other potential bus masters, such as DMA controllers, between transfers of parts of an unaligned operand, such as two bytes which form a word.

19. Interrupt vector table limit.

    The LIDT instruction can be used to set a limit on the size of the interrupt vector table. Shutdown occurs if an interrupt or exception attempts to read a vector beyond the limit. (The 8086 processor does not have a shutdown mode.)

20. If a stack operation wraps around the address limit, shutdown occurs. (The 8086 processor does not have a shutdown mode.)

21. Six new interrupt vectors.

    The 386 DX microprocessor adds six exceptions which are generated on an 8086 processor only by program bugs. Exception handlers should be added which treat these exceptions as invalid operations. This additional software does not significantly affect the existing 8086 processor software, because these interrupts do not occur normally. These interrupt identifiers should not be used by 8086 software, because they are reserved by Intel®. Table 14-2 describes the new 386 DX microprocessor exceptions.

14.8 DIFFERENCES FROM 80286 REAL-ADDRESS MODE

The few differences which exist between 386 DX microprocessor real-address mode and 80286 real-address mode are not likely to affect any existing 80286 programs except possibly the system initialization procedures.

Table 14-2. New 386™ DX Microprocessor Exceptions

Vector	Description
5	A BOUND instruction was executed with a register value outside the limit values.
6	A reserved opcode was encountered, or a LOCK prefix was used improperly.
7	The EM bit in the CR0 register was set when an ESC instruction executed, or the TS bit was set when a WAIT instruction was executed.
8	A vector indexes to an entry in the IDT which is beyond the segment limit for the IDT. This can only occur if the default limit has been changed.
12	A stack operation crossed the address limit.
13	An operation (other than a stack operation) exceeds the base or bounds of a segment, instruction execution is crossing the address limit (0FFFFH), or an instruction exceeds 15 bytes.

14.8.1 Bus Lock

The 80286 processor implements the bus lock function differently than the 386 DX microprocessor. Programs which use forms of memory locking specific to the 80286 processor may not run properly if transported to a specific application of the 386 DX microprocessor.

The LOCK prefix and its bus signal only should be used to prevent other bus masters from interrupting a data movement operation. The LOCK prefix only may be used with the following 386 DX microprocessor instructions when they modify memory. An invalid-opcode exception results from using the LOCK prefix before any other instruction, or with these instructions when no write operation is made to memory (i.e., when the destination operand is in a register).

- Bit test and change: the BTS, BTR, and BTC instructions.
- Exchange: the XCHG instruction.
- One-operand arithmetic and logical: the INC, DEC, NOT, NEG instructions.
- Two-operand arithmetic and logical: the ADD, ADC, SUB, SBB, AND, OR, and XOR instructions.

A locked instruction is guaranteed to lock only the area of memory defined by the destination operand, but may lock a larger memory area. For example, typical 8086 and 80286 configurations lock the entire physical memory space.

14.8.2 Location of First Instruction

The starting location is 0FFFFFFF0H (16 bytes from end of the 32-bit address space) on the 386 DX microprocessor rather than 0FFFFF0H (16 bytes from end of the 24-bit address space) as on the 80286 processor. Many 80286 ROM initialization programs will work correctly in this new environment. Others can be made to work correctly with external hardware to interpret the signals or the address signals A_{31-20}.

14.8.3 Initial Values of General Registers

On the 386 DX microprocessor, certain general registers may contain different values after reset initialization than on the 80286 processor. This should not cause compatibility problems, because the contents of 8086 registers after reset initialization are undefined. If self-test is requested during the reset sequence and errors are detected in the 386 DX microprocessor, the EAX register will contain a non-zero value. The EDX register contains the component and revision identifier. See Chapter 10 for more information.

14.8.4 MSW Initialization

The 80286 processor initializes the MSW register to 0FFF0H, but the 386 DX microprocessor initializes this register to 0000H. This difference should have no effect, because the bits which are different are reserved on the 80286 processor. Programs which read the value of the MSW will behave differently on the 386 DX microprocessor only if they depend on the setting of the undefined reserved bits.

14.8.5 Bus Hold

Unlike the 8086 and 80286 processors, the 386 DX microprocessor responds to requests for control of the bus from other potential bus masters, such as DMA controllers, between transfers of parts of an unaligned operand, such as two words which form a doubleword.

Virtual-8086 Mode 15

CHAPTER 15
VIRTUAL-8086 MODE

The 386™ DX microprocessor supports execution of one or more 8086, 8088, 80186, or 80188 programs in a 386 DX microprocessor protected-mode environment. An 8086 program runs in this environment as part of a virtual-8086 task. Virtual-8086 tasks take advantage of the hardware support of multitasking offered by the protected mode. Not only can there be multiple virtual-8086 tasks, each one running an 8086 program, but virtual-8086 tasks can run in multitasking with other 386 DX microprocessor tasks.

The purpose of a virtual-8086 task is to form a "virtual machine" for running programs written for the 8086 processor. A complete virtual machine consists of 386 DX microprocessor hardware and system software. The emulation of an 8086 processor is the result of software using hardware:

- The hardware provides a virtual set of registers (through the TSS), a virtual memory space (the first megabyte of the linear address space of the task), and directly executes all instructions which deal with these registers and with this address space.
- The software controls the external interfaces of the virtual machine (I/O, interrupts, and exceptions) in a manner consistent with the larger environment in which it runs. In the case of I/O, software can choose either to emulate I/O instructions or to let the hardware execute them directly without software intervention.

Software which supports virtual 8086 machines is called a virtual-8086 monitor.

15.1 EXECUTING 8086 PROCESSOR CODE

The processor runs in virtual-8086 mode when the VM (virtual machine) bit in the EFLAGS register is set. The processor tests this flag under two general conditions:

1. When loading segment registers, to know whether to use 8086-style address translation.
2. When decoding instructions, to determine which instructions are sensitive to IOPL.

Except for these two modifications to its normal operations, the 386 DX microprocessor in virtual-8086 mode operates similarly to protected mode.

15.1.1 Registers and Instructions

The register set available in virtual-8086 mode includes all the registers defined for the 8086 processor plus the new registers introduced by the 386 DX microprocessor: FS, GS, debug registers, control registers, and test registers. New instructions which explicitly operate on the segment registers FS and GS are available, and the new segment-override prefixes can be used to cause instructions to use the FS and GS registers for address calculations. Instructions can use 32-bit operands through the use of the operand size prefix.

Programs running as virtual-8086 tasks can take advantage of the new application-oriented instructions added to the architecture by the introduction of the 80186, 80188, 80286 and 386 DX microprocessors:

- New instructions introduced on the 80186, 80188, and 80286 processors.
  - PUSH immediate data
  - Push all and pop all (PUSHA and POPA)
  - Multiply immediate data
  - Shift and rotate by immediate count
  - String I/O
  - ENTER and LEAVE instruction
  - BOUND instruction
- New instructions introduced on the 386 DX microprocessor.
  - LSS, LFS, LGS instructions
  - Long-displacement conditional jumps
  - Single-bit instructions
  - Bit scan instructions
  - Double-shift instructions
  - Byte set on condition instruction
  - Move with sign/zero extension
  - Generalized multiply instruction
  - MOV to and from control registers
  - MOV to and from test registers
  - MOV to and from debug registers

15.1.2 Address Translation

In virtual-8086 mode, the 386 DX microprocessor does not interpret 8086 selectors by referring to descriptors; instead, it forms linear addresses as an 8086 processor would. It shifts the selector left by four bits to form a 20-bit base address. The effective address is extended with four clear bits in the upper bit positions and added to the base address to create a linear address, as shown in Figure 15-1.

Because of the possibility of a carry, the resulting linear address may have as many as 21 significant bits. An 8086 program may generate linear addresses anywhere in the range 0 to 10FFEFH (1 megabyte plus approximately 64K bytes) of the task's linear address space.

Virtual-8086 tasks generate 32-bit linear addresses. While an 8086 program only can use the lowest 21 bits of a linear address, the linear address can be mapped using paging to any 32-bit physical address.

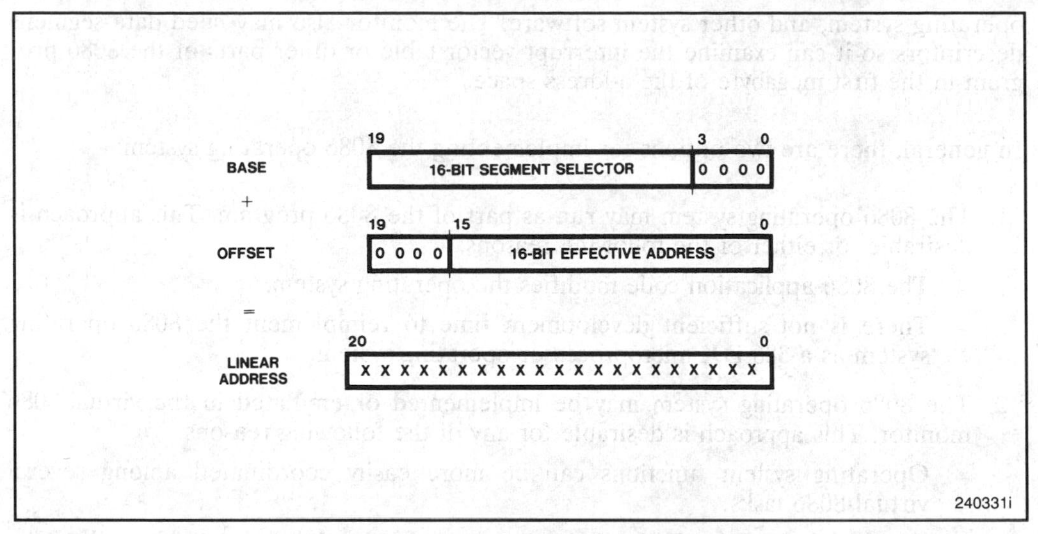

Figure 15-1. 8086 Address Translation

Unlike the 8086 and 80286 processors, the 386 DX microprocessor can generate 32-bit effective addresses using an address override prefix; however in virtual-8086 mode, the value of a 32-bit address may not exceed 65,535 without causing an exception. For full compatibility with 80286 real-address mode, pseudo-protection faults (interrupt 12 or 13 with no error code) occur if an effective address is generated outside the range 0 through 65,535.

15.2 STRUCTURE OF A VIRTUAL-8086 TASK

A virtual-8086 task consists of the 8086 program to be run and the 386 DX microprocessor "native mode" code which serves as the virtual-machine monitor. The task must be represented by a 386 DX microprocessor TSS (not an 80286 TSS). The processor enters virtual-8086 mode to run the 8086 program and returns to protected mode to run the monitor or other 386 DX CPU tasks.

To run in virtual-8086 mode, an existing 8086 processor program needs the following:

- A virtual-8086 monitor.
- Operating-system services.

The virtual-8086 monitor is 386 DX microprocessor protected-mode code which runs at privilege-level 0 (most privileged). The monitor mostly consists of initialization and exception-handling procedures. As with any other 386 DX microprocessor program, code-segment descriptors for the monitor must exist in the GDT or in the task's LDT. The linear addresses above 10FFEFH are available for the virtual-8086 monitor, the operating system, and other system software. The monitor also may need data-segment descriptors so it can examine the interrupt vector table or other parts of the 8086 program in the first megabyte of the address space.

In general, there are two options for implementing the 8086 operating system:

1. The 8086 operating system may run as part of the 8086 program. This approach is desirable for either of the following reasons:
   - The 8086 application code modifies the operating system.
   - There is not sufficient development time to reimplement the 8086 operating system as a 386 DX microprocessor operating system.
2. The 8086 operating system may be implemented or emulated in the virtual-8086 monitor. This approach is desirable for any of the following reasons:
   - Operating system functions can be more easily coordinated among several virtual-8086 tasks.
   - The functions of the 8086 operating system can be easily emulated by calls to the 386 DX microprocessor operating system.

Note that the approach chosen for implementing the 8086 processor operating system may have different virtual-8086 tasks using different 8086 operating systems.

15.2.1 Paging for Virtual-8086 Tasks

Paging is not necessary for a single virtual-8086 task, but paging is useful or necessary for any of the following reasons:

- Creating multiple virtual-8086 tasks. Each task must map the lower megabyte of linear addresses to different physical locations.
- Emulating the address wraparound which occurs at 1 megabyte. With members of the 8086 family, it is possible to specify addresses larger than 1 megabyte. For example, with a selector value of 0FFFFH and an offset of 0FFFFH, the effective address would be 10FFEFH (1 megabyte plus 65519 bytes). The 8086 processor, which can form addresses only up to 20 bits long, truncates the high-order bit, thereby "wrapping" this address to 0FFEFH. The 386 DX microprocessor, however, does not truncate such an address. If any 8086 processor programs depend on address wraparound, the same effect can be achieved in a virtual-8086 task by mapping linear addresses between 100000H and 110000H and linear addresses between 0 and 10000H to the same physical addresses.
- Creating a virtual address space larger than the physical address space.
- Sharing 8086 operating system or ROM code which is common to several 8086 programs running in multitasking.
- Redirecting or trapping references to memory-mapped I/O devices.

15.2.2 Protection within a Virtual-8086 Task

Protection is not enforced between the segments of an 8086 program. To protect the system software running in a virtual-8086 task from the 8086 application program, software designers may follow either of these approaches:

- Reserve the first megabyte (plus 64K bytes) of each task's linear address space for the 8086 processor program. An 8086 processor task cannot generate addresses outside this range.
- Use the U/S bit of page-table entries to protect the virtual-machine monitor and other system software in each virtual-8086 task's space. When the processor is in virtual-8086 mode, the CPL is 3 (least privileged). Therefore, an 8086 processor program has only user privileges. If the pages of the virtual-machine monitor have supervisor privilege, they cannot be accessed by the 8086 program.

15.3 ENTERING AND LEAVING VIRTUAL-8086 MODE

Figure 15-2 summarizes the ways to enter and leave an 8086 program. Virtual-8086 mode is entered by setting the VM flag. There are two ways to do this:

1. A task switch to a 386 DX microprocessor task loads the image of the EFLAGS register from the new TSS. The TSS of the new task must be a 386 DX microprocessor TSS, not an 80286 TSS, because the 80286 TSS does not load the high word of the EFLAGS register, which contains the VM flag. A set VM flag in the new contents of the EFLAGS register indicates that the new task is executing 8086 instructions; therefore, while loading the segment registers from the TSS, the 386 DX microprocessor forms base addresses in the 8086 style.
2. An IRET instruction from a procedure of a 386 DX task loads the EFLAGS register from the stack. A set VM flag indicates the procedure to which control is being returned to be an 8086 procedure. The CPL at the time the IRET instruction is executed must be 0, otherwise the processor does not change the state of the VM flag.

When a task switch is used to enter virtual-8086 mode, the segment registers are loaded from a TSS. But when an IRET instruction is used to set the VM flag, the segment registers keep the contents loaded during protected mode. Software should then reload these registers with segment selectors appropriate for virtual-8086 mode.

The processor leaves virtual-8086 mode when an interrupt or exception occurs. There are two cases:

1. The interrupt or exception causes a task switch. A task switch from a virtual-8086 task to any other task loads the EFLAGS register from the TSS of the new task. If the new TSS is a 386 DX microprocessor TSS and the VM flag in the new contents of the EFLAGS register is clear or if the new TSS is an 80286 TSS, the processor clears the VM flag of the EFLAGS register, loads the segment registers from the new TSS using 386 DX CPU-style address formation, and begins executing the instructions of the new task in 386 DX microprocessor protected mode.

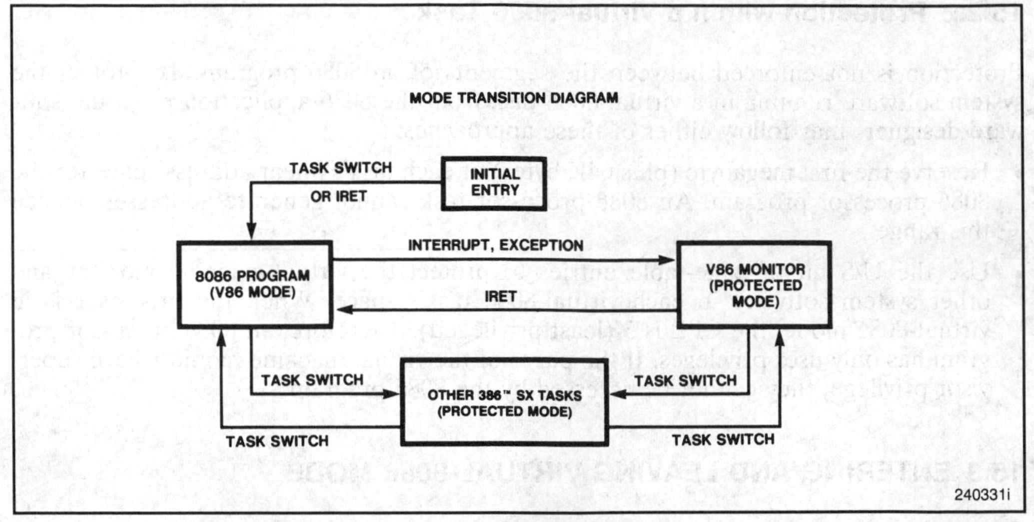

Figure 15-2. Entering and Leaving Virtual-8086 Mode

2. The interrupt or exception calls a privilege-level 0 procedure (most privileged). The processor stores the current contents of the EFLAGS register on the stack, then clears the VM flag. The interrupt or exception handler, therefore, runs as "native" 386 DX microprocessor protected-mode code. If an interrupt or exception calls a procedure in a conforming segment or in a segment at a privilege level other than 0 (most privileged), the processor generates a general-protection exception; the error code is the selector of the code segment to which a call was attempted.

System software does not change the state of the VM flag directly, but instead changes states in the image of the EFLAGS register stored on the stack or in the TSS. The virtual-8086 monitor sets the VM flag in the EFLAGS image on the stack or in the TSS when first creating a virtual-8086 task. Exception and interrupt handlers can examine the VM flag on the stack. If the interrupted procedure was running in virtual-8086 mode, the handler may need to call the virtual-8086 monitor.

15.3.1 Transitions Through Task Switches

A task switch to or from a virtual-8086 task may come from any of three causes:

1. An interrupt which calls a task gate.
2. An action of the scheduler of the 386 DX microprocessor operating system.
3. Executing an IRET instruction when the NT flag is set.

In any of these cases, the processor changes the VM flag in the EFLAGS register according to the image in the new TSS. If the new TSS is an 80286 TSS, the upper word of the EFLAGS register is not in the TSS; the processor clears the VM flag in this case. The processor updates the VM flag prior to loading the segment registers from their images in the new TSS. The new setting of the VM flag determines whether the processor interprets the new segment-register images as 8086 selectors or 80286 and 386 DX microprocessor selectors.

15.3.2 Transitions Through Trap Gates and Interrupt Gates

The 386 DX microprocessor leaves virtual-8086 mode as the result of an exception or interrupt which calls a trap or interrupt gate. The exception or interrupt handler returns to the 8086 program by executing an IRET instruction.

Because it was designed to run on an 8086 processor, an 8086 program in a virtual-8086 task will have an 8086-style interrupt table, which starts at linear address 0. However, the 386 DX microprocessor does not use this table directly. For all exceptions and interrupts which occur virtual-8086 mode, the processor calls handlers through the IDT. The IDT entry for an interrupt or exception in a virtual-8086 task must contain either:

- A task gate.
- A 386 DX trap gate (descriptor type 14) or 386 DX microprocessor interrupt gate (descriptor type 15), which must point to a nonconforming, privilege-level 0 (most privileged), code segment.

Interrupts and exceptions which call 386 DX microprocessor trap or interrupt gates use privilege-level 0. The contents of the segment registers are stored on the stack for this privilege level. Figure 15-3 shows the format of this stack after an exception or interrupt which occurs while a virtual-8086 task is running an 8086 program.

After the processor saves the 8086 segment registers on the stack for privilege level 0, it clears the segment registers before running the handler procedure. This lets the interrupt handler safely save and restore the DS, ES, FS, and GS registers as though they were 386 DX microprocessor selectors. Interrupt handlers, which may be called in the context of either a regular task or a virtual-8086 task, can use the same code sequences for saving and restoring the registers for any task. Clearing these registers before execution of the IRET instruction does not cause a trap in the interrupt handler. Interrupt procedures which expect values in the segment registers or which return values in the segment registers must use the register images saved on the stack for privilege level 0. Interrupt handlers which need to know whether the interrupt occurred in virtual-8086 mode can examine the VM flag in the stored contents of the EFLAGS register.

An interrupt handler passes control to the virtual-8086 monitor if the VM flag is set in the EFLAGS image stored on the stack and the interrupt or exception is one which the monitor needs to handle. The virtual-8086 monitor may either:

- Handle the interrupt within the virtual-8086 monitor.
- Call the 8086 program's interrupt handler.

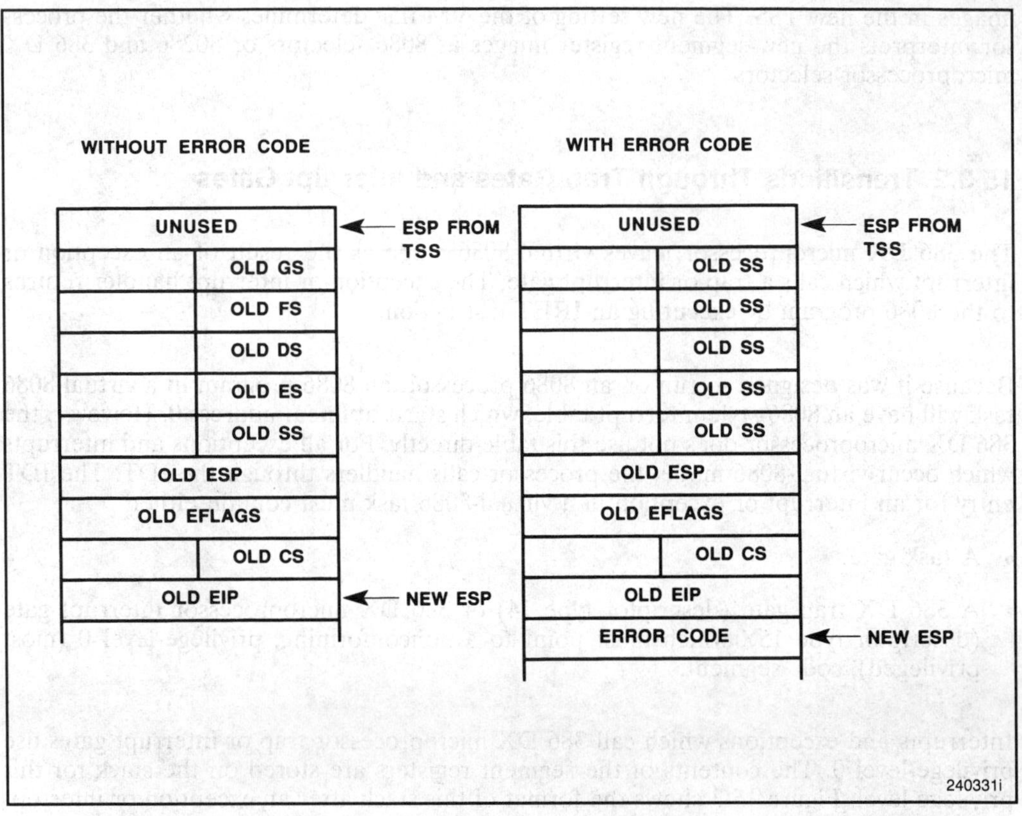

Figure 15-3. Privilege Level 0 Stack after Interrupt in Virtual-8086 Task

Sending an interrupt or exception back to the 8086 program involves the following steps:

1. Use the 8086 interrupt vector to locate the appropriate handler procedure.
2. Store the state of the 8086 program on the privilege-level 3 stack (least privileged).
3. Change the return link on the privilege-level 0 stack (most privileged) to point to the privilege-level 3 handler procedure.
4. Execute an IRET instruction to pass control to the handler.
5. When the IRET instruction from the privilege-level 3 handler again calls the virtual-8086 monitor, restore the return link on the privilege-level 0 stack to point to the original, interrupted, privilege-level 3 procedure.
6. Execute an IRET instruction to pass control back to the interrupted procedure.

15.4 ADDITIONAL SENSITIVE INSTRUCTIONS

When the 386 DX microprocessor is running in virtual-8086 mode, the PUSHF, POPF, INT *n* and IRET instructions are sensitive to IOPL. The IN, INS, OUT, and OUTS instructions, which are sensitive to IOPL in protected mode, are *not* sensitive in virtual-8086 mode. Following is a complete list of instructions which are sensitive in virtual-8086 mode:

CLI	– Clear Interrupt-Enable Flag
STI	– Set Interrupt-Enable Flag
PUSHF	– Push Flags
POPF	– Pop Flags
INT *n*	– Software Interrupt
IRET	– Interrupt Return

The CPL is always 3 while running in virtual-8086 mode; if the IOPL is less than 3, an attempt to use the instructions listed above will trigger a general-protection exception. These instructions are sensitive to the IOPL to give the virtual-8086 monitor a chance to emulate the facilities they affect.

15.4.1 Emulating 8086 Operating System Calls

The INT *n* instruction is sensitive to IOPL so a virtual-8086 monitor can intercept calls to the 8086 operating system. Many 8086 operating systems are called by pushing parameters onto the stack, then executing an INT *n* instruction. If the IOPL is less than 3, INT *n* instructions are intercepted by the virtual-8086 monitor. The virtual-8086 monitor then can emulate the function of the 8086 operating system or send the interrupt back to the 8086 operating system.

15.4.2 Emulating the Interrupt-Enable Flag

When the 386 DX microprocessor is running an 8086 program in a virtual-8086 task, the PUSHF, POPF, and IRET instructions are sensitive to the IOPL. This lets the virtual-8086 monitor protect the interrupt-enable flag (IF). Other instructions which affect the IF flag (such as the STI and CLI instructions) are sensitive to the IOPL in both 8086 and 386 DX microprocessor programs.

Many 8086 programs written for non-multitasking systems set and clear the IF flag to control interrupts. This may cause problems in a multitasking environment. If the IOPL is less than 3, all instructions which change or test the IF flag generate an exception. The virtual-8086 monitor then can control the IF flag in a manner compatible with the 386 DX microprocessor environment and transparent to 8086 programs.

15.5 VIRTUAL I/O

Many 8086 programs written for non-multitasking systems directly access I/O ports. This may cause problems in a multitasking environment. If more than one program accesses the same port, they may interfere with each other. Most multitasking systems require application programs to access I/O ports through the operating system. This results in simplified, centralized control.

The 386 DX microprocessor provides I/O protection for creating I/O which is compatible with the 386 DX microprocessor environment and transparent to 8086 programs. Designers may take any of several possible approaches to protecting I/O ports:

- Protect the I/O address space and generate exceptions for all attempts to perform I/O directly.
- Let the 8086 processor program perform I/O directly.
- Generate exceptions on attempts to access specific I/O ports.
- Generate exceptions on attempts to access specific memory-mapped I/O ports.

The method of controlling access to I/O ports depends upon whether they are I/O-mapped or memory-mapped.

15.5.1 I/O-Mapped I/O

The I/O address space in virtual-8086 mode differs from protected mode only because the IOPL is not checked. Only the I/O permission bit map is checked when virtual-8086 tasks access the I/O address space.

The I/O permission bit map can be used to generate exceptions on attempts to access specific I/O addresses. The I/O permission bit map of each virtual-8086 task determines which I/O addresses generate exceptions for that task. Because each task may have a different I/O permission bit map, the addresses which generate exceptions for one task may be different from the addresses for another task. See Chapter 8 for more information about the I/O permission bit map.

15.5.2 Memory-Mapped I/O

In systems which use memory-mapped I/O, the paging facilities of the 386 DX microprocessor can be used generate exceptions for attempts to access I/O ports. The virtual-8086 monitor may use paging to control memory-mapped I/O in these ways:

- Map part of the linear address space of each task which needs to perform I/O to the physical address space where I/O ports are placed. By putting the I/O ports at different addresses (in different pages), the paging mechanism can enforce isolation between tasks.
- Map part of the linear address space to pages which are not-present. This generates an exception whenever a task attempts to perform I/O to those pages. System software then can interpret the I/O operation being attempted.

Software emulation of the I/O space may require too much operating system intervention under some conditions. In these cases, it may be possible to generate an exception for only the first attempt to access I/O. The system software then may determine whether a program can be given exclusive control of I/O temporarily, the protection of the I/O space may be lifted, and the program allowed to run at full speed.

15.5.3 Special I/O Buffers

Buffers of intelligent controllers (for example, a bit-mapped frame buffer) also can be emulated using page mapping. The linear space for the buffer can be mapped to a different physical space for each virtual-8086 task. The virtual-8086 monitor then can control which virtual buffer to copy onto the real buffer in the physical address space.

15.6 DIFFERENCES FROM 8086 PROCESSOR

In general, virtual-8086 mode will run software written for the 8086, 8088, 80186, and 80188 processors. The following list shows the minor differences between the 8086 processor and the virtual-8086 mode of the 386 DX microprocessor.

1. Instruction clock counts.

   The 386 DX microprocessor takes fewer clocks for most instructions than the 8086 processor. The areas most likely to be affected are:

   - Delays required by I/O devices between I/O operations.
   - Assumed delays with 8086 processor operating in parallel with an 8087.

2. Divide exceptions point to the DIV instruction.

   Divide exceptions on the 386 DX microprocessor always leave the saved CS:IP value pointing to the instruction which failed. On the 8086 processor, the CS:IP value points to the next instruction.

3. Undefined 8086 processor opcodes.

   Opcodes which were not defined for the 8086 processor generate an invalid-opcode or execute as one of the new instructions defined for the 386 DX microprocessor.

4. Value written by PUSH SP.

   The 386 DX microprocessor pushes a different value on the stack for PUSH SP than the 8086 processor. The 386 DX microprocessor pushes the value in the SP register before it is incremented as part of the push operation; the 8086 processor pushes the value of the SP register after it is incremented. If the pushed value is important, replace PUSH SP instructions with the following three instructions:

   ```
   PUSH  BP
   MOV   BP, SP
   XCHG  BP, [BP]
   ```

   This code functions as the 8086 PUSH SP instruction on the 386 DX microprocessor.

5. Shift or rotate by more than 31 bits.

   The 386 DX microprocessor masks all shift and rotate counts to the lowest five bits. This limits the count to a maximum of 31 bit positions, thereby limiting the time that interrupt response is delayed while the instruction executes.

6. Redundant prefixes.

   The 386 DX microprocessor limits instructions to 15 bytes. The only way to violate this limit is with redundant prefixes before an instruction. A general-protection exception is generated if the limit on instruction length is violated. The 8086 processor has no instruction length limit.

7. Operand crossing offset 0 or 65,535.

   On the 8086 processor, an attempt to access a memory operand which crosses offset 65,535 (e.g., MOV a word to offset 65,535) or offset 0 (e.g., PUSH a word when the contents of the SP register are 1) causes the offset to wrap around modulo 65,536. The 386 DX microprocessor generates an exception in these cases, a general-protection exception if the segment is a data segment (i.e., if the CS, DS, ES, FS, or GS register is being used to address the segment), or a stack exception if the segment is a stack segment (i.e., if the SS register is being used).

8. Sequential execution across offset 65,535.

   On the 8086 processor, if sequential execution of instructions proceeds past offset 65,535, the processor fetches the next instruction byte from offset 0 of the same segment. On the 386 DX microprocessor, the processor generates a general-protection exception.

9. LOCK is restricted to certain instructions.

   The LOCK prefix and its output signal should only be used to prevent other bus masters from interrupting a data movement operation. The LOCK prefix only may be used with the following 386 DX microprocessor instructions when they modify memory. An invalid opcode exception results from using LOCK before any other instruction, or with these instructions when no write operation is made to memory.

   - Bit test and change: the BTS, BTR, and BTC instructions.
   - Exchange: the XCHG instruction.
   - One-operand arithmetic and logical: the INC, DEC, NOT, NEG instructions.
   - Two-operand arithmetic and logical: the ADD, ADC, SUB, SBB, AND, OR, and XOR instructions.

10. Single-stepping external interrupt handlers.

    The priority of the 386 DX microprocessor single-step exception is different from that of the 8086 processor. This change prevents an external interrupt handler from being single-stepped if the interrupt occurs while a program is being single-stepped. The 386 DX microprocessor single-step exception has higher priority than any external interrupt. The 386 DX microprocessor will still single-step through an interrupt handler called by the INT instruction or by an exception.

11. IDIV exceptions for quotients of 80H or 8000H.

    The 386 DX microprocessor can generate the largest negative number as a quotient from the IDIV instruction. The 8086 processor generates a divide-error exception instead.

12. Flags in stack.

    The contents of the EFLAGS register stored by the PUSHF instruction, by interrupts, and by exceptions is different from that stored by the 8086 processor in bit positions 12 through 15. On the 8086 processor these bits are stored as though they were set, but in virtual-8086 mode bit 15 is always clear, and bits 14 through 12 have the last value loaded into them.

13. NMI interrupting NMI handlers.

    After an NMI interrupt is accepted by the 386 DX microprocessor, the NMI interrupt is masked until an IRET instruction is executed.

14. Coprocessor errors generate interrupt 16.

    Any 386 DX microprocessor system with a coprocessor must use interrupt 16 for the coprocessor-error exception. If an 8086 system uses another vector for the 8087 interrupt, both vectors should point to the coprocessor-error exception handler.

15. Numeric exception handlers should allow prefixes.

    On the 386 DX microprocessor, the value of CS:IP saved for coprocessor exceptions points at any prefixes before an ESC instruction. On 8086 processor systems, the saved CS:IP points to the ESC instruction itself.

16. Coprocessor does not use interrupt controller.

    The coprocessor error signal to the 386 DX microprocessor does not pass through an interrupt controller (an 8087 INT signal does). Some instructions in a coprocessor error handler may need to be deleted if they deal with the interrupt controller.

17. Response to bus hold.

    Unlike the 8086 and 80286 processors, the 386 DX microprocessor responds to requests for control of the bus from other potential bus masters, such as DMA controllers, between transfers of parts of an unaligned operand, such as two words which form a doubleword.

18. CPL is 3 in virtual-8086 mode.

    The 8086 processor does not support protection, so it has no CPL. Virtual-8086 mode uses a CPL of 3, which prevents the execution of privileged instructions. These are:

    - LIDT instruction
    - LGDT instruction
    - LMSW instruction
    - special forms of the MOV instruction for loading and storing the control registers
    - CLTS instruction
    - HLT instruction

    These instructions may be executed while the processor is in real-address mode following reset initialization. They allow system data structures, such as descriptor tables, to be set up before entering protected mode. Virtual-8086 mode is entered from protected mode, so it has no need for these instructions.

15.7 DIFFERENCES FROM 80286 REAL-ADDRESS MODE

The 80286 processor implements the bus lock function differently than the 386 DX microprocessor. This fact may or may not be apparent to 8086 programs, depending on how the virtual-8086 monitor handles the LOCK prefix. Instructions with the LOCK prefix are sensitive to the IOPL; software designers can choose to emulate its function. If, however, 8086 programs are allowed to execute LOCK directly, programs which use forms of memory locking specific to the 8086 processor may not run properly when run on the 386 DX microprocessor.

The LOCK prefix and its bus signal only should be used to prevent other bus masters from interrupting a data movement operation. The LOCK prefix only may be used with the following 386 DX microprocessor instructions when they modify memory. An invalid-opcode exception results from using the LOCK prefix before any other instruction, or with these instructions when no write operation is made to memory (i.e., when the destination operand is in a register).

- Bit test and change: the BTS, BTR, and BTC instructions.
- Exchange: the XCHG instruction.
- One-operand arithmetic and logical: the INC, DEC, NOT, NEG instructions.
- Two-operand arithmetic and logical: the ADD, ADC, SUB, SBB, AND, OR, and XOR instructions.

A locked instruction is guaranteed to lock only the area of memory defined by the destination operand, but may lock a larger memory area. For example, typical 8086 and 80286 configurations lock the entire physical memory space.

Unlike the 8086 and 80286 processors, the 386 DX microprocessor responds to requests for control of the bus from other potential bus masters, such as DMA controllers, between transfers of parts of an unaligned operand, such as two words which form a doubleword.

Mixing 16-Bit and 32-Bit Code

16

CHAPTER 16
MIXING 16-BIT AND 32-BIT CODE

The 386™ DX microprocessor running in protected mode is a complete 32-bit architecture, but it supports programs written for the 16-bit architecture of earlier Intel® processors. There are three levels of this support:

1. Running 8086 and 80286 code with complete compatibility.
2. Mixing 16-bit modules with 32-bit modules.
3. Mixing 16-bit and 32-bit addresses and data within one module.

The first level is discussed in Chapter 13, Chapter 14, and Chapter 15. This chapter shows how 16-bit and 32-bit modules can cooperate with one another, and how one module can use both 16-bit and 32-bit operands and addressing.

The 386 DX microprocessor functions most efficiently when it is possible to distinguish between pure 16-bit modules and pure 32-bit modules. A pure 16-bit module has these characteristics:

- All segments occupy 64K bytes or less.
- Data items are either 8 bits or 16 bits wide.
- Pointers to code and data have 16-bit offsets.
- Control is transferred only among 16-bit segments.

A pure 32-bit module has these characteristics:

- Segments may occupy more than 64K bytes (0 bytes to 4 gigabytes).
- Data items are either 8 bits or 32 bits wide.
- Pointers to code and data have 32-bit offsets.
- Control is transferred only among 32-bit segments.

A program written for 16-bit processor would be pure 16-bit code. A new program written for the protected mode of the 386 DX microprocessor would be pure 32-bit code. As applications move from 16-bit processors to the 32-bit 386 DX microprocessor, there will be cases where 16-bit and 32-bit code will need to be mixed. Reasons for mixing code are:

- Modules will be converted one-by-one from 16-bit environments to 32-bit environments.
- Older, 16-bit compilers and software-development tools will be used in the new 32-bit operating environment until new 32-bit tools are available.
- The source code of 16-bit modules is not available for modification.
- The specific data structures used by a given module are fixed at 16-bit word size.
- The native word size of the source language is 16 bits.

16.1 USING 16-BIT AND 32-BIT ENVIRONMENTS

The features of the architecture which permit the 386 DX microprocessor to mix 16-bit and 32-bit address and operand size include:

- The D-bit (default bit) of code-segment descriptors, which determines the default choice of operand-size and address-size for the instructions of a code segment. (In real-address mode and virtual-8086 mode, which do not use descriptors, the default is 16 bits.) A code segment whose D-bit is set is a 32-bit segment; a code segment whose D-bit is clear is a 16-bit segment. The D-bit eliminates the need to put the operand size and address size in instructions when all instructions use operands and effective addresses of the same size.
- Instruction prefixes to override the default choice of operand size and address size (available in protected mode as well as in real-address mode and virtual-8086 mode).
- Separate 32-bit and 16-bit gates for intersegment control transfers (including call gates, interrupt gates, and trap gates). The operand size for the control transfer is determined by the type of gate, not by the D-bit or prefix of the transfer instruction.
- Registers which can be used both for 16-bit and 32-bit operands and effective-address calculations.
- The B bit (Big bit) of data-segment descriptors, which specifies the size of stack pointer (the 32-bit ESP register or the 16-bit SP register) used by the processor for implicit stack references.

16.2 MIXING 16-BIT AND 32-BIT OPERATIONS

The 386 DX microprocessor has two instruction prefixes which allow mixing of 32-bit and 16-bit operations within one segment:

- The operand-size prefix (66H)
- The address-size prefix (67H)

These prefixes *reverse* the default size selected by the Default bit. For example, the processor can interpret the MOV mem, reg instruction in any of four ways:

- In a 32-bit segment:
  1. Moves 32 bits from a 32-bit register to memory using a 32-bit effective address.
  2. If preceded by an operand-size prefix, moves 16 bits from a 16-bit register to memory using a 32-bit effective address.
  3. If preceded by an address-size prefix, moves 32 bits from a 32-bit register to memory using a 16-bit effective address.
  4. If preceded by both an address-size prefix and an operand-size prefix, moves 16 bits from a 16-bit register to memory using a 16-bit effective address.
- In a 16-bit segment:
  1. Moves 16 bits from a 16-bit register to memory using a 16-bit effective address.
  2. If preceded by an operand-size prefix, moves 32 bits from a 32-bit register to memory using a 16-bit effective address.

3. If preceded by an address-size prefix, moves 16 bits from a 16-bit register to memory using a 32-bit effective address.
4. If preceded by both an address-size prefix and an operand size prefix, moves 32 bits from a 32-bit register to memory using a 32-bit effective address.

These examples show that any instruction can generate any combination of operand size and address size regardless of whether the instruction is in a 16- or 32-bit segment. The choice of the 16- or 32-bit default for a code segment is based upon these criteria:

1. The need to address instructions or data in segments which are larger than 64K bytes.
2. The predominant size of operands.
3. The addressing modes desired. (See Chapter 17 for an explanation of the additional addressing modes available when 32-bit addressing is used.)

The Default bit should be given a setting which allows the predominant size of operands to be accessed without operand-size prefixes.

16.3 SHARING DATA AMONG MIXED-SIZE CODE SEGMENTS

Because the choice of operand size and address size is specified in code segments and their descriptors, data segments can be shared freely among both 16-bit and 32-bit code segments. The only limitation is imposed by pointers with 16-bit offsets, which only can point to the first 64K bytes of a segment. When a data segment with more than 64K bytes is to be shared among 16- and 32-bit segments, the data which is to be accessed by the 16-bit segments must be located within the first 64K bytes.

A stack which spans less than 64K bytes can be shared by both 16- and 32-bit code segments. This class of stacks includes:

- Stacks in expand-up segments with the Granularity and Big bits clear.
- Stacks in expand-down segments with the Granularity and Big bits clear.
- Stacks in expand-up segments with the Granularity bit set and the Big bit clear, in which the stack is contained completely within the lower 64K bytes. (Offsets greater than 0FFFFH can be used for data, other than the stack, which is not shared.)

The B-bit of a stack segment cannot, in general, be used to change the size of stack used by a 16-bit code segment. The size of stack pointer used by the processor for *implicit* stack references is controlled by the B-bit of the data-segment descriptor for the stack. Implicit references are those caused by interrupts, exceptions, and instructions such as the PUSH, POP, CALL, and RET instructions. Although it seems like the B bit could be used to increase the stack segment for 16-bit programs beyond 64K bytes, this may not be done. The B-bit does not control *explicit* stack references, such as accesses to parameters or local variables. A 16-bit code segment can use a "big" stack only if the code is modified so that all explicit references to the stack are preceded by the address-size prefix, causing those references to use 32-bit addressing.

In big, expand-down segments (the Granularity, Big, and Expand-down bits set), all offsets are greater than 64K, therefore 16-bit code cannot use this kind of stack segment unless the code segment is modified to use 32-bit addressing. (See Chapter 6 for more information about the G, B, and E bits.)

16.4 TRANSFERRING CONTROL AMONG MIXED-SIZE CODE SEGMENTS

When transferring control among procedures in 16-bit and 32-bit code segments, programmers must be aware of three points:

- Addressing limitations imposed by pointers with 16-bit offsets.
- Matching of operand-size attribute in effect for the CALL/RET instruction pair and the Interrupt/IRET pair for managing the stack correctly.
- Translation of parameters, especially pointer parameters.

Clearly, 16-bit effective addresses cannot be used to address data or code located beyond 0FFFFH in a 32-bit segment, nor can large 32-bit parameters be squeezed into a 16-bit word; however, except for these obvious limits, most interface problems between 16-bit and 32-bit modules can be solved. Some solutions involve inserting interface code between modules.

16.4.1 Size of Code-Segment Pointer

For control-transfer instructions which use a pointer to identify the next instruction (i.e., those which do not use gates), the size of the offset portion of the pointer is determined by the operand-size attribute. The implications of the use of two different sizes of code-segment pointer are:

- A JMP, CALL, or RET instruction from a 32-bit segment to a 16-bit segment is always possible using a 32-bit operand size.
- A JMP, CALL, or RET instruction from a 16-bit segment using a 16-bit operand size cannot address a destination in a 32-bit segment if the address of the destination is greater than 0FFFFH.

An interface procedure can provide a mechanism for transfers from 16-bit segments to destinations in 32-bit segments beyond 64K. The requirements for this kind of interface procedure are discussed later in this chapter.

16.4.2 Stack Management for Control Transfers

Because stack management is different for 16-bit CALL and RET instructions than for 32-bit CALL and RET instructions, the operand size of the RET instruction must match the CALL instruction. (See Figure 16-1.) A 16-bit CALL instruction pushes the contents of the 16-bit IP register and (for calls between privilege levels) the 16-bit SP register. The matching RET instruction also must use a 16-bit operand size to pop these 16-bit values from the stack into the 16-bit registers. A 32-bit CALL instruction pushes the

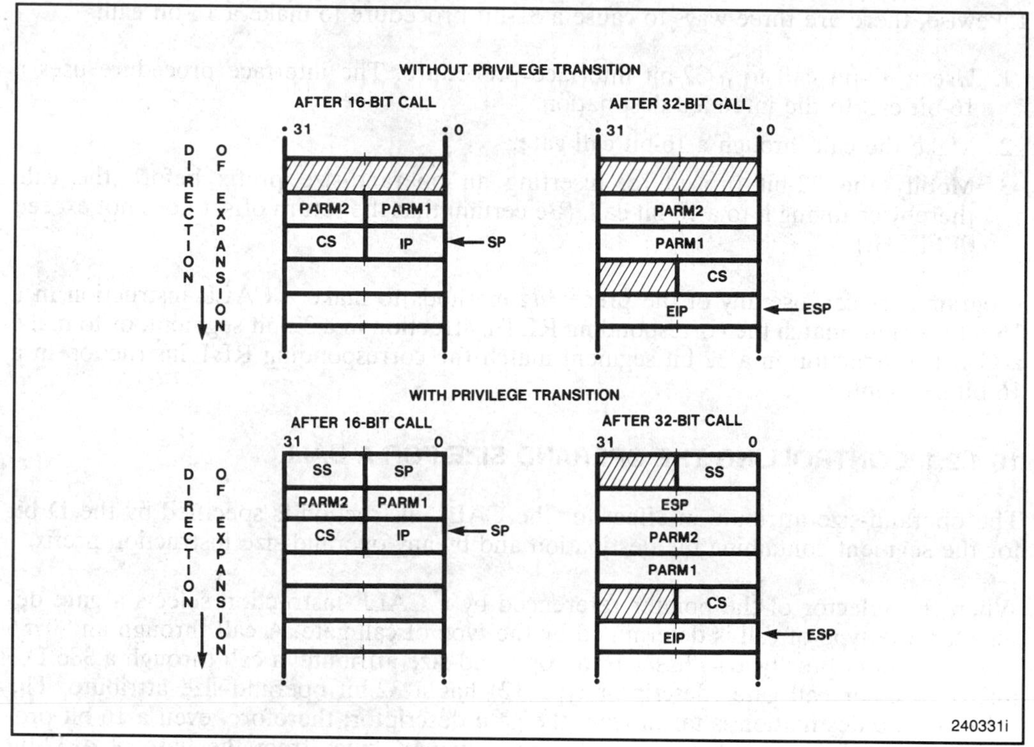

Figure 16-1. Stack after Far 16- and 32-Bit Calls

contents of the 32-bit EIP register and (for interlevel calls) the 32-bit ESP register. The matching RET instruction also must use a 32-bit operand size to pop these 32-bit values from the stack into the 32-bit registers. If the two parts of a CALL/RET instruction pair do not have matching operand sizes, the stack will not be managed correctly and the values of the instruction pointer and stack pointer will not be restored to correct values.

When the CALL instruction and its matching RET instruction are in segments which have D bits with the same values (i.e., both have 32-bit defaults or both havc 16-bit defaults), the default settings may be used. When the CALL instruction and its matching RET instruction are in segments which have different D-bit values, an operand size prefix must be used.

There are three ways for a 16-bit procedure to make a 32-bit call:

1. Use a 16-bit call to a 32-bit interface procedure. The interface procedure uses a 32-bit call to the intended destination.
2. Make the call through a 32-bit call gate.
3. Modify the 16-bit procedure, inserting an operand-size prefix before the call, to change it to a 32-bit call.

Likewise, there are three ways to cause a 32-bit procedure to make a 16-bit call:

1. Use a 32-bit call to a 32-bit interface procedure. The interface procedure uses a 16-bit call to the intended destination.
2. Make the call through a 16-bit call gate.
3. Modify the 32-bit procedure, inserting an operand-size prefix before the call, thereby changing it to a 16-bit call. (Be certain that the return offset does not exceed 0FFFFH.)

Programmers can use any of the preceding methods to make a CALL instruction in a 16-bit segment match the corresponding RET instruction in a 32-bit segment, or to make a CALL instruction in a 32-bit segment match the corresponding RET instruction in a 16-bit segment.

16.4.2.1 CONTROLLING THE OPERAND SIZE FOR A CALL

The operand-size attribute in effect for the CALL instruction is specified by the D bit for the segment containing the destination and by any operand-size instruction prefix.

When the selector of the pointer referenced by a CALL instruction selects a gate descriptor, the type of call is determined by the type of call gate. A call through an 80286 call gate (descriptor type 4) has a 16-bit operand-size attribute; a call through a 386 DX microprocessor call gate (descriptor type 12) has a 32-bit operand-size attribute. The offset to the destination is taken from the gate descriptor; therefore, even a 16-bit procedure can call a procedure located more than 64K bytes from the base of a 32-bit segment, because a 32-bit call gate contains a 32-bit offset.

An unmodified 16-bit code segment which has run successfully on an 8086 processor or in real-mode on an 80286 processor will have a D-bit which is clear and will not use operand-size override prefixes; therefore, it will use 16-bit versions of the CALL instruction. The only modification needed to make a 16-bit procedure produce a 32-bit call is to relink the call to a 386 DX microprocessor call gate.

16.4.2.2 CHANGING SIZE OF A CALL

When adding 32-bit gates to 16-bit procedures, it is important to consider the number of parameters. The count field of the gate descriptor specifies the size of the parameter string to copy from the current stack to the stack of the more privileged procedure. The count field of a 16-bit gate specifies the number of *words* to be copied, whereas the count field of a 32-bit gate specifies the number of *doublewords* to be copied; therefore, the 16-bit procedure must use an even number of words as parameters.

16.4.3 Interrupt Control Transfers

With a control transfer caused by an exception or interrupt, a gate is used. The operand-size attribute for the interrupt is determined by the gate descriptor in the interrupt descriptor table (IDT).

A 386 DX microprocessor interrupt or trap gate (descriptor type 14 or 15) to a 32-bit interrupt handler can be used to interrupt either 32-bit or 16-bit procedures. However, sometimes it is not practical to permit an interrupt or exception to call a 16-bit handler when 32-bit code is running, because a 16-bit interrupt procedure has a return offset of only 16 bits saved on its stack. If the 32-bit procedure is running at an address beyond 0FFFFH, the 16-bit interrupt procedure cannot provide the return address.

16.4.4 Parameter Translation

When segment offsets or pointers (which contain segment offsets) are passed as parameters between 16-bit and 32-bit procedures, some translation is required. If a 32-bit procedure passes a pointer to data located beyond 64K to a 16-bit procedure, the 16-bit procedure cannot use it. Except for this limitation, interface code can perform any format conversion between 32-bit and 16-bit pointers which may be needed.

Parameters passed by value between 32-bit and 16-bit code also may require translation between 32-bit and 16-bit formats. The form of the translation is application-dependent.

16.4.5 The Interface Procedure

Placing interface code between 32-bit and 16-bit procedures can be the solution to several interface problems:

- Allowing procedures in 16-bit segments to call procedures with offsets greater than 0FFFFH in 32-bit segments.
- Matching operand size between CALL and RET instructions.
- Translating parameters (data).

The interface code is simplified where these restrictions are followed.

- Interface code resides in a code segment whose D-bit is set, which indicates a default operand size of 32-bits.
- All procedures which may be called by 16-bit procedures have offsets which are not greater than 0FFFFH.
- All return addresses saved by 16-bit procedures also have offsets not greater than 0FFFFH.

The interface code becomes more complex if any of these restrictions are violated. For example, if a 16-bit procedure calls a 32-bit procedure with an entry point beyond 0FFFFH, the interface code will have to provide the offset to the entry point. The mapping between 16- and 32-bit addresses only is performed automatically when a call gate is used, because the descriptor for a call gate contains a 32-bit address. When a call gate is not used, the descriptor must provide the 32-bit address.

The interface code calls procedures in other segments. There may be two kinds of interface:

- Where 16-bit procedures call 32-bit procedures. The interface code is called by 16-bit CALL instructions and uses the operand-size prefix before RET instructions for performing a 16-bit RET instruction. Calls to 32-bit segments are 32-bit CALL instructions (by default, because the D-bit is set), and the 32-bit code returns with 32-bit RET instructions.

- Where 32-bit procedures call 16-bit procedures. The interface code is called by 32-bit CALL instructions, and returns with 32-bit RET instructions (by default, because the D-bit is set). CALL instructions to 16-bit procedures use the operand-size prefix; 16-bit procedures return with 16-bit RET instructions.

Part IV
Instruction Set

386™ DX Microprocessor Instruction Set

17

CHAPTER 17
386™ DX MICROPROCESSOR INSTRUCTION SET

This chapter presents instructions for the 386™ DX microprocessor in alphabetical order. For each instruction, the forms are given for each operand combination, including object code produced, operands required, execution time, and a description. For each instruction, there is an operational description and a summary of exceptions generated.

17.1 OPERAND-SIZE AND ADDRESS-SIZE ATTRIBUTES

When executing an instruction, the 386 DX microprocessor can address memory using either 16 or 32-bit addresses. Consequently, each instruction that uses memory addresses has associated with it an address-size attribute of either 16 or 32 bits. The use of 16-bit addresses implies both the use of 16-bit displacements in the instruction and the generation of 16-bit address offsets (segment relative addresses) as the result of the effective address calculation. The use of 32-bit addresses implies the use of 32-bit displacements and the generation of 32-bit address offsets. Similarly, an instruction that accesses words (16 bits) or doublewords (32 bits) has an operand-size attribute of either 16 or 32 bits.

The attributes are determined by a combination of defaults, instruction prefixes, and (for programs executing in protected mode) size-specification bits in segment descriptors.

17.1.1 Default Segment Attribute

For programs running in protected mode, the D bit in executable-segment descriptors specifies the default attribute for both address size and operand size. These default attributes apply to the execution of all instructions in the segment. A clear D bit sets the default address size and operand size to 16 bits; a set D bit, to 32 bits.

Programs that execute in real mode or virtual-8086 mode have 16-bit addresses and operands by default.

17.1.2 Operand-Size and Address-Size Instruction Prefixes

The internal encoding of an instruction can include two byte-long prefixes: the address-size prefix, 67H, and the operand-size prefix, 66H. (A later section, "Instruction Format," shows the position of the prefixes in an instruction's encoding.) These prefixes *override* the default segment attributes for the instruction that follows. Table 17-1 shows the effect of each possible combination of defaults and overrides.

Table 17-1. Effective Size Attributes

Segment Default D = ...	0	0	0	0	1	1	1	1
Operand-Size Prefix 66H	N	N	Y	Y	N	N	Y	Y
Address-Size Prefix 67H	N	Y	N	Y	N	Y	N	Y
Effective Operand Size	16	16	32	32	32	32	16	16
Effective Address Size	16	32	16	32	32	16	32	16

Y = Yes, this instruction prefix is present
N = No, this instruction prefix is not present

17.1.3 Address-Size Attribute for Stack

Instructions that use the stack implicitly (for example: POP EAX) also have a stack address-size attribute of either 16 or 32 bits. Instructions with a stack address-size attribute of 16 use the 16-bit SP stack pointer register; instructions with a stack address-size attribute of 32 bits use the 32-bit ESP register to form the address of the top of the stack.

The stack address-size attribute is controlled by the B-bit of the data-segment descriptor in the SS register. A value of zero in the B-bit selects a stack address-size attribute of 16; a value of one selects a stack address-size attribute of 32.

17.2 INSTRUCTION FORMAT

All instruction encodings are subsets of the general instruction format shown in Figure 17-1. Instructions consist of optional instruction prefixes, one or two primary opcode bytes, possibly an address specifier consisting of the ModR/M byte and the SIB (Scale Index Base) byte, a displacement, if required, and an immediate data field, if required.

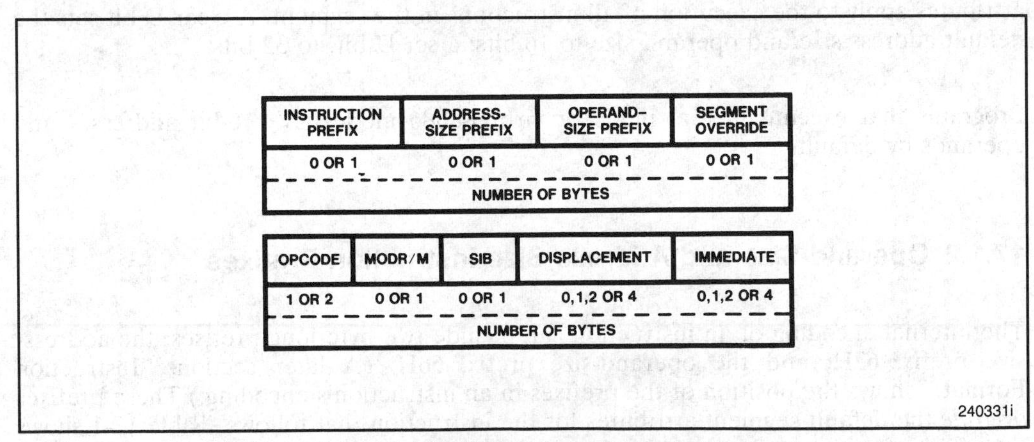

Figure 17-1. 386™ DX Microprocessor Instruction Format

Smaller encoding fields can be defined within the primary opcode or opcodes. These fields define the direction of the operation, the size of the displacements, the register encoding, or sign extension; encoding fields vary depending on the class of operation.

Most instructions that can refer to an operand in memory have an addressing form byte following the primary opcode byte(s). This byte, called the ModR/M byte, specifies the address form to be used. Certain encodings of the ModR/M byte indicate a second addressing byte, the SIB (Scale Index Base) byte, which follows the ModR/M byte and is required to fully specify the addressing form.

Addressing forms can include a displacement immediately following either the ModR/M or SIB byte. If a displacement is present, it can be 8-, 16- or 32-bits.

If the instruction specifies an immediate operand, the immediate operand always follows any displacement bytes. The immediate operand, if specified, is always the last field of the instruction.

The following are the allowable instruction prefix codes:

OF3H REP prefix (used only with string instructions)
OF3H REPE/REPZ prefix (used only with string instructions)
OF2H REPNE/REPNZ prefix (used only with string instructions)
OF0H LOCK prefix

The following are the segment override prefixes:

2EH CS segment override prefix
36H SS segment override prefix
3EH DS segment override prefix
26H ES segment override prefix
64H FS segment override prefix
65H GS segment override prefix
66H Operand-size override
67H Address-size override

17.2.1 ModR/M and SIB Bytes

The ModR/M and SIB bytes follow the opcode byte(s) in many of the 386 DX microprocessor instructions. They contain the following information:

- The indexing type or register number to be used in the instruction
- The register to be used, or more information to select the instruction
- The base, index, and scale information

The ModR/M byte contains three fields of information:

- The **mod** field, which occupies the two most significant bits of the byte, combines with the r/m field to form 32 possible values: eight registers and 24 indexing modes.

- The **reg** field, which occupies the next three bits following the mod field, specifies either a register number or three more bits of opcode information. The meaning of the reg field is determined by the first (opcode) byte of the instruction.

- The **r/m** field, which occupies the three least significant bits of the byte, can specify a register as the location of an operand, or can form part of the addressing-mode encoding in combination with the **mod** field as described above.

The based indexed and scaled indexed forms of 32-bit addressing require the SIB byte. The presence of the SIB byte is indicated by certain encodings of the ModR/M byte. The SIB byte then includes the following fields:

- The **ss** field, which occupies the two most significant bits of the byte, specifies the scale factor.

- The **index** field, which occupies the next three bits following the **ss** field and specifies the register number of the index register.

- The **base** field, which occupies the three least significant bits of the byte, specifies the register number of the base register.

Figure 17-2 shows the formats of the ModR/M and SIB bytes.

The values and the corresponding addressing forms of the ModR/M and SIB bytes are shown in Tables 17-2, 17-3, and 17-4. The 16-bit addressing forms specified by the ModR/M byte are in Table 17-2. The 32-bit addressing forms specified by the ModR/M are in Table 17-3. Table 17-4 shows the 32-bit addressing forms specified by the SIB byte.

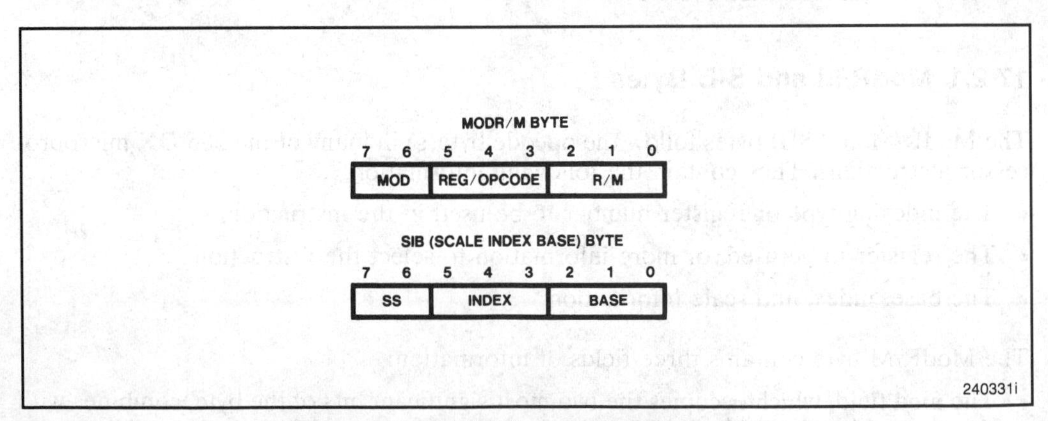

Figure 17-2. ModR/M and SIB Byte Formats

Table 17-2. 16-Bit Addressing Forms with the ModR/M Byte

r8(/r) r16(/r) r32(/r) /digit (Opcode) REG =		AL AX EAX 0 000	CL CX ECX 1 001	DL DX EDX 2 010	BL BX EBX 3 011	AH SP ESP 4 100	CH BP EBP 5 101	DH SI ESI 6 110	BH DI EDI 7 111
Effective Address	Mod R/M	ModR/M Values in Hexadecimal							
[BX+SI]	00 000	00	08	10	18	20	28	30	38
[BX+DI]	001	01	09	11	19	21	29	31	39
[BP+SI]	010	02	0A	12	1A	22	2A	32	3A
[BP+DI]	011	03	0B	13	1B	23	2B	33	3B
[SI]	100	04	0C	14	1C	24	2C	34	3C
[DI]	101	05	0D	15	1D	25	2D	35	3D
disp16	110	06	0E	16	1E	26	2E	36	3E
[BX]	111	07	0F	17	1F	27	2F	37	3F
[BX+SI]+disp8	01 000	40	48	50	58	60	68	70	78
[BX+DI]+disp8	001	41	49	51	59	61	69	71	79
[BP+SI]+disp8	010	42	4A	52	5A	62	6A	72	7A
[BP+DI]+disp8	011	43	4B	53	5B	63	6B	73	7B
[SI]+disp8	100	44	4C	54	5C	64	6C	74	7C
[DI]+disp8	101	45	4D	55	5D	65	6D	75	7D
[BP]+disp8	110	46	4E	56	5E	66	6E	76	7E
[BX]+disp8	111	47	4F	57	5F	67	6F	77	7F
[BX+SI]+disp16	10 000	80	88	90	98	A0	A8	B0	B8
[BX+DI]+disp16	001	81	89	91	99	A1	A9	B1	B9
[BX+SI]+disp16	010	82	8A	92	9A	A2	AA	B2	BA
[BX+DI]+disp16	011	83	8B	93	9B	A3	AB	B3	BB
[SI]+disp16	100	84	8C	94	9C	A4	AC	B4	BC
[DI]+disp16	101	85	8D	95	9D	A5	AD	B5	BD
[BP]+disp16	110	86	8E	96	9E	A6	AE	B6	BE
[BX]+disp16	111	87	8F	97	9F	A7	AF	B7	BF
EAX/AX/AL	11 000	C0	C8	D0	D8	E0	E8	F0	F8
ECX/CX/CL	001	C1	C9	D1	D9	EQ	E9	F1	F9
EDX/DX/DL	010	C2	CA	D2	DA	E2	EA	F2	FA
EBX/BX/BL	011	C3	CB	D3	DB	E3	EB	F3	FB
ESP/SP/AH	100	C4	CC	D4	DC	E4	EC	F4	FC
EBP/BP/CH	101	C5	CD	D5	DD	E5	ED	F5	FD
ESI/SI/DH	110	C6	CE	D6	DE	E6	EE	F6	FE
EDI/DI/BH	111	C7	CF	D7	DF	E7	EF	F7	FF

NOTES: **disp8** denotes an 8-bit displacement following the ModR/M byte, to be sign-extended and added to the index. **disp16** denotes a 16-bit displacement following the ModR/M byte, to be added to the index. Default segment register is SS for the effective addresses containing a BP index, DS for other effective addresses.

Table 17-3. 32-Bit Addressing Forms with the ModR/M Byte

r8(/r) r16(/r) r32(/r) /digit (Opcode) REG =			AL AX EAX 0 000	CL CX ECX 1 001	DL DX EDX 2 010	BL BX EBX 3 011	AH SP ESP 4 100	CH BP EBP 5 101	DH SI ESI 6 110	BH DI EDI 7 111
Effective Address	Mod	R/M	ModR/M Values in Hexadecimal							
[EAX]	00	000	00	08	10	18	20	28	30	38
[ECX]		001	01	09	11	19	21	29	31	39
[EDX]		010	02	0A	12	1A	22	2A	32	3A
[EBX]		011	03	0B	13	1B	23	2B	33	3B
[--][--]		100	04	0C	14	1C	24	2C	34	3C
disp32		101	05	0D	15	1D	25	2D	35	3D
[ESI]		110	06	0E	16	1E	26	2E	36	3E
[EDI]		111	07	0F	17	1F	27	2F	37	3F
disp8[EAX]	01	000	40	48	50	58	60	68	70	78
disp8[ECX]		001	41	49	51	59	61	69	71	79
disp8[EDX]		010	42	4A	52	5A	62	6A	72	7A
disp8[EPX];		011	43	4B	53	5B	63	6B	73	7B
disp8[--][--]		100	44	4C	54	5C	64	6C	74	7C
disp8[ebp]		101	45	4D	55	5D	65	6D	75	7D
disp8[ESI]		110	46	4E	56	5E	66	6E	76	7E
disp8[EDI]		111	47	4F	57	5F	67	6F	77	7F
disp32[EAX]	10	000	80	88	90	98	A0	A8	B0	B8
disp32[ECX]		001	81	89	91	99	A1	A9	B1	B9
disp32[EDX]		010	82	8A	92	9A	A2	AA	B2	BA
disp32[EBX]		011	83	8B	93	9B	A3	AB	B3	BB
disp32[--][--]		100	84	8C	94	9C	A4	AC	B4	BC
disp32[EBP]		101	85	8D	95	9D	A5	AD	B5	BD
disp32[ESI]		110	86	8E	96	9E	A6	AE	B6	BE
disp32[EDI]		111	87	8F	97	9F	A7	AF	B7	BF
EAX/AX/AL	11	000	C0	C8	D0	D8	E0	E8	F0	F8
ECX/CX/CL		001	C1	C9	D1	D9	E1	E9	F1	F9
EDX/DX/DL		010	C2	CA	D2	DA	E2	EA	F2	FA
EBX/BX/BL		011	C3	CB	D3	DB	E3	EB	F3	FB
ESP/SP/AH		100	C4	CC	D4	DC	E4	EC	F4	FC
EBP/BP/CH		101	C5	CD	D5	DD	E5	ED	F5	FD
ESI/SI/DH		110	C6	CE	D6	DE	E6	EE	F6	FE
EDI/DI/BH		111	C7	CF	D7	DF	E7	EF	F7	FF

NOTES: **[--][--]** means a SIB follows the ModR/M byte. **disp8** denotes an 8-bit displacement following the SIB byte, to be sign-extended and added to the index. **disp32** denotes a 32-bit displacement following the ModR/M byute, to be added to the index.

Table 17-4. 32-Bit Addressing Forms with the SIB Byte

r32 Base = Base =			EAX 0 000	ECX 1 001	EDX 2 010	EBX 3 011	ESP 4 100	[*] 5 101	ESI 6 110	EDI 7 111
Scaled Index	SS Index		ModR/M Values in Hexadecimal							
[EAX]	00	000	00	01	02	03	04	05	06	07
[ECX]		001	08	09	0A	0B	0C	0D	0E	0F
[EDX]		010	10	11	12	13	14	15	16	17
[EBX]		011	18	19	1A	1B	1C	1D	1E	1F
none		100	20	21	22	23	24	25	26	27
[EBP]		101	28	29	2A	2B	2C	2D	2E	2F
[ESI]		110	30	31	32	33	34	35	36	37
[EDI]		111	38	39	3A	3B	3C	3D	3E	3F
[EAX*2]	01	000	40	41	42	43	44	45	46	47
[ECX*2]		001	48	49	4A	4B	4C	4D	4E	4F
[ECX*2]		010	50	51	52	53	54	55	56	57
[EBX*2]		011	58	59	5A	5B	5C	5D	5E	5F
none		100	60	61	62	63	64	65	66	67
[EBP*2]		101	68	69	6A	6B	6C	6D	6E	6F
[ESI*2]		110	70	71	72	73	74	75	76	77
[EDI*2]		111	78	79	7A	7B	7C	7D	7E	7F
[EAX*4]	10	000	80	81	82	83	84	85	86	87
[ECX*4]		001	88	89	8A	8B	8C	8D	8E	8F
[EDX*4]		010	90	91	92	93	94	95	96	97
[EBX*4]		011	98	89	9A	9B	9C	9D	9E	9F
none		100	A0	A1	A2	A3	A4	A5	A6	A7
[EBP*4]		101	A8	A9	AA	AB	AC	AD	AE	AF
[ESI*4]		110	B0	B1	B2	B3	B4	B5	B6	B7
[EDI*4]		111	B8	B9	BA	BB	BC	BD	BE	BF
[EAX*8]	11	000	C0	C1	C2	C3	C4	C5	C6	C7
[ECX*8]		001	C8	C9	CA	CB	CC	CD	CE	CF
[EDX*8]		010	D0	D1	D2	D3	D4	D5	D6	D7
[EBX*8]		011	D8	D9	DA	DB	DC	DD	DE	DF
none		100	E0	E1	E2	E3	E4	E5	E6	E7
[EBP*8]		101	E8	E9	EA	EB	EC	ED	EE	EF
[ESI*8]		110	F0	F1	F2	F3	F4	F5	F6	F7
[EDI*8]		111	F8	F9	FA	FB	FC	FD	FE	FF

NOTES: [*] means a disp32 with no base if MOD is 00, [ESP] otherwise. This provides the following addressing modes:

disp32[index] (MOD = 00)
disp8[EBP][index] (MOD = 01)
disp32[EBP][index] (MOD = 10)

17.2.2 How to Read the Instruction Set Pages

The following is an example of the format used for each 386 DX microprocessor instruction description in this chapter:

CMC — Complement Carry Flag

Opcode	Instruction	Clocks	Description
F5	CMC	2	Complement carry flag

The above table is followed by paragraphs labelled "Operation," "Description," "Flags Affected," "Protected Mode Exceptions," "Real Address Mode Exceptions," and, optionally, "Notes." The following sections explain the notational conventions and abbreviations used in these paragraphs of the instruction descriptions.

17.2.2.1 OPCODE

The "Opcode" column gives the complete object code produced for each form of the instruction. When possible, the codes are given as hexadecimal bytes, in the same order in which they appear in memory. Definitions of entries other than hexadecimal bytes are as follows:

/digit: (digit is between 0 and 7) indicates that the ModR/M byte of the instruction uses only the r/m (register or memory) operand. The **reg** field contains the digit that provides an extension to the instruction's opcode.

/r: indicates that the ModR/M byte of the instruction contains both a register operand and an r/m operand.

cb, cw, cd, cp: a 1-byte (cb), 2-byte (cw), 4-byte (cd) or 6-byte (cp) value following the opcode that is used to specify a code offset and possibly a new value for the code segment register.

ib, iw, id: a 1-byte (ib), 2-byte (iw), or 4-byte (id) immediate operand to the instruction that follows the opcode, ModR/M bytes or scale-indexing bytes. The opcode determines if the operand is a signed value. All words and doublewords are given with the low-order byte first.

+rb, +rw, +rd: a register code, from 0 through 7, added to the hexadecimal byte given at the left of the plus sign to form a single opcode byte. The codes are—

rb		rw		rd	
AL	= 0	AX	= 0	EAX	= 0
CL	= 1	CX	= 1	ECX	= 1
DL	= 2	DX	= 2	EDX	= 2
BL	= 3	BX	= 3	EBX	= 3

rb			rw			rd		
AH	=	4	SP	=	4	ESP	=	4
CH	=	5	BP	=	5	EBP	=	5
DH	=	6	SI	=	6	ESI	=	6
BH	=	7	DI	=	7	EDI	=	7

17.2.2.2 INSTRUCTION

The "Instruction" column gives the syntax of the instruction statement as it would appear in an ASM386 program. The following is a list of the symbols used to represent operands in the instruction statements:

rel8: a relative address in the range from 128 bytes before the end of the instruction to 127 bytes after the end of the instruction.

rel16, rel32: a relative address within the same code segment as the instruction assembled. **rel16** applies to instructions with an operand-size attribute of 16 bits; **rel32** applies to instructions with an operand-size attribute of 32 bits.

ptr16:16, ptr16:32: a far pointer, typically in a code segment different from that of the instruction. The notation **16:16** indicates that the value of the pointer has two parts. The value to the right of the colon is a 16-bit selector or value destined for the code segment register. The value to the left corresponds to the offset within the destination segment. **ptr16:16** is used when the instruction's operand-size attribute is 16 bits; **ptr16:32** is used with the 32-bit attribute.

r8: one of the byte registers AL, CL, DL, BL, AH, CH, DH, or BH.

r16: one of the word registers AX, CX, DX, BX, SP, BP, SI, or DI.

r32: one of the doubleword registers EAX, ECX, EDX, EBX, ESP, EBP, ESI, or EDI.

imm8: an immediate byte value. **imm8** is a signed number between −128 and +127 inclusive. For instructions in which **imm8** is combined with a word or doubleword operand, the immediate value is sign-extended to form a word or doubleword. The upper byte of the word is filled with the topmost bit of the immediate value.

imm16: an immediate word value used for instructions whose operand-size attribute is 16 bits. This is a number between −32768 and +32767 inclusive.

imm32: an immediate doubleword value used for instructions whose operand-size attribute is 32-bits. It allows the use of a number between +2147483647 and −2147483648 inclusive.

r/m8: a one-byte operand that is either the contents of a byte register (AL, BL, CL, DL, AH, BH, CH, DH), or a byte from memory.

r/m16: a word register or memory operand used for instructions whose operand-size attribute is 16 bits. The word registers are: AX, BX, CX, DX, SP, BP, SI, DI. The contents of memory are found at the address provided by the effective address computation.

r/m32: a doubleword register or memory operand used for instructions whose operand-size attribute is 32-bits. The doubleword registers are: EAX, EBX, ECX, EDX, ESP, EBP, ESI, EDI. The contents of memory are found at the address provided by the effective address computation.

m8: a memory byte addressed by DS:SI or ES:DI (used only by string instructions).

m16: a memory word addressed by DS:SI or ES:DI (used only by string instructions).

m32: a memory doubleword addressed by DS:SI or ES:DI (used only by string instructions).

m16:16, m16:32: a memory operand containing a far pointer composed of two numbers. The number to the left of the colon corresponds to the pointer's segment selector. The number to the right corresponds to its offset.

m16&32, m16&16, m32&32: a memory operand consisting of data item pairs whose sizes are indicated on the left and the right side of the ampersand. All memory addressing modes are allowed. **m16&16** and **m32&32** operands are used by the BOUND instruction to provide an operand containing an upper and lower bounds for array indices. **m16&32** is used by LIDT and LGDT to provide a word with which to load the limit field, and a doubleword with which to load the base field of the corresponding Global and Interrupt Descriptor Table Registers.

moffs8, moffs16, moffs32: (memory offset) a simple memory variable of type BYTE, WORD, or DWORD used by some variants of the MOV instruction. The actual address is given by a simple offset relative to the segment base. No ModR/M byte is used in the instruction. The number shown with **moffs** indicates its size, which is determined by the address-size attribute of the instruction.

Sreg: a segment register. The segment register bit assignments are ES=0, CS=1, SS=2, DS=3, FS=4, and GS=5.

17.2.2.3 CLOCKS

The "Clocks" column gives the number of clock cycles the instruction takes to execute. The clock count calculations makes the following assumptions:

- The instruction has been prefetched and decoded and is ready for execution.
- Bus cycles do not require wait states.

- There are no local bus HOLD requests delaying processor access to the bus.
- No exceptions are detected during instruction execution.
- Memory operands are aligned.

Clock counts for instructions that have an r/m (register or memory) operand are separated by a slash. The count to the left is used for a register operand; the count to the right is used for a memory operand.

The following symbols are used in the clock count specifications:

- **n**, which represents a number of repetitions.
- **m**, which represents the number of components in the next instruction executed, where the entire displacement (if any) counts as one component, the entire immediate data (if any) counts as one component, and every other byte of the instruction and prefix(es) each counts as one component.
- **pm=**, a clock count that applies when the instruction executes in Protected Mode. **pm=** is not given when the clock counts are the same for Protected and Real Address Modes.

When an exception occurs during the execution of an instruction and the exception handler is in another task, the instruction execution time is increased by the number of clocks to effect a task switch. This parameter depends on several factors:

- The type of TSS used to represent the current task (386 DX TSS or 80286 TSS).
- The type of TSS used to represent the new task.
- Whether the current task is in V86 mode.
- Whether the new task is in V86 mode.

Table 17-5 summarizes the task switch times for exceptions.

Table 17-5. Task Switch Times for Exceptions

Old Task		New Task	
		386™ DX TSS VM = 0	80286 TSS
386 DX TSS	VM=0	309	282
386 DX TSS	VM=1	314	231
80286 TSS		307	282

17.2.2.4 DESCRIPTION

The "Description" column following the "Clocks" column briefly explains the various forms of the instruction. The "Operation" and "Description" sections contain more details of the instruction's operation.

17.2.2.5 OPERATION

The "Operation" section contains an algorithmic description of the instruction which uses a notation similar to the Algol or Pascal language. The algorithms are composed of the following elements:

Comments are enclosed within the symbol pairs "(*" and "*)".

Compound statements are enclosed between the keywords of the "if" statement (IF, THEN, ELSE, FI) or of the "do" statement (DO, OD), or of the "case" statement (CASE ... OF, ESAC).

A register name implies the contents of the register. A register name enclosed in brackets implies the contents of the location whose address is contained in that register. For example, ES:[DI] indicates the contents of the location whose ES segment relative address is in register DI. [SI] indicates the contents of the address contained in register SI relative to SI's default segment (DS) or overridden segment.

Brackets also used for memory operands, where they mean that the contents of the memory location is a segment-relative offset. For example, [SRC] indicates that the contents of the source operand is a segment-relative offset.

A ← B; indicates that the value of B is assigned to A.

The symbols =, < >, ≥, and ≤ are relational operators used to compare two values, meaning equal, not equal, greater or equal, less or equal, respectively. A relational expression such as A = B is TRUE if the value of A is equal to B; otherwise it is FALSE.

The following identifiers are used in the algorithmic descriptions:

- **OperandSize** represents the operand-size attribute of the instruction, which is either 16 or 32 bits. **AddressSize** represents the address-size attribute, which is either 16 or 32 bits. For example,

```
IF instruction = CMPSW
THEN OperandSize ← 16;
ELSE
    IF instruction = CMPSD
    THEN OperandSize ← 32;
    FI;
FI;
```

indicates that the operand-size attribute depends on the form of the CMPS instruction used. Refer to the explanation of address-size and operand-size attributes at the beginning of this chapter for general guidelines on how these attributes are determined.

- **StackAddrSize** represents the stack address-size attribute associated with the instruction, which has a value of 16 or 32 bits, as explained earlier in the chapter.
- **SRC** represents the source operand. When there are two operands, SRC is the one on the right.
- **DEST** represents the destination operand. When there are two operands, DEST is the one on the left.
- **LeftSRC, RightSRC** distinguishes between two operands when both are source operands.
- **eSP** represents either the SP register or the ESP register depending on the setting of the B-bit for the current stack segment.

The following functions are used in the algorithmic descriptions:

- **Truncate to 16 bits(value)** reduces the size of the value to fit in 16 bits by discarding the uppermost bits as needed.
- **Addr(operand)** returns the effective address of the operand (the result of the effective address calculation prior to adding the segment base).
- **ZeroExtend(value)** returns a value zero-extended to the operand-size attribute of the instruction. For example, if OperandSize = 32, ZeroExtend of a byte value of −10 converts the byte from F6H to doubleword with hexadecimal value 000000F6H. If the value passed to ZeroExtend and the operand-size attribute are the same size, ZeroExtend returns the value unaltered.
- **SignExtend(value)** returns a value sign-extended to the operand-size attribute of the instruction. For example, if OperandSize = 32, SignExtend of a byte containing the value −10 converts the byte from F6H to a doubleword with hexadecimal value FFFFFFF6H. If the value passed to SignExtend and the operand-size attribute are the same size, SignExtend returns the value unaltered.
- **Push(value)** pushes a value onto the stack. The number of bytes pushed is determined by the operand-size attribute of the instruction. The action of Push is as follows:

```
IF StackAddrSize = 16
THEN
    IF OperandSize = 16
    THEN
        SP ← SP − 2;
        SS:[SP] ← value; (* 2 bytes assigned starting at
                            byte address in SP *)
    ELSE (* OperandSize = 32 *)
        SP ← SP − 4;
        SS:[SP] ← value; (* 4 bytes assigned starting at
                            byte address in SP *)
    FI;
```

```
ELSE (* StackAddrSize = 32 *)
     IF OperandSize = 16
     THEN
          ESP ← ESP − 2;
          SS:[ESP] ← value; (* 2 bytes assigned starting at
                              byte address in ESP*)
     ELSE (* OperandSize = 32 *)
          ESP ← ESP − 4;
          SS:[ESP] ← value; (* 4 bytes assigned starting at
                              byte address in ESP*)
     FI;
FI;
```

- **Pop(value)** removes the value from the top of the stack and returns it. The statement EAX ← Pop( ); assigns to EAX the 32-bit value that Pop took from the top of the stack. Pop will return either a word or a doubleword depending on the operand-size attribute. The action of Pop is as follows:

```
IF StackAddrSize = 16
THEN
     IF OperandSize = 16
     THEN
          ret val ← SS:[SP]; (* 2-byte value *)
          SP ← SP + 2;
     ELSE (* OperandSize = 32 *)
          ret val ← SS:[SP]; (* 4-byte value *)
          SP ← SP + 4;
     FI;
ELSE (* StackAddrSize = 32 *)
     IF OperandSize = 16
     THEN
          ret val ← SS:[ESP]; (* 2 bytes value *)
          ESP ← ESP + 2;
     ELSE (* OperandSize = 32 *)
          ret val ← SS:[ESP]; (* 4 bytes value *)
          ESP ← ESP + 4;
     FI;
FI;
RETURN(ret val); (*returns a word or doubleword*)
```

- **Bit[BitBase, BitOffset]** returns the address of a bit within a bit string, which is a sequence of bits in memory or a register. Bits are numbered from low-order to high-order within registers and within memory bytes. In memory, the two bytes of a word are stored with the low-order byte at the lower address.

  If the base operand is a register, the offset can be in the range 0..31. This offset addresses a bit within the indicated register. An example, "BIT[EAX, 21]" is illustrated in Figure 17-3.

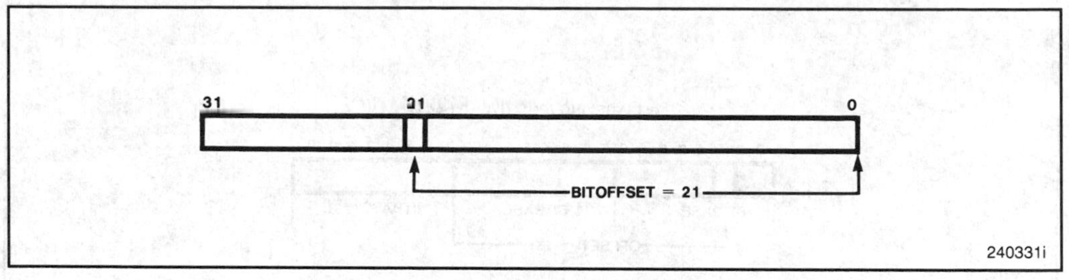

Figure 17-3. Bit Offset for BIT[EAX,21]

If BitBase is a memory address, BitOffset can range from −2 gigabits to 2 gigabits. The addressed bit is numbered (Offset MOD 8) within the byte at address (BitBase + (BitOffset DIV 8)), where DIV is signed division with rounding towards negative infinity, and MOD returns a positive number. This is illustrated in Figure 17-4.

- **I-O-Permission(I-O-Address, width)** returns TRUE or FALSE depending on the I/O permission bitmap and other factors. This function is defined as follows:

```
IF TSS type is 80286 THEN RETURN FALSE; FI;
Ptr ← [TSS + 66]; (* fetch bitmap pointer *)
BitStringAddr ← SHR (I-O-Address, 3) + Ptr;
MaskShift ← I-O-Address AND 7;
CASE width OF:
        BYTE: nBitMask ← 1;
        WORD: nBitMask ← 3;
        DWORD: nBitMask ← 15;
ESAC;
mask ← SHL (nBitMask, MaskShift);
CheckString ← [BitStringAddr] AND mask;
IF CheckString = 0
THEN RETURN (TRUE);
ELSE RETURN (FALSE);
FI;
```

- **Switch-Tasks** is the task switching function described in Chapter 7.

17.2.2.6 DESCRIPTION

The "Description" section contains further explanation of the instruction's operation.

17.2.2.7 FLAGS AFFECTED

The "Flags Affected" section lists the flags that are affected by the instruction, as follows:

- If a flag is always cleared or always set by the instruction, the value is given (0 or 1) after the flag name. Arithmetic and logical instructions usually assign values to the status flags in the uniform manner described in Appendix C. Nonconventional assignments are described in the "Operation" section.

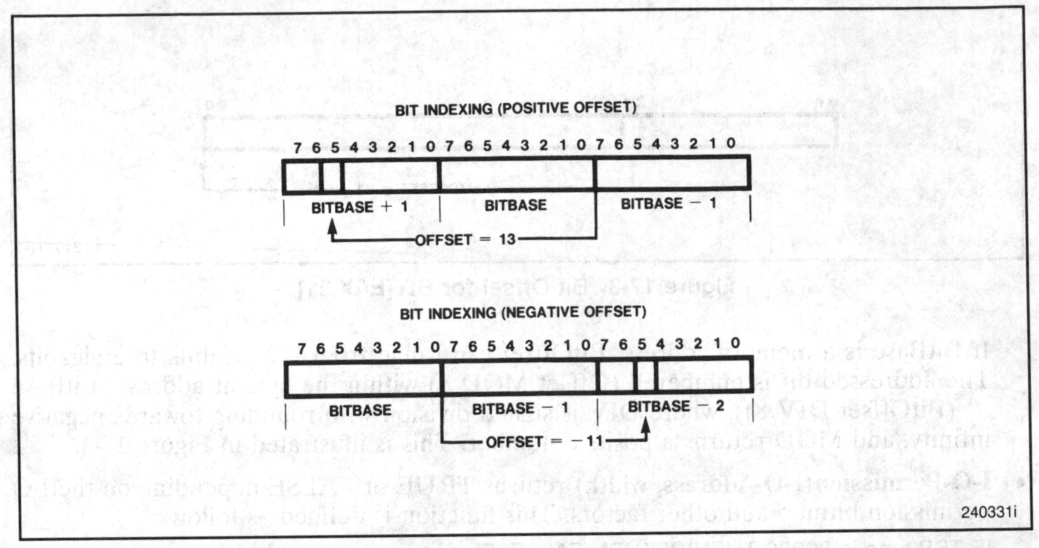

Figure 17-4. Memory Bit Indexing

- The values of flags listed as "undefined" may be changed by the instruction in an indeterminate manner.

All flags not listed are unchanged by the instruction.

17.2.2.8 PROTECTED MODE EXCEPTIONS

This section lists the exceptions that can occur when the instruction is executed in 386 DX microprocessor Protected Mode. The exception names are a pound sign (#) followed by two letters and an optional error code in parentheses. For example, #GP(0) denotes a general protection exception with an error code of 0. Table 17-6 associates each two-letter name with the corresponding interrupt number.

Chapter 9 describes the exceptions and the 386 DX microprocessor state upon entry to the exception.

Table 17-6. 386™ DX Microprocessor Exceptions

Mnemonic	Interrupt	Description
#UD	6	Invalid opcode
#NM	7	Coprocessor not available
#DF	8	Double fault
#TS	10	Invalid TSS
#NP	11	Segment or gate not present
#SS	12	Stack fault
#GP	13	General protection fault
#PF	14	Page fault
#MF	16	Math (coprocessor) fault

Application programmers should consult the documentation provided with their operating systems to determine the actions taken when exceptions occur.

17.2.2.9 REAL ADDRESS MODE EXCEPTIONS

Because less error checking is performed by the 386 DX microprocessor in Real Address Mode, this mode has fewer exception conditions. Refer to Chapter 14 for further information on these exceptions.

17.2.2.10 VIRTUAL-8086 MODE EXCEPTIONS

Virtual 8086 tasks provide the ability to simulate Virtual 8086 machines. Virtual 8086 Mode exceptions are similar to those for the 8086 processor, but there are some differences. Refer to Chapter 15 for details.

AAA—ASCII Adjust after Addition

Opcode	Instruction	Clocks	Description
37	AAA	4	ASCII adjust AL after addition

Operation

```
IF ((AL AND 0FH) > 9) OR (AF = 1)
THEN
   AL ← (AL + 6) AND 0FH;
   AH ← AH + 1;
   AF ← 1;
   CF ← 1;
ELSE
   CF ← 0;
   AF ← 0;
FI;
```

Description

Execute the AAA instruction only following an ADD instruction that leaves a byte result in the AL register. The lower nibbles of the operands of the ADD instruction should be in the range 0 through 9 (BCD digits). In this case, the AAA instruction adjusts the AL register to contain the correct decimal digit result. If the addition produced a decimal carry, the AH register is incremented, and the CF and AF flags are set. If there was no decimal carry, the CF and AF flags are cleared and the AH register is unchanged. In either case, the AL register is left with its top nibble set to 0. To convert the AL register to an ASCII result, follow the AAA instruction with OR AL, 30H.

Flags Affected

The AF and CF flags are set if there is a decimal carry, cleared if there is no decimal carry; the OF, SF, ZF, and PF flags are undefined

Protected Mode Exceptions

None

Real Address Mode Exceptions

None

Virtual 8086 Mode Exceptions

None

AAD—ASCII Adjust AX before Division

Opcode	Instruction	Clocks	Description
D5 0A	AAD	19	ASCII adjust AX before division

Operation

AL ← AH * 10 + AL;
AH ← 0;

Description

The AAD instruction is used to prepare two unpacked BCD digits (the least-significant digit in the AL register, the most-significant digit in the AH register) for a division operation that will yield an unpacked result. This is accomplished by setting the AL register to AL + (10 * AH), and then clearing the AH register. The AX register is then equal to the binary equivalent of the original unpacked two-digit number.

Flags Affected

The SF, ZF, and PF flags are set according to the result; the OF, AF, and CF flags are undefined

Protected Mode Exceptions

None

Real Address Mode Exceptions

None

Virtual 8086 Mode Exceptions

None

AAM — ASCII Adjust AX after Multiply

Opcode	Instruction	Clocks	Description
D4 0A	AAM	17	ASCII adjust AX after multiply

Operation

AH ← AL / 10;
AL ← AL MOD 10;

Description

Execute the AAM instruction only after executing a MUL instruction between two unpacked BCD digits that leaves the result in the AX register. Because the result is less than 100, it is contained entirely in the AL register. The AAM instruction unpacks the AL result by dividing AL by 10, leaving the quotient (most-significant digit) in the AH register and the remainder (least-significant digit) in the AL register.

Flags Affected

The SF, ZF, and PF flags are set according to the result; the OF, AF, and CF flags are undefined

Protected Mode Exceptions

None

Real Address Mode Exceptions

None

Virtual 8086 Mode Exceptions

None

AAS — ASCII Adjust AL after Subtraction

Opcode	Instruction	Clocks	Description
3F	AAS	4	ASCII adjust AL after subtraction

Operation

```
IF (AL AND 0FH) > 9 OR AF = 1
THEN
   AL ← AL − 6;
   AL ← AL AND 0FH;
   AH ← AH − 1;
   AF ← 1;
   CF ← 1;
ELSE
   CF ← 0;
   AF ← 0;
FI;
```

Description

Execute the AAS instruction only after a SUB instruction that leaves the byte result in the AL register. The lower nibbles of the operands of the SUB instruction must have been in the range 0 through 9 (BCD digits). In this case, the AAS instruction adjusts the AL register so it contains the correct decimal digit result. If the subtraction produced a decimal carry, the AH register is decremented, and the CF and AF flags are set. If no decimal carry occurred, the CF and AF flags are cleared, and the AH register is unchanged. In either case, the AL register is left with its top nibble set to 0. To convert the AL result to an ASCII result, follow the AAS instruction with OR AL, 30H.

Flags Affected

The AF and CF flags are set if there is a decimal carry, cleared if there is no decimal carry; the OF, SF, ZF, and PF flags are undefined

Protected Mode Exceptions

None

Real Address Mode Exceptions

None

Virtual 8086 Mode Exceptions

None

ADC — Add with Carry

Opcode	Instruction	Clocks	Description
14 *ib*	ADC AL,*imm8*	2	Add with carry immediate byte to AL
15 *iw*	ADC AX,*imm16*	2	Add with carry immediate word to AX
15 *id*	ADC EAX,*imm32*	2	Add with carry immediate dword to EAX
80 /2 *ib*	ADC *r/m8,imm8*	2/7	Add with carry immediate byte to *r/m* byte
81 /2 *iw*	ADC *r/m16,imm16*	2/7	Add with carry immediate word to *r/m* word
81 /2 *id*	ADC *r/m32,imm32*	2/7	Add with CF immediate dword to *r/m* dword
83 /2 *ib*	ADC *r/m16,imm8*	2/7	Add with CF sign-extended immediate byte to *r/m* word
83 /2 *ib*	ADC *r/m32,imm8*	2/7	Add with CF sign-extended immediate byte into *r/m* dword
10 /*r*	ADC *r/m8,r8*	2/7	Add with carry byte register to *r/m* byte
11 /*r*	ADC *r/m16,r16*	2/7	Add with carry word register to *r/m* word
11 /*r*	ADC *r/m32,r32*	2/7	Add with CF dword register to *r/m* dword
12 /*r*	ADC *r8,r/m8*	2/6	Add with carry *r/m* byte to byte register
13 /*r*	ADC *r16,r/m16*	2/6	Add with carry *r/m* word to word register
13 /*r*	ADC *r32,r/m32*	2/6	Add with CF *r/m* dword to dword register

Operation

DEST ← DEST + SRC + CF;

Description

The ADC instruction performs an integer addition of the two operands DEST and SRC and the carry flag, CF. The result of the addition is assigned to the first operand (DEST), and the flags are set accordingly. The ADC instruction is usually executed as part of a multi-byte or multi-word addition operation. When an immediate byte value is added to a word or doubleword operand, the immediate value is first sign-extended to the size of the word or doubleword operand.

Flags Affected

The OF, SF, ZF, AF, CF, and PF flags are set according to the result

Protected Mode Exceptions

#GP(0) if the result is in a nonwritable segment; #GP(0) for an illegal memory operand effective address in the CS, DS, ES, FS, or GS segments; #SS(0) for an illegal address in the SS segment; #PF(fault-code) for a page fault

Real Address Mode Exceptions

Interrupt 13 if any part of the operand would lie outside of the effective address space from 0 to 0FFFFH

Virtual 8086 Mode Exceptions

Same exceptions as in Real Address Mode; #PF(fault-code) for a page fault

ADD—Add

Opcode	Instruction	Clocks	Description
04 *ib*	ADD AL,*imm8*	2	Add immediate byte to AL
05 *iw*	ADD AX,*imm16*	2	Add immediate word to AX
05 *id*	ADD EAX,*imm32*	2	Add immediate dword to EAX
80 /0 *ib*	ADD *r/m8,imm8*	2/7	Add immediate byte to *r/m* byte
81 /0 *iw*	ADD *r/m16,imm16*	2/7	Add immediate word to *r/m* word
81 /0 *id*	ADD *r/m32,imm32*	2/7	Add immediate dword to *r/m* dword
83 /0 *ib*	ADD *r/m16,imm8*	2/7	Add sign-extended immediate byte to *r/m* word
83 /0 *ib*	ADD *r/m32,imm8*	2/7	Add sign-extended immediate byte to *r/m* dword
00 /*r*	ADD *r/m8,r8*	2/7	Add byte register to *r/m* byte
01 /*r*	ADD *r/m16,r16*	2/7	Add word register to *r/m* word
01 /*r*	ADD *r/m32,r32*	2/7	Add dword register to *r/m* dword
02 /*r*	ADD *r8,r/m8*	2/6	Add *r/m* byte to byte register
03 /*r*	ADD *r16,r/m16*	2/6	Add *r/m* word to word register
03 /*r*	ADD *r32,r/m32*	2/6	Add *r/m* dword to dword register

Operation

DEST ← DEST + SRC;

Description

The ADD instruction performs an integer addition of the two operands (DEST and SRC). The result of the addition is assigned to the first operand (DEST), and the flags are set accordingly.

When an immediate byte is added to a word or doubleword operand, the immediate value is sign-extended to the size of the word or doubleword operand.

Flags Affected

The OF, SF, ZF, AF, CF, and PF flags are set according to the result

Protected Mode Exceptions

#GP(0) if the result is in a nonwritable segment; #GP(0) for an illegal memory operand effective address in the CS, DS, ES, FS, or GS segments; #SS(0) for an illegal address in the SS segment; #PF(fault-code) for a page fault

Real Address Mode Exceptions

Interrupt 13 if any part of the operand would lie outside of the effective address space from 0 to 0FFFFH

Virtual 8086 Mode Exceptions

Same exceptions as in Real Address Mode; #PF(fault-code) for a page fault

AND — Logical AND

Opcode	Instruction	Clocks	Description
24 *ib*	AND AL,*imm8*	2	AND immediate byte to AL
25 *iw*	AND AX,*imm16*	2	AND immediate word to AX
25 *id*	AND EAX,*imm32*	2	AND immediate dword to EAX
80 /4 *ib*	AND *r/m8,imm8*	2/7	AND immediate byte to *r/m* byte
81 /4 *iw*	AND *r/m16,imm16*	2/7	AND immediate word to *r/m* word
81 /4 *id*	AND *r/m32,imm32*	2/7	AND immediate dword to *r/m* dword
83 /4 *ib*	AND *r/m16,imm8*	2/7	AND sign-extended immediate byte with *r/m* word
83 /4 *ib*	AND *r/m32,imm8*	2/7	AND sign-extended immediate byte with *r/m* dword
20 /*r*	AND *r/m8,r8*	2/7	AND byte register to *r/m* byte
21 /*r*	AND *r/m16,r16*	2/7	AND word register to *r/m* word
21 /*r*	AND *r/m32,r32*	2/7	AND dword register to *r/m* dword
22 /*r*	AND *r8,r/m8*	2/6	AND *r/m* byte to byte register
23 /*r*	AND *r16,r/m16*	2/6	AND *r/m* word to word register
23 /*r*	AND *r32,r/m32*	2/6	AND *r/m* dword to dword register

Operation

DEST ← DEST AND SRC;
CF ← 0;
OF ← 0;

Description

Each bit of the result of the AND instruction is a 1 if both corresponding bits of the operands are 1; otherwise, it becomes a 0.

Flags Affected

The CF and OF flags are cleared; the PF, SF, and ZF flags are set according to the result

Protected Mode Exceptions

#GP(0) if the result is in a nonwritable segment; #GP(0) for an illegal memory operand effective address in the CS, DS, ES, FS, or GS segments; #SS(0) for an illegal address in the SS segment; #PF(fault-code) for a page fault

Real Address Mode Exceptions

Interrupt 13 if any part of the operand would lie outside of the effective address space from 0 to 0FFFFH

Virtual 8086 Mode Exceptions

Same exceptions as in Real Address Mode; #PF(fault-code) for a page fault

ARPL—Adjust RPL Field of Selector

Opcode	Instruction	Clocks	Description
63 /r	ARPL *r/m16,r16*	pm=20/21	Adjust RPL of *r/m16* to not less than RPL of *r16*

Operation

```
IF RPL bits(0,1) of DEST < RPL bits(0,1) of SRC
THEN
   ZF ← 1;
   RPL bits(0,1) of DEST ← RPL bits(0,1) of SRC;
ELSE
   ZF ← 0;
FI;
```

Description

The ARPL instruction has two operands. The first operand is a 16-bit memory variable or word register that contains the value of a selector. The second operand is a word register. If the RPL field ("requested privilege level"—bottom two bits) of the first operand is less than the RPL field of the second operand, the ZF flag is set and the RPL field of the first operand is increased to match the second operand. Otherwise, the ZF flag is cleared and no change is made to the first operand.

The ARPL instruction appears in operating system software, not in application programs. It is used to guarantee that a selector parameter to a subroutine does not request more privilege than the caller is allowed. The second operand of the ARPL instruction is normally a register that contains the CS selector value of the caller.

Flags Affected

The ZF flag is set if the RPL field of the first operand is less than that of the second operand

Protected Mode Exceptions

#GP(0) if the result is in a nonwritable segment; #GP(0) for an illegal memory operand effective address in the CS, DS, ES, FS, or GS segments; #SS(0) for an illegal address in the SS segment; #PF(fault-code) for a page fault

Real Address Mode Exceptions

Interrupt 6; the ARPL instruction is not recognized in Real Address Mode

Virtual 8086 Mode Exceptions

Same exceptions as in Real Address Mode; #PF(fault-code) for a page fault

BOUND — Check Array Index Against Bounds

Opcode	Instruction	Clocks	Description
62 /r	BOUND *r16,m16&16*	10	Check if *r16* is within bounds (passes test)
62 /r	BOUND *r32,m32&32*	10	Check if *r32* is within bounds (passes test)

Operation

```
IF (LeftSRC < [RightSRC] OR LeftSRC > [RightSRC + OperandSize/8])
   (* Under lower bound or over upper bound *)
THEN Interrupt 5;
FI;
```

Description

The BOUND instruction ensures that a signed array index is within the limits specified by a block of memory consisting of an upper and a lower bound. Each bound uses one word when the operand-size attribute is 16 bits and a doubleword when the operand-size attribute is 32 bits. The first operand (a register) must be greater than or equal to the first bound in memory (lower bound), and less than or equal to the second bound in memory (upper bound) plus the number of bytes occupied for the operand size. If the register is not within bounds, an Interrupt 5 occurs; the return EIP points to the BOUND instruction.

The bounds limit data structure is usually placed just before the array itself, making the limits addressable via a constant offset from the beginning of the array.

Flags Affected

None

Protected Mode Exceptions

Interrupt 5 if the bounds test fails, as described above; #GP(0) for an illegal memory operand effective address in the CS, DS, ES, FS, or GS segments; #SS(0) for an illegal address in the SS segment; #PF(fault-code) for a page fault

The second operand must be a memory operand, not a register. If the BOUND instruction is executed with a ModR/M byte representing a register as the second operand, #UD occurs.

Real Address Mode Exceptions

Interrupt 5 if the bounds test fails; Interrupt 13 if any part of the operand would lie outside of the effective address space from 0 to 0FFFFH; Interrupt 6 if the second operand is a register

Virtual 8086 Mode Exceptions

Same exceptions as in Real Address Mode; #PF(fault-code) for a page fault

BSF — Bit Scan Forward

Opcode	Instruction	Clocks	Description
0F BC	BSF *r16,r/m16*	11+3*n*	Bit scan forward on *r/m* word
0F BC	BSF *r32,r/m32*	11+3*n*	Bit scan forward on *r/m* dword

Notes

n is the number of leading zero bits.

Operation

```
IF r/m = 0
THEN
  ZF ← 1;
  register ← UNDEFINED;
ELSE
  temp ← 0;
  ZF ← 0;
  WHILE BIT[r/m, temp = 0]
  DO
    temp ← temp + 1;
    register ← temp;
  OD;
FI;
```

Description

The BSF instruction scans the bits in the second word or doubleword operand starting with bit 0. The ZF flag is set if all the bits are 0; otherwise, the ZF flag is cleared and the destination register is loaded with the bit index of the first set bit.

Flags Affected

The ZF flag is set if all bits are 0; otherwise, the ZF flag is cleared

Protected Mode Exceptions

#GP(0) for an illegal memory operand effective address in the CS, DS, ES, FS, or GS segments; #SS(0) for an illegal address in the SS segment; #PF(fault-code) for a page fault

Real Address Mode Exceptions

Interrupt 13 if any part of the operand would lie outside of the effective address space from 0 to 0FFFFH

Virtual 8086 Mode Exceptions

Same exceptions as in Real Address Mode; #PF(fault-code) for a page fault

BSR — Bit Scan Reverse

Opcode	Instruction	Clocks	Description
0F BD	BSR *r16,r/m16*	9+3*n*	Bit scan reverse on *r/m* word
0F BD	BSR *r32,r/m32*	9+3*n*	Bit scan reverse on *r/m* dword

Operation

```
IF r/m = 0
THEN
  ZF ← 1;
  register ← UNDEFINED;
ELSE
  temp ← OperandSize − 1;
  ZF ← 0;
  WHILE BIT[r/m, temp] = 0
  DO
    temp ← temp − 1;
    register ← temp;
  OD;
FI;
```

Description

The BSR instruction scans the bits in the second word or doubleword operand from the most significant bit to the least significant bit. The ZF flag is set if all the bits are 0; otherwise, the ZF flag is cleared and the destination register is loaded with the bit index of the first set bit found when scanning in the reverse direction.

Flags Affected

The ZF flag is set if all bits are 0; otherwise, the ZF flag is cleared

Protected Mode Exceptions

#GP(0) if the result is in a nonwritable segment; #GP(0) for an illegal memory operand effective address in the CS, DS, ES, FS, or GS segments; #SS(0) for an illegal address in the SS segment; #PF(fault-code) for a page fault

Real Address Mode Exceptions

Interrupt 13 if any part of the operand would lie outside of the effective address space from 0 to 0FFFFH

Virtual 8086 Mode Exceptions

Same exceptions as in Real Address Mode; #PF(fault-code) for a page fault

BT — Bit Test

Opcode	Instruction	Clocks	Description
0F A3	BT *r/m16,r16*	3/12	Save bit in carry flag
0F A3	BT *r/m32,r32*	3/12	Save bit in carry flag
0F BA /4 *ib*	BT *r/m16,imm8*	3/6	Save bit in carry flag
0F BA /4 *ib*	BT *r/m32,imm8*	3/6	Save bit in carry flag

Operation

CF ← BIT[LeftSRC, RightSRC];

Description

The BT instruction saves the value of the bit indicated by the base (first operand) and the bit offset (second operand) into the CF flag.

Flags Affected

The CF flag contains the value of the selected bit

Protected Mode Exceptions

#GP(0) for an illegal memory operand effective address in the CS, DS, ES, FS, or GS segments; #SS(0) for an illegal address in the SS segment; #PF(fault-code) for a page fault

Real Address Mode Exceptions

Interrupt 13 if any part of the operand would lie outside of the effective address space from 0 to 0FFFFH

Virtual 8086 Mode Exceptions

Same exceptions as in Real Address Mode; #PF(fault-code) for a page fault

Notes

The index of the selected bit can be given by the immediate constant in the instruction or by a value in a general register. Only an 8-bit immediate value is used in the instruction. This operand is taken modulo 32, so the range of immediate bit offsets is 0..31. This allows any bit within a register to be selected. For memory bit strings, this immediate field gives only the bit offset within a word or doubleword. Immediate bit offsets larger than 31 are supported by using the immediate bit offset field in combination with the displacement field of the memory operand. The low-order 3 to 5 bits of the immediate bit offset are stored in the immediate bit offset field, and the high-order 27 to 29 bits are shifted and combined with the byte displacement in the addressing mode.

When accessing a bit in memory, the 386 DX microprocessor may access four bytes starting from the memory address given by:

Effective Address + (4 * (BitOffset DIV 32))

for a 32-bit operand size, or two bytes starting from the memory address given by:

Effective Address + (2 * (BitOffset DIV 16))

for a 16-bit operand size. It may do so even when only a single byte needs to be accessed in order to reach the given bit. You must therefore avoid referencing areas of memory close to address space holes. In particular, avoid references to memory-mapped I/O registers. Instead, use the MOV instructions to load from or store to these addresses, and use the register form of these instructions to manipulate the data.

BTC — Bit Test and Complement

Opcode	Instruction	Clocks	Description
0F BB	BTC *r/m16,r16*	6/13	Save bit in carry flag and complement
0F BB	BTC *r/m32,r32*	6/13	Save bit in carry flag and complement
0F BA /7 *ib*	BTC *r/m16,imm8*	6/8	Save bit in carry flag and complement
0F BA /7 *ib*	BTC *r/m32,imm8*	6/8	Save bit in carry flag and complement

Operation

CF ← BIT[LeftSRC, RightSRC];
BIT[LeftSRC, RightSRC] ← NOT BIT[LeftSRC, RightSRC];

Description

The BTC instruction saves the value of the bit indicated by the base (first operand) and the bit offset (second operand) into the CF flag and then complements the bit.

Flags Affected

The CF flag contains the complement of the selected bit

Protected Mode Exceptions

#GP(0) if the result is in a nonwritable segment; #GP(0) for an illegal memory operand effective address in the CS, DS, ES, FS, or GS segments; #SS(0) for an illegal address in the SS segment; #PF(fault-code) for a page fault

Real Address Mode Exceptions

Interrupt 13 if any part of the operand would lie outside of the effective address space from 0 to 0FFFFH

Virtual 8086 Mode Exceptions

Same exceptions as in Real Address Mode; #PF(fault-code) for a page fault

Notes

The index of the selected bit can be given by the immediate constant in the instruction or by a value in a general register. Only an 8-bit immediate value is used in the instruction. This operand is taken modulo 32, so the range of immediate bit offsets is 0..31. This allows any bit within a register to be selected. For memory bit strings, this immediate field gives only the bit offset within a word or doubleword. Immediate bit offsets larger than 31 are supported by using the immediate bit offset field in combination with the displacement field of the memory operand. The low-order 3 to 5 bits of the immediate bit offset are stored in the immediate bit offset field, and the high-order 27 to 29 bits are shifted and combined with the byte displacement in the addressing mode.

When accessing a bit in memory, the 386 DX microprocessor may access four bytes starting from the memory address given by:

Effective Address + (4 * (BitOffset DIV 32))

for a 32-bit operand size, or two bytes starting from the memory address given by:

Effective Address + (2 * (BitOffset DIV 16))

for a 16-bit operand size. It may do so even when only a single byte needs to be accessed in order to reach the given bit. You must therefore avoid referencing areas of memory close to address space holes. In particular, avoid references to memory-mapped I/O registers. Instead, use the MOV instructions to load from or store to these addresses, and use the register form of these instructions to manipulate the data.

BTR—Bit Test and Reset

Opcode	Instruction	Clocks	Description
0F B3	BTR *r/m16,r16*	6/13	Save bit in carry flag and reset
0F B3	BTR *r/m32,r32*	6/13	Save bit in carry flag and reset
0F BA /6 *ib*	BTR *r/m16,imm8*	6/8	Save bit in carry flag and reset
0F BA /6 *ib*	BTR *r/m32,imm8*	6/8	Save bit in carry flag and reset

Operation

```
CF ← BIT[LeftSRC, RightSRC];
BIT[LeftSRC, RightSRC] ← 0;
```

Description

The BTR instruction saves the value of the bit indicated by the base (first operand) and the bit offset (second operand) into the CF flag and then stores 0 in the bit.

Flags Affected

The CF flag contains the value of the selected bit

Protected Mode Exceptions

#GP(0) if the result is in a nonwritable segment; #GP(0) for an illegal memory operand effective address in the CS, DS, ES, FS, or GS segments; #SS(0) for an illegal address in the SS segment; #PF(fault-code) for a page fault

Real Address Mode Exceptions

Interrupt 13 if any part of the operand would lie outside of the effective address space from 0 to 0FFFFH

Virtual 8086 Mode Exceptions

Same exceptions as in Real Address Mode; #PF(fault-code) for a page fault

Notes

The index of the selected bit can be given by the immediate constant in the instruction or by a value in a general register. Only an 8-bit immediate value is used in the instruction. This operand is taken modulo 32, so the range of immediate bit offsets is 0..31. This allows any bit within a register to be selected. For memory bit strings, this immediate field gives only the bit offset within a word or doubleword. Immediate bit offsets larger than 31 (or 15) are supported by using the immediate bit offset field in combination with the displacement field of the memory operand. The low-order 3 to 5 bits of the immediate bit offset are stored in the immediate bit offset field, and the high-order 27 to 29 bits are shifted and combined with the byte displacement in the addressing mode.

When accessing a bit in memory, the 386 DX microprocessor may access four bytes starting from the memory address given by:

Effective Address + 4 * (BitOffset DIV 32)

for a 32-bit operand size, or two bytes starting from the memory address given by:

Effective Address + 2 * (BitOffset DIV 16)

for a 16-bit operand size. It may do so even when only a single byte needs to be accessed in order to reach the given bit. You must therefore avoid referencing areas of memory close to address space holes. In particular, avoid references to memory-mapped I/O registers. Instead, use the MOV instructions to load from or store to these addresses, and use the register form of these instructions to manipulate the data.

BTS—Bit Test and Set

Opcode	Instruction	Clocks	Description
0F AB	BTS *r/m16,r16*	6/13	Save bit in carry flag and set
0F AB	BTS *r/m32,r32*	6/13	Save bit in carry flag and set
0F BA /5 *ib*	BTS *r/m16,imm8*	6/8	Save bit in carry flag and set
0F BA /5 *ib*	BTS *r/m32,imm8*	6/8	Save bit in carry flag and set

Operation

CF ← BIT[LeftSRC, RightSRC];
BIT[LeftSRC, RightSRC] ← 1;

Description

The BTS instruction saves the value of the bit indicated by the base (first operand) and the bit offset (second operand) into the CF flag and then stores 1 in the bit.

Flags Affected

The CF flag contains the value of the selected bit

Protected Mode Exceptions

#GP(0) if the result is in a nonwritable segment; #GP(0) for an illegal memory operand effective address in the CS, DS, ES, FS, or GS segments; #SS(0) for an illegal address in the SS segment; #PF(fault-code) for a page fault

Real Address Mode Exceptions

Interrupt 13 if any part of the operand would lie outside of the effective address space from 0 to 0FFFFH

Virtual 8086 Mode Exceptions

Same exceptions as in Real Address Mode; #PF(fault-code) for a page fault

Notes

The index of the selected bit can be given by the immediate constant in the instruction or by a value in a general register. Only an 8-bit immediate value is used in the instruction. This operand is taken modulo 32, so the range of immediate bit offsets is 0..31. This allows any bit within a register to be selected. For memory bit strings, this immediate field gives only the bit offset within a word or doubleword. Immediate bit offsets larger than 31 are supported by using the immediate bit offset field in combination with the displacement field of the memory operand. The low-order 3 to 5 bits of the immediate bit offset are stored in the immediate bit offset field, and the high order 27 to 29 bits are shifted and combined with the byte displacement in the addressing mode.

When accessing a bit in memory, the 386 DX microprocessor may access four bytes starting from the memory address given by:

Effective Address + (4 * (BitOffset DIV 32))

for a 32-bit operand size, or two bytes starting from the memory address given by:

Effective Address + (2 * (BitOffset DIV 16))

for a 16-bit operand size. It may do this even when only a single byte needs to be accessed in order to get at the given bit. You must therefore be careful to avoid referencing areas of memory close to address space holes. In particular, avoid references to memory-mapped I/O registers. Instead, use the MOV instructions to load from or store to these addresses, and use the register form of these instructions to manipulate the data.

CALL — Call Procedure

Opcode	Instruction	Clocks	Description
E8 *cw*	CALL *rel16*	7+*m*	Call near, displacement relative to next instruction
FF /2	CALL *r/m16*	7+*m*/10+*m*	Call near, register indirect/memory indirect
9A *cd*	CALL *ptr16:16*	17+*m*,pm=34+*m*	Call intersegment, to full pointer given
9A *cd*	CALL *ptr16:16*	pm=52+*m*	Call gate, same privilege
9A *cd*	CALL *ptr16:16*	pm=86+*m*	Call gate, more privilege, no parameters
9A *cd*	CALL *ptr16:16*	pm=94+4*x*+*m*	Call gate, more privilege, *x* parameters
9A *cd*	CALL *ptr16:16*	ts	Call to task
FF /3	CALL *m16:16*	22+m,pm=38+*m*	Call intersegment, address at *r/m* dword
FF /3	CALL *m16:16*	pm=56+*m*	Call gate, same privilege
FF /3	CALL *m16:16*	pm=90+*m*	Call gate, more privilege, no parameters
FF /3	CALL *m16:16*	pm=98+4*x*+*m*	Call gate, more privilege, *x* parameters
FF /3	CALL *m16:16*	5 + ts	Call to task
E8 *cd*	CALL *rel32*	7+*m*	Call near, displacement relative to next instruction
FF /2	CALL *r/m32*	7+*m*/10+*m*	Call near, indirect
9A *cp*	CALL *ptr16:32*	17+*m*,pm=34+*m*	Call intersegment, to full pointer given
9A *cp*	CALL *ptr16:32*	pm=52+*m*	Call gate, same privilege
9A *cp*	CALL *ptr16:32*	pm=86+*m*	Call gate, more privilege, no parameters
9A *cp*	CALL *ptr32:32*	pm=94+4*x*+*m*	Call gate, more privilege, *x* parameters
9A *cp*	CALL *ptr16:32*	ts	Call to task
FF /3	CALL *m16:32*	22+*m*,pm=38+*m*	Call intersegment, address at *r/m* dword
FF /3	CALL *m16:32*	pm=56+*m*	Call gate, same privilege
FF /3	CALL *m16:32*	pm=90+*m*	Call gate, more privilege, no parameters
FF /3	CALL *m16:32*	pm=98+4*x*+*m*	Call gate, more privilege, *x* parameters
FF /3	CALL *m16:32*	5 + ts	Call to task

NOTE: Values of **ts** are given by the following table:

Old Task	New Task					
	386™ DX TSS VM = 0		386 DX TSS VM = 1		80286 TSS	
	Via Task Gate?					
	N	Y	N	Y	N	Y
386 DX TSS VM=0	392	401	309	321	285	294
80286 TSS	310	316	229	238	285	294

Operation

```
IF rel16 or rel32 type of call
THEN (* near relative call *)
   IF OperandSize = 16
   THEN
      Push(IP);
      EIP ← (EIP + rel16) AND 0000FFFFH;
   ELSE (* OperandSize = 32 *)
      Push(EIP);
      EIP ← EIP + rel32;
   FI;
FI;
```

```
IF r/m16 or r/m32 type of call
THEN (* near absolute call *)
  IF OperandSize = 16
  THEN
    Push(IP);
    EIP ← [r/m16] AND 0000FFFFH;
  ELSE (* OperandSize = 32 *)
    Push(EIP);
    EIP ← [r/m32];
  FI;
FI;

IF (PE = 0 OR (PE = 1 AND VM = 1))
(* real mode or virtual 8086 mode *)
  AND instruction = far CALL
  (* i.e., operand type is m16:16, m16:32, ptr16:16, ptr16:32 *)
THEN
  IF OperandSize = 16
  THEN
    Push(CS);
    Push(IP); (* address of next instruction; 16 bits *)
  ELSE
    Push(CS); (* padded with 16 high-order bits *)
    Push(EIP); (* address of next instruction; 32 bits *)
  FI;
  IF operand type is m16:16 or m16:32
  THEN (* indirect far call *)
    IF OperandSize = 16
    THEN
      CS:IP ← [m16:16];
      EIP ← EIP AND 0000FFFFH; (* clear upper 16 bits *)
    ELSE (* OperandSize = 32 *)
      CS:EIP ← [m16:32];
    FI;
  FI;
  IF operand type is ptr16:16 or ptr16:32
  THEN (* direct far call *)
    IF OperandSize = 16
    THEN
      CS:IP ← ptr16:16;
      EIP ← EIP AND 0000FFFFH; (* clear upper 16 bits *)
    ELSE (* OperandSize = 32 *)
      CS:EIP ← ptr16:32;
    FI;
  FI;
FI;

IF (PE = 1 AND VM = 0) (* Protected mode, not V86 mode *)
  AND instruction = far CALL
THEN
```

```
   If indirect, then check access of EA doubleword;
      #GP(0) if limit violation;
   New CS selector must not be null else #GP(0);
   Check that new CS selector index is within its
      descriptor table limits; else #GP(new CS selector);
   Examine AR byte of selected descriptor for various legal values;
      depending on value:
      go to CONFORMING-CODE-SEGMENT;
      go to NONCONFORMING-CODE-SEGMENT;
      go to CALL-GATE;
      go to TASK-GATE;
      go to TASK-STATE-SEGMENT;
   ELSE #GP(code segment selector);
FI;

CONFORMING-CODE-SEGMENT:
   DPL must be ≤ CPL ELSE #GP(code segment selector);
   Segment must be present ELSE #NP(code segment selector);
   Stack must be big enough for return address ELSE #SS(0);
   Instruction pointer must be in code segment limit ELSE #GP(0);
   Load code segment descriptor into CS register;
   Load CS with new code segment selector;
   Load EIP with zero-extend(new offset);
   IF OperandSize=16 THEN EIP ← EIP AND 0000FFFFH; FI;

NONCONFORMING-CODE-SEGMENT:
   RPL must be ≤ CPL ELSE #GP(code segment selector)
   DPL must be = CPL ELSE #GP(code segment selector)
   Segment must be present ELSE #NP(code segment selector)
   Stack must be big enough for return address ELSE #SS(0)
   Instruction pointer must be in code segment limit ELSE #GP(0)
   Load code segment descriptor into CS register
   Load CS with new code segment selector
   Set RPL of CS to CPL
   Load EIP with zero-extend(new offset);
   IF OperandSize=16 THEN EIP ← EIP AND 0000FFFFH; FI;

CALL-GATE:
   Call gate DPL must be ≥ CPL ELSE #GP(call gate selector)
   Call gate DPL must be ≥ RPL ELSE #GP(call gate selector)
   Call gate must be present ELSE #NP(call gate selector)
   Examine code segment selector in call gate descriptor:
      Selector must not be null ELSE #GP(0)
      Selector must be within its descriptor table
         limits ELSE #GP(code segment selector)
      AR byte of selected descriptor must indicate code
         segment ELSE #GP(code segment selector)
      DPL of selected descriptor must be ≤ CPL ELSE
         #GP(code segment selector)
```

```
    IF non-conforming code segment AND DPL < CPL
    THEN go to MORE-PRIVILEGE
    ELSE go to SAME-PRIVILEGE
    FI;

MORE-PRIVILEGE:
  Get new SS selector for new privilege level from TSS
    Check selector and descriptor for new SS:
      Selector must not be null ELSE #TS(0)
      Selector index must be within its descriptor
        table limits ELSE #TS(SS selector)
      Selector's RPL must equal DPL of code segment
        ELSE #TS(SS selector)
      Stack segment DPL must equal DPL of code
        segment ELSE #TS(SS selector)
      Descriptor must indicate writable data segment
        ELSE #TS(SS selector)
      Segment present ELSE #SS(SS selector)
    IF OperandSize=32
    THEN
      New stack must have room for parameters plus 16 bytes
        ELSE #SS(SS selector)
      EIP must be in code segment limit ELSE #GP(0)
      Load new SS:eSP value from TSS
      Load new CS:EIP value from gate
    ELSE
      New stack must have room for parameters plus 8 bytes

        ELSE #SS(SS selector)
      IP must be in code segment limit ELSE #GP(0)
      Load new SS:eSP value from TSS
      Load new CS:IP value from gate
    FI;
    Load CS descriptor
    Load SS descriptor
    Push long pointer of old stack onto new stack
    Get word count from call gate, mask to 5 bits
    Copy parameters from old stack onto new stack
    Push return address onto new stack
    Set CPL to stack segment DPL
    Set RPL of CS to CPL

SAME-PRIVILEGE:
  IF OperandSize=32
  THEN
    Stack must have room for 6-byte return address (padded to 8 bytes)
      ELSE #SS(0)
    EIP must be within code segment limit ELSE #GP(0)
    Load CS:EIP from gate
```

```
ELSE
   Stack must have room for 4-byte return address ELSE #SS(0)
   IP must be within code segment limit ELSE #GP(0)
   Load CS:IP from gate
FI;
Push return address onto stack
Load code segment descriptor into CS register
Set RPL of CS to CPL

TASK-GATE:
  Task gate DPL must be ≥ CPL ELSE #TS(gate selector)
  Task gate DPL must be ≥ RPL ELSE #TS(gate selector)
  Task Gate must be present ELSE #NP(gate selector)
  Examine selector to TSS, given in Task Gate descriptor:
     Must specify global in the local/global bit ELSE #TS(TSS selector)
     Index must be within GDT limits ELSE #TS(TSS selector)
     TSS descriptor AR byte must specify nonbusy TSS
        ELSE #TS(TSS selector)
     Task State Segment must be present ELSE #NP(TSS selector)
  SWITCH-TASKS (with nesting) to TSS
  IP must be in code segment limit ELSE #TS(0)

TASK-STATE-SEGMENT:
  TSS DPL must be ≥ CPL else #TS(TSS selector)
  TSS DPL must be ≥ RPL ELSE #TS(TSS selector)
  TSS descriptor AR byte must specify available TSS
     ELSE #GP(TSS selector)
  Task State Segment must be present ELSE #NP(TSS selector)
  SWITCH-TASKS (with nesting) to TSS
  IP must be in code segment limit ELSE #TS(0)
```

Description

The CALL instruction causes the procedure named in the operand to be executed. When the procedure is complete (a return instruction is executed within the procedure), execution continues at the instruction that follows the CALL instruction.

The action of the different forms of the instruction are described below.

Near calls are those with destinations of type *r/m16*, *r/m32*, *rel16*, *rel32*; changing or saving the segment register value is not necessary. The CALL *rel16* and CALL *rel32* forms add a signed offset to the address of the instruction following the CALL instruction to determine the destination. The *rel16* form is used when the instruction's operand-size attribute is 16 bits; *rel32* is used when the operand-size attribute is 32 bits. The result is stored in the 32-bit EIP register. With *rel16*, the upper 16 bits of the EIP register are cleared, resulting in an offset whose value does not exceed 16 bits. CALL *r/m16* and CALL *r/m32* specify a register or memory location from which the absolute segment offset is fetched. The offset fetched from *r/m* is 32 bits for an operand-size attribute of 32 (*r/m32*), or 16 bits for an operand-size of 16 (*r/m16*). The offset of the instruction following the CALL instruction is pushed onto the stack. It will be popped by a near RET instruction within the procedure. The CS register is not changed by this form of CALL.

The far calls, CALL *ptr16:16* and CALL *ptr16:32*, use a four-byte or six-byte operand as a long pointer to the procedure called. The CALL *m16:16* and *m16:32* forms fetch the long pointer from the memory location specified (indirection). In Real Address Mode or Virtual 8086 Mode, the long pointer provides 16 bits for the CS register and 16 or 32 bits for the EIP register (depending on the operand-size attribute). These forms of the instruction push both the CS and IP or EIP registers as a return address.

In Protected Mode, both long pointer forms consult the AR byte in the descriptor indexed by the selector part of the long pointer. Depending on the value of the AR byte, the call will perform one of the following types of control transfers:

- A far call to the same protection level
- An inter-protection level far call
- A task switch

For more information on Protected Mode control transfers, refer to Chapter 6 and Chapter 7.

Flags Affected

All flags are affected if a task switch occurs; no flags are affected if a task switch does not occur

Protected Mode Exceptions

For far calls: #GP, #NP, #SS, and #TS, as indicated in the "Operation" section

For near direct calls: #GP(0) if procedure location is beyond the code segment limits; #SS(0) if pushing the return address exceeds the bounds of the stack segment; #PF (fault-code) for a page fault

For a near indirect call: #GP(0) for an illegal memory operand effective address in the CS, DS, ES, FS, or GS segments; #SS(0) for an illegal address in the SS segment; #GP(0) if the indirect offset obtained is beyond the code segment limits; #PF(fault-code) for a page fault

Real Address Mode Exceptions

Interrupt 13 if any part of the operand would lie outside of the effective address space from 0 to 0FFFFH

Virtual 8086 Mode Exceptions

Same exceptions as in Real Address Mode; #PF(fault-code) for a page fault

Notes

Any far call from a 32-bit code segment to a 16-bit code segment should be made from the first 64K bytes of the 32-bit code segment, because the operand-size attribute of the instruction is set to 16, allowing only a 16-bit return address offset to be saved.

CBW/CWDE—Convert Byte to Word/Convert Word to Doubleword

Opcode	Instruction	Clocks	Description
98	CBW	3	AX ← sign-extend of AL
98	CWDE	3	EAX ← sign-extend of AX

Operation

```
IF OperandSize = 16 (* instruction = CBW *)
THEN AX ← SignExtend(AL);
ELSE (* OperandSize = 32, instruction = CWDE *)
  EAX ← SignExtend(AX);
FI;
```

Description

The CBW instruction converts the signed byte in the AL register to a signed word in the AX register by extending the most significant bit of the AL register (the sign bit) into all of the bits of the AH register. The CWDE instruction converts the signed word in the AX register to a doubleword in the EAX register by extending the most significant bit of the AX register into the two most significant bytes of the EAX register. Note that the CWDE instruction is different from the CWD instruction. The CWD instruction uses the DX:AX register pair rather than the EAX register as a destination.

Flags Affected

None

Protected Mode Exceptions

None

Real Address Mode Exceptions

None

Virtual 8086 Mode Exceptions

None

CLC — Clear Carry Flag

Opcode	Instruction	Clocks	Description
F8	CLC	2	Clear carry flag

Operation

CF ← 0;

Description

The CLC instruction clears the CF flag. It does not affect other flags or registers.

Flags Affected

The CF flag is cleared

Protected Mode Exceptions

None

Real Address Mode Exceptions

None

Virtual 8086 Mode Exceptions

None

CLD—Clear Direction Flag

Opcode	Instruction	Clocks	Description
FC	CLD	2	Clear direction flag; SI and DI will increment during string instructions

Operation

DF ← 0;

Description

The CLD instruction clears the direction flag. No other flags or registers are affected. After a CLD instruction is executed, string operations will increment the index registers (SI and/or DI) that they use.

Flags Affected

The DF flag is cleared

Protected Mode Exceptions

None

Real Address Mode Exceptions

None

Virtual 8086 Mode Exceptions

None

CLI—Clear Interrupt Flag

Opcode	Instruction	Clocks	Description
FA	CLI	8	Clear interrupt flag; interrupts disabled

Operation

IF ← 0;

Description

The CLI instruction clears the IF flag if the current privilege level is at least as privileged as IOPL. No other flags are affected. External interrupts are not recognized at the end of the CLI instruction or from that point on until the IF flag is set.

Flags Affected

The IF flag is cleared

Protected Mode Exceptions

#GP(0) if the current privilege level is greater (has less privilege) than the I/O privilege level in the flags register. The I/O privilege level specifies the least privileged level at which I/O can be performed.

Real Address Mode Exceptions

None

Virtual 8086 Mode Exceptions

#GP(0) as for Protected Mode

CLTS—Clear Task-Switched Flag in CR0

Opcode	Instruction	Clocks	Description
0F 06	CLTS	6	Clear task-switched flag

Operation

TS Flag in CR0 ← 0;

Description

The CLTS instruction clears the task-switched (TS) flag in the CR0 register. This flag is set by the 386 processor every time a task switch occurs. The TS flag is used to manage processor extensions as follows:

- Every execution of an ESC instruction is trapped if the TS flag is set.
- Execution of a WAIT instruction is trapped if the MP flag and the TS flag are both set.

Thus, if a task switch was made after an ESC instruction was begun, the processor extension's context may need to be saved before a new ESC instruction can be issued. The fault handler saves the context and clears the TS flag.

The CLTS instruction appears in operating system software, not in application programs. It is a privileged instruction that can only be executed at privilege level 0.

Flags Affected

The TS flag is cleared (the TS flag is in the CR0 register, not the flags register)

Protected Mode Exceptions

#GP(0) if the CLTS instruction is executed with a current privilege level other than 0

Real Address Mode Exceptions

None (valid in Real Address Mode to allow initialization for Protected Mode)

Virtual 8086 Mode Exceptions

None

CMC — Complement Carry Flag

Opcode	Instruction	Clocks	Description
F5	CMC	2	Complement carry flag

Operation

CF ← NOT CF;

Description

The CMC instruction reverses the setting of the CF flag. No other flags are affected.

Flags Affected

The CF flag contains the complement of its original value

Protected Mode Exceptions

None

Real Address Mode Exceptions

None

Virtual 8086 Mode Exceptions

None

CMP—Compare Two Operands

Opcode	Instruction	Clocks	Description
3C *ib*	CMP AL,*imm8*	2	Compare immediate byte to AL
3D *iw*	CMP AX,*imm16*	2	Compare immediate word to AX
3D *id*	CMP EAX,*imm32*	2	Compare immediate dword to EAX
80 /7 *ib*	CMP *r/m8,imm8*	2/5	Compare immediate byte to *r/m* byte
81 /7 *iw*	CMP *r/m16,imm16*	2/5	Compare immediate word to *r/m* word
81 /7 *id*	CMP *r/m32,imm32*	2/5	Compare immediate dword to *r/m* dword
83 /7 *ib*	CMP *r/m16,imm8*	2/5	Compare sign extended immediate byte to *r/m* word
83 /7 *ib*	CMP *r/m32,imm8*	2/5	Compare sign extended immediate byte to *r/m* dword
38 /*r*	CMP *r/m8,r8*	2/5	Compare byte register to *r/m* byte
39 /*r*	CMP *r/m16,r16*	2/5	Compare word register to *r/m* word
39 /*r*	CMP *r/m32,r32*	2/5	Compare dword register to *r/m* dword
3A /*r*	CMP *r8,r/m8*	2/6	Compare *r/m* byte to byte register
3B /*r*	CMP *r16,r/m16*	2/6	Compare *r/m* word to word register
3B /*r*	CMP *r32,r/m32*	2/6	Compare *r/m* dword to dword register

Operation

```
LeftSRC - SignExtend(RightSRC);
(* CMP does not store a result; its purpose is to set the flags *)
```

Description

The CMP instruction subtracts the second operand from the first but, unlike the SUB instruction, does not store the result; only the flags are changed. The CMP instruction is typically used in conjunction with conditional jumps and the SETcc instruction. (Refer to Appendix D for the list of signed and unsigned flag tests provided.) If an operand greater than one byte is compared to an immediate byte, the byte value is first sign-extended.

Flags Affected

The OF, SF, ZF, AF, PF, and CF flags are set according to the result

Protected Mode Exceptions

#GP(0) for an illegal memory operand effective address in the CS, DS, ES, FS, or GS segments; #SS(0) for an illegal address in the SS segment; #PF(fault-code) for a page fault

Real Address Mode Exceptions

Interrupt 13 if any part of the operand would lie outside of the effective address space from 0 to 0FFFFH

Virtual 8086 Mode Exceptions

Same exceptions as in Real Address Mode; #PF(fault-code) for a page fault

CMPS/CMPSB/CMPSW/CMPSD—Compare String Operands

Opcode	Instruction	Clocks	Description
A6	CMPS *m8,m8*	10	Compare bytes ES:[(E)DI] (second operand) with [(E)SI] (first operand)
A7	CMPS *m16,m16*	10	Compare words ES:[(E)DI] (second operand) with [(E)SI] (first operand)
A7	CMPS *m32,m32*	10	Compare dwords ES:[(E)DI] (second operand) with [(E)SI] (first operand)
A6	CMPSB	10	Compare bytes ES:[(E)DI] with DS:[SI]
A7	CMPSW	10	Compare words ES:[(E)DI] with DS:[SI]
A7	CMPSD	10	Compare dwords ES:[(E)DI] with DS:[SI]

Operation

```
IF (instruction = CMPSD) OR
  (instruction has operands of type DWORD)
THEN OperandSize ← 32;
ELSE OperandSize ← 16;
FI;
IF AddressSize = 16
THEN
  use SI for source-index and DI for destination-index
ELSE (* AddressSize = 32 *)
  use ESI for source-index and EDI for destination-index;
FI;
IF byte type of instruction
THEN
  [source-index] - [destination-index]; (* byte comparison *)
  IF DF = 0 THEN IncDec ← 1 ELSE IncDec ← −1; FI;
ELSE
  IF OperandSize = 16
  THEN
    [source-index] - [destination-index]; (* word comparison *)
    IF DF = 0 THEN IncDec ← 2 ELSE IncDec ← −2; FI;
  ELSE (* OperandSize = 32 *)
    [source-index] - [destination-index]; (* dword comparison *)
    IF DF = 0 THEN IncDec ← 4 ELSE IncDec ← −4; FI;
  FI;
FI;
source-index = source-index + IncDec;
destination-index = destination-index + IncDec;
```

Description

The CMPS instruction compares the byte, word, or doubleword pointed to by the source-index register with the byte, word, or doubleword pointed to by the destination-index register.

If the address-size attribute of this instruction is 16 bits, the SI and DI registers will be used for source- and destination-index registers; otherwise the ESI and EDI registers will be used. Load the correct index values into the SI and DI (or ESI and EDI) registers before executing the CMPS instruction.

The comparison is done by subtracting the operand indexed by the destination-index register from the operand indexed by the source-index register.

Note that the direction of subtraction for the CMPS instruction is [SI] – [DI] or [ESI] – [EDI]. The left operand (SI or ESI) is the source and the right operand (DI or EDI) is the destination. This is the reverse of the usual Intel® convention in which the left operand is the destination and the right operand is the source.

The result of the subtraction is not stored; only the flags reflect the change. The types of the operands determine whether bytes, words, or doublewords are compared. For the first operand (SI or ESI), the DS register is used, unless a segment override byte is present. The second operand (DI or EDI) must be addressable from the ES register; no segment override is possible.

After the comparison is made, both the source-index register and destination-index register are automatically advanced. If the DF flag is 0 (a CLD instruction was executed), the registers increment; if the DF flag is 1 (an STD instruction was executed), the registers decrement. The registers increment or decrement by 1 if a byte is compared, by 2 if a word is compared, or by 4 if a doubleword is compared.

The CMPSB, CMPSW and CMPSD instructions are synonyms for the byte, word, and doubleword CMPS instructions, respectively.

The CMPS instruction can be preceded by the REPE or REPNE prefix for block comparison of CX or ECX bytes, words, or doublewords. Refer to the description of the REP instruction for more information on this operation.

Flags Affected

The OF, SF, ZF, AF, PF, and CF flags are set according to the result

Protected Mode Exceptions

#GP(0) for an illegal memory operand effective address in the CS, DS, ES, FS, or GS segments; #SS(0) for an illegal address in the SS segment; #PF(fault-code) for a page fault

Real Address Mode Exceptions

Interrupt 13 if any part of the operand would lie outside of the effective address space from 0 to 0FFFFH

Virtual 8086 Mode Exceptions

Same exceptions as in Real Address Mode; #PF(fault-code) for a page fault

CWD/CDQ — Convert Word to Doubleword/Convert Doubleword to Quadword

Opcode	Instruction	Clocks	Description
99	CWD	2	DX:AX ← sign-extend of AX
99	CDQ	2	EDX:EAX ← sign-extend of EAX

Operation

```
IF OperandSize = 16 (* CWD instruction *)
THEN
   IF AX < 0 THEN DX ← 0FFFFH; ELSE DX ← 0; FI;
ELSE (* OperandSize = 32, CDQ instruction *)
   IF EAX < 0 THEN EDX ← 0FFFFFFFFH; ELSE EDX ← 0; FI;
FI;
```

Description

The CWD instruction converts the signed word in the AX register to a signed doubleword in the DX:AX register pair by extending the most significant bit of the AX register into all the bits of the DX register. The CDQ instruction converts the signed doubleword in the EAX register to a signed 64-bit integer in the register pair EDX:EAX by extending the most significant bit of the EAX register (the sign bit) into all the bits of the EDX register. Note that the CWD instruction is different from the CWDE instruction. The CWDE instruction uses the EAX register as a destination, instead of the DX:AX register pair.

Flags Affected

None

Protected Mode Exceptions

None

Real Address Mode Exceptions

None

Virtual 8086 Mode Exceptions

None

DAA — Decimal Adjust AL after Addition

Opcode	Instruction	Clocks	Description
27	DAA	4	Decimal adjust AL after addition

Operation

```
IF ((AL AND 0FH) > 9) OR (AF = 1)
THEN
   AL ← AL + 6;
   AF ← 1;
ELSE
   AF ← 0;
FI;
IF (AL > 9FH) OR (CF = 1)
THEN
   AL ← AL + 60H;
   CF ← 1;
ELSE CF ← 0;
FI;
```

Description

Execute the DAA instruction only after executing an ADD instruction that leaves a two-BCD-digit byte result in the AL register. The ADD operands should consist of two packed BCD digits. The DAA instruction adjusts the AL register to contain the correct two-digit packed decimal result.

Flags Affected

The AF and CF flags are set if there is a decimal carry, cleared if there is no decimal carry; the SF, ZF, PF, and CF flags are set according to the result.

Protected Mode Exceptions

None

Real Address Mode Exceptions

None

Virtual 8086 Mode Exceptions

None

DAS—Decimal Adjust AL after Subtraction

Opcode	Instruction	Clocks	Description
2F	DAS	4	Decimal adjust AL after subtraction

Operation

```
IF (AL AND 0FH) > 9 OR AF = 1
THEN
   AL ← AL − 6;
   AF ← 1;
ELSE
   AF ← 0;
FI;
IF (AL > 9FH) OR (CF = 1)
THEN
   AL ← AL − 60H;
   CF ← 1;
ELSE CF ← 0;
FI;
```

Description

Execute the DAS instruction only after a subtraction instruction that leaves a two-BCD-digit byte result in the AL register. The operands should consist of two packed BCD digits. The DAS instruction adjusts the AL register to contain the correct packed two-digit decimal result.

Flags Affected

The AF and CF flags are set if there is a decimal carry, cleared if there is no decimal carry; the SF, ZF, and PF flags are set according to the result.

Protected Mode Exceptions

None

Real Address Mode Exceptions

None

Virtual 8086 Mode Exceptions

None

DEC—Decrement by 1

Opcode	Instruction	Clocks	Description
FE /1	DEC r/m8	2/6	Decrement r/m byte by 1
FF /1	DEC r/m16	2/6	Decrement r/m word by 1
	DEC r/m32	2/6	Decrement r/m dword by 1
48+rw	DEC r16	2	Decrement word register by 1
48+rw	DEC r32	2	Decrement dword register by 1

Operation

DEST ← DEST − 1;

Description

The DEC instruction subtracts 1 from the operand. The DEC instruction does not change the CF flag. To affect the CF flag, use the SUB instruction with an immediate operand of 1.

Flags Affected

The OF, SF, ZF, AF, and PF flags are set according to the result.

Protected Mode Exceptions

#GP(0) if the result is a nonwritable segment; #GP(0) for an illegal memory operand effective address in the CS, DS, ES, FS, or GS segments; #SS(0) for an illegal address in the SS segment; #PF(fault-code) for a page fault

Real Address Mode Exceptions

Interrupt 13 if any part of the operand would lie outside of the effective address space from 0 to 0FFFFH

Virtual 8086 Mode Exceptions

Same exceptions as in Real Address Mode; #PF(fault-code) for a page fault

DIV — Unsigned Divide

Opcode	Instruction	Clocks	Description
F6 /6	DIV AL,*r/m8*	14/17	Unsigned divide AX by *r/m* byte (AL = Quo, AH = Rem)
F7 /6	DIV AX,*r/m16*	22/25	Unsigned divide DX:AX by *r/m* word (AX = Quo, DX = Rem)
F7 /6	DIV EAX,*r/m32*	38/41	Unsigned divide EDX:EAX by *r/m* dword (EAX = Quo, EDX = Rem)

Operation

```
temp ← dividend / divisor;
IF temp does not fit in quotient
THEN Interrupt 0;
ELSE
   quotient ← temp;
   remainder ← dividend MOD (r/m);
FI;
```

Note: Divisions are unsigned. The divisor is given by the *r/m* operand. The dividend, quotient, and remainder use implicit registers. Refer to the table under "Description."

Description

The DIV instruction performs an unsigned division. The dividend is implicit; only the divisor is given as an operand. The remainder is always less than the divisor. The type of the divisor determines which registers to use as follows:

Size	Dividend	Divisor	Quotient	Remainder
byte	AX	*r/m8*	AL	AH
word	DX:AX	*r/m16*	AX	DX
dword	EDX:EAX	*r/m32*	EAX	EDX

Flags Affected

The OF, SF, ZF, AF, PF, CF flags are undefined.

Protected Mode Exceptions

Interrupt 0 if the quotient is too large to fit in the designated register (AL, AX, or EAX), or if the divisor is 0; #GP(0) for an illegal memory operand effective address in the CS, DS, ES, FS, or GS segments; #SS(0) for an illegal address in the SS segment; #PF(fault-code) for a page fault

Real Address Mode Exceptions

Interrupt 0 if the quotient is too big to fit in the designated register (AL, AX, or EAX), or if the divisor is 0; Interrupt 13 if any part of the operand would lie outside of the effective address space from 0 to 0FFFFH

Virtual 8086 Mode Exceptions

Same exceptions as in Real Address Mode; #PF(fault-code) for a page fault

ENTER — Make Stack Frame for Procedure Parameters

Opcode	Instruction	Clocks	Description
C8 *iw* 00	ENTER *imm16*,0	10	Make procedure stack frame
C8 *iw* 01	ENTER *imm16*,1	12	Make stack frame for procedure parameters
C8 *iw* ib	ENTER *imm16*,*imm8*	15+4(*n*−1)	Make stack frame for procedure parameters

Operation

```
level ← level MOD 32
IF OperandSize = 16 THEN Push(BP) ELSE Push (EBP) FI;
  (* Save stack pointer *)
frame-ptr ← eSP
IF level > 0
THEN (* level is rightmost parameter *)
  FOR i ← 1 TO level − 1
  DO
    IF OperandSize = 16
    THEN
      BP ← BP − 2;
      Push[BP]
    ELSE (* OperandSize = 32 *)
      EBP ← EBP − 4;
      Push[EBP];
    FI;
  OD;
  Push(frame-ptr)
FI;
IF OperandSize = 16 THEN BP ← frame-ptr ELSE EBP ← frame-ptr; FI;
IF StackAddrSize = 16
THEN SP ← SP − First operand;
ELSE ESP ← ESP − ZeroExtend(First operand);
FI;
```

Description

The ENTER instruction creates the stack frame required by most block-structured high-level languages. The first operand specifies the number of bytes of dynamic storage allocated on the stack for the routine being entered. The second operand gives the lexical nesting level (0 to 31) of the routine within the high-level language source code. It determines the number of stack frame pointers copied into the new stack frame from the preceding frame. The BP register (or EBP, if the operand-size attribute is 32 bits) is the current stack frame pointer.

If the operand-size attribute is 16 bits, the 386 DX microprocessor uses the BP register as the frame pointer and the SP register as the stack pointer. If the operand-size attribute is 32 bits, the processor uses the EBP register for the frame pointer and the ESP register for the stack pointer.

If the second operand is 0, the ENTER instruction pushes the frame pointer (BP or EBP register) onto the stack; the ENTER instruction then subtracts the first operand from the stack pointer and sets the frame pointer to the current stack-pointer value.

For example, a procedure with 12 bytes of local variables would have an ENTER 12,0 instruction at its entry point and a LEAVE instruction before every RET instruction. The 12 local bytes would be addressed as negative offsets from the frame pointer.

Flags Affected

None

Protected Mode Exceptions

#SS(0) if the SP or ESP value would exceed the stack limit at any point during instruction execution; #PF(fault-code) for a page fault

Real Address Mode Exceptions

None

Virtual 8086 Mode Exceptions

None

HLT — Halt

Opcode	Instruction	Clocks	Description
F4	HLT	5	Halt

Operation

Enter Halt state;

Description

The HLT instruction stops instruction execution and places the 386 processor in a HALT state. An enabled interrupt, NMI, or a reset will resume execution. If an interrupt (including NMI) is used to resume execution after an HLT instruction, the saved CS:IP (or CS:EIP) value points to the instruction following the HLT instruction.

Flags Affected

None

Protected Mode Exceptions

The HLT instruction is a privileged instruction; #GP(0) if the current privilege level is not 0

Real Address Mode Exceptions

None

Virtual 8086 Mode Exceptions

#GP(0); the HLT instruction is a privileged instruction

IDIV—Signed Divide

Opcode	Instruction	Clocks	Description
F6 /7	IDIV *r/m8*	19	Signed divide AX by *r/m* byte (AL=Quo, AH=Rem)
F7 /7	IDIV AX,*r/m16*	27	Signed divide DX:AX by EA word (AX=Quo, DX=Rem)
F7 /7	IDIV EAX,*r/m32*	43	Signed divide EDX:EAX by DWORD byte (EAX=Quo, EDX=Rem)

Operation

```
temp ← dividend / divisor;
IF temp does not fit in quotient
THEN Interrupt 0;
ELSE
   quotient ← temp;
   remainder ← dividend MOD (r/m);
FI;
```

Notes: Divisions are signed. The divisor is given by the *r/m* operand. The dividend, quotient, and remainder use implicit registers. Refer to the table under "Description."

Description

The IDIV instruction performs a signed division. The dividend, quotient, and remainder are implicitly allocated to fixed registers. Only the divisor is given as an explicit *r/m* operand. The type of the divisor determines which registers to use as follows:

Size	Divisor	Quotient	Remainder	Dividend
byte	*r/m8*	AL	AH	AX
word	*r/m16*	AX	DX	DX:AX
dword	*r/m32*	EAX	EDX	EDX:EAX

If the resulting quotient is too large to fit in the destination, or if the division is 0, an Interrupt 0 is generated. Nonintegral quotients are truncated toward 0. The remainder has the same sign as the dividend and the absolute value of the remainder is always less than the absolute value of the divisor.

Flags Affected

The OF, SF, ZF, AF, PF, CF flags are undefined.

Protected Mode Exceptions

Interrupt 0 if the quotient is too large to fit in the designated register (AL or AX), or if the divisor is 0; #GP (0) for an illegal memory operand effective address in the CS, DS, ES, FS, or GS segments; #SS(0) for an illegal address in the SS segment; #PF(fault-code) for a page fault

Real Address Mode Exceptions

Interrupt 0 if the quotient is too large to fit in the designated register (AL or AX), or if the divisor is 0; Interrupt 13 if any part of the operand would lie outside of the effective address space from 0 to 0FFFFH

Virtual 8086 Mode Exceptions

Same exceptions as in Real Address Mode; #PF(fault-code) for a page fault

IMUL—Signed Multiply

Opcode	Instruction	Clocks	Description
F6 /5	IMUL *r/m8*	9-14/12-17	AX← AL * *r/m* byte
F7 /5	IMUL *r/m16*	9-22/12-25	DX:AX ← AX * *r/m* word
F7 /5	IMUL *r/m32*	9-38/12-41	EDX:EAX ← EAX * *r/m* dword
0F AF /r	IMUL *r16,r/m16*	9-22/12-25	word register ← word register * *r/m* word
0F AF /r	IMUL *r32,r/m32*	9-38/12-41	dword register ← dword register * *r/m* dword
6B /r ib	IMUL *r16,r/m16,imm8*	9-14/12-17	word register ← *r/m16* * sign-extended immediate byte
6B /r ib	IMUL *r32,r/m32,imm8*	9-14/12-17	dword register ← *r/m32* * sign-extended immediate byte
6B /r ib	IMUL *r16,imm8*	9-14/12-17	word register ← word register * sign-extended immediate byte
6B /r ib	IMUL *r32,imm8*	9-14/12-17	dword register ← dword register * sign-extended immediate byte
69 /r iw	IMUL *r16,r/m16,imm16*	9-22/12-25	word register ← *r/m16* * immediate word
69 /r id	IMUL *r32,r/m32,imm32*	9-38/12-41	dword register ← *r/m32* * immediate dword
69 /r iw	IMUL *r16,imm16*	9-22/12-25	word register ← *r/m16* * immediate word
69 /r id	IMUL *r32,imm32*	9-38/12-41	dword register ← *r/m32* * immediate dword

NOTES: The 386 DX microprocessor uses an early-out multiply algorithm. The actual number of clocks depends on the position of the most significant bit in the optimizing multiplier. The optimization occurs for positive and negative values. Because of the early-out algorithm, clock counts given are minimum to maximum. To calculate the actual clocks, use the following formula:

Actual clock = if $m <> 0$ then max(ceiling($\log_2$ | m |), 3) + 6 clocks
Actual clock = if $m = 0$ then 9 clocks
(where *m* is the multiplier)

Add three clocks if the multiplier is a memory operand.

Operation

result ← multiplicand * multiplier;

Description

The IMUL instruction performs signed multiplication. Some forms of the instruction use implicit register operands. The operand combinations for all forms of the instruction are shown in the "Description" column above.

The IMUL instruction clears the OF and CF flags under the following conditions:

Instruction Form	Condition for Clearing CF and OF
r/m8	AL = sign-extend of AL to 16 bits
r/m16	AX = sign-extend of AX to 32 bits
r/m32	EDX:EAX = sign-extend of EAX to 32 bits
r16,r/m16	Result exactly fits within *r16*
r/32,r/m32	Result exactly fits within *r32*
r16,r/m16,imm16	Result exactly fits within *r16*
r32,r/m32,imm32	Result exactly fits within *r32*

Flags Affected

The OF and CF flags as described in the table in the "Description" section above; the SF, ZF, AF, and PF flags are undefined

Protected Mode Exceptions

#GP(0) for an illegal memory operand effective address in the CS, DS, ES, FS, or GS segments; #SS(0) for an illegal address in the SS segment; #PF(fault-code) for a page fault

Real Address Mode Exceptions

Interrupt 13 if any part of the operand would lie outside of the effective address space from 0 to 0FFFFH

Virtual 8086 Mode Exceptions

Same exeptions as in Real Address Mode; #PF(fault-code) for a page fault

Notes

When using the accumulator forms (IMUL *r/m8*, IMUL *r/m16*, or IMUL *r/m32*), the result of the multiplication is available even if the overflow flag is set because the result is twice the size of the multiplicand and multiplier. This is large enough to handle any possible result.

IN—Input from Port

Opcode	Instruction	Clocks	Description
E4 *ib*	IN AL,*imm8*	12,pm=6*/26**	Input byte from immediate port into AL
E5 *ib*	IN AX,*imm8*	12,pm=6*/26**	Input word from immediate port into AX
E5 *ib*	IN EAX,*imm8*	14,pm=6*/26**	Input dword from immediate port into EAX
EC	IN AL,DX	13,pm=7*/27**	Input byte from port DX into AL
ED	IN AX,DX	13,pm=7*/27**	Input word from port DX into AX
ED	IN EAX,DX	13,pm=7*/27**	Input dword from port DX into EAX

NOTES: *If CPL ≤ IOPL
**If CPL > IOPL or if in virtual 8086 mode

Operation

```
IF (PE = 1) AND ((VM = 1) OR (CPL > IOPL))
THEN (* Virtual 8086 mode, or protected mode with CPL > IOPL *)
  IF NOT I-O-Permission (SRC, width(SRC))
  THEN #GP(0);
  FI;
FI;
DEST ← [SRC]; (* Reads from I/O address space *)
```

Description

The IN instruction transfers a data byte or data word from the port numbered by the second operand into the register (AL, AX, or EAX) specified by the first operand. Access any port from 0 to 65535 by placing the port number in the DX register and using an IN instruction with the DX instruction as the second parameter. These I/O instructions can be shortened by using an 8-bit port I/O in the instruction. The upper eight bits of the port address will be 0 when 8-bit port I/O is used.

Flags Affected

None

Protected Mode Exceptions

#GP(0) if the current privilege level is larger (has less privilege) than the I/O privilege level and any of the corresponding I/O permission bits in TSS equals 1

Real Address Mode Exceptions

None

Virtual 8086 Mode Exceptions

#GP(0) fault if any of the corresponding I/O permission bits in TSS equals 1

INC—Increment by 1

Opcode	Instruction	Clocks	Description
FE /0	INC *r/m8*	2/6	Increment *r/m* byte by 1
FF /0	INC *r/m16*	2/6	Increment *r/m* word by 1
FF /6	INC *r/m32*	2/10	Increment *r/m* dword by 1
40+ *rw*	INC *r16*	2	Increment word register by 1
40+ *rd*	INC *r32*	2	Increment dword register by 1

Operation

DEST ← DEST + 1;

Description

The INC instruction adds 1 to the operand. It does not change the CF flag. To affect the CF flag, use the ADD instruction with a second operand of 1.

Flags Affected

The OF, SF, ZF, AF, and PF flags are set according to the result

Protected Mode Exceptions

#GP(0) if the operand is in a nonwritable segment; #GP(0) for an illegal memory operand effective address in the CS, DS, ES, FS, or GS segments; #SS(0) for an illegal address in the SS segment; #PF(fault-code) for a page fault

Real Address Mode Exceptions

Interrupt 13 if any part of the operand would lie outside of the effective address space from 0 to 0FFFFH

Virtual 8086 Mode Exceptions

Same exceptions as in Real Address Mode; #PF(fault-code) for a page fault

INS/INSB/INSW/INSD — Input from Port to String

Opcode	Instruction	Clocks	Description
6C	INS *r/m8*,DX	15,pm=9*/29**	Input byte from port DX into ES:(E)DI
6D	INS *r/m16*,DX	15,pm=9*/29**	Input word from port DX into ES:(E)DI
6D	INS *r/m32*,DX	15,pm=9*/29**	Input dword from port DX into ES:(E)DI
6C	INSB	15,pm=9*/29**	Input byte from port DX into ES:(E)DI
6D	INSW	15,pm=9*/29**	Input word from port DX into ES:(E)DI
6D	INSD	15,pm=9*/29**	Input dword from port DX into ES:(E)DI

NOTES: *If CPL ≤ IOPL
**If CPL > IOPL or if in virtual 8086 mode

Operation

```
IF AddressSize = 16
THEN use DI for dest-index;
ELSE (* AddressSize = 32 *)
  use EDI for dest-index;
FI;
IF (PE = 1) AND ((VM = 1) OR (CPL > IOPL))
THEN (* Virtual 8086 mode, or protected mode with CPL > IOPL *)
  IF NOT I-O-Permission (SRC, width(SRC))
  THEN #GP(0);
  FI;
FI;
IF byte type of instruction
THEN
  ES:[dest-index] ← [DX]; (* Reads byte at DX from I/O address space *)
  IF DF = 0 THEN IncDec ← 1 ELSE IncDec ← −1; FI;
FI;
IF OperandSize = 16
THEN
  ES:[dest-index] ← [DX]; (* Reads word at DX from I/O address space *)
  IF DF = 0 THEN IncDec ← 2 ELSE IncDec ← −2; FI;
FI;
IF OperandSize = 32
THEN
  ES:[dest-index] ← [DX]; (* Reads dword at DX from I/O address space *)
  IF DF = 0 THEN IncDec ← 4 ELSE IncDec ← −4; FI;
FI;
dest-index ← dest-index + IncDec;
```

Description

The INS instruction transfers data from the input port numbered by the DX register to the memory byte or word at ES:dest-index. The memory operand must be addressable from the ES register; no segment override is possible. The destination register is the DI register if the address-size attribute of the instruction is 16 bits, or the EDI register if the address-size attribute is 32 bits.

The INS instruction does not allow the specification of the port number as an immediate value. The port must be addressed through the DX register value. Load the correct value into the DX register before executing the INS instruction.

The destination address is determined by the contents of the destination index register. Load the correct index into the destination index register before executing the INS instruction.

After the transfer is made, the DI or EDI register advances automatically. If the DF flag is 0 (a CLD instruction was executed), the DI or EDI register increments; if the DF flag is 1 (an STD instruction was executed), the DI or EDI register decrements. The DI register increments or decrements by 1 if a byte is input, by 2 if a word is input, or by 4 if a doubleword is input.

The INSB, INSW and INSD instructions are synonyms of the byte, word, and doubleword INS instructions. The INS instruction can be preceded by the REP prefix for block input of CX bytes or words. Refer to the REP instruction for details of this operation.

Flags Affected

None

Protected Mode Exceptions

#GP(0) if the current privilege level is numerically greater than the I/O privilege level and any of the corresponding I/O permission bits in TSS equals 1; #GP(0) if the destination is in a nonwritable segment; #GP(0) for an illegal memory operand effective address in the CS, DS, ES, FS, or GS segments; #SS(0) for an illegal address in the SS segment; #PF(fault-code) for a page fault

Real Address Mode Exceptions

Interrupt 13 if any part of the operand would lie outside of the effective address space from 0 to 0FFFFH

Virtual 8086 Mode Exceptions

#GP(0) fault if any of the corresponding I/O permission bits in TSS equals 1; #PF(fault-code) for a page fault

INT/INTO—Call to Interrupt Procedure

Opcode	Instruction	Clocks	Description
CC	INT 3	33	Interrupt 3—trap to debugger
CC	INT 3	*pm*=59	Interrupt 3—Protected Mode, same privilege
CC	INT 3	*pm*=99	Interrupt 3—Protected Mode, more privilege
CC	INT 3	*pm*=119	Interrupt 3—from V86 mode to PL 0
CC	INT 3	ts	Interrupt 3—Protected Mode, via task gate
CD *ib*	INT *imm8*	37	Interrupt numbered by immediate byte
CD *ib*	INT *imm8*	*pm*=59	Interrupt—Protected Mode, same privilege
CD *ib*	INT *imm8*	pm=99	Interrupt—Protected Mode, more privilege
CD *ib*	INT *imm8*	pm=119	Interrupt—from V86 mode to PL 0
CD *ib*	INT *imm8*	ts	Interrupt—Protected Mode, via task gate
CE	INTO	Fail:3,*pm*=3; Pass:35	Interrupt 4—if overflow flag is 1
CE	INTO	*pm*=59	Interrupt 4—Protected Mode, same privilege
CE	INTO	*pm*=99	Interrupt 4—Protected Mode, more privilege
CE	INTO	*pm*=119	Interrupt 4—from V86 mode to PL 0
CE	INTO	ts	Interrupt 4—Protected Mode, via task gate

NOTE: Approximate values of **ts** are given by the following table:

Old Task	New Task		
	386™ DX TSS VM = 0	**386 DX TSS VM = 1**	**80286 TSS**
386 DX TSS VM=0	309	226	282
386 DX TSS VM=1	314	231	287
80286 TSS	307	224	280

Operation

NOTE: The following operational description applies not only to the above instructions but also to external interrupts and exceptions.

```
IF PE = 0
THEN GOTO REAL-ADDRESS-MODE;
pELSE GOTO PROTECTED-MODE;
FI;

REAL-ADDRESS-MODE:
  Push (FLAGS);
  IF ← 0; (* Clear interrupt flag *)
  TF ← 0; (* Clear trap flag *)
  Push(CS);
  Push(IP);
  (* No error codes are pushed *)
  CS ← IDT[Interrupt number * 4].selector;
  IP ← IDT[Interrupt number * 4].offset;
```

```
PROTECTED-MODE:
  Interrupt vector must be within IDT table limits,
    else #GP(vector number * 8+2+EXT);
  Descriptor AR byte must indicate interrupt gate, trap gate, or task gate,
    else #GP(vector number * 8+2+EXT);
  IF software interrupt (* i.e. caused by INT n, INT 3, or INTO *)
  THEN
    IF gate descriptor DPL < CPL
    THEN #GP(vector number * 8+2+EXT);
    FI;
  FI;
  Gate must be present, else #NP(vector number * 8+2+EXT);
  IF trap gate OR interrupt gate
  THEN GOTO TRAP-GATE-OR-INTERRUPT-GATE;
  ELSE GOTO TASK-GATE;
  FI;

TRAP-GATE-OR-INTERRUPT-GATE:
  Examine CS selector and descriptor given in the gate descriptor;
  Selector must be non-null, else #GP (EXT);
  Selector must be within its descriptor table limits
    ELSE #GP(selector+EXT);
  Descriptor AR byte must indicate code segment
    ELSE #GP(selector + EXT);
  Segment must be present, else #NP(selector+EXT);

  IF code segment is non-conforming AND DPL < CPL
  THEN GOTO INTERRUPT-TO-INNER-PRIVILEGE;
  ELSE
    IF code segment is conforming OR code segment DPL = CPL
    THEN GOTO INTERRUPT-TO-SAME-PRIVILEGE-LEVEL;
    ELSE #GP(CS selector + EXT);
    FI;
  FI;

INTERRUPT-TO-INNER-PRIVILEGE:
  Check selector and descriptor for new stack in current TSS;
    Selector must be non-null, else #TS(EXT);
    Selector index must be within its descriptor table limits
      ELSE #TS(SS selector+EXT);
    Selector's RPL must equal DPL of code segment, else #TS(SS
      selector+EXT);
    Stack segment DPL must equal DPL of code segment, else #TS(SS
      selector+EXT);
    Descriptor must indicate writable data segment, else #TS(SS
      selector+EXT);
    Segment must be present, else #SS(SS selector+EXT);
  IF 32-bit gate
  THEN New stack must have room for 20 bytes else #SS(0)
```

```
  ELSE New stack must have room for 10 bytes else #SS(0)
  FI;
  Instruction pointer must be within CS segment boundaries else #GP(0);
  Load new SS and eSP value from TSS;
  IF 32-bit gate
  THEN CS:EIP ← selector:offset from gate;
  ELSE CS:IP ← selector:offset from gate;
  FI;
  Load CS descriptor into invisible portion of CS register;
  Load SS descriptor into invisible portion of SS register;
  IF 32-bit gate
  THEN
     Push (long pointer to old stack) (* 3 words padded to 4 *);
     Push (EFLAGS);
     Push (long pointer to return location) (* 3 words padded to 4*);
  ELSE
     Push (long pointer to old stack) (* 2 words *);
     Push (FLAGS);
     Push (long pointer to return location) (* 2 words *);
  FI;
  Set CPL to new code segment DPL;
  Set RPL of CS to CPL;
  IF interrupt gate THEN IF ← 0 (* interrupt flag to 0 (disabled) *); FI;
  TF ← 0;
  NT ← 0;


INTERRUPT-FROM-V86-MODE:
  TempEFlags ← EFLAGS;
  VM ← 0;
  TF ← 0;
  IF service through Interrupt Gate THEN IF ← 0;
  TempSS ← SS;
  TempESP ← ESP;
  SS ← TSS.SS0; (* Change to level 0 stack segment *)
  ESP ← TSS.ESP0; (* Change to level 0 stack pointer *)
  Push(GS); (* padded to two words *)
  Push(FS); (* padded to two words *)
  Push(DS); (* padded to two words *)
  Push(ES); (* padded to two words *)
  GS ← 0;
  FS ← 0;
  DS ← 0;
  ES ← 0;
  Push(TempSS); (* padded to two words *)
  Push(TempESP);
  Push(TempEFlags);
  Push(CS); (* padded to two words *)
  Push(EIP);
```

```
  CS:EIP ← selector:offset from interrupt gate;
  (* Starts execution of new routine in 386 DX Protected Mode *)

INTERRUPT-TO-SAME-PRIVILEGE-LEVEL:
  IF 32-bit gate
  THEN Current stack limits must allow pushing 10 bytes, else #SS(0);
  ELSE Current stack limits must allow pushing 6 bytes, else #SS(0);
  FI;
  IF interrupt was caused by exception with error code
  THEN Stack limits must allow push of two more bytes;
  ELSE #SS(0);
  FI;
  Instruction pointer must be in CS limit, else #GP(0);
  IF 32-bit gate
  THEN
    Push (EFLAGS);
    Push (long pointer to return location); (* 3 words padded to 4 *)
    CS:EIP ← selector:offset from gate;
  ELSE (* 16-bit gate *)
    Push (FLAGS);
    Push (long pointer to return location); (* 2 words *)
    CS:IP ← selector:offset from gate;
  FI;
  Load CS descriptor into invisible portion of CS register;
  Set the RPL field of CS to CPL;
  Push (error code); (* if any *)
  IF interrupt gate THEN IF ← 0; FI;
  TF ← 0;
  NT ← 0;

TASK-GATE:
  Examine selector to TSS, given in task gate descriptor;
    Must specify global in the local/global bit, else #TS(TSS selector);
    Index must be within GDT limits, else #TS(TSS selector);
    AR byte must specify available TSS (bottom bits 00001),
      else #TS(TSS selector;
    TSS must be present, else #NP(TSS selector);
  SWITCH-TASKS with nesting to TSS;
  IF interrupt was caused by fault with error code
  THEN
    Stack limits must allow push of two more bytes, else #SS(0);
    Push error code onto stack;
  FI;
  Instruction pointer must be in CS limit, else #GP(0);
```

Description

The INT *n* instruction generates via software a call to an interrupt handler. The immediate operand, from 0 to 255, gives the index number into the Interrupt Descriptor Table (IDT) of the interrupt routine to be called. In Protected Mode, the IDT consists of an array of eight-byte descriptors; the descriptor for the interrupt invoked must indicate an interrupt, trap, or task gate. In Real Address Mode, the IDT is an array of four byte-long pointers. In Protected and Real Address Modes, the base linear address of the IDT is defined by the contents of the IDTR.

The INTO conditional software instruction is identical to the INT *n* interrupt instruction except that the interrupt number is implicitly 4, and the interrupt is made only if the 386 DX microprocessor overflow flag is set.

The first 32 interrupts are reserved by Intel for system use. Some of these interrupts are use for internally generated exceptions.

The INT *n* instruction generally behaves like a far call except that the flags register is pushed onto the stack before the return address. Interrupt procedures return via the IRET instruction, which pops the flags and return address from the stack.

In Real Address Mode, the INT instruction *n* pushes the flags, the CS register, and the return IP onto the stack, in that order, then jumps to the long pointer indexed by the interrupt number.

Flags Affected

None

Protected Mode Exceptions

#GP, #NP, #SS, and #TS as indicated under "Operation" above

Real Address Mode Exceptions

None; if the SP or ESP register is 1, 3, or 5 before executing the INT or INTO instruction, the 386 DX microprocessor will shut down due to insufficient stack space

Virtual 8086 Mode Exceptions

#GP(0) fault if IOPL is less than 3, for the INT *n* instruction only, to permit emulation; Interrupt 3 (0CCH) generates a breakpoint exception; the INTO instruction generates an overflow exception if the OF flag is set

IRET/IRETD – Interrupt Return

Opcode	Instruction	Clocks	Description
CF	IRET	22,*pm*=38	Interrupt return (far return and pop flags)
CF	IRET	*pm*=82	Interrupt return to lesser privilege
CF	IRET	ts	Interrupt return, different task (NT = 1)
CF	IRETD	22,*pm*=38	Interrupt return (far return and pop flags)
CF	IRETD	*pm*=82	Interrupt return to lesser privilege
CF	IRETD	*pm*=60	Interrupt return to V86 mode
CF	IRETD	ts	Interrupt return, different task (NT = 1)

NOTE: Values of **ts** are given by the following table:

Old Task	New Task		
	386™ DX TSS VM = 0	**386 DX TSS VM = 1**	**80286 TSS**
386 DX TSS VM=0	275	223	271
80286 TSS	265	213	232

Operation

```
IF PE = 0
THEN (* Real-address mode *)
  IF OperandSize = 32 (* Instruction = IRETD *)
  THEN EIP ← Pop();
  ELSE (* Instruction = IRET *)
    IP ← Pop();
  FI;
  CS ← Pop();
  IF OperandSize = 32 (* Instruction = IRETD *)
  THEN EFLAGS ← Pop();
  ELSE (* Instruction = IRET *)
    FLAGS ← Pop();
  FI;
ELSE (* Protected mode *)
  IF VM = 1
  THEN #GP(0);
  ELSE
    IF NT = 1
    THEN GOTO TASK-RETURN;
    ELSE
      IF VM = 1 in flags image on stack
      THEN GO TO STACK-RETURN-TO-V86;
      ELSE GOTO STACK-RETURN;
      FI;
    FI;
  FI;
```

```
FI;STACK-RETURN-TO-V86: (* Interrupted procedure was in V86 mode *)
  IF top 36 bytes of stack not within limits
  THEN #SS(0);
  FI;
  IF instruction pointer not within code segment limit   THEN #GP(0);
  FI;

  EFLAGS ← SS:[ESP + 8]; (* Sets VM in interrupted routine *)
  EIP ← Pop();
  CS ← Pop(); (* CS behaves as in 8086, due to VM = 1 *)
  throwaway ← Pop(); (* pop away EFLAGS already read *)
  TempESP ← Pop();
  TempSS ← Pop();
  ES ← Pop(); (* pop 2 words; throw away high-order word *)
  DS ← Pop(); (* pop 2 words; throw away high-order word *)
  FS ← Pop(); (* pop 2 words; throw away high-order word *)
  GS ← Pop(); (* pop 2 words; throw away high-order word *)
    SS:ESP ← TempSS:TempESP;

  (* Resume execution in Virtual 8086 mode *)

TASK-RETURN:
  Examine Back Link Selector in TSS addressed by the current task
    register:
    Must specify global in the local/global bit, else #TS(new TSS selector);
    Index must be within GDT limits, else #TS(new TSS selector);
    AR byte must specify TSS, else #TS(new TSS selector);
    New TSS must be busy, else #TS(new TSS selector);
    TSS must be present, else #NP(new TSS selector);
  SWITCH-TASKS without nesting to TSS specified by back link selector;
  Mark the task just abandoned as NOT BUSY;
  Instruction pointer must be within code segment limit ELSE #GP(0);

STACK-RETURN:
  IF OperandSize=32
  THEN Third word on stack must be within stack limits, else #SS(0);
  ELSE Second word on stack must be within stack limits, else #SS(0);
  FI;
  Return CS selector RPL must be ≥ CPL, else #GP(Return selector);
  IF return selector RPL = CPL
  THEN GOTO RETURN-SAME-LEVEL;
  ELSE GOTO RETURN-OUTER-LEVEL;
  FI;

RETURN-SAME-LEVEL:
  IF OperandSize=32
  THEN
    Top 12 bytes on stack must be within limits, else #SS(0);
    Return CS selector (at eSP+4) must be non-null, else #GP(0);
```

```
ELSE
  Top 6 bytes on stack must be within limits, else #SS(0);
  Return CS selector (at eSP+2) must be non-null, else #GP(0);
FI;
Selector index must be within its descriptor table limits, else #GP
  (Return selector);
AR byte must indicate code segment, else #GP(Return selector);
IF non-conforming
THEN code segment DPL must = CPL;
ELSE #GP(Return selector);
FI;
IF conforming
THEN code segment DPL must be ≤ CPL, else #GP(Return selector);
Segment must be present, else #NP(Return selector);
Instruction pointer must be within code segment boundaries, else #GP(0);
FI;
IF OperandSize=32
THEN
  Load CS:EIP from stack;
  Load CS-register with new code segment descriptor;
  Load EFLAGS with third doubleword from stack;
  Increment eSP by 12;
ELSE
  Load CS-register with new code segment descriptor;
  Load FLAGS with third word on stack;
  Increment eSP by 6;
FI;

RETURN-OUTER-LEVEL:
  IF OperandSize=32
  THEN Top 20 bytes on stack must be within limits, else #SS(0);
  ELSE Top 10 bytes on stack must be within limits, else #SS(0);
  FI;
  Examine return CS selector and associated descriptor:
    Selector must be non-null, else #GP(0);
    Selector index must be within its descriptor table limits;
      ELSE #GP(Return selector);
    AR byte must indicate code segment, else #GP(Return selector);
    IF non-conforming
    THEN code segment DPL must = CS selector RPL;
    ELSE #GP(Return selector);
    FI;
    IF conforming
    THEN code segment DPL must be > CPL;
    ELSE #GP(Return selector);
    FI;
    Segment must be present, else #NP(Return selector);

  Examine return SS selector and associated descriptor:
    Selector must be non-null, else #GP(0);
```

```
    Selector index must be within its descriptor table limits
      ELSE #GP(SS selector);
    Selector RPL must equal the RPL of the return CS selector
      ELSE #GP(SS selector);
    AR byte must indicate a writable data segment, else #GP(SS selector);
    Stack segment DPL must equal the RPL of the return CS selector
      ELSE #GP(SS selector);
    SS must be present, else #NP(SS selector);

Instruction pointer must be within code segment limit ELSE #GP(0);
IF OperandSize=32
THEN
    Load CS:EIP from stack;
    Load EFLAGS with values at (eSP+8);
ELSE
    Load CS:IP from stack;
    Load FLAGS with values at (eSP+4);
FI;
Load SS:eSP from stack;
Set CPL to the RPL of the return CS selector;
Load the CS register with the CS descriptor;
Load the SS register with the SS descriptor;
FOR each of ES, FS, GS, and DS
DO;
   IF the current value of the register is not valid for the outer level;
   THEN zero the register and clear the valid flag;
   FI;
   To be valid, the register setting must satisfy the following properties:
      Selector index must be within descriptor table limits;
      AR byte must indicate data or readable code segment;
      IF segment is data or non-conforming code,
      THEN DPL must be ≥ CPL, or DPL must be ≥ RPL;
OD;
```

Description

In Real Address Mode, the IRET instruction pops the instruction pointer, the CS register, and the flags register from the stack and resumes the interrupted routine.

In Protected Mode, the action of the IRET instruction depends on the setting of the nested task flag (NT) bit in the flag register. When the new flag image is popped from the stack, the IOPL bits in the flag register are changed only when CPL equals 0.

If the NT flag is cleared, the IRET instruction returns from an interrupt procedure without a task switch. The code returned to must be equally or less privileged than the interrupt routine (as indicated by the RPL bits of the CS selector popped from the stack). If the destination code is less privileged, the IRET instruction also pops the stack pointer and SS from the stack.

If the NT flag is set, the IRET instruction reverses the operation of a CALL or INT that caused a task switch. The updated state of the task executing the IRET instruction is saved in its task state segment. If the task is reentered later, the code that follows the IRET instruction is executed.

Flags Affected

All flags are affected; the flags register is popped from stack

Protected Mode Exceptions

#GP, #NP, or #SS, as indicated under "Operation" above

Real Address Mode Exceptions

Interrupt 13 if any part of the operand being popped lies beyond address 0FFFFH

Virtual 8086 Mode Exceptions

#GP(0) fault if the I/O privilege level is less than 3, to permit emulation

Jcc—Jump if Condition is Met

Opcode	Instruction	Clocks	Description
77 *cb*	JA *rel8*	7+*m*,3	Jump short if above (CF=0 and ZF=0)
73 *cb*	JAE *rel8*	7+*m*,3	Jump short if above or equal (CF=0)
72 *cb*	JB *rel8*	7+*m*,3	Jump short if below (CF=1)
76 *cb*	JBE *rel8*	7+*m*,3	Jump short if below or equal (CF=1 or ZF=1)
72 *cb*	JC *rel8*	7+*m*,3	Jump short if carry (CF=1)
E3 *cb*	JCXZ *rel8*	9+*m*,5	Jump short if CX register is 0
E3 *cb*	JECXZ *rel8*	9+*m*,5	Jump short if ECX register is 0
74 *cb*	JE *rel8*	7+*m*,3	Jump short if equal (ZF=1)
74 *cb*	JZ *rel8*	7+*m*,3	Jump short if 0 (ZF=1)
7F *cb*	JG *rel8*	7+*m*,3	Jump short if greater (ZF=0 and SF=OF)
7D *cb*	JGE *rel8*	7+*m*,3	Jump short if greater or equal (SF=OF)
7C *cb*	JL *rel8*	7+*m*,3	Jump short if less (SF< >OF)
7E *cb*	JLE *rel8*	7+*m*,3	Jump short if less or equal (ZF=1 or SF< >OF)
76 *cb*	JNA *rel8*	7+*m*,3	Jump short if not above (CF=1 or ZF=1)
72 *cb*	JNAE *rel8*	7+*m*,3	Jump short if not above or equal (CF=1)
73 *cb*	JNB *rel8*	7+*m*,3	Jump short if not below (CF=0)
77 *cb*	JNBE *rel8*	7+*m*,3	Jump short if not below or equal (CF=0 and ZF=0)
73 *cb*	JNC *rel8*	7+*m*,3	Jump short if not carry (CF=0)
75 *cb*	JNE *rel8*	7+*m*,3	Jump short if not equal (ZF=0)
7E *cb*	JNG *rel8*	7+*m*,3	Jump short if not greater (ZF=1 or SF< >OF)
7C *cb*	JNGE *rel8*	7+*m*,3	Jump short if not greater or equal (SF< >OF)
7D *cb*	JNL *rel8*	7+*m*,3	Jump short if not less (SF=OF)
7F *cb*	JNLE *rel8*	7+*m*,3	Jump short if not less or equal (ZF=0 and SF=OF)
71 *cb*	JNO *rel8*	7+*m*,3	Jump short if not overflow (OF=0)
7B *cb*	JNP *rel8*	7+*m*,3	Jump short if not parity (PF=0)
79 *cb*	JNS *rel8*	7+*m*,3	Jump short if not sign (SF=0)
75 *cb*	JNZ *rel8*	7+*m*,3	Jump short if not zero (ZF=0)
70 *cb*	JO *rel8*	7+*m*,3	Jump short if overflow (OF=1)
7A *cb*	JP *rel8*	7+*m*,3	Jump short if parity (PF=1)
7A *cb*	JPE *rel8*	7+*m*,3	Jump short if parity even (PF=1)
7B *cb*	JPO *rel8*	7+*m*,3	Jump short if parity odd (PF=0)
78 *cb*	JS *rel8*	7+*m*,3	Jump short if sign (SF=1)
74 *cb*	JZ *rel8*	7+*m*,3	Jump short if zero (ZF = 1)
0F 87 *cw/cd*	JA *rel16/32*	7+*m*,3	Jump near if above (CF=0 and ZF=0)
0F 83 *cw/cd*	JAE *rel16/32*	7+*m*,3	Jump near if above or equal (CF=0)
0F 82 *cw/cd*	JB *rel16/32*	7+*m*,3	Jump near if below (CF=1)
0F 86 *cw/cd*	JBE *rel16/32*	7+*m*,3	Jump near if below or equal (CF=1 or ZF=1)
0F 82 *cw/cd*	JC *rel16/32*	7+*m*,3	Jump near if carry (CF=1)
0F 84 *cw/cd*	JE *rel16/32*	7+*m*,3	Jump near if equal (ZF=1)
0F 84 *cw/cd*	JZ *rel16/32*	7+*m*,3	Jump near if 0 (ZF=1)
0F 8F *cw/cd*	JG *rel16/32*	7+*m*,3	Jump near if greater (ZF=0 and SF=OF)
0F 8D *cw/cd*	JGE *rel16/32*	7+*m*,3	Jump near if greater or equal (SF=OF)
0F 8C *cw/cd*	JL *rel16/32*	7+*m*,3	Jump near if less (SF< >OF)
0F 8E *cw/cd*	JLE *rel16/32*	7+*m*,3	Jump near if less or equal (ZF=1 or SF< >OF)
0F 86 *cw/cd*	JNA *rel16/32*	7+*m*,3	Jump near if not above (CF=1 or ZF=1)
0F 82 *cw/cd*	JNAE *rel16/32*	7+*m*,3	Jump near if not above or equal (CF=1)
0F 83 *cw/cd*	JNB *rel16/32*	7+*m*,3	Jump near if not below (CF=0)
0F 87 *cw/cd*	JNBE *rel16/32*	7+*m*,3	Jump near if not below or equal (CF=0 and ZF=0)
0F 83 *cw/cd*	JNC *rel16/32*	7+*m*,3	Jump near if not carry (CF=0)
0F 85 *cw/cd*	JNE *rel16/32*	7+*m*,3	Jump near if not equal (ZF=0)
0F 8E *cw/cd*	JNG *rel16/32*	7+*m*,3	Jump near if not greater (ZF=1 or SF< >OF)
0F 8C *cw/cd*	JNGE *rel16/32*	7+*m*,3	Jump near if not greater or equal (SF< >OF)
0F 8D *cw/cd*	JNL *rel16/32*	7+*m*,3	Jump near if not less (SF=OF)
0F 8F *cw/cd*	JNLE *rel16/32*	7+*m*,3	Jump near if not less or equal (ZF=0 and SF=OF)
0F 81 *cw/cd*	JNO *rel16/32*	7+*m*,3	Jump near if not overflow (OF=0)
0F 8B *cw/cd*	JNP *rel16/32*	7+*m*,3	Jump near if not parity (PF=0)
0F 89 *cw/cd*	JNS *rel16/32*	7+*m*,3	Jump near if not sign (SF=0)
0F 85 *cw/cd*	JNZ *rel16/32*	7+*m*,3	Jump near if not zero (ZF=0)
0F 80 *cw/cd*	JO *rel16/32*	7+*m*,3	Jump near if overflow (OF=1)
0F 8A *cw/cd*	JP *rel16/32*	7+*m*,3	Jump near if parity (PF=1)
0F 8A *cw/cd*	JPE *rel16/32*	7+*m*,3	Jump near if parity even (PF=1)
0F 8B *cw/cd*	JPO *rel16/32*	7+*m*,3	Jump near if parity odd (PF=0)
0F 88 *cw/cd*	JS *rel16/32*	7+*m*,3	Jump near if sign (SF=1)
0F 84 *cw/cd*	JZ *rel16/32*	7+*m*,3	

NOTES: The first clock count is for the true condition (branch taken); the second clock count is for the false condition (branch not taken). *rel16/32* indicates that these instructions map to two; one with a 16-bit relative displacement, the other with a 32-bit relative displacement, depending on the operand-size attribute of the instruction.

Operation

```
IF condition
THEN
  EIP ← EIP + SignExtend(rel8/16/32);
  IF OperandSize = 16
  THEN EIP ← EIP AND 0000FFFFH;
  FI;
FI;
```

Description

Conditional jumps (except the JCXZ instruction) test the flags which have been set by a previous instruction. The conditions for each mnemonic are given in parentheses after each description above. The terms "less" and "greater" are used for comparisons of signed integers; "above" and "below" are used for unsigned integers.

If the given condition is true, a jump is made to the location provided as the operand. Instruction coding is most efficient when the target for the conditional jump is in the current code segment and within −128 to +127 bytes of the next instruction's first byte. The jump can also target −32768 thru +32767 (segment size attribute 16) or -2^{31} thru $+2^{31}-1$ (segment size attribute 32) relative to the next instruction's first byte. When the target for the conditional jump is in a different segment, use the opposite case of the jump instruction (i.e., the JE and JNE instructions), and then access the target with an unconditional far jump to the other segment. For example, you cannot code—

```
JZ FARLABEL;
```

You must instead code—

```
   JNZ BEYOND;
   JMP FARLABEL;
BEYOND:
```

Because there can be several ways to interpret a particular state of the flags, ASM386 provides more than one mnemonic for most of the conditional jump opcodes. For example, if you compared two characters in AX and want to jump if they are equal, use the JE instruction; or, if you ANDed the AX register with a bit field mask and only want to jump if the result is 0, use the JZ instruction, a synonym for the JE instruction.

The JCXZ instruction differs from other conditional jumps because it tests the contents of the CX or ECX register for 0, not the flags. The JCXZ instruction is useful at the beginning of a conditional loop that terminates with a conditional loop instruction (such as `LOOPNE TARGET LABEL`. The JCXZ instruction prevents entering the loop with the CX or ECX register equal to zero, which would cause the loop to execute 64K or 32G times instead of zero times.

Flags Affected

None

Protected Mode Exceptions

#GP(0) if the offset jumped to is beyond the limits of the code segment

Real Address Mode Exceptions

None

Virtual 8086 Mode Exceptions

None

JMP—Jump

Opcode	Instruction	Clocks	Description
EB *cb*	JMP *rel8*	7+*m*	Jump short
E9 *cw*	JMP *rel16*	7+*m*	Jump near, displacement relative to next instruction
FF /4	JMP *r/m16*	7+*m*/10+*m*	Jump near indirect
EA *cd*	JMP *ptr16:16*	12+*m*,pm=27+*m*	Jump intersegment, 4-byte immediate address
EA *cd*	JMP *ptr16:16*	*pm*=45+*m*	Jump to call gate, same privilege
EA *cd*	JMP *ptr16:16*	ts	Jump via task state segment
EA *cd*	JMP *ptr16:16*	ts	Jump via task gate
FF /5	JMP *m16:16*	43+*m*,pm=31+*m*	Jump *r/m16:16* indirect and intersegment
FF /5	JMP *m16:16*	*pm*=49+*m*	Jump to call gate, same privilege
FF /5	JMP *m16:16*	5 + ts	Jump via task state segment
FF /5	JMP *m16:16*	5 + ts	Jump via task gate
E9 *cd*	JMP *rel32*	7+*m*	Jump near, displacement relative to next instruction
FF /4	JMP *r/m32*	7+*m*/10+*m*	Jump near, indirect
EA *cp*	JMP *ptr16:32*	12+*m*,pm=27+*m*	Jump intersegment, 6-byte immediate address
EA *cp*	JMP *ptr16:32*	*pm*=45+*m*	Jump to call gate, same privilege
EA *cp*	JMP *ptr16:32*	ts	Jump via task state segment
EA *cp*	JMP *ptr16:32*	ts	Jump via task gate
FF /5	JMP *m16:32*	43+*m*,pm=31+*m*	Jump intersegment, address at *r/m* dword
FF /5	JMP *m16:32*	*pm*=49+*m*	Jump to call gate, same privilege
FF /5	JMP *m16:32*	5 + ts	Jump via task state segment
FF /5	JMP *m16:32*	5 + ts	Jump via task gate

NOTE: Values of **ts** are given by the following table:

Old Task	New Task					
	386™ DX TSS VM = 0		386 DX TSS VM = 1		80286 TSS	
	Via Task Gate?					
	N	Y	N	Y	N	Y
386 DX TSS VM=0	392	401	309	321	285	294
80286 TSS	310	316	229	238	285	294

Operation

IF instruction = relative JMP
   (* i.e. operand is *rel8*, *rel16*, or *rel32* *)
THEN
   EIP ← EIP + *rel8/16/32*;
   IF OperandSize = 16
   THEN EIP ← EIP AND 0000FFFFH;
   FI;
FI;

```
IF instruction = near indirect JMP
  (* i.e. operand is r/m16 or r/m32 *)
THEN
  IF OperandSize = 16
  THEN
    EIP ← [r/m16 AND 0000FFFFH;
  ELSE (* OperandSize = 32 *)
    EIP ← [r/m32;
  FI;
FI;

IF (PE = 0 OR (PE = 1 AND VM = 1)) (* real mode or V86 mode *)
  AND instruction = far JMP
  (* i.e., operand type is m16:16, m16:32, ptr16:16, ptr16:32 *)
THEN GOTO REAL-OR-V86-MODE;
  IF operand type = m16:16 or m16:32
  THEN (* indirect *)
    IF OperandSize = 16
    THEN
      CS:IP ← [m16:16;
      EIP ← EIP AND 0000FFFFH; (* clear upper 16 bits *)
    ELSE (* OperandSize = 32 *)
      CS:EIP ← [m16:32;
    FI;
  FI;
  IF operand type = ptr16:16 or ptr16:32
  THEN
    IF OperandSize = 16
    THEN
      CS:IP ← ptr16:16;
      EIP ← EIP AND 0000FFFFH; (* clear upper 16 bits *)
    ELSE (* OperandSize = 32 *)
      CS:EIP ← ptr16:32;
    FI;
  FI;
FI;

IF (PE = 1 AND VM = 0) (* Protected mode, not V86 mode *)
  AND instruction = far JMP
THEN
  IF operand type = m16:16 or m16:32
  THEN (* indirect *)
    check access of EA dword;
    #GP(0) or #SS(0) IF limit violation;
  FI;
  Destination selector is not null ELSE #GP(0)
  Destination selector index is within its descriptor table limits ELSE
#GP(selector)
  Depending on AR byte of destination descriptor:
```

```
    GOTO CONFORMING-CODE-SEGMENT;
    GOTO NONCONFORMING-CODE-SEGMENT;
    GOTO CALL-GATE;
    GOTO TASK-GATE;
    GOTO TASK-STATE-SEGMENT;
  ELSE #GP(selector); (* illegal AR byte in descriptor *)
FI;

CONFORMING-CODE-SEGMENT:
  Descriptor DPL must be ≤ CPL ELSE #GP(selector);
  Segment must be present ELSE #NP(selector);
  Instruction pointer must be within code-segment limit ELSE #GP(0);
  IF OperandSize = 32
  THEN Load CS:EIP from destination pointer;
  ELSE Load CS:IP from destination pointer;
  FI;
  Load CS register with new segment descriptor;

NONCONFORMING-CODE-SEGMENT:
  RPL of destination selector must be ≤ CPL ELSE #GP(selector);
  Descriptor DPL must be = CPL ELSE #GP(selector);
  Segment must be present ELSE # NP(selector);
  Instruction pointer must be within code-segment limit ELSE #GP(0);
  IF OperandSize = 32
  THEN Load CS:EIP from destination pointer;
  ELSE Load CS:IP from destination pointer;
  FI;
  Load CS register with new segment descriptor;
  Set RPL field of CS register to CPL;

CALL-GATE:
  Descriptor DPL must be ≥ CPL ELSE #GP(gate selector);
  Descriptor DPL must be ≥ gate selector RPL ELSE #GP(gate selector);
  Gate must be present ELSE #NP(gate selector);
  Examine selector to code segment given in call gate descriptor:
    Selector must not be null ELSE #GP(0);
    Selector must be within its descriptor table limits ELSE
      #GP(CS selector);
    Descriptor AR byte must indicate code segment
      ELSE #GP(CS selector);
    IF non-conforming
    THEN code-segment descriptor, DPL must = CPL
    ELSE #GP(CS selector);
    FI;
    IF conforming
    THEN code-segment descriptor DPL must be ≤ CPL;
    ELSE #GP(CS selector);
    Code segment must be present ELSE #NP(CS selector);
    Instruction pointer must be within code-segment limit ELSE #GP(0);
```

```
      IF OperandSize = 32
      THEN Load CS:EIP from call gate;
      ELSE Load CS:IP from call gate;
      FI;
   Load CS register with new code-segment descriptor;
   Set RPL of CS to CPL

TASK-GATE:
   Gate descriptor DPL must be ≥ CPL ELSE #GP(gate selector);
   Gate descriptor DPL must be ≥ gate selector RPL ELSE #GP(gate selector);
   Task Gate must be present ELSE #NP(gate selector);
   Examine selector to TSS, given in Task Gate descriptor:
      Must specify global in the local/global bit ELSE #GP(TSS selector);
      Index must be within GDT limits ELSE #GP(TSS selector);
      Descriptor AR byte must specify available TSS (bottom bits 00001);
         ELSE #GP(TSS selector);
      Task State Segment must be present ELSE #NP(TSS selector);
   SWITCH-TASKS (without nesting) to TSS;
   Instruction pointer must be within code-segment limit ELSE #GP(0);

TASK-STATE-SEGMENT:
   TSS DPL must be ≥ CPL ELSE #GP(TSS selector);
   TSS DPL must be ≥ TSS selector RPL ELSE #GP(TSS selector);
   Descriptor AR byte must specify available TSS (bottom bits 00001)
      ELSE #GP(TSS selector);
   Task State Segment must be present ELSE #NP(TSS selector);
   SWITCH-TASKS (without nesting) to TSS;
   Instruction pointer must be within code-segment limit ELSE #GP(0);
```

Description

The JMP instruction transfers control to a different point in the instruction stream without recording return information.

The action of the various forms of the instruction are shown below.

Jumps with destinations of type *r/m16*, *r/m32*, *rel16*, and *rel32* are near jumps and do not involve changing the segment register value.

The JMP *rel16* and JMP *rel32* forms of the instruction add an offset to the address of the instruction following the JMP to determine the destination. The *rel16* form is used when the instruction's operand-size attribute is 16 bits (segment size attribute 16 only); *rel32* is used when the operand-size attribute is 32 bits (segment size attribute 32 only). The result is stored in the 32-bit EIP register. With *rel16*, the upper 16 bits of the EIP register are cleared, which results in an offset whose value does not exceed 16 bits.

The JMP *r/m16* and JMP *r/m32* forms specify a register or memory location from which the absolute offset from the procedure is fetched. The offset fetched from *r/m* is 32 bits for an operand-size attribute of 32 bits (*r/m32*), or 16 bits for an operand-size attribute of 16 bits (*r/m16*).

The JMP *ptr16:16* and *ptr16:32* forms of the instruction use a four-byte or six-byte operand as a long pointer to the destination. The JMP *m16:16* and *m16:32* forms fetch the long pointer from the memory location specified (indirection). In Real Address Mode or Virtual 8086 Mode, the long pointer provides 16 bits for the CS register and 16 or 32 bits for the EIP register (depending on the operand-size attribute). In Protected Mode, both long pointer forms consult the Access Rights (AR) byte in the descriptor indexed by the selector part of the long pointer. Depending on the value of the AR byte, the jump will perform one of the following types of control transfers:

- A jump to a code segment at the same privilege level
- A task switch

For more information on protected mode control transfers, refer to Chapter 6 and Chapter 7.

Flags Affected

All if a task switch takes place; none if no task switch occurs

Protected Mode Exceptions

Far jumps: #GP, #NP, #SS, and #TS, as indicated in the list above.

Near direct jumps: #GP(0) if procedure location is beyond the code segment limits.

Near indirect jumps: #GP(0) for an illegal memory operand effective address in the CS, DS, ES, FS, or GS segments: #SS(0) for an illegal address in the SS segment; #GP if the indirect offset obtained is beyond the code segment limits; #PF(fault-code) for a page fault.

Real Address Mode Exceptions

Interrupt 13 if any part of the operand would be outside of the effective address space from 0 to 0FFFFH

Virtual 8086 Mode Exceptions

Same exceptions as under Real Address Mode; #PF(fault-code) for a page fault

LAHF—Load Flags into AH Register

Opcode	Instruction	Clocks	Description
9F	LAHF	2	Load: AH = flags SF ZF xx AF xx PF xx CF

Operation

AH ← SF:ZF:xx:AF:xx:PF:xx:CF;

Description

The LAHF instruction transfers the low byte of the flags word to the AH register. The bits, from MSB to LSB, are sign, zero, indeterminate, auxiliary, carry, indeterminate, parity, indeterminate, and carry.

Flags Affected

None

Protected Mode Exceptions

None

Real Address Mode Exceptions

None

Virtual 8086 Mode Exceptions

None

LAR — Load Access Rights Byte

Opcode	Instruction	Clocks	Description
0F 02 /r	LAR *r16,r/m16*	pm = 15/16	*r16* ← *r/m16* masked by FF00
0F 02 /r	LAR *r32,r/m32*	pm = 15/16	*r32* ← *r/m32* masked by 00FxFF00

Description

The LAR instruction stores a marked form of the second doubleword of the descriptor for the source selector if the selector is visible at the current privilege level (modified by the selector's RPL) and is a valid descriptor type. The destination register is loaded with the high-order doubleword of the descriptor masked by 00FxFF00, and the ZF flag is set. The x indicates that the four bits corresponding to the upper four bits of the limit are undefined in the value loaded by the LAR instruction. If the selector is invisible or of the wrong type, the ZF flag is cleared.

If the 32-bit operand size is specified, the entire 32-bit value is loaded into the 32-bit destination register. If the 16-bit operand size is specified, the lower 16-bits of this value are stored in the 16-bit destination register.

All code and data segment descriptors are valid for the LAR instruction.

The valid special segment and gate descriptor types for the LAR instruction are given in the following table:

Type	Name	Valid/Invalid
0	Invalid	Invalid
1	Available 80286 TSS	Valid
2	LDT	Valid
3	Busy 80286 TSS	Valid
4	80286 call gate	Valid
5	80286/386™ DX task gate	Valid
6	80286 trap gate	Valid
7	80286 interrupt gate	Valid
8	Invalid	Invalid
9	Available 386 DX TSS	Valid
A	Invalid	Invalid
B	Busy 386 DX TSS	Valid
C	386 DX call gate	Valid
D	Invalid	Invalid
E	386 DX trap gate	Valid
F	386 DX interrupt gate	Valid

Flags Affected

The ZF flag is set unless the selector is invisible or of the wrong type, in which case the ZF flag is cleared.

Protected Mode Exceptions

#GP(0) for an illegal memory operand effective address in the CS, DS, ES, FS, or GS segments, #SS(0) for an illegal address in the SS segment; #PF(fault-code) for a page fault

Real Address Mode Exceptions

Interrupt 6; the LAR instruction is unrecognized in Real Address Mode

Virtual 8086 Mode Exceptions

Same exceptions as in Real Address Mode

LEA—Load Effective Address

Opcode	Instruction	Clocks	Description
8D /r	LEA *r16,m*	2	Store effective address for *m* in register *r16*
8D /r	LEA *r32,m*	2	Store effective address for *m* in register *r32*
8D /r	LEA *r16,m*	2	Store effective address for *m* in register *r16*
8D /r	LEA *r32,m*	2	Store effective address for *m* in register *r32*

Operation

```
IF OperandSize = 16 AND AddressSize = 16
THEN r16 ← Addr(m);
ELSE
  IF OperandSize = 16 AND AddressSize = 32
  THEN
    r16 ← Truncate_to_16bits(Addr(m));      (* 32-bit address *)
  ELSE
    IF OperandSize = 32 AND AddressSize = 16
    THEN
      r32 ← Truncate_to_16bits(Addr(m));
    ELSE
      IF OperandSize = 32 AND AddressSize = 32
      THEN    r32 ← Addr(m);
      FI;
    FI;
  FI;
FI;
```

Description

The LEA instruction calculates the effective address (offset part) and stores it in the specified register. The operand-size attribute of the instruction (represented by OperandSize in the algorithm under "Operation" above) is determined by the chosen register. The address-size attribute (represented by AddressSize) is determined by the USE attribute of the segment containing the second operand. The address-size and operand-size attributes affect the action performed by the LEA instruction, as follows:

Operand Size	Address Size	Action Performed
16	16	16-bit effective address is calculated and stored in requested 16-bit register destination.
16	32	32-bit effective address is calculated. The lower 16 bits of the address are stored in the requested 16-bit register destination.
32	16	16-bit effective address is calculated. The 16-bit address is zero-extended and stored in the requested 32-bit register destination.

Operand Size	Address Size	Action Performed
32	32	32-bit effective address is calculated and stored in the requested 32-bit register destination.

Flags Affected

None

Protected Mode Exceptions

#UD if the second operand is a register

Real Address Mode Exceptions

Interrupt 6 if the second operand is a register

Virtual 8086 Mode Exceptions

Same exceptions as in Real Address Mode

LEAVE — High Level Procedure Exit

Opcode	Instruction	Clocks	Description
C9	LEAVE	4	Set SP to BP, then pop BP
C9	LEAVE	4	Set ESP to EBP, then pop EBP

Operation

```
IF StackAddrSize = 16
THEN
   SP ← BP;
ELSE (* StackAddrSize = 32 *)
   ESP ← EBP;
FI;
IF OperandSize = 16
THEN
   BP ← Pop();
ELSE (* OperandSize = 32 *)
   EBP ← Pop();
FI;
```

Description

The LEAVE instruction reverses the actions of the ENTER instruction. By copying the frame pointer to the stack pointer, the LEAVE instruction releases the stack space used by a procedure for its local variables. The old frame pointer is popped into the BP or EBP register, restoring the caller's frame. A subsequent RET *nn* instruction removes any arguments pushed onto the stack of the exiting procedure.

Flags Affected

None

Protected Mode Exceptions

#SS(0) if the BP register does not point to a location within the limits of the current stack segment

Real Address Mode Exceptions

Interrupt 13 if any part of the operand would lie outside of the effective address space from 0 to 0FFFFH

Virtual 8086 Mode Exceptions

Same exceptions as in Real Address Mode

LGDT/LIDT — Load Global/Interrupt Descriptor Table Register

Opcode	Instruction	Clocks	Description
0F 01 /2	LGDT *m16&32*	11	Load *m* into GDTR
0F 01 /3	LIDT *m16&32*	11	Load *m* into IDTR

Operation

```
IF instruction = LIDT
THEN
  IF OperandSize = 16
  THEN IDTR.Limit:Base ← m16:24 (* 24 bits of base loaded *)
  ELSE IDTR.Limit:Base ← m16:32
  FI;
ELSE (* instruction = LGDT *)
  IF OperandSize = 16
  THEN GDTR.Limit:Base ← m16:24 (* 24 bits of base loaded *)
  ELSE GDTR.Limit:Base ← m16:32;
  FI;
FI;
```

Description

The LGDT and LIDT instructions load a linear base address and limit value from a six-byte data operand in memory into the GDTR or IDTR, respectively. If a 16-bit operand is used with the LGDT or LIDT instruction, the register is loaded with a 16-bit limit and a 24-bit base, and the high-order eight bits of the six-byte data operand are not used. If a 32-bit operand is used, a 16-bit limit and a 32-bit base is loaded; the high-order eight bits of the six-byte operand are used as high-order base address bits.

The SGDT and SIDT instructions always store into all 48 bits of the six-byte data operand. With the 80286, the upper eight bits are undefined after the SGDT or SIDT instruction is executed. With the 386 DX microprocessor, the upper eight bits are written with the high-order eight address bits, for both a 16-bit operand and a 32-bit operand. If the LGDT or LIDT instruction is used with a 16-bit operand to load the register stored by the SGDT or SIDT instruction, the upper eight bits are stored as zeros.

The LGDT and LIDT instructions appear in operating system software; they are not used in application programs. They are the only instructions that directly load a linear address (i.e., not a segment relative address) in 386 DX microprocessor Protected Mode.

Flags Affected

None

Protected Mode Exceptions

#GP(0) if the current privilege level is not 0; #UD if the source operand is a register; #GP(0) for an illegal memory operand effective address in the CS, DS, ES, FS, or GS segments; #SS(0) for an illegal address in the SS segment; #PF(fault-code) for a page fault

Real Address Mode Exceptions

Interrupt 13 if any part of the operand would lie outside of the effective address space from 0 to 0FFFFH; Interrupt 6 if the source operand is a register

Note: These instructions are valid in Real Address Mode to allow power-up initialization for Protected Mode

Virtual 8086 Mode Exceptions

Same exceptions as in Real Address Mode; #PF(fault-code) for a page fault

LGS/LSS/LDS/LES/LFS — Load Full Pointer

Opcode	Instruction	Clocks	Description
C5 /r	LDS *r16,m16:16*	7,*pm*=26	Load DS:*r16* with pointer from memory
C5 /r	LDS *r32,m16:32*	7,*pm*=28	Load DS:*r32* with pointer from memory
0F B2 /r	LSS *r16,m16:16*	7,*pm*=26	Load SS:*r16* with pointer from memory
0F B2 /r	LSS *r32,m16:32*	7,*pm*=28	Load SS:*r32* with pointer from memory
C4 /r	LES *r16,m16:16*	7,*pm*=26	Load ES:*r16* with pointer from memory
C4 /r	LES *r32,m16:32*	7,*pm*=28	Load ES:*r32* with pointer from memory
0F B4 /r	LFS *r16,m16:16*	7,*pm*=29	Load FS:*r16* with pointer from memory
0F B4 /r	LFS *r32,m16:32*	7,*pm*=31	Load FS:*r32* with pointer from memory
0F B5 /r	LGS *r16,m16:16*	7,*pm*=29	Load GS:*r16* with pointer from memory
0F B5 /r	LGS *r32,m16:32*	7,*pm*=31	Load GS:*r32* with pointer from memory

Operation

```
CASE instruction OF
  LSS: Sreg is SS; (* Load SS register *)
  LDS: Sreg is DS; (* Load DS register *)
  LES: Sreg is ES; (* Load ES register *)
  LFS: Sreg is FS; (* Load FS register *)
  LGS: Sreg is DS; (* Load GS register *)
ESAC;
IF (OperandSize = 16)
THEN
  r16 ← [Effective Address]; (* 16-bit transfer *)
  Sreg ← [Effective Address + 2]; (* 16-bit transfer *)
  (* In Protected Mode, load the descriptor into the segment register *)
ELSE (* OperandSize = 32 *)
  r32 ← [Effective Address]; (* 32-bit transfer *)
  Sreg ← [Effective Address + 4]; (* 16-bit transfer *)
  (* In Protected Mode, load the descriptor into the segment register *)
FI;
```

Description

The LGS, LSS, LDS, LES, and LFS instructions read a full pointer from memory and store it in the selected segment register:register pair. The full pointer loads 16 bits into the segment register SS, DS, ES, FS, or GS. The other register loads 32 bits if the operand-size attribute is 32 bits, or loads 16 bits if the operand-size attribute is 16 bits. The other 16- or 32-bit register to be loaded is determined by the *r16* or *r32* register operand specified.

When an assignment is made to one of the segment registers, the descriptor is also loaded into the segment register. The data for the register is obtained from the descriptor table entry for the selector given.

A null selector (values 0000-0003) can be loaded into DS, ES, FS, or GS registers without causing a protection exception. (Any subsequent reference to a segment whose corresponding segment register is loaded with a null selector to address memory causes a #GP(0) exception. No memory reference to the segment occurs.)

The following is a listing of the Protected Mode checks and actions taken in the loading of a segment register:

```
IF SS is loaded:
  IF selector is null THEN #GP(0); FI;
  Selector index must be within its descriptor table limits ELSE
     #GP(selector);
  Selector's RPL must equal CPL ELSE #GP(selector);
  AR byte must indicate a writable data segment ELSE #GP(selector);
  DPL in the AR byte must equal CPL ELSE #GP(selector);
  Segment must be marked present ELSE #SS(selector);
  Load SS with selector;
  Load SS with descriptor;

IF DS, ES, FS, or GS is loaded with non-null selector:
  Selector index must be within its descriptor table limits ELSE
     #GP(selector);
  AR byte must indicate data or readable code segment ELSE
     #GP(selector);
  IF data or nonconforming code
  THEN both the RPL and the CPL must be less than or equal to DPL in
     AR byte;
  ELSE #GP(selector);
  Segment must be marked present ELSE #NP(selector);
Load segment register with selector and RPL bits;
Load segment register with descriptor;

IF DS, ES, FS or GS is loaded with a null selector:
  Load segment register with selector;
  Clear descriptor valid bit;
```

Flags Affected

None

Protected Mode Exceptions

#GP(0) for an illegal memory operand effective address in the CS, DS, ES, FS, or GS segments; #SS(0) for an illegal address in the SS segment; the second operand must be a memory operand, not a register; #GP(0) if a null selector is loaded into SS; #PF(fault-code) for a page fault

Real Address Mode Exceptions

The second operand must be a memory operand, not a register; Interrupt 13 if any part of the operand would lie outside of the effective address space from 0 to 0FFFFH

Virtual 8086 Mode Exceptions

Same exceptions as in Real Address Mode; #PF(fault-code) for a page fault

LLDT—Load Local Descriptor Table Register

Opcode	Instruction	Clocks	Description
0F 00 /2	LLDT *r/m16*	20	Load selector *r/m16* into LDTR

Operation

LDTR ← SRC;

Description

The LLDT instruction loads the Local Descriptor Table register (LDTR). The word operand (memory or register) to the LLDT instruction should contain a selector to the Global Descriptor Table (GDT). The GDT entry should be a Local Descriptor Table. If so, then the LDTR is loaded from the entry. The descriptor registers DS, ES, SS, FS, GS, and CS are not affected. The LDT field in the task state segment does not change.

The selector operand can be 0; if so, the LDTR is marked invalid. All descriptor references (except by the LAR, VERR, VERW or LSL instructions) cause a #GP fault.

The LLDT instruction is used in operating system software; it is not used in application programs.

Flags Affected

None

Protected Mode Exceptions

#GP(0) if the current privilege level is not 0; #GP(selector) if the selector operand does not point into the Global Descriptor Table, or if the entry in the GDT is not a Local Descriptor Table; #NP(selector) if the LDT descriptor is not present; #GP(0) for an illegal memory operand effective address in the CS, DS, ES, FS, or GS segments; #SS(0) for an illegal address in the SS segment; #PF(fault-code) for a page fault

Real Address Mode Exceptions

Interrupt 6; the LLDT instruction is not recognized in Real Address Mode

Virtual 8086 Mode Exceptions

Same exceptions as in Real Address Mode (because the instruction is not recognized, it will not execute or perform a memory reference)

Note

The operand-size attribute has no effect on this instruction.

LMSW—Load Machine Status Word

Opcode	Instruction	Clocks	Description
0F 01 /6	LMSW *r/m16*	11/14	Load *r/m16* in machine status word

Operation

MSW ← *r/m16*; (* 16 bits is stored in the machine status word *)

Description

The LMSW instruction loads the machine status word (part of the CR0 register) from the source operand. This instruction can be used to switch to Protected Mode; if so, it must be followed by an intrasegment jump to flush the instruction queue. The LMSW instruction will not switch back to Real Address Mode.

The LMSW instruction is used only in operating system software. It is not used in application programs.

Flags Affected

None

Protected Mode Exceptions

#GP(0) if the current privilege level is not 0; #GP(0) for an illegal memory operand effective address in the CS, DS, ES, FS, or GS segments; #SS(0) for an illegal address in the SS segment; #PF(fault-code) for a page fault

Real Address Mode Exceptions

Interrupt 13 if any part of the operand would lie outside of the effective address space from 0 to 0FFFFH

Virtual 8086 Mode Exceptions

Same exceptions as in Real Address Mode; #PF(fault-code) for a page fault

Notes

The operand-size attribute has no effect on this instruction. This instruction is provided for compatibility with the 80286; 386 DX microprocessor programs should use the MOV CR0, ... instruction instead. The LMSW instruction does not affect the PG or ET bits, and it cannot be used to clear the PE bit.

LOCK—Assert LOCK# Signal Prefix

Opcode	Instruction	Clocks	Description
F0	LOCK	0	Assert LOCK# signal for the next instruction

Description

The LOCK prefix causes the LOCK# signal of the 386 DX microprocessor to be asserted during execution of the instruction that follows it. In a multiprocessor environment, this signal can be used to ensure that the 386 DX microprocessor has exclusive use of any shared memory while LOCK# is asserted. The read-modify-write sequence typically used to implement test-and-set on the 386 DX microprocessor is the BTS instruction.

The LOCK prefix functions only with the following instructions:

BTS, BTR, BTC	mem, reg/imm
XCHG	reg, mem
XCHG	mem, reg
ADD, OR, ADC, SBB, AND, SUB, XOR	mem, reg/imm
NOT, NEG, INC, DEC	mem

An undefined opcode trap will be generated if a LOCK prefix is used with any instruction not listed above.

The XCHG instruction always asserts LOCK# regardless of the presence or absence of the LOCK prefix.

The integrity of the LOCK prefix is not affected by the alignment of the memory field. Memory locking is observed for arbitrarily misaligned fields.

Flags Affected

None

Protected Mode Exceptions

#UD if the LOCK prefix is used with an instruction not listed in the "Description" section above; other exceptions can be generated by the subsequent (locked) instruction

Real Address Mode Exceptions

Interrupt 6 if the LOCK prefix is used with an instruction not listed in the "Description" section above; exceptions can still be generated by the subsequent (locked) instruction

Virtual 8086 Mode Exceptions

#UD if the LOCK prefix is used with an instruction not listed in the "Description" section above; exceptions can still be generated by the subsequent (locked) instruction

LODS/LODSB/LODSW/LODSD – Load String Operand

Opcode	Instruction	Clocks	Description
AC	LODS *m8*	5	Load byte [(E)SI] into AL
AD	LODS *m16*	5	Load word [(E)SI] into AX
AD	LODS *m32*	5	Load dword [(E)SI] into EAX
AC	LODSB	5	Load byte DS:[(E)SI] into AL
AD	LODSW	5	Load word DS:[(E)SI] into AX
AD	LODSD	5	Load dword DS:[(E)SI] into EAX

Operation

```
AddressSize = 16
THEN use SI for source-index
ELSE (* AddressSize = 32 *)
  use ESI for source-index;
FI;
IF byte type of instruction
THEN
  AL ← [source-index]; (* byte load *)
  IF DF = 0 THEN IncDec ← 1 ELSE IncDec ← −1; FI;
ELSE
  IF OperandSize = 16
  THEN
    AX ← [source-index]; (* word load *)
    IF DF = 0 THEN IncDec ← 2 ELSE IncDec ← −2; FI;
  ELSE (* OperandSize = 32 *)
    EAX ← [source-index]; (* dword load *)
    IF DF = 0 THEN IncDec ← 4 ELSE IncDec ← −4; FI;
  FI;
FI;
source-index ← source-index + IncDec
```

Description

The LODS instruction loads the AL, AX, or EAX register with the memory byte, word, or doubleword at the location pointed to by the source-index register. After the transfer is made, the source-index register is automatically advanced. If the DF flag is 0 (the CLD instruction was executed), the source index increments; if the DF flag is 1 (the STD instruction was executed), it decrements. The increment or decrement is 1 if a byte is loaded, 2 if a word is loaded, or 4 if a doubleword is loaded.

If the address-size attribute for this instruction is 16 bits, the SI register is used for the source-index register; otherwise the address-size attribute is 32 bits, and the ESI register is used. The address of the source data is determined solely by the contents of the ESI or SI register. Load the correct index value into the SI register before executing the LODS instruction. The LODSB, LODSW, and LODSD instructions are synonyms for the byte, word, and doubleword LODS instructions.

The LODS instruction can be preceded by the REP prefix; however, the LODS instruction is used more typically within a LOOP construct, because further processing of the data moved into the EAX, AX, or AL register is usually necessary.

Flags Affected

None

Protected Mode Exceptions

#GP(0) for an illegal memory operand effective address in the CS, DS, ES, FS, or GS segments; #SS(0) for an illegal address in the SS segment; #PF(fault-code) for a page fault

Real Address Mode Exceptions

Interrupt 13 if any part of the operand would lie outside of the effective address space from 0 to 0FFFFH

Virtual 8086 Mode Exceptions

Same exceptions as in Real Address Mode; #PF(fault-code) for a page fault

LOOP/LOOPcond — Loop Control with CX Counter

Opcode	Instruction	Clocks	Description
E2 *cb*	LOOP *rel8*	11+*m*	DEC count; jump short if count < > 0
E1 *cb*	LOOPE *rel8*	11+*m*	DEC count; jump short if count < > 0 and ZF=1
E1 *cb*	LOOPZ *rel8*	11+*m*	DEC count; jump short if count < > 0 and ZF=1
E0 *cb*	LOOPNE *rel8*	11+*m*	DEC count; jump short if count < > 0 and ZF=0
E0 *cb*	LOOPNZ *rel8*	11+*m*	DEC count; jump short if count < > 0 and ZF=0

Operation

```
IF AddressSize = 16 THEN CountReg is CX ELSE CountReg is ECX; FI;
CountReg ← CountReg − 1;

IF instruction < > LOOP
THEN
   IF (instruction = LOOPE) OR (instruction = LOOPZ)
   THEN BranchCond ← (ZF = 1) AND (CountReg < > 0);
   FI;
   IF (instruction = LOOPNE) OR (instruction = LOOPNZ)
   THEN BranchCond ← (ZF = 0) AND (CountReg < > 0);
   FI;
FI;

IF BranchCond
THEN
   IF OperandSize = 16
   THEN
      IP ← IP + SignExtend(rel8);
   ELSE (* OperandSize = 32 *)
      EIP ← EIP + SignExtend(rel8);
   FI;
FI;
```

Description

The LOOP instruction decrements the count register without changing any of the flags. Conditions are then checked for the form of the LOOP instruction being used. If the conditions are met, a short jump is made to the label given by the operand to the LOOP instruction. If the address-size attribute is 16 bits, the CX register is used as the count register; otherwise the ECX register is used. The operand of the LOOP instruction must be in the range from 128 (decimal) bytes before the instruction to 127 bytes ahead of the instruction.

The LOOP instructions provide iteration control and combine loop index management with conditional branching. Use the LOOP instruction by loading an unsigned iteration count into the count register, then code the LOOP instruction at the end of a series of instructions to be iterated. The destination of the LOOP instruction is a label that points to the beginning of the iteration.

Flags Affected

None

Protected Mode Exceptions

#GP(0) if the offset jumped to is beyond the limits of the current code segment

Real Address Mode Exceptions

None

Virtual 8086 Mode Exceptions

None

LSL — Load Segment Limit

Opcode	Instruction	Clocks	Description
0F 03 /r	LSL *r16,r/m16*	pm = 21/22	Load: *r16* ← segment limit, selector *r/m16* (byte granular)
0F 03 /r	LSL *r32,r/m32*	pm = 21/22	Load: *r32* ← segment limit, selector *r/m32* (byte granular)
0F 03 /r	LSL *r16,r/m16*	pm = 25/26	Load: *r16* ← segment limit, selector *r/m16* (page granular)
0F 03 /r	LSL *r32,r/m32*	pm = 25/26	Load: *r32* ← segment limit, selector *r/m32* (page granular)

Description

The LSL instruction loads a register with an unscrambled segment limit, and sets the ZF flag, provided that the source selector is visible at the current privilege level and RPL, and that the descriptor is a type accepted by the LSL instruction. Otherwise, the ZF flag is cleared, and the destination register is unchanged. The segment limit is loaded as a byte granular value. If the descriptor has a page granular segment limit, the LSL instruction will translate it to a byte limit before loading it in the destination register (shift left 12 the 20-bit "raw" limit from descriptor, then OR with 00000FFFH).

The 32-bit forms of the LSL instruction store the 32-bit byte granular limit in the 16-bit destination register.

Code and data segment descriptors are valid for the LSL instruction.

The valid special segment and gate descriptor types for the LSL instruction are given in the following table:

Type	Name	Valid/Invalid
0	Invalid	Invalid
1	Available 80286 TSS	Valid
2	LDT	Valid
3	Busy 80286 TSS	Valid
4	80286 call gate	Invalid
5	80286/386™ DX task gate	Invalid
6	80286 trap gate	Invalid
7	80286 interrupt gate	Invalid
8	Invalid	Valid
9	Available 386 DX TSS	Valid
A	Invalid	Invalid
B	Busy 386 DX TSS	Valid
C	386 DX call gate	Invalid
D	Invalid	Invalid
E	386 DX trap gate	Invalid
F	386 DX interrupt gate	Invalid

Flags Affected

The ZF flag is set unless the selector is invisible or of the wrong type, in which case the ZF flag is cleared

Protected Mode Exceptions

#GP(0) for an illegal memory operand effective address in the CS, DS, ES, FS, or GS segments; #SS(0) for an illegal address in the SS segment; #PF(fault-code) for a page fault

Real Address Mode Exceptions

Interrupt 6; the LSL instruction is not recognized in Real Address Mode

Virtual 8086 Mode Exceptions

Same exceptions as in Real Address Mode

LTR — Load Task Register

Opcode	Instruction	Clocks	Description
0F 00 /3	LTR r/m16	pm=23/27	Load EA word into task register

Description

The LTR instruction loads the task register from the source register or memory location specified by the operand. The loaded TSS is marked busy. A task switch does not occur.

The LTR instruction is used only in operating system software; it is not used in application programs.

Flags Affected

None

Protected Mode Exceptions

#GP(0) for an illegal memory operand effective address in the CS, DS, ES, FS, or GS segments; #SS(0) for an illegal address in the SS segment; #GP(0) if the current privilege level is not 0; #GP(selector) if the object named by the source selector is not a TSS or is already busy; #NP(selector) if the TSS is marked "not present"; #PF(fault-code) for a page fault

Real Address Mode Exceptions

Interrupt 6; the LTR instruction is not recognized in Real Address Mode

Virtual 8086 Mode Exceptions

Same exceptions as in Real Address Mode

Notes

The operand-size attribute has no effect on this instruction.

MOV — Move Data

Opcode	Instruction	Clocks	Description
88 /r	MOV *r/m8,r8*	2/2	Move byte register to *r/m* byte
89 /r	MOV *r/m16,r16*	2/2	Move word register to *r/m* word
89 /r	MOV *r/m32,r32*	2/2	Move dword register to *r/m* dword
8A /r	MOV *r8,r/m8*	2/4	Move *r/m* byte to byte register
8B /r	MOV *r16,r/m16*	2/4	Move *r/m* word to word register
8B /r	MOV *r32,r/m32*	2/4	Move *r/m* dword to dword register
8C /r	MOV *r/m16,Sreg*	2/2	Move segment register to *r/m* word
8E /r	MOV *Sreg,r/m16*	2/5,*pm*=18/19	Move *r/m* word to segment register
A0	MOV AL,*moffs8*	4	Move byte at (*seg:offset*) to AL
A1	MOV AX,*moffs16*	4	Move word at (*seg:offset*) to AX
A1	MOV EAX,*moffs32*	4	Move dword at (*seg:offset*) to EAX
A2	MOV *moffs8*,AL	2	Move AL to (*seg:offset*)
A3	MOV *moffs16*,AX	2	Move AX to (*seg:offset*)
A3	MOV *moffs32*,EAX	2	Move EAX to (*seg:offset*)
B0+ *rb*	MOV *reg8,imm8*	2	Move immediate byte to register
B8+ *rw*	MOV *reg16,imm16*	2	Move immediate word to register
B8+ *rd*	MOV *reg32,imm32*	2	Move immediate dword to register
C6	MOV *r/m8,imm8*	2/2	Move immediate byte to *r/m* byte
C7	MOV *r/m16,imm16*	2/2	Move immediate word to *r/m* word
C7	MOV *r/m32,imm32*	2/2	Move immediate dword to *r/m* dword

NOTES: *moffs8*, *moffs16*, and *moffs32* all consist of a simple offset relative to the segment base. The *8*, *16*, and *32* refer to the size of the data. The address-size attribute of the instruction determines the size of the offset, either 16 or 32 bits.

Operation

DEST ← SRC;

Description

The MOV instruction copies the second operand to the first operand.

If the destination operand is a segment register (DS, ES, SS, etc.), then data from a descriptor is also loaded into the register. The data for the register is obtained from the descriptor table entry for the selector given. A null selector (values 0000-0003) can be loaded into the DS and ES registers without causing an exception; however, use of the DS or ES register causes a #GP(0) exception, and no memory reference occurs.

A MOV into SS instruction inhibits all interrupts until after the execution of the next instruction (which is presumably a MOV into ESP instruction).

Loading a segment register under 386 DX Protected Mode results in special checks and actions, as described in the following listing:

```
IF SS is loaded;
THEN
   IF selector is null THEN #GP(0);
FI;
   Selector index must be within its descriptor table limits else #GP(selector);
   Selector's RPL must equal CPL else #GP(selector);
```

```
AR byte must indicate a writable data segment else #GP(selector);
   DPL in the AR byte must equal CPL else #GP(selector);
   Segment must be marked present else #SS(selector);
   Load SS with selector;
   Load SS with descriptor.
FI;
IF DS, ES, FS or GS is loaded with non-null selector;
THEN
   Selector index must be within its descriptor table limits
      else #GP(selector);
   AR byte must indicate data or readable code segment else #GP(selector);
   IF data or nonconforming code segment
   THEN both the RPL and the CPL must be less than or equal to DPL in AR byte;
   ELSE #GP(selector);
   FI;
   Segment must be marked present else #NP(selector);
   Load segment register with selector;
   Load segment register with descriptor;
FI;
IF DS, ES, FS or GS is loaded with a null selector;
THEN
   Load segment register with selector;
   Clear descriptor valid bit;
FI;
```

Flags Affected

None

Protected Mode Exceptions

#GP, #SS, and #NP if a segment register is being loaded; otherwise, #GP(0) if the destination is in a nonwritable segment; #GP(0) for an illegal memory operand effective address in the CS, DS, ES, FS, or GS segments; #SS(0) for an illegal address in the SS segment; #PF(fault-code) for a page fault

Real Address Mode Exceptions

Interrupt 13 if any part of the operand would lie outside of the effective address space from 0 to 0FFFFH

Virtual 8086 Mode Exceptions

Same exceptions as in Real Address Mode; #PF(fault-code) for a page fault

MOV—Move to/from Special Registers

Opcode	Instruction	Clocks	Description
0F 20 /r	MOV *r32*,CR0/CR2/CR3	6	Move (control register) to (register)
0F 22 /r	MOV CR0/CR2/CR3,*r32*	11/4/5	Move (register) to (control register)
0F21 /r	MOV *r32*,DR0 – 3	22	Move (debug register) to (register)
0F 21 /r	MOV *r32*,DR6/DR7	14	Move (debug register) to (register)
0F 23 /r	MOV DR0 – 3,*r32*	22	Move (register) to (debug register)
0F 23 /r	MOV DR6/DR7,*r32*	16	Move (register) to (debug register)
0F 24 /r	MOV *r32*,TR6/TR7	12	Move (test register) to (register)
0F 26 /r	MOV TR6/TR7,*r32*	12	Move (register) to (test register)

Operation

DEST ← SRC;

Description

The above forms of the MOV instruction store or load the following special registers in or from a general purpose register:

- Control registers CR0, CR2, and CR3
- Debug Registers DR0, DR1, DR2, DR3, DR6, and DR7
- Test Registers TR6 and TR7

Thirty-two bit operands are always used with these instructions, regardless of the operand-size attribute.

Flags Affected

The OF, SF, ZF, AF, PF, and CF flags are undefined

Protected Mode Exceptions

#GP(0) if the current privilege level is not 0

Real Address Mode Exceptions

None

Virtual 8086 Mode Exceptions

#GP(0) if instruction execution is attempted

Notes

The instructions must be executed at privilege level 0 or in real-address mode; otherwise, a protection exception will be raised.

The *reg* field within the ModR/M byte specifies which of the special registers in each category is involved. The two bits in the *mod* field are always 11. The *r/m* field specifies the general register involved.

MOVS/MOVSB/MOVSW/MOVSD—Move Data from String to String

Opcode	Instruction	Clocks	Description
A4	MOVS *m8,m8*	8	Move byte [(E)SI] to ES:[(E)DI]
A5	MOVS *m16,m16*	8	Move word [(E)SI] to ES:[(E)DI]
A5	MOVS *m32,m32*	8	Move dword [(E)SI] to ES:[(E)DI]
A4	MOVSB	8	Move byte DS:[(E)SI] to ES:[(E)DI]
A5	MOVSW	8	Move word DS:[(E)SI] to ES:[(E)DI]
A5	MOVSD	8	Move dword DS:[(E)SI] to ES:[(E)DI]

Operation

```
IF (instruction = MOVSD) OR (instruction has doubleword operands)
THEN OperandSize ← 32;
ELSE OperandSize ← 16;
IF AddressSize = 16
THEN use SI for source-index and DI for destination-index;
ELSE (* AddressSize = 32 *)
  use ESI for source-index and EDI for destination-index;
FI;
IF byte type of instruction
THEN
  [destination-index] ← [source-index]; (* byte assignment *)
  IF DF = 0 THEN IncDec ← 1 ELSE IncDec ← −1; FI;
ELSE
  IF OperandSize = 16
  THEN
    [destination-index] ← [source-index]; (* word assignment *)
    IF DF = 0 THEN IncDec ← 2 ELSE IncDec ← −2; FI;
  ELSE (* OperandSize = 32 *)
    [destination-index] ← [source-index]; (* doubleword assignment *)
    IF DF = 0 THEN IncDec ← 4 ELSE IncDec ← −4; FI;
  FI;
FI;
source-index ← source-index + IncDec;
destination-index ← destination-index + IncDec;
```

Description

The MOVS instruction copies the byte or word at [(E)SI] to the byte or word at ES-:[(E)DI]. The destination operand must be addressable from the ES register; no segment override is possible for the destination. A segment override can be used for the source operand; the default is the DS register.

The addresses of the source and destination are determined solely by the contents of the (E)SI and (E)DI registers. Load the correct index values into the (E)SI and (E)DI registers before executing the MOVS instruction. The MOVSB, MOVSW, and MOVSD instructions are synonyms for the byte, word, and doubleword MOVS instructions.

After the data is moved, both the (E)SI and (E)DI registers are advanced automatically. If the DF flag is 0 (the CLD instruction was executed), the registers are incremented; if the DF flag is 1 (the STD instruction was executed), the registers are decremented. The registers are incremented or decremented by 1 if a byte was moved, 2 if a word was moved, or 4 if a doubleword was moved.

The MOVS instruction can be preceded by the REP prefix for block movement of CX bytes or words. Refer to the REP instruction for details of this operation.

Flags Affected

None

Protected Mode Exceptions

#GP(0) if the result is in a nonwritable segment; #GP(0) for an illegal memory operand effective address in the CS, DS, ES, FS, or GS segments; #SS(0) for an illegal address in the SS segment; #PF(fault-code) for a page fault

Real Address Mode Exceptions

Interrupt 13 if any part of the operand would lie outside of the effective address space from 0 to 0FFFFH

Virtual 8086 Mode Exceptions

Same exceptions as in Real Address Mode; #PF(fault-code) for a page fault

MOVSX — Move with Sign-Extend

Opcode	Instruction	Clocks	Description
0F BE /r	MOVSX *r16,r/m8*	3/6	Move byte to word with sign-extend
0F BE /r	MOVSX *r32,r/m8*	3/6	Move byte to dword, sign-extend
0F BF /r	MOVSX *r32,r/m16*	3/6	Move word to dword, sign-extend

Operation

DEST ← SignExtend(SRC);

Description

The MOVSX instruction reads the contents of the effective address or register as a byte or a word, sign-extends the value to the operand-size attribute of the instruction (16 or 32 bits), and stores the result in the destination register.

Flags Affected

None

Protected Mode Exceptions

#GP(0) for an illegal memory operand effective address in the CS, DS, ES, FS or GS segments; #SS(0) for an illegal address in the SS segment; #PF(fault-code) for a page fault

Real Address Mode Exceptions

Interrupt 13 if any part of the operand would lie outside of the effective address space from 0 to 0FFFFH

Virtual 8086 Mode Exceptions

Same exceptions as in Real Address Mode; #PF(fault-code) for a page fault

MOVZX — Move with Zero-Extend

Opcode	Instruction	Clocks	Description
0F B6 /r	MOVZX *r16,r/m8*	3/6	Move byte to word with zero-extend
0F B6 /r	MOVZX *r32,r/m8*	3/6	Move byte to dword, zero-extend
0F B7 /r	MOVZX *r32,r/m16*	3/6	Move word to dword, zero-extend

Operation

DEST ← ZeroExtend(SRC);

Description

The MOVZX instruction reads the contents of the effective address or register as a byte or a word, zero extends the value to the operand-size attribute of the instruction (16 or 32 bits), and stores the result in the destination register.

Flags Affected

None

Protected Mode Exceptions

#GP(0) for an illegal memory operand effective address in the CS, DS, ES, FS, or GS segments; #SS(0) for an illegal address in the SS segment; #PF(fault-code) for a page fault

Real Address Mode Exceptions

Interrupt 13 if any part of the operand would lie outside of the effective address space from 0 to 0FFFFH

Virtual 8086 Mode Exceptions

Same exceptions as in Real Address Mode; #PF(fault-code) for a page fault

MUL—Unsigned Multiplication of AL or AX

Opcode	Instruction	Clocks	Description
F6 /4	MUL AL,*r/m8*	9-14/12-17	Unsigned multiply (AX ← AL * *r/m* byte)
F7 /4	MUL AX,*r/m16*	9-22/12-25	Unsigned multiply (DX:AX ← AX * *r/m* word)
F7 /4	MUL EAX,*r/m32*	9-38/12-41	Unsigned multiply (EDX:EAX ← EAX * *r/m* dword)

NOTES: The 386 DX uses an early-out multiply algorithm. The actual number of clocks depends on the position of the most significant bit in the optimizing multiplier. The optimization occurs for positive and negative multiplier values. Because of the early-out algorithm, clock counts given are minimum to maximum. To calculate the actual clocks, use the following formula:

Actual clock = if **m** < > 0 then max(ceiling($\log_2$ | **m** |), 3) + 6 clocks;

Actual clock = if **m** = 0 then 9 clocks

where **m** is the multiplier.

Operation

```
IF byte-size operation
THEN AX ← AL * r/m8
ELSE (* word or doubleword operation *)
  IF OperandSize = 16
  THEN DX:AX ← AX * r/m16
  ELSE (* OperandSize = 32 *)
    EDX:EAX ← EAX * r/m32
  FI;
FI;
```

Description

The MUL instruction performs unsigned multiplication. Its actions depend on the size of its operand, as follows:

- A byte operand is multiplied by the AL value; the result is left in the AX register. The CF and OF flags are cleared if the AH value is 0; otherwise, they are set.
- A word operand is multiplied by the AX value; the result is left in the DX:AX register pair. The DX register contains the high-order 16 bits of the product. The CF and OF flags are cleared if the DX value is 0; otherwise, they are set.
- A doubleword operand is multiplied by the EAX value and the result is left in the EDX:EAX register. The EDX register contains the high-order 32 bits of the product. The CF and OF flags are cleared if the EDX value is 0; otherwise, they are set.

Flags Affected

The OF and CF flags are cleared if the upper half of the result is 0; otherwise they are set; the SF, ZF, AF, PF, and CF flags are undefined

Protected Mode Exceptions

#GP(0) for an illegal memory operand effective address in the CS, DS, ES, FS, or GS segments; #SS(0) for an illegal address in the SS segment; #PF(fault-code) for a page fault

Real Address Mode Exceptions

Interrupt 13 if any part of the operand would lie outside of the effective address space from 0 to 0FFFFH

Virtual 8086 Mode Exceptions

Same exceptions as in Real Address Mode; #PF(fault-code) for a page fault

NEG — Two's Complement Negation

Opcode	Instruction	Clocks	Description
F6 /3	NEG *r/m8*	2/6	Two's complement negate *r/m* byte
F7 3	NEG *r/m16*	2/6	Two's complement negate *r/m* word
F7 /3	NEG *r/m32*	2/6	Two's complement negate *r/m* dword

Operation

IF *r/m* = 0 THEN CF ← 0 ELSE CF ← 1; FI;
r/m ← − *r/m*

Description

The NEG instruction replaces the value of a register or memory operand with its two's complement. The operand is subtracted from zero, and the result is placed in the operand.

The CF flag is set, unless the operand is zero, in which case the CF flag is cleared.

Flags Affected

The CF flag is set unless the operand is zero, in which case the CF flag is cleared; the OF, SF, ZF, and PF flags are set according to the result

Protected Mode Exceptions

#GP(0) if the result is in a nonwritable segment; #GP(0) for an illegal memory operand effective address in the CS, DS, ES, FS, or GS segments; #SS(0) for an illegal address in the SS segment; #PF(fault-code) for a page fault

Real Address Mode Exceptions

Interrupt 13 if any part of the operand would lie outside of the effective address space from 0 to 0FFFFH

Virtual 8086 Mode Exceptions

Same exceptions as in real-address mode; #PF(fault-code) for a page fault

NOP — No Operation

Opcode	Instruction	Clocks	Description
90	NOP	3	No operation

Description

The NOP instruction performs no operation. The NOP instruction is a one-byte instruction that takes up space but affects none of the machine context except the (E)IP register.

The NOP instruction is an alias mnemonic for the XCHG (E)AX, (E)AX instruction.

Flags Affected

None

Protected Mode Exceptions

None

Real Address Mode Exceptions

None

Virtual 8086 Mode Exceptions

None

NOT — One's Complement Negation

Opcode	Instruction	Clocks	Description
F6 /2	NOT *r/m8*	2/6	Reverse each bit of *r/m* byte
F7 /2	NOT *r/m16*	2/6	Reverse each bit of *r/m* word
F7 /2	NOT *r/m32*	2/6	Reverse each bit of *r/m* dword

Operation

r/m ← NOT *r/m*;

Description

The NOT instruction inverts the operand; every 1 becomes a 0, and vice versa.

Flags Affected

None

Protected Mode Exceptions

#GP(0) if the result is in a nonwritable segment; #GP(0) for an illegal memory operand effective address in the CS, DS, ES, FS, or GS segments; #SS(0) for an illegal address in the SS segment; #PF(fault-code) for a page fault

Real Address Mode Exceptions

Interrupt 13 if any part of the operand would lie outside of the effective address space from 0 to 0FFFFH

Virtual 8086 Mode Exceptions

Same exceptions as in real-address mode; #PF(fault-code) for a page fault

OR – Logical Inclusive OR

Opcode	Instruction	Clocks	Description
0C *ib*	OR AL,*imm8*	2	OR immediate byte to AL
0D *iw*	OR AX,*imm16*	2	OR immediate word to AX
0D *id*	OR EAX,*imm32*	2	OR immediate dword to EAX
80 /1 *ib*	OR *r/m8,imm8*	2/7	OR immediate byte to *r/m* byte
81 /1 *iw*	OR *r/m16,imm16*	2/7	OR immediate word to *r/m* word
81 /1 *id*	OR *r/m32,imm32*	2/7	OR immediate dword to *r/m* dword
83 /1 *ib*	OR *r/m16,imm8*	2/7	OR sign-extended immediate byte with *r/m* word
83 /1 *ib*	OR *r/m32,imm8*	2/7	OR sign-extended immediate byte with *r/m* dword
08 /*r*	OR *r/m8,r8*	2/6	OR byte register to *r/m* byte
09 /*r*	OR *r/m16,r16*	2/6	OR word register to *r/m* word
09 /*r*	OR *r/m32,r32*	2/6	OR dword register to *r/m* dword
0A /*r*	OR *r8,r/m8*	2/7	OR byte register to *r/m* byte
0B /*r*	OR *r16,r/m16*	2/7	OR word register to *r/m* word
0B /*r*	OR *r32,r/m32*	2/7	OR dword register to *r/m* dword

Operation

DEST ← DEST OR SRC;
CF ← 0;
OF ← 0

Description

The OR instruction computes the inclusive OR of its two operands and places the result in the first operand. Each bit of the result is 0 if both corresponding bits of the operands are 0; otherwise, each bit is 1.

Flags Affected

The OF and CF flags are cleared; the SF, ZF, and PF flags are set according to the result; the AF flag is undefined

Protected Mode Exceptions

#GP(0) if the result is in a nonwritable segment; #GP(0) for an illegal memory operand effective address in the CS, DS, ES, FS, or GS segments; #SS(0) for an illegal address in the SS segment; #PF(fault-code) for a page fault

Real Address Mode Exceptions

Interrupt 13 if any part of the operand would lie outside of the effective address space from 0 to 0FFFFH

Virtual 8086 Mode Exceptions

Same exceptions as in real-address mode; #PF(fault-code) for a page fault

OUT—Output to Port

Opcode	Instruction	Clocks	Description
E6 *ib*	OUT *imm8*,AL	10,pm=4*/24**	Output byte AL to immediate port number
E7 *ib*	OUT *imm8*,AX	10,pm=4*/24**	Output word AL to immediate port number
E7 *ib*	OUT *imm8*,EAX	10,pm=4*/24**	Output dword AL to immediate port number
EE	OUT DX,AL	11,pm=5*/25**	Output byte AL to port number in DX
EF	OUT DX,AX	11,pm=5*/25**	Output word AL to port number in DX
EF	OUT DX,EAX	11,pm=5*/25**	Output dword AL to port number in DX

NOTES: *If CPL ≤ IOPL
**If CPL > IOPL or if in virtual 8086 mode

Operation

```
IF (PE = 1) AND ((VM = 1) OR (CPL > IOPL))
THEN (* Virtual 8086 mode, or protected mode with CPL > IOPL *)
  IF NOT I-O-Permission (DEST, width(DEST))
  THEN #GP(0);
  FI;
FI;
[DEST] ← SRC; (* I/O address space used *)
```

Description

The OUT instruction transfers a data byte or data word from the register (AL, AX, or EAX) given as the second operand to the output port numbered by the first operand. Output to any port from 0 to 65535 is performed by placing the port number in the DX register and then using an OUT instruction with the DX register as the first operand. If the instruction contains an eight-bit port ID, that value is zero-extended to 16 bits.

Flags Affected

None

Protected Mode Exceptions

#GP(0) if the current privilege level is higher (has less privilege) than the I/O privilege level and any of the corresponding I/O permission bits in the TSS equals 1

Real Address Mode Exceptions

None

Virtual 8086 Mode Exceptions

#GP(0) fault if any of the corresponding I/O permission bits in the TSS equals 1

OUTS/OUTSB/OUTSW/OUTSD—Output String to Port

Opcode	Instruction	Clocks	Description
6E	OUTS DX,*r/m8*	14,pm=8*/28**	Output byte [(E)SI] to port in DX
6F	OUTS DX,*r/m16*	14,pm=8*/28**	Output word [(E)SI] to port in DX
6F	OUTS DX,*r/m32*	14,pm=8*/28**	Output dword [(E)SI] to port in DX
6E	OUTSB	14,pm=8*/28**	Output byte DS:[(E)SI] to port in DX
6F	OUTSW	14,pm=8*/28**	Output word DS:[(E)SI] to port in DX
6F	OUTSD	14,pm=8*/28**	Output dword DS:[(E)SI] to port in DX

NOTES: *If CPL ≤ IOPL
**If CPL > IOPL or if in virtual 8086 mode

Operation

```
IF AddressSize = 16
THEN use SI for source-index;
ELSE (* AddressSize = 32 *)
  use ESI for source-index;
FI;

IF (PE = 1) AND ((VM = 1) OR (CPL > IOPL))
THEN (* Virtual 8086 mode, or protected mode with CPL > IOPL *)
  IF NOT I-O-Permission (DEST, width(DEST))
  THEN #GP(0);
  FI;
FI;
IF byte type of instruction
THEN
  [DX] ← [source-index]; (* Write byte at DX I/O address *)
  IF DF = 0 THEN IncDec ← 1 ELSE IncDec ← –1; FI;
FI;
IF OperandSize = 16
THEN
  [DX] ← [source-index]; (* Write word at DX I/O address *)
  IF DF = 0 THEN IncDec ← 2 ELSE IncDec ← –2; FI;
FI;
IF OperandSize = 32
THEN
  [DX] ← [source-index]; (* Write dword at DX I/O address *)
  IF DF = 0 THEN IncDec ← 4 ELSE IncDec ← –4; FI;
  FI;
FI;
source-index ← source-index + IncDec;
```

Description

The OUTS instruction transfers data from the memory byte, word, or doubleword at the source-index register to the output port addressed by the DX register. If the address-size attribute for this instruction is 16 bits, the SI register is used for the source-index register; otherwise, the address-size attribute is 32 bits, and the ESI register is used for the source-index register.

The OUTS instruction does not allow specification of the port number as an immediate value. The port must be addressed through the DX register value. Load the correct value into the DX register before executing the OUTS instruction.

The address of the source data is determined by the contents of source-index register. Load the correct index value into the SI or ESI register before executing the OUTS instruction.

After the transfer, source-index register is advanced automatically. If the DF flag is 0 (the CLD instruction was executed), the source-index register is incremented; if the DF flag is 1 (the STD instruction was executed), it is decremented. The amount of the increment or decrement is 1 if a byte is output, 2 if a word is output, or 4 if a doubleword is output.

The OUTSB, OUTSW, and OUTSD instructions are synonyms for the byte, word, and doubleword OUTS instructions. The OUTS instruction can be preceded by the REP prefix for block output of CX bytes or words. Refer to the REP instruction for details on this operation.

Flags Affected

None

Protected Mode Exceptions

#GP(0) if the current privilege level is greater than the I/O privilege level and any of the corresponding I/O permission bits in TSS equals 1; #GP(0) for an illegal memory operand effective address in the CS, DS, or ES segments; #SS(0) for an illegal address in the SS segment; #PF(fault-code) for a page fault

Real Address Mode Exceptions

Interrupt 13 if any part of the operand would lie outside of the effective address space from 0 to 0FFFFH

Virtual 8086 Mode Exceptions

#GP(0) fault if any of the corresponding I/O permission bits in TSS equals 1; #PF(fault-code) for a page fault

POP—Pop a Word from the Stack

Opcode	Instruction	Clocks	Description
8F /0	POP *m16*	5	Pop top of stack into memory word
8F /0	POP *m32*	5	Pop top of stack into memory dword
58+ *rw*	POP *r16*	4	Pop top of stack into word register
58+ *rd*	POP *r32*	4	Pop top of stack into dword register
1F	POP DS	7,*pm*=21	Pop top of stack into DS
07	POP ES	7,*pm*=21	Pop top of stack into ES
17	POP SS	7,*pm*=21	Pop top of stack into SS
0F A1	POP FS	7,*pm*=21	Pop top of stack into FS
0F A9	POP GS	7,*pm*=21	Pop top of stack into GS

Operation

```
IF StackAddrSize = 16
THEN
  IF OperandSize = 16
  THEN
    DEST ← (SS:SP); (* copy a word *)
    SP ← SP + 2;
  ELSE (* OperandSize = 32 *)
    DEST ← (SS:SP); (* copy a dword *)
    SP ← SP + 4;
  FI;

ELSE (* StackAddrSize = 32 * )
  IF OperandSize = 16
  THEN
    DEST ← (SS:ESP); (* copy a word *)
    ESP ← ESP + 2;
  ELSE (* OperandSize = 32 *)
    DEST ← (SS:ESP); (* copy a dword *)
    ESP ← ESP + 4;
  FI;
FI;
```

Description

The POP instruction replaces the previous contents of the memory, the register, or the segment register operand with the word on the top of the 386 DX microprocessor stack, addressed by SS:SP (address-size attribute of 16 bits) or SS:ESP (address-size attribute of 32 bits). The stack pointer SP is incremented by 2 for an operand-size of 16 bits or by 4 for an operand-size of 32 bits. It then points to the new top of stack.

The POP CS instruction is not a 386 DX microprocessor instruction. Popping from the stack into the CS register is accomplished with a RET instruction.

If the destination operand is a segment register (DS, ES, FS, GS, or SS), the value popped must be a selector. In protected mode, loading the selector initiates automatic loading of the descriptor information associated with that selector into the hidden part of the segment register; loading also initiates validation of both the selector and the descriptor information.

A null value (0000-0003) may be popped into the DS, ES, FS, or GS register without causing a protection exception. An attempt to reference a segment whose corresponding segment register is loaded with a null value causes a #GP(0) exception. No memory reference occurs. The saved value of the segment register is null.

A POP SS instruction inhibits all interrupts, including NMI, until after execution of the next instruction. This allows sequential execution of POP SS and POP eSP instructions without danger of having an invalid stack during an interrupt. However, use of the LSS instruction is the preferred method of loading the SS and eSP registers.

Loading a segment register while in protected mode results in special checks and actions, as described in the following listing:

```
IF SS is loaded:
   IF selector is null THEN #GP(0);
   Selector index must be within its descriptor table limits ELSE
      #GP(selector);
   Selector's RPL must equal CPL ELSE #GP(selector);
   AR byte must indicate a writable data segment ELSE #GP(selector);
   DPL in the AR byte must equal CPL ELSE #GP(selector);
   Segment must be marked present ELSE #SS(selector);
   Load SS register with selector;
   Load SS register with descriptor;

IF DS, ES, FS or GS is loaded with non-null selector:
   AR byte must indicate data or readable code segment ELSE
      #GP(selector);
   IF data or nonconforming code
   THEN both the RPL and the CPL must be less than or equal to DPL in
      AR byte
   ELSE #GP(selector);
   FI;
   Segment must be marked present ELSE #NP(selector);
   Load segment register with selector;
   Load segment register with descriptor;

IF DS, ES, FS, or GS is loaded with a null selector:
   Load segment register with selector
   Clear valid bit in invisible portion of register
```

Flags Affected

None

Protected Mode Exceptions

#GP, #SS, and #NP if a segment register is being loaded; #SS(0) if the current top of stack is not within the stack segment; #GP(0) if the result is in a nonwritable segment; #GP(0) for an illegal memory operand effective address in the CS, DS, ES, FS, or GS segments; #SS(0) for an illegal address in the SS segment; #PF(fault-code) for a page fault

Real Address Mode Exceptions

Interrupt 13 if any part of the operand would lie outside of the effective address space from 0 to 0FFFFH

Virtual 8086 Mode Exceptions

Same exceptions as in real-address mode; #PF(fault-code) for a page fault

POPA/POPAD—Pop all General Registers

Opcode	Instruction	Clocks	Description
61	POPA	24	Pop DI, SI, BP, SP, BX, DX, CX, and AX
61	POPAD	24	Pop EDI, ESI, EBP, ESP, EDX, ECX, and EAX

Operation

```
IF OperandSize = 16 (* instruction = POPA *)
THEN
   DI ←Pop();
   SI ← Pop();
   BP ← Pop();
   throwaway ← Pop (); (* Skip SP *)
   BX ← Pop();
   DX ← Pop();
   CX ← Pop();
   AX ← Pop();
ELSE (* OperandSize = 32, instruction = POPAD *)
   EDI ← Pop();
   ESI ← Pop();
   EBP ← Pop();
   throwaway ← Pop (); (* Skip ESP *)
   EBX ← Pop();
   EDX ← Pop();
   ECX ← Pop();
   EAX ← Pop();
FI;
```

Description

The POPA instruction pops the eight 16-bit general registers. However, the SP value is discarded instead of loaded into the SP register. The POPA instruction reverses a previous PUSHA instruction, restoring the general registers to their values before the PUSHA instruction was executed. The first register popped is the DI register.

The POPAD instruction pops the eight 32-bit general registers. The ESP value is discarded instead of loaded into the ESP register. The POPAD instruction reverses the previous PUSHAD instruction, restoring the general registers to their values before the PUSHAD instruction was executed. The first register popped is the EDI register.

Flags Affected

None

Protected Mode Exceptions

#SS(0) if the starting or ending stack address is not within the stack segment; #PF(fault-code) for a page fault

Real Address Mode Exceptions

Interrupt 13 if any part of the operand would lie outside of the effective address space from 0 to 0FFFFH

Virtual 8086 Mode Exceptions

Same exceptions as in real-address mode; #PF(fault-code) for a page fault

POPF/POPFD — Pop Stack into FLAGS or EFLAGS Register

Opcode	Instruction	Clocks	Description
9D	POPF	5	Pop top of stack FLAGS
9D	POPFD	5	Pop top of stack into EFLAGS

Operation

Flags ← Pop();

Description

The POPF and POPFD instructions pop the word or doubleword on the top of the stack and store the value in the flags register. If the operand-size attribute of the instruction is 16 bits, then a word is popped and the value is stored in the FLAGS register. If the operand-size attribute is 32 bits, then a doubleword is popped and the value is stored in the EFLAGS register.

Refer to Chapter 2 and Chapter 4 for information about the FLAGS and EFLAGS registers. Note that bits 16 and 17 of the EFLAGS register, called the VM and RF flags, respectively, are not affected by the POPF or POPFD instruction.

The I/O privilege level is altered only when executing at privilege level 0. The interrupt flag is altered only when executing at a level at least as privileged as the I/O privilege level. (Real-address mode is equivalent to privilege level 0.) If a POPF instruction is executed with insufficient privilege, an exception does not occur, but the privileged bits do not change.

Flags Affected

All flags except the VM and RF flags

Protected Mode Exceptions

#SS(0) if the top of stack is not within the stack segment

Real Address Mode Exceptions

Interrupt 13 if any part of the operand would lie outside of the effective address space from 0 to 0FFFFH

Virtual 8086 Mode Exceptions

#GP(0) fault if the I/O privilege level is less than 3, to permit emulation

PUSH — Push Operand onto the Stack

Opcode	Instruction	Clocks	Description
FF /6	PUSH *m16*	5	Push memory word
FF /6	PUSH *m32*	5	Push memory dword
50+ /r	PUSH *r16*	2	Push register word
50+ /r	PUSH *r32*	2	Push register dword
6A	PUSH *imm8*	2	Push immediate byte
68	PUSH *imm16*	2	Push immediate word
68	PUSH *imm32*	2	Push immediate dword
0E	PUSH CS	2	Push CS
16	PUSH SS	2	Push SS
1E	PUSH DS	2	Push DS
06	PUSH ES	2	Push ES
0F A0	PUSH FS	2	Push FS
0F A8	PUSH GS	2	Push GS

Operation

```
IF StackAddrSize = 16
THEN
  IF OperandSize = 16 THEN
    SP ← SP − 2;
    (SS:SP) ← (SOURCE); (* word assignment *)
  ELSE
    SP ← SP − 4;
    (SS:SP) ← (SOURCE); (* dword assignment *)
  FI;
ELSE (* StackAddrSize = 32 *)
  IF OperandSize = 16
  THEN
    ESP ← ESP − 2;
    (SS:ESP) ← (SOURCE); (* word assignment *)
  ELSE
    ESP ← ESP − 4;
    (SS:ESP) ← (SOURCE); (* dword assignment *)
  FI;
FI;
```

Description

The PUSH instruction decrements the stack pointer by 2 if the operand-size attribute of the instruction is 16 bits; otherwise, it decrements the stack pointer by 4. The PUSH instruction then places the operand on the new top of stack, which is pointed to by the stack pointer.

The 386 DX microprocessor PUSH ESP instruction pushes the value of the ESP register as it existed before the instruction. This differs from the 8086, where the PUSH SP instruction pushes the new value (decremented by 2).

Flags Affected

None

Protected Mode Exceptions

#SS(0) if the new value of the SP or ESP register is outside the stack segment limit; #GP(0) for an illegal memory operand effective address in the CS, DS, ES, FS, or GS segments; #SS(0) for an illegal address in the SS segment; #PF(fault-code) for a page fault

Real Address Mode Exceptions

None; if the SP or ESP register is 1, the 386 DX microprocessor shuts down due to a lack of stack space

Virtual 8086 Mode Exceptions

Same exceptions as in real-address mode; #PF(fault-code) for a page fault

PUSHA/PUSHAD—Push all General Registers

Opcode	Instruction	Clocks	Description
60	PUSHA	18	Push AX, CX, DX, BX, original SP, BP, SI, and DI
00	PUSHAD	18	Push EAX, ECX, EDX, EBX, original ESP, EBP, ESI, and EDI

Operation

```
IF OperandSize = 16 (* PUSHA instruction *)
THEN
   Temp ← (SP);
   Push(AX);
   Push(CX);
   Push(DX);
   Push(BX);
   Push(Temp);
   Push(BP);
   Push(SI);
   Push(DI);
ELSE (* OperandSize = 32, PUSHAD instruction *)
   Temp ← (ESP);
   Push(EAX);
   Push(ECX);
   Push(EDX);
   Push(EBX);
   Push(Temp);
   Push(EBP);
   Push(ESI);
   Push(EDI);
FI;
```

Description

The PUSHA and PUSHAD instructions save the 16-bit or 32-bit general registers, respectively, on the 386 DX stack. The PUSHA instruction decrements the stack pointer (SP) by 16 to hold the eight word values. The PUSHAD instruction decrements the stack pointer (ESP) by 32 to hold the eight doubleword values. Because the registers are pushed onto the stack in the order in which they were given, they appear in the 16 or 32 new stack bytes in reverse order. The last register pushed is the DI or EDI register.

Flags Affected

None

Protected Mode Exceptions

#SS(0) if the starting or ending stack address is outside the stack segment limit; #PF(fault-code) for a page fault

Real Address Mode Exceptions

Before executing the PUSHA or PUSHAD instruction, the 386 DX microprocessor shuts down if the SP or ESP register equals 1, 3, or 5; if the SP or ESP register equals 7, 9, 11, 13, or 15, exception 13 occurs

Virtual 8086 Mode Exceptions

Same exceptions as in real-address mode; #PF(fault-code) for a page fault

PUSHF/PUSHFD—Push Flags Register onto the Stack

Opcode	Instruction	Clocks	Description
9C	PUSHF	4	Push FLAGS
9C	PUSHFD	4	Push EFLAGS

Operation

```
IF OperandSize = 32
THEN push(EFLAGS);
ELSE push(FLAGS);
FI;
```

Description

The PUSHF instruction decrements the stack pointer by 2 and copies the FLAGS register to the new top of stack; the PUSHFD instruction decrements the stack pointer by 4, and the 386 DX microprocessor EFLAGS register is copied to the new top of stack which is pointed to by SS:ESP. Refer to Chapter 2 and to Chapter 4 for information on the EFLAGS register.

Flags Affected

None

Protected Mode Exceptions

#SS(0) if the new value of the ESP register is outside the stack segment boundaries

Real Address Mode Exceptions

None; the 386 DX microprocessor shuts down due to a lack of stack space

Virtual 8086 Mode Exceptions

#GP(0) fault if the I/O privilege level is less than 3, to permit emulation

RCL/RCR/ROL/ROR-—Rotate

Opcode	Instruction	Clocks	Description
D0 /2	RCL *r/m8*,1	9/10	Rotate 9 bits (CF,*r/m* byte) left once
D2 /2	RCL *r/m8*,CL	9/10	Rotate 9 bits (CF,*r/m* byte) left CL times
C0 /2 *ib*	RCL *r/m8,imm8*	9/10	Rotate 9 bits (CF,*r/m* byte) left *imm8* times
D1 /2	RCL *r/m16*,1	9/10	Rotate 17 bits (CF,*r/m* word) left once
D3 /2	RCL *r/m16*,CL	9/10	Rotate 17 bits (CF,*r/m* word) left CL times
C1 /2 *ib*	RCL *r/m16,imm8*	9/10	Rotate 17 bits (CF,*r/m* word) left *imm8* times
D1 /2	RCL *r/m32*,1	9/10	Rotate 33 bits (CF,*r/m* dword) left once
D3 /2	RCL *r/m32*,CL	9/10	Rotate 33 bits (CF,*r/m* dword) left CL times
C1 /2 *ib*	RCL *r/m32,imm8*	9/10	Rotate 33 bits (CF,*r/m* dword) left *imm8* times
D0 /3	RCR *r/m8*,1	9/10	Rotate 9 bits (CF,*r/m* byte) right once
D2 /3	RCR *r/m8*,CL	9/10	Rotate 9 bits (CF,*r/m* byte) right CL times
C0 /3 *ib*	RCR *r/m8,imm8*	9/10	Rotate 9 bits (CF,*r/m* byte) right *imm8* times
D1 /3	RCR *r/m16*,1	9/10	Rotate 17 bits (CF,*r/m* word) right once
D3 /3	RCR *r/m16*,CL	9/10	Rotate 17 bits (CF,*r/m* word) right CL times
C1 /3 *ib*	RCR *r/m16,imm8*	9/10	Rotate 17 bits (CF,*r/m* word) right *imm8* times
D1 /3	RCR *r/m32*,1	9/10	Rotate 33 bits (CF,*r/m* dword) right once
D3 /3	RCR *r/m32*,CL	9/10	Rotate 33 bits (CF,*r/m* dword) right CL times
C1 /3 *ib*	RCR *r/m32,imm8*	9/10	Rotate 33 bits (CF,*r/m* dword) right *imm8* times
D0 /0	ROL *r/m8*,1	3/7	Rotate 8 bits *r/m* byte left once
D2 /0	ROL *r/m8*,CL	3/7	Rotate 8 bits *r/m* byte left CL times
C0 /0 *ib*	ROL *r/m8,imm8*	3/7	Rotate 8 bits *r/m* byte left *imm8* times
D1 /0	ROL *r/m16*,1	3/7	Rotate 16 bits *r/m* word left once
D3 /0	ROL *r/m16*,CL	3/7	Rotate 16 bits *r/m* word left CL times
C1 /0 *ib*	ROL *r/m16,imm8*	3/7	Rotate 16 bits *r/m* word left *imm8* times
D1 /0	ROL *r/m32*,1	3/7	Rotate 32 bits *r/m* dword left once
D3 /0	ROL *r/m32*,CL	3/7	Rotate 32 bits *r/m* dword left CL times
C1 /0 *ib*	ROL *r/m32,imm8*	3/7	Rotate 32 bits *r/m* dword left *imm8* times
D0 /1	ROR *r/m8*,1	3/7	Rotate 8 bits *r/m* byte right once
D2 /1	ROR *r/m8*,CL	3/7	Rotate 8 bits *r/m* byte right CL times
C0 /1 *ib*	ROR *r/m8,imm8*	3/7	Rotate 8 bits *r/m* word right *imm8* times
D1 /1	ROR *r/m16*,1	3/7	Rotate 16 bits *r/m* word right once
D3 /1	ROR *r/m16*,CL	3/7	Rotate 16 bits *r/m* word right CL times
C1 /1 *ib*	ROR *r/m16,imm8*	3/7	Rotate 16 bits *r/m* word right *imm8* times
D1 /1	ROR *r/m32*,1	3/7	Rotate 32 bits *r/m* dword right once
D3 /1	ROR *r/m32*,CL	3/7	Rotate 32 bits *r/m* dword right CL times
C1 /1 *ib*	ROR *r/m32,imm8*	3/7	Rotate 32 bits *r/m* dword right *imm8* times

Operation

```
(* ROL - Rotate Left *)
temp ← COUNT;
WHILE (temp < > 0)
DO
  tmpcf ← high-order bit of (r/m);
  r/m ← r/m * 2 + (tmpcf);
  temp ← temp − 1;
OD;
IF COUNT = 1
THEN
  IF high-order bit of r/m < > CF
  THEN OF ← 1;
  ELSE OF ← 0;
  FI;
ELSE OF ← undefined;
FI;
```

```
(* ROR - Rotate Right *)
temp ← COUNT;
WHILE (temp < > 0 )
DO
   tmpct ← low-order bit of (r/m);
   r/m ← r/m / 2 + (tmpcf * 2^width(r/m));
   temp ← temp − 1;
DO;
IF COUNT = 1
THEN
   IF (high-order bit of r/m) < > (bit next to high-order bit of r/m)
   THEN OF ← 1;
   ELSE OF ← 0;
   FI;
ELSE OF ← undefined;
FI;
```

Description

Each rotate instruction shifts the bits of the register or memory operand given. The left rotate instructions shift all the bits upward, except for the top bit, which is returned to the bottom. The right rotate instructions do the reverse: the bits shift downward until the bottom bit arrives at the top.

For the RCL and RCR instructions, the CF flag is part of the rotated quantity. The RCL instruction shifts the CF flag into the bottom bit and shifts the top bit into the CF flag; the RCR instruction shifts the CF flag into the top bit and shifts the bottom bit into the CF flag. For the ROL and ROR instructions, the original value of the CF flag is not a part of the result, but the CF flag receives a copy of the bit that was shifted from one end to the other.

The rotate is repeated the number of times indicated by the second operand, which is either an immediate number or the contents of the CL register. To reduce the maximum instruction execution time, the 386 DX microprocessor does not allow rotation counts greater than 31. If a rotation count greater than 31 is attempted, only the bottom five bits of the rotation are used. The 8086 does not mask rotation counts. The 386 DX microprocessor in Virtual 8086 Mode does mask rotation counts.

The OF flag is defined only for the single-rotate forms of the instructions (second operand is a 1). It is undefined in all other cases. For left shifts/rotates, the CF bit after the shift is XORed with the high-order result bit. For right shifts/rotates, the high-order two bits of the result are XORed to get the OF flag.

Flags Affected

The OF flag is affected only for single-bit rotates; the OF flag is undefined for multi-bit rotates; the CF flag contains the value of the bit shifted into it; the SF, ZF, AF, and PF flags are not affected

Protected Mode Exceptions

#GP(0) if the result is in a nonwritable segment; #GP(0) for an illegal memory operand effective address in the CS, DS, ES, FS, or GS segments; #SS(0) for an illegal address in the SS segment; #PF(fault-code) for a page fault

Real Address Mode Exceptions

Interrupt 13 if any part of the operand would lie outside of the effective address space from 0 to 0FFFFH

Virtual 8086 Mode Exceptions

Same exceptions as in Real Address Mode; #PF(fault-code) for a page fault

REP/REPE/REPZ/REPNE/REPNZ — Repeat Following String Operation

Opcode	Instruction	Clocks	Description
F3 6C	REP INS *r/m8*, DX	14+6*(E)CX, pm=8+6*(E)CX*1/ 28+6*(E)CX*2	Input (E)CX bytes from port DX into ES:[(E)DI]
F3 6D	REP INS *r/m16*,DX	14+6*(E)CX, pm=8+6*(E)CX*1/ 28+6*(E)CX*2	Input (E)CX words from port DX into ES:[(E)DI]
F3 6D	REP INS *r/m32*,DX	14+6*(E)CX, pm=8+6*(E)CX*1/ 28+6*(E)CX*2	Input (E)CX dwords from pot DX into ES:[(E)DI]
F3 A4	REP MOVS *m8,m8*	8+4*(E)CX	Move (E)CX bytes from [(E)SI] to ES:[(E)DI]
F3 A5	REP MOVS *m16,m16*	8+4*(E)CX	Move (E)CX words from [(E)SI] to ES:[(E)DI]
F3 A5	REP MOVS *m32,m32*	8+4*(E)CX	Move (E)CX dwords from [(E)SI] to ES:[(E)DI]
F3 6E	REP OUTS DX,*r/m8*	12+5*(E)CX, pm=6+5*(E)CX*1/ 26+5*(E)CX*2	Output (E)CX bytes from [(E)SI] to port DX
F3 6F	REP OUTS DX,*r/m16*	12+5*(E)CX, pm=6+5*(E)CX*1/ 26+5*(E)CX*2	Output (E)CX words from [(E)SI] to port DX
F3 6F	REP OUTS DX,*r/m32*	12+5*(E)CX, pm=6+5*(E)CX*1/ 26+5*(E)CX*2	Output (E)CX dwords from [(E)SI] to port DX
F2 AC	REP LODS *m8*	5+6*(E)CX	Load (E)CX bytes from [(E)SI] to AL
F2 AD	REP LODS *m16*	5+6*(E)CX	Load (E)CX words from [(E)SI] to AX
F2 AD	REP LODS *m32*	5+6*(E)CX	Load (E)CX dwords from [(E)SI] to EAX
F3 AA	REP STOS *m8*	5+5*(E)CX	Fill (E)CX bytes at ES:[(E)DI] with AL
F3 AB	REP STOS *m16*	5+5*(E)CX	Fill (E)CX words at ES:[(E)DI] with AX
F3 AB	REP STOS *m32*	5+5*(E)CX	Fill (E)CX dwords at ES:[(E)DI] with EAX
F3 A6	REPE CMPS *m8,m8*	5+9*N	Find nonmatching bytes in ES:[(E)DI] and [(E)SI]
F3 A7	REPE CMPS *m16,m16*	5+9*N	Find nonmatching words in ES:[(E)DI] and [(E)SI]
F3 A7	REPE CMPS *m32,m32*	5+9*N	Find nonmatching dwords in ES:[(E)DI] and [(E)SI]
F3 AE	REPE SCAS *m8*	5+8*N	Find non-AL byte starting at ES:[(E)DI]
F3 AF	REPE SCAS *m16*	5+8*N	Find non-AX word starting at ES:[(E)DI]
F3 AF	REPE SCAS *m32*	5+8*N	Find non-EAX dword starting at ES:[(E)DI]
F2 A6	REPNE CMPS *m8,m8*	5+9*N	Find matching bytes in ES:[(E)DI] and [(E)SI]
F2 A7	REPNE CMPS *m16,m16*	5+9*N	Find matching words in ES:[(E)DI] and [(E)SI]
F2 A7	REPNE CMPS *m32,m32*	5+9*N	Find matching dwords in ES:[(E)DI] and [(E)SI]
F2 AE	REPNE SCAS *m8*	5+8*N	Find AL, starting at ES:[(E)DI]
F2 AF	REPNE SCAS *m16*	5+8*N	Find AX, starting at ES:[(E)DI]
F2 AF	REPNE SCAS *m32*	5+8*N	Find EAX, starting at ES:[(E)DI]

NOTES: *1 If CPL ≤ IOPL
*2 If CPL > IOPL or if in virtual 8086 mode

Operation

```
IF AddressSize = 16
THEN use CX for CountReg;
ELSE (* AddressSize = 32 *) use ECX for CountReg;
FI;
WHILE CountReg <> 0
DO
  service pending interrupts (if any);
  perform primitive string instruction;
  CountReg ← CountReg − 1;
  IF primitive operation is CMPB, CMPW, SCAB, or SCAW
  THEN
    IF (instruction is REP/REPE/REPZ) AND (ZF=1)
```

```
      THEN exit WHILE loop
      ELSE
         IF (instruction is REPNZ or REPNE) AND (ZF=0)
         THEN exit WHILE loop;
         FI;
      FI;
   FI;
OD;
```

Description

The REP, REPE (repeat while equal), and REPNE (repeat while not equal) prefixes are applied to string operation. Each prefix causes the string instruction that follows to be repeated the number of times indicated in the count register or (for the REPE and REPNE prefixes) until the indicated condition in the ZF flag is no longer met.

Synonymous forms of the REPE and REPNE prefixes are the REPZ and REPNZ prefixes, respectively.

The REP prefixes apply only to one string instruction at a time. To repeat a block of instructions, use the LOOP instruction or another looping construct.

The precise action for each iteration is as follows:

1. If the address-size attribute is 16 bits, use the CX register for the count register; if the address-size attribute is 32 bits, use the ECX register for the count register.
2. Check the CX register. If it is zero, exit the iteration, and move to the next instruction.
3. Acknowledge any pending interrupts.
4. Perform the string operation once.
5. Decrement the CX or ECX register by one; no flags are modified.
6. Check the ZF flag if the string operation is a SCAS or CMPS instruction. If the repeat condition does not hold, exit the iteration and move to the next instruction. Exit the iteration if the prefix is REPE and the ZF flag is 0 (the last comparison was not equal), or if the prefix is REPNE and the ZF flag is one (the last comparison was equal).
7. Return to step 1 for the next iteration.

Repeated CMPS and SCAS instructions can be exited if the count is exhausted or if the ZF flag fails the repeat condition. These two cases can be distinguished by using either the JCXZ instruction, or by using the conditional jumps that test the ZF flag (the JZ, JNZ, and JNE instructions).

Flags Affected

The ZF flag is affected by the REP CMPS and REP SCAS as described above

Protected Mode Exceptions

Exceptions can be generated when the string operation is executed; refer to the descrip tions of the string instructions themselves

Real Address Mode Exceptions

Exceptions can be generated when the string operation is executed; refer to the descriptions of the string instructions themselves

Virtual 8086 Mode Exceptions

Exceptions can be generated when the string operation is executed; refer to the descriptions of the string instructions themselves

Notes

Not all I/O ports can handle the rate at which the REP INS and REP OUTS instructions execute.

The repeat prefix is ignored when it is used with a non-string instruction.

RET—Return from Procedure

Opcode	Instruction	Clocks	Description
C3	RET	10+*m*	Return (near) to caller
CB	RET	18+*m*,*pm*=32+*m*	Return (far) to caller, same privilege
CB	RET	*pm*=69	Return (far), lesser privilege, switch stacks
C2 *iw*	RET *imm16*	10+*m*	Return (near), pop *imm16* bytes of parameters
CA *iw*	RET *imm16*	18+*m*,*pm*=32+*m*	Return (far), same privilege, pop *imm16* bytes
CA *iw*	RET *imm16*	pm=69	Return (far), lesser privilege, pop *imm16* bytes

Operation

```
IF instruction = near RET
THEN;
  IF OperandSize = 16
  THEN
    IP ← Pop();
    EIP ← EIP AND 0000FFFFH;
  ELSE (* OperandSize = 32 *)
    EIP ← Pop();
  FI;
  IF instruction has immediate operand THEN eSP ← eSP + imm16; FI;
FI;

IF (PE = 0 OR (PE = 1 AND VM = 1))
  (* real mode or virtual 8086 mode *)
  AND instruction = far RET
THEN;
  IF OperandSize = 16
  THEN
    IP ← Pop();
    EIP ← EIP AND 0000FFFFH;
    CS ← Pop(); (* 16-bit pop *)
  ELSE (* OperandSize = 32 *)
    EIP ← Pop();
    CS ← Pop(); (* 32-bit pop, high-order 16-bits discarded *)
  FI;
  IF instruction has immediate operand THEN eSP ← eSP + imm16; FI;
FI;

IF (PE = 1 AND VM = 0) (* Protected mode, not V86 mode *)
  AND instruction = far RET
THEN
  IF OperandSize=32
  THEN Third word on stack must be within stack limits else #SS(0);
  ELSE Second word on stack must be within stack limits else #SS(0);
  FI;
  Return selector RPL must be ≥ CPL ELSE #GP(return selector)
  IF return selector RPL = CPL
```

```
  THEN GOTO SAME-LEVEL;
  ELSE GOTO OUTER-PRIVILEGE-LEVEL;
  FI;
FI;

SAME-LEVEL:
  Return selector must be non-null ELSE #GP(0)
  Selector index must be within its descriptor table limits ELSE
    #GP(selector)
  Descriptor AR byte must indicate code segment ELSE #GP(selector)
  IF non-conforming
  THEN code segment DPL must equal CPL;
  ELSE #GP(selector);
  FI;
  IF conforming
  THEN code segment DPL must be ≤ CPL;
  ELSE #GP(selector);
  FI;
  Code segment must be present ELSE #NP(selector);
  Top word on stack must be within stack limits ELSE #SS(0);
  IP must be in code segment limit ELSE #GP(0);
  IF OperandSize=32
  THEN
    Load CS:EIP from stack
    Load CS register with descriptor
    Increment eSP by 8 plus the immediate offset if it exists
  ELSE (* OperandSize=16 *)
    Load CS:IP from stack
    Load CS register with descriptor
    Increment eSP by 4 plus the immediate offset if it exists
  FI;

OUTER-PRIVILEGE-LEVEL:
  IF OperandSize=32
  THEN Top (16+immediate) bytes on stack must be within stack limits
    ELSE #SS(0);
  ELSE Top (8+immediate) bytes on stack must be within stack limits ELSE
    #SS(0);
  FI;
  Examine return CS selector and associated descriptor:
    Selector must be non-null ELSE #GP(0);
    Selector index must be within its descriptor table limits ELSE
      #GP(selector)
    Descriptor AR byte must indicate code segment ELSE #GP(selector);
    IF non-conforming
    THEN code segment DPL must equal return selector RPL
    ELSE #GP(selector);
    FI;
    IF conforming
```

```
    THEN code segment DPL must be ≤ return selector RPL;
    ELSE #GP(selector);
    FI;
    Segment must be present ELSE #NP(selector)
  Examine return SS selector and associated descriptor:
    Selector must be non-null ELSE #GP(0);
    Selector index must be within its descriptor table limits
       ELSE #GP(selector);
    Selector RPL must equal the RPL of the return CS selector ELSE
       #GP(selector);
    Descriptor AR byte must indicate a writable data segment ELSE
       #GP(selector);
    Descriptor DPL must equal the RPL of the return CS selector ELSE
       #GP(selector);
    Segment must be present ELSE #NP(selector);
  IP must be in code segment limit ELSE #GP(0);
  Set CPL to the RPL of the return CS selector;
  IF OperandMode=32
  THEN
    Load CS:EIP from stack;
    Set CS RPL to CPL;
    Increment eSP by 8 plus the immediate offset if it exists;
    Load SS:eSP from stack;
  ELSE (* OperandMode=16 *)
    Load CS:IP from stack;
    Set CS RPL to CPL;
    Increment eSP by 4 plus the immediate offset if it exists;
    Load SS:eSP from stack;
  FI;
  Load the CS register with the return CS descriptor;
  Load the SS register with the return SS descriptor;
  For each of ES, FS, GS, and DS
  DO
    IF the current register setting is not valid for the outer level,
       set the register to null (selector ← AR ← 0);
    To be valid, the register setting must satisfy the following properties:
       Selector index must be within descriptor table limits;
       Descriptor AR byte must indicate data or readable code segment;
       IF segment is data or non-conforming code, THEN
          DPL must be ≥ CPL, or DPL must be ≥ RPL;
       FI;
  OD;
```

Description

The RET instruction transfers control to a return address located on the stack. The address is usually placed on the stack by a CALL instruction, and the return is made to the instruction that follows the CALL instruction.

The optional numeric parameter to the RET instruction gives the number of stack bytes (OperandMode=16) or words (OperandMode=32) to be released after the return address is popped. These items are typically used as input parameters to the procedure called.

For the intrasegment (near) return, the address on the stack is a segment offset, which is popped into the instruction pointer. The CS register is unchanged. For the intersegment (far) return, the address on the stack is a long pointer. The offset is popped first, followed by the selector.

In real mode, the CS and IP registers are loaded directly. In Protected Mode, an intersegment return causes the processor to check the descriptor addressed by the return selector. The AR byte of the descriptor must indicate a code segment of equal or lesser privilege (or greater or equal numeric value) than the current privilege level. Returns to a lesser privilege level cause the stack to be reloaded from the value saved beyond the parameter block.

The DS, ES, FS, and GS segment registers can be cleared by the RET instruction during an interlevel transfer. If these registers refer to segments that cannot be used by the new privilege level, they are cleared to prevent unauthorized access from the new privilege level.

Flags Affected

None

Protected Mode Exceptions

#GP, #NP, or #SS, as described under "Operation" above; #PF(fault-code) for a page fault

Real Address Mode Exceptions

Interrupt 13 if any part of the operand would be outside the effective address space from 0 to 0FFFFH

Virtual 8086 Mode Exceptions

Same exceptions as in Real Address Mode; #PF(fault-code) for a page fault

SAHF—Store AH into Flags

Opcode	Instruction	Clocks	Description
9E	SAHF	3	Store AH into flags SF ZF xx AF xx PF xx CF

Operation

SF:ZF:xx:AF:xx:PF:xx:CF ← AH;

Description

The SAHF instruction loads the SF, ZF, AF, PF, and CF flags with values from the AH register, from bits 7, 6, 4, 2, and 0, respectively.

Flags Affected

The SF, ZF, AF, PF, and CF flags are loaded with values form the AH register

Protected Mode Exceptions

None

Real Address Mode Exceptions

None

Virtual 8086 Mode Exceptions

None

SAL/SAR/SHL/SHR — Shift Instructions

Opcode	Instruction	Clocks	Description
D0 /4	SAL *r/m8*,1	3/7	Multiply *r/m* byte by 2, once
D2 /4	SAL *r/m8*,CL	3/7	Multiply *r/m* byte by 2, CL times
C0 /4 *ib*	SAL *r/m8,imm8*	3/7	Multiply *r/m* byte by 2, *imm8* times
D1 /4	SAL *r/m16*,1	3/7	Multiply *r/m* word by 2, once
D3 /4	SAL *r/m16*,CL	3/7	Multiply *r/m* word by 2, CL times
C1 /4 *ib*	SAL *r/m16,imm8*	3/7	Multiply *r/m* word by 2, *imm8* times
D1 /4	SAL *r/m32*,1	3/7	Multiply *r/m* dword by 2, once
D3 /4	SAL *r/m32*,CL	3/7	Multiply *r/m* dword by 2, CL times
C1 /4 *ib*	SAL *r/m32,imm8*	3/7	Multiply *r/m* dword by 2, *imm8* times
D0 /7	SAR *r/m8*,1	3/7	Signed divide[1] *r/m* byte by 2, once
D2 /7	SAR *r/m8*,CL	3/7	Signed divide[1] *r/m* byte by 2, CL times
C0 /7 *ib*	SAR *r/m8,imm8*	3/7	Signed divide[1] *r/m* byte by 2, *imm8* times
D1 /7	SAR *r/m16*,1	3/7	Signed divide[1] *r/m* word by 2, once
D3 /7	SAR *r/m16*,CL	3/7	Signed divide[1] *r/m* word by 2, CL times
C1 /7 *ib*	SAR *r/m16,imm8*	3/7	Signed divide[1] *r/m* word by 2, *imm8* times
D1 /7	SAR *r/m32*,1	3/7	Signed divide[1] *r/m* dword by 2, once
D3 /7	SAR *r/m32*,CL	3/7	Signed divide[1] *r/m* dword by 2, CL times
C1 /7 *ib*	SAR *r/m32,imm8*	3/7	Signed divide[1] *r/m* dword by 2, *imm8* times
D0 /4	SHL *r/m8*,1	3/7	Multiply *r/m* byte by 2, once
D2 /4	SHL *r/m8*,CL	3/7	Multiply *r/m* byte by 2, CL times
C0 /4 *ib*	SHL *r/m8,imm8*	3/7	Multiply *r/m* byte by 2, *imm8* times
D1 /4	SHL *r/m16*,1	3/7	Multiply *r/m* word by 2, once
D3 /4	SHL *r/m16*,CL	3/7	Multiply *r/m* word by 2, CL times
C1 /4 *ib*	SHL *r/m16,imm8*	3/7	Multiply *r/m* word by 2, *imm8* times
D1 /4	SHL *r/m32*,1	3/7	Multiply *r/m* dword by 2, once
D3 /4	SHL *r/m32*,CL	3/7	Multiply *r/m* dword by 2, CL times
C1 /4 *ib*	SHL *r/m32,imm8*	3/7	Multiply *r/m* dword by 2, *imm8* times
D0 /5	SHR *r/m8*,1	3/7	Unsigned divide *r/m* byte by 2, once
D2 /5	SHR *r/m8*,CL	3/7	Unsigned divide *r/m* byte by 2, CL times
C0 /5 *ib*	SHR *r/m8,imm8*	3/7	Unsigned divide *r/m* byte by 2, *imm8* times
D1 /5	SHR *r/m16*,1	3/7	Unsigned divide *r/m* word by 2, once
D3 /5	SHR *r/m16*,CL	3/7	Unsigned divide *r/m* word by 2, CL times
C1 /5 *ib*	SHR *r/m16,imm8*	3/7	Unsigned divide *r/m* word by 2, *imm8* times
D1 /5	SHR *r/m32*,1	3/7	Unsigned divide *r/m* dword by 2, once
D3 /5	SHR *r/m32*,CL	3/7	Unsigned divide *r/m* dword by 2, CL times
C1 /5 *ib*	SHR *r/m32,imm8*	3/7	Unsigned divide *r/m* dword by 2, *imm8* times

Not the same division as IDIV; rounding is toward negative infinity.

Operation

```
(* COUNT is the second parameter *)
(temp) ← COUNT;
WHILE (temp < > 0)
DO
   IF instruction is SAL or SHL
   THEN CF ← high-order bit of r/m;
   FI;
   IF instruction is SAR or SHR
   THEN CF ← low-order bit of r/m;
   FI;
   IF instruction = SAL or SHL
   THEN r/m ← r/m * 2;
   FI;
   IF instruction = SAR
   THEN r/m ← r/m /2 (*Signed divide, rounding toward negative infinity*);
```

```
   FI;
   IF instruction = SHR
   THEN r/m ← r/m / 2; (* Unsigned divide *);
   FI;
   temp ← temp − 1;
OD;
(* Determine overflow for the various instructions *)
IF COUNT = 1
THEN
   IF instruction is SAL or SHL
   THEN OF ← high-order bit of r/m <> (CF);
   FI;
   IF instruction is SAR
   THEN OF ← 0;
   FI;
   IF instruction is SHR
   THEN OF ← high-order bit of operand;
   FI;
ELSE OF ← undefined;
FI;
```

Description

The SAL instruction (or its synonym, SHL) shifts the bits of the operand upward. The high-order bit is shifted into the CF flag, and the low-order bit is cleared.

The SAR and SHR instructions shift the bits of the operand downward. The low-order bit is shifted into the CF flag. The effect is to divide the operand by two. The SAR instruction performs a signed divide with rounding toward negative infinity (not the same as the IDIV instruction); the high-order bit remains the same. The SHR instruction performs an unsigned divide; the high-order bit is cleared.

The shift is repeated the number of times indicated by the second operand, which is either an immediate number or the contents of the CL register. To reduce the maximum execution time, the 386 DX microprocessor does not allow shift counts greater than 31. If a shift count greater than 31 is attempted, only the bottom five bits of the shift count are used. (The 8086 uses all eight bits of the shift count.)

The OF flag is affected only if the single-shift forms of the instructions are used. For left shifts, the OF flag is cleared if the high bit of the answer is the same as the result of the CF flag (i.e., the top two bits of the original operand were the same); the OF flag is set if they are different. For the SAR instruction, the OF flag is cleared for all single shifts. For the SHR instruction, the OF flag is set to the high-order bit of the original operand.

Flags Affected

The OF flag is affected for single shifts; the OF flag is undefined for multiple shifts; the CF, ZF, PF, and SF flags are set according to the result

Protected Mode Exceptions

#GP(0) if the result is in a nonwritable segment; #GP(0) for an illegal memory operand effective address in the CS, DS, ES, FS, or GS segments; #SS(0) for an illegal address in the SS segment; #PF(fault-code) for a page fault

Real Address Mode Exceptions

Interrupt 13 if any part of the operand would lie outside of the effective address space from 0 to 0FFFFH

Virtual 8086 Mode Exceptions

Same exceptions as in Real Address Mode; #PF(fault-code) for a page fault

SBB—Integer Subtraction with Borrow

Opcode	Instruction	Clocks	Description
1C *ib*	SBB AL,*imm8*	2	Subtract with borrow immediate byte from AL
1D *iw*	SBB AX,*imm16*	2	Subtract with borrow immediate word from AX
1D *id*	SBB EAX,*imm32*	2	Subtract with borrow immediate dword from EAX
80 /3 *ib*	SBB *r/m8,imm8*	2/7	Subtract with borrow immediate byte from *r/m* byte
81 /3 *iw*	SBB *r/m16,imm16*	2/7	Subtract with borrow immediate word from *r/m* word
81 /3 *id*	SBB *r/m32,imm32*	2/7	Subtract with borrow immediate dword from *r/m* dword
83 /3 *ib*	SBB *r/m16,imm8*	2/7	Subtract with borrow sign-extended immediate byte from *r/m* word
83 /3 *ib*	SBB *r/m32,imm8*	2/7	Subtract with borrow sign-extended immediate byte from *r/m* dword
18 /*r*	SBB *r/m8,r8*	2/6	Subtract with borrow byte register from *r/m* byte
19 /*r*	SBB *r/m16,r16*	2/6	Subtract with borrow word register from *r/m* word
19 /*r*	SBB *r/m32,r32*	2/6	Subtract with borrow dword register from *r/m* dword
1A /*r*	SBB *r8,r/m8*	2/7	Subtract with borrow byte register from *r/m* byte
1B /*r*	SBB *r16,r/m16*	2/7	Subtract with borrow word register from *r/m* word
1B /*r*	SBB *r32,r/m32*	2/7	Subtract with borrow dword register from *r/m* dword

Operation

IF SRC is a byte and DEST is a word or dword
THEN DEST = DEST − (SignExtend(SRC) + CF)
ELSE DEST ← DEST − (SRC + CF);

Description

The SBB instruction adds the second operand (SRC) to the CF flag and subtracts the result from the first operand (DEST). The result of the subtraction is assigned to the first operand (DEST), and the flags are set accordingly.

When an immediate byte value is subtracted from a word operand, the immediate value is first sign-extended.

Flags Affected

The OF, SF, ZF, AF, PF, and CF flags are set according to the result

Protected Mode Exceptions

#GP(0) if the result is in a nonwritable segment; #GP(0) for an illegal memory operand effective address in the CS, DS, ES, FS, or GS segments; #SS(0) for an illegal address in the SS segment; #PF(fault-code) for a page fault

Real Address Mode Exceptions

Interrupt 13 if any part of the operand would lie outside of the effective address space from 0 to 0FFFFH

Virtual 8086 Mode Exceptions

Same exceptions as in Real Address Mode; #PF(fault-code) for a page fault

SCAS/SCASB/SCASW/SCASD – Compare String Data

Opcode	Instruction	Clocks	Description
AE	SCAS *m8*	8	Compare bytes AL-ES:[DI], update (E)DI
AF	SCAS *m16*	8	Compare words AX-ES:[DI], update (E)DI
AF	SCAS *m32*	8	Compare dwords EAX-ES:[DI], update (E)DI
AE	SCASB	8	Compare bytes AL-ES:[DI], update (E)DI
AF	SCASW	8	Compare words AX-ES:[DI], update (E)DI
AF	SCASD	8	Compare dwords EAX-ES:[DI], update (E)DI

Operation

```
IF AddressSize = 16
THEN use DI for dest-index;
ELSE (* AddressSize = 32 *) use EDI for dest-index;
FI;
IF byte type of instruction
THEN
  AL − [dest-index]; (* Compare byte in AL and dest *)
  IF DF = 0 THEN IndDec ← 1 ELSE IncDec ← −1; FI;
ELSE
  IF OperandSize = 16
  THEN
    AX − [dest-index]; (* compare word in AL and dest *)
    IF DF = 0 THEN IncDec ← 2 ELSE IncDec ← −2; FI;
  ELSE (* OperandSize = 32 *)
    EAX − [dest-index];(* compare dword in EAX & dest *)
    IF DF = 0 THEN IncDec ← 4 ELSE IncDec ← −4; FI;
  FI;
FI;
dest-index = dest-index + IncDec
```

Description

The SCAS instruction subtracts the memory byte or word at the destination register from the AL, AX or EAX register. The result is discarded; only the flags are set. The operand must be addressable from the ES segment; no segment override is possible.

If the address-size attribute for this instruction is 16 bits, the DI register is used as the destination register; otherwise, the address-size attribute is 32 bits and the EDI register is used.

The address of the memory data being compared is determined solely by the contents of the destination register, not by the operand to the SCAS instruction. The operand validates ES segment addressability and determines the data type. Load the correct index value into the DI or EDI register before executing the SCAS instruction.

After the comparison is made, the destination register is automatically updated. If the direction flag is 0 (the CLD instruction was executed), the destination register is incremented; if the direction flag is 1 (the STD instruction was executed), it is decremented. The increments or decrements are by 1 if bytes are compared, by 2 if words are compared, or by 4 if doublewords are compared.

The SCASB, SCASW, and SCASD instructions are synonyms for the byte, word and doubleword SCAS instructions that don't require operands. They are simpler to code, but provide no type or segment checking.

The SCAS instruction can be preceded by the REPE or REPNE prefix for a block search of CX or ECX bytes or words. Refer to the REP instruction for further details.

Flags Affected

The OF, SF, ZF, AF, PF, and CF flags are set according to the result

Protected Mode Exceptions

#GP(0) for an illegal memory operand effective address in the CS, DS, ES, FS, or GS segments; #SS(0) for an illegal address in the SS segment; #PF(fault-code) for a page fault

Real Address Mode Exceptions

Interrupt 13 if any part of the operand would lie outside of the effective address space from 0 to 0FFFFH

Virtual 8086 Mode Exceptions

Same exceptions as in Real Address Mode; #PF(fault-code) for a page fault

SETcc—Byte Set on Condition

Opcode	Instruction	Clocks	Description
0F 97	SETA *r/m8*	4/5	Set byte if above (CF=0 and ZF=0)
0F 93	SETAE *r/m8*	4/5	Set byte if above or equal (CF=0)
0F 92	SETB *r/m8*	4/5	Set byte if below (CF=1)
0F 96	SETBE *r/m8*	4/5	Set byte if below or equal (CF=1 or (ZF=1)
0F 92	SETC *r/m8*	4/5	Set if carry (CF=1)
0F 94	SETE *r/m8*	4/5	Set byte if equal (ZF=1)
0F 9F	SETG *r/m8*	4/5	Set byte if greater (ZF=0 or SF=OF)
0F 9D	SETGE *r/m8*	4/5	Set byte if greater or equal (SF=OF)
0F 9C	SETL *r/m8*	4/5	Set byte if less (SF< >OF)
0F 9E	SETLE *r/m8*	4/5	Set byte if less or equal (ZF=1 or SF< >OF)
0F 96	SETNA *r/m8*	4/5	Set byte if not above (CF=1)
0F 92	SETNAE *r/m8*	4/5	Set byte if not above or equal (CF=1)
0F 93	SETNB *r/m8*	4/5	Set byte if not below (CF=0)
0F 97	SETNBE *r/m8*	4/5	Set byte if not below or equal (CF=0 and ZF=0)
0F 93	SETNC *r/m8*	4/5	Set byte if not carry (CF=0)
0F 95	SETNE *r/m8*	4/5	Set byte if not equal (ZF=0)
0F 9E	SETNG *r/m8*	4/5	Set byte if not greater (ZF=1 or SF< >OF)
0F 9C	SETNGE *r/m8*	4/5	Set if not greater or equal (SF< >OF)
0F 9D	SETNL *r/m8*	4/5	Set byte if not less (SF=OF)
0F 9F	SETNLE *r/m8*	4/5	Set byte if not less or equal (ZF=0 and SF=OF)
0F 91	SETNO *r/m8*	4/5	Set byte if not overflow (OF=0)
0F 9B	SETNP *r/m8*	4/5	Set byte if not parity (PF=0)
0F 99	SETNS *r/m8*	4/5	Set byte if not sign (SF=0)
0F 95	SETNZ *r/m8*	4/5	Set byte if not zero (ZF=0)
0F 90	SETO *r/m8*	4/5	Set byte if overflow (OF=1)
0F 9A	SETP *r/m8*	4/5	Set byte if parity (PF=1)
0F 9A	SETPE *r/m8*	4/5	Set byte if parity even (PF=1)
0F 9B	SETPO *r/m8*	4/5	Set byte if parity odd (PF=0)
0F 98	SETS *r/m8*	4/5	Set byte if sign (SF=1)
0F 94	SETZ *r/m8*	4/5	Set byte if zero (ZF=1)

Operation

IF condition THEN *r/m8* ← 1 ELSE *r/m8* ← 0; FI;

Description

The SETcc instruction stores a byte at the destination specified by the effective address or register if the condition is met, or a 0 byte if the condition is not met.

Flags Affected

None

Protected Mode Exceptions

#GP(0) if the result is in a non-writable segment; #GP(0) for an illegal memory operand effective address in the CS, DS, ES, FS, or GS segments; #SS(0) for an illegal address in the SS segment; #PF(fault-code) for a page fault

Real Address Mode Exceptions

Interrupt 13 if any part of the operand would lie outside of the effective address space from 0 to 0FFFFH

Virtual 8086 Mode Exceptions

Same exceptions as in Real Address Mode; #PF(fault-code) for a page fault

SGDT/SIDT — Store Global/Interrupt Descriptor Table Register

Opcode	Instruction	Clocks	Description
0F 01 /0	SGDT *m*	9	Store GDTR to *m*
0F 01 /1	SIDT *m*	9	Store IDTR to *m*

Operation

DEST ← 48-bit BASE/LIMIT register contents;

Description

The SGDT and SIDT instructions copy the contents of the descriptor table register to the six bytes of memory indicated by the operand. The LIMIT field of the register is assigned to the first word at the effective address. If the operand-size attribute is 32 bits, the next three bytes are assigned the BASE field of the register, and the fourth byte is written with zero. The last byte is undefined. Otherwise, if the operand-size attribute is 16 bits, the next four bytes are assigned the 32-bit BASE field of the register.

The SGDT and SIDT instructions are used only in operating system software; they are not used in application programs.

Flags Affected

None

Protected Mode Exceptions

Interrupt 6 if the destination operand is a register; #GP(0) if the destination is in a nonwritable segment; #GP(0) for an illegal memory operand effective address in the CS, DS, ES, FS, or GS segments; #SS(0) for an illegal address in the SS segment; #PF(fault-code) for a page fault

Real Address Mode Exceptions

Interrupt 6 if the destination operand is a register; Interrupt 13 if any part of the operand would lie outside of the effective address space from 0 to 0FFFFH

Virtual 8086 Mode Exceptions

Same exceptions as in Real Address Mode; #PF(fault-code) for a page fault

Compatibility Note

The 16-bit forms of the SGDT and SIDT instructions are compatible with the 80286, if the value in the upper eight bits is not referenced. The 80286 stores 1's in these upper bits, whereas the 386 DX microprocessor stores 0's if the operand-size attribute is 16 bits. These bits were specified as undefined by the SGDT and SIDT instructions in the *iAPX 286 Programmer's Reference Manual*.

SHLD—Double Precision Shift Left

Opcode	Instruction	Clocks	Description
0F A4	SHLD *r/m16,r16,imm8*	3/7	*r/m16* gets SHL of *r/m16* concatenated with *r16*
0F A4	SHLD *r/m32,r32,imm8*	3/7	*r/m32* gets SHL of *r/m32* concatenated with *r32*
0F A5	SHLD *r/m16,r16*,CL	3/7	*r/m16* gets SHL of *r/m16* concatenated with *r16*
0F A5	SHLD *r/m32,r32*,CL	3/7	*r/m32* gets SHL of *r/m32* concatenated with *r32*

Operation

```
(* count is an unsigned integer corresponding to the last operand of the instruction, either an
immediate byte or the byte in register CL *)
ShiftAmt ← count MOD 32;
inBits ← register; (* Allow overlapped operands *)
IF ShiftAmt = 0
THEN no operation
ELSE
  IF ShiftAmt ≥ OperandSize
  THEN (* Bad parameters *)
    r/m ← UNDEFINED;
    CF, OF, SF, ZF, AF, PF ← UNDEFINED;
  ELSE (* Perform the shift *)
    CF ← BIT[Base, OperandSize - ShiftAmt];
      (* Last bit shifted out on exit *)
    FOR i ← OperandSize - 1 DOWNTO ShiftAmt
    DO
      BIT[Base, i] ← BIT[Base, i - ShiftAmt];
    OF;
    FOR i ← ShiftAmt - 1 DOWNTO 0
    DO
      BIT[Base, i] ← BIT[inBits, i - ShiftAmt + OperandSize];
    OD;
    Set SF, ZF, PF (r/m);
      (* SF, ZF, PF are set according to the value of the result *)
    AF ← UNDEFINED;
  FI;
FI;
```

Description

The SHLD instruction shifts the first operand provided by the *r/m* field to the left as many bits as specified by the count operand. The second operand (*r16* or *r32*) provides the bits to shift in from the right (starting with bit 0). The result is stored back into the *r/m* operand. The register remains unaltered.

The count operand is provided by either an immediate byte or the contents of the CL register. These operands are taken MODULO 32 to provide a number between 0 and 31 by which to shift. Because the bits to shift are provided by the specified registers, the operation is useful for multiprecision shifts (64 bits or more). The SF, ZF and PF flags are set according to the value of the result. The CF flag is set to the value of the last bit shifted out. The OF and AF flags are left undefined.

Flags Affected

The SF, ZF, and PF, flags are set according to the result; the CF flag is set to the value of the last bit shifted out; after a shift of one bit position, the OF flag is set if a sign change occurred, otherwise it is cleared; after a shift of more than one bit position, the OF flag is undefined; the AF flag is undefined, except for a shift count of zero, which does not affect any flags.

Protected Mode Exceptions

#GP(0) if the result is in a nonwritable segment; #GP(0) for an illegal memory operand effective address in the CS, DS, ES, FS, or GS segments; #SS(0) for an illegal address in the SS segment; #PF(fault-code) for a page fault

Real Address Mode Exceptions

Interrupt 13 if any part of the operand would lie outside of the effective address space from 0 to 0FFFFH

Virtual 8086 Mode Exceptions

Same exceptions as in Real Address Mode; #PF(fault-code) for a page fault

SHRD—Double Precision Shift Right

Opcode	Instruction	Clocks	Description
0F AC	SHRD *r/m16,r16,imm8*	3/7	*r/m16* gets SHR of *r/m16* concatenated with *r16*
0F AC	SHRD *r/m32,r32,imm8*	3/7	*r/m32* gets SHR of *r/m32* concatenated with *r32*
0F AD	SHRD *r/m16,r16*,CL	3/7	*r/m16* gets SHR of *r/m16* concatenated with *r16*
0F AD	SHRD *r/m32,r32*,CL	3/7	*r/m32* gets SHR of *r/m32* concatenated with *r32*

Operation

```
(* count is an unsigned integer corresponding to the last operand of the instruction, either an
   immediate byte or the byte in register CL *)
ShiftAmt ← count MOD 32;
inBits ← register; (* Allow overlapped operands *)
IF ShiftAmt = 0
THEN no operation
ELSE
  IF ShiftAmt ≥ OperandSize
  THEN (* Bad parameters *)
    r/m ← UNDEFINED;
    CF, OF, SF, ZF, AF, PF ← UNDEFINED;
  ELSE (* Perform the shift *)
    CF ← BIT[r/m, ShiftAmt − 1]; (* last bit shifted out on exit *)
    FOR i ← 0 TO OperandSize − 1 − ShiftAmt
    DO
      BIT[r/m, i] ← BIT[r/m, i − ShiftAmt];
    OD;
    FOR i ← OperandSize − ShiftAmt TO OperandSize − 1
    DO
      BIT[r/m,i] ← BIT[inBits,i + ShiftAmt − OperandSize];
    OD;
    Set SF, ZF, PF (r/m);
      (* SF, ZF, PF are set according to the value of the result *)
    Set SF, ZF, PF (r/m);
    AF ←UNDEFINED;
  FI;
FI;
```

Description

The SHRD instruction shifts the first operand provided by the *r/m* field to the right as many bits as specified by the count operand. The second operand (*r16* or *r32*) provides the bits to shift in from the left (starting with bit 31). The result is stored back into the *r/m* operand. The register remains unaltered.

The count operand is provided by either an immediate byte or the contents of the CL register. These operands are taken MODULO 32 to provide a number between 0 and 31 by which to shift. Because the bits to shift are provided by the specified register, the operation is useful for multi-precision shifts (64 bits or more). The SF, ZF and PF flags are set according to the value of the result. The CF flag is set to the value of the last bit shifted out. The OF and AF flags are left undefined.

Flags Affected

The SF, ZF, and PF flags are set according to the result; the CF flag is set to the value of the last bit shifted out; after a shift of one bit position, the OF flag is set if a sign change occurred, otherwise it is cleared; after a shift of more than one bit position, the OF flag is undefined; the AF flag is undefined, except for a shift count of zero, which does not affect any flags.

Protected Mode Exceptions

#GP(0) if the result is in a nonwritable segment; #GP(0) for an illegal memory operand effective address in the CS, DS, ES, FS, or GS segments; #SS(0) for an illegal address in the SS segment; #PF(fault-code) for a page fault

Real Address Mode Exceptions

Interrupt 13 if any part of the operand would lie outside of the effective address space from 0 to 0FFFFH

Virtual 8086 Mode Exceptions

Same exceptions as in Real Address Mode; #PF(fault-code) for a page fault

SLDT — Store Local Descriptor Table Register

Opcode	Instruction	Clocks	Description
0F 00 /0	SLDT *r/m16*	*pm*=2/2	Store LDTR to EA word

Operation

r/m16 ← LDTR;

Description

The SLDT instruction stores the Local Descriptor Table Register (LDTR) in the two-byte register or memory location indicated by the effective address operand. This register is a selector that points into the Global Descriptor Table.

The SLDT instruction is used only in operating system software. It is not used in application programs.

Flags Affected

None

Protected Mode Exceptions

#GP(0) if the result is in a nonwritable segment; #GP(0) for an illegal memory operand effective address in the CS, DS, ES, FS, or GS segments; #SS(0) for an illegal address in the SS segment; #PF(fault-code) for a page fault

Real Address Mode Exceptions

Interrupt 6; the SLDT instruction is not recognized in Real Address Mode

Virtual 8086 Mode Exceptions

Same exceptions as in Real Address Mode; #PF(fault-code) for a page fault

Notes

The operand-size attribute has no effect on the operation of the instruction.

SMSW—Store Machine Status Word

Opcode	Instruction	Clocks	Description
0F 01 /4	SMSW *r/m16*	2/3,pm=2/2	Store machine status word to EA word

Operation

r/m16 ← MSW;

Description

The SMSW instruction stores the machine status word (part of the CR0 register) in the two-byte register or memory location indicated by the effective address operand.

Flags Affected

None

Protected Mode Exceptions

#GP(0) if the result is in a nonwritable segment; #GP(0) for an illegal memory operand effective address in the CS, DS, ES, FS, or GS segments; #SS(0) for an illegal address in the SS segment; #PF(fault-code) for a page fault

Real Address Mode Exceptions

Interrupt 13 if any part of the operand would lie outside of the effective address space from 0 to 0FFFFH

Virtual 8086 Mode Exceptions

Same exceptions as in Real Address Mode; #PF(fault-code) for a page fault

Notes

This instruction is provided for compatibility with the 80286; 386 DX microprocessor programs should use the MOV ..., CR0 instruction.

STC — Set Carry Flag

Opcode	Instruction	Clocks	Description
F9	STC	2	Set carry flag

Operation

CF ← 1;

Description

The STC instruction sets the CF flag.

Flags Affected

The CF flag is set

Protected Mode Exceptions

None

Real Address Mode Exceptions

None

Virtual 8086 Mode Exceptions

None

STD—Set Direction Flag

Opcode	Instruction	Clocks	Description
FD	STD	£	Set direction flag so (E)SI and/or (E)DI decrement

Operation

DF ← 1;

Description

The STD instruction sets the direction flag, causing all subsequent string operations to decrement the index registers, (E)SI and/or (E)DI, on which they operate.

Flags Affected

The DF flag is set

Protected Mode Exceptions

None

Real Address Mode Exceptions

None

Virtual 8086 Mode Exceptions

None

STI—Set Interrupt Flag

Opcode	Instruction	Clocks	Description
F13	STI	8	Set interrupt flag; interrupts enabled at the end of the next instruction

Operation

IF ← 1

Description

The STI instruction sets the IF flag. The 386 DX microprocessor then responds to external interrupts after executing the next instruction if the next instruction allows the IF flag to remain enabled. If external interrupts are disabled and you code the STI instruction followed by the RET instruction (such as at the end of a subroutine), the RET instruction is allowed to execute before external interrupts are recognized. Also, if external interrupts are disabled and you code the STI instruction followed by the CLI instruction, then external interrupts are not recognized because the CLI instruction clears the IF flag during its execution.

Flags Affected

The IF flag is set

Protected Mode Exceptions

#GP(0) if the current privilege level is greater (has less privilege) than the I/O privilege level

Real Address Mode Exceptions

None

Virtual 8086 Mode Exceptions

None

STOS/STOSB/STOSW/STOSD — Store String Data

Opcode	Instruction	Clocks	Description
AA	STOS *m8*	5	Store AL in byte ES:[(E)DI], update (E)DI
AB	STOS *m16*	5	Store AX in word ES:[(E)DI], update (E)DI
AB	STOS *m32*	5	Store EAX in dword ES:[(E)DI], update (E)DI
AA	STOSB	5	Store AL in byte ES:[(E)DI], update (E)DI
AB	STOSW	5	Store AX in word ES:[(E)DI], update (E)DI
AB	STOSD	5	Store EAX in dword ES:[(E)DI], update (E)DI

Operation

```
IF AddressSize = 16
THEN use ES:DI for DestReg
ELSE (* AddressSize = 32 *) use ES:EDI for DestReg;
FI;
IF byte type of instruction
THEN
  (ES:DestReg) ← AL;
  IF DF = 0
  THEN DestReg ← DestReg + 1;
  ELSE DestReg ← DestReg − 1;
  FI;
ELSE IF OperandSize = 16
  THEN
    (ES:DestReg) ← AX;
    IF DF = 0
    THEN DestReg ← DestReg + 2;
    ELSE DestReg ← DestReg − 2;
    FI;
  ELSE (* OperandSize = 32 *)
    (ES:DestReg) ←EAX;
    IF DF = 0
    THEN DestReg ← DestReg + 4;
    ELSE DestReg ← DestReg − 4;
    FI;
  FI;
FI;
```

Description

The STOS instruction transfers the contents of the AL, AX, or EAX register to the memory byte or word given by the destination register relative to the ES segment. The destination register is the DI register for an address-size attribute of 16 bits or the EDI register for an address-size attribute of 32 bits.

The destination operand must be addressable from the ES register. A segment override is not possible.

The address of the destination is determined by the contents of the destination register, not by the explicit operand of the STOS instruction. This operand is used only to validate ES segment addressability and to determine the data type. Load the correct index value into the destination register before executing the STOS instruction.

After the transfer is made, the DI register is automatically updated. If the DF flag is 0 (the CLD instruction was executed), the DI register is incremented; if the DF flag is 1 (the STD instruction was executed), the DI register is decremented. The DI register is incremented or decremented by 1 if a byte is stored, by 2 if a word is stored, or by 4 if a doubleword is stored.

The STOSB, STOSW, and STOSD instructions are synonyms for the byte, word, and doubleword STOS instructions, that do not require an operand. They are simpler to use, but provide no type or segment checking.

The STOS instruction can be preceded by the REP prefix for a block fill of CX or ECX bytes, words, or doublewords. Refer to the REP instruction for further details.

Flags Affected

None

Protected Mode Exceptions

#GP(0) if the result is in a nonwritable segment; #GP(0) for an illegal memory operand effective address in the CS, DS, ES, FS, or GS segments; #SS(0) for an illegal address in the SS segment; #PF(fault-code) for a page fault

Real Address Mode Exceptions

Interrupt 13 if any part of the operand would lie outside of the effective address space from 0 to 0FFFFH

Virtual 8086 Mode Exceptions

Same exceptions as in Real Address Mode; #PF(fault-code) for a page fault

STR — Store Task Register

Opcode	Instruction	Clocks	Description
0F 00 /1	STR *r/m16*	pm=23/27	Store task register to EA word

Operation

r/m ← task register;

Description

The contents of the task register are copied to the two-byte register or memory location indicated by the effective address operand.

The STR instruction is used only in operating system software. It is not used in application programs.

Flags Affected

None

Protected Mode Exceptions

#GP(0) if the result is in a nonwritable segment; #GP(0) for an illegal memory operand effective address in the CS, DS, ES, FS, or GS segments; #SS(0) for an illegal address in the SS segment; #PF(fault-codc) for a page fault

Real Address Mode Exceptions

Interrupt 6; the STR instruction is not recognized in Real Address Mode

Virtual 8086 Mode Exceptions

Same exceptions as in Real Address Mode

Notes

The operand-size attribute has no effect on this instruction.

SUB — Integer Subtraction

Opcode	Instruction	Clocks	Description
2C *ib*	SUB AL,*imm8*	2	Subtract immediate byte from AL
2D *iw*	SUB AX,*imm16*	2	Subtract immediate word from AX
2D *id*	SUB EAX,*imm32*	2	Subtract immediate dword from EAX
80 /5 *ib*	SUB *r/m8,imm8*	2/7	Subtract immediate byte from *r/m* byte
81 /5 *iw*	SUB *r/m16,imm16*	2/7	Subtract immediate word from *r/m* word
81 /5 *id*	SUB *r/m32,imm32*	2/7	Subtract immediate dword from *r/m* dword
83 /5 *ib*	SUB *r/m16,imm8*	2/7	Subtract sign-extended immediate byte from *r/m* word
83 /5 *ib*	SUB *r/m32,imm8*	2/7	Subtract sign-extended immediate byte from *r/m* dword
28 /*r*	SUB *r/m8,r8*	2/6	Subtract byte register from *r/m* byte
29 /*r*	SUB *r/m16,r16*	2/6	Subtract word register from *r/m* word
29 /*r*	SUB *r/m32,r32*	2/6	Subtract dword register from *r/m* dword
2A /*r*	SUB *r8,r/m8*	2/7	Subtract *r/m* byte from byte register
2B /*r*	SUB *r16,r/m16*	2/7	Subtract *r/m* word from word register
2B /*r*	SUB *r32,r/m32*	2/7	Subtract *r/m* dword from dword register

Operation

```
IF SRC is a byte and DEST is a word or dword
THEN DEST = DEST - SignExtend(SRC);
ELSE DEST ← DEST - SRC;
FI;
```

Description

The SUB instruction subtracts the second operand (SRC) from the first operand (DEST). The first operand is assigned the result of the subtraction, and the flags are set accordingly.

When an immediate byte value is subtracted from a word operand, the immediate value is first sign-extended to the size of the destination operand.

Flags Affected

The OF, SF, ZF, AF, PF, and CF flags are set according to the result

Protected Mode Exceptions

#GP(0) if the result is in a nonwritable segment; #GP(0) for an illegal memory operand effective address in the CS, DS, ES, FS, or GS segments; #SS(0) for an illegal address in the SS segment; #PF(fault-code) for a page fault

Real Address Mode Exceptions

Interrupt 13 if any part of the operand would lie outside of the effective address space from 0 to 0FFFFH

Virtual 8086 Mode Exceptions

Same exceptions as in Real Address Mode; #PF(fault-code) for a page fault

TEST — Logical Compare

Opcode	Instruction	Clocks	Description
A8 *ib*	TEST AL,*imm8*	2	AND immediate byte with AL
A9 *iw*	TEST AX,*imm16*	2	AND immediate word with AX
A9 *id*	TEST EAX,*imm32*	2	AND immediate dword with EAX
F6 /0 *ib*	TEST *r/m8,imm8*	2/5	AND immediate byte with *r/m* byte
F7 /0 *iw*	TEST *r/m16,imm16*	2/5	AND immediate word with *r/m* word
F7 /0 *id*	TEST *r/m32,imm32*	2/5	AND immediate dword with *r/m* dword
84 /*r*	TEST *r/m8,r8*	2/5	AND byte register with *r/m* byte
85 /*r*	TEST *r/m16,r16*	2/5	AND word register with *r/m* word
85 /*r*	TEST *r/m32,r32*	2/5	AND dword register with *r/m* dword

Operation

DEST : = LeftSRC AND RightSRC;
CF ← 0;
OF ← 0;

Description

The TEST instruction computes the bit-wise logical AND of its two operands. Each bit of the result is 1 if both of the corresponding bits of the operands are 1; otherwise, each bit is 0. The result of the operation is discarded and only the flags are modified.

Flags Affected

The OF and CF flags are cleared; the SF, ZF, and PF flags are set according to the result

Protected Mode Exceptions

#GP(0) for an illegal memory operand effective address in the CS, DS, ES, FS, or GS segments; #SS(0) for an illegal address in the SS segment; #PF(fault-code) for a page fault

Real Address Mode Exceptions

Interrupt 13 if any part of the operand would lie outside of the effective address space from 0 to 0FFFFH

Virtual 8086 Mode Exceptions

Same exceptions as in Real Address Mode; #PF(fault-code) for a page fault

VERR, VERW—Verify a Segment for Reading or Writing

Opcode	Instruction	Clocks	Description
0F 00 /4	VERR *r/m16*	pm=10/11	Set ZF=1 if segment can be read, selector in *r/m16*
0F 00 /5	VERW *r/m16*	pm=15/16	Set ZF=1 if segment can be written, selector in *r/m16*

Operation

```
IF segment with selector at (r/m) is accessible
  with current protection level
  AND ((segment is readable for VERR) OR
    (segment is writable for VERW))
THEN ZF ← 1;
ELSE ZF ← 0;
FI;
```

Description

The two-byte register or memory operand of the VERR and VERW instructions contains the value of a selector. The VERR and VERW instructions determine whether the segment denoted by the selector is reachable from the current privilege level and whether the segment is readable (VERR) or writable (VERW). If the segment is accessible, the ZF flag is set; if the segment is not accessible, the ZF flag is cleared. To set the ZF flag, the following conditions must be met:

- The selector must denote a descriptor within the bounds of the table (GDT or LDT); the selector must be "defined."
- The selector must denote the descriptor of a code or data segment (not that of a task state segment, LDT, or a gate).
- For the VERR instruction, the segment must be readable. For the VERW instruction, the segment must be a writable data segment.
- If the code segment is readable and conforming, the descriptor privilege level (DPL) can be any value for the VERR instruction. Otherwise, the DPL must be greater than or equal to (have less or the same privilege as) both the current privilege level and the selector's RPL.

The validation performed is the same as if the segment were loaded into the DS, ES, FS, or GS register, and the indicated access (read or write) were performed. The ZF flag receives the result of the validation. The selector's value cannot result in a protection exception, enabling the software to anticipate possible segment access problems.

Flags Affected

The ZF flag is set if the segment is accessible, cleared if it is not

Protected Mode Exceptions

Faults generated by illegal addressing of the memory operand that contains the selector; the selector is not loaded into any segment register, and no faults attributable to the selector operand are generated

#GP(0) for an illegal memory operand effective address in the CS, DS, ES, FS, or GS segments; #SS(0) for an illegal address in the SS segment; #PF(fault-code) for a page fault

Real Address Mode Exceptions

Interrupt 6; the VERR and VERW instructions are not recognized in Real Address Mode

Virtual 8086 Mode Exceptions

Same exceptions as in Real Address Mode; #PF(fault-code) for a page fault

WAIT — Wait until BUSY# Pin is Inactive (HIGH)

Opcode	Instruction	Clocks	Description
9B	WAIT	7 minimum	Wait until BUSY pin is inactive (HIGH)

Description

The WAIT instruction suspends execution of the 386 DX microprocessor instructions until the BUSY# pin is inactive (high). The BUSY# pin is driven by the 387™ DX numeric coprocessor.

Flags Affected

None

Protected Mode Exceptions

#NM if the task-switched flag in the machine status word (the lower 16 bits of the CR0 register) is set; #MF if the ERROR# input pin is asserted (i.e., the 387 math coprocessor has detected an unmasked numeric error)

Real Address Mode Exceptions

Same exceptions as in Protected Mode

Virtual 8086 Mode Exceptions

Same exceptions as in Protected Mode

XCHG — Exchange Register/Memory with Register

Opcode	Instruction	Clocks	Description
90+ *r*	XCHG AX,*r16*	3	Exchange word register with AX
90+ *r*	XCHG *r16*,AX	3	Exchange word register with AX
90+ *r*	XCHG EAX,*r32*	3	Exchange dword register with EAX
90+ *r*	XCHG *r32*,EAX	3	Exchange dword register with EAX
86 /*r*	XCHG *r/m8,r8*	3	Exchange byte register with EA byte
86 /*r*	XCHG *r8,r/m8*	3/5	Exchange byte register with EA byte
87 /*r*	XCHG *r/m16,r16*	3	Exchange word register with EA word
87 /*r*	XCHG *r16,r/m16*	3/5	Exchange word register with EA word
87 /*r*	XCHG *r/m32,r32*	3	Exchange dword register with EA dword
87 /*r*	XCHG *r32,r/m32*	3/5	Exchange dword register with EA dword

Operation

temp ← DEST
DEST ← SRC
SRC ← temp

Description

The XCHG instruction exchanges two operands. The operands can be in either order. If a memory operand is involved, the LOCK# signal is asserted for the duration of the exchange, regardless of the presence or absence of the LOCK prefix or of the value of the IOPL.

Flags Affected

None

Protected Mode Exceptions

#GP(0) if either operand is in a nonwritable segment; #GP(0) for an illegal memory operand effective address in the CS, DS, ES, FS, or GS segments; #SS(0) for an illegal address in the SS segment; #PF(fault-code) for a page fault

Real Address Mode Exceptions

Interrupt 13 if any part of the operand would lie outside of the effective address space from 0 to 0FFFFH

Virtual 8086 Mode Exceptions

Same exceptions as in Real Address Mode; #PF(fault-code) for a page fault

XLAT/XLATB — Table Look-up Translation

Opcode	Instruction	Clocks	Description
D7	XLAT *m8*	5	Set AL to memory byte DS:[(E)BX + unsigned AL]
D7	XLATB	5	Set AL to memory byte DS:[(E)BX + unsigned AL]

Operation

```
IF AddressSize = 16
THEN
  AL ← (BX + ZeroExtend(AL))
ELSE (* AddressSize = 32 *)
  AL ← (EBX + ZeroExtend(AL));
FI;
```

Description

The XLAT instruction changes the AL register from the table index to the table entry. The AL register should be the unsigned index into a table addressed by the DS:BX register pair (for an address-size attribute of 16 bits) or the DS:EBX register pair (for an address-size attribute of 32 bits).

The operand to the XLAT instruction allows for the possibility of a segment override. The XLAT instruction uses the contents of the BX register even if they differ from the offset of the operand. The offset of the operand should have been moved into the BX or EBX register with a previous instruction.

The no-operand form, the XLATB instruction, can be used if the BX or EBX table will always reside in the DS segment.

Flags Affected

None

Protected Mode Exceptions

#GP(0) for an illegal memory operand effective address in the CS, DS, ES, FS, or GS segments; #SS(0) for an illegal address in the SS segment; #PF(fault-code) for a page fault

Real Address Mode Exceptions

Interrupt 13 if any part of the operand would lie outside of the effective address space from 0 to 0FFFFH

Virtual 8086 Mode Exceptions

Same exceptions as in Real Address Mode; #PF(fault-code) for a page fault

XOR — Logical Exclusive OR

Opcode	Instruction	Clocks	Description
34 *ib*	XOR AL,*imm8*	2	Exclusive-OR immediate byte to AL
35 *iw*	XOR AX,*imm16*	2	Exclusive-OR immediate word to AX
35 *id*	XOR EAX,*imm32*	2	Exclusive-OR immediate dword to EAX
80 /6 *ib*	XOR *r/m8,imm8*	2/7	Exclusive-OR immediate byte to *r/m* byte
81 /6 *iw*	XOR *r/m16,imm16*	2/7	Exclusive-OR immediate word to *r/m* word
81 /6 *id*	XOR *r/m32,imm32*	2/7	Exclusive-OR immediate dword to *r/m* dword
83 /6 *ib*	XOR *r/m16,imm8*	2/7	XOR sign-extended immediate byte with *r/m* word
83 /6 *ib*	XOR *r/m32,imm8*	2/7	XOR sign-extended immediate byte with *r/m* dword
30 /*r*	XOR *r/m8,r8*	2/6	Exclusive-OR byte register to *r/m* byte
31 /*r*	XOR *r/m16,r16*	2/6	Exclusive-OR word register to *r/m* word
31 /*r*	XOR *r/m32,r32*	2/6	Exclusive-OR dword register to *r/m* dword
32 /*r*	XOR *r8,r/m8*	2/7	Exclusive-OR byte register to *r/m* byte
33 /*r*	XOR *r16,r/m16*	2/7	Exclusive-OR word register to *r/m* word
33 /*r*	XOR *r32,r/m32*	2/7	Exclusive-OR dword register to *r/m* dword

Operation

DEST ← LeftSRC XOR RightSRC
CF ← 0
OF ← 0

Description

The XOR instruction computes the exclusive OR of the two operands. Each bit of the result is 1 if the corresponding bits of the operands are different; each bit is 0 if the corresponding bits are the same. The answer replaces the first operand.

Flags Affected

The CF and OF flags are cleared; the SF, ZF, and PF flags are set according to the result; the AF flag is undefined

Protected Mode Exceptions

#GP(0) if the result is in a nonwritable segment; #GP(0) for an illegal memory operand effective address in the CS, DS, ES, FS, or GS segments; #SS(0) for an illegal address in the SS segment; #PF(fault-code) for a page fault

Real Address Mode Exceptions

Interrupt 13 if any part of the operand would lie outside of the effective address space from 0 to 0FFFFH

Virtual 8086 Mode Exceptions

Same exceptions as in Real Address Mode; #PF(fault-code) for a page fault

Opcode Map

A

APPENDIX A
OPCODE MAP

The opcode tables that follow aid in interpreting 386™ DX microprocessor object code. Use the high-order four bits of the opcode as an index to a row of the opcode table; use the low-order four bits as an index to a column of the table. If the opcode is 0FH, refer to the two-byte opcode table and use the second byte of the opcode to index the rows and columns of that table.

A.1 KEY TO ABBREVIATIONS

Operands are identified by a two-character code of the form Zz. The first character, an uppercase letter, specifies the addressing method; the second character, a lowercase letter, specifies the type of operand.

A.2 CODES FOR ADDRESSING METHOD

A Direct address; the instruction has no modR/M byte; the address of the operand is encoded in the instruction; no base register, index register, or scaling factor can be applied; e.g., far JMP (EA).

C The reg field of the modR/M byte selects a control register; e.g., MOV (0F20, 0F22).

D The reg field of the modR/M byte selects a debug register; e.g., MOV (0F21,0F23).

E A modR/M byte follows the opcode and specifies the operand. The operand is either a general register or a memory address. If it is a memory address, the address is computed from a segment register and any of the following values: a base register, an index register, a scaling factor, a displacement.

F Flags Register.

G The reg field of the modR/M byte selects a general register; e.g., ADD (00).

I Immediate data. The value of the operand is encoded in subsequent bytes of the instruction.

J The instruction contains a relative offset to be added to the instruction pointer register; e.g., JMP short, LOOP.

M The modR/M byte may refer only to memory; e.g., BOUND, LES, LDS, LSS, LFS, LGS.

O The instruction has no modR/M byte; the offset of the operand is coded as a word or double word (depending on address size attribute) in the instruction. No base register, index register, or scaling factor can be applied; e.g., MOV (A0–A3).

R The mod field of the modR/M byte may refer only to a general register; e.g., MOV (0F20–0F24, 0F26).

S The reg field of the modR/M byte selects a segment register; e.g., MOV (8C,8E).

T The reg field of the modR/M byte selects a test register; e.g., MOV (0F24,0F26).

X Memory addressed by the DS:SI register pair; e.g., MOVS, COMPS, OUTS, LODS, SCAS.

Y Memory addressed by the ES:DI register pair; e.g., MOVS, CMPS, INS, STOS.

A.3 CODES FOR OPERAND TYPE

a Two one-word operands in memory or two double-word operands in memory, depending on operand size attribute (used only by BOUND).

b Byte (regardless of operand size attribute)

c Byte or word, depending on operand size attribute.

d Double word (regardless of operand size attribute)

p Thirty-two bit or 48-bit pointer, depending on operand size attribute.

s Six-byte pseudo-descriptor

v Word or double word, depending on operand size attribute.

w Word (regardless of operand size attribute)

A.4 REGISTER CODES

When an operand is a specific register encoded in the opcode, the register is identified by its name; e.g., AX, CL, or ESI. The name of the register indicates whether the register is 32-, 16-, or 8-bits wide. A register identifier of the form eXX is used when the width of the register depends on the operand size attribute; for example, eAX indicates that the AX register is used when the operand size attribute is 16 and the EAX register is used when the operand size attribute is 32.

One-Byte Opcode Map

	0	1	2	3	4	5	6	7
0	ADD						PUSH ES	POP ES
	Eb,Gb	Ev,Gv	Gb,Eb	Gv,Ev	AL,Ib	eAX,Iv		
1	ADC						PUSH SS	POP SS
	Eb,Gb	Ev,Gv	Gb,Eb	Gv,Ev	AL,Ib	eAX,Iv		
2	AND						SEG =ES	DAA
	Eb,Gb	Ev,Gv	Gb,Eb	Gv,Ev	AL,Ib	eAX,Iv		
3	XOR						SEG =SS	AAA
	Eb,Gb	Ev,Gv	Gb,Eb	Gb,Ev	AL,Ib	eAX,Iv		
4	INC general register							
	eAX	eCX	eDX	eBX	eSP	eBP	eSI	eDI
5	PUSH general register							
	eAX	eCX	eDX	eBX	eSP	eBP	eSI	eDI
6	PUSHA	POPA	BOUND Gv,Ma	ARPL Ew,Rw	SEG =FS	SEG =GS	Operand Size	Address Size
7	Short-displacement jump on condition (Jb)							
	JO	JNO	JB	JNB	JZ	JNZ	JBE	JNBE
8	Immediate Grpl		MOVB	Grpl Ev,Ib	TEST		XCHG	
	Eb,Ib	Ev,Iv	AL,imm8		Eb,Gb	Ev,Gv	Eb,Gb	Ev,Gv
9	NOP	XCHG word or double-word register with eAX						
		eCX	eDX	eBX	eSP	eBP	eSI	eDI
A	MOV				MOVSB Xb,Yb	MOVSW/D Xv,Yv	CMPSB Xb,Yb	CMPSW/D Xv,Yv
	AL,Ob	eAX,Ov	Ob,AL	Ov,eAX				
B	MOV immediate byte into byte register							
	AL	CL	DL	BL	AH	CH	DH	BH
C	Shift Grp2		RET near		LES Gv,Mp	LDS Gv,Mp	MOV	
	Eb,Ib	Ev,Ib	Iw				Eb,Ib	Ev,Iv
D	Shift Grp2				AAM	AAD		XLAT
	Eb,1	Ev,1	Eb,CL	Ev,CL				
E	LOOPNE Jb	LOOPE Jb	LOOP Jb	JCXZ Jb	IN		OUT	
					Al,Ib	eAX,Ib	Ib,AL	Ib,eAX
F	LOCK		REPNE	REP REPE	HLT	CMC	Unary Grp3	
							Eb	Ev

One-Byte Opcode Map

	8	9	A	B	C	D	E	F
0	OR						PUSH CS	2-byte escape
	Eb,Gb	Ev,Gv	Gb,Eb	Gv,Ev	AL,Ib	eAX,Iv		
1	SBB						PUSH DS	POP DS
	Eb,Gb	Ev,Gv	Gb,Eb	Gv,Ev	AL,Ib	eAX,Iv		
2	SUB						SEG =CS	DAS
	Eb,Gb	Ev,Gv	Gb,Eb	Gv,Ev	AL,Ib	eAX,Iv		
3	CMP						SEG =DS	AAS
	Eb,Gb	Ev,Gv	Gb,Eb	Gv,Ev	AL,Ib	eAX,Iv		
4	DEC general register							
	eAX	eCX	eDX	eBX	eSP	eBP	eSI	eDI
5	POP into general register							
	eAX	eCX	eDX	eBX	eSP	eBP	eSI	eDI
6	PUSH Iv	IMUL GvEvIv	PUSH Ib	IMUL GvEvIb	INSB Yb,DX	INSW/D Yv,DX	OUTSB DX,Xb	OUTSW/D DX,Xv
7	Short-displacement jump on condition (Jb)							
	JS	JNS	JP	JNP	JL	JNL	JLE	JNLE
8	MOV				MOV Ew,Sw	LEA Gv,M	MOV Sw,Ew	POP Ev
	Eb,Gb	Ev,Gv	Gb,Eb	Gv,Ev				
9	CBW	CWD	CALL Ap	WAIT	PUSHF Fv	POPF Fv	SAHF	LAHF
A	TEST		STOSB Yb,AL	STOSW/D Yv,eAX	LODSB AL,Xb	LODSW/D eAX,Xv	SCASB AL,Xb	SCASW/D eAX,Xv
	AL,Ib	eAX,Iv						
B	MOV immediate word or double into word or double register							
	eAX	eCX	eDX	eBX	eSP	eBP	eSI	eDI
C	ENTER Iw,IB	LEAVE	RET far		INT 3	INT Ib	INTO	IRET
			Iw					
D	ESC (Escape to coprocessor instruction set)							
E	CALL Jv	JMP			IN		OUT	
		Jv	Ap	Jb	AL,DX	eAX,DX	DX,AL	DX,eAX
F	CLC	STC	CLI	STI	CLD	STD	INC/DEC Grp4	INC/DEC Grp5

Two-Byte Opcode Map (first byte is 0FH)

	0	1	2	3	4	5	6	7
0	Grp6	Grp7	LAR Gv,Ew	LSL Gv,Ew			CLTS	
1								
2	MOV Rd,Cd	MOV Rd,Dd	MOV Cd,Rd	MOV Dd,Rd	MOV Rd,Td		MOV Td,Rd	
3								
4								
5								
6								
7								
8	Long-displacement jump on condition (Jv)							
	JO	JNO	JB	JNB	JZ	JNZ	JBE	JNBE
9	Byte Set on condition (Eb)							
	SETO	SETNO	SETB	SETNB	SETZ	SETNZ	SETBE	SETNBE
A	PUSH FS	POP FS		BT Ev,Gv	SHLD EvGvIb	SHLD EvGvCL		
B			LSS Mp	BTR Ev,Gv	LFS Mp	LGS Mp	MOVZX	
							Gv,Eb	Gv,Ew
C								
D								
E								
F								

Two-Byte Opcode Map (first byte is 0FH)

	8	9	A	B	C	D	E	F
0								
1								
2								
3								
4								
5								
6								
7								
8	Long-displacement jump on condition (Jv)							
	JS	JNS	JP	JNP	JL	JNL	JLE	JNLE
9	SETS	SETNS	SETP	SETNP	SETL	SETNL	SETLE	SETNLE
A	PUSH GS	POP GS		BTS Ev,Gv	SHRD EvGvIb	SHRD EvGvCL		IMUL Gv,Ev
B			Grp-8 Ev,Ib	BTC Ev,Gv	BSF Gv,Ev	BSR Gv,Ev	MOVSX	
							Gv,Eb	Gv,Ew
C								
D								
E								
F								

Opcodes determined by bits 5,4,3 of modR/M byte:

mod	nnn	R/M

	000	001	010	011	100	101	110	111
1	ADD	OR	ADC	SBB	AND	SUB	XOR	CMP
2	ROL	ROR	RCL	RCR	SHL	SHR	SHL	SAR
3	TEST Ib/Iv	TEST Ib/Iv	NOT	NEG	MUL AL/eAX	IMUL AL/eAX	DIV AL/eAX	IDIV AL/eAX
4	INC Eb	DEC Eb						
5	INC Ev	DEC Ev	CALL Ev	CALL eP	JMP Ev	JMP Ep	PUSH Ev	

Opcodes determined by bits 5,4,3 of modR/M byte:

mod	nnn	R/M

	000	001	010	011	100	101	110	111
6	SLDT Ew	STR Ew	LLDT Ew	LTR Ew	VERR Ew	VERW Ew		
7	SGDT Ms	SIDT Ms	LGDT Ms	LIDT Ms	SMSW Ew		LMSW Ew	
8					BT	BTS	BTR	BTC

Complete Flag Cross-Reference

B

APPENDIX B
COMPLETE FLAG CROSS-REFERENCE

B.1 KEY TO CODES

T	= instruction tests flag
M	= instruction modifies flag (either sets or resets depending on operands)
0	= instruction resets flag
1	= instruction sets flag
—	= instruction's effect on flag is undefined
R	= instruction restores prior value of flag
blank	= instruction does not affect flag

Instruction	OF	SF	ZF	AF	PF	CF	TF	IF	DF	NT	RF
AAA	—	—	—	TM	—	M					
AAD	—	M	M	—	M	—					
AAM	—	M	M	—	M	—					
AAS	—	—	—	TM	—	M					
ADC	M	M	M	M	M	TM					
ADD	M	M	M	M	M	M					
AND	0	M	M	—	M	0					
ARPL			M								
BOUND											
BSF/BSR	—	—	M	—	—	—					
BT/BTS/BTR/BTC	—	—	—	—	—	M					
CALL											
CBW											
CLC						0					
CLD									0		
CLI								0			
CLTS											
CMC						M					
CMP	M	M	M	M	M	M					
CMPS	M	M	M	M	M	M			T		
CWD											
DAA	—	M	M	TM	M	TM					
DAS	—	M	M	TM	M	TM					
DEC	M	M	M	M	M						
DIV	—	—	—	—	—	—					
ENTER											
ESC											
HLT											
IDIV	—	—	—	—	—	—					
IMUL	M	—	—	—	—	M					
IN											
INC	M	M	M	M	M						
INS									T		
INT							0			0	
INTO	T						0			0	
IRET	R	R	R	R	R	R	R	R	R	T	
Jcond	T	T	T		T	T					

Instruction	OF	SF	ZF	AF	PF	CF	TF	IF	DF	NT	RF
JCXZ											
JMP											
LAHF											
LAR			M								
LDS/LES/LSS/LFS/LGS											
LEA											
LEAVE											
LGDT/LIDT/LLDT/LMSW											
LOCK											
LODS									T		
LOOP											
LOOPE/LOOPNE			T								
LSL			M								
LTR											
MOV											
MOV control, debug	—	—	—	—	—	—					
MOVS									T		
MOVSX/MOVZX											
MUL	M	—	—	—	—	M					
NEG	M	M	M	M	M	M					
NOP											
NOT											
OR	0	M	M	—	M	0					
OUT											
OUTS									T		
POP/POPA											
POPF	R	R	R	R	R	R	R	R	R	R	
PUSH/PUSHA/PUSHF											
RCL/RCR 1	M					TM					
RCL/RCR count	—					TM					
REP/REPE/REPNE											
RET											
ROL/ROR 1	M					M					
ROL/ROR count	—					M					
SAHF		R	R	R	R	R					
SAL/SAR/SHL/SHR 1	M	M	M	—	M	M					
SAL/SAR/SHL/SHR count	—	M	M	—	M	M					
SBB	M	M	M	M	M	TM					
SCAS	M	M	M	M	M	M			T		
SET cond	T	T	T		T	T					
SGDT/ SIDT/SLDT/SMSW											
SHLD/SHRD	—	M	M	—	M	M					
STC						1					
STD									1		
STI								1			
STOS									T		
STR											
SUB	M	M	M	M	M	M					
TEST	0	M	M	—	M	0					
VERR/VERRW			M								
WAIT											
XCHG											
XLAT											
XOR	0	M	M	—	M	0					

Status Flag Summary

C

APPENDIX C
STATUS FLAG SUMMARY

C.1 STATUS FLAGS' FUNCTIONS

Bit	Name	Function
0	CF	Carry Flag – Set on high-order bit carry or borrow; cleared otherwise.
2	PF	Parity Flag – Set if low-order eight bits of result contain an even number of 1 bits; cleared otherwise.
4	AF	Adjust flag – Set on carry from or borrow to the low order four bits of AL; cleared otherwise. Used for decimal arithmetic.
6	ZF	Zero Flag – Set if result is zero; cleared otherwise.
7	SF	Sign Flag – Set equal to high-order bit of result (0 is positive, 1 if negative).
11	OF	Overflow Flag – Set if result is too large a positive number or too small a negative number (excluding sign-bit) to fit in destination operand; cleared otherwise.

C.2 KEY TO CODES

Code	Meaning
T	= instruction tests flag
M	= instruction modifies flag (either sets or resets depending on operands)
0	= instruction resets flag
—	= instruction's effect on flag is undefined
blank	= instruction does not affect flag

Instruction	OF	SF	ZF	AF	PF	CF
AAA	—	—	—	TM	—	M
AAS	—	—	—	TM	—	M
AAD	—	M	M	—	M	—
AAM	—	M	M	—	M	—
DAA	—	M	M	TM	M	TM
DAS	—	M	M	TM	M	TM
ADC	M	M	M	M	M	TM
ADD	M	M	M	M	M	M
SBB	M	M	M	M	M	TM
SUB	M	M	M	M	M	M
CMP	M	M	M	M	M	M
CMPS	M	M	M	M	M	M
SCAS	M	M	M	M	M	M
NEG	M	M	M	M	M	M
DEC	M	M	M	M	M	
INC	M	M	M	M	M	
IMUL	M	—	—	—	—	M
MUL	M	—	—	—	—	M
RCL/RCR 1	M					TM
RCL/RCR count	—					TM
ROL/ROR 1	M					M
ROL/ROR count	—					M
SAL/SAR/SHL/SHR 1	M	M	M	—	M	M
SAL/SAR/SHL/SHR count	—	M	M		M	M
SHLD/SHRD	—	M	M	—	M	M
BSF/BSR	—	—	M	—	—	—
BT/BTS/BTR/BTC	—	—	—	—	—	M
AND	0	M	M	—	M	0
OR	0	M	M	—	M	0
TEST	0	M	M	—	M	0
XOR	0	M	M	—	M	0

Condition Codes D

APPENDIX D
CONDITION CODES

Note: The terms "above" and "below" refer to the relation between two unsigned values (neither the SF flag nor the OF flag is tested). The terms "greater" and "less" refer to the relation between two signed values (the SF and OF flags are tested).

D.1 DEFINITION OF CONDITIONS

(For conditional instructions Jcond, and SETcond)

Mnemonic	Meaning	Instruction Subcode	Condition Tested
O	Overflow	0000	OF = 1
NO	No overflow	0001	OF = 0
B NAE	Below Neither above nor equal	0010	CF = 1
NB AE	Not below Above or equal	0011	CF = 0
E Z	Equal Zero	0100	ZF = 1
NE NZ	Not equal Not zero	0101	ZF = 0
BE NA	Below or equal Not above	0110	(CF or ZF) = 1
NBE A	Neither below nor equal Above	0111	(CF or ZF) = 0
S	Sign	1000	SF = 1
NS	No sign	1001	SF = 0
P PE	Parity Parity even	1010	PF = 1
NP PO	No parity Parity odd	1011	PF = 0
L NGE	Less Neither greater nor equal	1100	(SF xor OF) = 1
NL GE	Not less Greater or equal	1101	(SF xor OF) = 0
LE NG	Less or equal Not greater	1110	((SF xor OF) or ZF) = 1
NLE G	Neither less nor equal Greater	1111	((SF xor OF) or ZF) = 0

Instruction Format and Timing

E

APPENDIX E
INSTRUCTION FORMAT AND TIMING

This appendix is an excerpt from Section 6 of the 386™ DX Microprocessor Data Sheet.

6. INSTRUCTION SET

This section describes the 386™ DX Microprocessor instruction set. A table lists all instructions along with instruction encoding diagrams and clock counts. Further details of the instruction encoding are then provided in the following sections, which completely describe the encoding structure and the definition of all fields occurring within 386 DX Microprocessor instructions.

6.1 386™ DX MICROPROCESSOR INSTRUCTION ENCODING AND CLOCK COUNT SUMMARY

To calculate elapsed time for an instruction, multiply the instruction clock count, as listed in Table 6-1 below, by the processor clock period (e.g. 50 ns for a 20 MHz 386 DX Microprocessor, 40 ns for a 25 MHz 386 DX Microprocessor, and 30 ns for a 33 MHz 386 DX Microprocessor).

For more detailed information on the encodings of instructions refer to Section 6.2 Instruction Encodings. Section 6.2 explains the general structure of instruction encodings, and defines exactly the encodings of all fields contained within the instruction.

Instruction Clock Count Assumptions

1. The instruction has been prefetched, decoded, and is ready for execution.
2. Bus cycles do not require wait states.
3. There are no local bus HOLD requests delaying processor access to the bus.
4. No exceptions are detected during instruction execution.
5. If an effective address is calculated, it does not use two general register components. One register, scaling and displacement can be used within the clock counts shown. However, if the effective address calculation uses two general register components, add 1 clock to the clock count shown.

Instruction Clock Count Notation

1. If two clock counts are given, the smaller refers to a register operand and the larger refers to a memory operand.
2. n = number of times repeated.
3. m = number of components in the next instruction executed, where the entire displacement (if any) counts as one component, the entire immediate data (if any) counts as one component, and each of the **other** bytes of the instruction and prefix(es) each count as one component.

Table 6-1. 386 DX™ Microprocessor Instruction Set Clock Count Summary

INSTRUCTION	FORMAT	Clk Count Virtual 8086 Mode	CLOCK COUNT Real Address Mode or Virtual 8086 Mode	CLOCK COUNT Protected Virtual Address Mode	NOTES Real Address Mode or Virtual 8086 Mode	NOTES Protected Virtual Address Mode
GENERAL DATA TRANSFER						
MOV = Move:						
Register to Register/Memory	1000100w · mod reg r/m		2/2	2/2	b	h
Register/Memory to Register	1000101w · mod reg r/m		2/4	2/4	b	h
Immediate to Register/Memory	1100011w · mod 000 r/m · immediate data		2/2	2/2	b	h
Immediate to Register (short form)	1011 w reg · immediate data		2	2	b	h
Memory to Accumulator (short form)	1010000w · full displacement		4	4	b	h
Accumulator to Memory (short form)	1010001w · full displacement		2	2	b	h
Register Memory to Segment Register	10001110 · mod sreg3 r/m		2/5	18/19	b	h, i, j
Segment Register to Register/Memory	10001100 · mod sreg3 r/m		2/2	2/2	b	h
MOVSX = Move With Sign Extension						
Register From Register/Memory	00001111 · 1011111w · mod reg r/m		3/6	3/6	b	h
MOVZX = Move With Zero Extension						
Register From Register/Memory	00001111 · 1011011w · mod reg r/m		3/6	3/6	b	h
PUSH = Push:						
Register/Memory	11111111 · mod 110 r/m		5	5	b	h
Register (short form)	01010 reg		2	2	b	h
Segment Register (ES, CS, SS or DS)	000 sreg2 110		2	2	b	h
Segment Register (FS or GS)	00001111 · 10 sreg3 000		2	2	b	h
Immediate	011010s0 · immediate data		2	2	b	h
PUSHA = Push All	01100000		18	18	b	h
POP = Pop						
Register/Memory	10001111 · mod 000 r/m		5	5	b	h
Register (short form)	01011 reg		4	4	b	h
Segment Register (ES, SS or DS)	000 sreg 2 111		7	21	b	h, i, j
Segment Register (FS or GS)	00001111 · 10 sreg 3 001		7	21	b	h, i, j
POPA = Pop All	01100001		24	24	b	h
XCHG = Exchange						
Register/Memory With Register	1000011w · mod reg r/m		3/5	3/5	b, f	f, h
Register With Accumulator (short form)	10010 reg		3	3		
IN = Input from:						
Fixed Port	1110010w · port number	†26	12	6*/26**		m
Variable Port	1110110w	†27	13	7*/27**		m
OUT = Output to:						
Fixed Port	1110011w · port number	†24	10	4*/24**		m
Variable Port	1110111w	†25	11	5*/25**		m
LEA = Load EA to Register	10001101 · mod reg r/m		2	2		

* If CPL ≤ IOPL   ** If CPL > IOPL

Table 6-1. 386 DX™ Microprocessor Instruction Set Clock Count Summary (contd.)

INSTRUCTION	FORMAT				CLOCK COUNT		NOTES	
					Real Address Mode or Virtual 8086 Mode	Protected Virtual Address Mode	Real Address Mode or Virtual 8086 Mode	Protected Virtual Address Mode
SEGMENT CONTROL								
LDS = Load Pointer to DS	11000101	mod reg r/m			7	22	b	h, i, j
LES = Load Pointer to ES	11000100	mod reg r/m			7	22	b	h, i, j
LFS = Load Pointer to FS	00001111	10110100	mod reg r/m		7	25	b	h, i, j
LGS = Load Pointer to GS	00001111	10110101	mod reg r/m		7	25	b	h, i, j
LSS = Load Pointer to SS	00001111	10110010	mod reg r/m		7	22	b	h, i, j
FLAG CONTROL								
CLC = Clear Carry Flag	11111000				2	2		
CLD = Clear Direction Flag	11111100				2	2		
CLI = Clear Interrupt Enable Flag	11111010				8	8		m
CLTS = Clear Task Switched Flag	00001111	00000110			6	6	c	l
CMC = Complement Carry Flag	11110101				2	2		
LAHF = Load AH into Flag	10011111				2	2		
POPF = Pop Flags	10011101				5	5	b	h, n
PUSHF = Push Flags	10011100				4	4	b	h
SAHF = Store AH into Flags	10011110				3	3		
STC = Set Carry Flag	11111001				2	2		
STD = Set Direction Flag	11111101				2	2		
STI = Set Interrupt Enable Flag	11111011				8	8		m
ARITHMETIC								
ADD = Add								
Register to Register	000000dw	mod reg r/m			2	2		
Register to Memory	0000000w	mod reg r/m			7	7	b	h
Memory to Register	0000001w	mod reg r/m			6	6	b	h
Immediate to Register/Memory	100000sw	mod 000 r/m	immediate data		2/7	2/7	b	h
Immediate to Accumulator (short form)	0000010w	immediate data			2	2		
ADC = Add With Carry								
Register to Register	000100dw	mod reg r/m			2	2		
Register to Memory	0001000w	mod reg r/m			7	7	b	h
Memory to Register	0001001w	mod reg r/m			6	6	b	h
Immediate to Register/Memory	100000sw	mod 010 r/m	immediate data		2/7	2/7	b	h
Immediate to Accumulator (short form)	0001010w	immediate data			2	2		
INC = Increment								
Register/Memory	1111111w	mod 000 r/m			2/6	2/6	b	h
Register (short form)	01000 reg				2	2		
SUB = Subtract								
Register from Register	001010dw	mod reg r/m			2	2		

Table 6-1. 386 DX™ Microprocessor Instruction Set Clock Count Summary (contd.)

INSTRUCTION	FORMAT	CLOCK COUNT: Real Address Mode or Virtual 8086 Mode	CLOCK COUNT: Protected Virtual Address Mode	NOTES: Real Address Mode or Virtual 8086 Mode	NOTES: Protected Virtual Address Mode
ARITHMETIC (Continued)					
Register from Memory	0010100w | mod reg r/m	7	7	b	h
Memory from Register	0010101w | mod reg r/m	6	6	b	h
Immediate from Register/Memory	100000sw | mod 101 r/m | immediate data	2/7	2/7	b	h
Immediate from Accumulator (short form)	0010110w | immediate data	2	2		
SBB = Subtract with Borrow					
Register from Register	000110dw | mod reg r/m	2	2		
Register from Memory	0001100w | mod reg r/m	7	7	b	h
Memory from Register	0001101w | mod reg r/m	6	6	b	h
Immediate from Register/Memory	100000sw | mod 011 r/m | immediate data	2/7	2/7	b	h
Immediate from Accumulator (short form)	0001110w | immediate data	2	2		
DEC = Decrement					
Register/Memory	1111111w | reg 001 r/m	2/6	2/6	b	h
Register (short form)	01001 reg	2	2		
CMP = Compare					
Register with Register	001110dw | mod reg r/m	2	2		
Memory with Register	0011100w | mod reg r/m	5	5	b	h
Register with Memory	0011101w | mod reg r/m	6	6	b	h
Immediate with Register/Memory	100000sw | mod 111 r/m | immediate data	2/5	2/5	b	h
Immediate with Accumulator (short form)	0011110w | immediate data	2	2		
NEG = Change Sign	1111011w | mod 011 r/m	2/6	2/6	b	h
AAA = ASCII Adjust for Add	00110111	4	4		
AAS = ASCII Adjust for Subtract	00111111	4	4		
DAA = Decimal Adjust for Add	00100111	4	4		
DAS = Decimal Adjust for Subtract	00101111	4	4		
MUL = Multiply (unsigned)					
Accumulator with Register/Memory	1111011w | mod 100 r/m				
Multiplier-Byte		12–17/15–20	12–17/15–20	b, d	d, h
-Word		12–25/15–28	12–25/15–28	b, d	d, h
-Doubleword		12–41/15–44	12–41/15–44	b, d	d, h
IMUL = Integer Multiply (signed)					
Accumulator with Register/Memory	1111011w | mod 101 r/m				
Multiplier-Byte		12–17/15–20	12–17/15–20	b, d	d, h
-Word		12–25/15–28	12–25/15–28	b, d	d, h
-Doubleword		12–41/15–44	12–41/15–44	b, d	d, h
Register with Register/Memory	00001111 | 10101111 | mod reg r/m				
Multiplier-Byte		12–17/15–20	12–17/15–20	b, d	d, h
-Word		12–25/15–28	12–25/15–28	b, d	d, h
-Doubleword		12–41/15–44	12–41/15–44	b, d	d, h
Register/Memory with Immediate to Register	011010s1 | mod reg r/m | immediate data				
-Word		13–26/14–27	13–26/14–27	b, d	d, h
-Doubleword		13–42/14–43	13–42/14–43	b, d	d, h

Table 6-1. 386 DX™ Microprocessor Instruction Set Clock Count Summary (contd.)

INSTRUCTION	FORMAT	CLOCK COUNT: Real Address Mode or Virtual 8086 Mode	CLOCK COUNT: Protected Virtual Address Mode	NOTES: Real Address Mode or Virtual 8086 Mode	NOTES: Protected Virtual Address Mode
ARITHMETIC (Continued)					
DIV = Divide (Unsigned)					
Accumulator by Register/Memory	1111011w | mod 110 r/m				
Divisor—Byte		14/17	14/17	b,e	e,h
—Word		22/25	22/25	b,e	e,h
—Doubleword		38/41	38/41	b,e	e,h
IDIV = Integer Divide (Signed)					
Accumulator By Register/Memory	1111011w | mod 111 r/m				
Divisor—Byte		19/22	19/22	b,e	e,h
—Word		27/30	27/30	b,e	e,h
—Doubleword		43/46	43/46	b,e	e,h
AAD = ASCII Adjust for Divide	11010101 | 00001010	19	19		
AAM = ASCII Adjust for Multiply	11010100 | 00001010	17	17		
CBW = Convert Byte to Word	10011000	3	3		
CWD = Convert Word to Double Word	10011001	2	2		
LOGIC					
Shift Rotate Instructions					
Not Through Carry **(ROL, ROR, SAL, SAR, SHL, and SHR)**					
Register/Memory by 1	1101000w | mod TTT r/m	3/7	3/7	b	h
Register/Memory by CL	1101001w | mod TTT r/m	3/7	3/7	b	h
Register/Memory by Immediate Count	1100000w | mod TTT r/m | immed 8-bit data	3/7	3/7	b	h
Through Carry **(RCL and RCR)**					
Register/Memory by 1	1101000w | mod TTT r/m	9/10	9/10	b	h
Register/Memory by CL	1101001w | mod TTT r/m	9/10	9/10	b	h
Register/Memory by Immediate Count	1100000w | mod TTT r/m | immed 8-bit data	9/10	9/10	b	h
	TTT Instruction 000 ROL 001 ROR 010 RCL 011 RCR 100 SHL/SAL 101 SHR 111 SAR				
SHLD = Shift Left Double					
Register/Memory by Immediate	00001111 | 10100100 | mod reg r/m | immed 8-bit data	3/7	3/7		
Register/Memory by CL	00001111 | 10100101 | mod reg r/m	3/7	3/7		
SHRD = Shift Right Double					
Register/Memory by Immediate	00001111 | 10101100 | mod reg r/m | immed 8-bit data	3/7	3/7		
Register/Memory by CL	00001111 | 10101101 | mod reg r/m	3/7	3/7		
AND = And					
Register to Register	001000dw | mod reg r/m	2	2		

Table 6-1. 386 DX™ Microprocessor Instruction Set Clock Count Summary (contd.)

INSTRUCTION	FORMAT			Clk Count Virtual 8086 Mode	CLOCK COUNT: Real Address Mode or Virtual 8086 Mode	CLOCK COUNT: Protected Virtual Address Mode	NOTES: Real Address Mode or Virtual 8086 Mode	NOTES: Protected Virtual Address Mode
LOGIC (Continued)								
Register to Memory	0010000w	mod reg r/m			7	7	b	h
Memory to Register	0010001w	mod reg r/m			6	6	b	h
Immediate to Register/Memory	1000000w	mod 100 r/m	immediate data		2/7	2/7	b	h
Immediate to Accumulator (Short Form)	0010010w	immediate data			2	2		
TEST = And Function to Flags, No Result								
Register/Memory and Register	1000010w	mod reg r/m			2/5	2/5	b	h
Immediate Data and Register/Memory	1111011w	mod 000 r/m	immediate data		2/5	2/5	b	h
Immediate Data and Accumulator (Short Form)	1010100w	immediate data			2	2		
OR = Or								
Register to Register	000010dw	mod reg r/m			2	2		
Register to Memory	0000100w	mod reg r/m			7	7	b	h
Memory to Register	0000101w	mod reg r/m			6	6	b	h
Immediate to Register/Memory	1000000w	mod 001 r/m	immediate data		2/7	2/7	b	h
Immediate to Accumulator (Short Form)	0000110w	immediate data			2	2		
XOR = Exclusive Or								
Register to Register	001100dw	mod reg r/m			2	2		
Register to Memory	0011000w	mod reg r/m			7	7	b	h
Memory to Register	0011001w	mod reg r/m			6	6	b	h
Immediate to Register/Memory	1000000w	mod 110 r/m	immediate data		2/7	2/7	b	h
Immediate to Accumulator (Short Form)	0011010w	immediate data			2	2		
NOT = Invert Register/Memory	1111011w	mod 010 r/m			2/6	2/6	b	h
STRING MANIPULATION								
CMPS = Compare Byte Word	1010011w				10	10	b	h
INS = Input Byte/Word from DX Port	0110110w			†29	15	9*/29**	b	h, m
LODS = Load Byte/Word to AL/AX/EAX	1010110w				5	5	b	h
MOVS = Move Byte Word	1010010w				8	8	b	h
OUTS = Output Byte/Word to DX Port	0110111w			†28	14	8*/28**	b	h, m
SCAS = Scan Byte Word	1010111w				8	8	b	h
STOS = Store Byte/Word from AL/AX/EX	1010101w				5	5	b	h
XLAT = Translate String	11010111				5	5		h
REPEATED STRING MANIPULATION								
Repeated by Count in CX or ECX								
REPE CMPS = Compare String (Find Non-Match)	11110011	1010011w			5+9n	5+9n	b	h

* If CPL ≤ IOPL ** If CPL > IOPL

Table 6-1. 386 DX™ Microprocessor Instruction Set Clock Count Summary (contd.)

INSTRUCTION	FORMAT	Clk Count Virtual 8086 Mode	CLOCK COUNT: Real Address Mode or Virtual 8086 Mode	CLOCK COUNT: Protected Virtual Address Mode	NOTES: Real Address Mode or Virtual 8086 Mode	NOTES: Protected Virtual Address Mode
REPEATED STRING MANIPULATION (Continued)						
REPNE CMPS = Compare String						
(Find Match)	11110010 1010011w		5+9n	5+9n	b	h
REP INS = Input String	11110010 0110110w	†28+6n	14+6n	8+6n*/28+6n**	b	h, m
REP LODS = Load String	11110010 1010110w		5+6n	5+6n	b	h
REP MOVS = Move String	11110010 1010010w		8+4n	8+4n	b	h
REP OUTS = Output String	11110010 0110111w	†26+5n	12+5n	6+5n*/26+5n**	b	h, m
REPE SCAS = Scan String						
(Find Non-AL/AX/EAX)	11110011 1010111w		5+8n	5+8n	b	h
REPNE SCAS = Scan String						
(Find AL/AX/EAX)	11110010 1010111w		5+8n	5+8n	b	h
REP STOS = Store String	11110010 1010101w		5+5n	5+5n	b	h
BIT MANIPULATION						
BSF = Scan Bit Forward	00001111 10111100 mod reg r/m		11+3n	11+3n	b	h
BSR = Scan Bit Reverse	00001111 10111101 mod reg r/m		9+3n	9+3n	b	h
BT = Test Bit						
Register/Memory, Immediate	00001111 10111010 mod 100 r/m immed 8-bit data		3/6	3/6	b	h
Register/Memory, Register	00001111 10100011 mod reg r/m		3/12	3/12	b	h
BTC = Test Bit and Complement						
Register/Memory, Immediate	00001111 10111010 mod 111 r/m immed 8-bit data		6/8	6/8	b	h
Register/Memory, Register	00001111 10111011 mod reg r/m		6/13	6/13	b	h
BTR = Test Bit and Reset						
Register/Memory, Immediate	00001111 10111010 mod 110 r/m immed 8-bit data		6/8	6/8	b	h
Register/Memory, Register	00001111 10110011 mod reg r/m		6/13	6/13	b	h
BTS = Test Bit and Set						
Register/Memory, Immediate	00001111 10111010 mod 101 r/m immed 8-bit data		6/8	6/8	b	h
Register/Memory, Register	00001111 10101011 mod reg r/m		6/13	6/13	b	h
CONTROL TRANSFER						
CALL = Call						
Direct Within Segment	11101000 full displacement		7+m	7+m	b	r
Register/Memory						
Indirect Within Segment	11111111 mod 010 r/m		7+m/ 10+m	7+m/ 10+m	b	h, r
Direct Intersegment	10011010 unsigned full offset, selector		17+m	34+m	b	j,k,r

NOTES:

† Clock count shown applies if I/O permission allows I/O to the port in virtual 8086 mode. If I/O bit map denies permission exception 13 fault occurs; refer to clock counts for INT 3 instruction.

* If CPL ≤ IOPL ** If CPL > IOPL

Table 6-1. 386 DX™ Microprocessor Instruction Set Clock Count Summary (contd.)

INSTRUCTION	FORMAT	CLOCK COUNT: Real Address Mode or Virtual 8086 Mode	CLOCK COUNT: Protected Virtual Address Mode	NOTES: Real Address Mode or Virtual 8086 Mode	NOTES: Protected Virtual Address Mode
CONTROL TRANSFER (Continued)					
Protected Mode Only (Direct Intersegment)					
Via Call Gate to Same Privilege Level			52+m		h,j,k,r
Via Call Gate to Different Privilege Level, (No Parameters)			86+m		h,j,k,r
Via Call Gate to Different Privilege Level, (x Parameters)			94+4x+m		h,j,k,r
From 80286 Task to 80286 TSS			273		h,j,k,r
From 80286 Task to 386DX™ CPU TSS			298		h,j,k,r
From 80286 Task to Virtual 8086 Task (386DX™ CPU TSS)			218		h,j,k,r
From 386DX™ CPU Task to 80286 TSS			273		h,j,k,r
From 386DX™ CPU Task to 386DX™ CPU TSS			300		h,j,k,r
From 386DX™ CPU Task to Virtual 8086 Task (386DX™ CPU TSS)			218		h,j,k,r
Indirect Intersegment	11111111 mod 011 r/m	22+m	38+m	b	h,j,k,r
Protected Mode Only (Indirect Intersegment)					
Via Call Gate to Same Privilege Level			56+m		h,j,k,r
Via Call Gate to Different Privilege Level, (No Parameters)			90+m		h,j,k,r
Via Call Gate to Different Privilege Level, (x Parameters)			98+4x+m		h,j,k,r
From 80286 Task to 80286 TSS			278		h,j,k,r
From 80286 Task to 386DX™ CPU TSS			303		h,j,k,r
From 80286 Task to Virtual 8086 Task (386DX™ CPU TSS)			222		h,j,k,r
From 386DX™ CPU Task to 80286 TSS			278		h,j,k,r
From 386DX™ CPU Task to 386DX™ CPU TSS			305		h,j,k,r
From 386DX™ CPU Task to Virtual 8086 Task (386DX™ CPU TSS)			222		h,j,k,r
JMP = Unconditional Jump					
Short	11101011 8-bit displacement	7+m	7+m		r
Direct within Segment	11101001 full displacement	7+m	7+m		r
Register/Memory Indirect within Segment	11111111 mod 100 r/m	7+m/ 10+m	7+m/ 10+m	b	h,r
Direct Intersegment	11101010 unsigned full offset, selector	12+m	27+m		j,k,r
Protected Mode Only (Direct Intersegment)					
Via Call Gate to Same Privilege Level			45+m		h,j,k,r
From 80286 Task to 80286 TSS			274		h,j,k,r
From 80286 Task to 386DX™ CPU TSS			301		h,j,k,r
From 80286 Task to Virtual 8086 Task (386DX™ CPU TSS)			219		h,j,k,r
From 386DX™ CPU Task to 80286 TSS			270		h,j,k,r
From 386DX™ CPU Task to 386DX™ CPU TSS			303		h,j,k,r
From 386DX™ CPU Task to Virtual 8086 Task (386DX™ CPU TSS)			221		h,j,k,r
Indirect Intersegment	11111111 mod 101 r/m	17+m	31+m	b	h,j,k,r
Protected Mode Only (Indirect Intersegment)					
Via Call Gate to Same Privilege Level			49+m		h,j,k,r
From 80286 Task to 80286 TSS			279		h,j,k,r
From 80286 Task to 386DX™ CPU TSS			306		h,j,k,r
From 80286 Task to Virtual 8086 Task (386DX™ CPU TSS)			223		h,j,k,r
From 386DX™ CPU Task to 80286 TSS			275		h,j,k,r
From 386DX™ CPU Task to 386DX™ CPU TSS			308		h,j,k,r
From 386DX™ CPU Task to Virtual 8086 Task (386DX™ CPU TSS)			225		h,j,k,r

Table 6-1. 386 DX™ Microprocessor Instruction Set Clock Count Summary (contd.)

INSTRUCTION	FORMAT			Clock Count: Real Address Mode or Virtual 8086 Mode	Clock Count: Protected Virtual Address Mode	Notes: Real Address Mode or Virtual 8086 Mode	Notes: Protected Virtual Address Mode
CONTROL TRANSFER (Continued)							
RET = Return from CALL:							
Within Segment	11000011			10 + m	10 + m	b	g, h, r
Within Segment Adding Immediate to SP	11000010	16-bit displ		10 + m	10 + m	b	g, h, r
Intersegment	11001011			18 + m	32+m	b	g, h, j, k, r
Intersegment Adding Immediate to SP	11001010	16-bit displ		18 + m	32+m	b	g, h, j, k, r
Protected Mode Only (RET):							
to Different Privilege Level							
Intersegment					69		h, j, k, r
Intersegment Adding Immediate to SP					69		h, j, k, r
CONDITIONAL JUMPS							
NOTE: Times Are Jump "Taken or Not Taken"							
JO = Jump on Overflow							
8-Bit Displacement	01110000	8-bit displ		7 + m or 3	7 + m or 3		r
Full Displacement	00001111	10000000	full displacement	7 + m or 3	7 + m or 3		r
JNO = Jump on Not Overflow							
8-Bit Displacement	01110001	8-bit displ		7 + m or 3	7 + m or 3		r
Full Displacement	00001111	10000001	full displacement	7 + m or 3	7 + m or 3		r
JB/JNAE = Jump on Below/Not Above or Equal							
8-Bit Displacement	01110010	8-bit displ		7 + m or 3	7 + m or 3		r
Full Displacement	00001111	10000010	full displacement	7 + m or 3	7 + m or 3		r
JNB/JAE = Jump on Not Below/Above or Equal							
8-Bit Displacement	01110011	8-bit displ		7 + m or 3	7 + m or 3		r
Full Displacement	00001111	10000011	full displacement	7 + m or 3	7 + m or 3		r
JE/JZ = Jump on Equal/Zero							
8-Bit Displacement	01110100	8-bit displ		7 + m or 3	7 + m or 3		r
Full Displacement	00001111	10000100	full displacement	7 + m or 3	7 + m or 3		r
JNE/JNZ = Jump on Not Equal/Not Zero							
8-Bit Displacement	01110101	8-bit displ		7 + m or 3	7 + m or 3		r
Full Displacement	00001111	10000101	full displacement	7 + m or 3	7 + m or 3		r
JBE/JNA = Jump on Below or Equal/Not Above							
8-Bit Displacement	01110110	8-bit displ		7 + m or 3	7 + m or 3		r
Full Displacement	00001111	10000110	full displacement	7 + m or 3	7 + m or 3		r
JNBE/JA = Jump on Not Below or Equal/Above							
8-Bit Displacement	01110111	8-bit displ		7 + m or 3	7 + m or 3		r
Full Displacement	00001111	10000111	full displacement	7 + m or 3	7 + m or 3		r
JS = Jump on Sign							
8-Bit Displacement	01111000	8-bit displ		7 + m or 3	7 + m or 3		r
Full Displacement	00001111	10001000	full displacement	7 + m or 3	7 + m or 3		r

Table 6-1. 386 DX™ Microprocessor Instruction Set Clock Count Summary (contd.)

INSTRUCTION	FORMAT				CLOCK COUNT: Real Address Mode or Virtual 8086 Mode	CLOCK COUNT: Protected Virtual Address Mode	NOTES: Real Address Mode or Virtual 8086 Mode	NOTES: Protected Virtual Address Mode
CONDITIONAL JUMPS (Continued)								
JNS = Jump on Not Sign								
8-Bit Displacement	01111001	8-bit displ			7 + m or 3	7 + m or 3		r
Full Displacement	00001111	10001001	full displacement		7 + m or 3	7 + m or 3		r
JP/JPE = Jump on Parity/Parity Even								
8-Bit Displacement	01111010	8-bit displ			7 + m or 3	7 + m or 3		r
Full Displacement	00001111	10001010	full displacement		7 + m or 3	7 + m or 3		r
JNP/JPO = Jump on Not Parity/Parity Odd								
8-Bit Displacement	01111011	8-bit displ			7 + m or 3	7 + m or 3		r
Full Displacement	00001111	10001011	full displacement		7 + m or 3	7 + m or 3		r
JL/JNGE = Jump on Less/Not Greater or Equal								
8-Bit Displacement	01111100	8-bit displ			7 + m or 3	7 + m or 3		r
Full Displacement	00001111	10001100	full displacement		7 + m or 3	7 + m or 3		r
JNL/JGE = Jump on Not Less/Greater or Equal								
8-Bit Displacement	01111101	8-bit displ			7 + m or 3	7 + m or 3		r
Full Displacement	00001111	10001101	full displacement		7 + m or 3	7 + m or 3		r
JLE/JNG = Jump on Less or Equal/Not Greater								
8-Bit Displacement	01111110	8-bit displ			7 + m or 3	7 + m or 3		r
Full Displacement	00001111	10001110	full displacement		7 + m or 3	7 + m or 3		r
JNLE/JG = Jump on Not Less or Equal/Greater								
8-Bit Displacement	01111111	8-bit displ			7 + m or 3	7 + m or 3		r
Full Displacement	00001111	10001111	full displacement		7 + m or 3	7 + m or 3		r
JCXZ = Jump on CX Zero	11100011	8-bit displ			9 + m or 5	9 + m or 5		r
JECXZ = Jump on ECX Zero	11100011	8-bit displ			9 + m or 5	9 + m or 5		r
(Address Size Prefix Differentiates JCXZ from JECXZ)								
LOOP = Loop CX Times	11100010	8-bit displ			11 + m	11 + m		r
LOOPZ/LOOPE = Loop with Zero/Equal	11100001	8-bit displ			11 + m	11 + m		r
LOOPNZ/LOOPNE = Loop While Not Zero	11100000	8-bit displ			11 + m	11 + m		r
CONDITIONAL BYTE SET								
NOTE: Times Are Register/Memory								
SETO = Set Byte on Overflow								
To Register/Memory	00001111	10010000	mod 000	r/m	4/5	4/5		h
SETNO = Set Byte on Not Overflow								
To Register/Memory	00001111	10010001	mod 000	r/m	4/5	4/5		h
SETB/SETNAE = Set Byte on Below/Not Above or Equal								
To Register/Memory	00001111	10010010	mod 000	r/m	4/5	4/5		h

Table 6-1. 386 DX™ Microprocessor Instruction Set Clock Count Summary (contd.)

INSTRUCTION	FORMAT	CLOCK COUNT: Real Address Mode or Virtual 8086 Mode	CLOCK COUNT: Protected Virtual Address Mode	NOTES: Real Address Mode or Virtual 8086 Mode	NOTES: Protected Virtual Address Mode
CONDITIONAL BYTE SET (Continued)					
SETNB = Set Byte on Not Below/Above or Equal					
To Register/Memory	00001111 | 10010011 | mod 000 r/m	4/5	4/5		h
SETE/SETZ = Set Byte on Equal/Zero					
To Register/Memory	00001111 | 10010100 | mod 000 r/m	4/5	4/5		h
SETNE/SETNZ = Set Byte on Not Equal/Not Zero					
To Register/Memory	00001111 | 10010101 | mod 000 r/m	4/5	4/5		h
SETBE/SETNA = Set Byte on Below or Equal/Not Above					
To Register/Memory	00001111 | 10010110 | mod 000 r/m	4/5	4/5		h
SETNBE/SETA = Set Byte on Not Below or Equal/Above					
To Register/Memory	00001111 | 10010111 | mod 000 r/m	4/5	4/5		h
SETS = Set Byte on Sign					
To Register/Memory	00001111 | 10011000 | mod 000 r/m	4/5	4/5		h
SETNS = Set Byte on Not Sign					
To Register/Memory	00001111 | 10011001 | mod 000 r/m	4/5	4/5		h
SETP/SETPE = Set Byte on Parity/Parity Even					
To Register/Memory	00001111 | 10011010 | mod 000 r/m	4/5	4/5		h
SETNP/SETPO = Set Byte on Not Parity/Parity Odd					
To Register/Memory	00001111 | 10011011 | mod 000 r/m	4/5	4/5		h
SETL/SETNGE = Set Byte on Less/Not Greater or Equal					
To Register/Memory	00001111 | 10011100 | mod 000 r/m	4/5	4/5		h
SETNL/SETGE = Set Byte on Not Less/Greater or Equal					
To Register/Memory	00001111 | 01111101 | mod 000 r/m	4/5	4/5		h
SETLE/SETNG = Set Byte on Less or Equal/Not Greater					
To Register/Memory	00001111 | 10011110 | mod 000 r/m	4/5	4/5		h
SETNLE/SETG = Set Byte on Not Less or Equal/Greater					
To Register/Memory	00001111 | 10011111 | mod 000 r/m	4/5	4/5		h
ENTER = Enter Procedure	11001000 | 16-bit displacement, 8-bit level				
L = 0		10	10	b	h
L = 1		12	12	b	h
L > 1		15 + 4(n − 1)	15 + 4(n − 1)	b	h
LEAVE = Leave Procedure	11001001	4	4	b	h

Table 6-1. 386 DX™ Microprocessor Instruction Set Clock Count Summary (contd.)

INSTRUCTION	FORMAT	CLOCK COUNT: Real Address Mode or Virtual 8086 Mode	CLOCK COUNT: Protected Virtual Address Mode	NOTES: Real Address Mode or Virtual 8086 Mode	NOTES: Protected Virtual Address Mode
INTERRUPT INSTRUCTIONS					
INT = Interrupt:					
Type Specified	11001101 | type	37		b	
Type 3	11001100	33		b	
INTO = Interrupt 4 if Overflow Flag Set	11001110				
If OF = 1		35		b, e	
If OF = 0		3	3	b, e	
Bound = Interrupt 5 if Detect Value Out of Range	01100010 | mod reg r/m				
If Out of Range		44		b, e	e, g, h, j, k, r
If In Range		10	10	b, e	e, g, h, j, k, r
Protected Mode Only (INT)					
INT: Type Specified					
Via Interrupt or Trap Gate to Same Privilege Level			59		g, j, k, r
Via Interrupt or Trap Gate to Different Privilege Level			99		g, j, k, r
From 80286 Task to 80286 TSS via Task Gate			282		g, j, k, r
From 80286 Task to 386DX™ CPU TSS via Task Gate			309		g, j, k, r
From 80286 Task to virt 8086 md via Task Gate			226		g, j, k, r
From 386DX™ CPU Task to 80286 TSS via Task Gate			284		g, j, k, r
From 386DX™ CPU Task to 386DX™ CPU TSS via Task Gate			311		g, j, k, r
From 386DX™ CPU Task to virt 8086 md via Task Gate			228		g, j, k, r
From virt 8086 md to 80286 TSS via Task Gate			289		g, j, k, r
From virt 8086 md to 386DX™ CPU TSS via Task Gate			316		g, j, k, r
From virt 8086 md to priv level 0 via Trap Gate or Interrupt Gate			119		
INT: TYPE 3					
Via Interrupt or Trap Gate to Same Privilege Level			59		g, j, k, r
Via Interrupt or Trap Gate to Different Privilege Level			99		g, j, k, r
From 80286 Task to 80286 TSS via Task Gate			278		g, j, k, r
From 80286 Task to 386DX™ CPU TSS via Task Gate			305		g, j, k, r
From 80286 Task to Virt 8086 md via Task Gate			222		g, j, k, r
From 386DX™ CPU Task to 80286 TSS via Task Gate			280		g, j, k, r
From 386DX™ CPU Task to 386DX™ CPU TSS via Task Gate			307		g, j, k, r
From 386DX™ CPU Task to Virt 8086 md via Task Gate			224		g, j, k, r
From virt 8086 md to 80286 TSS via Task Gate			285		g, j, k, r
From virt 8086 md to 386DX™ CPU TSS via Task Gate			312		g, j, k, r
From virt 8086 md to priv level 0 via Trap Gate or Interrupt Gate			119		
INTO:					
Via Interrupt or Trap Grate to Same Privilege Level			59		g, j, k, r
Via Interrupt or Trap Gate to Different Privilege Level			99		g, j, k, r
From 80286 Task to 80286 TSS via Task Gate			280		g, j, k, r
From 80286 Task to 386DX™ CPU TSS via Task Gate			307		g, j, k, r
From 80286 Task to virt 8086 md via Task Gate			224		g, j, k, r
From 386DX™ CPU Task to 80286 TSS via Task Gate			282		g, j, k, r
From 386DX™ CPU Task to 386DX™ CPU TSS via Task Gate			309		g, j, k, r
From 386DX™ CPU Task to virt 8086 md via Task Gate			225		g, j, k, r
From virt 8086 md to 80286 TSS via Task Gate			287		g, j, k, r
From virt 8086 md to 386DX™ CPU TSS via Task Gate			314		g, j, k, r
From virt 8086 md to priv level 0 via Trap Gate or Interrupt Gate			119		

Table 6-1. 386 DX™ Microprocessor Instruction Set Clock Count Summary (contd.)

INSTRUCTION	FORMAT			CLOCK COUNT		NOTES	
				Real Address Mode or Virtual 8086 Mode	Protected Virtual Address Mode	Real Address Mode or Virtual 8086 Mode	Protected Virtual Address Mode
INTERRUPT INSTRUCTIONS (Continued)							
BOUND:							
Via Interrupt or Trap Gate to Same Privilege Level					59		g, j, k, r
Via Interrupt or Trap Gate to Different Privilege Level					99		g, j, k, r
From 80286 Task to 80286 TSS via Task Gate					254		g, j, k, r
From 80286 Task to 386DX™ CPU TSS via Task Gate					284		g, j, k, r
From 80268 Task to virt 8086 Mode via Task Gate					231		g, j, k, r
From 386DX™ CPU Task to 80286 TSS via Task Gate					264		g, j, k, r
From 386DX™ CPU Task to 386DX™ CPU TSS via Task Gate					294		g, j, k, r
From 80368 Task to virt 8086 Mode via Task Gate					243		g, j, k, r,
From virt 8086 Mode to 80286 TSS via Task Gate					264		g, j, k, r
From virt 8086 Mode to 386DX™ CPU TSS via Task Gate					294		g, j, k, r
From virt 8086 md to priv level 0 via Trap Gate or Interrupt Gate					119		
INTERRUPT RETURN							
IRET = Interrupt Return	11001111			22			g, h, j, k, r
Protected Mode Only (IRET)							
To the Same Privilege Level (within task)					38		g, h, j, k, r
To Different Privilege Level (within task)					82		g, h, j, k, r
From 80286 Task to 80286 TSS					232		h, j, k, r
From 80286 Task to 386DX™ CPU TSS					265		h, j, k, r
From 80286 Task to Virtual 8086 Task					213		h, j, k, r
From 80286 Task to Virtual 8086 Mode (within task)					60		
From 386DX™ CPU Task to 80286 TSS					271		h, j, k, r
From 386DX™ CPU Task to 386DX™ CPU TSS					275		h, j, k, r
From 386DX™ CPU Task to Virtual 8086 Task					223		h, j, k, r
From 386DX™ CPU Task to Virtual 8086 Mode (within task)					60		
PROCESSOR CONTROL							
HLT = HALT	11110100			5	5		l
MOV = Move to and From Control/Debug/Test Registers							
CR0/CR2/CR3 from register	00001111	00100010	11 eee reg	11/4/5	11/4/5		l
Register From CR0–3	00001111	00100000	11 eee reg	6	6		l
DR0–3 From Register	00001111	00100011	11 eee reg	22	22		l
DR6–7 From Register	00001111	00100011	11 eee reg	16	16		l
Register from DR6–7	00001111	00100001	11 eee reg	14	14		l
Register from DR0–3	00001111	00100001	11 eee reg	22	22		l
TR6–7 from Register	00001111	00100110	11 eee reg	12	12		l
Register from TR6–7	00001111	00100100	11 eee reg	12	12		l
NOP = No Operation	10010000			3	3		
WAIT = Wait until BUSY# pin is negated	10011011			7	7		

Table 6-1. 386 DX™ Microprocessor Instruction Set Clock Count Summary (contd.)

INSTRUCTION	FORMAT			CLOCK COUNT: Real Address Mode or Virtual 8086 Mode	CLOCK COUNT: Protected Virtual Address Mode	NOTES: Real Address Mode or Virtual 8086 Mode	NOTES: Protected Virtual Address Mode
PROCESSOR EXTENSION INSTRUCTIONS							
Processor Extension Escape	11011TTT	mod LLL r/m		See 80287/80387 data sheets for clock counts			h
	TTT and LLL bits are opcode information for coprocessor.						
PREFIX BYTES							
Address Size Prefix	01100111			0	0		
LOCK = Bus Lock Prefix	11110000			0	0		m
Operand Size Prefix	01100110			0	0		
Segment Override Prefix							
CS:	00101110			0	0		
DS:	00111110			0	0		
ES:	00100110			0	0		
FS:	01100100			0	0		
GS:	01100101			0	0		
SS:	00110110			0	0		
PROTECTION CONTROL							
ARPL = Adjust Requested Privilege Level							
From Register/Memory	01100011	mod reg r/m		N/A	20/21	a	h
LAR = Load Access Rights							
From Register/Memory	00001111	00000010	mod reg r/m	N/A	15/16	a	g, h, j, p
LGDT = Load Global Descriptor Table Register	00001111	00000001	mod 010 r/m	11	11	b, c	h, l
LIDT = Load Interrupt Descriptor Table Register	00001111	00000001	mod 011 r/m	11	11	b, c	h, l
LLDT = Load Local Descriptor							
Table Register to Register/Memory	00001111	00000000	mod 010 r/m	N/A	20/24	a	g, h, j, l
LMSW = Load Machine Status Word							
From Register/Memory	00001111	00000001	mod 110 r/m	11/14	11/14	b, c	h, l
LSL = Load Segment Limit							
From Register/Memory	00001111	00000011	mod reg r/m				
Byte-Granular Limit				N/A	21/22	a	g, h, j, p
Page-Granular Limit				N/A	25/26	a	g, h, j, p
LTR = Load Task Register							
From Register/Memory	00001111	00000000	mod 001 r/m	N/A	23/27	a	g, h, j, l
SGDT = Store Global Descriptor Table Register	00001111	00000001	mod 000 r/m	9	9	b, c	h
SIDT = Store Interrupt Descriptor Table Register	00001111	00000001	mod 001 r/m	9	9	b, c	h
SLDT = Store Local Descriptor Table Register							
To Register/Memory	00001111	00000000	mod 000 r/m	N/A	2/2	a	h

Table 6-1. 386 DX™ Microprocessor Instruction Set Clock Count Summary (contd.)

INSTRUCTION	FORMAT			CLOCK COUNT: Real Address Mode or Virtual 8086 Mode	CLOCK COUNT: Protected Virtual Address Mode	NOTES: Real Address Mode or Virtual 8086 Mode	NOTES: Protected Virtual Address Mode
SMSW = **Store Machine Status Word**	00001111	00000001	mod 100 r/m	2/2	2/2	b, c	h, l
STR = **Store Task Register**							
To Register/Memory	00001111	00000000	mod 001 r/m	N/A	2/2	a	h
VERR = **Verify Read Access**							
Register/Memory	00001111	00000000	mod 100 r/m	N/A	10/11	a	g, h, j, p
VERW = **Verify Write Access**	00001111	00000000	mod 101 r/m	N/A	15/16	a	g, h, j, p

INSTRUCTION NOTES FOR TABLE 6-1

Notes a through c apply to 386DX Microprocessor Real Address Mode only:

a. This is a Protected Mode instruction. Attempted execution in Real Mode will result in exception 6 (invalid opcode).

b. Exception 13 fault (general protection) will occur in Real Mode if an operand reference is made that partially or fully extends beyond the maximum CS, DS, ES, FS or GS limit, FFFFH. Exception 12 fault (stack segment limit violation or not present) will occur in Real Mode if an operand reference is made that partially or fully extends beyond the maximum SS limit.

c. This instruction may be executed in Real Mode. In Real Mode, its purpose is primarily to initialize the CPU for Protected Mode.

Notes d through g apply to 386DX Microprocessor Real Address Mode and 386DX Microprocessor Protected Virtual Address Mode:

d. The 386DX Microprocessor uses an early-out multiply algorithm. The actual number of clocks depends on the position of the most significant bit in the operand (multiplier).

Clock counts given are minimum to maximum. To calculate actual clocks use the following formula:

Actual Clock = if $m < > 0$ then max $([\log_2 |m|], 3) + b$ clocks:

if $m = 0$ then $3 + b$ clocks

In this formula, m is the multiplier, and

$b = 9$ for register to register,

$b = 12$ for memory to register,

$b = 10$ for register with immediate to register,

$b = 11$ for memory with immediate to register.

e. An exception may occur, depending on the value of the operand.

f. LOCK# is automatically asserted, regardless of the presence or absence of the LOCK# prefix.

g. LOCK# is asserted during descriptor table accesses.

Notes h through r apply to 386DX Microprocessor Protected Virtual Address Mode only:

h. Exception 13 fault (general protection violation) will occur if the memory operand in CS, DS, ES, FS or GS cannot be used due to either a segment limit violation or access rights violation. If a stack limit is violated, an exception 12 (stack segment limit violation or not present) occurs.

i. For segment load operations, the CPL, RPL, and DPL must agree with the privilege rules to avoid an exception 13 fault (general protection violation). The segment's descriptor must indicate "present" or exception 11 (CS, DS, ES, FS, GS not present). If the SS register is loaded and a stack segment not present is detected, an exception 12 (stack segment limit violation or not present) occurs.

j. All segment descriptor accesses in the GDT or LDT made by this instruction will automatically assert LOCK# to maintain descriptor integrity in multiprocessor systems.

k. JMP, CALL, INT, RET and IRET instructions referring to another code segment will cause an exception 13 (general protection violation) if an applicable privilege rule is violated.

l. An exception 13 fault occurs if CPL is greater than 0 (0 is the most privileged level).

m. An exception 13 fault occurs if CPL is greater than IOPL.

n. The IF bit of the flag register is not updated if CPL is greater than IOPL. The IOPL and VM fields of the flag register are updated only if CPL = 0.

o. The PE bit of the MSW (CR0) cannot be reset by this instruction. Use MOV into CR0 if desiring to reset the PE bit.

p. Any violation of privilege rules as applied to the selector operand does not cause a protection exception; rather, the zero flag is cleared.

q. If the coprocessor's memory operand violates a segment limit or segment access rights, an exception 13 fault (general protection exception) will occur before the ESC instruction is executed. An exception 12 fault (stack segment limit violation or not present) will occur if the stack limit is violated by the operand's starting address.

r. The destination of a JMP, CALL, INT, RET or IRET must be in the defined limit of a code segment or an exception 13 fault (general protection violation) will occur.

6.2 INSTRUCTION ENCODING

6.2.1 Overview

All instruction encodings are subsets of the general instruction format shown in Figure 6-1. Instructions consist of one or two primary opcode bytes, possibly an address specifier consisting of the "mod r/m" byte and "scaled index" byte, a displacement if required, and an immediate data field if required.

Within the primary opcode or opcodes, smaller encoding fields may be defined. These fields vary according to the class of operation. The fields define such information as direction of the operation, size of the displacements, register encoding, or sign extension.

Almost all instructions referring to an operand in memory have an addressing mode byte following the primary opcode byte(s). This byte, the mod r/m byte, specifies the address mode to be used. Certain encodings of the mod r/m byte indicate a second addressing byte, the scale-index-base byte, follows the mod r/m byte to fully specify the addressing mode.

Addressing modes can include a displacement immediately following the mod r/m byte, or scaled index byte. If a displacement is present, the possible sizes are 8, 16 or 32 bits.

If the instruction specifies an immediate operand, the immediate operand follows any displacement bytes. The immediate operand, if specified, is always the last field of the instruction.

Figure 6-1 illustrates several of the fields that can appear in an instruction, such as the mod field and the r/m field, but the Figure does not show all fields. Several smaller fields also appear in certain instructions, sometimes within the opcode bytes themselves. Table 6-2 is a complete list of all fields appearing in the 386DX Microprocessor instruction set. Further ahead, following Table 6-2, are detailed tables for each field.

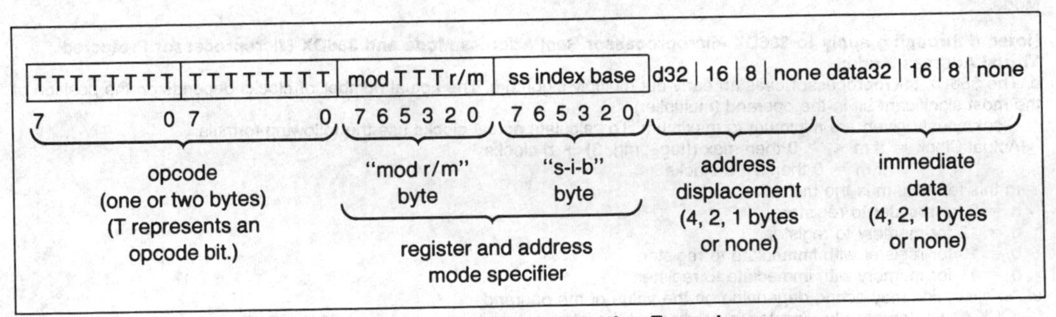

Figure 6-1. General Instruction Format

Table 6-2. Fields within 386 DX™ Microprocessor Instructions

Field Name	Description	Number of Bits
w	Specifies if Data is Byte or Full Size (Full Size is either 16 or 32 Bits	1
d	Specifies Direction of Data Operation	1
s	Specifies if an Immediate Data Field Must be Sign-Extended	1
reg	General Register Specifier	3
mod r/m	Address Mode Specifier (Effective Address can be a General Register)	2 for mod; 3 for r/m
ss	Scale Factor for Scaled Index Address Mode	2
index	General Register to be used as Index Register	3
base	General Register to be used as Base Register	3
sreg2	Segment Register Specifier for CS, SS, DS, ES	2
sreg3	Segment Register Specifier for CS, SS, DS, ES, FS, GS	3
tttn	For Conditional Instructions, Specifies a Condition Asserted or a Condition Negated	4

Note: Table 6-1 shows encoding of individual instructions.

6.2.2 32-Bit Extensions of the Instruction Set

With the 386DX Microprocessor, the 8086/80186/80286 instruction set is extended in two orthogonal directions: 32-bit forms of all 16-bit instructions are added to support the 32-bit data types, and 32-bit addressing modes are made available for all instructions referencing memory. This orthogonal instruction set extension is accomplished having a Default (D) bit in the code segment descriptor, and by having 2 prefixes to the instruction set.

Whether the instruction defaults to operations of 16 bits or 32 bits depends on the setting of the D bit in the code segment descriptor, which gives the default length (either 32 bits or 16 bits) for both operands and effective addresses when executing that code segment. In the Real Address Mode or Virtual 8086 Mode, no code segment descriptors are used, but a D value of 0 is assumed internally by the 386DX Microprocessor when operating in those modes (for 16-bit default sizes compatible with the 8086/80186/80286).

Two prefixes, the Operand Size Prefix and the Effective Address Size Prefix, allow overriding individually the Default selection of operand size and effective address size. These prefixes may precede any opcode bytes and affect only the instruction they precede. If necessary, one or both of the prefixes may be placed before the opcode bytes. The presence of the Operand Size Prefix and the Effective Address Prefix will toggle the operand size or the effective address size, respectively, to the value "opposite" from the Default setting. For example, if the default operand size is for 32-bit data operations, then presence of the Operand Size Prefix toggles the instruction to 16-bit data operation. As another example, if the default effective address size is 16 bits, presence of the Effective Address Size prefix toggles the instruction to use 32-bit effective address computations.

These 32-bit extensions are available in all 386DX Microprocessor modes, including the Real Address Mode or the Virtual 8086 Mode. In these modes the default is always 16 bits, so prefixes are needed to specify 32-bit operands or addresses. For instructions with more than one prefix, the order of prefixes is unimportant.

Unless specified otherwise, instructions with 8-bit and 16-bit operands do not affect the contents of the high-order bits of the extended registers.

6.2.3 Encoding of Instruction Fields

Within the instruction are several fields indicating register selection, addressing mode and so on. The exact encodings of these fields are defined immediately ahead.

6.2.3.1 ENCODING OF OPERAND LENGTH (w) FIELD

For any given instruction performing a data operation, the instruction is executing as a 32-bit operation or a 16-bit operation. Within the constraints of the operation size, the w field encodes the operand size as either one byte or the full operation size, as shown in the table below.

w Field	Operand Size During 16-Bit Data Operations	Operand Size During 32-Bit Data Operations
0	8 Bits	8 Bits
1	16 Bits	32 Bits

6.2.3.2 ENCODING OF THE GENERAL REGISTER (reg) FIELD

The general register is specified by the reg field, which may appear in the primary opcode bytes, or as the reg field of the "mod r/m" byte, or as the r/m field of the "mod r/m" byte.

Encoding of reg Field When w Field is not Present in Instruction

reg Field	Register Selected During 16-Bit Data Operations	Register Selected During 32-Bit Data Operations
000	AX	EAX
001	CX	ECX
010	DX	EDX
011	BX	EBX
100	SP	ESP
101	BP	EBP
101	SI	ESI
101	DI	EDI

Encoding of reg Field When w Field is Present in Instruction

reg	Register Specified by reg Field During 16-Bit Data Operations:	
	Function of w Field	
	(when w = 0)	(when w = 1)
000	AL	AX
001	CL	CX
010	DL	DX
011	BL	BX
100	AH	SP
101	CH	BP
110	DH	SI
111	BH	DI

Register Specified by reg Field During 32-Bit Data Operations		
reg	Function of w Field	
	(when w = 0)	(when w = 1)
000	AL	EAX
001	CL	ECX
010	DL	EDX
011	BL	EBX
100	AH	ESP
101	CH	EBP
110	DH	ESI
111	BH	EDI

6.2.3.3 ENCODING OF THE SEGMENT REGISTER (sreg) FIELD

The sreg field in certain instructions is a 2-bit field allowing one of the four 80286 segment registers to be specified. The sreg field in other instructions is a 3-bit field, allowing the 386DX Microprocessor FS and GS segment registers to be specified.

2-Bit sreg2 Field

2-Bit sreg2 Field	Segment Register Selected
00	ES
01	CS
10	SS
11	DS

3-Bit sreg3 Field

3-Bit sreg3 Field	Segment Register Selected
000	ES
001	CS
010	SS
011	DS
100	FS
101	GS
110	do not use
111	do not use

6.2.3.4 ENCODING OF ADDRESS MODE

Except for special instructions, such as PUSH or POP, where the addressing mode is pre-determined, the addressing mode for the current instruction is specified by addressing bytes following the primary opcode. The primary addressing byte is the "mod r/m" byte, and a second byte of addressing information, the "s-i-b" (scale-index-base) byte, can be specified.

The s-i-b byte (scale-index-base byte) is specified when using 32-bit addressing mode and the "mod r/m" byte has r/m = 100 and mod = 00, 01 or 10. When the sib byte is present, the 32-bit addressing mode is a function of the mod, ss, index, and base fields.

The primary addressing byte, the "mod r/m" byte, also contains three bits (shown as TTT in Figure 6-1) sometimes used as an extension of the primary opcode. The three bits, however, may also be used as a register field (reg).

When calculating an effective address, either 16-bit addressing or 32-bit addressing is used. 16-bit addressing uses 16-bit address components to calculate the effective address while 32-bit addressing uses 32-bit address components to calculate the effective address. When 16-bit addressing is used, the "mod r/m" byte is interpreted as a 16-bit addressing mode specifier. When 32-bit addressing is used, the "mod r/m" byte is interpreted as a 32-bit addressing mode specifier.

Tables on the following three pages define all encodings of all 16-bit addressing modes and 32-bit addressing modes.

Encoding of 16-bit Address Mode with "mod r/m" Byte

mod r/m	Effective Address
00 000	DS:[BX+SI]
00 001	DS:[BX+DI]
00 010	SS:[BP+SI]
00 011	SS:[BP+DI]
00 100	DS:[SI]
00 101	DS:[DI]
00 110	DS:d16
00 111	DS:[BX]
01 000	DS:[BX+SI+d8]
01 001	DS:[BX+DI+d8]
01 010	SS:[BP+SI+d8]
01 011	SS:[BP+DI+d8]
01 100	DS:[SI+d8]
01 101	DS:[DI+d8]
01 110	SS:[BP+d8]
01 111	DS:[BX+d8]

mod r/m	Effective Address
10 000	DS:[BX+SI+d16]
10 001	DS:[BX+DI+d16]
10 010	SS:[BP+SI+d16]
10 011	SS:[BP+DI+d16]
10 100	DS:[SI+d16]
10 101	DS:[DI+d16]
10 110	SS:[BP+d16]
10 111	DS:[BX+d16]
11 000	register—see below
11 001	register—see below
11 010	register—see below
11 011	register—see below
11 100	register—see below
11 101	register—see below
11 110	register—see below
11 111	register—see below

Register Specified by r/m During 16-Bit Data Operations

mod r/m	Function of w Field	
	(when w=0)	(when w =1)
11 000	AL	AX
11 001	CL	CX
11 010	DL	DX
11 011	BL	BX
11 100	AH	SP
11 101	CH	BP
11 110	DH	SI
11 111	BH	DI

Register Specified by r/m During 32-Bit Data Operations

mod r/m	Function of w Field	
	(when w=0)	(when w =1)
11 000	AL	EAX
11 001	CL	ECX
11 010	DL	EDX
11 011	BL	EBX
11 100	AH	ESP
11 101	CH	EBP
11 110	DH	ESI
11 111	BH	EDI

Encoding of 32-bit Address Mode with "mod r/m" byte (no "s-i-b" byte present):

mod r/m	Effective Address
00 000	DS:[EAX]
00 001	DS:[ECX]
00 010	DS:[EDX]
00 011	DS:[EBX]
00 100	s-i-b is present
00 101	DS:d32
00 110	DS:[ESI]
00 111	DS:[EDI]
01 000	DS:[EAX + d8]
01 001	DS:[ECX + d8]
01 010	DS:[EDX + d8]
01 011	DS:[EBX + d8]
01 100	s-i-b is present
01 101	SS:[EBP + d8]
01 110	DS:[ESI + d8]
01 111	DS:[EDI + d8]

mod r/m	Effective Address
10 000	DS:[EAX + d32]
10 001	DS:[ECX + d32]
10 010	DS:[EDX + d32]
10 011	DS:[EBX + d32]
10 100	s-i-b is present
10 101	SS:[EBP + d32]
10 110	DS:[ESI + d32]
10 111	DS:[EDI + d32]
11 000	register—see below
11 001	register—see below
11 010	register—see below
11 011	register—see below
11 100	register—see below
11 101	register—see below
11 110	register—see below
11 111	register—see below

Register Specified by reg or r/m during 16-Bit Data Operations:

mod r/m	function of w field	
	(when w = 0)	(when w = 1)
11 000	AL	AX
11 001	CL	CX
11 010	DL	DX
11 011	BL	BX
11 100	AH	SP
11 101	CH	BP
11 110	DH	SI
11 111	BH	DI

Register Specified by reg or r/m during 32-Bit Data Operations:

mod r/m	function of w field	
	(when w = 0)	(when w = 1)
11 000	AL	EAX
11 001	CL	ECX
11 010	DL	EDX
11 011	BL	EBX
11 100	AH	ESP
11 101	CH	EBP
11 110	DH	ESI
11 111	BH	EDI

Encoding of 32-bit Address Mode ("mod r/m" byte and "s-i-b" byte present):

mod base	Effective Address
00 000	DS:[EAX + (scaled index)]
00 001	DS:[ECX + (scaled index)]
00 010	DS:[EDX + (scaled index)]
00 011	DS:[EBX + (scaled index)]
00 100	SS:[ESP + (scaled index)]
00 101	DS:[d32 + (scaled index)]
00 110	DS:[ESI + (scaled index)]
00 111	DS:[EDI + (scaled index)]
01 000	DS:[EAX + (scaled index) + d8]
01 001	DS:[ECX + (scaled index) + d8]
01 010	DS:[EDX + (scaled index) + d8]
01 011	DS:[EBX + (scaled index) + d8]
01 100	SS:[ESP + (scaled index) + d8]
01 101	SS:[EBP + (scaled index) + d8]
01 110	DS:[ESI + (scaled index) + d8]
01 111	DS:[EDI + (scaled index) + d8]
10 000	DS:[EAX + (scaled index) + d32]
10 001	DS:[ECX + (scaled index) + d32]
10 010	DS:[EDX + (scaled index) + d32]
10 011	DS:[EBX + (scaled index) + d32]
10 100	SS:[ESP + (scaled index) + d32]
10 101	SS:[EBP + (scaled index) + d32]
10 110	DS:[ESI + (scaled index) + d32]
10 111	DS:[EDI + (scaled index) + d32]

NOTE:
Mod field in "mod r/m" byte; ss, index, base fields in "s-i-b" byte.

ss	Scale Factor
00	x1
01	x2
10	x4
11	x8

index	Index Register
000	EAX
001	ECX
010	EDX
011	EBX
100	no index reg**
101	EBP
110	ESI
111	EDI

****IMPORTANT NOTE:**
When index field is 100, indicating "no index register," then ss field MUST equal 00. If index is 100 and ss does not equal 00, the effective address is undefined.

6.2.3.5 ENCODING OF OPERATION DIRECTION (d) FIELD

In many two-operand instructions the d field is present to indicate which operand is considered the source and which is the destination.

d	Direction of Operation
0	Register/Memory <- - Register "reg" Field Indicates Source Operand; "mod r/m" or "mod ss index base" Indicates Destination Operand
1	Register <- - Register/Memory "reg" Field Indicates Destination Operand; "mod r/m" or "mod ss index base" Indicates Source Operand

6.2.3.6 ENCODING OF SIGN-EXTEND (s) FIELD

The s field occurs primarily to instructions with immediate data fields. The s field has an effect only if the size of the immediate data is 8 bits and is being placed in a 16-bit or 32-bit destination.

s	Effect on Immediate Data8	Effect on Immediate Data 16|32
0	None	None
1	Sign-Extend Data8 to Fill 16-Bit or 32-Bit Destination	None

6.2.3.7 ENCODING OF CONDITIONAL TEST (tttn) FIELD

For the conditional instructions (conditional jumps and set on condition), tttn is encoded with n indicating to use the condition (n=0) or its negation (n=1), and ttt giving the condition to test.

Mnemonic	Condition	tttn
O	Overflow	0000
NO	No Overflow	0001
B/NAE	Below/Not Above or Equal	0010
NB/AE	Not Below/Above or Equal	0011
E/Z	Equal/Zero	0100
NE/NZ	Not Equal/Not Zero	0101
BE/NA	Below or Equal/Not Above	0110
NBE/A	Not Below or Equal/Above	0111
S	Sign	1000
NS	Not Sign	1001
P/PE	Parity/Parity Even	1010
NP/PO	Not Parity/Parity Odd	1011
L/NGE	Less Than/Not Greater or Equal	1100
NL/GE	Not Less Than/Greater or Equal	1101
LE/NG	Less Than or Equal/Greater Than	1110
NLE/G	Not Less or Equal/Greater Than	1111

6.2.3.8 ENCODING OF CONTROL OR DEBUG OR TEST REGISTER (eee) FIELD

For the loading and storing of the Control, Debug and Test registers.

When Interpreted as Control Register Field

eee Code	Reg Name
000	CR0
010	CR2
011	CR3
Do not use any other encoding	

When Interpreted as Debug Register Field

eee Code	Reg Name
000	DR0
001	DR1
010	DR2
011	DR3
110	DR6
111	DR7
Do not use any other encoding	

When Interpreted as Test Register Field

eee Code	Reg Name
110	TR6
111	TR7
Do not use any other encoding	

DOMESTIC SALES OFFICES

ALABAMA

†Intel Corp.
5015 Bradford Dr., #2
Huntsville 35805
Tel: (205) 830-4010
FAX: (205) 837-2640

ARIZONA

†Intel Corp.
11225 N. 28th Dr.
Suite D-214
Phoenix 85029
Tel: (602) 869-4980
FAX: (602) 869-4294

Intel Corp.
1161 N. El Dorado Place
Suite 301
Tucson 85715
Tel: (602) 299-6815
FAX: (602) 296-8234

CALIFORNIA

†Intel Corp.
21515 Vanowen Street
Suite 116
Canoga Park 91303
Tel: (818) 704-8500
FAX: (818) 340-1144

†Intel Corp.
2250 E. Imperial Highway
Suite 218
El Segundo 90245
Tel: (213) 640-6040
FAX: (213) 640-7133

Intel Corp.
1510 Arden Way
Suite 101
Sacramento 95815
Tel: (916) 920-8096
FAX: (916) 920-8253

†Intel Corp.
9665 Chesapeake Dr.
Suite 325
San Diego 95123
Tel: (619) 292-8086
FAX: (619) 292-0628

†Intel Corp.*
400 N. Tustin Avenue
Suite 450
Santa Ana 92705
Tel: (714) 835-9642
TWX: 910-595-1114
FAX: (714) 541-9157

†Intel Corp.*
San Tomas 4
2700 San Tomas Expressway
2nd Floor
Santa Clara 95051
Tel: (408) 986-8086
TWX: 910-338-0255
FAX: (408) 727-2620

COLORADO

Intel Corp.
4445 Northpark Drive
Suite 100
Colorado Springs 80907
Tel: (719) 594-6622
FAX: (303) 594-0720

†Intel Corp.*
650 S. Cherry St.
Suite 915
Denver 80222
Tel: (303) 321-8086
TWX: 910-931-2289
FAX: (303) 322-8670

CONNECTICUT

†Intel Corp.
301 Lee Farm Corporate Park
83 Wooster Heights Rd.
Danbury 06810
Tel: (203) 748-3130
FAX: (203) 794-0339

FLORIDA

†Intel Corp.
6363 N.W. 6th Way
Suite 100
Ft. Lauderdale 33309
Tel: (305) 771-0600
TWX: 510-956-9407
FAX: (305) 772-8193

†Intel Corp.
5850 T.G. Lee Blvd.
Suite 340
Orlando 32822
Tel: (407) 240-8000
FAX: (407) 240-8097

Intel Corp.
11300 4th Street North
Suite 170
St. Petersburg 33716
Tel: (813) 577-2413
FAX: (813) 578-1607

GEORGIA

Intel Corp.
20 Technology Parkway, N.W.
Suite 150
Norcross 30092
Tel: (404) 449-0541
FAX: (404) 605-9762

ILLINOIS

†Intel Corp.*
300 N. Martingale Road
Suite 400
Schaumburg 60173
Tel: (312) 605-8031
FAX: (312) 706-9762

INDIANA

†Intel Corp.
8777 Purdue Road
Suite 125
Indianapolis 46268
Tel: (317) 875-0623
FAX: (317) 875-8938

IOWA

Intel Corp.
1930 St. Andrews Drive N.E.
2nd Floor
Cedar Rapids 52402
Tel: (319) 393-1294

KANSAS

†Intel Corp.
10985 Cody St.
Suite 140, Bldg. D
Overland Park 66210
Tel: (913) 345-2727
FAX: (913) 345-2076

MARYLAND

†Intel Corp.*
10010 Junction Dr.
Suite 200
Annapolis Junction 20701
Tel: (301) 206-2860
FAX: (301) 206-3677
(301) 206-3678

MASSACHUSETTS

†Intel Corp.*
Westford Corp. Center
3 Carlisle Road
2nd Floor
Westford 01886
Tel: (508) 692-3222
TWX: 710-343-6333
FAX: (508) 692-7867

MICHIGAN

†Intel Corp.
7071 Orchard Lake Road
Suite 100
West Bloomfield 48322
Tel: (313) 851-8096
FAX: (313) 851-8770

MINNESOTA

†Intel Corp.
3500 W. 80th St.
Suite 360
Bloomington 55431
Tel: (612) 835-6722
TWX: 910-576-2867
FAX: (612) 831-6497

MISSOURI

†Intel Corp.
4203 Earth City Expressway
Suite 131
Earth City 63045
Tel: (314) 291-1990
FAX: (314) 291-4341

NEW JERSEY

†Intel Corp.*
Parkway 109 Office Center
328 Newman Springs Road
Red Bank 07701
Tel: (201) 747-2233
FAX: (201) 747-0983

†Intel Corp.
280 Corporate Center
75 Livingston Avenue
First Floor
Roseland 07068
Tel: (201) 740-0111
FAX: (201) 740-0626

NEW YORK

Intel Corp.*
850 Cross Keys Office Park
Fairport 14450
Tel: (716) 425-2750
TWX: 510-253-7391
FAX: (716) 223-2561

†Intel Corp.*
2950 Expressway Dr., South
Suite 130
Islandia 11722
Tel: (516) 231-3300
TWX: 510-227-6236
FAX: (516) 348-7939

†Intel Corp.
Westage Business Center
Bldg. 300, Route 9
Fishkill 12524
Tel: (914) 897-3860
FAX: (914) 897-3125

NORTH CAROLINA

†Intel Corp.
5800 Executive Center Dr.
Suite 105
Charlotte 28212
Tel: (704) 568-8966
FAX: (704) 535-2236

Intel Corp.
5540 Centerview Dr.
Suite 215
Raleigh 27606
Tel: (919) 851-9537
FAX: (919) 851-8974

OHIO

†Intel Corp.*
3401 Park Center Drive
Suite 220
Dayton 45414
Tel: (513) 890-5350
TWX: 810-450-2528
FAX: (513) 890-8658

†Intel Corp.*
25700 Science Park Dr.
Suite 100
Beachwood 44122
Tel: (216) 464-2736
TWX: 810-427-9298
FAX: (804) 282-0673

OKLAHOMA

Intel Corp.
6801 N. Broadway
Suite 115
Oklahoma City 73162
Tel: (405) 848-8086
FAX: (405) 840-9819

OREGON

†Intel Corp.
15254 N.W. Greenbrier Parkway
Building B
Beaverton 97005
Tel: (503) 645-8051
TWX: 910-467-8741
FAX: (503) 645-8181

PENNSYLVANIA

†Intel Corp.*
455 Pennsylvania Avenue
Suite 230
Fort Washington 19034
Tel: (215) 641-1000
TWX: 510-661-2077
FAX: (215) 641-0785

†Intel Corp.*
400 Penn Center Blvd.
Suite 610
Pittsburgh 15235
Tel: (412) 823-4970
FAX: (412) 829-7578

PUERTO RICO

†Intel Corp.
South Industrial Park
P.O. Box 910
Las Piedras 00671
Tel: (809) 733-8616

TEXAS

Intel Corp.
8911 Capital of Texas Hwy.
Austin 78759
Tel: (512) 794-8086
FAX: (512) 338-9335

†Intel Corp.*
12000 Ford Road
Suite 400
Dallas 75234
Tel: (214) 241-8087
FAX: (214) 484-1180

†Intel Corp.*
7322 S.W. Freeway
Suite 1490
Houston 77074
Tel: (713) 988-8086
TWX: 910-881-2490
FAX: (713) 988-3660

UTAH

†Intel Corp.
428 East 6400 South
Suite 104
Murray 84107
Tel: (801) 263-8051
FAX: (801) 268-1457

VIRGINIA

†Intel Corp.
1504 Santa Rosa Road
Suite 108
Richmond 23288
Tel: (804) 282-5668
FAX: (216) 464-2270

WASHINGTON

†Intel Corp.
155 108th Avenue N.E.
Suite 386
Bellevue 98004
Tel: (206) 453-8086
TWX: 910-443-3002
FAX: (206) 451-9556

Intel Corp.
408 N. Mullan Road
Suite 102
Spokane 99206
Tel: (509) 928-8086
FAX: (509) 928-9467

WISCONSIN

Intel Corp.
330 S. Executive Dr.
Suite 102
Brookfield 53005
Tel: (414) 784-8087
FAX: (414) 796-2115

CANADA

BRITISH COLUMBIA

Intel Semiconductor of
Canada, Ltd.
4585 Canada Way
Suite 202
Burnaby V5G 4L6
Tel: (604) 298-0387
FAX: (604) 298-8234

ONTARIO

†Intel Semiconductor of
Canada, Ltd.
2650 Queensview Drive
Suite 250
Ottawa K2B 8H6
Tel: (613) 829-9714
FAX: (613) 820-5936

†Intel Semiconductor of
Canada, Ltd.
190 Attwell Drive
Suite 500
Rexdale M9W 6H8
Tel: (416) 675-2105
FAX: (416) 675-2438

QUEBEC

Intel Semiconductor of
Canada, Ltd.
620 St. Jean Boulevard
Pointe Claire H9R 3K2
Tel: (514) 694-9130
FAX: 514-694-0064

†Sales and Service Office
*Field Application Location

DOMESTIC DISTRIBUTORS

ALABAMA

Arrow Electronics, Inc.
1015 Henderson Road
Huntsville 35805
Tel: (205) 837-6955

†Hamilton/Avnet Electronics
4940 Research Drive
Huntsville 35805
Tel: (205) 837-7210
TWX: 810-726-2162

Pioneer/Technologies Group, Inc.
4825 University Square
Huntsville 35805
Tel: (205) 837-9300
TWX: 810-726-2197

ARIZONA

†Hamilton/Avnet Electronics
505 S. Madison Drive
Tempe 85281
Tel: (602) 231-5140
TWX: 910-950-0077

Hamilton/Avnet Electronics
30 South McKiemy
Chandler 85226
Tel: (602) 961-6669
TWX: 910-950-0077

Arrow Electronics, Inc.
4134 E. Wood Street
Phoenix 85040
Tel: (602) 437-0750
TWX: 910-951-1550

Wyle Distribution Group
17855 N. Black Canyon Hwy.
Phoenix 85023
Tel: (602) 249-2232
TWX: 910-951-4282

CALIFORNIA

Arrow Electronics, Inc.
10824 Hope Street
Cypress 90630
Tel: (714) 220-6300

Arrow Electronics, Inc.
19748 Dearborn Street
Chatsworth 91311
Tel: (213) 701-7500
TWX: 910-493-2086

†Arow Electronics, Inc.
521 Weddell Drive
Sunnyvale 94086
Tel: (408) 745-6600
TWX: 910-339-9371

Arrow Electronics, Inc.
9511 Ridgehaven Court
San Diego 92123
Tel: (619) 565-4800
TWX: 888-064

†Arrow Electronics, Inc.
2961 Dow Avenue
Tustin 92680
Tel: (714) 838-5422
TWX: 910-595-2860

†Avnet Electronics
350 McCormick Avenue
Costa Mesa 92626
Tel: (714) 754-6071
TWX: 910-595-1928

†Hamilton/Avnet Electronics
1175 Bordeaux Drive
Sunnyvale 94086
Tel: (408) 743-3300
TWX: 910-339-9332

†Hamilton/Avnet Electronics
4545 Ridgeview Avenue
San Diego 92123
Tel: (619) 571-7500
TWX: 910-595-2638

†Hamilton/Avnet Electronics
9650 Desoto Avenue
Chatsworth 91311
Tel: (818) 700-1161

†Hamilton Electro Sales
10950 W. Washington Blvd.
Culver City 20230
Tel: (213) 558-2458
TWX: 910-340-6364

Hamilton Electro Sales
1361B West 190th Street
Gardena 90248
Tel: (213) 217-6700

†Hamilton/Avnet Electronics
3002 'G' Street
Ontario 91761
Tel: (714) 989-9411

†Avnet Electronics
20501 Plummer
Chatsworth 91351
Tel: (213) 700-6271
TWX: 910-494-2207

†Hamilton Electro Sales
3170 Pullman Street
Costa Mesa 92626
Tel: (714) 641-4150
TWX: 910-595-2638

†Hamilton/Avnet Electronics
4103 Northgate Blvd.
Sacramento 95834
Tel: (916) 920-3150

Wyle Distribution Group
124 Maryland Street
El Segundo 90254
Tel: (213) 322-8100

Wyle Distribution Group
7382 Lampson Ave.
Garden Grove 92641
Tel: (714) 891-1717
TWX: 910-348-7140 or 7111

Wyle Distribution Group
11151 Sun Center Drive
Rancho Cordova 95670
Tel: (916) 638-5282

†Wyle Distribution Group
9525 Chesapeake Drive
San Diego 92123
Tel: (619) 565-9171
TWX: 910-335-1590

†Wyle Distribution Group
3000 Bowers Avenue
Santa Clara 95051
Tel: (408) 727-2500
TWX: 910-338-0296

†Wyle Distribution Group
17872 Cowan Avenue
Irvine 92714
Tel: (714) 863-9953
TWX: 910-595-1572

Wyle Distribution Group
26677 W. Agoura Rd.
Calabasas 91302
Tel: (818) 880-9000
TWX: 372-0232

COLORADO

Arrow Electronics, Inc.
7060 South Tucson Way
Englewood 80112
Tel: (303) 790-4444

†Hamilton/Avnet Electronics
8765 E. Orchard Road
Suite 708
Englewood 80111
Tel: (303) 740-1017
TWX: 910-935-0787

†Wyle Distribution Group
451 E. 124th Avenue
Thornton 80241
Tel: (303) 457-9953
TWX: 910-936-0770

CONNECTICUT

†Arrow Electronics, Inc.
12 Beaumont Road
Wallingford 06492
Tel: (203) 265-7741
TWX: 710-476-0162

Hamilton/Avnet Electronics
Commerce Industrial Park
Commerce Drive
Danbury 06810
Tel: (203) 797-2800
TWX: 710-456-9974

†Pioneer Electronics
112 Main Street
Norwalk 06851
Tel: (203) 853-1515
TWX: 710-468-3373

FLORIDA

†Arrow Electronics, Inc.
400 Fairway Drive
Suite 102
Deerfield Beach 33441
Tel: (305) 429-8200
TWX: 510-955-9456

Arrow Electronics, Inc.
37 Skyline Drive
Suite 3101
Lake Marv 32746
Tel: (407) 323-0252
TWX: 510-959-6337

†Hamilton/Avnet Electronics
6801 N.W. 15th Way
Ft. Lauderdale 33309
Tel: (305) 971-2900
TWX: 510-956-3097

†Hamilton/Avnet Electronics
3197 Tech Drive North
St. Petersburg 33702
Tel: (813) 576-3930
TWX: 810-863-0374

†Hamilton/Avnet Electronics
6947 University Boulevard
Winter Park 32792
Tel: (305) 628-3888
TWX: 810-853-0322

†Pioneer/Technologies Group, Inc.
337 S. Lake Blvd.
Alta Monte Springs 32701
Tel: (407) 834-9090
TWX: 810-853-0284

Pioneer/Technologies Group, Inc.
674 S. Military Trail
Deerfield Beach 33442
Tel: (305) 428-8877
TWX: 510-955-9653

GEORGIA

†Arrow Electronics, Inc.
3155 Northwoods Parkway
Suite A
Norcross 30071
Tel: (404) 449-8252
TWX: 810-766-0439

†Hamilton/Avnet Electronics
5825 D Peachtree Corners
Norcross 30092
Tel: (404) 447-7500
TWX: 810-766-0432

Pioneer/Technologies Group, Inc.
3100 F Northwoods Place
Norcross 30071
Tel: (404) 448-1711
TWX: 810-766-4515

ILLINOIS

Arrow Electronics, Inc.
1140 W. Thorndale
Itasca 60143
Tel: (312) 250-0500
TWX: 312-250-0916

†Hamilton/Avnet Electronics
1130 Thorndale Avenue
Bensenville 60106
Tel: (312) 860-7780
TWX: 910-227-0060

MTI Systems Sales
1100 W. Thorndale
Itasca 60143
Tel: (312) 773-2300

†Pioneer Electronics
1551 Carmen Drive
Elk Grove Village 60007
Tel: (312) 437-9680
TWX: 910-222-1834

INDIANA

†Arrow Electronics, Inc.
2495 Directors Row, Suite H
Indianapolis 46241
Tel: (317) 243-9353
TWX: 810-341-3119

Hamilton/Avnet Electronics
485 Gradle Drive
Carmel 46032
Tel: (317) 844-9333
TWX: 810-260-3966

†Pioneer Electronics
6408 Castleplace Drive
Indianapolis 46250
Tel: (317) 849-7300
TWX: 810-260-1794

IOWA

Hamilton/Avnet Electronics
915 33rd Avenue, S.W.
Cedar Rapids 52404
Tel: (319) 362-4757

KANSAS

Arrow Electronics
8208 Melrose Dr., Suite 210
Lenexa 66214
Tel: (913) 541-9542

†Hamilton/Avnet Electronics
9219 Quivera Road
Overland Park 66215
Tel: (913) 888-8900
TWX: 910-743-0005

Pioneer/Tec Gr.
10551 Lockman Rd.
Lenexa 66215
Tel: (913) 492-0500

KENTUCKY

Hamilton/Avnet Electronics
1051 D. Newton Park
Lexington 40511
Tel: (606) 259-1475

MARYLAND

Arrow Electronics, Inc.
8300 Guilford Drive
Suite H, River Center
Columbia 21046
Tel: (301) 995-0003
TWX: 710-236-9005

Hamilton/Avnet Electronics
6822 Oak Hall Lane
Columbia 21045
Tel: (301) 995-3500
TWX: 710-862-1861

†Mesa Technology Corp.
9720 Patuxent Woods Dr.
Columbia 21046
Tel: (301) 290-8150
TWX: 710-828-9702

†Pioneer/Technologies Group, Inc.
9100 Gaither Road
Gaithersburg 20877
Tel: (301) 921-0660
TWX: 710-828-0545

Arrow Electronics, Inc.
7524 Standish Place
Rockville 20855
Tel: 301-424-0244

MASSACHUSETTS

Arrow Electronics, Inc.
25 Upton Dr.
Wilmington 01887
Tel: (617) 935-5134

†Hamilton/Avnet Electronics
10D Centennial Drive
Peabody 01960
Tel: (617) 531-7430
TWX: 710-393-0382

MTI Systems Sales
83 Cambridge St.
Burlington 01813

Pioneer Electronics
44 Hartwell Avenue
Lexington 02173
Tel: (617) 861-9200
TWX: 710-326-6617

MICHIGAN

Arrow Electronics, Inc.
755 Phoenix Drive
Ann Arbor 48104
Tel: (313) 971-8220
TWX: 810-223-6020

Hamilton/Avnet Electronics
2215 29th Street S.E.
Space A5
Grand Rapids 49508
Tel: (616) 243-8805
TWX: 810-274-6921

Pioneer Electronics
4504 Broadmoor S.E.
Grand Rapids 49508
FAX: 616-698-1831

†Hamilton/Avnet Electronics
32487 Schoolcraft Road
Livonia 48150
Tel: (313) 522-4700
TWX: 810-282-8775

†Pioneer/Michigan
13485 Stamford
Livonia 48150
Tel: (313) 525-1800
TWX: 810-242-3271

MINNESOTA

†Arrow Electronics, Inc.
5230 W. 73rd Street
Edina 55435
Tel: (612) 830-1800
TWX: 910-576-3125

†Hamilton/Avnet Electronics
12400 Whitewater Drive
Minnetonka 55434
Tel: (612) 932-0600

†Pioneer Electronics
7625 Golden Triange Dr.
Suite G
Eden Prairi 55343
Tel: (612) 944-3355

MISSOURI

†Arrow Electronics, Inc.
2380 Schuetz
St. Louis 63141
Tel: (314) 567-6888
TWX: 910-764-0882

†Hamilton/Avnet Electronics
13743 Shoreline Court
Earth City 63045
Tel: (314) 344-1200
TWX: 910-762-0684

NEW HAMPSHIRE

†Arrow Electronics, Inc.
3 Perimeter Road
Manchester 03103
Tel: (603) 668-6968
TWX: 710-220-1684

†Hamilton/Avnet Electronics
444 E. Industrial Drive
Manchester 03103
Tel: (603) 624-9400

†Microcomputer System Technical Distributor Center

DOMESTIC DISTRIBUTORS (Contd.)

NEW JERSEY

†Arrow Electronics, Inc.
Four East Stow Road
Unit 11
Marlton 08053
Tel: (609) 596-8000
TWX: 710-897-0829

†Arrow Electronics
6 Century Drive
Parsipanny 07054
Tel: (201) 538-0900

†Hamilton/Avnet Electronics
1 Keystone Ave., Bldg. 36
Cherry Hill 08003
Tel: (609) 424-0110
TWX: 710-940-0262

†Hamilton/Avnet Electronics
10 Industrial
Fairfield 07006
Tel: (201) 575-5300
TWX: 710-734-4388

†MTI Systems Sales
37 Kulick Rd.
Fairfield 07006
Tel: (201) 227-5552

†Pioneer Electronics
45 Route 46
Pinebrook 07058
Tel: (201) 575-3510
TWX: 710-734-4382

NEW MEXICO

Alliance Electronics Inc.
11030 Cochiti S.E.
Albuquerque 87123
Tel: (505) 292-3360
TWX: 910-989-1151

Hamilton/Avnet Electronics
2524 Baylor Drive S.E.
Albuquerque 87106
Tel: (505) 765-1500
TWX: 910-989-0614

NEW YORK

†Arrow Electronics, Inc.
3375 Brighton Henrietta
Townline Rd.
Rochester 14623
Tel: (716) 275-0300
TWX: 510-253-4766

Arrow Electronics, Inc.
20 Oser Avenue
Hauppauge 11788
Tel: (516) 231-1000
TWX: 510-227-6623

Hamilton/Avnet
933 Motor Parkway
Hauppauge 11788
Tel: (516) 231-9800
TWX: 510-224-6166

†Hamilton/Avnet Electronics
333 Metro Park
Rochester 14623
Tel: (716) 475-9130
TWX: 510-253-5470

†Hamilton/Avnet Electronics
103 Twin Oaks Drive
Syracuse 13206
Tel: (315) 437-0288
TWX: 710-541-1560

†MTI Systems Sales
38 Harbor Park Drive
Port Washington 11050
Tel: (516) 621-6200

†Pioneer Electronics
68 Corporate Drive
Binghamton 13904
Tel: (607) 722-9300
TWX: 510-252-0893

Pioneer Electronics
40 Oser Avenue
Hauppauge 11787
Tel: (516) 231-9200

†Pioneer Electronics
60 Crossway Park West
Woodbury, Long Island 11797
Tel: (516) 921-8700
TWX: 510-221-2184

†Pioneer Electronics
840 Fairport Park
Fairport 14450
Tel: (716) 381-7070
TWX: 510-253-7001

NORTH CAROLINA

†Arrow Electronics, Inc.
5240 Greensdairy Road
Raleigh 27604
Tel: (919) 876-3132
TWX: 510-928-1856

†Hamilton/Avnet Electronics
3510 Spring Forest Drive
Raleigh 27604
Tel: (919) 878-0819
TWX: 510-928-1836

Pioneer/Technologies Group, Inc.
9801 A-Southern Pine Blvd.
Charlotte 28210
Tel: (919) 527-8188
TWX: 810-621-0366

OHIO

Arrow Electronics, Inc.
7620 McEwen Road
Centerville 45459
Tel: (513) 435-5563
TWX: 810-459-1611

†Arrow Electronics, Inc.
6238 Cochran Road
Solon 44139
Tel: (216) 248-3990
TWX: 810-427-9409

†Hamilton/Avnet Electronics
954 Senate Drive
Dayton 45459
Tel: (513) 439-6733
TWX: 810-450-2531

Hamilton/Avnet Electronics
4588 Emery Industrial Pkwy.
Warrensville Heights 44128
Tel: (216) 349-5100
TWX: 810-427-9452

†Hamilton/Avnet Electronics
777 Brooksedge Blvd.
Westerville 43081
Tel: (614) 882-7004

†Pioneer Electronics
4433 Interpoint Boulevard
Dayton 45424
Tel: (513) 236-9900
TWX: 810-459-1622

†Pioneer Electronics
4800 E. 131st Street
Cleveland 44105
Tel: (216) 587-3600
TWX: 810-422-2211

OKLAHOMA

Arrow Electronics, Inc.
1211 E. 51st St., Suite 101
Tulsa 74146
Tel: (918) 252-7537

†Hamilton/Avnet Electronics
12121 E. 51st St., Suite 102A
Tulsa 74146
Tel: (918) 252-7297

OREGON

†Almac Electronics Corp.
1885 N.W. 169th Place
Beaverton 97005
Tel: (503) 629-8090
TWX: 910-467-8746

†Hamilton/Avnet Electronics
6024 S.W. Jean Road
Bldg. C, Suite 10
Lake Oswego 97034
Tel: (503) 635-7848
TWX: 910-455-8179

Wyle Distribution Group
5250 N.E. Elam Young Parkway
Suite 600
Hillsboro 97124
Tel: (503) 640-6000
TWX: 910-460-2203

PENNSYLVANIA

Arrow Electronics, Inc.
650 Seco Road
Monroeville 15146
Tel: (412) 856-7000

Hamilton/Avnet Electronics
2800 Liberty Ave.
Pittsburgh 15238
Tel: (412) 281-4150

Pioneer Electronics
259 Kappa Drive
Pittsburgh 15238
Tel: (412) 782-2300
TWX: 710-795-3122

†Pioneer/Technologies Group, Inc.
Delaware Valley
261 Gibraltar Road
Horsham 19044
Tel: (215) 674-4000
TWX: 510-665-6778

TEXAS

†Arrow Electronics, Inc.
3220 Commander Drive
Carrollton 75006
Tel: (214) 380-6464
TWX: 910-860-5377

†Arrow Electronics, Inc.
10899 Kinghurst
Suite 100
Houston 77099
Tel: (713) 530-4700
TWX: 910-880-4439

†Arrow Electronics, Inc.
2227 W. Braker Lane
Austin 78758
Tel: (512) 835-4180
TWX: 910-874-1348

†Hamilton/Avnet Electronics
1807 W. Braker Lane
Austin 78758
Tel: (512) 837-8911
TWX: 910-874-1319

†Hamilton/Avnet Electronics
2111 W. Walnut Hill Lane
Irving 75038
Tel: (214) 550-6111
TWX: 910-860-5929

†Hamilton/Avnet Electronics
4850 Wright Rd., Suite 190
Stafford 77477
Tel: (713) 240-7733
TWX: 910-881-5523

†Pioneer Electronics
18260 Kramer
Austin 78758
Tel: (512) 835-4000
TWX: 910-874-1323

†Pioneer Electronics
13710 Omega Road
Dallas 75234
Tel: (214) 386-7300
TWX: 910-850-5563

†Pioneer Electronics
5853 Point West Drive
Houston 77036
Tel: (713) 988-5555
TWX: 910-881-1606

Wyle Distribution Group
1810 Greenville Avenue
Richardson 75081
Tel: (214) 235-9953

UTAH

Arrow Electronics
1946 Parkway Blvd.
Salt Lake City 84119
Tel: (801) 973-6913

†Hamilton/Avnet Electronics
1585 West 2100 South
Salt Lake City 84119
Tel: (801) 972-2800
TWX: 910-925-4018

Wyle Distribution Group
1325 West 2200 South
Suite E
West Valley 84119
Tel: (801) 974-9953

WASHINGTON

†Almac Electronics Corp.
14360 S.E. Eastgate Way
Bellevue 98007
Tel: (206) 643-9992
TWX: 910-444-2067

Arrow Electronics, Inc.
19540 68th Ave. South
Kent 98032
Tel: (206) 575-4420

†Hamilton/Avnet Electronics
14212 N.E. 21st Street
Bellevue 98005
Tel: (206) 643-3950
TWX: 910-443-2469

Wyle Distribution Group
15385 N.E. 90th Street
Redmond 98052
Tel: (206) 881-1150

WISCONSIN

Arrow Electronics, Inc.
200 N. Patrick Blvd., Ste. 100
Brookfield 53005
Tel: (414) 767-6600
TWX: 910-262-1193

Hamilton/Avnet Electronics
2975 Moorland Road
New Berlin 53151
Tel: (414) 784-4510
TWX: 910-262-1182

CANADA

ALBERTA

Hamilton/Avnet Electronics
2816 21st Street N.E.
Calgary T2E 6Z3
Tel: (403) 230-3586
TWX: 03-827-642

Zentronics
Bay No. 1
3300 14th Avenue N.E.
Calgary T2A 6J4
Tel: (403) 272-1021

BRITISH COLUMBIA

†Hamilton/Avnet Electronics
105-2550 Boundary
Burmalay V5M 3Z3
Tel: (604) 437-6667

Zentronics
108-11400 Bridgeport Road
Richmond V6X 1T2
Tel: (604) 273-5575
TWX: 04-5077-89

MANITOBA

Zentronics
60-1313 Border Unit 60
Winnipeg R3H 0X4
Tel: (204) 694-1957

ONTARIO

Arrow Electronics, Inc.
36 Antares Dr.
Nepean K2E 7W5
Tel: (613) 226-6903

Arrow Electronics, Inc.
1093 Meyerside
Mississauga L5T 1M4
Tel: (416) 673-7769
TWX: 06-218213

†Hamilton/Avnet Electronics
6845 Rexwood Road
Units 3-4-5
Mississauga L4T 1R2
Tel: (416) 677-7432
TWX: 610-492-8867

Hamilton/Avnet Electronics
6845 Rexwood Rd., Unit 6
Mississauga L4T 1R2
Tel: (416) 277-0484

†Hamilton/Avnet Electronics
190 Colonnade Road South
Nepean K2E 7L5
Tel: (613) 226-1700
TWX: 05-349-71

†Zentronics
8 Tilbury Court
Brampton L6T 3T4
Tel: (416) 451-9600
TWX: 06-976-78

†Zentronics
155 Colonnade Road
Unit 17
Nepean K2E 7K1
Tel: (613) 226-8840

Zentronics
60-1313 Border St.
Winnipeg R3H 0I4
Tel: (204) 694-7957

QUEBEC

†Arrow Electronics Inc.
4050 Jean Talon Quest
Montreal H4P 1W1
Tel: (514) 735-5511
TWX: 05-25590

Arrow Electronics, Inc.
500 Avenue St-Jean Baptiste
Suite 280
Quebec G2E 5R9
Tel: (418) 871-7500
FAX: 418-871-6816

Hamilton/Avnet Electronics
2795 Halpern
St. Laurent H2E 7K1
Tel: (514) 335-1000
TWX: 610-421-3731

Zentronics
817 McCaffrey
St. Laurent H4T 1M3
Tel: (514) 737-9700
TWX: 05-827-535

†Microcomputer System Technical Distributor Center

DOMESTIC SERVICE OFFICES

ALABAMA

*Intel Corp.
5015 Bradford Dr., Suite 2
Huntsville 35805
Tel: (205) 830-4010

ALASKA

Intel Corp.
c/o TransAlaska Data Systems
300 Old Steese Hwy.
Fairbanks 99701-3120
Tel: (907) 452-4401

Intel Corp.
c/o TransAlaska Data Systems
1551 Lore Road
Anchorage 99507
Tel: (907) 522-1776

ARIZONA

*Intel Corp.
11225 N. 28th Dr.
Suite D-214
Phoenix 85029
Tel: (602) 869-4980

*Intel Corp.
500 E. Fry Blvd., Suite M-15
Sierra Vista 85635
Tel: (602) 459-5010

CALIFORNIA

†Intel Corp.
21515 Vanowen St., Ste. 116
Canoga Park 91303
Tel: (818) 704-8500

*Intel Corp.
2250 E. Imperial Hwy., Ste. 218
El Segundo 90245
Tel: (213) 640-6040

*Intel Corp.
1900 Prairie City Rd.
Folsom 95630-9597
Tel: (916) 351-6143
1-800-468-3548

Intel Corp.
9665 Cheasapeake Dr., Suite 325
San Diego 92123-1326
Tel: (619) 292-8086

**Intel Corp.
400 N. Tustin Avenue
Suite 450
Santa Ana 92705
Tel: (714) 835-9642

**†Intel Corp.
San Tomas 4
2700 San Tomas Exp., 2nd Floor
Santa Clara 95051
Tel: (408) 986-8086

COLORADO

*Intel Corp.
650 S. Cherry St., Suite 915
Denver 80222
Tel: (303) 321-8086

CONNECTICUT

*Intel Corp.
301 Lee Farm Corporate Park
83 Wooster Heights Rd.
Danbury 06810
Tel: (203) 748-3130

FLORIDA

**Intel Corp.
6363 N.W. 6th Way, Ste. 100
Ft. Lauderdale 33309
Tel: (305) 771-0600

*Intel Corp.
5850 T.G. Lee Blvd., Ste. 340
Orlando 32822
Tel: (407) 240-8000

GEORGIA

*Intel Corp.
3280 Pointe Pkwy., Ste. 200
Norcross 30092
Tel: (404) 449-0541

HAWAII

*Intel Corp.
U.S.I.S.C. Signal Batt.
Building T-1521
Shafter Plats
Shafter 96856

ILLINOIS

**†Intel Corp.
300 N. Martingale Rd., Ste. 400
Schaumburg 60173
Tel: (312) 605-8031

INDIANA

*Intel Corp.
8777 Purdue Rd., Ste. 125
Indianapolis 46268
Tel: (317) 875-0623

KANSAS

*Intel Corp.
10985 Cody, Suite 140
Overland Park 66210
Tel: (913) 345-2727

MARYLAND

**†Intel Corp.
10010 Junction Dr., Suite 200
Annapolis Junction 20701
Tel: (301) 206-2860
FAX: 301-206-3677

MASSACHUSETTS

**†Intel Corp.
3 Carlisle Rd., 2nd Floor
Westford 01886
Tel: (508) 692-1060

MICHIGAN

*†Intel Corp.
7071 Orchard Lake Rd., Ste. 100
West Bloomfield 48322
Tel: (313) 851-8905

MINNESOTA

*†Intel Corp.
3500 W. 80th St., Suite 360
Bloomington 55431
Tel: (612) 835-6722

MISSOURI

*Intel Corp.
4203 Earth City Exp., Ste. 131
Earth City 63045
Tel: (314) 291-1990

NEW JERSEY

**Intel Corp.
300 Sylvan Avenue
Englewood Cliffs 07632
Tel: (201) 567-0821

*Intel Corp.
Parkway 109 Office Center
328 Newman Springs Road
Red Bank 07701
Tel: (201) 747-2233

*Intel Corp.
280 Corporate Center
75 Livingston Ave., 1st Floor
Roseland 07068
Tel: (201) 740-0111

NEW YORK

*†Intel Corp.
2950 Expressway Dr. South
Islandia 11722
Tel: (516) 231-3300

*Intel Corp.
Westage Business Center
Bldg. 300, Route 9
Fishkill 12524
Tel: (914) 897-3860

NORTH CAROLINA

*Intel Corp.
5800 Executive Dr., Ste. 105
Charlotte 28212
Tel: (704) 568-8966

**Intel Corp.
2700 Wycliff Road
Suite 102
Raleigh 27607
Tel: (919) 781-8022

OHIO

**†Intel Corp.
3401 Park Center Dr., Ste. 220
Dayton 45414
Tel: (513) 890-5350

*†Intel Corp.
25700 Science Park Dr., Ste. 100
Beachwood 44122
Tel: (216) 464-2736

OREGON

Intel Corp.
15254 N.W. Greenbrier Parkway
Building B
Beaverton 97005
Tel: (503) 645-8051

*Intel Corp.
5200 N.E. Elam Young Parkway
Hillsboro 97123
Tel: (503) 681-8080

PENNSYLVANIA

*†Intel Corp.
455 Pennsylvania Ave., Ste. 230
Fort Washington 19034
Tel: (215) 641-1000

†Intel Corp.
400 Penn Center Blvd., Ste. 610
Pittsburgh 15235
Tel: (412) 823-4970

Intel Corp.
1513 Cedar Cliff Dr.
Camp Hill 17011
Tel: (717) 761-0860

PUERTO RICO

Intel Corp.
South Industrial Park
P.O. Box 910
Las Piedras 00671
Tel: (809) 733-8616

TEXAS

Intel Corp.
8815 Dyer St., Suite 225
El Paso 79904
Tel: (915) 751-0186

*Intel Corp.
313 E. Anderson Lane, Suite 314
Austin 78752
Tel: (512) 454-3628

**†Intel Corp.
12000 Ford Rd., Suite 401
Dallas 75234
Tel: (214) 241-8087

*Intel Corp.
7322 S.W. Freeway, Ste. 1490
Houston 77074
Tel: (713) 988-8086

UTAH

Intel Corp.
428 East 6400 South, Ste. 104
Murray 84107
Tel: (801) 263-8051

VIRGINIA

*Intel Corp.
1504 Santa Rosa Rd., Ste. 108
Richmond 23288
Tel: (804) 282-5668

WASHINGTON

*Intel Corp.
155 108th Avenue N.E., Ste. 386
Bellevue 98004
Tel: (206) 453-8086

CANADA

ONTARIO

Intel Semiconductor of
Canada, Ltd.
2650 Queensview Dr., Ste. 250
Ottawa K2B 8H6
Tel: (613) 829-9714
FAX: 613-820-5936

Intel Semiconductor of
Canada, Ltd.
190 Attwell Dr., Ste. 102
Rexdale M9W 6H8
Tel: (416) 675-2105
FAX: 416-675-2438

CUSTOMER TRAINING CENTERS

CALIFORNIA

2700 San Tomas Expressway
Santa Clara 95051
Tel: (408) 970-1700
1-800-421-0386

ILLINOIS

300 N. Martingale Road
Suite 300
Schaumburg 60173
Tel: (708) 706-5700
1-800-421-0386

MASSACHUSETTS

3 Carlisle Road, First Floor
Westford 01886
Tel: (301) 220-3380
1-800-328-0386

MARYLAND

10010 Junction Dr.
Suite 200
Annapolis Junction 20701
Tel: (301) 206-2860
1-800-328-0386

SYSTEMS ENGINEERING MANAGERS OFFICES

MINNESOTA

3500 W. 80th Street
Suite 360
Bloomington 55431
Tel: (612) 835-6722

NEW YORK

2950 Expressway Dr., South
Islandia 11722
Tel: (506) 231-3300

†System Engineering locations
*Carry-in locations
**Carry-in/mail-in locations

EUROPEAN SALES OFFICES

DENMARK

Intel Denmark A/S
Glentevej 61, 3rd Floor
2400 Copenhagen NV
Tel: (45) (31) 19 80 33
TLX: 19567

FINLAND

Intel Finland OY
Ruosilantie 2
00390 Helsinki
Tel: (358) 0 544 644
TLX: 123332

FRANCE

Intel Corporation S.A.R.L.
1, Rue Edison-BP 303
78054 St. Quentin-en-Yvelines
Cedex
Tel: (33) (1) 30 57 70 00
TLX: 699016

WEST GERMANY

Intel Semiconductor GmbH*
Dornacher Strasse 1
8016 Feldkirchen bei Muenchen
Tel: (49) 089/90992-0
TLX: 5-23177

Intel Semiconductor GmbH
Hohenzollern Strasse 5
3000 Hannover 1
Tel: (49) 0511/344081
TLX: 9-23625

Intel Semiconductor GmbH
Abraham Lincoln Strasse 16-18
6200 Wiesbaden
Tel: (49) 06121/7605-0
TLX: 4-186183

Intel Semiconductor GmbH
Zettachring 10A
7000 Stuttgart 80
Tel: (49) 0711/7287-280
TLX: 7-254826

ISRAEL

Intel Semiconductor Ltd.*
Atidim Industrial Park-Neve Sharet
P.O. Box 43202
Tel-Aviv 61430
Tel: (972) 03-498080
TLX: 371215

ITALY

Intel Corporation Italia S.p.A.*
Milanofiori Palazzo E
20090 Assago
Milano
Tel: (39) (02) 89200950
TLX: 341286

NETHERLANDS

Intel Semiconductor B.V.*
Postbus 84130
3099 CC Rotterdam
Tel: (31) 10.407.11.11
TLX: 22283

NORWAY

Intel Norway A/S
Hvamveien 4-PO Box 92
2013 Skjetten
Tel: (47) (6) 842 420
TLX: 78018

SPAIN

Intel Iberia S.A.
Zurbaran, 28
28010 Madrid
Tel: (34) (1) 308.25.52
TLX: 46880

SWEDEN

Intel Sweden A.B.*
Dalvagen 24
171 36 Solna
Tel: (46) 8 734 01 00
TLX: 12261

SWITZERLAND

Intel Semiconductor A.G.
Zuerichstrasse
8185 Winkel-Rueti bei Zuerich
Tel: (41) 01/860 62 62
TLX: 825977

UNITED KINGDOM

Intel Corporation (U.K.) Ltd.*
Pipers Way
Swindon, Wiltshire SN3 1RJ
Tel: (44) (0793) 696000
TLX: 444447/8

EUROPEAN DISTRIBUTORS/REPRESENTATIVES

AUSTRIA

Bacher Electronics G.m.b.H.
Rotenmuehlgasse 26
1120 Wien
Tel: (43) (0222) 83 56 46
TLX: 31532

BELGIUM

Inelco Belgium S.A.
Av. des Croix de Guerre 94
1120 Bruxelles
Oorlogskruisenlaan, 94
1120 Brussel
Tel: (32) (02) 216 01 60
TLX: 64475 or 22090

DENMARK

ITT-Multikomponent
Naverland 29
2600 Glostrup
Tel: (45) (0) 2 45 66 45
TLX: 33 355

FINLAND

OY Fintronic AB
Melkonkatu 24A
00210 Helsinki
Tel: (358) (0) 6926022
TLX: 124224

FRANCE

Almex
Zone industrielle d'Antony
48, rue de l'Aubepine
BP 102
92164 Antony cedex
Tel: (33) (1) 46 66 21 12
TLX: 250067

Jermyn-Generim
60, rue des Gemeaux
Silic 580
94653 Rungis cedex
Tel: (33) (1) 49 78 49 78
TLX: 261585

Metrologie
Tour d'Asnieres
4, av. Laurent-Cely
92606 Asnieres Cedex
Tel: (33) (1) 47 90 62 40
TLX: 611448

Tekelec-Airtronic
Cite des Bruyeres
Rue Carle Vernet - BP 2
92310 Sevres
Tel: (33) (1) 45 34 75 35
TLX: 204552

WEST GERMANY

Electronic 2000 AG
Stahlgruberring 12
8000 Muenchen 82
Tel: (49) 089/42001-0
TLX: 522561

ITT Multikomponent GmbH
Postfach 1265
Bahnhofstrasse 44
7141 Moeglingen
Tel: (49) 07141/4879
TLX: 7264472

Jermyn GmbH
Im Dachsstueck 9
6250 Limburg
Tel: (49) 06431/508-0
TLX: 415257-0

Metrologie GmbH
Meglingerstrasse 49
8000 Muenchen 71
Tel: (49) 089/78042-0
TLX: 5213189

Proelectron Vertriebs GmbH
Max Planck Strasse 1-3
6072 Dreieich
Tel: (49) 06103/30434-3
TLX: 417903

IRELAND

Micro Marketing Ltd.
Glenageary Office Park
Glenageary
Co. Dublin
Tel: (21) (353) (01) 85 63 25
TLX: 31584

ISRAEL

Eastronics Ltd.
11 Rozanis Street
P.O.B. 39300
Tel-Aviv 61392
Tel: (972) 03-475151
TLX: 33638

ITALY

Intesi
Divisione ITT Industries GmbH
Viale Milanofiori
Palazzo E/5
20090 Assago (MI)
Tel: (39) 02/824701
TLX: 311351

Lasi Elettronica S.p.A.
V. le Fulvio Testi, 126
20092 Cinisello Balsamo (MI)
Tel: (39) 02/2440012
TLX: 352040

Telcom S.r.l.
Via M. Civitali 75
20148 Milano
Tel: (39) 02/4049046
TLX: 335654

ITT Multicomponents
Viale Milanofiori E/5
20090 Assago (MI)
Tel: (39) 02/824701
TLX: 311351

Silverstar
Via Dei Gracchi 20
20146 Milano
Tel: (39) 02/49961
TLX: 332189

NETHERLANDS

Koning en Hartman Elektrotechniek B.V.
Energieweg 1
2627 AP Delft
Tel: (31) (0) 15/609906
TLX: 38250

NORWAY

Nordisk Elektronikk (Norge) A/S
Postboks 123
Smedsvingen 4
1364 Hvalstad
Tel: (47) (02) 84 62 10
TLX: 77546

PORTUGAL

ATD Portugal LDA
Rua Dos Lusiados, 5 Sala B
1300 Lisboa
Tel: (35) (1) 64 80 91
TLX: 61562

Ditram
Avenida Miguel Bombarda, 133
1000 Lisboa
Tel: (35) (1) 54 53 13
TLX: 14182

SPAIN

ATD Electronica, S.A.
Plaza Ciudad de Viena, 6
28040 Madrid
Tel: (34) (1) 234 40 00
TLX: 42477

ITT-SESA
Calle Miguel Angel, 21-3
28010 Madrid
Tel: (34) (1) 419 09 57
TLX: 27461

Metrologia Iberica, S.A.
Ctra. de Fuencarral, n.80
28100 Alcobendas (Madrid)
Tel: (34) (1) 653 86 11

SWEDEN

Nordisk Elektronik AB
Torshamnsgatan 39
Box 36
164 93 Kista
Tel: (46) 08-03 46 30
TLX: 105 47

SWITZERLAND

Industrade A.G.
Hertistrasse 31
8304 Wallisellen
Tel: (41) (01) 8328111
TLX: 56788

TURKEY

EMPA Electronic
Lindwurmstrasse 95A
8000 Muenchen 2
Tel: (49) 089/53 80 570
TLX: 528573

UNITED KINGDOM

Accent Electronic Components Ltd.
Jubilee House, Jubilee Road
Letchworth, Herts SG6 1TL
Tel: (44) (0462) 686666
TLX: 826293

Bytech-Comway Systems
3 The Western Centre
Western Road
Bracknell RG12 1RW
Tel: (44) (0344) 55333
TLX: 847201

Jermyn
Vestry Estate
Otford Road
Sevenoaks
Kent TN14 5EU
Tel: (44) (0732) 450144
TLX: 95142

MMD
Unit 8 Southview Park
Caversham
Reading
Berkshire RG4 0AF
Tel: (44) (0734) 481666
TLX: 846669

Rapid Silicon
Rapid House
Denmark Street
High Wycombe
Buckinghamshire HP11 2ER
Tel: (44) (0494) 442266
TLX: 837931

Rapid Systems
Rapid House
Denmark Street
High Wycombe
Buckinghamshire HP11 2ER
Tel: (44) (0494) 450244
TLX: 837931

YUGOSLAVIA

H.R. Microelectronics Corp.
2005 de la Cruz Blvd., Ste. 223
Santa Clara, CA 95050
U.S.A.
Tel: (1) (408) 988-0286
TLX: 387452

Rapido Electronic Components S.p.a.
Via C. Beccaria, 8
34133 Trieste
Italia
Tel: (39) 040/360555
TLX: 460461

*Field Application Location

INTERNATIONAL SALES OFFICES

AUSTRALIA

Intel Australia Pty. Ltd.*
Spectrum Building
200 Pacific Hwy., Level 6
Crows Nest, NSE, 2065
Tel: 612-957-2744
FAX: 612-923-2632

BRAZIL

Intel Semicondutores do Brazil LTDA
Av. Paulista, 1159-CJS 404/405
01311 - Sao Paulo - S.P.
Tel: 55-11-287-5899
TLX: 3911153146 ISDB
FAX: 55-11-287-5119

CHINA/HONG KONG

Intel PRC Corporation
15/F, Office 1, Citic Bldg.
Jian Guo Men Wai Street
Beijing, PRC
Tel: (1) 500-4850
TLX: 22947 INTEL CN
FAX: (1) 500-2953

Intel Semiconductor Ltd.*
10/F East Tower
Bond Center
Queensway, Central
Hong Kong
Tel: (5) 8444-555
TLX: 63869 ISHLHK HX
FAX: (5) 8681-989

INDIA

Intel Asia Electronics, Inc.
4/2, Samrah Plaza
St. Mark's Road
Bangalore 560001
Tel: 011-91-812-215065
TLX: 9538452875 DCBY
FAX: 091-812-215067

JAPAN

Intel Japan K.K.
5-6 Tokodai, Tsukuba-shi
Ibaraki, 300-26
Tel: 0298-47-8511
TLX: 3656-160
FAX: 029747-8450

Intel Japan K.K.*
Daiichi Mitsugi Bldg.
1-8889 Fuchu-cho
Fuchu-shi, Tokyo 183
Tel: 0423-60-7871
FAX: 0423-60-0315

Intel Japan K.K.*
Bldg. Kumagaya
2-69 Hon-cho
Kumagaya-shi, Saitama 360
Tel: 0485-24-6871
FAX: 0485-24-7518

Intel Japan K.K.*
Mitsui-Seimei Musashi-kosugi Bldg.
915 Shinmaruko, Nakahara-ku
Kawasaki-shi, Kanagawa 211
Tel: 044-733-7011
FAX: 044-733-7010

Intel Japan K.K.
Nihon Seimei Atsugi Bldg.
1-2-1 Asahi-machi
Atsugi-shi, Kanagawa 243
Tel: 0462-29-3731
FAX: 0462-29-3781

Intel Japan K.K.*
Ryokuchi-Eki Bldg.
2-4-1 Terauchi
Toyonaka-shi, Osaka 560
Tel: 06-863-1091
FAX: 06-863-1084

Intel Japan K.K.
Shinmaru Bldg.
1-5-1 Marunouchi
Chiyoda-ku, Tokyo 100
Tel: 03-201-3621
FAX: 03-201-6850

Intel Japan K.K.
Green Bldg.
1-16-20 Nishiki
Naka-ku, Nagoya-shi
Aichi 450
Tel: 052-204-1261
FAX: 052-204-1285

KOREA

Intel Technology Asia, Ltd.
16th Floor, Life Bldg.
61 Yoido-dong, Youngdeungpo-Ku
Seoul 150-010
Tel: (2) 784-8186, 8286, 8386
TLX: K29312 INTELKO
FAX: (2) 784-8096

SINGAPORE

Intel Singapore Technology, Ltd.
101 Thomson Road #21-05/06
United Square
Singapore 1130
Tel: 250-7811
TLX: 39921 INTEL
FAX: 250-9256

TAIWAN

Intel Technology Far East Ltd.
8th Floor, No. 205
Bank Tower Bldg.
Tung Hua N. Road
Taipei
Tel: 886-2-716-9660
FAX: 886-2-717-2455

INTERNATIONAL DISTRIBUTORS/REPRESENTATIVES

ARGENTINA

DAFSYS S.R.L.
Chacabuco, 90-6 PISO
1069-Buenos Aires
Tel: 54-1-334-7726
FAX: 54-1-334-1871

AUSTRALIA

Email Electronics
15-17 Hume Street
Huntingdale, 3166
Tel: 011-61-3-544-8244
TLX: AA 30895
FAX: 011-61-3-543-8179

NSD-Australia
205 Middleborough Rd.
Box Hill, Victoria 3128
Tel: 03 8900970
FAX: 03 8990819

BRAZIL

Elebra Microelectronica S.A.
Rua Geraldo Flausina Gomes, 78
10th Floor
04575 - Sao Paulo - S.P.
Tel: 55-11-534-9641
TLX: 55-11-54593/54591
FAX: 55-11-534-9424

CHILE

DIN Instruments
Suecia 2323
Casilla 6055, Correo 22
Santiago
Tel: 56-2-225-8139
TLX: 240.846 RUD

CHINA/HONG KONG

Novel Precision Machinery Co., Ltd.
Flat D, 20 Kingsford Ind. Bldg.
Phase 1, 26 Kwai Hei Street
N.T., Kowloon
Hong Kong
Tel: 852-0-4223222
TWX: 39114 JINMI HX
FAX: 852-0-4261602

INDIA

Micronic Devices
Arun Complex
No. 65 D.V.G. Road
Basavanagudi
Bangalore 560 004
Tel: 011-91-812-600-631
011-91-812-611-365
TLX: 9538458332 MDBG

Micronic Devices
No. 516 5th Floor
Swastik Chambers
Sion, Trombay Road
Chembur
Bombay 400 071
TLX: 9531 171447 MDEV

Micronic Devices
25/8, 1st Floor
Bada Bazaar Marg
Old Rajinder Nagar
New Delhi 110 060
Tel: 011-91-11-5723509
011-91-11-589771
TLX: 031-63253 MDND IN

Micronic Devices
6-3-348/12A Dwarakapuri Colony
Hyderabad 500 482
Tel: 011-91-842-226748

S&S Corporation
1587 Kooser Road
San Jose, CA 95118
Tel: (408) 978-6216
TLX: 820281
FAX: (408) 978-8635

JAPAN

Asahi Electronics Co. Ltd.
KMM Bldg. 2-14-1 Asano
Kokurakita-ku
Kitakyushu-shi 802
Tel: 093-511-6471
FAX: 093-551-7861

C. Itoh Techno-Science Co., Ltd.
4-8-1 Dobashi, Miyamae-ku
Kawasaki-shi, Kanagawa 213
Tel: 044-852-5121
FAX: 044-877-4268

Dia Semicon Systems, Inc.
Flower Hill Shinmachi Higashi-kan
1-23-9 Shinmachi, Setagaya-ku
Tokyo 154
Tel: 03-439-1600
FAX: 03-439-1601

Okaya Koki
2-4-18 Sakae
Naka-ku, Nagoya-shi 460
Tel: 052-204-2916
FAX: 052-204-2901

Ryoyo Electro Corp.
Konwa Bldg.
1-12-22 Tsukiji
Chuo-ku, Tokyo 104
Tel: 03-546-5011
FAX: 03-546-5044

KOREA

J-Tek Corporation
6th Floor, Government Pension Bldg.
24-3 Yoido-dong
Youngdeungpo-ku
Seoul 150-010
Tel: 82-2-780-8039
TLX: 25299 KODIGIT
FAX: 82-2-784-8391

Samsung Electronics
150 Taepyungro-2 KA
Chungku, Seoul 100-102
Tel: 82-2-751-3985
TLX: 27970 KORSST
FAX: 82-2-753-0967

MEXICO

SSB Electronics, Inc.
675 Palomar Street, Bldg. 4, Suite A
Chula Vista, CA 92011
Tel: (619) 585-3253
TLX: 287751 CBALL UR
FAX: (619) 585-8322

Dicopel S.A.
Tochtli 368 Fracc. Ind. San Antonio
Azcapotzalco
C.P. 02760-Mexico, D.F.
Tel: 52-5-561-3211
TLX: 177 3790 Dicome
FAX: 52-5-561-1279

PSI de Mexico
Francisco Villas Esq. Ajusto
Cuernavaca – Morelos – CEP 62130
Tel: 52-73-13-9412
FAX: 52-73-17-5333

NEW ZEALAND

Email Electronics
36 Olive Road
Penrose, Auckland
Tel: 011-64-9-591-155
FAX: 011-64-9-592-681

SINGAPORE

Electronic Resources Pte, Ltd.
17 Harvey Road #04-01
Singapore 1336
Tel: 283-0888
TWX: 56541 ERS
FAX: 2895327

SOUTH AFRICA

Electronic Building Elements
178 Erasmus Street (off Watermeyet Street)
Meyerspark, Pretoria, 0184
Tel: 011-2712-803-7680
FAX: 011-2712-803-8294

TAIWAN

Micro Electronics Corporation
5/F 587, Ming Shen East Rd.
Taipei, R.O.C.
Tel: 886-2-501-8231
FAX: 886-2-505-6609

Sertek
15/F 135, Section 2
Chien Juo North Rd.
Taipei 10479, R.O.C.
Tel: (02) 5010055
FAX: (02) 5012521
(02) 5058414

VENEZUELA

P. Benavides S.A.
Avilanes a Rio
Residencia Kamarata
Locales 4 AL 7
La Candelaria, Caracas
Tel: 58-2-574-6338
TLX: 28450
FAX: 58-2-572-3321

*Field Application Location